Automatic Text Processing

The Transformation, Analysis, and Retrieval of Information by Computer

Gerard Salton

Cornell University

ADDISON-WESLEY PUBLISHING COMPANY
Reading, Massachusetts • Menlo Park, California
New York • Don Mills, Ontario • Wokingham, England
Amsterdam • Bonn • Sydney • Singapore
Tokyo • Madrid • San Juan

This book is in the Addison-Wesley Series in Computer Science

Michael A. Harrison, Consulting Editor

Library of Congress Cataloging-in-Publication Data

Salton, Gerard.
    Automatic text processing: the transformation, analysis, and retrieval of information by computer / by Gerard Salton.
        p.   cm.
    Bibliography: p.
    Includes index.
    ISBN 0-201-12227-8
    1. Text processing (Computer science)   I. Title.
QA76.9.T48S25 1989
005—dc19   88-467
                                                                            CIP

Reprinted with corrections December, 1988

3 4 5 6 7 8 9 10 HA 95949392

Preface

The current period is known as the information age because more information is generated about more topics than ever before. In this complex world, relevant information is often needed to carry out the tasks at hand and to make intelligent decisions. When large data banks of information are collected and stored, it is difficult to find the data actually needed at a given time, and to distinguish relevant from extraneous data. For this reason, electronic search aids are widely used to process, store, and retrieve information items on demand.

The information of interest at any particular time takes various forms. In particular, standard written data and natural-language texts must be distinguished from spoken utterances and speech sounds, and from graphical and pictorial data. Textual information is primarily important because text is used universally to convey information and to communicate. In addition, text can be automatically processed more easily and less expensively than either speech or pictures.

This book deals with the whole area of automatic text-processing — that is, the handling of texts using automatic equipment. The aim is not to teach laymen or humanists how to program computers to manipulate text, nor to teach scientists language-processing skills. Instead, the book examines the area of text processing as a whole, describing various text-processing methodologies and identifying those tasks now undertaken routinely, while also discussing more experimental procedures not yet ready for operation. For example, it is conceptually easy to take the English text which makes up this book and determine the number of occurrences in the text of the word "information." It is more difficult to identify all the sections in the book that deal with "information storage and retrieval," in part because the words "information" and "retrieval" do not occur explicitly in some relevant sections. It is even more difficult to find the sections exhibiting stylistic similarities with the style used in this preface. Indeed, such a request cannot be processed without specifying the perceived stylistic features characterizing the preface. Analogously, it is very difficult to devise effective methods for retrieving from a library all books whose opinions about the mechanization of text processing reflect the opinions expressed here.

This should be a useful reference for users of text-processing systems and designers of text-processing routines. It can also serve as a textbook in programs of computer science and engineering, library and information science, computational linguistics, as well as programs about relations among science, technology, and society. Various parts of the text have been used in a text-processing course taught at Cornell University to upper-level computer-science undergraduates and first-year graduate students.

The book is divided into four main parts. The introduction, Chapters 1, 2, and 3, covers the existing computer environment and the automated office situation, in which text processing is of particular interest. The second part, Chapters 4 to 7, covers the main word-processing areas, which treat texts on the level of individual words. This includes text editing and formatting, properly termed "word processing" in the standard literature. Also included in Part 2 are text-compression methods designed to reduce the size of stored texts, text encryption methods designed to hide the meaning of the texts, and file-accessing methods used to access and search mechanized text files.

Part 3, Chapters 8, 9, and 10, covers text-retrieval systems whose operations are normally based on text units larger than single, individual word forms. Included is an examination of conventional text-retrieval systems based on automatic text scanning as well as conventional indexed text searches. Simple text analysis, and so-called automatic indexing systems designed to assign content identifiers to texts, are also described. Finally, advanced text-retrieval systems are considered that may be based on automatic text classification and complex Boolean query formulations.

Part 4, Chapters 11, 12, and 13, covers the main language-analysis and language-processing topics in which text meaning and text understanding are of principal concern: syntactic and semantic language-analysis methods that determine language structure and text content, and modern knowledge-based text processing. Various applications of linguistic procedures are also described including automatic text extracting and abstracting, text generation, and text translation. The book ends with an examination of paperless information systems that process speech and graphics information as well as text. Various electronic-information systems are covered such as electronic mail and message systems, automatic publication systems, and electronic books and libraries.

Each chapter can be read independently, but not every chapter will be equally accessible to every reader. In particular, the more mathematical treatment of text compression and encryption in Chapters 5 and 6 and some of the advanced retrieval methods of Chapter 10 are intended for those with technical training. Specialized sections or subsections, or those that require a mathematical background, are appropriately marked.

The following chapter arrangement can be used for a one-semester course for upper-level undergraduate and beginning graduate students in various disciplines (see also the figures on pages vi and vii):

Computer science and related subjects	Part 2 (Chapters 4–7) on compression, encryption and file access; Part 3 (Chapters 8–10) on automatic information retrieval
Linguistics and language processing	Part 1 (Chapters 1–3); Part 3 (Chapter 9, on document analysis), Part 4 (Chapters 11–13) on language processing
Library and information science, science and technology programs	Part 1 (Chapters 1–3); Chapter 4 of Part 2 on word processing; Part 3 (Chapters 8 and 9) on conventional retrieval; Part 4 (Chapters 11 and 13) on language analysis and paperless information systems

Part 1. The Information-Processing Environment

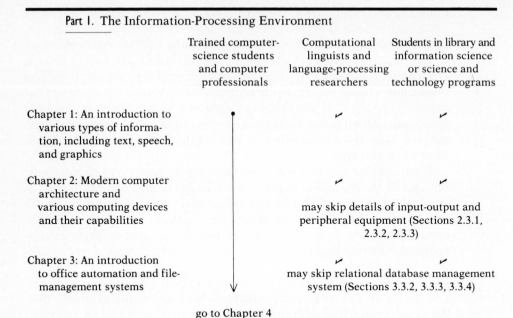

	Trained computer-science students and computer professionals	Computational linguists and language-processing researchers	Students in library and information science or science and technology programs
Chapter 1: An introduction to various types of information, including text, speech, and graphics	•	✔	✔
Chapter 2: Modern computer architecture and various computing devices and their capabilities		✔	✔
		may skip details of input-output and peripheral equipment (Sections 2.3.1, 2.3.2, 2.3.3)	
Chapter 3: An introduction to office automation and file-management systems		✔	✔
		may skip relational database management system (Sections 3.3.2, 3.3.3, 3.3.4)	

go to Chapter 4

Part 2. Word Processing and File Access

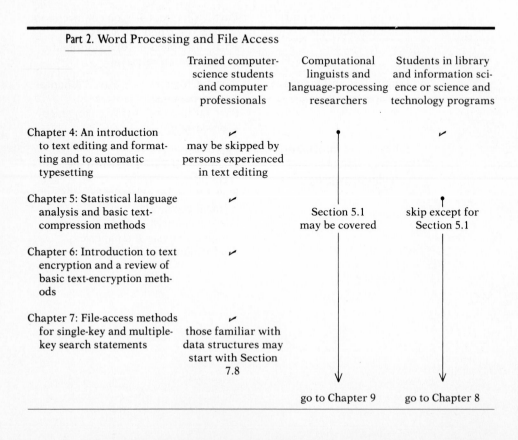

	Trained computer-science students and computer professionals	Computational linguists and language-processing researchers	Students in library and information science or science and technology programs
Chapter 4: An introduction to text editing and formatting and to automatic typesetting	✔ may be skipped by persons experienced in text editing	•	✔
Chapter 5: Statistical language analysis and basic text-compression methods	✔	Section 5.1 may be covered	skip except for Section 5.1
Chapter 6: Introduction to text encryption and a review of basic text-encryption methods	✔		
Chapter 7: File-access methods for single-key and multiple-key search statements	✔ those familiar with data structures may start with Section 7.8		
		go to Chapter 9	go to Chapter 8

Part 3. Information Retrieval Systems

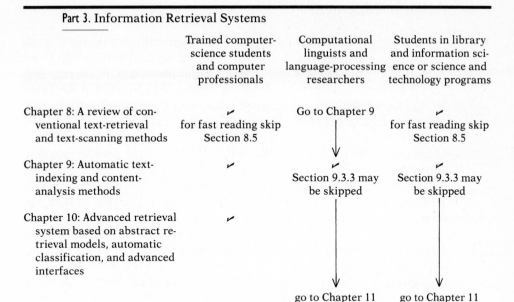

	Trained computer-science students and computer professionals	Computational linguists and language-processing researchers	Students in library and information science or science and technology programs
Chapter 8: A review of conventional text-retrieval and text-scanning methods	✔ for fast reading skip Section 8.5	Go to Chapter 9	✔ for fast reading skip Section 8.5
Chapter 9: Automatic text-indexing and content-analysis methods	✔	✔ Section 9.3.3 may be skipped	✔ Section 9.3.3 may be skipped
Chapter 10: Advanced retrieval system based on abstract retrieval models, automatic classification, and advanced interfaces	✔		
		go to Chapter 11	go to Chapter 11

Part 4. Text Analysis and Language Processing

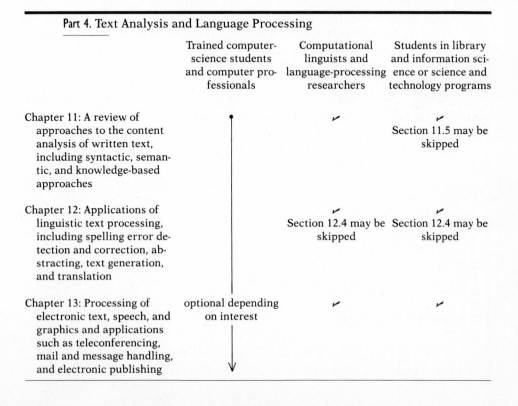

	Trained computer-science students and computer professionals	Computational linguists and language-processing researchers	Students in library and information science or science and technology programs
Chapter 11: A review of approaches to the content analysis of written text, including syntactic, semantic, and knowledge-based approaches		✔	✔ Section 11.5 may be skipped
Chapter 12: Applications of linguistic text processing, including spelling error detection and correction, abstracting, text generation, and translation		Section 12.4 may be skipped	Section 12.4 may be skipped
Chapter 13: Processing of electronic text, speech, and graphics and applications such as teleconferencing, mail and message handling, and electronic publishing	optional depending on interest	✔	✔

Acknowledgements

I am deeply indebted to a number of individuals who have made valuable suggestions about the content and form of this material, especially Dr. Michael E. Lesk of Bell Communications Research, Professor Michael A. Harrison of the University of California at Berkeley, Dr. Michael Lebowitz of Morgan Stanley and Company, Dr. Richard J. Beach of Xerox Palo Alto Research Center, and a number of former and present graduate students in information retrieval at Cornell, including Dr. Edward A. Fox, Dr. Ellen Voorhees, Dr. Joel Fagan, and Christopher Buckley. I am also most grateful to Professor Giovanni Coray of the Mathematics Department at the Ecole Polytechnique Federale in Lausanne (EPFL) and to Professor Charles Stuart, the chairman of that department, for having made available the exceptionally nice surroundings of the EPFL during a sabbatical year in Lausanne in 1984-85 when I wrote the first chapters of this book. Special thanks are due to my colleagues at Cornell, especially the two recent chairmen of the Computer Science Department, Professor David Gries and Professor John Hopcroft, for giving me the time to write a book when many other departmental matters might have taken precedence. Finally, I am deeply grateful to Geri Pinkham for once again spending much time to prepare this manuscript on the departmental word-processing equipment with her usual diligence and competence, and to Margaret Schimizzi and Teresa Leidenfrost, who helped draw the figures and prepare the typescript. I thank all these individuals for their guidance and assistance.

Ithaca, New York   Gerard Salton

Contents

Part 1

The Information-Processing Environment

Chapter 1

The Information Environment

1.1 Automatic Information Processing

It has been claimed that we live in the information age, and our society is often called the information society. More information is produced and collected in our time than ever before: thousands of books, tens of thousands of journal articles, and innumerable informal studies and reports. Our capacity to absorb this information and use it in reaching intelligent decisions is stretched not only by the amount and variety of the available data, but also by the complex relationships among different types of information, and the resulting difficulties in interpreting the data.

Fortunately, although we are inundated by all sorts of information, improvements are being made in the ways in which information is stored and processed. In particular, modern information-processing equipment can organize and store large amounts of information and provide fast access to the stored records. Communications networks, used increasingly to reach the available information sources, also connect different information stores to large, often far-flung groups of users.

The use of modern computing equipment to process information has had a two-fold effect. On the one hand, it facilitates the generation, collection, and storage of more information, complicating the task of absorbing and using the available data. [1] On the other hand, modern equipment somewhat simplifies the problems of access to information by providing useful ways to search for and retrieve it.

This book deals with modern information processing, that is, the methods used to generate, analyze, store, retrieve, and handle information items using automatic equipment. Current capabilities in information processing are examined, and difficulties and conceptual problems in analyzing and understanding information are described. By distinguishing relatively routine tasks from more experimental, laboratory-type endeavors, and by considering future developments, the book also outlines the information-processing world of the future.

1.2 Types of Information

Information can take three forms: written texts, spoken utterances, and graphs and images. Text, the basic medium for formal communications between human beings, consists of notes, messages, letters, memoranda, books, newspapers, magazines, and so on. Speech is more informal than text and, unlike text, is also accessible to people who cannot read or write. Graphs and images may accompany written texts, but can also be used alone as illustrations, displays, movies, or paintings.

In dealing with these information types it is useful to consider two principal aspects of information processing. The first area is the *technical* problem of information representation and manipulation, including methods of introducing and storing information in computers, and of transferring the data and making them accessible to interested users. The second area relates to the *semantic* and *behavioral* aspects of information processing: the accuracy with which the stored information conveys intended meanings, and the effectiveness with which it affects users' conduct as intended.

From a technical point of view, stored information can be treated simply as collections of disconnected elements — for example, individual words in given texts, individual characters in particular words, or picture elements in graphs and pictures. For processing purposes, the information elements are not assumed to convey specific meanings or to be tied to particular contexts. Thus a text can be reproduced or copied without the text content ever being considered. In actual fact, however, the information elements do carry meaning, and are expected to generate specific responses by the information users. Ultimately the meaning of the information tends to be more important than the form of representation and the manner in which the data are manipulated.

Because meaning is often ill-defined and elusive, semantic and behavioral information-processing tasks are far more difficult to carry out than technical aspects of information processing. [2]

1.2.1 Text Processing

Processing problems are much simpler and better understood for text than for other types of information. For one thing, natural language text can be represented as one-dimensional character strings, whereas speech and pictures are inherently two-dimensional. Speech utterances are often represented by two-dimensional waveforms, known as spectrograms, which can be transformed into digital form for computer storage. Images and pictures are similarly two-dimensional; they can usually be decomposed into picture elements for processing purposes. A picture can then be represented in computer storage by the properties of the individual picture elements. Certain well-defined picture components — consisting for example of special lines and curves — can be described by mathematical equations.

The relatively simpler mode of representing text is reflected in substantially greater storage efficiencies. Table 1.1 gives the storage requirements for one page of information in terms of equivalent numbers of characters, or bytes of storage. It is assumed that a printed page contains about 500 words of text and that the average word consists of six characters, with each character encoded as one byte of eight binary digits (bits) — thus one printed page requires about 3000 bytes of storage. That page of information read aloud produces about four minutes or 240 seconds of speech. A typical conversion of spoken information to digital form takes place at a rate of 9600 bits of information per second of speech — equivalent to about 300,000 bytes of information. Spoken information thus requires a storage capacity two

Table 1.1 Storage requirements per page of information.

Type of Information	Amount of Information per Page	Assumptions	Total Information in Bytes per Page
Text	500 words per page	6 characters or bytes per word	3000 bytes per page
Speech	4 minutes (240 seconds) to read 500 words	9600 bit-per-second sampling rate of speech input	2.3M bits (about 300,000 bytes) per page
Pictures	500 bits per inch (250,000 bits per square inch)	93 square inches per page	23M bits (about 3,000,000 bytes) per page

orders of magnitude larger than required for the comparable written text. The situation is even less favorable for high-resolution graphic data, which typically can be represented by 250,000 picture points per square inch. Assuming that a typical page includes 93 square inches, 3 million bytes are needed to store a full page of pictorial information — three orders of magnitude larger than required for a comparable page of written text.

Given the simpler representation and much greater storage efficiency available for text, not surprisingly it is much easier to manipulate text than speech or graphics. Indeed a wide range of text operations that depend principally on the recognition of individual text words, and individual characters within text words, are now used routinely in many types of applications. [3,4] These operations include automatic editing and formatting methods for texts; detection and sometimes correction of spelling errors; compression of text into reduced representations requiring much less than 3000 bytes of storage per page; encryption of text into a form that hides the normal appearance of the text words; comparison of words occurring in texts with stored dictionary information to determine such word properties as the syntactic functions or translated forms of the words; and retrieval of texts containing certain words or combinations of words.

1.2.2 Speech Processing

The text manipulations just mentioned depend on the presence or absence of words or word patterns in texts, and possibly on statistical properties of texts such as the frequencies with which particular text words or patterns of words occur. It appears simple in principle to extend these methods to speech and graphics information. This is unfortunately not true: There is no single, standard form of representation for all speech utterances and picture components, and these components are much harder to isolate and recognize than individual characters and words of text.

In speech processing, it is necessary to deal with many different forms of speech input, which depend on the type of speaker and the environment in which the speech sample is produced. The same spoken utterance can be represented by different wave patterns, and many otherwise clear utterances are difficult to capture under noisy conditions. In addition, distinct words such as "seen" and "seem" exhibit similar speech forms. [5,6] Since speech is normally produced without detectable pauses between sounds or between the words of an utterance, identifying separate units of spoken information is also a major problem.

It is also necessary to distinguish between speech *synthesis* and speech *recognition*. Synthesis, the production of speech output obtained from various forms of stored information, is used in such applications as talking instrument panels and question-answering systems — for example, automatic stock-quotation systems, which furnish the values of particular stocks over telephone lines on demand. Speech synthesis is also used in reading machines for visually impaired people, which automatically convert written texts into spoken output.

Conversely, speech-recognition systems use spoken utterances or speech waveforms as input, producing written versions of the input — or at least analyzed forms specifying the structure and possibly the meaning of the input utterances. Speech recognition can be used in telephone transaction systems in which goods are ordered by telephone, but input keyboards are not available to the user. In other applications, machinery is controlled by speech when the operators' hands are not free to use an input keyboard.

Speech synthesis is obviously much simpler than speech recognition: In a synthesis system only one type of voice with known characteristics must be produced, and the desired properties of the voice output can be accurately specified. In speech-recognition applications, however, the quality of the voice input may not be under the control of the designers. In such a case the system must be adjusted to many different input forms, some difficult to handle and analyze. Applications of speech synthesis are therefore much further advanced than those of speech recognition.

Speech synthesis is now possible for particular voice types, especially in environments where the input is limited to particular types of voices and particular classes of vocabulary. But synthesis applications are not always straightforward: In addition to producing individual speech sounds, the "glue" that relates the sound units must also be supplied, as must other speech characteristics that give ordinary speech its human quality — stress, pitch, and intonation for example. The disadvantage of speech recognition systems is that they are available only for small vocabularies (up to a few hundred words). Moreover, the preferable input consists of discrete, as opposed to continuous, speech in which pauses are forcibly introduced between adjacent words of the utterance. Also, the recognition equipment must be trained in advance to the particular qualities of the input voices.

1.2.3 Graphics Processing

The problems of speech processing also apply to graphic information. It is usually difficult to decompose pictures and images into discrete, recognizable elements, and hence manipulations that depend on identifying individual characters or words cannot be easily used in graphic-information environments. As in speech handling, image synthesis must be distinguished from image recognition, and synthesis is again much easier than recognition. Many applications require only simple images to be produced: For example, bar charts showing variations over time in the price or quantity of goods, or curves outlining statistical data. In such cases, it is relatively easy to process the corresponding graphic elements and substructures, and to transform the pictures by processes like translation, rotation, reflection, duplication, or superposition of certain elements. [7,8] Some applications allow even relatively complex pictures such as shapes of automobile bodies or airplanes to be generated from component parts; image-synthesis programs can then be used for the computer-aided design of these products.

Image recognition presents a much more complicated situation. As in the speech environment, it is difficult to standardize picture input. Thus many different kinds of images, ostensibly representing the same input, must be dealt with. For example, in recognizing handwritten alphabetic characters, as many distinct forms of input may have to be processed as the number of subjects submitting handwritten samples. Furthermore, as in the speech illustration, the individual picture elements appear in context with specific background data. The context may substantially affect the ease with which the elements can be recognized.

Picture-generation systems are usable when there are only a small number of different picture elements and when individual components are well defined. Picture recognition is usually limited to special situations and controlled environments. The technical processing environment for text, speech, and pictures is summarized in Table 1.2.

1.2.4 Semantic and Behavioral Processing

In many applications the detection of words and features within document texts will not solve the problem at hand. A deeper analysis of document content, one dealing with the meaning and the intent of the items, may then be required. Thus in information search and retrieval, it is not always sufficient to identify items containing particular text words. Instead the attempt must be to find records that actually cover a particular topic.

To determine document or record content, a broad background is necessary. Obviously the subject area under consideration must be mastered. Thus when requesting records dealing with information retrieval, the user must be aware that information retrieval is related to library science and to information organization and classification. Further, because information searches leading to retrieval are often carried out automatically, information retrieval is also related to aspects of computer processing. In addition to knowing specific subject areas, an interpretation of document content also requires common-sense knowledge and the wide background normally available to people in the world-at-large. Unfortunately, methods are not yet available for identifying the information actually needed in a particular case and for introducing apparently unlimited stores of knowledge into computer memory.

Attempts have been made to design structured *knowledge bases* for particular areas of discourse by specifying the main entities of interest in each area and then presenting specific relationships between entities — synonym relations, whole-part relations, cause-effect relations, and so on. Also, rules have been developed to relate record contents and document texts to the entities included in the knowledge base. However, little success has been achieved in actually analyzing the content of unrestricted texts by computer acceptably: Document content cannot usually be captured by means of limited and circumscribed amounts of prestored knowledge.

Table 1.2 Problem characterization for various information types.

	Technical Problem: Transmission or Processing	Semantic and Behavioral Problem: Conveying Meaning and Affecting Conduct
Text	generally under control for areas such as editing, formatting, compression, encryption, message handling, dictionary preparation, storing, retrieving	tractable for severely constrained subject areas or for special-purpose documents in particular environments
Speech	spoken utterances take on many forms *synthesis*: under control for limited vocabularies and limited voice types *recognition*: restricted to limited vocabularies and discrete speech, with training sequences	may be tractable in severely constrained subject areas; more difficult than for text
Pictures	*generation*: easy when needed components are prestored; understood somewhat for graphs *transformation*: difficulties arise in transforming two-dimensional representations to three-dimensional forms *recognition*: difficult in general; easier for limited predefined objects	more difficult than for text because of wider variety of possible relationships among components

For practical purposes, then, content-based information processing is possible only in special circumstances: [9]

1. When the environment is severely limited and can be represented adequately by a few entities and their relationships, or

2. When the documents fulfill special functions that automatically place the texts in particular contexts from which most of the usual ambiguities in interpretation are absent.

Content analyses have thus been carried out for certain controlled *microworlds*, but there is no indication that the methods applicable in these special circumstances can be extended to more realistic situations.

Content analysis of speech samples and pictures is even more elusive than the analysis of written texts because the basic entities and the relationships among them are more difficult to determine. Once again, content analysis is much simplified when the origin and context of the incoming samples are specified in advance. A baby's cry, inherently unintelligible, is often easily interpreted by the mother, who knows the child and the environment in which he or she cries. The same is true of drawings produced by four-year olds: They may appear to be jumbles of lines to uninitiated outsiders, but are accessible to informed observers.

Because written texts are basic to human information processing and can be manipulated easily by computer, text processing is emphasized in the rest of this book. There are three main sections: word processing, including text editing, document preparation, text compression and encryption, and file accessing (Chapters 4–7); information storage and retrieval, including document organization and retrieval modeling (Chapters 8–10); and language processing, including the syntactic and semantic aspects of language manipulation, as well as text transformations such as abstracting and text translation (Chapters 11–12.) In Chapter 13, the processing of multimedia items consisting of text, speech, and images is again examined, together with the design of electronic communication systems, such as mail and messaging systems, electronic conferencing, and automatic library and publication systems. The material of Chapters 4–13 is introduced by an examination of the existing computer hardware (Chapter 2) and modern office environments (Chapter 3).

References

1. I. de Sola Pool, Tracking the Flow of Information, *Science*, 221:4611, 12 August 1983, 609–613.

2. C.E. Shannon and W. Weaver, *The Mathematical Theory of Communication*, University of Illinois Press, Urbana, IL, 1949.

3. A.B. Tucker, *Text Processing: Algorithms, Languages and Applications*, Academic Press, New York, 1979.

4. G. Sampath, *An Introduction to Text Processing*, River Valley Publishing Co., Jeffersontown, KY, 1985.

5. H.L. Andrews, Speech Processing, *Computer*, 17:10, October 1984, 315–324.

6. D.H. Klatt, Review of the ARPA Speech Understanding Project, *Journal of the Acoustical Society of America*, 62:6, December 1977, 1345–1366.

7. J.D. Foley and A. van Dam, *Fundamentals of Interactive Computer Graphics*, Addison-Wesley Publishing Co., Reading, MA, 1982.

8. W.M. Newman and R.F. Sproull, *Principles of Interactive Computer Graphics*, McGraw-Hill Book Co., New York, 1979.

9. P.J. Hayes and J.G. Carbonell, *A Tutorial on Techniques and Applications for Natural Language Processing*, Carnegie-Mellon University, Report CS 83-158, Pittsburgh, PA, October 1983.

Chapter 2

The Computer Environment

2.1 Computer Architecture

Over the past 25 years, remarkable changes have occurred in computer architecture and in the ways information is processsed on computers. Vacuum tubes, principal components in early computers, have been replaced by semiconductors, and bulk processes are now used to assemble thousands of components on small computer chips. Along with large-scale reductions in size, current equipment offers increases in both memory capacity and processor speed by factors of several thousand compared with the capabilities of earlier equipment. Further, a great variety of equipment allows many processes to be carried out under the user's direct control. Finally, parallelism now makes it possible for many users to share computing equipment, carrying out a number of different tasks more or less simultaneously. [1]

2.1.1 Large versus Small Machines

Until the mid-1970s, most computing was done by large centralized machines known as *mainframes*. The operations were generally performed off-line — that is, without direct intervention by human beings

— because the expensive equipment could not economically be controlled by individual users in an interactive mode. When a multiprocessing system was available, it usually consisted of a duplicate pair of processors for reliability, allowing an exact twin to continue processing whenever an original unit failed.

Recent advances in large-scale integration (LSI), which have reduced computer costs dramatically, without substantially decreasing performance, have resulted in much smaller machines that are more easily installed and manipulated. These small machines can be directly controlled by users, leading to interactive computations carried out "online." Instead of sharing a central processing unit (CPU) and sending necessary data to the processing sites, many users now have personal machines at their individual sites, and the computing is done where the data are located. [2] The use of smaller machines has also led to specialization of components in the sense that equipment with specialized architectures can be constructed for special-purpose tasks. Specialized small machines are then used for such tasks as connecting a number of terminals to larger *host* machines or controlling message distribution in computer networks.

The simultaneous availability of large mainframe machines and small mini- or microcomputers implies that existing computational needs are no longer automatically met by the powerful, large-scale processing units. Large machines are of course useful when high performance is needed: They can execute many millions of instructions per second (MIPS); they offer a large main memory, an elaborate instruction set, and sophisticated software systems; and they can usually be shared by many users. Smaller machines, however, are more economical. They are also easier to use, require less user training, and are immediately available when needed. Further, the computing power of even small single-chip processors is by no means negligible, rivaling that available on older mainframes. For many day-to-day applications, such as word processing and text manipulation, the small machines provide an ideal online processing environment.

In the future, as both large processing units and small microprocessors become more powerful, the smaller units will be favored for more and more applications.

2.1.2 Sequential versus Parallel Computing

Until recently, computer design was controlled by the von Neumann principle, which provides a single communications *bus* to interconnect a number of different computer units. A typical computer of this type consists of:

1. A command (instruction) processor and a data processor, together constituting the central processing unit;

2. A memory unit for storing of programs and data;

3. An input-output processor to handle communications between the computer and the environment; and

4. Internal data paths using the communications bus to enable information to be interchanged among components.

A simplified design of the von Neumann computer organization is shown in Fig. 2.1. [3]

The operating principle of the conventional computer is based on a two-phase processing system:

1. The contents of a memory cell are obtained and then stored in a command register to be interpreted as a command.

2. The contents of another memory cell specified in that command are then processed in accordance with the specifications given in the command register.

The operations are thus carried out sequentially, using the communications bus to move first a command and later the corresponding data item from one unit to another. Because the connecting path can carry only a single piece of information at one time, it has been called the von Neumann "bottleneck." Recent attempts have been made to speed up operations by removing this bottleneck, either by using memory-

Figure 2.1 Conventional computer organization.

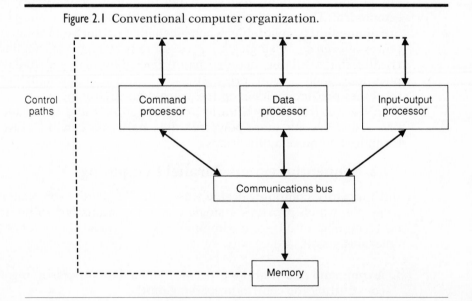

access techniques to stored data that do not require a conventional memory address, or by employing parallelism, which allows several data items to be handled simultaneously.

Several types of parallelism can be distinguished. The *fine-grained* approach consists of improving the efficiency of instruction handling and instruction execution. By providing several different operations units — for example, an adder, a multiplier, and a memory-fetch unit — the corresponding addition, multiplication, and memory-fetch operations can be carried out simultaneously. Further, the execution of complex operations, such as multiplication and division, can often be broken down into smaller steps. In such a *pipeline*, several data elements might occupy an operations unit simultaneously, each situated at a different stage of the operation. Figure 2.2 depicts a four-stage operation of this type: Four different data items can be held in the pipeline at once; when item i is at stage 4 of the operation, item $i+1$ will be at stage 3, item $i+2$ at stage 2, and item $i+3$ at stage 1. Thus five complete four-stage operations can be carried out in the eight time cycles normally needed to handle two sequential four-stage operations. Special-purpose processors, known as *array processors*, are sometimes attached to conventional host machines to provide the fine-grained parallelism inherent in pipelined operations and multiple-operations units.

Figure 2.2 Sequential and pipelined operation for a four-stage instruction.

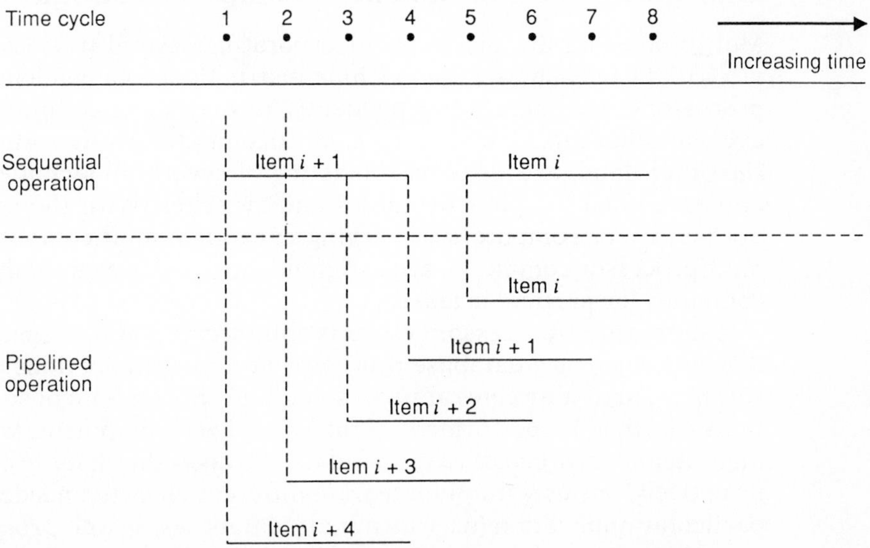

At the other end of the parallelism spectrum is the *coarse-grained* approach, which takes a complete process — say a payroll application or an information-retrieval process — and identifies subprocesses that can be carried out independently. These independent processes can then be overlapped and executed simultaneously on different processors. When several independent processors are used, connections must be provided between them so that the results of independent operations can be passed from one to another as needed.

Many intermediate forms of parallelism are also possible. For example, the memory accesses needed to fetch data elements from memory can be overlapped with the memory accesses used to handle instructions. Alternatively, information transfer to and from disk or other bulk storage devices can be executed independently of the operations of the CPU, making it possible to carry out input-output operations in parallel with normal internal processing. Finally, for certain applications, the number of processors available for parallel use can be increased to several hundred or even several thousand.

Highly parallel machines, consisting of numerous CPUs, primary storage memories, and input-output channels, will no doubt be designed in the near future. Switching arrangements will make it possible to connect each unit of a given type to all units of the other types; in principle, assuming proper program organization, all units will be able to operate simultaneously. A simplifed arrangement of this type is shown in Fig. 2.3.

2.1.3 Multiprocessor and Multicomputer Configurations

Multiprocessors are machines incorporating several processing devices that can each execute machine instructions independently. The processors may operate independently, or may share computer storage and other machine resources. Multicomputer configurations, on the other hand, are systems consisting of several independent machines hooked together by cables and switches. With the growing availability of computers of varying capability, multicomputer and multiprocessor complexes are assembled to provide exactly the right computer for particular tasks.

A simple multiprocessor system is obtained by adding a specialized machine, such as a database processor or a communications processor, to a particular central processing unit. Special-purpose operations can then be performed on the specialized equipment, with the high-capability processors reserved for the tasks they handle best. Alternatively, one can simply integrate different elements needed for a particular application (user terminals, databases, search processors, printing units, and so on) and supply appropriate connections among the various units. Finally, it is possible to interrelate independent machines of varying capabilities, most conspicuously small personal computers and large mainframe machines. In this case, the personal computer user is given access to the memory banks and large databases of the big machine, while the mainframe user can off-load simple user transactions to the smaller personal machines, allowing the large processor to handle the complicated tasks. [4]

Several complex matters must be considered if multiprocessor or multicomputer installations are to be used effectively. First, an ideal mix of machines must be chosen to solve a particular problem. Second, the components must be interconnected to allow the equipment to be best used. Finally, the processing must be organized to use the available resources as effectively as possible. For example, local storage should be used for frequently used data and programs, with summaries or results forwarded from place to place as needed.

In view of the problems that often arise in recognizing independent program fragments and their allocation to different processors, an alternative *data-level* parallel-processing approach has been advocated to solve certain problems. The data-level approach uses a large num-

Figure 2.3 Highly parallel machine, consisting of a variable number of memory units, central processors, and input-output units.

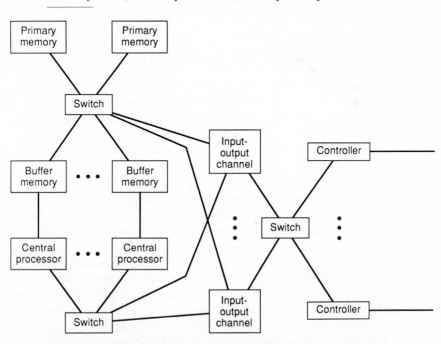

ber of suitably interconnected, identical processing units; instead of executing distinct, independent program fragments, however, each processor, using different sets of data, performs exactly the same processing sequence. The control problems that arise in implementating data-level parallelism are relatively simple: In general it suffices to store a common program in each processor, and to allocate the distinct data elements to the individual processing units as needed. Provisions must also be made to collect the results of computations from the processing units. Data-level parallel processing methods have been suggested, for example, for the analysis of geographic features corresponding to different locations in a given environment. Each processor then handles the data for a different geographic location. In information retrieval, a distinct record could be stored in each processor, allowing the comparisons between the stored records and a given search request to be carried out simultaneously for a large number of records. [5] However, the use of a very large number of processors tends to be expensive, and therefore cost considerations, not technical limitations, may restrict the application of large-scale multiprocessing systems.

2.1.4 Types of Computers

Formerly, computers were considered indivisible equipment complexes with specific capabilities, designed to carry out particular types of tasks. More recently, computers have been assembled in a modular fashion, with the number of subunits varying according to the requirements of particular processing environments. Further, the capabilities of subunits such as processors and memory banks have been substantially improved, to the point where distinctions among different types of computers are now blurred. At present, no clear-cut distinction exists among microcomputers, workstations, superminicomputers, and mainframe computers — other than the obvious fact that the machines at the upper end of the scale are faster, support more users simultaneously, and cost more.

Technically, the principal difference among the various types of computers consists of the degree of parallelism inherent in the design, which in turn affects price and performance. Microcomputers use only fine-grained parallelism with instruction pipelines, and fast intermediate buffer memories, known as *caches*, to speed up access to data storage and instruction memory. Intermediate-size workstations may in addition use direct memory-access methods, which provide memory accesses through separate paths, independent of the CPU. Superminicomputers may use "smart" peripheral parallelism, in which each input-output channel operates its own channel program to control the input-output operations. Finally, large mainframes use duplicated units of many kinds, including many CPUs and various coarse-grained as well as fine-grained parallel approaches.

The parallel-processing capabilities of some typical machines in each category are listed in Table 2.1, together with approximate prices and a processing benchmark number that represents the relative power of the equipment for certain computation-intensive problems. [6] The benchmark figures are computed for single-user tasks, thus underrating the power of the larger machines, which can accommodate many simultaneous users performing many parallel tasks.

2.2 Storage Technology

To allow computers to manipulate information automatically, the necessary data and programs must be stored in machine-readable form. In principle, the medium used for that purpose should have a high storage capacity; in addition, speed of access to the information should be high, and storage costs should be low. In practice, all three criteria are not met by a single device: Instead, the faster the access to the stored information, the higher the cost, and hence usually the lower the storage capacity. Thus most systems use a hierarchy of storage devices, ranging from low-capacity, fast-access, high-cost devices

Table 2.1 Typical computer capabilities.

Machine Type	Example	Approximate Cost	Type of Parallelism	CPU Benchmark
Micro-computer	Apple Macintosh	$1500	fine-grained; fast intermediate buffers for memory access	600
Workstation	SUN-3	$16,000	more pipelined operations than Macintosh; direct memory access to disk without involving CPU; supports 10–20 users	3200
Supermini	Gould 9080	$500,000	full dual processors that can work independently; floating-point operations implemented in hardware; intelligent input-output channels; supports 150 users	5000
Mainframe	IBM 3090	$2,000,000+	all kinds	31,000

for internal storage; to medium-capacity, medium-access, medium-speed devices for secondary storage; to high-capacity, relatively low-cost, low-speed devices for bulk storage. [7]

Internal memory is used to store data and programs that must be immediately available during a process. Because data are modified in the course of the operations, the internal memory must have both read and write capabilities, and random access should be provided — that is, the time required to access each memory cell should be approximately the same. Devices that provide access to stored data in some particular, prespecified order cannot be used to implement internal memory.

Until the 1970s, most internal memories consisted of ferrite cores, arranged in a plane and threaded by wires to allow read and write operations. Core planes were available at reasonable cost and provided acceptably fast access. However, core memories were relatively bulky, required sophisticated read-write circuitry, and had to be manufactured by discrete processes. More recently, semiconductor memories have been developed using integrated circuit techniques that manufacture the complete memory as a bulk process. In the usual MOS (metal oxide semiconductor) technology, one switch is used per memory cell, and chips containing 64K (64 thousand) or 256K bits are now current. The cost per bit is between 1 and 10 cents; access time is of the order of 100 nanoseconds (ns). Future substantial advances in semiconductor technology are expected that will further reduce price and increase storage capacity.

External memories are usually implemented by magnetic storage devices such as disks, drums, cartridges, or cassettes. The information is recorded along tracks arranged on the magnetically coated surface of the device. On disks and drums, the tracks are circular and the information is read as the device spins and the recording surface passes under a read head. Magnetic storage devices do not provide random access because the information recorded on a particular track is available only in the order in which it was recorded originally.

At present, the disk — or the disk pack, consisting of several disks mounted on the same assembly — is most popular for storing large masses of data. Many kinds of disks are available, ranging in diameter from 3 to 14 inches. The disks may be fixed, or may be removable from their drive for external storage away from the machine. In the latter case, the recording densities and storage capacities are smaller because the reading equipment (head) cannot be placed very close to the disk surface. Disks may be hard (that is, rigid) or floppy (flexible). Recording densities, and hence reading speeds, are higher for hard disks than for floppies, as is cost. In many cases, a single read-write assembly is provided for each disk surface, and the read head is physically moved to the proper track before read or write operations can begin;

this method is used to access individual disk sections on certain automatic record players. A faster but more expensive solution consists of providing a separate, fixed read-write head for each disk track, thereby avoiding the delay due to the head movements.

Typical storage capacities are from 150K bytes to 1M (one million) bytes for floppy disks, and from 5M to 600M bytes for large, high-capacity hard disks. The recording densities range from 10^6 to 10^7 bits per square inch, and reading rates of 1M to 3M bits per second (bps) are achievable. A typical random-access rate is 15 to 30 milliseconds to access an item located at a specified address. Disk costs range from a few dollars for small floppies to well over $10,000 for high-capacity, high-performance hard disks.

Disks are used for online storage of large files, in which case they are permanently connected to the computing equipment. They are also used to back up components and replace them if they fail, or for *bulk storage* of files that are not needed continually. In the latter case, the disks are stored away from the machine until needed. Magnetic tape devices also can be used for bulk storage; longitudinal tracks along the length of the tape replace the circular tracks of information used with disks and drums. A standard tape is usually 1/2-inch wide; seven to nine tracks are recorded and read in parallel. Recording densities for high-performance tapes range from 800 to 6250 bits per inch (bpi), and reading speeds are up to 250 inches per second, corresponding to a data rate of over 1M bits per second. Prices for tape transports range from a few hundred dollars to well over $50,000 for high-performance devices. Because the information is recorded along the length of the tape, the stored data must be read sequentially. Thus tapes cannot be used when an application demands fast access to specific data items.

The storage capacity of tape devices can be increased by using a number of tapes in parallel, and providing either reading equipment that moves from tape to tape as needed or a separate fixed head for each tape. Multiple tape cartridges and multiple tape strips both give relatively fast access to very large stores of data. A more recent technique for large-scale bulk storage uses *optical disks*, on which information is recorded by burning microscopic pits with a laser beam. The recorded information is played back by directing another laser beam on the information surface and monitoring the intensity and duration of the reflected light pulses. The bit density within a track is comparable to that obtained with advanced magnetic disks, but the track density is at least 10 times greater — more than 1000M bytes can be stored on one side of a 12-inch disk. Typically, several hundred thousand pages of typed text fit on one side of an optical disk, and text and images can be interspersed. The reading rate may be as high as 3M bits per second, producing random-access rates of 100 to 200 milliseconds, somewhat lower than with magnetic disks.

The great advantage of optical disks is their large storage capacity and relatively low cost. Producing the master copy of a disk costs a few thousand dollars, but duplication costs only $10 to $20. Thus a vendor can ship large recorded data banks to individual end users, letting each user access the files locally, a system that replaces expensive information networks. Because the sharply focused laser beam used for reading and recording need not be placed close to the disk surface (unlike magnetic read-write heads), the laser disks can be easily removed from their device, exchanged, or shipped.

The major disadvantage of optical technology is its nonerasability — the recorded information is physically burned into the surface. This restricts the use of laser disks to storing static information; the introduction of changes in the stored data currently requires another recording of a complete disk. Another temporary disadvantage, the lack of standards for optical technology, makes it difficult to build complete systems incorporating the optical equipment. One fairly widespread implementation consists of using a small compact disk capable of storing 600M bytes, corresponding to about 275,000 pages of printed text, or about 1000 floppy disks. *CD ROM* (compact-disk readonly memory) disk drives cost about $1000 while complete databases, such as word dictionaries or encyclopedias recorded on compact disks, cost between $3000 and $4000 (including the disk player). The recorded information is usually accessed by using a prerecorded index, stored at the beginning of the disk, that identifies the track or tracks containing the corresponding information. Optical technology is expected to replace magnetic devices for the bulk storage of text and images in many applications. [8,9]

Typical performance measures for several storage devices are shown in Table 2.2.

Table 2.2 Performance characteristics of sample storage devices.

Storage Device	Storage Capacity	Approximate Cost (cents per bit)	Random-access Time
Internal semiconductor memory	64K–256K bits	1–10	100 ms
Magnetic high-performance disk	5M–600M bytes	0.1	15–30 ms
Magnetic floppy disk	150K–1M bytes	0.001	20 ms
Optical disk for bulk storage	600M–4000M bytes	0.0001	100–200 ms

2.3 Input-Output and Peripheral Equipment

In the modern computer environment, where users control the computational process from individual terminals, the characteristics of the input-output equipment used to communicate with the processors are crucial. This is especially true because peripheral equipment may account for as much as 75 percent of the cost of the typical modern small computer. Peripheral equipment specifically intended to be used with computing equipment was first constructed in the 1950s; it consisted of magnetic tapes and drums and of devices to transfer data between punched cards and magnetic tapes and, for data entry, between keyboard and tape. During the 1960s, the first online systems were created — for example, for airline reservations — and special-purpose hardware was soon designed for direct interaction with the computer. This development continued in the 1970s with the design of intelligent terminals (those including some processing and storage facilities), high-speed printing equipment, and sophisticated magnetic tape and disk devices.

Two types of input-output devices can be distinguished: those that perform input-output functions but can also be used for external or bulk storage (such as magnetic and paper tape drives and magnetic or optical disk equipment), and those especially designed to transcribe data from a given medium into computer-readable digital form, or vice versa (such as terminal equipment, printing equipment, plotting and display devices, and certain character-handling devices). This second kind of peripheral equipment is examined in the remainder of this section.

❖ 2.3.1 Terminal Equipment

From the user's point of view, the workstation, terminal, or console device is the most important component of a computer system: That device is directly responsible for user satisfaction, or perhaps discomfort. Modern workstations can process many different types of information, including text, business records, graphic images, and possibly speech signals, and can also control the various information-processing operations, such as displaying, creating, editing, storing, retrieving, and transmitting data.

User terminals can be classified according to their processing capability: [10]

- *Voice systems*, such as standard telephones and dictation equipment, and telephones with added answering, message-storing, and message-forwarding capabilities.

- *Word-processing devices*, which generally consist of keyboards and cathode-ray tube (CRT) display systems, together with storage and possibly communications equipment controlled by a micro-processor.

- *Data-processing terminals* designed to enter alphanumeric or text data to host computers or to display data from host computers; these include line-at-a-time typewriters, CRT equipment, and key-to-disk or key-to-tape data-entry stations.

- *Graphics systems*, capable of handling graphics and alphanumeric data, including equipment for storing, displaying, and refreshing graphic data.

- *Image systems*, designed to process images in digital or analog form; such systems have the capability of television sets with additional image-processing facilities.

- *Personal computers* that offer data-processing and word-processing functions in addition to other applications using text data and graphics.

In terms of appearance, the major distinction is between keyboard-printer terminals, which process mostly text and alphanumeric data and provide keyboard input and hard copy output, and, generally more expensive, terminals that can also display graphics. The latter usually include a CRT display and facilities for interaction between the user and the displayed information. [11]

The ideal terminal design is flexible, allowing the user to specify the mode that most suits a particular application by changing only the internal software and possibly the external equipment, such as printers or communications lines, connected to the device. Regardless of their use, all workstations provide the following main components: an input section to introduce information and processing instructions; an output and display section; a file component for local storage and retrieval of data or instructions; a processing component that handles user applications; and a communications component to interface with processors and networks. [11,12]

A great variety of input devices are used with computer terminals, the most common being numeric keypads and alphanumeric keyboards. The terminal keyboard is still the primary means by which textual data are entered into the machine. Such keyboards are similar to those on ordinary typewriters, but may include special keys such as those used to move a position indicator (cursor) on a display screen.

In addition to the keyboard, several kinds of analog devices are used as pointers to designate display-screen locations during text editing and information manipulation. The *mouse*, a popular device, includes buttons and rollers: When the mouse is rolled on a tabletop or other surface near the display device, the cursor automatically moves in the corresponding direction on the screen. *Joy sticks* are levers used to control both the cursor and the information display. *Light pens* are pointing devices that can be directed at the screen to identify particular screen positions. *Graphic pads* may also be used to identify screen location, as well as to specify freehand drawings and handwriting for later introduction into computer storage. Finally, *touch-sensitive displays* allow the user to define objects and screen locations by touching the screen.

Limited voice input is available in some situations. Because of the difficulties inherent in the automatic recognition of speech, however, at present these devices are restricted to small vocabularies, and to message processing using telephone-type equipment.

For information *output*, separate printing equipment may be used (see the next subsection). In addition, the console keyboard is sometimes used for hard copy output, while the display screen serves to present text or graphic output. A standard display provides 24 to 60 lines of text 80 characters wide; it has limited graphics capability. In *bitmapped* displays, each point position on a screen can be specified separately. Thus, instead of a letter of the alphabet being specified as a complete, nondecomposable unit, a letter can be drawn by identifying the individual points of its shape. This makes it possible to display multifont texts and to intersperse text and graphics freely in the same display. The current trend is to offer increasingly greater resolution, that is, increasingly more detailed picture specifications: Some applications provide screens with several hundred thousand to more than a million separately addressable picture points (pixels).

To avoid flicker, CRT displays require refreshing, or regeneration, of the picture some 30 to 60 times a minute. For high-resolution displays, the task of storing and repeatedly moving the image from storage to screen is substantial, requiring considerable storage and processing power.

Many computer terminals are now available as complete workstations with separate file storage components, such as local floppy disk or hard disk drives, or single-chip microprocessors and communication facilities to connect the workstation to local-area networks, including other workstations. Local storage and processing facilities minimize the communications costs, and the use of local connections among workstations also allows equipment to be shared. For example, a common internal memory can be used to service several workstations in parallel. Figure 2.4 shows the components of a typical workstation. [13]

❖ 2.3.2 Printing Equipment

Console terminals are used to input data and to control the data during processing. When permanent, hard copy is needed for large masses of data, however, ordinary consoles cannot be used for output purposes. Printing equipment is an essential component of most data-processing systems; one printer may service a single user or may be shared by many users in parallel.

High-speed printing devices were developed in the 1950s and 1960s to help cope with the output of modern computers. Since then much progress has been made in the design of printing equipment, most recently in color and nonimpact printing. From the point of view of the user and the application, the following printer characteristics are most important: whether impact printing or more modern nonimpact methods produce the printed page; whether the output is produced serially (one character at a time), or a complete line or page is printed simultaneously; whether colored output can be produced; and whether the printer can operate in several different modes (such as with or without color) depending on specifications. [7,14,15]

Until the 1950s, printed output was produced by the well-known *impact technologies*: Typeface characters are brought into contact with paper and ribbon by a moving hammer. The typeface characters may be fully formed when the hammer strikes, or each character may be formed by choosing a number of individual wires or needles from an array of needles (a wire matrix). Figure 2.5 shows how the letter B is formed using a wire matrix of dimension 7 by 5 (7 rows and 5 columns of wires).

The best-known typing elements are the type ball, a golf-ball-sized sphere on which preformed characters are arranged around the cir-

Figure 2.4 Workstation components (adapted from [13]).

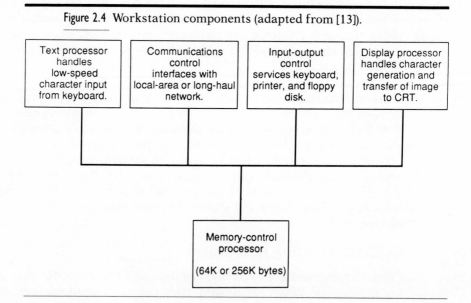

cumference, and the daisywheel, an arrangement of spokes or arms, each carrying a preformed character. For both devices, the hub is rotated until the desired character faces the paper, and then the hammer strikes. There are also belt, band, and chain printers, in which the characters are arranged on a rotating belt and the hammer strikes when the proper character is in position in front of the paper. A disadvantage of all impact printers is the noise created by the striking hammers.

Impact printers can produce multiple copies using carbons or specially prepared paper stock, and many of these printers produce complete lines at a time instead of single characters. For example, a separate 7 by 5 wire matrix, or a separate print wheel with preformed characters, can be provided for each print position across a line, all operating simultaneously. In a serial mode, impact printers produce up to 300 or 400 characters per second; in a line mode, up to 3000 lines per minute. The costs range from a few thousand dollars to more than $100,000, depending on model and capabilities.

Nonimpact printers, which operate without hammers, are therefore relatively free of noise. However, such printers can produce only one copy at a time. Some nonimpact technologies use multilayered paper in which the top layer is vaporized when the writing element applies a current, leaving a visible black image. Other technologies use coated paper that changes color when voltage is applied to the writing element. In thermal-transfer printers, a heat-sensitive paper changes color when heat is applied by the print head.

Newer nonimpact printers use ordinary paper. In the well-known electrophotographic (xerographic) method, for example, a light-sensitive surface is selectively exposed, by using either a photographic image of the characters to be printed or a laser beam, which burns off selected areas. The images are then developed by applying a toner of black or colored particles to the exposed areas; finally, heat is used to transfer the image from the light-sensitive surface to the paper. The process is illustrated in simplified form in Fig. 2.6. Laser printing is

Figure 2.5 Letter B, formed by choosing certain picture points from a 7-by-5 wire matrix.

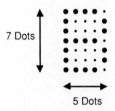

7 Dots

5 Dots

advantageous when high-quality output is needed for a number of different typefonts, or for graphics interspersed with text. Currently, low-speed laser printers producing from 15 to 30 pages per minute cost less than $20,000; printers with speeds of several hundred pages per minute may cost $300,000 or more.

When only standard characters must be printed, simpler, less expensive technologies are available. For example, magnetic printers use magnetic printheads, possibly in the form of a wire matrix, to print characters on a magnetic belt. The information is then developed by using a magnetic toner attracted to the magnetized areas before the transfer onto plain paper. The magnetic belt must be erased before it can be reused. Another nonimpact printer uses ink-jet technology, in which droplets of ink are ejected from a nozzle. In the drop-on-demand process, a separate nozzle is provided for each dot position in a dot matrix; nozzles are activated as needed to form individual characters. In the continuous-stream process, a nozzle produces a continuous stream of droplets, which are deflected by charged plates before they hit the paper. Although ink-jet printers use plain paper, they are not yet competitive in price with impact printers or in quality with methods using preshaped characters.

Both impact and nonimpact technologies can be adapted to line-at-a-time operation by providing a number of print elements operating in parallel. Colored characters also can be printed — for example, by using multicolor ribbons with impact printers. (The correct ribbon must then be in position before the hammer or needle strikes the ribbon.) In ink-jet technology, multiple spray nozzles can be used, one for each color; in transfer technology, several toners of different color can be used serially to produce the final colored output. Color printers are still much more expensive than black-on-white ones. They also are relatively slow and may be unreliable. For example, one must ensure that the multicolor ribbons are not contaminated by overprinting with several colors.

Figure 2.6 Simplified electrophotographic printing process.

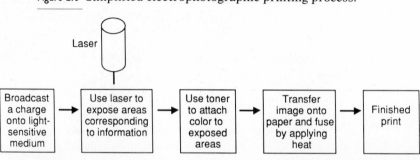

There is a tradeoff between printing speed, on the one hand, and quality or resolution, on the other. Multimode printers help solve this problem by offering different print qualities at distinct speed settings. Thus data-processing quality may be obtainable at high speed, while word-processing or business-letter quality is furnished at lower speeds. In general, engraved (preformed) letter printers offer higher quality than do the wire-matrix printers, and the toned technologies offer higher speed than either the engraved or wire-matrix methods.

In the future, printers with better resolution at high speeds will be available, as will printers that produce output by image formation using bit-mapped screens on which every dot position is separately addressable and printable.

❖ 2.3.3 Document Input

Before an automatic information process can be carried out, the required data must be available in machine-readable form. Document input is becoming much simpler, at least for text, because of the widespread use of word-processing equipment to produce original documents. Many existing older document collections are not available in machine-readable form, however, and certain kinds of materials — for example, pictures and speech — are not easily handled by currently available word-processing methods.

Already existing text materials can be treated in two ways. First, the text can be typed into a machine using a manual keying operation. For large quantities of text, this method is unappealing. Alternatively, some form of character or pattern recognition can be used to distinguish the characters and recreate the text in the machine. Three main character-recognition methods are available: [16,17]

1. A *template match*, in which sample forms of the characters to be recognized are stored in a special file of templates, and the unknown incoming characters are compared with the prestored forms.

2. A *decision-theoretic method*, in which a number of features are isolated for each unknown pattern, and the resulting feature vector is then assigned to the character class that best fits the given feature values.

3. A *syntactic process*, in which complex patterns are decomposed into simpler subpatterns, and the recognition process proceeds hierarchically by first recognizing individual strokes, followed by a determination of the interconnection pattern of the strokes, until a complete character is eventually identified.

Decision-theoretic pattern-recognition methods consist of four parts: feature selection, feature extraction, pattern classification, and learning. In feature selection, known sample patterns are analyzed and those character features are identified that are likely to distinguish a particular type of character from all other characters in the given character set. For alphabetic characters, typical features might be the number of times a given straight line crosses the strokes that form a character, or the maximum height of a character stroke above the baseline of the character, or the length of the longest horizontal or vertical stroke.

After desirable features are identified, each unknown incoming pattern is analyzed, and the values of the corresponding features are computed. Finally, a pattern-classification method is used to assign each unknown pattern to a class — that is, an unknown pattern may be recognized as being a sample of the letter a or the letter c, based on the feature vectors computed for that pattern. A learning procedure also can be built into the recognition process to improve the classification, based on analyzing the results of a given pattern-recognition system.

The procedure for syntactic pattern recognition is similar, except that complex patterns must be broken down into more primitive patterns, and the relationship between primitive features must be recognized before a pattern classification is possible. There exists no general solution to the problem of selecting useful primitive patterns, or of designing effective pattern-classification systems based on the identification of primitives and their relationships.

A complete document-scanning process thus can be subdivided into the following steps: [17,18]

1. The document pages are scanned using, for example, a photodiode array; this produces an analog signal that corresponds to the amount of light reflected from each point position on the document.

2. A segmentation logic then finds individual lines of text on the page, and individual character positions within each line. For individual text characters, the character-segmentation system must take into account imperfections in the input product such as touching or overlapping character sequences.

3. Following character segmentation, the individual character images are registered, and the recognition logic is used to classify each character into a particular character class.

4. Finally, the identified text elements are assembled for computer storage or printout.

Optical character recognition appears to operate satisfactorily when simple typefonts are used for a limited character set and when care is taken to distinguish character combinations with similar shapes, such as e–c, a–ce, a–u, d–ce, g–y, and n–u. Usually ordinary printed texts cannot be controlled sufficiently to permit many text portions to be recognized unambiguously. This is especially true of texts including multiple typefonts and of handwritten text materials. [19–22] Graphic data are normally recognized separately from text, and compression techniques must be used to reduce the number of scanned picture points prior to storage. Graphs and other line art are normally easier to recognize than continuous-tone art such as paintings and photographs.

Typical optical-scanning equipment operating at a rate of one to two pages per minute costs between $2000 and $6000. High-performance equipment that can be used for a large number of different type fonts operating at a rate of six to eight pages per minute may cost $40,000 or more.

The situation is less complicated when documents must be transmitted from place to place but not stored or modified by computer processing. The input problem may then be solved by a *facsimile* process, which does not involve the recognition of individual characters. [23,24] In that case, the document pages can be scanned globally, converting the graphic images to an electrical representation in the form of analog or digital signals. These signals are then transmitted over a common-carrier facility such as a telephone line, and reconverted at the receiving end into the complete image of a printed page.

The facsimile process does not have to distinguish between text and picture portions of a page because the pages are scanned one line at a time. Further, it is easy to achieve high scanning rates — several hundred lines per minute. The main disadvantage is that the output of a facsimile recorder is not machine readable, and thus computer processing of the transmitted information is not possible.

2.4 Computer Networks

Computer networks are collections of computers that use accepted conventions, known as *protocols*, to communicate over connecting transmission media. Computer networks allow users to share resources by making available remotely located processors and data files on demand. A network also serves as a communications medium between users, making it possible for them to forward messages and carry out joint computing activities. Among the more obvious applications of networking are electronic mail and messaging systems, computer conferencing systems connecting diverse sets of participants, remotely located databases such as those used in credit authorization systems, and corporate networks to connect the different components of a single organization. [25]

Network types can be distinguished according to the distance between their components and the amount of information that can be transmitted from one component to another in a given period of time. When the components are separated by more than a few miles, the network is a *long-haul* or *wide-area* network. The transmission rate of data is then relatively low — generally less than 100Kbps. In *local-area* networks (LANs) the separation between components is between 0.1 km and 10 km, and the transmission rate of the data may be as high as 10 million bits per second (10Mbps). Finally, in multiprocessing environments, all computing components are typically located in the same building and very high transmission rates — more than 10Mbps — are possible.

A network consists of two main types of components, *nodes* and *circuits*. A node is an attachment point for a computer system or a terminal that can process new information or simply forward existing information along some path in the network. A circuit is a path from one point in a network to another that supports communications in one or both directions. Operations of computer networks can be described by various characteristics, including the network architecture (the layout of the paths between individual nodes); the individual node composition; the methods used to route information along the network; the channel characteristics, including transmission rate and delay and error characteristics; and the method of control used to set up and break connections and to specify and decode address information. [26]

In generating a network configuration, it is necessary to limit the cost of interconnecting components. This implies that the length of the cables needed to connect the network components must be limited. In these circumstances, a completely *centralized* system, in which one master station is used to control all network operations, is not attractive because the cost of interconnection may be quite high. Centralized networks typically are used for simple inquiry-response systems, in which a number of user terminals are connected to a single teleprocessing system. When two or more users at different stations want to communicate, the master station must first allocate a communications path in a centralized control network. A centralized (star) network configuration is shown in Fig. 2.7(a).

In a *serial* network, each node receives messages from one incoming node and delivers messages to one outgoing node. A ring configuration of this type (see Fig. 2.7b) may then be used. Although the cable length is minimized in a serial organization, the network is difficult to maintain because an error condition at a single site may disable the complete configuration. Alternative network arrangements are often used, such as the *bus* configuration of Fig. 2.7(c) or the *concentration-point* system of Fig. 2.7(d), in which a number of concentrator nodes are connected and each concentrator is a control point for a number of other local nodes.

In a partially decentralized network, no single node controls the communications facilities. Various methods are then available to co-ordinate the access to the network. In a *contention network*, any node can become the master node charged with temporary control, following an exchange of special control messages that ensure that no other station has control of the network. The well-known *token-ring* access system is a ring configuration in which a special message sequence, known as the token, circulates from node to node around the ring. Each node holds the token for a given time period, and is authorized to originate messages during that time, before passing the token to the next node in sequence. [27]

Another decentralized access-control system is the passive broadcasting system used in *Ethernet*. [28] In that network, a message broadcast from an originating station is heard by all other stations, but is copied only by certain destination nodes according to the message ad-

Figure 2.7 Typical network configurations. (a) Star. (b) Ring. (c) Bus. (d) Concentration points.

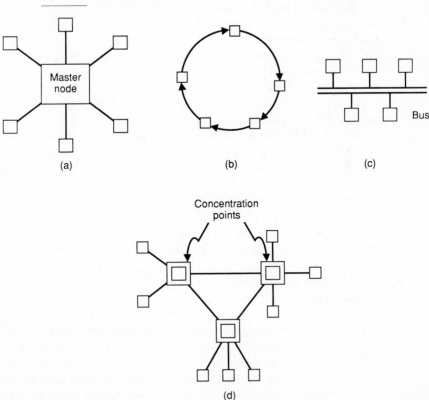

dress. When a *collision* is detected by a node that wishes to transmit a message — that is, when the network is busy with a previously transmitted message — the attempt to transmit the new message is abandoned, and a statistical arbitration system is used that allows the abandoned message to be retransmitted after a dynamically chosen random time period. Normally, the mean retransmission interval is adjusted in proportion to the frequency of collisions.

The connection patterns between nodes in part determines the routing methods used to forward messages. For example, when several possible paths exist between two points in a network, appropriate routing decisions must be made before a message is actually sent. On the other hand, when one communications channel is shared by all nodes, a message sent by one node may be received by all others. No special routing decision is then required; however, all nodes must look at the destination labels of all incoming messages to determine which messages can be ignored and which must be processed.

Communications channels are characterized by various properties, including the error and delay characteristics of the channel, the directional properties of the transmission lines (whether a line can carry information in both directions or in one direction only), and especially the data rates of the channel. Low-speed Teletype transmission operates at between 60 and 100 bps. Medium-speed lines of the kind used for voice-grade communication in a telephone system operate from 300 to 10,000 bps. High-speed lines, known as broadband or wideband, are generally used for computer-to-computer communications and have data rates of 100,000 bps or more; they use advanced transmission media such as microwave links, fiber optics, and satellite links.

The transmission mode used between network points depends on the characteristics of the node (terminal), and on transmission speeds. Asynchronous transmission may be used for low-speed transmission from simple terminals that carry no internal storage. In that case, to permit easy decoding at the receiving end, start and stop codes are inserted before and after each transmitted character. For higher speed transmission, data may be grouped and sent in synchronous mode over a communications channel; the beginning and end of characters are determined by timing mechanisms during character conversion. Synchronous transmission can be used for voice-grade and broadband transmission.

Because modern communications networks are used in large part to transmit mail (messages), special systems have been devised to ensure that messages are properly addressed and distributed at the point of origin, and assembled and received at the destination. [29,30] In the conceptually simple *circuit-switching* system, a circuit is established between two points, as in a conventional telephone network, and for a specified time that circuit is dedicated to two-way communications between the points. This ensures continuity of transmission and reception, but leads to a low utilization of the equipment because of the uneven nature of transmission requirements in a typical two-way communication. In circuit switching, any unused transmission capability cannot be shared by other users or messages.

In *message switching*, discrete entities called messages are broken up into data blocks, and are accepted, transmitted, and delivered as a whole. No physical path exists in advance between source and destination; instead, an address is transmitted at the beginning of each message, and the message-switching system uses this address to guide the message through the network. A message-switching system allows network resources to be used better even though each message is still treated as an entity.

Packet switching is even more flexible: Messages are broken up into independent packets, each carrying identical routing information. The packets can be routed independently to their destinations over different links; at the receiving end, they are reassembled into complete messages before being delivered to users. When the last packet pertaining to a message is received, an acknowledgment packet may be returned to the originating node to terminate the transmission for that message. The packet-switching mode allows available transmission facilities to be utilized efficiently, because in many cases packets can be transmitted in parallel. Further, there are fewer delays because individual packets can be transmitted as soon as they are received, without having to wait for complete messages. Figure 2.8 shows the decomposition of message blocks and packets in message switching and packet switching, respectively.

Figure 2.8 Message decomposition. (a) Decomposition of first transmitted block in a message-switching system. (b) Decomposition of first transmitted packet in a packet-switching system.

Block identifier	Total blocks	Destination address	Sender address	Block 1	Text of block	Block-control character

(a)

Packet identifier	Total packets	Destination address	Sender address	Packet 1	Text of package	Redundancy check

(b)

For network operations, the tasks needed to transform an incoming message into a stream of information bits ready for transmission are specified by the communications protocol, and carried out by a communications controller interposed between network nodes and transmission lines. The controller can be charged with message transformation, using, for example, compression of data, decomposition of messages into blocks, addition of control information, choice of outgoing transmission lines, and final linking to particular lines.

Many of the network characterizations already outlined apply to all types of networks, including the long-haul networks designed for large, dispersed user populations as well as the local networks that connect personnel and computers within a single organization. The short transmission distances of LANs allow very high bandwidth, with transmission of large amounts of information between nodes, as well as low transmission delay and good reliability. [31,32]

A typical LAN is implemented as a packet-switched contention network, in which each node can gain master control and collisions between nodes are detected and resolved. Because of the expansion of automated mail systems, and the increasing need to process electronic information files, the number and size of available computer networks are expected to increase.

2.5 Integrated Computing Systems

The preceding sections covered current developments in the design of individual computing components, the organization of information-processing systems, and the structure of computer networks. When all these components are used in a single computing environment, the result is a powerful system that performs many operations locally and uses remote databases and facilities when needed. [33]

The modern system consists of a hierarchy of components, outlined in Fig. 2.9:

1. Local workstations with keyboards, display screens, pointing devices, and printers;

2. Connections from each set of workstations to local files and high-speed printers;

3. Local-area networks that connect various processing devices and workstations within a limited geographic area; and

4. Long-distance networks that provide access to large processing resources and to expensive databases that cannot be duplicated locally.

Although such a system gives the user powerful processing capability, using it effectively can be burdensome. The many components and modes of operation allow many operating choices, requiring the user to have considerable expertise. To give less sophisticated users access to the system, various mechanisms have been designed, including tutorial learning sequences, diagnostic systems designed to detect questionable user behavior, sequences (menus) of possible operations to guide users through critical areas in the processing cycle, and user-friendly display systems based on simple object displays and understandable mnemonic designations. In the future, attempts to incorporate into the computational process knowledge derived from human expert informers may help streamline many data-processing activities such as file accessing and file searches. [34,35] For now, the barrier faced by the nonprofessional in using available processing resources effectively and efficiently remains formidable, and flexible user-system interfaces and automated programming aids must help to bridge the gap between increasingly sophisticated processing complexes and the relatively limited expertise of many potential users.

Figure 2.9 Components of a modern computing system.

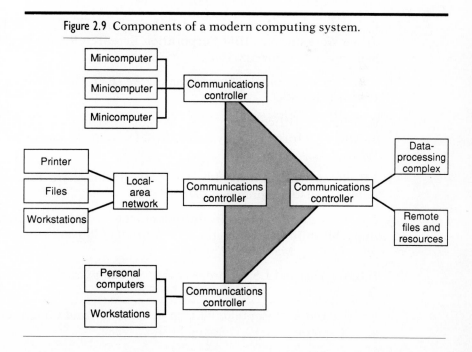

References

1. J.L. Baer, Computer Architecture, *Computer*, 17:10, October 1984, 77–86.

2. H. Gerola and R.E. Gomory, Computers in Science and Technology: Early Indications, *Science*, 6 July 1984, 225:4657, 11–18.

3. W.K. Giloi, *Rechnerarchitektur*, Springer-Verlag, Berlin, 1981.

4. B.C. Goldstein, A.R. Heller, F.H. Moss, and I. Wladawky-Berger, Directions in Cooperative Processing between Workstations and Hosts, *IBM Systems Journal*, 23:3, 1984, 236–244.

5. D.L. Waltz, Applications of the Connection Machine, *Computer*, 20:1, January 1987, 85–97.

6. S. Spanier, SUN-3 Benchmarks, Internal Memorandum, August 1985.

7. L.C. Hobbs, Printing and Storage Peripherals: Past, Present, and Future, *Computer*, 17:10, October 1984, 225–241.

8. F.E. Marsh, Jr., Videodisc Technology, *Journal of the ASIS*, 33:4, July 1982, 237–244.

9. C.M. Goldstein, Optical Disk Technology and Information Science, *Science*, 215:12, February 1982, 862–868.

10. R.D. Selinger, A.M. Patlack, and E.D. Carlson, The 925 Family of Office Workstations, IBM Corporation Research Report RJ 3406, San Jose, CA, February 1982.

11. L.C. Hobbs, Terminals, *Proceedings of the IEEE*, 60:11, November 1972, 1273–1283.

12. B. Scheurer, Office Workstation Design, International Workshop on Office Information Systems, St. Maximin, France, October 1981.

13. J.E. Shemer and J.R. Keddy, The Soft Display Word Processor, *Computer*, 11:9, September 1978, 39–48.

14. R.A. Myers and J.C. Tamulis, Introduction to Topical Issue on Non-Impact Printing Technologies, *IBM Journal of Research and Development*, 28:3, May 1984, 234–240.

15. H.S. Watkins and J.S. Moore, A Survey of Color Graphics Printing, *IEEE Spectrum*, 21:7, July 1984, 26–37.

16. K.S. Fu and A. Rosenfeld, Pattern Recognition and Computer Vision, *Computer*, 17:10, October 1984, 274–282.

17. R.G. Casey and C.R. Jih, A Processor-based OCR System, *IBM Journal of Research and Development*, 27:4, July 1983, 387–399.

18. K.Y. Wong, R.G. Casey and F.M. Wahl, Document Analysis System, *IBM Journal of Research and Development*, 26:6, November 1982, 647–656.

19. C.C. Tappert, Cursive Script Recognition by Elastic Matching, *IBM Journal of Research and Development*, 26:6, November 1982, 765–771.

20. M. Eden, Handwriting Generation and Recognition, in *Recognizing Patterns*, MIT Press, Cambridge, MA, 1968.

21. N. Lindgren, Machine Recognition of Human Language, Part 3 — Cursive Script Recognition, *IEEE Spectrum*, 2, May 1965, 104-116.

22. L.D. Harmon, Automatic Recognition of Print and Script, *Proceedings of the IEEE*, 60:10, October 1972, 1165–1176.

23. D.H. Axner, The Facts about Facsimile, *Data Processing Magazine*, 10:5, May 1968, 42–51.

24. T.B. Holmes, A Facsimile Primer, AFIPS Office Automation Conference, Houston, TX, March 1981.

25. J.S. Quarterman and J.C. Hoskins, Notable Computer Networks, *Communications of the ACM*, 29:10, October 1986, 932–971.

26. T.N. Pyke, Jr., and R.P. Blanc, Computer Network Technology — A State of the Art Review, *Computer*, 6:8, August 1973, 12–19.

27. R.C. Dixon, N.C. Strole, and J.D. Markov, A Token-Ring Network for Local Data Communications, *IBM Systems Journal*, 22:1 and 2, 1983, 47–62.

28. R.M. Metcalfe and D.R. Boggs, Ethernet: Distributed Packet Switching for Local Computer Networks, *Communications of the ACM*, 19:7, July 1976, 395–404.

29. R.E. Kahn, Resource Sharing Computer Communications Networks, *Proceedings of the IEEE*, 60:11, November 1972, 1397–1407.

30. L.G. Roberts, Data by the Packet, *IEEE Spectrum*, 11:2, February 1974, 46–51.

31. N.C. Strole, A Local Communications Network Based on Interconnected Token Access Rings: A Tutorial, *IBM Journal of Research and Development*, 27:5, September 1983, 481–496.

32. J.F. Shoch, Y.K. Dalal, and D.D. Redell, Evolution of the Ethernet Local Computer Network, *Computer*, 15:8, August 1982, 10–27.

33. R.J. Spinrad, Office Automation, *Science*, 215:4534, 12 February 1982, 808–813.

34. B. Shneiderman, The Future of Interactive Systems and the Emergence of Direct Manipulation, Computer Science Department, University of Maryland, Technical Report TR 1156, College Park, MD, April 1982.

35. H. Mozeico, A Human/Computer Interface to Accommodate User Learning Stages, *Communications of the ACM*, 25:2, February 1982, 100–104.

Chapter 3

The Automated Office

3.1 The Office Environment

The new computing environment has substantially changed the way in which many information-processing problems are solved. In particular, hands-on computing now makes it possible for users to directly control complex operations in a dynamic environment. As a result, new approaches are being taken not only in many scientific and technological applications, but also in most commercial and data-processing tasks. The conventional business office provides a particularly good example of the changed information-processing situation — an office is a complex environment for processing many diverse objects, involving interactions and communications among different classes of participants. In the modern office, all the well-known processing tasks, including dictating, typing, editing, mailing, and filing, have been eliminated, or at least substantially altered, by new systems and procedures.

Because of the complexity of the office situation, a global approach must be used in analyzing tasks and introducing new methods, taking into account the many factors that influence the office environment. Introducing new procedures necessarily involves the hardware

described in the last chapter, including especially intelligent workstations and small computers, imaging and printing equipment, the local
networking systems, and communications equipment for remote data
access. In addition, a complicated software environment must be dealt
with that integrates various classes of information, including the
natural-language text of business forms and letters, the structured
data of normal business files, and the graphic and pictorial information often used to characterize and illustrate business situations. In
certain modern office environments, voice responses may be provided
in answer to certain inquiries, in which case voice data must also be
processed. Much of the rest of this book stresses the processing of
natural-language text. In this chapter the emphasis is on manipulating
structured data files of the type prevalent in business environments.

New office environments may result in the following advantages
and improvements in productivity: [1,2]

- Rationalized office procedures, including better throughput, less
  time required to perform various tasks, fewer data transformations,
  increased control over operations, and speedier decision making;

- Efficient mail-handling methods, including speedy intra- and inter-
  office communications, fast outside communications, and few
  wasted steps;

- Effective conferencing facilities, such as telephone interactions enhanced by automatically supplied visual aids;

- Effective information storage and retrieval facilities, providing fast
  access to correspondence, memoranda, contracts, and data;

- Mechanized calendar functions, including automated reminder procedures and the management of scheduled activities; and

- Decision-support facilities providing a choice of methodologies
  based on a thorough understanding of the existing situation, fast responses to unexpected happenings, and better utilization of resources and data.

The success of any analysis and rationalization effort in a complex
environment depends on completely understanding the various elements included in the environment and the interactions among them.
In the office environment, three main factors must be distinguished:
participants such as managers, professional people, secretaries, and
clerks; *objects* such as furniture, file cabinets, bulletin boards, waste-
paper baskets, clocks, calendars, and many kinds of machines; and the
activities carried out by the participants. [3–7] Relations among these
three factors must be considered. For example, secretaries devote substantial time to preparing and manipulating office forms; clerks file

documents; and managers may spend much time on the telephone, or away from the office. Office objects are physically related by various containment properties: Desks contain note pads that in turn contain messages; file drawers contain folders that contain office forms; forms contain information, broken down into rows and columns of data listed in a particular order. Office activities can be characterized by their overall purpose, the priority of the tasks, the time involved, the resources needed, and the frequency of the tasks. In general, complete tasks can be broken down into small steps, involving the transformation of particular data items and the manipulation of specific office forms.

Mechanization and rationalization might be restricted to high-activity components such as the handling of the payroll, cash transactions, and office correspondence. An exhaustive analysis might also affect the less conventional, normally hidden activities, such as preparing periodic reports, filing patent disclosures, and scheduling vacation periods for office personnel.

Because people work in offices, human factors must be considered in any mechanization and rationalization effort. Particularly important are the possibility of increased stress on the office workers, as well as their possible alienation as a result of the changed office environment.

3.2 Analyzing Office Systems

Corresponding to the important factors in office environments — especially participants, objects, and activities — several kinds of office models have been proposed: *agent-based*, *data-based*, and *process-based* models. [8, 9]

In agent-based models, the viewpoint is that of active participants in the system and of their activities. Each agent is presumed to be responsible for a number of tasks involving the use of various objects. A process can then be represented as a sequence of actions initiated by certain individuals and of reactions from the outside. Because of the dynamic nature of the office environment, the changing nature of work assignments, and the multiple interactions among persons and objects, however, agent-based models do not always provide a simple, easily understandable picture of the office environment.

Data-based models are characterized by the flow of information through office systems, and by the data transformations carried out to achieve certain desired results. For example, the number of hours worked in a period of time can be used to obtain salary as well as withholding figures for tax and other purposes. Because office procedures are often accompanied by form manipulations, a detailed data-based view may also be based on operations performed with office forms. [10–12]

A form consists of background text, plus special elements, called *fields*, containing the data items that represent the values of attributes characterizing the form. For example, an order form can be characterized by attributes such as name and address of the person placing the order, the name and address of the organization to whom the order is sent, and the names, quantities, and prices of the items ordered. To generate a particular type of form, it is necessary to use the background information associated with forms of that type, known as the *template*, and to supply specific values for the attributes associated with the open fields of the template. [11] Sample form-template and form-type specifications are contained in Table 3.1.

Table 3.1 Sample form characterization and form template (adapted from [11]).

Invoice Attributes

Invoice number, Customer name, Customer address, Invoice date, Order number, Order date, Item name, Unit cost, Number of items, Total cost, Sales tax, Item weight, Total weight, Shipping charge, Amount payable, Status

Invoice Operations

Verify customer name from customer order
Check item availability and inventory status
Calculate shipping weight from unit weight and number of items ordered
Calculate amount payable from unit cost, number of items, sales tax and shipping charge

Template for Shipping Notice

[Customer Name]
[Customer Address]

Dear Customer:

In accordance with your earlier order [order number] we are sending you the following items

[number of items] of [item name]

by express mail. We appreciate receiving your order.

Sincerely yours,

Special form-processing systems have been constructed that offer facilities for form specification and generation, as well as form processing, manipulation, and routing. Varying degrees of sophistication can be built into a form-processing system, depending on the variety of data classes to be manipulated. Some systems accept only vector-type data structures — for example, objects characterized by sets of attributes. Alternatively, tree-type or network-type objects may be allowed, where hierarchical or other relations among attributes are defined. The user interface may consist of individual forms and of simple screen operations sufficient to display short programs. On the other hand, facilities may be provided for overlapping several forms on a single screen, and for relating particular form operations to dynamic changes on the display screen. Different kinds of programming interfaces may be available, including ordinary programming languages with embedded commands for special-purpose form operations, or complete form-processing languages that operate separately from the ordinary programs. In the latter case, the process specification may be command driven, or menus of possible operations may be provided from which the user chooses appropriate entries at each point.

Program executions and data manipulations may depend on the occurrence of prior events. Thus acknowledgment letters can be automatically generated upon receipt of orders; at the same time a filing process may be used to file the orders, and notices may be sent to check an inventory file before the orders are filled. A so-called *trigger operations manager*, controlled by the occurrence of certain scheduled or unscheduled events, is normally used to initiate the generation and routing of forms.

Many form-processing systems provide access to underlying utilities, such as database management systems and storage and retrieval systems, that access stored files to obtain the information needed by the form-processing system. Most form-processing systems also check for correctness: first for the contents and appearance of individual forms, then for their processing and routing, and finally for the interactions among them. The main components of form-processing systems are shown in Table 3.2; a typical form system is outlined in Fig. 3.1.

The left side of Fig. 3.1 shows the form-specification system, based on a form directory that defines form templates and form structures, and a data dictionary that contains the specifications for the data items that are added to the form templates to build a completed form. The actual form-manipulation system is shown on the right side of the figure. The operations may include the creation, alteration, dissemination, condensation, and display of forms, as well as the retrieval of information included on the forms in answer to users' queries. All

Figure 3.1 Typical form-processing system (adapted from [10]). (S.B. Yao, A.R. Hevner, Z. Shi, and D. Luo, Formanager: An Office Forms Management System, *ACM Transactions on Office Informations Systems*, Vol. 2, July 1984. Reprinted with permission.)

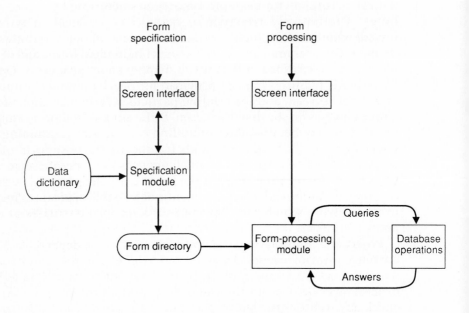

these operations can be controlled by a file-management system of the type described in the next section.

Table 3.2 Components of form-processing system.

Menu-processing system: displays allowed operations

User help and tutorial system: displays advice and tutorial sequences

Form-processing system: creates, alters, stores, retrieves, disseminates, receives, condenses, lists, and displays forms

Trigger-operation manager: initiates scheduled or unscheduled events at particular times

Operation-control system: when certain commands are executed, initiates additional programs

Integrity and correctness-checking system: verifies completeness and correctness of data

Complete process-based models are also used to represent the office environment. A carefully prepared process-based model may eliminate existing inefficiences and redundancies and produce a rational and streamlined set of operations. In such a model, an activity is broken down into individual steps, and transitions from step to step are controlled by specific preconditions. Given that a particular step has just been performed, the preconditions for the successor steps are verified, and the subsequent actions are performed when the corresponding preconditions become true. A process-based model can be represented in network form, with nodes corresponding to actions or activities, and branches indicating transitions from one activity to another controlled by stated conditions attached to the branches. [13,14]

Normally the synchronization structure between activities is defined when a procedure is specified. For example, whenever an order is received for a given product, the inventory may be checked and, provided sufficient quantities of the product are on hand, a shipping order may be generated. A process-based model may also support dynamic communication between procedures, where the conditions depend on abnormal situations, or on events that are themselves dynamically controlled. For example, a product-order procedure may be automatically initiated whenever an inventory item falls below a certain level as a result of earlier order-filling actions. Alternatively, a process may be changed depending on the vacation schedule of the personnel or the availability of important documents.

Figure 3.2, representing a simplified editorial process for articles submitted by authors to journal editors, depicts a typical dynamic processing environment. [13] Certain *triggers* will "fire" after a certain time upon fulfillment of the trigger conditions. For the process of Fig. 3.2 this will happen if either referees or authors do not reply to requests by a fixed time. A real editing process, of course, must prevent the endless loops in Fig. 3.2 produced by continuous inaction on the part of authors or referees.

3.3 File-management Systems

3.3.1 System Characteristics

All abstract office models, whether agent based, data based, or process based, must eventually concern themselves with operations performed on individual data items in the office files. Special processing systems — known as *file-processing*, or *database management* systems — have been created to manage operations on collections of data, and to simplify file access for the users. [15–17] Database management systems usually create and manipulate files, ensure smooth interactions between users and file system through special file-processing languages and control procedures, maintain data correctness and consistency using the available syntactic and semantic definitions of the data, provide appropriate file organizations for the stored data, and preserve the integrity and security of the file system in the face of errors and breakdowns.

A simplified view of a database management system (DBMS) appears in Fig. 3.3. As the figure shows, the DBMS is interposed between users and the stored files. When a DBMS is used, the file structure is usually specified abstractly by a set of file-composition statements known as a *schema*, which hide the details of the physical file arrangement. A high-level *data-definition* language is often used to specify the file schema, and a corresponding *data-manipulation* language to access and manipulate the files. The DBMS uses stored data dictionaries

Figure 3.2 Simplified dynamic processing system for handling articles submitted by authors to journal editors.

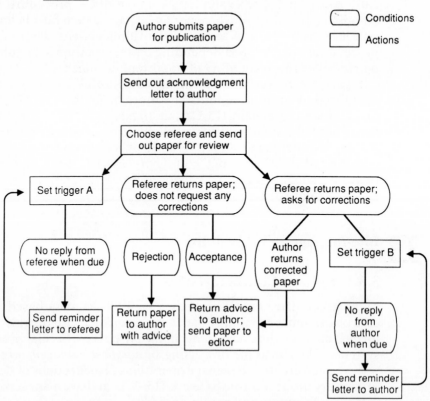

and physical file specifications to translate the statements in the high-level data-definition and data-manipulation languages into actual file operations. The DBMS thus provides physical data independence, in the sense that the physical file arrangement can be altered without affecting the user's applications programs. Logical data independence is also provided: The conceptual schema that specifies file structure is maintained independently of the user programs.

The success of database management systems rests with the relatively simple structure of many business files. A typical file is composed of a set of records characterized by file attributes, also known as file *domains*. A particular record in a file is identified by specific values for each of the attribute domains characterizing the file. Table 3.3(a) gives the attribute domains used to characterize the records in a sample Publications file, and Table 3.3(b) contains the actual *attribute values* for three sample records in that file. As the example shows, each record represents a published article identified by the relevant bibliographic information for the article.

Figure 3.3 Typical database management system.

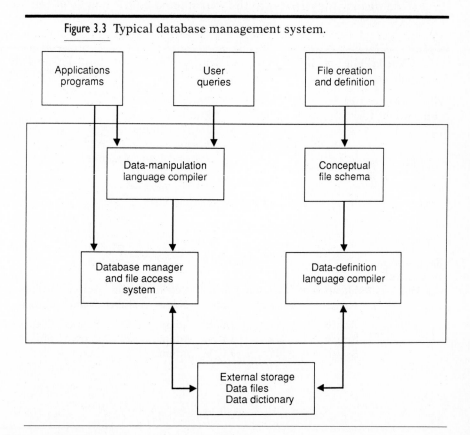

In a structured file environment such as that of Table 3.3, the content analysis and content representation of a record are reduced to the choice of appropriate values for the objective attributes used to characterize the file. This contrasts with the treatment of unstructured files of natural-language text, where content analysis is a major problem, and objective attributes are not usually appropriate to represent content.

❖ 3.3.2 Relational Database Systems

In early database management systems, a special order was normally imposed on the elements of each file, and that order was used in providing appropriate file access. A hierarchical arrangement of file attributes might be imposed, or perhaps a network structure, and hierarchically superior file elements would be accessed first before other, subordinate elements could be reached. A hierarchical view of the Publications file is shown in Fig. 3.4, where the set of publishers constitutes the primary file element. In this example, each publisher name provides access to the journal and editor names of the journals

Table 3.3 File specification for Publications file. (a) Attribute domains. (b) Sample records.

File attributes for Publications file	Publisher Name
	Publisher Address
	Journal Name
	Editor Name
	Journal Issue Number
	Author Name
	Author Address
	Article Title

(a)

Sample Records in Publications File

Publication Name	Publication Address	Journal Name	Editor Name	Issue Number	Author Name	Author Address	Article Title
Smith	NY	JACM	Adams	23	Brown	Phila.	ABC
Smith	NY	JACM	Adams	23	Brown	Phila.	DEF
Smith	NY	JACM	Adams	23	Cod	NY	GHI
				.			
				.			
				.			

(b)

belonging to that publisher. Journal names are used in turn to obtain information about individual journal issues, and about the authors and the titles of articles appearing in particular issues.

As Fig. 3.4 makes clear, a file hierarchy, or file network, can provide simple and inexpensive access to the primary attribute information located at the top of the file structure, but that access is much less convenient to the information listed at the bottom of the structure. In the file represented, access to the publisher information can be rapid because the corresponding information occurs early in the access structure. On the other hand, in the absence of specially constructed supplementary indexes, access to the author information will be inconvenient, because the authors cannot be accessed unless the corresponding publishers and journals are known first.

The *relational database,* an approach developed over the past 10 to 15 years, gives up the advantages of especially rapid access to certain file components. In the relational system, a file is considered to be a two-dimensional table known as a *relation*, such as that illustrated in Table 3.3(b). In the table, each record, or *tuple*, appears as a row, while each column represents the assignment of values of some file attribute

Figure 3.4 Hierarchical access to publication file.

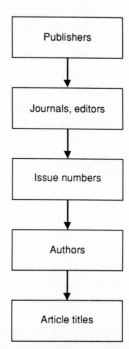

to the records of the collection. In the relational view all attributes are treated as equally important, and there is no preferred file-access order.

The file arrangement of Table 3.3(b) appears to be extraordinarily inefficient in terms of storage space because publisher names and addresses must apparently be stored repeatedly for each journal article pertaining to a particular publisher. The same appears true for the editor names, repeated for each article edited by an editor, and for the author addresses, included for each article written by an author. However, much of the storage redundancy apparently inherent in the relational approach can be eliminated by taking into account dependencies among file attributes, and storing the data for dependent attributes in separate files.

A file attribute B is said to be *functionally dependent* on another file attribute A (written $A \rightarrow B$), if each value of attribute A uniquely determines the corresponding value of B: That is, distinct values of B must correspond to distinct values of A. In the example of Table 3.3, the publisher names functionally determine the publisher addresses (or publisher addresses are functionally dependent on publisher names) because each publisher lives at a particular address; similarly, the author names and article titles jointly determine the journal names and issue numbers in which the articles are published. Note, however, that the author names alone do not determine the journal names — an author may of course write many articles published in various places.

Whether functional dependencies exist is determined by using the semantic properties of the attributes in a given file environment. For example, in situations where a publisher or author may own two different homes, the corresponding functional dependency between names and addresses must be eliminated. Similarly, if the publication system is designed to ensure that all published articles have unique titles, a functional dependency is defined between article titles and the corresponding journal names and issue numbers.

Dependencies among file attributes can be used to decompose the Publications file of Table 3.3(b) into the four subfiles of Table 3.4: Publisher, Journal, Author, and Article. The decomposition of Table 3.4 separates publisher information from author information, and both publisher and author information from journal and article information. Each publisher and author address is now listed only once, as are the names of journal editors. In decomposed form, the separate relations can be independently manipulated and updated — for example, a new publisher name and address can be added to the Publisher relation even if the corresponding author or journal information are not available.

Not all file decompositions are equally desirable. In practice, the decomposition should preserve dependency — the dependencies between attributes that exist in the full relation should also be present in the decomposed relations. Further, it should be possible to recover the full relation without loss or extraneous information from the decomposed form, a property known as *lossless join*.

When two relations contain at least one common attribute, they can be joined to form a combined relation. The combined relation is formed by juxtaposing all pairs of tuples from the individual relations for which the attribute values of the common attributes (known as the *join attributes*) agree in each case. Thus the Publisher and Journal relations of Table 3.4 can be joined using the join attribute Publisher Name to form the combined Publisher-Journal relation shown in Table 3.5. The Publisher-Journal relation contains only two tuples, because only one common publisher name (Smith) exists that matches the first tuple of the Publisher relation with the first two tuples of the Journal relation. The combined Publisher-Journal relation can in turn be joined to the Article relation using join attribute Journal Name to form the Publisher-Journal-Article relation shown in Table 3.5. When this last relation is joined to the Author relation using Author Name, the original relation of Table 3.3(b) is restored. The file decomposition of Table 3.4 thus exhibits the lossless-join property.

In a relational database, the tuples in a relation must be distinct. Hence each relation includes a subset of attributes — known as key attributes, or *keys* — whose values distinguish the tuples from each other. For the Publisher, Journal, Author, and Article relations of Table 3.4, the key attributes are Publisher Name, Journal Name, Author Name, and the combination of Article Title and Author Name, respectively. In a form of file decomposition known as the third normal form, all the existing functional determinants (that is, the left sides of all functional dependency formulas) are either keys or parts of keys. For a relation not already in third normal form, a lossless-join, dependency-

Table 3.4 Subfile decomposition for Publications file of Table 3.3(b).

Publisher	Publisher Name	Publisher Address	Journal	Journal Name	Publisher Name	Editor Name
	Smith	NY		CACM	Smith	Wolf
	Stanton	NY		JACM	Smith	Adams
	Taylor	Boston		JASIS	Evans	Black

Author	Author Name	Author Address	Article	Article Title	Author Name	Journal Name	Issue Number
	Brown	Phila.		ABC	Brown	JACM	23
	Blue	NY		DEF	Brown	JACM	23
	Cod	NY		GHI	Cod	JACM	23

preserving decomposition into third normal form can always be found. [15–17]

❖ 3.3.3 Relational Data Manipulations

Relational databases are conceptually attractive because, at least in principle, they provide standard access procedures for any combination of variables. Two main types of data-manipulation languages have been proposed, known as *relational algebra* and *relational calculus*. Relational algebra is a procedural language that provides the following main operations:

1. The *select* operation $\sigma(A)$ chooses certain tuples of a relation A (certain rows of the file) according to a logical condition P imposed on the attributes of the relation. For example, $\sigma_{\text{Publisher Name} = \text{'Smith'}}$ (Journal) produces the first two rows of the Journal relation of Table 3.4.

2. The *project* operation $\Pi(A)$ chooses certain designated columns of a relation A. For example, $\Pi_{\text{Author Name, Journal Name}}$ (Article) produces the two tuples

> (Brown JACM)
> (Cod JACM) .

when applied to the relations of Table 3.4.

Table 3.5 Natural join of relations of Table 3.4(a). (a) Join of Publisher and Journal. (b) Join of Publisher, Journal, and Article.

Publisher, Journal	Publisher Name	Publisher Address	Journal Name	Editor Name
	Smith	NY	CACM	Wolf
	Smith	NY	JACM	Adams

(a)

Publisher, Journal, Article	Publisher Name	Publisher Address	Journal Name	Editor Name	Article Name	Author Name	Issue Number
	Smith	NY	JACM	Adams	ABC	Brown	23
	Smith	NY	JACM	Adams	DEF	Brown	23
	Smith	NY	JACM	Adams	GHI	Cod	23

(b)

3. The *Cartesian product* of two relations A and B, written $A \times B$, produces a new relation with all possible tuple combinations (a,b), where a is a tuple in A, and b a tuple in B. For example, if

$$A = \begin{bmatrix} a_1b_1 \\ a_1b_2 \end{bmatrix} \text{ and } B = \begin{bmatrix} c_1c_1d_1 \\ c_2c_2d_2 \end{bmatrix}, \text{ then } A \times B = \begin{bmatrix} a_1b_1c_1d_1 \\ a_1b_1c_2d_2 \\ a_1b_2c_1d_1 \\ a_1b_2c_2d_2 \end{bmatrix}$$

4. The *union* of two relations $(A \cup B)$ with identical sets of attributes is the relation C of distinct tuples t such that t is an element of A or t is an element of B.

5. The *difference* between two relations $(A - B)$ with identical sets of attributes is the relation C of all tuples in A that are not also in B.

Additional algebraic operations can be derived from the five basic ones, including the intersection between two relations A and B with identical attributes, consisting of the common tuples contained in both relations, and the previously mentioned join operation, a restricted Cartesian product whose tuples obey a stated logical condition. Thus the join of Publisher and Author with (Publisher Address = NY and Author Address = NY) is the relation

Smith	NY	Blue	NY
Smith	NY	Cod	NY
Stanton	NY	Blue	NY
Stanton	NY	Cod	NY

Instead of using procedural relational algebra to specify file-processing operations, several forms of a nonprocedural relational calculus are available. In *tuple-relational calculus*, the variables represent tuples. The general form of search statement is $\{t|P(t)\}$ representing all tuples t that obey the logical formula $P(t)$. For example, $\{t \mid t \in$ Publisher and Address = 'Boston'$\}$ retrieves the tuple (Taylor, Boston) from the Publisher relation of Table 3.4. In the equivalent *domain-relational calculus*, the variables refer to the domains of relations rather than to the tuples. In domain-relational calculus, the previous query would be expressed as $\{(pn, pa) \mid (pn, pa) \in$ Publisher and pa = 'Boston'$\}$, where the variables pn and pa designate the domains Publisher Name and Publisher Address, respectively.

A processing language that is at least as powerful as relational calculus is said to be *relationally complete*. Relational algebra is known to be relationally complete because a reduction procedure exists that transforms any calculus expression into an equivalent expression in relational algebra. In principle, then, it is immaterial whether a processing language is based on the algebra or the calculus since the two are equivalent.

One well-known data-manipulation language, SQL (formerly called Sequel), combines relational algebra and relational calculus. [18] The basic statement in SQL is a SELECT-FROM-WHERE combination, where SELECT specifies a projection, FROM designates the relevant relations, and WHERE introduces a logical condition statement. In SQL, the previous sample query concerning the publishers living in Boston would be expressed as

```
SELECT    Publisher Name, Publisher Address
FROM      Publisher
WHERE     Publisher Address = 'Boston'
```

When an attribute name *A* appears in more than one relation, ambiguity is avoided by writing R.A to refer to attribute *A* of relation *R*. This makes it possible to express a natural join operation in SQL as a standard SELECT-FROM-WHERE combination. For example, a query requesting the names and addresses of authors of articles in the *Journal of the Association for Computing Machinery (JACM)* can be implemented as a Cartesian product between the Author and Article relations of Table 3.4:

```
SELECT    Author Name, Author Address
FROM      Author, Article
WHERE     Author.Author Name = Article.Author Name
          AND Journal Name = 'JACM'
```

An alternative formulation for the join in SQL is based on the IN operator. This implementation first chooses a subset of tuples from one relation, and then restricts the chosen tuples by conditions that operate on a different relation. Thus the previous query can also be written as

```
SELECT    Author Name, Author Address:
FROM      Author
WHERE     Author Name IN
              SELECT    Author Name
              FROM      Article
              WHERE     Journal Name = JACM
```

In SQL, tuple variables can be used as in relational calculus; output ordering can be specified using an ORDER BY operator; and aggregate operators are available, including AVG, MIN, MAX, SUM, and

COUNT. An example of the use of tuple variables is provided by a request for the names of publishers located in the same city as publisher Stanton. In that case, only one relation is involved (Publisher), but two tuple variables can be used to relate the unknown publishers to publisher Stanton. The query can be expressed using tuple variables S and T:

```
SELECT    S. Publisher Name
FROM      Publisher.S, Publisher.T
WHERE     S. Publisher Address    = T. Publisher Address
          AND T. Publisher Name   = 'Stanton'
```

Alternatively, one can write

```
SELECT    Publisher Name
FROM      Publisher
WHERE     Publisher Address IN
              SELECT    Publisher Address
              FROM      Publisher
              WHERE     Publisher Name = 'Stanton'
```

Another well-known data-manipulation language, somewhat different from SQL, is QUEL, which uses a form of tuple-relational calculus. [19] The basic form of QUEL is a RANGE OF-RETRIEVE-WHERE combination, where RANGE OF takes the place of FROM in SQL by designating the relations for which particular tuple variables are defined; RETRIEVE is equivalent to the SELECT in SQL; and WHERE introduces a logical condition.

SQL statements using tuple variables are very similar to the corresponding QUEL statements. For example, to find author names and addresses for authors publishing in *JACM*, one can write

```
RANGE OF    t is Author
RANGE OF    s is Article
RETRIEVE    t. Author Name, t.Author Address
WHERE       t.Author Name = s.Author Name
            AND s.Journal Name = 'JACM'
```

QUEL has special facilities not available in other data-manipulation languages. For example, temporary files can be defined to collect partial results from several different relations. Thus, when retrieving the names of publishers and authors living in New York, one might first collect the publisher names in a temporary file (temp), and then add the author names:

RANGE OF	s is Publisher
RETRIEVE INTO	temp (s.Publisher Name)
WHERE	s.Publisher Address = 'New York'
RANGE OF	t is Author
APPEND TO	temp (t.Author Name)
WHERE	t.Author Address = 'New York'
RANGE OF	u is temp
RETRIEVE	u.Publisher Name

Most data manipulations performed in business environments are carried out interactively under user control. This suggests the advantage for practical application of a data-manipulation language with a built-in graphic interface. The well-known Query-by-Example (QBE) language uses a tabular display with a two-dimensional syntax as an interface between user and system, combining this with formulations from domain-relational calculus. [20,21] A query is constructed by first displaying a table that identifies the attribute domains of the relation. The complete query formulation is then prepared by filling the empty columns of the table with suitable variables, constants, and commands. Thus to retrieve publisher names for publishers living in Boston, one writes

Publisher	Publisher Name	Publisher Address
	P. x	Boston

In the preceding table, Boston represents the constant publisher address, and x is a variable that covers all publisher names, subject to the specified publisher address. The command P. stands for print out, or retrieve.

When a query covers more than one relation, several tables appear on the screen simulanteously. Thus the following formulation is used to print the names and addresses of authors publishing in *JACM*:

Author	Author Name	Author Address
	P. x	P.

Article	Article Title	Author Name	Journal Name	Issue Number
		x	JACM	

Note that the variable name x must be the same in both tables to indicate that the author names in the two relations must correspond.

Conditions can be entered directly into the displayed tables, if necessary by repeating certain attribute columns. Alternatively, separate "condition boxes" can be used to formulate the logical conditions. For example, to retrieve the names of authors of *JACM* articles published in volumes 20–24, one can write

Article	Article Title	Author Name	Journal Name	Issue Number	Issue Number
		P.	JACM	≥ 20	≤ 24

The same query can be formulated with separate condition boxes:

Article	Article Title	Author Name	Journal Name	Issue Number
		P.	JACM	x

conditions
$x \geq 20$ AND $x \leq 24$

The tabular display system of QBE is easy to learn and use. The system therefore enjoys widespread popularity for file generation, editing, updating, and retrieval, as well as for general form processing in offices. [22,23] In this last application, displayed tables can be used to define the contents of a particular form and to specify the conditions under which the forms are generated and routed. Table 3.6 shows a "journal issue report" generated for all authors of articles in a particu-

Table 3.6 Form specification and routing.

		Journal Issue Report			
	Input				**Output**
Article	Author Name	Article Title	Journal Name	Issue Number	To Recipients
	x	y	JACM	23	Smith Stanton

lar journal issue. The figure specifies both the form composition and the routing details.

By suitably combining an automatic file-management system with one of the office-analysis models considered, a flexible environment can be created to specify and execute office procedures.

❖ 3.3.4 Data Security, Integrity, and Recovery

Most database management systems devote substantial attention to maintaining smooth operations in a multiuser environment. For purposes of this discussion, a list of the more important facilities usually provided in the area of data security and integrity will suffice:

- Special *authorization* mechanisms that allow users to perform only certain types of operations for certain specified files.

- *User-view* mechanisms that entitle a user to access only those file portions that are specifically included in his or her personal view of the file.

- *Assertion* mechanisms specifying particular integrity constraints for certain data items. These assertions are then verified by the system at specified intervals to ensure data correctness. Thus if a data item is identified as a file key, the system will verify that all key values in the file are unique. In the same way, one can verify that all journal issues contain a minimum number of articles, or that each author publishes no more than a stated number of articles in each journal.

- Sensitive items of data can be automatically encrypted using an available *privacy-transformation* system. Alternatively, only aggregates of data may be retrievable from a file to protect data privacy. For example, it may be possible to obtain average salary figures for a class of employees, but not the salary of a particular individual.

In addition to ensuring data security, special methods may be invoked to restore file consistency in the event of system crashes or malfunctions. In particular, special program units known as *transactions* may be defined whose execution leaves the database in a consistent state. When the system crashes, transactions interrupted before termination or *commitment* must be rolled back, or undone. File consistency can be assured by using a special file, known as the *log*, to record all file changes made by each transaction. The database can be maintained in a consistent state after a system malfunction by consulting the log and undoing the effect of uncommitted transactions.

One of the most important functions of a DBMS is the control of multiple users who, in principle, may wish to access the same files at the same time. In these circumstances, the users must be prevented from interfering with each other's programs. Such unwanted interference can be prevented by insisting that transaction executions be *serializable*. Transaction serializability implies that the outcome of several transactions run simultaneously by different users is the same as the outcome produced by running the transactions serially in some order. (Obviously, in a serial execution, no interference can occur between transactions.)

Serializability is obtained by using *locking* protocols that force users to lock files before updating them. Locked files are generally accessible only to users who actually hold the file lock. Several file-locking protocols have been developed, designed to insure serializability of transactions; unfortunately some of these protocols can produce file-*deadlock* conditions. A deadlock between users arises when user A waits for release of a lock held by user B, while at the same time B waits for release of a lock held by A. In these circumstances, neither user can proceed and complete his or her transaction. A viable concurrency-control system must ensure transaction serializability, while at the same time preventing or resolving deadlock conditions.

Integrity and concurrency-control systems are much more complex in distributed database environments, where files are allocated to a number of different processing sites, than in centralized file systems. In a distributed environment, data may have to be moved from one location to another in accordance with user requirements. Alternatively, some of the heavily accessed file portions may have to be replicated and stored in several different locations.

3.4 Office Display Systems

The office-analysis systems discussed earlier model a well-structured environment composed of specific operations performed on specific data at particular times. These systems emphasize operational control, as well as the well formedness and integrity of objects and procedures. The operational environment within which these systems operate, however, can be relatively free and more flexible than suggested by a given detailed representation of procedures, or by specific form and document transformations. In fact, the automated office is sometimes conceived as an open, unstructured environment in which "electronic desks" perform a multiplicity of operations, their scope limited by only the skill and imagination of the operators. [24–27]

Typically, such an electronic desk consists of a microcomputer with substantial processing capabilities, a sufficient amount of internal storage and a disk space for back-up storage, a high-resolution display with appropriate positional controls to permit the displayed information to be manipulated easily, a keyboard or equivalent console input, and connections to networks offering facilities for filing or printing, as well as for mail operations. In such an environment, office objects such as documents, file drawers, and in-out baskets may be represented by pictorial displays, or *icons*, each object being associated with a set of allowable operations. In particular, objects may be selected, moved, copied, deleted, altered, and so on, by simply choosing the appropriate displayed icon, and performing symbolic operations on the displayed images. For example, to print out a document, the corresponding document icon can be moved to a printer icon on the display screen. Similarly, to file an item, the displayed object can be moved to a file-basket icon on the display screen.

The operations performed with individual displayed objects can be extended to complete files of records. Thus a file item might be chosen by displaying the record set on the screen and pointing to the particular file element. Likewise, elements from several files could be combined by performing appropriate processing operations on displayed images. The correctness of the operations can be verified in each case by viewing the resulting image on the screen. Whenever possible, the display should be lifelike. Hence it is necessary to specify appropriate properties for the content and appearance of each type of object. Documents may be characterized by type, background information, open fields, range of the variables filling the fields, and set of possible operations that can be performed. Similarly, characters are identified by font type (italic, bold, and so on), typeface, size, and position. Other objects are characterized by style, size, and other properties.

With a flexible display system, the user usually manipulates a multiwindow screen, showing a menu of icons from which to choose, plus the actual objects and documents being worked on. The following are among the operations that suggest themselves:

1. Data definition — performed, for example, by displaying an empty record file to open the file, or copying an empty document with particular properties to create the document.

2. Data display — exhibiting a complete document, or limiting the display to certain fields plus the related processing options.

3. Data transfer — establishing a correspondence between particular fields in different records or in different files.

4. Display scrolling — interactively moving through a particular document or through the records in a given file.

5. Data alteration and updating — performing a variety of word-processing operations.

Table 3.7 Operations controlled by icon manipulation.

Display of objects:	file cabinet; envelope; appointment calendar; desk pad; clock; telephone set; in-basket; out-basket; memo pad; wastepaper basket
Operational sequence	point to in-basket to see display of items; select first item and place it on the desk; select next page of item; select records from a file in record cabinet; place previous displayed item in pending box; display selected record; generate new document using file information; select mailing envelope; insert memorandum in envelope; place in out-box and put copy in pending box; file document in records file

---

6. Data interrogation — scanning through a given file and choosing the items that obey particular search specifications, or else using a query language to formulate the search queries.

7. Data ordering — arranging the records or objects in a particular order for storage or display.

Table 3.7 shows a sample operational sequence that can be performed by suitable icon manipulations. [26] To perform operations such as those included in the table, an interactive input controller is needed that recognizes the objects being selected and responds by displaying appropriate recognition symbols, such as flashing or boldface images; a display generator that transfers the displayed objects to the screen; a set of processing routines based on a specified data model with relationship indicators between data items; and a message handler.

When connections are available to local or long-distance networks, mail-forwarding operations can be implemented to allow transfers between workstations within an office, and between different offices. [28–31] In that case, individual mail boxes are created for each system participant, and messages, appropriately labeled by message type, sender, receiver, message number, and content, can be processed. The communications system is responsible for decomposing messages before forwarding them, and for reassembling them before distributing them, while the file-handling system is charged with message identification, filing, search, and retrieval.

3.5 Office-Information Retrieval

To the extent that office information consists of structured data of the type stored in ordinary business files, the database management component of an office system usually takes care of the retrieval operations using commands provided by the data-manipulation language. In most office environments, however, text and graphic data must also be processed, and special provisions must then be made to store and retrieve these unstructured data.

When text items are present, the retrieval function includes analyzing the content of texts and assigning content identifiers to individual text items; classifying texts, (that is, creating affinity classes between documents according to various criteria); filing texts; searching text files, and retrieving texts in response to user search requests; and constructing user interfaces to simplify file searches.

These problems are examined in more detail in Chapters 8–10. Here some special characteristics are mentioned that affect the processing of texts in office situations:

- Many texts are quite short, consisting of small items of correspondence and short messages.

- Many items are not abstracted, so that the main text of the item must necessarily serve for purposes of content analysis.

- Some text databases may be small, and a sequential scan through the texts might find the wanted items.

- Office items are characterized by special structures, including special headers and trailers, and bodies consisting of both text and numeric data and tables.

- The office environment is highly interactive and requires flexible search and retrieval facilities that allow browsing through collections of items and retrieval of items according to different criteria.

In response to these special circumstances, proposals have been made to eliminate the content analysis of office texts entirely by representing content by all text words not included in a special dictionary of excluded words. [32,33] Such a solution may be reasonable for short documents of approximately equal length, and for sufficiently standardized vocabularies when document text words are also expected to be used to formulate queries.

In a more general situation, some form of text-content analysis may be required, designed to recognize the affinity between different word forms such as "analyzer" and "analysis" and to identify synonyms and related words. One proposed system uses a tailormade business thesaurus that includes conventional formulations for references, salutations, courtesies, and closing statements, of the kind found in items of business correspondence. This thesaurus could serve for a special analysis of the heading and trailing statements in business letters, to be performed before, or in addition to, the standard analysis of the text body. [34] An excerpt from such a thesaurus appears in Table 3.8; and the corresponding simplified analysis system is represented in Fig. 3.5.

In the office, three different types of content identifiers for text items can be distinguished:

1. Identifiers normally derived from the text body that refer to the purpose and meaning of the text.

2. Objective identifiers dealing with the context within which the items are placed, such as sender, receiver, and date for correspondence, or author, journal, publisher, and date of publication for published items.

3. References or citations to other, related documents that may be derived from the text body or specified in a formal reference list.

This multiplicity of content descriptions means that mixed queries containing different types of identifiers must be handled. Also, multiple item classifications must be constructed in which the classes contain items of similar content, or items related by citation or reference,

---

Table 3.8 Typical entries in business thesaurus. [34]

Type of Phrase	Phrase Formulation
References	attach, enclose, inclose, letter dated..., letter of..., note dated..., note of...., recent letter..., recent note...
Salutations	Dear..., Madam, Sir, To whom it may concern
Closing forms	Best wishes, Best regards, Cordially (yours), Sincerely (yours), Very truly yours, Yours truly,...
Courtesies	all good wishes, all your help, at your service, favorable consideration, for your consideration, hope that this, how do you, look forward to, looking forward to, many thanks, personal regards, please let me know, remember me to, take pleasure, thank you, with all good wishes...

or items exhibiting common objective identifiers such as common author specifications, or items that would be placed in a common folder in a conventional office. [35,36]

These requirements are sometimes fulfilled by systems permitting search formulations in natural-language form. Methods of language-analysis are needed in that case to choose proper query terms, and to transform initial queries into suitable search statements. [37,38] Alternatively, extended vector systems can be used to represent documents and queries, where the individual text items are identified by sets of terms, but distinct term types receive distinct treatment. [39] For example, a given document could be identified by sets of objective identifiers of the type used in data-management systems, as well as additional automatically derived content identifiers, and references to related bibliographic citations. A different term-matching process

Figure 3.5 Simplified analysis system for business letters.

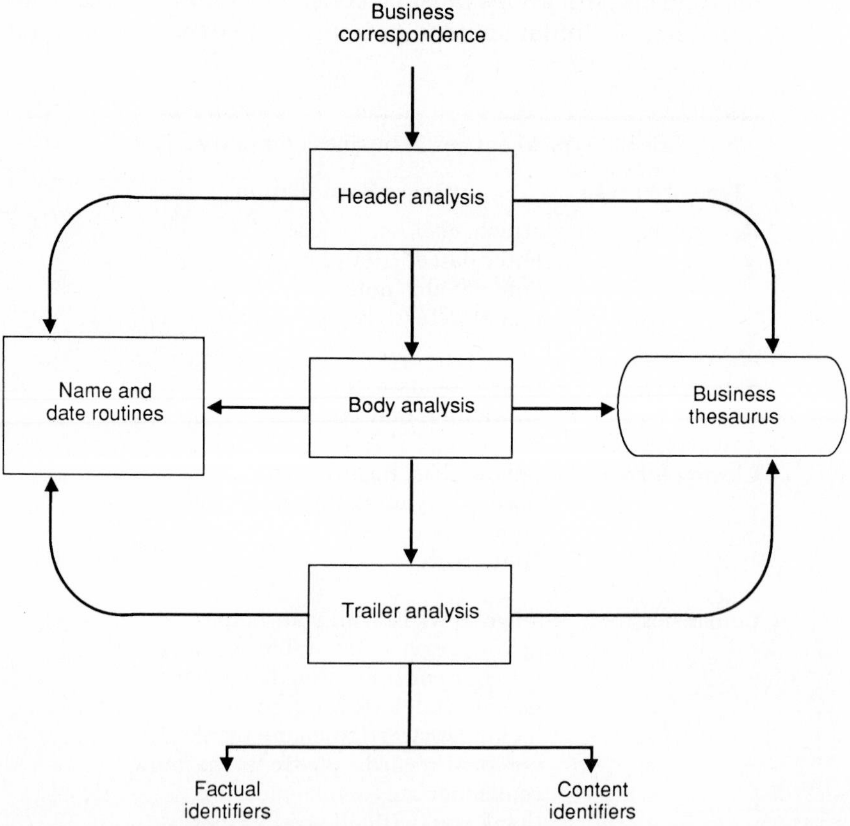

would then be used for the objective identifiers, content terms, and bibliographic references.

In another approach to processing complex office items, the conventional Boolean query formulations that exist in ordinary retrieval environments could be preserved, while assigning special values to the Boolean operators depending on the type of terms they connect. Extended systems of Boolean logic are available in which strictness parameters can be attached to Boolean operators. Such systems offer a relaxed interpretation in which tentative terms are used in query formulation, while maintaining a strict, conventional interpretation for terms considered compulsory. For the mixed-item identifications arising in office environments, one might then use relaxed interpretations for the identifiers related to item content, but stricter interpretations for the objective identifiers. [40] Still another approach consists of applying a relational system, or other DBMS, extended to handle natural-language text elements. Such extensions and related methods are further described in Chapter 10, while multimedia documents that include text as well as images are considered further in Chapter 13.

References

1. M. Hammer and M. Sirbu, What Is Office Automation?, *1980 Office Information Digest*, AFIPS Press, Montvale, NJ, 1980, 37–49.

2. S. Rohlfs, Office Communications: Promises, Problems, and Pitfalls, *International Computing Symposium 1983*, H.J. Schneider, editor, B.G. Teubner, Stuttgart, Germany, 1983, 249–267.

3. T.W. Malone, How Do People Organize Their Desks? Implications for the Design of Office Information Systems, *ACM Transactions on Office Information Systems*, 1:1, January 1983, 99–112.

4. G.H. Engel, J. Groppuso, R.A. Lowenstein, and W.G Traub, An Office Communication System, *IBM Systems Journal*, 18:3, 1979, 402–431.

5. H. Mintzberg, *The Nature of Managerial Work*, Harper and Row, New York, 1973.

6. C.V. Bullen, J.L. Bennett, and E.D. Carlson, A Case Study of Office Workstation Use, IBM Research Laboratory, Research Report RJ 3405, San Jose, CA, March 1982.

7. M. Hammer, R. Ilson, T. Anderson, E. Gilbert, M. Good, B. Niamir, L. Rosenstein, and S. Schoichet, Etude: An Integrated Document Processing System, *AFIPS Office Automation Conference*, AFIPS Press, Montvale, NJ, 1981, 209–220.

8. G. Bracchi and B. Pernici, The Design Requirements of Office Systems, *ACM Transactions on Data Base Systems*, 2:2, April 1984, 151–170.

9. G. Bracchi and B. Pernici, SOS: A Conceptual Model for Office Information Systems, *Data Base*, 15:2, Winter 1984, 11–18.

10. S.B. Yao, A.R. Hevner, Z. Shi, and D. Luo, Formanager: An Office Forms Management System, *ACM Transactions on Office Information Systems*, 2:3, July 1984, 235–262.

11. D. Tsichritzis, Form Management, *Communications of the ACM*, 25:7, July 1982, 453–478.

12. V.Y. Lum, D.M. Choy, and N.C. Shu, OPAS: An Office Procedure Automation System, *IBM Systems Journal*, 21:3, 1982, 327–350.

13. W.K. Lin, D.R. Ries, B.T. Blaustein, and K.M. Chilenskas, Office Procedures on a Distributed Data Base Application, *Data Base*, 15:2, Winter 1984, 5–10.

14. C.A. Ellis and G.J. Nutt, Office Information Systems and Computer Science, *Computing Surveys*, 12:1, March 1980, 27–60.

15. C.J. Date, *An Introduction to Database Systems*, Vol. 1, Fourth Edition, Addison-Wesley Publishing Co., Reading, MA, 1986.

16. J.D. Ullman, *Principles of Data Base Systems*, Computer Science Press, Rockville, MD, Second Edition, 1982.

17. H.F. Korth and A. Silberschatz, *Database System Concepts*, McGraw-Hill Book Co., New York, 1986.

18. D.D. Chamberlin, M.M. Astrahan, K.P. Eswaran, P.P. Griffiths, R.A. Lorie, J.W. Mehl, T. Reimer, and B.W. Wade, Sequel 2: A Unified Approach to Data Definition, Manipulation, and Control, *IBM Journal of Research and Development*, 20:6, November 1976, 560–575.

19. G. Held and M. Stonebraker, Storage Structures and Access Methods in the Relational Data Base Management System Ingres, Electronics Research Laboratory, University of California, Memorandum ERL-M505, Berkeley, CA, March 1975.

20. M.M. Zloof, Query-by-Example, A Database Language, *IBM Systems Journal*, 16:4, 1977, 324–343.

21. M.M. Zloof, Office-by-Example: A Business System that Unifies Data and Word Processing and Electronic Mail, *IBM Systems Journal*, 21:3, 1982, 272–304.

22. P. De Jong, The System for Business Automation (SBA): A Unified Application Development System, *Information Processing '80*, S.H. Lavington, editor, North Holland Publishing Co., Amsterdam, 1980, 433–438.

23. D. Luo and S.B. Yao, Form Operation by Example — A Language for Office Information Processing, *Proceedings ACM SIGMOD Meeting*, Association for Computing Machinery, New York, 1981, 212–233.

24. L. Yedwab, C.F. Herot, R.L. Rosenberg, and C. Gross, The Automated Desk, *ACM SIGSMALL Newsletter*, October 1981, 102–108.

25. R. Purvy, J. Farrell, and P. Klose, The Design of Star's Records Processing: Data Processing for the Noncomputer Professional, *ACM Transactions on Office Information Systems*, 1:1, January 1983, 3–24.

26. W. Schild, L.R. Power, and M. Karnaugh, Pictureworld: A Concept for Future Office Systems, IBM Corporation, IBM Research Report RC 8384, White Plains, NY, July 1980.

27. H.P. Frei and J.F. Jauslin, Graphical Presentation of Information and Services: A User Oriented Interface, *Information Technology Research and Development*, 21, January 1983, 23–42.

28. N. Naffah, Communications Protocols for Intergrated Office Systems, Project Kayak, Report ARC 2.515, INRIA, Rocquencourt, France, September 1981.

29. H.T. Smith, D.A. Waterman, and W.S. Faught, An Office Communication System Design, Rand Corporation, Rand Memorandum P-6393, Santa Monica, CA, September 1979.

30. D.B. Terry and S. Andler, The Cosie Communication Subsystem: Support for Distributed Office Applications, *ACM Transactions on Office Information Systems*, 2:2, April 1984, 79–95.

31. D.J. Moore, Teletex — A Worldwide Link among Office Systems for Electronic Document Exchange, *IBM Systems Journal*, 22:1 and 2, 1983, 30–45.

32. D. Tsichritzis and S. Christodoulakis, Message Files, *ACM Transactions on Data Base Systems*, 1:1, January 1983, 88–98.

33. J. Slonin, L.J. MacRae, W.E. Mennie, and N. Diamond, NDX-100: An Electronic Filing Machine for the Office of the Future, *Computer*, May 1981, 24–36.

34. E. Nodtvedt, Information Retrieval in the Business Environment, Department of Computer Science, Cornell University, Technical Report TR 80-447, Ithaca, NY, December 1980.

35. W.B. Croft and M.T. Pezarro, Text Retrieval Techniques for the Automated Office, *Proceedings of the International Workshop on Office Information Systems*, St. Maximin, France, 1981.

36. G. Salton, Some Notions About Information Retrieval in Automated Office Environments, Department of Computer Science, Cornell University, Technical Report TR 84-609, Ithaca, NY, May 1984.

37. G.G. Hendrix, E.D. Sacerdoti, D. Sagalowicz, and J. Slocum, Developing a Natural Language Interface to Complex Data, *ACM Transactions on Database Systems*, 3:2, June 1978, 105–147.

38. B.K. Boguraev and K. Sparck Jones, A Natural Language Analyzer for Database Access, *Information Technology: Research and Development*, 1:1, 1982, 23–39.

39. E.A. Fox, Extending the Boolean and Vector Space Models of Information Retrieval with P-Norm Queries and Multiple Concept Types, Doctoral Dissertation, Cornell University, August 1983.

40. G. Salton, E.A. Fox, and H. Wu, Extended Boolean Information Retrieval, *Communications of the ACM*, 26:11, November 1983, 1022–1036.

Part 2

Word Processing and File Access

Chapter 4

Text Editing and Formatting

4.1 Introduction

Three main types of text-processing activities must be distinguished: word processing, text storage and retrieval, and text-processing applications requiring a deep understanding of language structure and text content. In terms of immediate usefulness and acceptability, word processing is by far the most important application.

Word processing literally means processing at the level of words. However, many procedures based on individual word manipulations, such as statistical text analysis using word-counting methods, are not considered word processing. Other tasks, however, such as the detection or correction of spelling errors, may be included in some word-processing packages even though they may require complex linguistic methods.

Word processing usually includes text generation (including initial text preparation), text modification, and text correction, as well as the text-arranging and -formatting operations that precede output printing or display. The main word-processing activities are briefly described in this chapter, including text-alteration and text-editing systems, document-structuring and -formatting operations, and text design. Other text-correction systems involving more substantial linguistic techniques, such as style and syntax checking and automatic text-writing aids, are covered in Chapter 12, along with additional language-processing applications.

4.2 Approaches to Word Processing

A word-processing system consists of equipment and procedures for the preparation, alteration, formatting, and storage of text items. Nearly everyone deals with text at one time or another, and thus word-processing systems are potentially useful to many groups — professional people preparing analyses and reports, teachers and students dealing with educational materials, secretaries and office personnel manipulating correspondence files and other office items, and so on.

Several main classes of word-processing systems can be distinguished. [1–5] First, text manipulations can be carried out in a batch-processing mode by marking up the complete texts, much as in a manual editing environment, with text-transformation and text-formatting commands supplied in advance. At some later time, the raw texts are turned into suitable formatted output without additional input from the user. The alternative is to work in an interactive environment, where text-transformation operations are performed one at a time, and a display system lets the user see the results of each operation.

In some word-processing systems only the text is processed, as would be done by conventional copy editors of text materials. Alternatively, computer storage may also be provided for digitized graphic images and pictures, in which case editing and formatting procedures may also be available to transform and insert the graphic portions.

A third distinction is based on the types of operations used to perform the text manipulations. In procedural systems, the operator immediately controls the text-alteration system by using low-level operations that specify spacing, indentation, paragraphing, underscoring, and so on. In declarative systems, on the other hand, a high-level environment is initially specified for each type of document, and the details of the editing and formatting operations are globally assumed by the system in accordance with the particular environmental specifications.

The following goals apply to the design of word-processing systems: [1]

- The system should be powerful enough to allow the user to carry out all the text transformations that would normally be performed by using pencil, scissors, and tape.

- The system should respond fast enough to allow the user to transform texts at "normal" speeds: In interactive situations, this implies that the text-manipulation operations should be performed in real time while the user sits at a workstation or computer terminal.

- The computer interface should be easy to use. Thus the amount of detail to be mastered should be limited, and simple methods should be provided to perform common operations.

- Global text-search and text-alteration methods should be available, capable of finding user-specified patterns in the text and of performing uniform text transformations everywhere a given text pattern occurs.

- When display screens are used, the text editor should supply updated document views, permitting the user to review the current composition and complexion of the text as the operations are carried out.

- On the same input-output device, multiple contexts should be provided that allow text operations at various levels of detail, and provide protocols of the text operations already performed, with menus, or lists, of new operations that suggest themselves at particular points in the processing chain.

The early word processors were typewriter-like devices, providing machine-language commands to manipulate the text, generally on a line-by-line basis. Each individual operation would be separately specified, and trouble arose when the altered form of a line exceeded the maximum line length provided. The line editors eventually evolved into stream editors, where the text was treated as a single stream of data, and new lines were automatically formed to conform to the requirements of the actual text elements.

During the 1970s, *structured* formatters became available: A document was treated as a complete structured entity, and global operations applying to particular structural elements could be performed. Thus documents could typically be broken down hierarchically into chapters, which themselves were broken down into sections, and paragraphs, and sentences, and words. An abstract tree (see Fig. 4.1) would then represent the document structure, and global operations could be specified that would apply to all nodes on a particular level of the tree — for example all chapter headings or all paragraphs. Further, the various text-transformation operations could be represented by corresponding transformations in the abstract graphical representation. Thus new paragraphs could be inserted by creating new subtrees; sentence orders could be changed by permuting tree nodes, and nodes could be deleted, copied, moved, split, or merged.

Figure 4.1 Partial document structure in tree form.

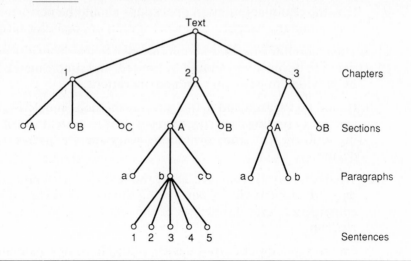

Alternatively, a document could be considered as a series of freely linked blocks producing a network (see Fig. 4.2). In such a *hypertext* environment, blocks could be attached to other blocks to simulate the sequence of sections of a document, and blocks could be inserted for inserts, annotations, and footnotes. The environment for a given block

Figure 4.2 Document block structure.

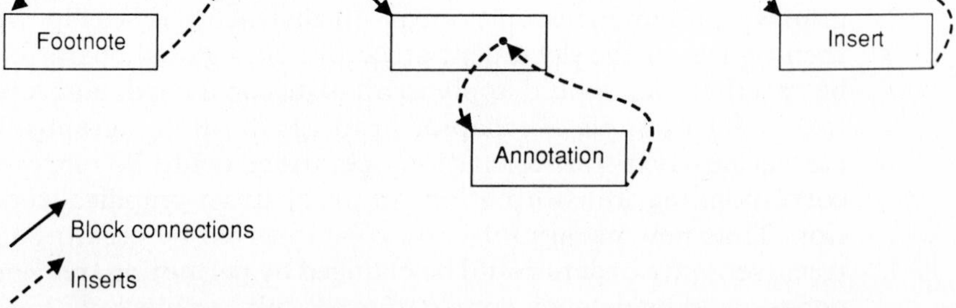

Footnote

Insert

Annotation

Block connections

Inserts

inserts, annotations, and footnotes. The environment for a given block could be specified by "begin" and "end" markers, and particular text operations could then be applied globally within the confines of the specified blocks.

Like the document structure, the text-processing model can be structured and based on the syntax of the particular environment. Thus a particular set of operations may be allowed only if it is compatible with the given structural conditions. For example, fixed ordering relations may be defined between sets of substatements and the main statements to which they refer. Similarly, inserts such as footnotes or references may be forbidden in chapter or section heads, and section numbers may be assignable only to text portions at least two paragraphs long.

In recent years, structured text-editing and -formatting operations have been incorporated into *integrated* editor-formatting systems, often based on advanced graphic display systems operating in an interactive mode. Such systems combine editing and formatting operations with viewing, filing, and other text-processing operations such as mail handling and document-typesetting facilities. By associating particular views with specific document portions, parts of the text can be continuously displayed on the screen, giving the user an up-to-date record of the current state of the process. In such a situation, the text transformations become physically obvious, and remedies can be supplied before a document is accepted in final form.

When high-resolution bit-mapped display screens are used, picture elements as well as text can be stored and displayed. Picture-editing and -transformation operations may be able to treat the image and text parts simultaneously on an equal basis. Texts and figures can then be integrated on the display, producing a final document representation ready for printing or typesetting.

4.3 Text Editing and Formatting

A simplified *text-editing* system is shown in Fig. 4.3. [1] It has four principal components used for editing, traveling, viewing, and display, respectively. The editing component includes the modules dealing with the actual text processing. The starting place for each editing operation is determined by an editing pointer set by the traveling component. By moving the editing pointer from place to place, it is possible to carry out text insertion, deletion, moving, and other text transformations. The viewing component creates an up-to-date image of the text after each text-editing operation. Portions of the updated text may be selected, as specified by viewing pointers, and transferred by the display component to an output device for printing and display. The output component of the text-editing system usually includes filtering operations designed to select the text elements needed for display, as well as formatting operations to transform the text into suitable output form.

In Fig. 4.3 the editing system is connected to a file-storage facility that saves texts and documents. Specified text portions can then be chosen and transferred to the editing buffer for processing, or the editing buffer can be filled by new input text. Edited texts can also be stored in the files or readied for output and display.

The following types of operations are often used in text editing:

- Moving through a text file starting at a location specified by the file pointer.

- Searching for a pattern in a text file based on a matching pattern of text elements.

- Browsing through a structured document by following pointers from one text block to the next.

- Viewing text portions by selecting the desired text parts, formatting the text for output, and mapping the text to a window or a physical output device.

Figure 4.3 Typical architecture for text editing (adapted from [1]).

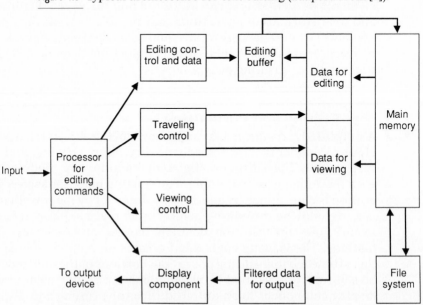

- Creating documents by displaying a sample frame for the desired document type (such as a letter, contract, or proposal) and inserting appropriate text portions into the blank spaces provided. Alternatively, customized documents can be created without a standard preestablished format.

- Selecting the size of the text to be manipulated by setting the editing pointer (or cursor) to the appropriate text portions.

- Deleting, changing, or substituting text portions while preserving the original text in a buffer from which it can be recalled if necessary.

- Moving text items from a source to a destination location, or copying text items (that is, moving text portions without deleting the original).

- Undoing or canceling previously executed editing operations, or interrupting an editing session while saving the content for later resumption.

- Providing automatic document profiles by using default instead of user-specified parameters to control complex conditions.

- Providing coded macro operations representing editing scripts for complex text-transformation operations.

- Supplying help facilities for users who need them and writing aids such as spelling checkers and style monitors to improve readability.

The production of written texts requires not only editing facilities, but also formatting facilities. Traditionally, *text-formatting* operations are performed by human experts who lay out pages, strip in negatives for graphs and pictures, and pass on the completed layout for platemaking and reproduction. In automatic text-formatting systems, however, a text is treated as a collection of blocks with height, width, sequence, and preferred placement conditions, and the blocks are packed into pages automatically. Block sizes might be automatically altered by changing the spacing between adjacent pages, or, when splitting is not permitted, blocks might be integrally moved to a different page.

Interactive text-formatting systems may display complete pages on a screen, and the user may take an active part in either accepting or overriding the layout provided by the automated system. A typical system of this type is outlined in Fig. 4.4. [3] The document formatter first takes the text portions obtained from the text editor, together with the corresponding digitized form of images and figures, and prepares a tentative layout. In the system of Fig. 4.4 the tentative layout is shown to the user on a full-page display system. Accepted pages are released for printing or typesetting, while pages requiring revision are treated by an interactive layout override system before being reformatted. The override system can in principle be used several times until a satisfactory format is obtained.

The following kinds of formatting functions are most important:

- Selecting basic elements to be used in formatting, such as characters in a particular typeface.

- Horizontally and vertically placing elements, including specification of indentations, skips, centering, spacing, and so on.

- Horizontally and vertically aligning, that is, horizontal or vertical placement of the elements relative to each other.

- Breaking up blocks of text elements into paged sets, including page headers and footnotes.

- Scaling elements, or blocks, to achieve appropriate increases or reductions in size.

- Providing automatic document-management aids, such as cross-referencing, annotating, and locating document features that require special handling.

Text-editing and -formatting procedures can be carried out using a wide variety of equipment configurations. Stand-alone word processors can be used, as can shared-logic systems where a central processing unit controls a number of attached word-processing stations. Early word-processing units consisted of typewriter keyboards used

Figure 4.4 Interactive text-formatting system.

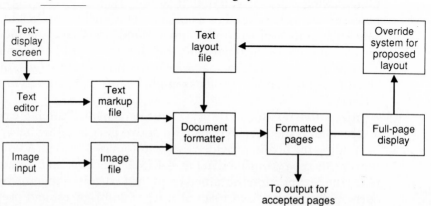

for data and command entry, and printing equipment to produce hard-copy output. Later, cathode ray tube technology was added for display purposes, and magnetic disks or diskettes for image and text storage.

Many of the advanced input and output devices discussed in Chapter 2 are used advantageously in word processing. In addition to keyboard and display units, these devices include special-function keys that generate appropriate interrupts when pushed; "pick" devices, such as light pens, that point to a place on a screen and tell the program to read the position of the selected point; and locator devices, such as cursor keys, trackballs, or mice, that position a cursor symbol at a particular point on a display to control subsequent text manipulations.

Various methods are used to manage the interaction between user and editing facilities. In the most basic situation, a keyboard/printer is used to enter data and editing commands. This requires substantial familiarity by the user with the system and the text-processing language. Function-oriented keyboards may be helpful because they allow the main editing and formatting instructions to be initiated using the special-function keys. Menu-oriented systems display the possible operations at each point in an editing session; the user can select the proper operation from the displayed menu. Finally, multiple window displays contain various text portions together with pop-up menus of operations superimposed on the corresponding texts.

The usefulness of a text-manipulation system is often based on the ease with which various document portions can be modified, the methods used to point to particular text positions where changes must take place, and the type of document display provided. [6] Among the features considered especially useful are automatic line handling (the system automatically sets line lengths, and the user is not concerned with "carriage" returns to move from one line to the next); direct addressing systems (screen positions are addressed without reference to the current position); continuous page displays (portions of the edited text are continuously displayed); and recognition of higher-level text units such as sentences and paragraphs, not only individual words or lines of text.

4.4 Typical Processing Systems

4.4.1 Off-Line Text-Editing Systems

The SCRIPT system, a typical editing and formatting facility, uses a text editor to create input files consisting of text elements interspersed with SCRIPT commands. [7] In SCRIPT, detailed low-level formatting instructions can be supplied, and formatting specifications are directly specified by the user. Table 4.1 gives a list of typical SCRIPT commands; a few simple formatting examples are shown in Table 4.2. The basic commands appear in a *.xy* form, and commands may be used singly, or in paired sets. In the latter case, the two appearances are used to bracket the text portion affected by the command. As shown in Tables 4.1 and 4.2, SCRIPT includes all the usual formatting instructions, such as margin specification, indentation, underscoring, and spacing. In addition, complete text blocks can be identified and processed as units.

Text-editing and -formatting programs may be included in general utility packages for the preparation and manipulation of written texts, notably the case in environments using the UNIX operating system. A document-preparation facility includes normal text-editing and text-alteration methods, as well as writer's aids such as the detection of spelling errors and index preparation; formatting instructions with special provisions for difficult text portions such as tables, equations, and bibliographic references; and output facilities for document production on printers and typesetters. [8–10]

In interactive editing systems, a pointer or cursor is moved through the text, and the editing operation — for example, substitution, inser-

Table 4.1 Typical SCRIPT formatting commands.

Typical Command	Explanation
.ll line length	absolute line length in numbers of characters, or relative to current length
.ds double space	
.pp paragraph	skips line, indents three spaces
.us underscore	line of text to be underscored
.up capitalize	
.pa start new page	.pa +5 starts new page and skips five page numbers
.sp blank line	
.em empty page	
.rm right margin	
.bm bottom margin	
.co concatenated	places as much text on a line as will fit
.cp conditional page control	keeps a block of text on one page
.fk floating keep	denotes text portions used to fill leftover space
.ce centering	centers lines of text

tion, or deletion — takes place at the pointer position. Alternatively, a "current-line" pointer can be used, and the text-alteration area specified with respect to the current line position. A third possibility consists of using a text-search system to find the text area where a given word or character sequence occurs. The editing operation will then use the particular pattern occurrence as a reference. In the *ed* editor included in UNIX the current-line and pattern-match positioning devices are used. A particular operation may be confined to a single line or to a set of specified lines, or may apply to a complete text. In the latter case, a global (g) environment is defined that makes additional position specifications unnecessary.

The UNIX document-formatting system provides the same basic parameters as SCRIPT for specifying character size, page length, spacing, indentation, and so on. In addition, UNIX uses special functions to generate vertical or horizontal motions, and to produce symbols such as brackets, boxes, circles, and ellipses. An attempt is made to decouple the content of a document from its format as much as possible. This is achieved by using special-purpose languages applica-

---

Table 4.2 SCRIPT formatting examples.

Example	Explanation
.us line | of text | to be underscored	| is escape character; will print <u>line</u> of text <u>to be underscored</u>
.cp conditional page control (begin) input text .cp conditional page control (end)	keeps a block of text together on one page; that is, starts a new page if complete text does not fit on current page
.fk floating keep (begin) input text .fk floating keep (end)	text labeled "floating keep" can be used to fill leftover space on a page
.ce centering (begin) input text .ce centering (end)	centers the corresponding lines of text
.fn (begin) .of 1 text .of -1 .fn (end)	defines footnote, offset by one space relative to current text indent; footnote text can be placed anywhere, but system will eventually place footnote at bottom of current page
.bx 1 60 .sp .in $+3$ -3 input text .in -3 $+3$	places box of 60-character width around a block of text; text is left and right indented by three character widths

ble to particular text portions, such as mathematical equations and tables of data, and by introducing higher-level subroutines (macros) that furnish complex output applicable to specified text portions.

Basic text formatting under UNIX is performed by a common, largely device-independent, program known as NROFF (for the output of workstations and printers) and TROFF (for the output of typesetting machines). Output-device-description tables are used to specify the exact nature of the printing device in use. Table 4.3 includes a number of typical TROFF formatting commands as well as a list of special characters. Special characters are obtained by using a two-character identifier preceded by \(. Thus \(ga designates the French accent grave ` . Two different characters are superimposed by inhibiting the horizontal motion following the printing of the first character using the \o indicator. Thus \o"e\(ga" produces è. Special strings can also be defined using a string definition operator .ds. Such strings can later be referred to in the text by using *. Command sequences can be interspersed with ordinary text by using "escape" characters (normally reverse slashes) to distinguish the command positions following the slash from the text sequences. Examples of this type are shown in Table 4.4.

The availability of macro operations is an important feature of UNIX document preparation. Macros are normally used to specify the format for the major text portions, such as titles, abstracts, footnotes, paragraphs, and bibliographic references. Each macro operation must be defined, using a .de operator, before being used; the .de operator introduces the TROFF or NROFF program necessary to carry out the corresponding formatting operations. Some typical macro commands are listed in Table 4.5; the NP (new page) macro is defined in the lower half of the table. (This macro is used to place a particular caption at the top of each new page using specified type-font, point-size, and line-length indicators.)

UNIX makes special provisions for the preparation of tables, mathematical expressions, and graphs using the TBL, EQN, and PIC programs. [11–13] Tables are rectangular arrays in which table positions are made available to be filled with items of information. A table definition uses .TS and .TE (table start and table end) indicators, plus a set of options and formats as well as data. The options determine placement and size of the table and specify whether certain table entries or the entire table are to be surrounded by boxes. The formatting instructions, on the other hand, describe the nature and form of each table entry. A typical table format appears in Table 4.6.

In the example of Table 4.6, the table is to be centered on the page, and the complete table (but not the individual entries) is to be boxed. (The option allbox would have to be used to achieve the latter result.) One line of formatting specifications is needed for each line of data, except that all the table entries in the body of the table with the same format are specified by a single formatting line. In Table 4.6, the specification "css" indicates that the first table entry is centered on the

Table 4.3 Typical TROFF formatting commands.

Command	Example	Explanation
Point Size		
.ps	.ps 36	point size 36
Vertical Space		
.vs	.vs 11p	vertical space of 11 points
.sp	.sp 2i	two inches of vertical space
Fonts		
.ft	.ftB	switch to bold
	.ftI	switch to italics
.bd		"synthetic" bold by overstriking
Special Characters		
\(	\(14	1/4
	\(#a	α
\l	\l'1i'	horizontal line of one inch
\L	\L'1i'	vertical line of one inch
Line Formats		
.ll	.ll 6i	six-inch length
.po	.po 0	page offset as far left as possible
.in	.in 0.3i	indent of 0.3 inches
.ti	.ti 3 in	temporary indent for one line
\l	\l'1i'	horizontal line of one inch
\L	\L'1i'	vertical line of one inch
Tabs and Local Motions		
.ta	.ta 1i 2i	tab at one inch and two inch positions
\u	r\u2	up motion gives "r^2"
\d	m\d2	down motion give "m$_2$"
\v	\v'0.1i'	vertical space of 0.1 inch
\h	\h '−0.3'	horizontal motion by −0.3 units
\0		blank space of width of digit 0
\z		suppress horizontal motion
\o		overstriking (inhibits horizontal motion after character printing)
String Definition		
.ds	.ds e \o"e\'"	defines e as é; refer to string as *e

Table 4.4 TROFF formatting examples with escape characters.

Example	Explanation
\s8 UNIX \s10 runs on a \s8 PDP \s10 11/45	prints as "UNIX runs on a PDP 11/45" 8pt 10pt 8pt 10pt
\fB bold \fI face \fR text	prints as "**bold** *face* text" with words in bold, italics, and roman, respectively
\o 'set'	overstriking of word "set"
>\h '−0.3 m'>	prints as "> >" close together
syst \o "e \(ga" me	prints as "système"; \(ga is accent grave `)
t*el*e phone	prints as "téléphone"

page, and the complete table (but not the individual entries) is to be boxed. The corresponding data entry "Position of Major Cities" is included at the bottom of the table specification. The remaining rows of

Table 4.5 Macro definition in TROFF.

Typical macros:	.TL	title
	.AU	author
	.AI	author's institution
	.AB	abstract
	.AE	abstract end
	.NH	numbered section headings
	.FS	footnote
	.FE	footnote end
	.PP	paragraph
	.LP	left-aligned block
Definition of new page macro:	.de NP	new page macro definition
	.bp	skip to beginning of page
	.sp 0.5i	vertical space of one-half inch
	.ft R	set table font to roman
	.ps 10	set size to 10 point
	.ll 6i	set line length to 6 inches
	.tl'left'center'right'	define what goes left, center, and right at top of page
	.ps	revert to previous size
	.ft P	revert to previous font
	.sp 0.3i	vertical space of 0.3 inches

the table are all formatted by the "lnn" specification. This provides a left-adjusted entry in column 1 for the city name, and numeric entries for columns 2 and 3 corresponding to the city's latitude and longitude, respectively. Numeric entries are normally centered and aligned by decimal point or some other punctuation sign. The final output is shown at the bottom of Table 4.6.

Formatting mathematical expressions is more complex because the information is not neatly arranged in row and column form. The EQN program, usually used to format mathematical expressions in UNIX, approaches the problem by using English-like designations to replace mathematical symbols, and by maintaining the usual conventions of operator precedence in evaluating mathematical expressions. Thus "partial" is used to represent a partial derivative, "int" is an integral, and "sqrt" a square root. Terms such as "over" and "sup" designate division and exponentiation operations, and "sub" is used for subscripting variables. Parentheses and brackets are reproduced in the final output, but braces are used as special symbols indicating group-

Table 4.6 Typical table format.

Table Formatting

.TS	table start
options	
format	
data	
.TE	table end

Example
.TS

center,box;	place in center inside a box
css	one line centered and spanned
lnn	three fields, first one is left adjusted, the other two numeric

Position of Major Cities
Tokyo T 35° 45′ N T 139° 46′E
New York T 40° 43′ N T 74° 01′W
.TE

Position of Major Cities		
Tokyo	35°45′N	139°46′E
New York	40°43′N	74°01′W

ing of symbols when necessary; thus, in the input form

{ −b + − sqrt { b sup 2 − 4ac } } over 2a

the inside braces specify the scope of the square root, and the outside braces indicate that the divisor 2a extends over the whole expression. The corresponding output appears as

$$\frac{-b + - \sqrt{b^2 - 4ac}}{2a}$$

In EQN, the size of printed parentheses and brackets is automatically adjusted to correspond to the size of the enclosed expression. This same facility also produces object "piles" — where homogeneous data appear on several lines appropriately aligned one above the other. The special term "above" is used in EQN to specify the object placement.

Some typical examples of the EQN conventions are included in Table 4.7, illustrating the use of special terminology, mathematical precedence, and built-up brackets. The table also includes a sample text with appropriate EQN instructions. Mathematical expressions to be displayed are introduced by .EQ. On the other hand, expressions to be reproduced as part of the linear text are bracketed by @. Ordinary formatting commands are used for the conventional text portions.

A third useful program, known as PIC, is used to specify the format for graphic elements. PIC provides various basic objects such as lines, arrows, arcs, boxes, circles, ellipses, and splines, and generates complex graphs by appropriately combining basic objects. Pictures are thus created by writing descriptions of the desired objects, rather than by drawing as on a display screen. Typical examples of the PIC facilities are included in Table 4.8.

In PIC, a number of useful conventions simplify picture specification, among them the existence of default dimensions and default motions. Unless otherwise noted, the direction of motion in a picture specification is left to right, and default sizes are half-inch radii for circles arcs, and half-inch line lengths. Standard boxes are 3/4-inch wide by 1/2-inch high. Different lengths can be specified by stating the length in inches, and nonstandard motions are described by using terms such as "top," "bottom," "left," "right," "north," "northeast," and "southwest." Objects can also be labeled for later reference, and captions, specified within quotation marks, can be placed inside enclosed objects.

The UNIX document-processing system provides low-level operations for specifying document formats. Such a system is particularly attractive to expert users who can cope with the details of the format specifications. Another low-level document-specification system with impressive facilities is known as TeX. [14] TeX uses character specifications fairly similar to those available in TROFF, but adds new factors concerning the arrangement of objects within documents. Especially affected are the ways in which lines of text are broken up and words are hyphenated, as well as the ways in which complete paragraphs are constructed and placed.

In TeX, the document objects — that is characters, words, lines, paragraphs and pages — are considered to be two-dimensional boxes

---

Table 4.7 Typical facilities in EQN system.

Mathematical expressions:

.EQ   EQN program converts mathematical portions into TROFF
       commands

  .

  .

  .

.EN

Special terms (pi, int, omega, sin): $2\pi \int \sin(\omega t)dt$
  2 pi int sin (omega t) dt

Fractions (use "over") $\dfrac{a + b}{c + d + e} = 1$
  {a + b} over {c + d + e} = 1

Superscripts and subscripts ("sup", "sub") $x^2 + y^2 = z^2$
  x sup 2 + y sup 2 = z sup 2

Mathematical procedure $\dfrac{a^2}{b}$ not $a^{2/b}$
  a sup 2 over b

Brackets, braces of proper height ("left", $\left[\dfrac{x+y}{2a}\right] = 1$
  "right", "˜" for space)
  left [x+y over 2a right]˜= ˜1

Piles of objects ("above")
  sign (x) ˜= =˜left {
    rpile {1 above 0 above −1} $sign(x) \equiv \begin{cases} 1 \text{ if } x > 0 \\ 0 \text{ if } x = 0 \\ -1 \text{ if } x < 0 \end{cases}$
    ˜˜lpile {if above if above if}
    ˜˜lpile {x>0 above x=0 above x <0}

Input example ("ˆ" for "close-up")
  When @pˆ=ˆ1@
  this becomes the sum of absolute values
  .EQ
  ||x vec|| sub 1˜=˜sum from i =1 to n|x sub i|
  .EN

Output example: When p = 1 this becomes the sum of absolute values

$$||\vec{x}||_1 = \sum_{i=1}^{n} |x_i|$$

connected by a variable amount of free space known as "glue." The glue has a natural size corresponding to the ideally desired space between objects, but it can be stretched or shrunk if necessary. The glue

---

Table 4.8 Typical PIC specification for graphic objects.

PIC creates pictures by writing, using boxes, arrows, circles, ellipses, arcs, and splines

Input

.PS

.

.

.

.PE

Specifications can be given in detail:

Input	**Output**
box height 0.3i width 0.5i at 0.25i, 0.15i line from 0.25i, 0.15i to 0.75i, 0.15i	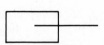

The commands "up," "down," "left," "right" are used; "then" separates motions.

Input	**Output**
line up right then down right then down left then up left	

Default motion is left to right; cw denotes clockwise

Input	**Output**
arrow ; arc ; arc cw ; arrow	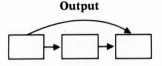

Objects are labeled for later reference

Input	**Output**
B1 : box ; arrow ; box ; arrow B3 : box arc : cw from top of B1 to top of B3	

Captions are enclosed in quotation marks; se denotes southeast; nw, northwest

Input	**Output**
ellipse "1" ellipse "2" with nw at last ellipse se	

between the individual letters of a word is normally of zero width, but the ideal glue between individual words may, for example, be equal to the width of the letter e, with a maximum stretch to 2e and a maximum shrink to 1/2 e. When all the glue is concentrated at the beginning of a line, right justification is obtained; that is, the line appears flush against the right margin. When the glue appears at both ends of a line, the text is centered. Special stretch factors are used after commas and periods, and both stretch and shrink factors can be introduced above and below mathematical equations.

Using the notion of boxes connected by glue, it is convenient to process complete paragraphs at a time so that they will have a pleasing appearance. [15] In particular, one wants to avoid excessive stretching or shrinking of individual lines of text, as well as too many hyphenated word endings. Two adjacent lines each ending in a hyphenated word are especially objectionable, as is a hyphenation in the next-to-last line of a paragraph. A dynamic program may be used to determine line lengths based on available box lengths, stretch and shrink factors, and identification of places where line breaks are possible. The actual line breaks are then chosen so as to simultaneously minimize the overall discrepancy between real line lengths compared with ideally desirable line lengths, and reduce the number of hyphenated words as much as possible. [15]

A similar philosophy guides the placement of paragraphs within pages: TeX exploits discretionary space that can be inserted between adjacent paragraphs, and above and below mathematical equations. The objective is to avoid bad paragraph breaks between pages, such as breaks after a hyphenated word, or breaks that leave a single line alone on a page.

It is difficult to hyphenate English words automatically because of the many exceptions to the basic rules. Examples are provided by word pairs such as rec-ord (noun) and re-cord (verb), hy-phen-a-tion and con-cat-e-na-tion, a-part and ap-er-ture, and aph-o-rism and a-pha-sia. As in the case of word stemming, the simplest way to handle the hyphenation problem is to formulate basic laws that operate in most cases, while using exception dictionaries for words that do not follow these rules. Each candidate word for hyphenation is then checked against the dictionary; the normal hyphenation rules are used if the word is not found on the list. TeX uses an exception dictionary of about 350 entries and four basic rules: [14]

1. Remove suffix and insert a permissible hyphen if the word ends in one of a number of specific suffixes such as -able, -ary, -ment, and -ness.

2. Remove prefixes and insert a hyphen if the word begins in one of a number of recognized prefixes such as com-, con-, dis-, and equi-.

3. Study the consonant pairs in the remaining word stems and combine certain pairs into a single unit (such as ch, sh, and th); insert breaks between noncombined consonant pairs in particular contexts.

4. Discard breaks produced by the preceding rules when only one or two letters are left after the break, or only one letter appears before the break, or only one letter appears between prefix and suffix.

Clearly the best way to avoid questionable hyphenations is to avoid hyphenation altogether, which is what the TeX line-break system attempts to do.

Both the UNIX and TeX document-formatting systems provide refined tools for document preparation. Attempts have also been made to decouple document content from formatting details much more radically than in UNIX and TeX by using higher-level operations and separating text and formatting data. In the SCRIBE system, the text does not contain specific formatting instructions. [16] Instead, a document *environment* is provided for each type of document, and for each distinguished document portion. Such an environment is characterized by variables for spacing, indentations, type font, and so on, and by appropriate value assignments for these variables. The automated system then carries out the details of the formatting tasks using information about document type and environment. In SCRIBE, detailed format operations — including page, chapter and footnote numberings, as well as the preparation of glossaries, tables of contents, and tables of figures — are all handled by the system itself, with only minimal inputs by the user. The advantage is a much lower ratio of required formatting commands to text length, and a faster processing time — at the cost of some loss of control by the user.

4.4.2 Interactive Graphics-Editing Systems

The alternative approach to off-line text editing and formatting is taken in the popular microcomputer-based systems, such as Final-Word, WordPerfect, WordStar, and MacWrite. These systems use flexible graphics-interface methods to manipulate text interactively, under the WYSIWYG ("what you see is what you get") principle. Instead of stripping low-level editing and formatting commands into the text, and letting the computer rearrange text globally, the operations are performed singly under direct user control, and the effect of each operation is verified immediately using the available graphic display. The microcomputer-based systems do not usually provide elaborate programs for manipulating complex text items such as tables and equations, and no attempt is made to optimize paragraph placement and hyphenation. Instead, the user is asked to judge the effect of each operation, and to remedy the situation if a particular operation produces unsatisfactory results.

Consider, for example, the text manipulations available on the Macintosh computer using programs such as MacWrite, MacDraw, and MacPaint. [17,18] These packages use a mixture of icon displays, standard command menus displayed on a menu "bar", and pop-up menus that appear superimposed on the current display when the user chooses a particular high-level operation. The following main facilities are available on the basic display screen:

- A menu bar that lists basic choices such as font style and format. When an entry is chosen from the menu bar, an additional lower-level menu appears that provides a font menu, or a style menu from which further choices must be made.

- A scroll bar that makes it possible to move the displayed list up or down, one line at a time, or continuously, as desired.

- Spacing and tab rules that are used to set margins, spaces between lines, and tabs.

All these operations are performed by a movable hand-held mouse provided with buttons that the user can depress. When the mouse is moved on a table in front of the screen, a cursor moves in synchronism and points to particular objects displayed on the screen. Three main mouse-handling techniques are used:

1. A button is clicked, that is, pushed down and immediately released when the cursor points to an object. The clicking action selects the particular object seen by the cursor.

2. A button is pressed, that is, pushed down and held in the down position. Normally, this maintains the desired effect for as long as the button is pressed.

3. The mouse is "dragged" by first pointing it to an object, then pressing a button, and then moving the mouse while keeping the button depressed. This usually moves the clicked object to a new position on the screen.

Thus to specify the margin width for a particular text portion, a margin setter is chosen from the basic display (by clicking the button of the mouse pointing to the margin setter); by dragging the mouse in the correct direction, the margin setter is placed into the proper position next to the wanted text portion.

The MacWrite program provides six basic screen windows:

1. A document window that displays a text excerpt to create or update a document.

2. Separate header and footer windows that contain specifications for document headings and endings.

3. A find window to locate text portions containing particular key-word configurations. The search pattern used may contain up to 45 characters, and the text can be searched continuously, or within specified limits.

4. A change window that makes it possible to cut and paste new text portions at places previously located by a find operation.

5. A clipboard window to save text or to store text before filing it away in designated files. A special file menu is used to store text, and various intermediate storage areas are provided for special use, including a "scrapbook" to store text excerpts that are frequently needed.

All windows can be moved on the screen, changed in size, and closed when no longer required.

New text is normally generated by choosing an appropriate insertion point, and simply typing it in. The system uses an automatic "wraparound" feature to start a new line of text whenever the margin is reached on the previous line. Spacing is provided by clicking the mouse at the proper place, and the text can be filed or printed when complete. In the latter case, printing formats and paper choice must be specified using a special printing menu.

The MacDraw and MacPaint programs extend the text preparation strategies to include drawings and pictures. In MacDraw, graph components such as straight lines and various curves, furnished on an icon display, are used to construct the desired graph patterns. In MacPaint, freehand images are generated, rather than graphs containing preset patterns. Various drawing tools are then provided, including paint cans with specified colors, background patterns of many kinds, erasers to remove displayed portions of pictures, and various paintbrush shapes. To form a given picture, a particular paintbrush can be chosen together with specified paint cans and backgound patterns, and the paint can be spread across the designated areas by dragging the mouse appropriately. Pictures can also be edited by copying picture portions, or by inversion, edge tracing, horizontal or vertical flipping, rotation, and so on.

Because of the small display screen on the standard Macintosh machine, the displayed picture does not provide the fine detail required for complete viewing. Indeed the picure is restricted to 1M picture points per screen, whereas 300 by 300 (or 90,000) dots per square inch are usually needed for proper resolution. Thus for a full-page display 5.8M dots are desirable instead of the 1M actually available. Even with the reduced resolution, however, the general picture arrangement is easily visible.

In addition to microcomputer-based text-processing systems, certain elaborate document-preparation systems have been designed using high-resolution graphic displays for document and command sequences. [5,19,20] These systems may provide high-level operational sequences based on the use of "property sheets" to specify needed variables. Alternatively, sample texts can be displayed whose properties and formats are then transferred to the new documents currently under construction.

Typical displays of document forms and property sheets for character and paragraph production are shown in Table 4.9. To specify a formatting environment, one of the possible values is chosen from each line of the appropriate property list before the corresponding operation is performed.

An interactive editing and formatting system gives the user easily learnable contexts and a friendly interface. As fancy, high-resolution displays become more widespread in the future, the use of interactive systems is expected to increase.

4.5 Automatic Typesetting Systems

4.5.1 Typesetting Systems

In the conventional "hot type" typesetting environments used for several hundred years, a metal stamp was prepared for each page by cutting out the required size and shape of the type in a metal bar. Ink was then applied, and an impression was created on paper or some other hard-copy medium. In the late 19th century, Ottmar Mergenthaler introduced a keyboard-operated typesetting machine, known as the Linotype, that set type a line at a time. The Monotype machine, invented almost simultaneously, represented an advance in typsetting because it allowed each character to be cast separately.

In the 1930s and 1940s, another major typesetting advance occurred with the introduction of advanced photo-offset technology — "cold type" — that no longer required raised type or setting characters in metal. Today most phototypesetters are computer driven, in the sense that the instructions to choose the proper character set and the arrangement of characters in lines are provided by computer rather than a human operator.

Two types of technologies are current in automatic phototypesetting systems. [21,22] First is an analog procedure: Preformed characters, usually stored on a rotating film disk, are individually copied, transformed in size, and positioned by a system of lenses and prisms. Eventually the characters are recorded on film or another photosensitive medium, from which the printing plates are produced. Such a system is shown in simplified form in Fig. 4.5. The other type of technol-

Table 4.9 Sample display configurations. (a) Display configuration. (b) Character property sheet. (c) Paragraph property sheet.

Document excerpt	Icons for: files of records folders of records individual records in and out-boxes file drawers user terminals

(a)

Display	CHAR | PARA
Font	CLASSIC | MODERN | TITAN | BOLD
Size	8 | 10 | 12 | 14 | 18 | 24
Font	BOLD | ITALICS | UNDERLINE
Position	CENTER | UPPER RIGHT | LOWER RT.

(b)

Display	CHARACTER | PARAGRAPH
Alignment	FLUSH LEFT | CENTERED | FLUSH RT.
Hyphenation	USE HYPHENATION
Margins	LEFT \[\] RIGHT \[\]
Line Height	SINGLE | 11/2 | DOUBLE | TRIPLE | OTHER \[\]

(c)

Figure 4.5 Typical phototypesetting process.

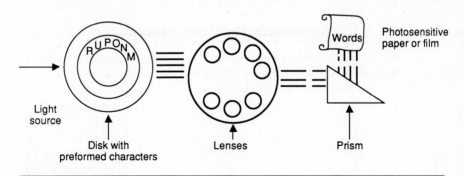

ogy is digital: The images of the characters are represented by a set of black or white point positions on a screen. These digitized images can be kept in a computer store and appropriately modified before the actual printing takes place. The digitized form of the characters can be obtained by scanning a set of prerecorded characters and storing the resulting black and white pulses. Alternatively, the characters can be generated by machine, using appropriate parameters stored for that purpose. When the computer is used to design fonts, each character can be generated "on the fly", as needed, or the digitized forms of the characters can be prestored and brought out from memory when required. A sample digitized character is shown in Fig. 4.6.

In phototypesetting, almost any typefont or character design can be used. Further, in digitized phototypesetting there are few moving parts compared with letterpress technologies, and typesetting speed

Figure 4.6 Typical digitized character.

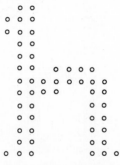

is correspondingly much greater, ranging from about 50 to many hundreds of characters per second.

❖ 4.5.2 Automatic Typefont Design

While photocomposition allows for many different typeface designs, including the use of joined and overlapping characters, some prerecorded characters may prove unappealing when transformed by simple enlarging or compression operations. Trouble may also arise when small point sizes are used with devices of limited resolution, that is, with few available point positions per inch. In that case, sawtooth effects are obtained for diagonal portions of the output (see Fig. 4.7).

The problems arising from inadequate resolution can be eliminated by using larger point densities, although at the cost of increased storage requirements and decreased production speeds. Using higher resolution devices, however, does not remedy the problem of unappealing or limited character designs. This problem has been attacked by using the computer itself as a tool in producing interesting and pleasing designs. [23–25] In one approach, an artist designs an ideal picture of a particular character, using a high-resolution graphic display. Such a design can be interactively modified, and the image can be scanned to produce a digitized point map representing the character. In another computer-based approach, the type design is based on mathematical descriptions of the needed lines and curves, rather than initial artwork. Specified point location and equations are used to represent the curves that join particular points. Thus the amount of data needed to describe a given character is much smaller than required for a digitized point map. However, the designer is obliged to manipulate mathematical formulas instead of graphic images. In principle, computerized character design can be performed in a batch-

Figure 4.7 Staircase effect for low-resolution character.

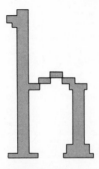

processing mode by supplying the required parameter lists in advance and having a computer generate the characters off-line. Alternatively, an interactive method can be used in which the finished designs are displayed and modified on the spot by adjusting parameters.

All character-design systems, whether based on batch-processing or interactive methodologies, use basic utilities that allow the following: A choice among given typefaces; the matching of type characteristics (such as serifs and stems) in a single design; the generation of derivative fonts, such as italics or bold, from a basic font; the generation of type of various point sizes; the derivation of smooth curves joining pairs or sets of multiple points; the generation of strokes starting at a given point and following specified directions; and so on.

The METAFONT system is probably the best noninteractive type-design system. [23] In METAFONT the characters are drawn using sets of virtual pens with circular, vertical, or horizontal outlines (see Fig. 4.8). Character descriptions are given in terms of motions between specified character points rather than by following stroke boundaries. This makes possible more parsimonious descriptions, as shown in Fig. 4.8 by the straight line between points 1 and 2 drawn by a circular pen. In addition to the various pens, a set of "erasers" cleans off ink at critical points where different strokes overlap.

It is important to choose pleasing designs for the curvilinear parts of characters. In METAFONT a curve passing through three points will take a direction at the middle point equivalent to the arc of the circle joining the three points. Further, when two points are connected by a curve exhibiting specific tangential directions at those points, a cubic spline (described by a cubic equation) is used. Consider the heart design in Fig. 4.9. A satisfactory design can be obtained by using a horizontal tangent at points 2 and 6 and a vertical tangent at points 3 and 5, and by specifying the initial directions of the curves at points 1 and 4.

The METAFONT system was used to develop a new typeface: Computer Modern. Twenty-eight principal parameters were used to describe the letter shapes, plus three additional parameters affecting

Figure 4.8 Metafont pens and strategy. (a) Pen types. (b) Straight line obtained with circular pen.

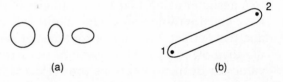

(a)   (b)

Figure 4.9 Heart design.

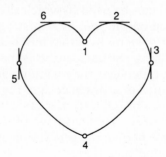

letter spacing. [23] The parameters types can be grouped into the following:

- Parameters controlling the vertical dimension of the letters such as the x height (the height of the letter x); the height of ascenders above x of letters such as d, t, and b; the height of descenders below x of letters such as p, q, and y; and the e height (the height of the horizontal part of e).

- Parameters controlling the horizontal dimension of the letters, that is, the widths of the characters.

- Parameters controlling the shape of elliptical pens, such as the aspect ratio between horizontal and vertical pen dimensions, and the size of hairlines and stems drawn with these pens.

- The amount of overshoot by which curves and sharp corners are allowed to go above the mean line or below the baseline.

- Serif parameters controlling the shear and bracketing of serifs.

- Slant parameters that specify the amount of slanting in italic fonts.

- The so-called "square root of 2," which designates the 45-degree points of elliptical curves, and allows the generation of rounder or flatter curves resulting from the corresponding parameter changes.

A designer using a large multiplicity of parameters obviously must have considerable knowledge about the availability of design tools and their effect. Interactive font-design systems may be more forgiving than off-line methods because unfortunate choices of parameter values or design operations are reflected immediately in unsatisfactory output displays. In interactive design systems, mathematical insights about parameter values and their effects are replaced by artistic sense and design expertise. [24]

A recently developed interactive font-design system includes the following principal facilities: [25]

- A system for drawing contours on a screen, or for mathematically specifying the contour lines, followed by the automatic digitizing of the contour in terms of black and white picture points.

- A contour editing system with a "zoom" mode for magnifying various picture portions and carrying out picture transformations such as copying character parts from one figure to another, and stretching, translating, rotating, mirroring, and otherwise adjusting character designs.

- A curve-generation system that produces specified curves connecting particular points.

- An interactive display controller capable of showing character layouts, font design parameters, dialogue excerpts from earlier design sessions, and command menus for new operations that may suggest themselves.

The area of computer-aided font-design is relatively new. As it develops further, font-design packages may be incorporated into general-purpose word-processing systems. In time, an integrated automated document-processing system may be available that customizes the complete document-production cycle, from initial text generation to final output in typeset form.

References

1. N. Meyrowitz and A. van Dam, Interactive Editing Systems, in *Document Preparation Systems*, J. Nievergelt, G. Coray, J.D. Nicoud, and A.C. Shaw, editors, North Holland Publishing Company, Amsterdam, 1982, 21–123.

2. K.Y. Wong, R.G. Casey, and F.M. Wahl, Document Analysis System, *IBM Journal of Research and Development*, 26:6, November 1982, 647–656.

3. D.D. Chamberlin, O.P. Bertrand, M.J. Goodfellow, J.C. King, D.R. Slutz, S.J.P. Todd, and B.W. Wade, Janus — An Interactive Document Formatter Based on Declarative Tags, *IBM Systems Journal*, 21:3, 1982, 250–271.

4. J. Furuta, J. Scofield, and A. Shaw, Document Formatting Systems: Survey, Concepts, and Issues, *Computing Surveys*, 14:3, September 1982, 417–472.

5. M. Hammer, R. Ilson, T. Anderson, M. Good, L. Rosenstein, B. Niamir, S. Schoichet, and E. Gilbert, The Implementation of Etude, an Integrated and Interactive Document Preparation System, *Proceedings of the ACM SIGPLAN-SIGOA Symposium on Text Manipulation*, Association for Computing Machinery, New York, June 1981, 137–146.

6. T.L. Roberts and T.P Moran, The Evaluation of Text Editors: Methodology and Empirical Results, *Communications of the ACM*, 26:4, April 1983, 265–283.

7. Introduction to Waterloo SCRIPT, University of Waterloo Computing Center, Waterloo, Ontario, October 1977.

8. B.W. Kernighan and M.E. Lesk, UNIX Document Preparation, in *Document Preparation Systems*, J. Nievergelt, G. Coray, J.D. Nicoud, and A.C. Shaw, editors, North Holland Publishing Company, Amsterdam, 1982, 1–20.

9. J.F. Ossana, NROFF/TROFF User's Manual, Bell Laboratories, Computer Science Technical Report 54, Murray Hill, NJ, October 1981.

10. B.W. Kernighan and P. J. Plauger, *Software Tools*, Addison-Wesley Publishing Company, Reading, MA, 1976.

11. M.E. Lesk, TBL — A Program to Format Tables, Bell Laboratories, Technical Report No. 49, Murray Hill, NJ, 1976.

12. B.W. Kernighan and L.L. Cherry, A System for Typesetting Mathematics, *Communications of the ACM*, 18:3, March 1975, 182–193.

13. B.W. Kernighan, PIC — A Language for Typesetting Graphics, *Proceedings of the SIGPLAN-SIGOA Symposium on Text Manipulation*, Association for Computing Machinery, New York, June 1981, 92–98.

14. D.E. Knuth, *TeX and Metafont; New Directions in Typesetting*, American Mathematical Society and Digital Press, Bedford, MA, 1979.

15. M.F. Plass and D.E. Knuth, Choosing Better Line Breaks, in *Computer Preparation Systems*, J. Nievergelt, G. Coray, J.D. Nicoud, and A.C. Shaw, editors, North Holland Publishing Company, Amsterdam, 1982, 221–242.

16. B.K. Reid, A High-Level Approach to Computer Document Formatting, *Proceedings of Seventh Annual ACM Conference on Principles of Programming Languages*, Association for Computing Machinery, New York, 1980, 24–31.

17. Apple Computer Inc, MacWrite, Manual M1502, Cupertino, CA, 1985.

18. Apple Computer Inc, MacPaint, Manual M1501, Cupertino, CA, 1983.

19. B.W. Lampson, Bravo Manual — Alto User's Handbook, Xerox Corporation, Palo Alto, CA, 1978.

20. J. Gutknecht, Concepts of the Text Editor Lara, *Communications of the ACM*, 28:9, September 1985, 942–960.

21. M.P. Barnett, *Computer Typesetting — Experiments and Prospects*, MIT Press, Cambridge, MA, 1965.

22. J.N. Akkerhuis, Typesetting and Troff, Stichting Mathematisch Centrum, Computer Science Report IW 247/83, Amsterdam, December 1983.

23. D.E. Knuth, The Concept of a Metafont, Computer Science Department, Stanford University, Report STAN-CS 81-886, Stanford, CA, October 1980.

24. J. Flowers, Digital Type Manufacture: An Interactive Approach, *Computer*, 17:5 May 1984, 40–48.

25. E. Kohen, An Interactive Method for Middle Resolution Font Design on Personal Workstations, Institute fur Informatik, Swiss Federal Institute of Technology, Zurich, Switzerland, 1985.

Chapter 5

Text Compression

The usefulness and efficiency of text-processing systems can often be improved greatly by converting normal natural-language text representations into a new form better adapted to computer manipulation. For example, storage space and processing time are saved in many applications by using short document abstracts, or summaries, instead of full document texts. Alternatively, the texts can be stored and processed in encrypted form, rather than the usual format, to preserve the secrecy of the content.

One obvious factor usable in text transformations is the redundancy built into normal natural-language representation. By eliminating redundancies — a method known as *text compression* — it is often possible to reduce text sizes considerably without any loss of text content. Compression was especially attractive in earlier years, when computers of restricted size and capability were used to manipulate text. Today large disk arrays are usually available, but using short texts and small dictionary sizes saves processing time in addition to storage space and still remains attractive.

5.1 Statistical Language Characteristics

❖ 5.1.1 Frequency Considerations

A study of the composition of text samples shows the unevenness with which linguistic text elements occur. Thus for languages of Western Europe, the 15 alphabetic characters occurring most frequently in running text account for 85 to 95 percent of all letter occurrences. [1] In English, the 10 most frequent alphabetic characters (e, t, a, i, s, o, n, h, r, and d) together account for over 70 percent of letter occurrences.

Letter combinations and complete words also occur unevenly. Thus many two-letter combinations (digrams) do not occur at all in English (e.g., qz), while others, such as th are quite frequent. The 10 most frequent words in English, taken from a sample of over 1 million words of text, are shown in Table 5.1. [2] It can be seen that the two words the and of account for over 10 percent of the word occurrences of English text, while the first six words (the, of, and, to, a, and in) account for over 20 percent of all word occurrences in English. The 50 most frequent words cover more than half of all word occurrences in ordinary text.

The words used frequently in English are short: The average word length for distinct English words is 8.1 characters, whereas the average length of word occurrences in ordinary English text, where frequent words are repeated many times, is 4.7 characters. This same fact is demonstrated by considering lists of distinct English words arranged in order of decreasing frequency. To find a word eight-

Table 5.1 Illustration of rank frequency law.

Rank r	Word	Frequency $f(r)$ $N \sim 1$ million	$r \cdot \dfrac{f(r)}{N}$
1	the	69,971	0.070
2	of	36,411	0.073
3	and	28,852	0.086
4	to	26,149	0.104
5	a	23,237	0.116
6	in	21,341	0.128
7	that	10,595	0.074
8	is	10.049	0.081
9	was	9,816	0.088
10	he	9,543	0.095

characters long, one must go down to the 162nd entry for the word American. [2]

The frequency characteristics of text words are of interest in fields such as communications theory and psycholinguistics. One psycholinguist, George Zipf, has observed that when the distinct words in some sample texts are arranged in decreasing frequency order, and rank orders are assigned (that is, rank 1 is assigned to the most frequent word, rank 2 to the next most frequent word, and so on), then the frequency of occurrence $f(r)$ of the rth word in frequency order multiplied by rank r is approximately constant, or

$$r \cdot f(r) \sim \text{constant} \qquad (5.1)$$

The rank-frequency formulation can also be expressed in probabilistic terms because $p(r)$, the probability of occurrence of the rth ranked word in frequency order, is $f(r)/N$ for N total word occurrences. If t is the number of distinct words, one also has $\sum_{i=1}^{t} p(i) = 1$. Table 5.1 illustrates the Zipf law for the 10 most frequent words in English, as taken from a sample of more than 1 million text words. It is seen that the constant for $r \cdot p(r)$ lies in the vicinity of 0.1. [3]

Zipf has rationalized his observations of word occurrence as an instance of a general logarithmic law of ecology that demands that the least effort be expended to handle the words used most frequently, with more effort required to process rarer words. The most frequent words must necessarily be short.

Word-frequency statistics can be used to compute the reduction in text size that can be achieved by text compression and text encryption. One can also estimate storage requirements for word lists and dictionaries. For example, in information retrieval, tables of distinct text words are often built in, giving the locations of each word in the text. The sizes of such tables can be estimated as follows. [4-5]

Suppose that a word occurs exactly n times in a text. Then for a total of N word occurrences in the text one has, according to Zipf,

$$r_n = A \frac{N}{n} \qquad (A \sim 0.1). \qquad (5.2)$$

Several words can be expected to occur the same number of times. Let r_n designate the rank of the last of the terms occurring exactly n times. Then r_n terms occur n times or more, while r_{n+1} terms occur $(n+1)$ times or more. Hence if I_n designates the number of terms that occur exactly n times, one has

$$I_n = r_n - r_{n+1} = A \frac{N}{n} - A \frac{N}{n+1} = A \cdot \frac{N}{n(n+1)} . \qquad (5.3)$$

Since the highest-ranking term (rank t) may be assumed to occur only once, $t = A \cdot N/1$. Also, the number of words occurring exactly once is

$$I_1 = r_1 - r_2 = A \cdot \frac{N}{1} - A \cdot \frac{N}{2} = A \cdot \frac{N}{2}. \qquad (5.4)$$

From (3) and (4) one concludes that

$$\frac{I_n}{t} = \frac{1}{n(n+1)} \quad \text{and} \quad \frac{I_1}{I_n} = \frac{2}{n(n+1)}.^1 \qquad (5.5)$$

These formulas can be used to estimate the number of occurrences of low-frequency words in English texts. Table 5.2 shows the predicted number of occurrences of words of frequency n for n from 1 to 10 using the formulas of expression (5.5). The table also shows the actual proportion and number of occurrences of low-frequency words for the sample of more than 1 million English word occurrences already cited. In that case t, the number of distinct words in the sample was equal to 50,406. Table 5.2 shows that about 50 percent of the distinct words in ordinary text occur only once, about 16 percent occur twice, and

Table 5.2 Occurrence frequencies of low-frequency words.

Number of Occurrences (n)	Predicted Proportion of Occurrences $1/n(n+1)$	Actual Proportion of Terms Occurring n Times I_n/t	Actual Number of Terms I_n Occurring n Times ($t = 50,406$)
1	0.500	0.447	22,543
2	0.167	0.143	7,233
3	0.083	0.078	3,947
4	0.050	0.049	2,465
5	0.033	0.036	1,820
6	0.024	0.025	1,279
7	0.018	0.022	1,121
8	0.014	0.016	824
9	0.011	0.014	695
10	0.009	0.011	559

1. Formulas (5.3)–(5.5) were derived by Booth [5] and described by Heaps [4].

about 8 percent occur three times. About 80 percent of the distinct words occur not more than four times. This confirms the general understanding that for normal text a very small number of distinct words occur very often; a very large number of words are extremely rare.

Vocabulary growth can also be related to the length of text examined. If t is the number of distinct words in a given text, and N is the total number of word occurrences, a typical relationship between t and N is given by

$$t = k N^\beta \tag{5.6}$$

where the constants k and β are determined by the text under consideration. Typical values for k are between 10 and 20; for β, between 0.5 and 0.6. Table 5.3 contains the vocabulary growth data (t versus N) for $\beta=0.5$ and $k=10$, demonstrating that, as text size increases the number of new words found very rapidly becomes smaller.

❖ 5.1.2 Entropy Measurements

The occurrence characteristics of linguistic elements also form the basis of statistical communications theory, which estimates the value, or information content, of messages sent from message sources to message receivers. In communications theory, the value of a message is assumed to be inversely proportional to the probability with which the message text could have been predicted by the receiver before the

Table 5.3 Vocabulary growth data (expression (5.6) with $\beta = 0.5$, $k=10$).

Number of Word Occurrences N	Number of Distinct Words t
500	223.6
1000	316.2
2000	447.2
4000	632.5 (+185.3)
6000	774.6 (+142.1)
8000	894.4 (+119.8)
10000	1000.0 (+105.6)
12000	1095.4 (+95.4)

message arrived. [6] Thus given a partial message consisting of the character pair th, the value of the character e, received subsequently, is very small because the probability of e following th is very large; on the other hand, the value of y following th is much higher because its occurrence probability in that context is low.

The information content H of a message, or partial message, is then defined as a decreasing function $H(p)$ of the probability p of that message. Because the information content of two messages should be an additive function of their individual content values, that is, $H(p_1 p_2) = H(p_1) + H(p_2)$, and the value of a message received with probability 1 should be null (that is, $H(1) = 0$), the information content of a message can be defined as

$$H(p) = -\log(p) = \log 1/p \qquad (5.7)$$

$H(p)$, also known as the *entropy* of a message received with probability p, measures the quantity by which the receiver's uncertainty is reduced when the message is received. Given that k possible messages are predictable with probabilities $p_1, p_2, ..., p_k$, the average or expected information content gained through the receipt of one of the k messages is

$$\bar{H} = -\sum_{i=1}^{k} p_i \log p_i, \qquad (5.8)$$

where $\sum_{i=1}^{k} p_i = 1$. It can be shown that $\bar{H}$ is maximized when the occurrence probabilities for the k messages are all equal, with value $1/k$. Thus when a message is received, and nothing is known about the occurrence characteristics of the individual characters or letters, one may assume that each character occurs with probability 1/26. In that case the occurrence of a given character provides an information content of

$$H_o = -\log 1/26 = 4.70 \text{ bits.}^2 \qquad (5.9a)$$

When the characters have the actual probabilities of the letters in English text, one finds that

2. Number of bits (binary digits) is used to measure the value of the entropy, because it is known that n equiprobable characters can be encoded by using $\log_2 n$ bits per character. This is the same quantity previously used to measure information content $(-\log_2 1/n)$.

$$H_1 = - \sum_{i=1}^{26} p_i \log p_i = 4.29 \text{ bits.} \qquad (5.9b)$$

The skewed occurrence probabilities of the characters in English text, then, are worth 0.41 bits per received character in a message.

The uncertainty, or entropy, of a character is also reduced by specifying the context in which the character occurs. Thus when the preceding characters are specified, the entropy of the following characters is smaller than the entropy of a single character alone. Let p_{rs} designate the probability of the character pair rs. The entropy of character s, if preceded by the character r, is then given by

$$-\log(p_{rs}/p_r) = -\log p_{rs} + \log p_r,$$

a quantity smaller than that obtainable from p_s alone. [4]

The entrophy of full words, as opposed to individual characters, is also reduced when the occurrence characteristics of the words are uneven, or when the context of the words is known. Table 5.4 shows the average entrophy per word when vocabulary size varies from 10,000 to 100,000 distinct words. When the word occurrences are all equal, $\bar{H} = -\log 1/t$. On the other hand, when the words occur with the probabilities suggested by Zipf's rank-frequency expression, $p_i = A/r_i$ and

$$\bar{H} = - \sum_{i=1}^{t} p_i \log p_i = - \sum_{i=1}^{t} \frac{A}{i} \log \frac{A}{i} . \qquad (5.10)$$

The data of Table 5.4 show that the high occurrence probabilities, and hence low entropies, of certain words reduce the average information content of the words by nearly four bits per word for a vocabulary of 10,000 distinct words, and by more than five bits per word for vocabularies of 100,000 words. [4]

Table 5.4 Average entropy for vocabularies of various sizes.

Vocabulary size t	Average Entropy for Equal Occurrence Probability $-\log (1/t)$	Average Entropy for Occurrence Probabilities According to Zipf (5.10)
10,000	13.3 bits	9.5 bits
50,000	15.6 bits	10.9 bits
100,000	16.6 bits	11.4 bits

Mandelbrot used statistical communications theory to generate improved indicators of relationships between ranks and frequencies of linguistic elements. [7] In particular, consider the word-frequency distribution $f(r)$, or equivalently the word-probability distribution $p(r)$, which produces the smallest mean number of letters per word for a particular value of the entropy $\bar{H}$. To obtain such a distribution, one must minimize

$$\sum_{r=1}^{t} p(r)\, m(r)$$

for t distinct words, where $m(r)$ represents the length of the rth ranked word. When the restrictions

$$\sum_{r=1}^{t} p(r) = 1 \text{ and } \bar{H} = -\sum_{r=1}^{t} p(r) \log p(r) = \text{constant}$$

are used, one obtains the solution

$$p(r) = \frac{A}{(r+B)^{\beta}}, \qquad\qquad (5.11)$$

where the constants A, B, and β are fixed for vocabularies of a given subject. Values of β around 1.2 appear reasonable for English. Expression (5.11), which has the form previously given in (5.1) produces approximations closer than those illustrated for the basic formula in the right-most column of Table 5.1.

Statistical methodologies are used extensively in many text-processing applications. For example, the value of a word as an indicator of text content is often taken to be an inverse function of its frequency of occurrence in the documents of a collection. This agrees with the observation that the most frequent words exhibit the smallest entropy and contribute little to the characterization of individual texts. When the full scope of automatic text-processing applications is considered, however, the statistical component provides only limited information. Structural and semantic considerations must also be taken into account.

5.2 Rationale for Text Compression

Statistical text characterization shows that the normal use of a natural-language text to convey text meaning involves substantial redundancies. These redundancies are of two main types: First, the statistical redundancy arising from the uneven frequencies of alphabetic characters or speech sounds, and from dependencies between character groups, and second, the structural and semantic redundancies produced by the use of complex turns of phrases instead of equivalent, more straightforward modes of expression.

With regard to statistical redundancies, inefficiencies are obviously present when the same amount of effort or space is used to represent a high-frequency symbol like e and a low-frequency character like z. The same is true when character combinations such as qu are used instead of the simpler, nearly equivalent q. These effects are even more important in computer processing of texts, in which fixed-length strings of binary digits usually represent each alphabetic or numeric character, regardless of the frequency or usage characteristics of the characters. Because the information content of the high-frequency characters is low, as previously explained, it is obviously wasteful to devote as much space to represent them as to represent elements with a higher information content.

The structural and semantic redundancies in normal text are illustrated by the existence of abbreviated representations such as 11/12/85 to represent 12 November 1985, or by the standard utilization of telegraphic style to reduce the cost of messages transmitted over long distances.

In ordinary language, redundancy serves many important purposes. For example, repetition and circuitous locutions can simplify comprehension in some circumstances; further, redundant elements often indicate ambiguity or vagueness, increasing the flexibility of the available linguistic tools. However, linguistic redundancies substantially increase the cost of processing data by computer, and for this reason substantial efforts have been devoted to devising text transformations that eliminate redundancy.

All text-transformation systems are based on *data-encoding* methods, which map into code values a collection of encoding units — for example, individual text characters, or individual words and word combinations. In conventional computer representations, each text character is normally mapped into a sequence of six or eight binary digits, known as a byte. If the mapping is one to one — that is, if each encoding unit corresponds to a unique code value and vice versa — the mapping is reversible. A reverse transformation is then easily defined from encoded forms back to the original texts.

Some text-transformation systems provide *data-compaction* by reducing the data size of the encoded form compared with the original, nevertheless preserving the essential information. Data-compaction systems that are also reversible are known as *compression* systems. In most practical text-processing systems, the original text must be preserved for output purposes. Hence irreversible data-compaction methods are not relevant here.

The purpose of data compression is to reduce file size without any resulting loss of information content. The basic measure of compression effectiveness is the compression ratio, which relates the original data length to the encoded length as follows: [8]

$$\text{Compression ratio} = \frac{\text{Original length} - \text{Encoded length}}{\text{Original length}}$$

Many text-compression systems produce compression ratios of 50 percent or more, which produces substantial advantages in practical processing systems:

- Storage costs and the size of the buffer stores needed for text processing may be substantially reduced.

- Many text-processing operations, such as text scanning, file merging, and text sorting, are performed much more rapidly for small files than for large ones.

- Data transmission costs are smaller for compressed files than for the originals; this reduces the cost of text-distribution systems that send files to local areas for searching and manipulation.

- When compressed files are used, many text-processing applications can be performed using small machines with limited memory size and processing capability.

The disadvantages of text compression relate to the added layer of processing needed to carry out the compression and decompression, as well as to the complexities inherent in certain compression methods:

- Compression and decompression take extra time, and many systems require special code tables that must be stored and maintained.

- Some compression methods produce variable-length records, more difficult to process than fixed-length records.

- Some compression methods require manipulation at the bit level rather than the normal character level, substantially complicating the processing operations.

- Various kinds of approximate text-matching operations that could be useful for correcting errors are impossible for texts in compressed form because very similar input forms may then exhibit completely dissimilar compressed versions.

Whether to use data compression depends on many factors, including the size of the database, the amount and type of redundancy in the data, the nature and frequency of the required file accesses, the availability of extra memory to store any conversion tables that may be needed to compress or decompress, the efficiency and complexity of the particular data-compression method, and the cost and availability of the required processing time. In general, compression is attractive when the net storage space saved is substantial, and the resources needed for coding and decoding are relatively modest. In practice, compression techniques are often avoided because the system designer underestimates the amount of compression actually achievable, while overestimating the complexity in time and space of the added operations.

5.3 Text-Compression Methods

Two main principles are involved in data compression. First, the encoded form of the characters, or character strings, may better reflect the information content of the elements — notably the case in *variable-length coding* systems, which assign long codes to low-frequency encoding units with high information content, and short codes to high-frequency units with low information value. Second, the encoded text form may take into account dependencies among characters by using complex *encoding* units representing several dependent characters instead of only single characters.

When the characters to be encoded have even occurrence frequencies or probabilities, the use of fixed-length codes of length $\log_2 n$ (equal to $\bar{H}$) for n encoding units is in fact optimal. On the other hand, when the characters exhibit uneven occurrence probabilities — as do alphabetic characters in natural-language texts — a variable-length coding system is more efficient. Alternatively, a fixed-length code can be used, but applied to variable-length encoding units, that is, to character sets of variable-length, so chosen as to even out the occurrence probabilities of the various encoding units.

❖ 5.3.1 Special-purpose Compression Systems

Before treating the compression problem for general text files it is useful to discuss briefly a specialized problem arising in certain kinds of commercial files. Two main file characteristics are apparent in that environment:

1. The data may be mainly numerical, instead of alphabetic, and many entries are vacuous, consisting of zeros or blanks.

2. The data appearing adjacently in the file may be related, as in the case of alphabetically ordered dictionaries in which only a few terminal characters may differ in adjacent word entries.

In files consisting only of numeric information, an immediate 50 percent compression ratio may be achieved by simply packing two numeric digits per information byte. A half-bite encoding and decoding system accommodates all numeric data in such coding systems as EBCDIC and ASCII because they use eight-bit bytes to encode each character, whereas only four bits are needed to encode each of the 10 decimal digits. Five bits per character are required for strictly alphabetic data ($2^5 = 32$ different combinations of five binary digits are available, of which only 26 are needed for the alphabetic characters). Using five instead of eight bits per character produces a compression ratio of 37.5 percent. However, the decoding operation must then be performed at the bit level because many five-bit chunks will straddle adjacent bytes.

When the data records take the form of *sparse* vectors, consisting of elements almost all of which are zero or null, the null elements can be suppressed. The compressed form will then consist of nonzero components together with information about the position of each nonzero component in the vector. Some examples of sparse-vector representation are included in Table 5.5. A typical sparse record appears at the top of the table, followed by three sample compressed representations. The following information is shown in these three cases:

1. The nonzero digits together with a column number for each digit.

2. The nonzero digits together with a binary number indicating the positions of the respective nonzero digits from left to right.

Table 5.5 Sparse-vector representation.

1	0	0	8	0	0	0	5	0	0	0	0	2	0	basic record
14	13	12	11	10	9	8	7	6	5	4	3	2	1	column numbers

1. 2, 2; 5, 7; 8, 11; 1, 14 — Nonzero elements plus column number

2. 1 0 0 1 0 0 0 1 0 0 0 0 1 0
1, 8, 5, 2 — Nonzero elements plus binary vector

3. 9 2 8 2
1, 8, 5, 2 — Nonzero elements plus decimal number

4. 1, 2, 8, 3, 5, 4, 2, 1 — Nonzero elements followed by number of suppressed zeros

3. The nonzero digits together with the binary number used in the previous representation converted to decimal form (that is, $(10010001000010)_2 = (9282)_{10}$).

The last representation in Table 5.5 differs in that no reference is made to the vector positions of the nonzero elements. Instead each nonzero digit is followed by another digit giving the number of suppressed zeros that follow at that point. Thus the digit 1 is followed by two zeros, followed by the digit 8 and three zeros, and so on. This technique, known as *run-length encoding*, is said to achieve up to 70 percent compression for some files. [9] More generally, all sparse-vector representations gain in efficiency as the original data become sparser. Further, no special decoding tables are required for decompression.

In many alphabetic dictionary files, adjacent entries differ only in a few terminal characters. In such a case a *differential-coding* technique can be used in which a complete entry is replaced by the difference between the current entry and the preceding one. When differential coding is used, correct decoding requires the dictionary file to be read sequentially.

When specialized compression techniques are used based on the suppression of null or repeating characters, compressed forms of variable length are obtained depending on the amount of suppressed material. In some circumstances it may be inconvenient to process variable-length codes; when equivalent compression ratios can be obtained, fixed-length codes are usually preferred.

5.3.2 Basic Fixed-Length Codes

In normal fixed-length character coding, a six- or eight-bit byte represents each character. When eight-bit bytes are used, 2^8 or 256 different characters can be encoded even though normal character sets include only about 80 different characters. The coding efficiency can then be improved by making use of the normally unused capacity of the code. Code combinations can be assigned to encoding units more densely, either by reducing the length of the codes (the number of binary digits used to represent each character), or by increasing the number of encoding units. In the first approach, a short byte, consisting typically of five bits, is used for each character, and each code combination represents several different characters. One implementation of this idea uses a *base case* to encode the most frequent characters, and an auxiliary *shift case* to accommodate the remaining less frequently encoded units. For example, the base case may use 30 of 32 possible five-bit codes to represent the 30 characters of greatest frequency. Two code combinations — say 00000 and 11111 — are used to indicate shifts from the base to the auxiliary case, and vice versa. The same 30-code combinations already used in the base case are then reassigned in the auxiliary case to 30 new, less frequent characters.

The efficiency of the multiple-case approach depends on the infrequent use of the shift characters that cannot be used to represent information. When the character frequencies for the auxiliary case are small, a single *temporary shift* character can be used to switch from the base to the auxiliary case. Such a temporary shift may be valid for only one character at a time. That is, following the occurrence of a low-frequency character belonging to an auxiliary case, the base case automatically resumes decoding subsequent characters. When a temporary shift is used, no reverse shift symbol is needed.

An alternative to the multiple-case approach is to accommodate a larger character set within the single-case byte structure by exploiting otherwise-unused code combinations. One possibility consists of using frequently occurring digrams as encoding units, in addition to the needed single characters. In one implementation, 88 code combinations of the 256 eight-bit codes are used for single characters, leaving 168 codes for frequently occurring character pairs. [8,10]

Consider a byte representation in which each byte is divided into two half bytes of four bits each. If the 16 code combinations in each half byte are designated by the digits 0 to 9 and the characters A to F, respectively (see Table 5.6(a)), each eight-bit code can be identified by the character pair corresponding to the two half bytes — for example, 67 for the bit string 01100111 or A3 for the string 10100011. The encoding system of Table 5.6 specifies the following code assignment: The first 88 code combinations are used for single characters, leaving 168 codes to be assigned to character pairs. The 168 pairs are obtained by designating 8 particular characters as master characters and 21 additional characters as combining characters. Each character pair that can be represented by a special bit string is then defined as the combination of a master character followed by a combining character (see Table 5.6(b)). Thus the pair TH is represented by a particular eight-bit byte because T is a master character and H a combining character; however, the pair HT must be encoded by using two single character codes because H is not a master character.

The following string-encoding method can then be used to produce a compressed text representation: [8]

1. The text is scanned left to right on a character-by-character basis.

2. If the initial character is not a master character, it is encoded normally using a single-character code.

3. Otherwise, if the next string character is not a combining character, the initial character is again encoded by a normal single-character code.

Table 5.6 Encoding system for single characters and pairs. (a) Half-byte representation and single-character assignment. (b) Master and combining characters. (c) Typical string subdivision.

Code combination	Representation	Characters	Number of Codes
0000	0	# blank	1
0001	1		
0010	2	uppercase alphabetics	26
0011	3		
0100	4		
0101	5		
0110	6	lowercase alphabetics	26
0111	7		
1000	8		
1001	9	decimal digits	10
1010	A		
1011	B	special symbols	25
1100	C		
1101	D		———
1110	E		88
1111	F		

(a)

Master Characters	Combining Characters		
#	#	H	S
A	A	I	T
E	B	L	U
I	C	M	V
O	D	N	W
N	E	O	
T	F	P	
U	G	R	

(b)

AM	ON	G	#T	H	E#	P	EO	P	L	E#

(c)

4. Otherwise, if the initial character pair consists of a master character followed by a combining character, the two characters are encoded as a pair.

5. The process is repeated for the remaining string characters.

A sample string subdivision obtained with this method is shown in Table 5.6(c), where a 17-character string is encoded by using 6 character pairs and 5 single characters, producing a compression ratio of 35 percent. The digram encoding and decoding process is advantageous because it requires only a minimal coding table — 268 entries together with corresponding code assignments. However, the compression ratio is limited to 50 percent because at best every pair of string characters is represented by a combined one-byte code.

Numeric coding extends this idea by assigning fixed-length codes to larger subsets of adjacent characters. For example, the character strings in a text can be broken down into subgroups of n adjacent characters, each subgroup represented by a fixed-length code string. Numerical coding methods have been developed in which each m-digit character string is mapped into an m-digit number expressed in a base-b number system. [8] Very high compression ratios can be obtained using this method, but the encoding and decoding require substantial effort. [11]

5.3.3 Restricted Variable-length Codes

The multicase-coding method is in effect a restricted variable-length code because the shift symbol needed to switch from one case to another, and hence from one code transformation to another, constitutes overhead that effectively lengthens the representations for the symbols included in the auxiliary cases. In view of the skewed frequency characteristics of the characters in natural-language texts, it appears especially attractive to use codes of different length to represent encoding units of varying frequency. However, instead of choosing a freely varying code length and thereby complicating encoding and decoding, it might be possible to use only a few distinct code lengths that could be related to the byte length provided by available computing equipment. In normal environments this implies code lengths consisting of an integral number of bytes or half bytes.

Consider as an example the standard computer environment providing eight-bit bytes. In these circumstances one might use half bytes to represent a few very frequent characters, and full bytes for the remaining characters. Since it is necessary to use a one-bit prefix to distinguish the half-byte from the full-byte codes — for example, 0 to designate the half-byte codes and 1 for the full-byte codes — three bits are left to carry the half-byte information, and seven bits the full-byte data. In this system the seven most-frequent characters can therefore be encoded using a three-bit code with a 0 prefix; 128 additional, less-frequent characters are assigned seven-bit codes with a 1 prefix. [12] A sample string encoded in this system is shown in Fig. 5.1. In the example, the characters T and E are high-frequency characters, whereas H and Y are of lower frequency. Since the seven most-frequent characters account for 65 percent of letter occurrences in English text, the expected code length will be 5.4 bits per character, producing a 32.8 percent saving over text encoded in a standard eight-bit code.

It is possible to generalize the preceding by using a larger number of subdivisions whose corresponding code length increases by an even number of bits. Suppose that n distinct encoding units are available in a system. By subdividing the encoding units into r groups in decreasing order of their occurrence frequency, one could use the following code assignment, in which a code length of n_1 bits is used for group 1, n_2 bits for group 2, and so on, up to n_r bits for group r ($n_1 < n_2 < ... < n_r$): [13]

1. The 2^{n_1-1} most-frequent characters are assigned codes of length n_1, beginning with a 1 digit to indicate that the coded string belongs to the initial class; this leaves $n_1 - 1$ bits to carry the information. If $n_1 = 4$, the corresponding codes will range from 1000 to 1111.

Figure 5.1 Restricted variable-length encoding for THEY.

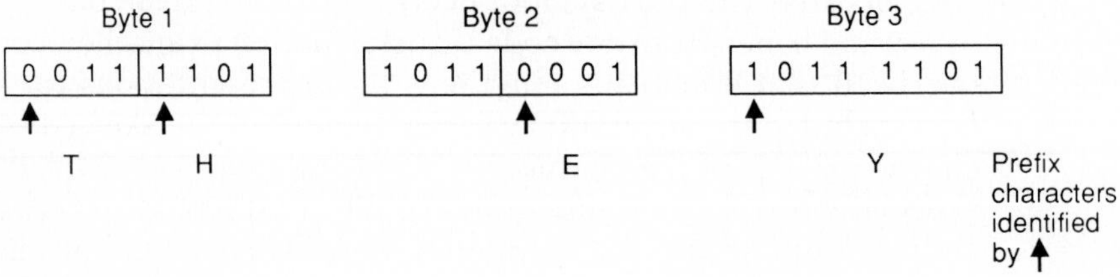

Byte 1	Byte 2	Byte 3
0 0 1 1 | 1 1 0 1	1 0 1 1 | 0 0 0 1	1 0 1 1 1 1 0 1

T   H   E   Y   Prefix characters identified by ↑

Coding

E	001	
T	011	
H	101	1011
Y	011	1101

2. The next 2^{n_2-2} characters are assigned codes of length n_2 by appending code increments of length $n_2 - n_1$ to the previous codes; the initial prefix must now be 0 to indicate that an additional code portion follows. If $n_2 = 8$ and $n_1 = 4$, any additional 2^6 characters can be accommodated with codes of the form 0xxx1xxx.

3. The next 2^{n_3-3} terms are assigned codes of length n_3 by appending code increments of length $n_3 - n_2$ to the previous set of codes. If $n_3 = 12$ this produces code combinations for 2^9 additional characters of the form 0xxx0xxx1xxx.

If the code lengths increase in even increments related to the byte size, coding and decoding are easily accomplished, and the size of the decoding tables relating the encoding units to the corresponding codes remains small when the number of different encoding units is limited.

In addition to individual characters, a restricted variable-length coding system can encode complete text words. In that case, one might choose length increments of one byte, and use a single byte for the 2^7 (128) most frequent words in the language, two bytes for the next 2^{14} (equal to 16,384) words in frequency order, and three bytes for the remaining words. If the vocabulary exhibits the usual Zipf distribution characteristics, the average code length will be between 12 and 13 bits per word for vocabularies between 20,000 and 50,000 words, compared with an optimal length of 10 to 11 bits for a completely variable length code. [12] While the word-encoding method produces close to optimal compression ratios, the large size of the decoding dictionaries makes the compression process at the word level impractical in most environments.

5.3.4 Variable-length Codes

As mentioned earlier, fixed-length codes work well with data of equal probability of occurrence. When the encoding units exhibit uneven occurrence characteristics, two possible strategies suggest themselves:

1. Variable-length encoding units might be used, constructed so as to even out the occurrence frequencies of the various encoding units. In such a case, fixed-length codes are best assigned to the encoding units. This approach was used earlier in the system providing fixed, byte-length codes for both single characters and selected character pairs.

2. Alternatively, the normal fixed-length encoding units can be preserved, but the lengths of the corresponding codes can be made to vary by using an inverse relationship between code length and occurrence probability of the corresponding encoding unit. A step in

this direction was taken by increasing the length of the codes in fixed increments (see the preceding subsection).

Completely variable-length codes are even more efficient than codes with restricted length variations. The best-known of the former type is the Huffman code, which yields minimum redundancy for a given collection of encoding units with known and unchanging occurrence probabilities. [14] The Huffman code does not take into account dependencies between different encoding units, that is, between the terms or characters to be encoded, but it yields minimum average code length when the characters occur independently of each other, and when each character is encoded by an integral number of bits. In some variable-length encoding systems, each symbol is not encoded by an integral number of bits. Such systems allow improvements in coding efficiency beyond those possible with the conventional Huffman code. [15]

A Huffman code is generated recursively by combining at each step the two characters (or two encoding units) with the lowest occurrence probability while generating a new combined encoding unit whose occurrence probability is then equal to the sum of the probabilities for the two component units. Each component of a combined unit is distinguished by the assignment of code digits 0 and 1, respectively (see Fig. 5.2(a)). This character-combining operation is then repeated for the two encoding units (or combined encoding units) with the next higher occurrence frequencies, until eventually only a single combination of encoding units remains, which includes all individual units. The occurrence frequency of the final combined unit then equals 1.

The construction of a sample Huffman code is illustrated by the tree of Fig. 5.2(b), built for some frequently occurring English words. The encoding units appear as leaves of the tree; the code assignment to each unit is obtained by following the path from the root of the tree down to the corresponding leaf and reading off the code values (binary digits) attached to the tree branches. The tree was constructed by using the word-occurrence characteristics shown in column 2 of Table 5.7. The two units with the lowest probability of occurrence are ON and IT, with assumed probabilities of 0.033 and 0.040, respectively. First, these units are combined into a unit ON-IT with a total probability of 0.073. In the example of Fig. 5.2(b), a 0 is assigned to ON and a 1 to IT. The next pair of characters to be combined is IS and THAT, with a combined probability of 0.095. Once again these characters are distinguished by code digits 0 and 1, respectively. The next step combines the joint ON-IT (0.073) with the character IN (0.074), producing a combined ON-IT-IN unit, with an occurrence probability of 0.147. The last step combines ON-IT-IN-OF-THE with A-IS-THAT-TO-AND, and the resulting final combined probability equals 1.

Figure 5.2 Huffman coding tree. (a) Combined encoding unit 1-2, with occurrence probability equal to sum of probabilities of unit 1 and unit 2. (b) Generation of sample Huffman code.

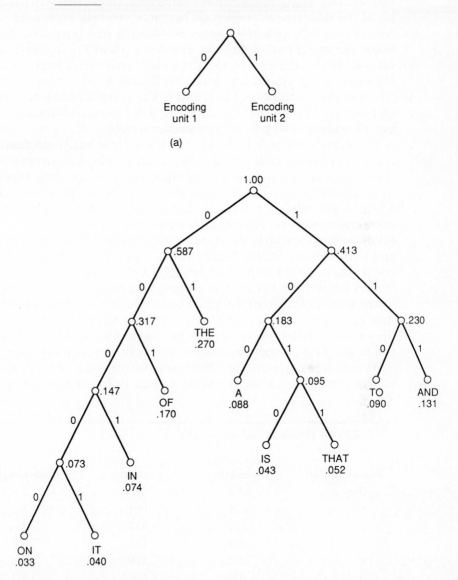

As Table 5.7 shows, the code length varies from 2 for THE to 5 for IT and ON. The average code length is given by $\sum_{i=1}^{n} p_i l_i$, where n is the number of encoding units, and p_i and l_i are the occurrence probability and the code length for the ith encoding unit, respectively. In the example of the table, the average code length is 3.05 bits, compared with a minimal code length of 4 to encode 10 units in a fixed-length code. When the individual alphabetic characters (A to Z) are encoded in a variable-length Huffman code, the code length varies from 3 bits for high-frequency characters such as E and A, to 10 bits for low-frequency characters such as Q and Z. The average code length is 4.12 bits, compared with the 8-bit code length for normal character encoding. This yields a 48 percent compression ratio.

The variable-length Huffman coding system has some disadvantages, which concern the need to use predetermined occurrence probabilities for all encoding units, and the expense of decoding. When frequency information is not available, it may be possible to compute adequate probabilities on the fly using available text samples. [16] The decoding operation requires a bit by bit scan of the encoded strings, followed by a look-up in a code table containing lists of encoding units and their corresponding binary codes. Special tree data structures could also be used for the decoding. [17] A Huffman code is characterized by its prefixes because an assigned character code is never used as the prefix of another assigned code. The decoding operation will then produce a unique result, assuming that no errors are present in the encoded string. However, the bit-wise left-to-right scan of the encoded text may be onerous in some computing environments.

As with other systems, in a Huffman system more compression can be obtained by encoding complete words. Unfortunately, the size of

Table 5.7 Huffman coding example.

Encoding Unit	Occurrence Probability	Code Value	Code Length
the	.270	01	2
of	.170	001	3
and	.137	111	3
to	.099	110	3
a	.088	100	3
in	.074	0001	4
that	.052	1011	4
is	.043	1010	4
it	.040	00001	5
on	.033	00000	5

the decoding tables makes this possibility impracticable in most situations. A compromise consists of using special codes for a subset of high-frequency words in English, while using the conventional eight-bit character representations for the remaining words. When the 800 most-frequent English words are given special codes and conventional single-character codes are used for the other words, only a small decoding table is needed, and compression ratios of 40 to 50 percent can be obtained. [18]

5.3.5 Word-Fragment Encoding

Unrestricted variable-length codes are not used as extensively as might be expected because of the relative inefficiency of the decoding operations required to transform the compressed forms back to the original plain text. Further, character dependencies, so prevalent and noticeable in natural-language texts, are not taken into account in a normal Huffman code assignment. Thus the possibility of applying fixed-length codes to variable-length encoding units should be given further attention. In such a system, the principal character dependencies can be taken into account by choosing encoding units that include groupings of dependent characters. Also when the encoding units are chosen so as to exhibit approximately even occurrence probabilities p, a fixed-length code of length $\log_2 (1/p)$ bits will in fact be optimal.

When variable-length encoding units are used at the word or phrase level, the number of possible encoding units becomes very large. The size of the coding tables, or dictionaries, needed to specify the correspondence between codes and encoding units may then become unmanageable. This suggests that the encoding units should be reasonably short, consisting principally of *word fragments*. There exist only 26^n different alphabetic character strings of length n (that is, 676 different pairs, 17,576 different triples, and so on), and most character combinations do not occur in the language, or are rare enough to be disregarded in a multicharacter system. The number of multicharacter combinations to be included in a fragment-encoding system is therefore small, and the decoding dictionaries are easily managed. Finally, as in other compression systems based on the use of multicharacter encoding units, relatively high compression ratios can be expected. [19–21]

In choosing a set of word fragments for use in a compression system, ideally the frequency of occurrence of each fragment should be close to some initially chosen target frequency. In addition, the available fragment set should permit all possible words in the language to be formed, and hence encoded; this effectively implies that all single-character symbols must be included in the given fragment set together with certain multicharacter symbols. Also, the fragment set should be chosen so as to maximize the average length of the fragments; that is, longer fragments consisting of the more frequent character combinations are given preference over shorter fragments. Finally, for ease of decoding, the text decomposition into fragments should be carried out within individual words and not across word boundaries.

Two main strategies are used to form a word-fragment set for use in compression: (1) an agglomerative method, in which single characters are taken initially to be successively combined to form strings of several characters with occurrence frequencies close to the target frequency; [22] and (2) a divisive method, in which complete words or multicharacter strings are successively divided until shorter character strings are obtained that once again meet the restrictions of the target frequency. [23] A typical string-decomposition process of the second kind might operate in the following way:

1. The words in a set of sample texts are decomposed into word fragments in all possible ways, as shown in Fig. 5.3 for the word "cats."

2. Frequency counts are generated for all fragments, reflecting the number of fragment occurrences in the text sample. Typical frequency counts for the character sequences are shown in the figure.

3. Let i be the length of the longest available word fragment. From among all fragments of length i, choose for inclusion in the fragment set that fragment whose frequency exceeds the threshold frequency by the smallest amount. If no fragment qualifies, i is decremented by 1, and the process is repeated until $i = 1$.

Figure 5.3 Decomposition into word fragments.

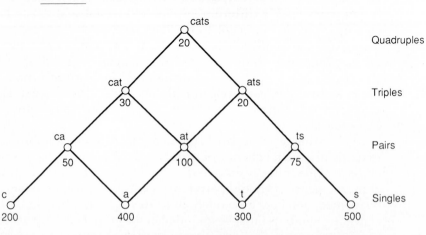

4. When a selected fragment is included in the symbol set, the frequencies of its descendants in the decomposition graph are reduced by the frequency of the selected fragment. (Thus in the graph of Fig. 5.3 the choice of "at" reduces the frequency of "a" and "t" by 100.) The fragment-selection process is repeated starting with step 3 until no further fragments qualify.

5. The size of the fragment set can be reduced to a predetermined total such as 256 (thus permitting the use of one eight-bit byte per fragment to be encoded) by eliminating redundant fragments that are included in larger fragments already chosen. However, all single-character fragments are preserved in the final set.

A list of sample word fragments from a typical set of 256 fragments is shown in Table 5.8. The fragment set shown in the table consists of character combinations ranging from one to four characters, including many high-frequency function words and word endings. When the fragment-generation method is extended to include spaces between words and at the beginning of new words, multiword fragments may be formed. This method is shown in Table 5.9, where high-frequency word combinations such as "in the," "of the," and "on the" are included, as well as many words with terminal spaces.

In actually representing a text string by fragment codes, the aim is make the resulting code as efficient as possible. Code efficiency can be

Table 5.8 Typical word fragments included in a set of 256 symbols.

Four characters	Three characters		Two characters		
ATIO	AND	NOT	AC	BA	DA
FROM	BUT	OUT	AD	BE	DE
PRES	COM	PLA	AG	BO	DI
THAT	CON	PRO	AI	BY	many other
THER	FOR	TED	AL	CA	pairs starting
TION	GHT	TER	AM	CE	with E,F,G
WERE	HAS	THE	AN	CH	H,I,L,M,N,
WILL	HER	VER	AR	CI	O,P,R,S,T,
WITH	HIS	WAS	AS	CK	U,V, and W
	ING	WHO	AT	CO	
				CT	

defined as the ratio of the average optimal code length per word divided by average actual code length, or

$$\text{Efficiency} = \frac{\Sigma \, p_i \log_2 p_i}{\Sigma \, p_i \, b_i}$$

where p_i is the probability of occurrence of the ith word and b_i is the length in bits of the fragment representation of the ith word. This suggests once again that each text word should be represented by the fewest possible number of word fragments, or alternatively that fragments corresponding to longer character strings should be assigned in preference to codes for shorter strings. The following methods are possible:

1. Given a text word, assign first the code covering the longest possible substring of that word; continue with the code for the longest substring included in the remaining characters of the word.

2. Instead of starting at an arbitrary character position in a word, perform a left-to-right scan and use successively the longest possible word prefix that matches a given fragment.

3. Subdivide a text word into the smallest possible number of different fragments.

The fastest encoding method (method 2) uses the left-to-right scan process, but is not necessarily the most efficient method. In practice, there are no large differences among the compression ratios obtainable with the encoding systems discussed: With a fragment set of 256

Table 5.9 Word fragments, including terminal spaces.

A-	ED-	HIS-	OF-	THE-
AL-	EN-	IN-THE-	ON-THE-	TION-
AND-	ER-	ING-	ON-	TO-THE-
AS-	ES-	IN-	OR-	VE-
BE-	FOR-	IS-	OUT-	WAS-
BUT-	FROM-	IT-	S-	WERE-
CE-	GHT-	LY-	SS-	WHO-
CH-	HAS-	NG-	TED-	WILL-
D-	HER-	NOT-	TER-	WITH-
E-	HE-	OF-THE-	THAT-	Y-

symbols, the compression ratio is usually 50 to 55 percent. [24] This shows that a fragment-encoding system incorporating the effect of both varying character frequencies and character dependency factors leads to higher compression ratios than do other compression systems, including the variable-length single-character Huffman code, or the fixed-length digram-encoding system described earlier. Further, when the number of fragments is limited, fragment-encoding and -decoding operations require only a small coding table. The effectiveness of the fragment encoding, however, depends on the availability of accurate frequency information for the various text fragments.

References

1. G. Herdan, *Language as Choice and Chance*, Noordhoff, Groningen, Holland, 1956.

2. H. Kucera and W.N. Francis, *Computational Analysis of Present-day American English*, Brown University Press, Providence, RI, 1967.

3. G.K. Zipf, *Human Behavior and the Principle of Least Effort*, Addison-Wesley Publishing Co., Reading, MA, 1949.

4. H.S. Heaps, *Information Retrieval — Computational and Theoretical Aspects*, Academic Press, New York, 1978.

5. A.D. Booth, A Law of Occurrence for Words of Low Frequency, *Information and Control*, 10:4, April 1967, 386–393.

6. C.E. Shannon, A Mathematical Theory of Communications, *Bell System Technical Journal*, 27:3,4, 1948, 379–423, 623–656.

7. B. Mandelbrot, Information Theory and Psycholinguistics: A Theory of Word Frequencies, *Readings in Mathematical Social Science*, P.F. Lazarsfeld and N.W. Henry, editors, Science Research Associates, Chicago, IL, 1966, 350–368.

8. D.G. Severance, A Practitioner's Guide to Database Compression, *Information Systems*, 8:1, 1983, 51–62.

9. J. Martin, *Data Compaction in Computer Database Organization*, Second Edition, Chapter 32, Prentice-Hall, Englewood Cliffs, NJ, 1977, 572–587.

10. M. Synderman and B. Hunt, The Myriad Virtues of Text Compression, *Datamation*, 16:12, December 1970, 36–40.

11. B. Hahn, A New Technique for Compression and Storage of Data, *Communications of the ACM*, 17:8, August 1974, 434–436.

12. H.S. Heaps, Storage Analysis of a Compression Coding for a Document Database, *INFOR*, 10:1, February 1972, 47–61.

13. L.H. Thiel and H.S. Heaps, Program Design for Retrospective Search on Large Data Bases, *Information Storage and Retrieval*, 8:1, 1972, 1–20.

14. D.A. Huffman, A Method for the Construction of Minimum-Redundancy Codes, *Proceedings of the IRE*, 40:9, 1952, 1098–1101.

15. I.H. Whitten, R.M. Neal, and J.G. Cleary, Arithmetic Coding for Data Compression, *Communications of the ACM*, 30:6, June 1987, 520–540.

16. J. Ziv and A. Lempel, A Universal Algorithm for Sequential Data Compression, *IEEE Transactions on Information Theory*, 23:3, May 1977, 337–343 and 24:5, September 1978, 530–536.

17. M. Pechura, File Archival Techniques Using Data Compression, *Communications of the ACM*, 25:9, September 1982, 605–611.

18. S.F. Weiss and R.L. Vernor, A Word-based Compression Technique for Text Files, *Journal of Library Automation*, 11:2, 1978, 97–105.

19. D. Cooper and M.F. Lynch, Text Compression Using Variable to Fixed Length Encodings, *Journal of the ASIS*, 33:1 January 1982, 18–31.

20. E.J. Schuegraf and H.S. Heaps, Selection of Equifrequent Word Fragments for Information Retrieval, *Information Storage and Retrieval*, 9:12, 1973, 697–711.

21. E.J. Schuegraf and H.S. Heaps, A Comparison of Algorithms for Data Base Compression by Use of Fragments as Language Elements, *Information Storage and Retrieval*, 10:9/10, 1974, 309–319.

22. D. Cooper and M.F. Lynch, Compression of Wiswesser Line Notations Using Variety Generation, *Journal of Chemical Information and Computer Sciences*, 19:3, 1979, 165–169.

23. I.J. Barton, S.E. Creasey, M.F. Lynch, and M.J. Snell, An Information Theoretic Approach to Text Searching in Direct Access Systems, *Communications of the ACM*, 17:6, June 1974, 345–350.

24. J.E. Burnett, D. Cooper, M.F. Lynch, P. Willet, and M. Wycherley, Document Retrieval Experiments Using Indexing Vocabularies of Varying Size, I. Variety Generation Symbols Assigned to the Fronts of Index Terms, *Journal of Documentation*, 35:3, 1979, 197–206.

Chapter 6

Text Encryption

6.1 Basic Cryptographic Concepts

Text-encryption methods are reversible text transformations designed to obscure the meaning of a text and render its data useless to unauthorized persons. [1–5] Cryptography can be traced back to antiquity, and has been used for diplomatic and government correspondence since the 12th century. Until this century, cryptography was used primarily to ensure the confidentiality of messages sent over channels where eavesdropping and message interception could occur. Modern methods of electronic communication mean that opportunities to interfere with the normal message flow have considerably increased; this has led to more use of cryptographic transformations. While previously encryption was used primarily for government and military communications, today secrecy transformations are often applied to business and commercial information, as well as to personal data about individuals that may be stored in computer systems or sent over electronic communications lines.

Cryptographic transformations can provide both *privacy* and *authentication*. Information remains private when a prospective opponent is prevented from extracting useful information from a communications channel. Authentication, on the other hand, makes it impossible for an opponent to alter the data or to inject false data into the channel without detection.

A cryptographic transformation consists of taking an ordinary unciphered text, also known as *plaintext P*, and applying a reversible transformation S_k to produce the encrypted *ciphertext C*. Thus

$$C = S_k(P).$$

When a legitimate receiver obtains an enciphered text C, he or she deciphers, or decrypts, it using a reverse transformation S_k^{-1} to restore the original text *P*. Thus

$$S_k^{-1}(C) = S_k^{-1}(S_k(P)) = P. \tag{6.1}$$

The actual transformation that turns plaintext into ciphertext and vice versa is determined by a special parameter known as the *key k*.

Cryptographic transformations are related to compression because they attempt to even out the occurrence characteristics of the components of the enciphered text, making unauthorized decryption more difficult. As in compression, the basic text-transformation method S used to encipher may be known to all participants in the communications system, in the same sense that the operations of a combination lock may be generally known. In carrying out privacy transformations, however, the basic aim is not to reduce the size of the message space, although such reduction may be inherent in some encryption systems. Instead the objective is to safeguard the confidentiality of the data. Further, in the case of cryptography, the reverse transformation S^{-1} cannot be easily executed without access to the normally secret key information, just as a particular combination lock cannot usually be opened without knowing the combination for that lock.

At present, most cryptographic enciphering and deciphering operations are carried out automatically by using computers to encipher or decipher the texts. Computers are also used in attempts to break a cipher by performing a *cryptanalysis*. A successful cryptanalysis makes it possible to decipher a cryptogram C and restore the plaintext *P*, or alternatively to encrypt an inauthentic plaintext P' and obtain an acceptable cryptogram C without knowing the applicable key k. Cryptographic systems are secure when a cryptanalysis cannot be performed successfully. With the increasing use of computational devices for cryptanalysis, two kinds of cryptographic security can be distinguished:

1. Normal unconditional security: The amount of information available to the cryptanalyst is insufficient to determine the enciphering and deciphering transformations.

2. Computational security: The deciphering task can be achieved with a finite amount of computation, but the computations are so extensive that the deciphering cannot be carried out quickly enough.

Practical cryptographic systems rely on computational security since it is impossible to prove that any cryptanalysis problem is in principle unsolvable.

The usefulness of cryptographic systems depends on preserving the secrecy of the key k used in the text-transformation system. Two main methods suggest themselves for this purpose. In conventional cryptographic systems, encrypting and decrypting are closely tied together, consisting normally of inverse operations performed with the same key information. In that case, the sender and receiver must agree on the use of a common key before any message transmission takes place, or a safe communications channel must exist between sender and receiver to permit the key information to be transmitted without risk of detection by outside parties. Such a key-distribution system is represented in Fig. 6.1(a). The need to transmit keys from place to place limits conventional cryptographic systems severely, especially because long, frequently changing keys must usually be used to increase the security of the system and lessen the chance of key detection.

Figure 6.1 Key management in cryptographic systems. (a) Key-distribution system. (b) Public key cryptosystem.

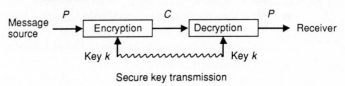

(a)

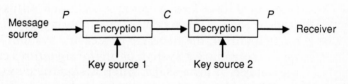

(b)

An alternative system consists of separating the enciphering and deciphering operations and using different key sources for those purposes, thus foregoing key transmission. If different functions are used for enciphering and deciphering, one of the two keys can be made public, provided that it is impossible to generate one key from the other. In *public key cryptosystems*, also known as *asymmetric cryptosystems*, random pairs of inverse keys E_k and D_k are used for enciphering and deciphering, respectively, based on a key value k chosen from among a set of possible keys K operating on a message set M. Each pair E_k and D_k must exhibit the following properties: [2]

- For each $k \in K$, D_k is the inverse of E_k; that is, for each message m, $D_k(E_k(m)) = m$

- For each $k \in K$, and $m \in M$, the values $E_k(m)$ and $D_k(m)$ are easy to compute.

- For most values of $k \in K$, it is computationally impossible to compute D_k from a known value of E_k.

- For every value of $k \in K$, it is feasible to generate the inverse pair E_k and D_k.

In a public key cryptosystem, each participant is assigned a pair of inverse keys E and D; E can be made public, but D is kept secret. This substantially simplifies the key-manipulation system because normal key transmission between senders and receivers can be replaced by an open directory of enciphering keys, containing the keys E for all participants. When person A wishes to send a message to person B, the receiver's enciphering key E_B is used to generate the ciphertext $E_B(m)$. Since the key E_B is freely available, anyone can then encipher a message destined for B. However, only the recipient B with access to the deciphering key D_B can regenerate the original text by performing the inverse transformation $D_B(E_B(m))$.

In conventional cryptography, in which a common key is used for enciphering and deciphering, a forgery by an unauthorized person can be prevented because a tampered message cannot be properly deciphered. However, a decipherable message is not properly identified as to the actual sender, the assumption being that only the one person sharing the key k with the receiver could have sent the message. In public key cryptosystems such an assumption cannot be made, because the receiver's enciphering key E is now known to all participants in the message-processing system. It is therefore important to introduce a system of *digital signatures* capable of identifying the source of a message. Such a signature system is analogous to the normal handwritten signatures that appear on conventional legal documents. [6,7]

Figure 6.2 Privacy and signature transformations in public key cryptosystems.

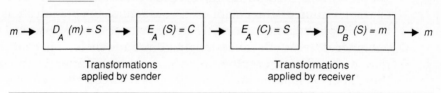

| Transformations applied by sender | Transformations applied by receiver |

Public key cryptosystems can satisfy the need for signatures if both deciphering and enciphering keys can be applied to any message m, and if the order in which an inverse pair E and D is applied is immaterial. In that case, the following equality applies for each key and message pair k and m: [8–10]

$$D_k\,(E_k(m)) = E_k\,(D_k(m)) = m. \tag{6.2}$$

When equation (6.2) is satisfied, the following system can be used to authenticate messages between sender A and receiver B. The message m is first transformed using the sender's private key D_A to produce $S = D_A(m)$. The normal deciphering key D_A is thus used as a signing key by sender A. When receiver B wishes to read the message, the sender's public key E_A can be used to restore the message as follows:

$$E_A\,(D_A(m)) = m.$$

Such an encoding system satisfies the need for signatures since no one except sender A could have produced the enciphered message S. Privacy is not assured, however, because if the sender's name is known, anyone can decipher the message. Signatures as well as privacy are provided by using a double transformation involving the keys of both the sender and the receiver. In particular, sender A may encipher a message m using first his or her private decryption key D_A for signature, followed by receiver B's public encryption key E_B, to produce the encrypted message $E_B\,(D_A(m)) = E_B(S)$. Receiver B now uses his or her private decryption key D_B to obtain the signed message $D_B(E_B(S)) = S$, followed by the sender's public key E_A, to obtain the original message $E_A(S) = E_A(D_A(m)) = m$. This chain of message transformations is summarized in Fig. 6.2.

6.2 Conventional Cryptographic Systems

In cryptography, as in compression, an attempt is made to remove language redundancies by reducing the uneven occurrence characteristics of the language elements and eliminating character dependencies as much as possible. Indeed, any attempt at code breaking is much simpler when substantial differences exist among the occurrence characteristics of the enciphered characters. Cryptanalysis is similarly simplified when character dependencies can be observed in the enciphered texts. Because language redundancies may not be removed completely, cryptographic systems must attempt to confuse the reader by making any dependencies between characters as complex as possible, and to diffuse or spread out the dependencies over long substrings of the enciphered text. [11]

Two main types of transformations are used for this purpose in conventional cryptography. The confusion factor is taken into account by substituting new characters for the original plaintext characters in such a way that the substituted characters depend not only on the original plaintext characters, but also on the position of the characters in the original message. Substitution operations are carried out using so-called substitution boxes (S-boxes). The diffusion problem is treated by permuting the characters of the input in such a way as to remove obvious dependencies between adjacent sets of characters. Permutations are normally carried out on blocks of characters using so-called permutation boxes (P-boxes).

A permutation box is a device with n input and n output wires connected one to one in such a way that the ith input is attached to the jth output. A typical P-box appears in simplified form in Fig. 6.3. To specify the construction of a P-box, it is necessary to give the position of the output wire corresponding to each of the n input wires in order. The specification of one output of n requires $\log_2 n$ bits; hence a total of $n \log_2 n$ bits of key information is required. In practice, preconstructed P-boxes corresponding to random permutations of the inputs are used to provide the required diffusion without reference to, or storage of, key information.

Specifying character substitutions is more complex than specifying permutations because any input character can be transformed into

Figure 6.3 Typical *P*-box.

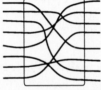

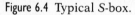

Figure 6.4 Typical S-box.

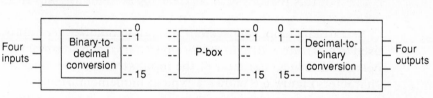

any given output character. A box with n input wires can accept 2^n different input quantities. Assuming that the replacement of two different inputs by the same output must be avoided, $(2^n)!$ different substitution wirings must be allowed for. Thus to specify a given substitution wiring $\log_2 [(2^n)!]$, or about $n \cdot 2^n$, bits are required. To reduce the amount of key information needed to specify S-boxes, each S-box may be designed to operate on a small input segment — typically four bits of input — and several S-boxes may be used in parallel.

A typical S-box design is shown in Fig. 6.4, in which a slice of four binary inputs is transformed into one of 16 decimal outputs, which are reconverted into binary form after permutation. Sets of parallel S-boxes and P-boxes can be used consecutively, as shown in Fig. 6.5. Such a sequential arrangement is known as a *product cipher*. In product ciphers, the same key handles both enciphering and deciphering: The arrangement of S- and P-boxes used for enciphering is simply reversed for deciphering.

In most practical situations, machine-aided rather than manual encryption and decryption methods are used. Machine-aided operations can be made more complex by using a cipher in which the generated output depends on the available input as well as on an internal machine state. The characters are then not treated independently — the

Figure 6.5 Typical product cipher.

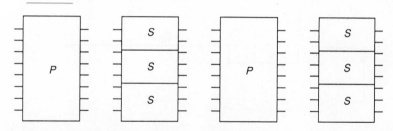

position of each character in the input stream is also taken into account. For this reason, such enciphering systems are known as *stream ciphers*.

In a stream-ciphering system, a random number generator may be used to generate a stream of key characters, each character of the key being added to a character of the input stream to produce an output character. Figure 6.6 shows a typical implementation of such a system, using a shift register with an exclusive-or (modulo 2 addition) operator $\oplus$ to add particular bits of the key stream to the source text. When exclusive-or operations are used, the same shift register arrangement can produce the key stream for both enciphering and deciphering, because two consecutive exclusive-or operations with the same key restore the original data. Thus

$$1010 \oplus 0110 = 1100$$
$$1100 \oplus 0110 = 1010$$

Stream-ciphering systems are easily implemented because they are memoryless in the sense that encrypting a character does not depend on any preceding or following character but only on the character position. However, the key stream produced by a random number generator necessarily repeats itself after a certain time. For example, in the shift-register implementation of Fig. 6.6, the contents of the register are shifted right by one character position in each iteration, replacing the right-most character by the exclusive-or sum of the two right-most characters. Thus if the bit stream 1010 is stored in the shift register, a right shift produces 101, and the left-most character is generated as 1 $\oplus$ 0=1. The new contents will then be 1101. This will be modified in turn to produce 1110, 1111, 0111, and so on, until after 15 iterations the original 1010 reappears and the entire cycle is repeated.

Figure 6.6 Typical stream-ciphering system.

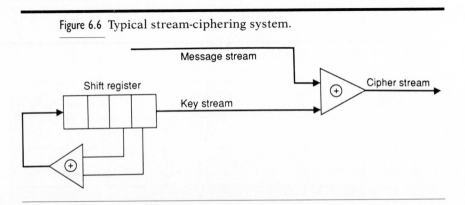

The periodicity built into random number generators weakens stream ciphers and, when the length of the cycle is known, helps the cryptanalyst. For this reason, the original plaintext is often subdivided into blocks of data, and independent substitution operations are carried out on each block of data. When the block size is large enough, *block ciphers* provide character substitutions on very large alphabets — for example, a block size of 64 bits represents an alphabet of 2^{64} different characters. In that case, an attempt to break the code by performing a frequency analysis of the enciphered characters is much more difficult than for alphabets of normal size.

6.3 Sample Cryptographic Ciphers

In the basic *substitution* cipher, the key consists simply of a permutation of the normal alphabet that specifies a replacement character for each character in the original text. Encryption is then carried out by replacing each plaintext character by the corresponding character in the permuted alphabet. Alternatively, the rank orders of the original and the key characters (in normal alphabetic order) can be added to obtain the order number for the substituted character. In the sample substitution alphabet of Table 6.1, the letter A is replaced by W, B is replaced by E, and so on. The original text "THE CAT ATE THE RAT" is then replaced by "XYF BWX WXF XYF PWX."

A simple substitution cipher is easy to solve by performing a frequency analysis of characters, or character groups, or by looking for frequently occurring words, such as "the," that are always replaced by "xyf" in the sample code. As the size of the alphabet is increased, substitution ciphers become more secure as previously suggested. Both the enciphering and the deciphering operations are more expensive to perform, however, because larger coding tables are then needed. [12]

In a *permutation* cipher, the positions of the plaintext characters are permuted instead of the characters themselves. The key is then a permutation that specifies the new position in the enciphered text corresponding to each character position in the original text. Assuming

Table 6.1 Simple substitution cipher.

Original alphabet	A B C D E F G H I J K L M N O P Q R S T U V W X Y Z
Key alphabet	W E B Q F K V Y M L U A O N C H S P D X I R G T J Z

that groups of five characters are permuted in one operation, a typical code specification may then appear as

```
1  2  3  4  5
2  5  1  4  3
```

indicating that the first character in each group appears in position 2, that the second character moves to position 5, the third moves to position 1, and so on. Using that permutation, the sample text, which appears as "THE#C AT#AT E#THE #RAT#" when grouped into five-character segments with spaces represented by #, is transformed into "ETC#H #ATAT TEEH# A##TR."

A frequency analysis of characters will easily break the simple substitution or permutation ciphers. For this reason, product ciphers are used because they provide series of substitutions and permutations and even out the character frequencies. An alternative is to use *polyalphabetic* ciphers, in which several different substitution alphabets are used periodically to encipher a message. For example, if five different substitution alphabets of the kind shown in Table 6.1 are used, characters in positions $5n + i$ for $n \geq 0$ can be enciphered in the ith alphabet. Thus the characters in positions 1, 6, 11, 16, etc. are enciphered in alphabet 1; those in positions 2, 7, 12, 17, etc. use alphabet 2; and so on.

The frequency count of the characters is much more even in polyalphabetic ciphers than in single substitution ciphers because a given plaintext character is replaced by a variety of different characters in the ciphertext, depending on the original character position. However, a polyalphabetic cipher can still be attacked by noting regularities in the enciphered text and using them to determine the period, that is, the number of different alphabets used. A frequency analysis for each distinct alphabet can then be used to break the cipher. For example, if four different alphabets are used consecutively to encipher the text "THE# CAT# ATE# THE# RAT#," the two occurrences of "THE#" will be converted into identical strings in the ciphertext. A possible solution to such an attack consists of using the polyalphabetic enciphering process several times — that is, first converting the plaintext into a ciphertext using p_1 substitution alphabets, then converting the ciphertext into a supercipher using a polyalphabetic cipher of period p_2. When p_1 and p_2 are relatively prime, the period of the supercipher is $p_1 \cdot p_2$.

The remaining regularities in the polyalphabetic ciphers can be eliminated by using so-called *running-key* ciphers. Running-key alphabetics are aperiodic polyalphabetics in which a continuously changing alphabetic key sequence is used for enciphering. Typically the text at a particular point in a known document is used as a key sequence. Each character in the key sequence is then combined with a corresponding character of the plaintext to generate the enciphered character. For example, one might add the rank orders of the characters modulo 26, with A = 1, B = 2, C = 3, etc. to obtain the rank order of the enciphered character. An example of this process appears in Table 6.2 for the key sequence "an example of this process appears in," without spaces. This example shows that the six occurrences of the letter T are replaced by six different characters in the ciphertext; similarly five different characters are obtained for the seven original occurrences of the letter E.

Running-key ciphers are easy to decrypt when the key sequence is known since the plaintext can be obtained by simply subtracting the key sequences from the ciphertext modulo 26. When the key sequence is not known, a cryptanalysis could be attempted by guessing a probable common word in the plaintext. When that word is subtracted from the ciphertext in all possible locations, a part of the key sequence is produced that can be extended in both directions. Alternatively, one might note that when different aperiodically selected alphabets are used to transform the plaintext into ciphertext, certain combinations of letter pairs are much more likely to occur than others. For example, the plaintext-key combination E-E occurs in positions 3 and 9 of the example of Table 6.2, producing the ciphertext character J both times. Similarly, the combination of E and P occurs twice, producing the ciphertext letter U. When certain digram solutions are available they might be extended to larger character sequences. [13] Multiple encipherings with running keys are relatively safe, but long key sequences

---

Table 6.2 Running key cipher.

Alphabet

A B C D E F G H I J K L M N O P Q R S T U V W X Y Z

Rank order

1 2 3 4 5 6 7 8 9 10 11 12 13 14 15 16 17 18 19 20 21 22 23 24 25 26

Plaintext
THE CAT ATE THE RAT AND THE CHEESE

Key sequence

ANE XAM PLE OFT HIS PRO CES SAPPEA

**Sum of
rank order
modulo 26**

21,22,10 1,2,7 17,6,10 9,14,25 26,10,13 17,6,19 23,13,24 22,9,21 21,24,6

Ciphertext

U V J A B G Q F J I N Y Z J M Q F R W M X V I U U X F

must be stored and manipulated, and the resulting enciphering and deciphering processes are expensive to perform.

Attempts have been made to provide the equivalent of running-key ciphers by using ciphering machines, which generate a stream of key characters that can be added to plaintext to produce ciphertext. The period of repetition of the keystream is made sufficiently long — normally millions of characters — to prevent easy detection. The *Hagelin machine*, used by the United States during World War II, is a typical running-key ciphering machine. In the Hagelin machine, six keywheels are provided that carry 26, 25, 23, 21, 19 and 17 character positions, respectively. These positions can be labeled from A to Z for the first wheel, from A to Y for the second wheel, and so on down to A to Q for the last wheel. A particular position of the six keywheels can then be represented by a combination of six characters such as AAAAAA.

Since there are no common factors in the number of character positions on each keywheel, the number of different character combinations obtained by rotating each keywheel by one position in each iteration is $26 \cdot 25 \cdot 23 \cdot 21 \cdot 19 \cdot 17$, or over 101 million. A few character combinations, starting with AAAAAA, are shown in Table 6.3. The key digits corresponding to each character combination on the Hagelin machine are obtained by placing a retractable pin next to each character position on each wheel of the machine. Each pin represents the digits 1 and 0 in the extended or retracted states, respectively. For example, a particular character combination with extended pins for wheels 1, 3, and 5 would produce the key character 101010.

Table 6.3 Character combinations of Hagelin machine.

1	AAAAAA
2	BBBBBB
.	
.	
.	
17	QQQQQQ
18	RRRRRA
19	SSSSSB
20	TTTTAC
21	UUUUBD
22	VVVACE
23	WWWBDF
24	XXACEG
25	YYBDFH
26	ZACEGI
27	ABDFHJ

The Hagelin machine could be prepared for transmission by specifying an initial character combination for the keywheels, and arranging the settings for the 131 different pins. The machine used at the receiving end would receive identical pin settings, but the operation with the keystream would be inverted by subtracting the keystream from the ciphertext to restore the original plaintext. Attempts to break the Hagelin stream cipher must be based on noticing regularities in sequences of 17 adjacent characters for the last column corresponding to the right-most key wheel, 19 adjacent characters for the next to last column, 21 adjacent characters for the next column, and so on. A cryptanalysis can be foiled once again by changing the pin settings frequently. [14,15]

The *rotor* enciphering machines, also used by various countries during World War II, differ from the Hagelin implementation in two important respects. First, each keywheel can be rotated by an arbitrary amount instead of by only one character position in going from one iteration to the next. Second, the keywheels, or rotors, provide an additional character permutation by placing contacts next to each character position, and wiring pairs of contacts together. Assuming, for example, that input A is wired to output G, an input signal received as A is transmitted and read out as a new character G.

When the rotors are moved from one position to another, the permutations produced on an incoming signal change. If R represents the permutation wired into the rotor, then the new permutation P obtained by a cyclic shift of j character positions C^j can be denoted as $P = C^j R C^{j-1}$. Thus if the wired permutation $R(A)$ produces the letter G, a cyclic shift of the rotor by three positions ($j=3$) transforms the plaintext character D into the ciphertext character J as follows: [2]

$$P(D) = C^3 R C^{-3}(D) = C^3 R(A) = C^3(G) = J. \qquad (6.3)$$

In a rotor machine, several rotors are typically connected in such a way that an input signal is permuted several times before it leaves the system. The transformation can then be represented as

$$P = C^{j_1} R_1 C^{-j_1} C^{j_2} R_2 C^{-j_2} \cdots C^{j_n} R_n C^{-j_n}$$

$$(6.4)$$

$$= C^{j_1} R_1 C^{j_2-j_1} R_2 C^{j_3-j_2} \cdots C^{j_{n-1}} R_n C^{-j_n}.$$

A strong system is obtained when the period of repetition between cycles is large and when the state of the rotors is changed after each character in such a way that most exponents ($j_i - j_{i-1}$) are nonzero.

The best-known rotor machine is the German Enigma. The Enigma code was believed to be unbreakable, but was eventually solved by

British cryptanalysts. [16–17] The Enigma was especially versatile because many different factors could be varied independently, including the type of rotor in use with all the possible wirings, the order in which the rotors were introduced in the machine, the pattern of motion of the rotors (clockwise or counterclockwise), the initial rotor positions, and the stopping places for each rotor following a given motion.

The Enigma consisted of a keyboard used to enter characters, a plugboard performing a single, constant, pairwise letter transformation, a scrambling unit consisting of three connected rotors with 26 character positions each (labeled 1 to 3 in Fig. 6.7), a reversing drum, and a light-board array. When the Enigma operator punched a letter key, the current flowed through the apparatus, as shown in Fig. 6.7, and a light bulb corresponding to the enciphered character lit up. The

Figure 6.7 Basic design of the Enigma ciphering machine.

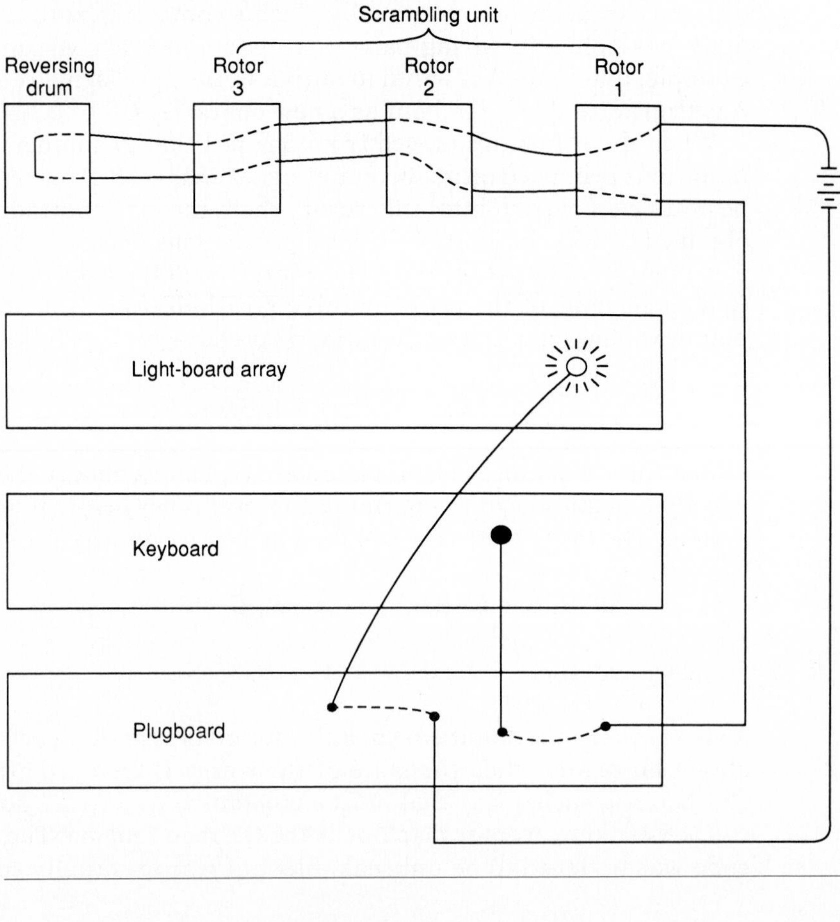

reversing drum ensured that the coding was reversible. That is, if the sending operator transformed a keyboard key A into an output signal G, the receiving operator could restore the original output A by punching the encrypted character G.

The Enigma key consisted of three components in addition to the plugboard:

1. The rotor type and the order in which the rotors were placed in the machine, which allowed for 60 possible rotor arrangements.

2. The ring settings on the rotors, used to specify a home position for each rotor. Each rotor had 26 possible ring positions, providing a total of $26^3 = 17,576$ different ring settings.

3. The text setting, which specified the initial position for each rotor used in enciphering a message.

Different rotor arrangements and ring settings were specified by the authorities for each day of operation. The text setting, on the other hand, varied from one text to the next.

During text enciphering, the right-most rotor would rotate to the next stopping point whenever a letter key was punched by the operator. When a rotor moved through the home position, the next rotor to the left would also rotate. The stopping points of the rotors were controlled by an outer ring inserted in each rotor with stopping points appropriately marked. In principle, the home positions for each rotor could always be specified as a starting point prior to enciphering a text. Because the rotors could be moved freely, the use of any standard initial position would have unnecessarily restricted the capabilities of the machine. A different initial text setting chosen by the Enigma operators was therefore used for each encoded text, and this setting would be transmitted with the text in enciphered form to permit decoding by the receiving operator.

In principle, for each message more than 1 million settings were possible using the Enigma machine ($60 \cdot 17,576 = 1,054,560$), plus the plugboard transformation, plus the variable text settings for the messages. The British were able to break the code by exploiting the Germans' habit in the early war years of transmitting two versions of the text setting at the beginning of each message. For many text settings, repeating characters occurred in the enciphered form. The Germans apparently failed to realize that only about half the initial rotor orders and ring settings could produce identical pairs of characters in certain positions of the enciphered text setting, corresponding in each case to the same character of the plaintext. By accumulating enough messages, and finding enough identical pairs for the encoded text settings, the British were able to reduce the number of possible initial machine settings used on a particular day to about 250, and these 250 possible settings could be individually tested to find the correct one.

As the war progressed, the Germans gave up the double encoding of the text settings, but the British cryptanalysts were able to capitalize on the habits of the German cipher clerks — such as choosing similar text and ring settings. Toward the end of the war, decrypting became comparatively simple, and the German Enigma encoding was less and less effective.

Over the years, most encryption and decryption efforts have been devoted to converting single plaintext characters into single cipher-text characters. However, secrecy transformations can also be applied to voice or facsimile data or to larger text units, where the input is not available in the form of single characters. When large text excerpts are transformed as a unit, normal ciphering methods are conveniently replaced by *code books* consisting of lists of words and phrases together with corresponding randomly chosen groups of ciphertext letters and numbers, known as *code groups*. A typical code book may contain many tens of thousands of entries. Ciphertext produced by a code-book transformation is usually substantially compressed, in addition to being nearly impossible to break without access to the code book. However, the use of large dictionaries is necessarily expensive, even when computers are used for enciphering, especially because code books must be changed periodically for the sake of security. For this reason, codes are rarely used.

6.4 The Data Encryption Standard (DES)

The best-known practical data-enciphering system, the Data Encryption Standard (DES), transforms blocks of data using conventional permutation and substitution methods. Since too much key information is needed to specify substitutions on large data blocks, the block length actually used is small, and the security of the DES cipher is obtained by using a product cipher built up from collections of individually weak components. [18–22]

Specifically, the system is based on a series of simple cryptographic substitution operations B_i performed on four-bit groups of the input, with unkeyed mixing permutations M following each substitution. The substitutions provide the necessary confusion, while the permutations furnish diffusion. The complete system is represented as a series of B and M transformations $B_1 - M - B_2 - ... - M - B_n$, indicating that the output of stage i is used as input to stage $i+1$ (see Fig. 6.8). The system uses 16 stages, which operate on blocks of 64 plaintext bits. Each plaintext block is subdivided into sets of four-bit bytes that are acted on by different substitution boxes. The permutations between adjacent S-box transformations serve to mix the information obtained from different S-boxes.

Such a system is inconvenient to implement because of the large amount of required key information. Assuming that each S-box provides a 4-bit to 4-bit mapping, each box could accommodate a total of $2^4 = 16$ different words. For each input word a different 4-bit output must be specified. If 16 different S-boxes were used per stage to transform the 64-bit input, the required key length would be

$$16 \text{ words} \cdot 4 \text{ bits} \cdot 16 \text{ S-boxes} \cdot 16 \text{ stages} = 16{,}384 \text{ bits}.$$

The large amount of required key information can be reduced by providing only a small number of different S-boxes, and by using fewer S-boxes in parallel. If only two different S-boxes were available, labeled S_0 and S_1, respectively, a single bit per box would be sufficient to specify the applicable box type at each point.

The DES algorithm actually used is illustrated in simplified form in Fig. 6.9. The structure of each stage is shown in Fig. 6-9(a). Each 64-bit input block is broken down into a left half and a right half ($L(i)$ and $R(i)$). The right subblock is subjected to a transformation (identified as the S–P transformation in the figure) involving substitutions, permutations, and a modulo 2 addition with portions of the key implementation. Following the S–P operations, the 32 left-half bits ($L(i)$) are added to the transformed 32 right-half bits using an exclusive-or operation. The right-half input for a given stage $R(i)$ is then used as left-half input for the following stage $L(i+1)$, and the operations are repeated for the next stage.

Details of the S–P transformation are given in Fig. 6.9(b). The 32 bits of input are first expanded to a 48-bit width by repeating the edge bits

Figure 6.8 Basic DES enciphering strategy.

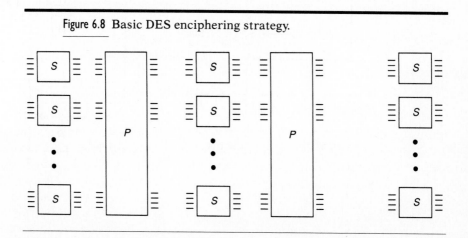

of each 4-bit byte (that is, bits 1 and 4, 5 and 8, 9 and 12, and so on). By slightly permuting some of these bits, eight 6-bit bytes are obtained consisting of bit groups $b_{32}b_1b_2b_3b_4b_5, b_4b_5$ $b_6b_7b_8b_9,....,b_{28}b_{29}b_{30}b_{31}b_{32}b_1$, where b_i is the bit appearing in position i of the original 32-bit string. The resulting 48 information bits are next added to a set of 48 key bits using modulo 2 addition, followed by a substitution transformation using eight S-boxes that provide 6-bit to 4-bit substitutions. Finally, the resulting 32 bits are permuted in a P-box before being added to the left-half information as previously explained.

In principle, each of the 16 stages requires a different 48-bit key, which would normally use a key length of $16 \cdot 48 = 768$ bits. However, only 56 bits of key information are actually used, divided into halves of 28 bits each. These are loaded into two shift registers with 24 taps

Figure 6.9 DES enciphering algorithm. (a) Two basic stages. (b) S-P function.

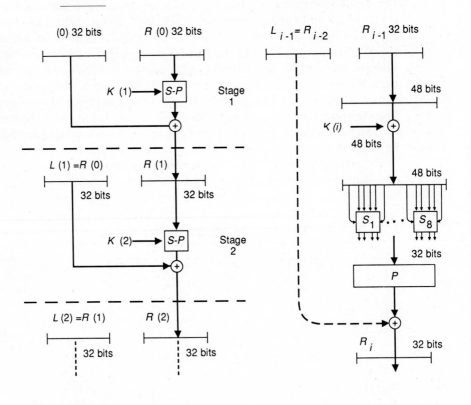

(a)

(b)

each. After each stage the shift registers are cyclically shifted to provide the next 48 key bits.

The DES system ensures that the transformations produce adequate confusion, as well as adequate diffusion across all bit positions in each block. Thus the S-boxes are designed so that a change of one input bit alters at least 2 output bits. Also, the four outputs of any S-box appear as input to six different S-boxes in the next stage. The DES system has nevertheless been criticized as weak because the 16 stages of input transformations can easily be tried on any available ciphertext to produce the plaintext, given that only 56 bits of key information are used. With 56 bits, 2^{56} or about 10^{17} different keys are available. Large-scale integration chips can be built that will search one key in a microsecond. With one million chips, about 10^{12} keys could be tried per second, implying that the entire key space could be searched exhaustively in 10^5 seconds, or about a day. Of course, by using multiple encipherments and longer keys, the DES system might be strengthened without giving up its basic enciphering strategy.

6.5 ❖ Ciphers Based on Computationally Difficult Problems

In algorithm analysis, there is a class of problems known as NP-complete, which appear impossible to solve in useful time. That is, for these problems a systematic deterministic solution is likely to require exponential time in the number of inputs. It has been suggested that the NP-completeness property could provide interesting ciphering strategies because potential intruders would have no simple deciphering process. In particular, if the insights provided by the theory of computational complexity are to be used, a simple encrypting process is needed. The corresponding decrypting process, however, would have to be computationally difficult except in special cases when supplementary information (such as decrypting keys) is available.

These requirements are fulfilled by the so-called *one-way* functions, where a simple transformation in one direction $C = f(P)$ can transform a plaintext P into a ciphertext C, while a much more difficult reverse transformation $P = f^{-1}(C)$ must be used to restore the original plaintext P. When special *trapdoor* information is available, however, the reverse transformation is as simple as the direct operation. Examples of one-way functions are multiplication and factoring, or exponentiation and the computation of logarithms. In both cases, the initial transformation — multiplying a number of factors or raising a quantity to a power — is simple, but the reverse process of generating the individual factors contained in a product, or computing a logarithm, is more time consuming.

The following process was suggested by Diffie and Hellman as a basis for a public-key cryptosystem. [2,3] A pair of keys X_i and Y_i is assigned to each user i in the system, where

$$Y_i = \alpha^{X_i} \bmod q \qquad 1 \le X \le q-1, \qquad 1 \le \alpha \le q-1 \qquad (6.5)$$

for some prime number q. Given X_i, it is easy to compute Y_i; in fact, the exponentiation takes at most $2 \cdot \log_2 q$ multiplications (for example, for $X_i = 18$, $\alpha^{18} = ((((\alpha^2)^2)^2)^2 \cdot \alpha^2)$. On the other hand, the reverse transformation

$$X_i = \log_\alpha Y_i \qquad 1 \le Y_i \le q-1 \qquad (6.6)$$

may take on the order of $q^{1/2}$ operations. If q is a prime number slightly less than 2^b, all quantities can be represented as b-bit numbers. For $b = 200$, about 400 ($2 \cdot b$) multiplications are needed for the exponentiation, but the reverse logarithmic transformation will require $2^{b/2} = 2^{100}$ or about 10^{30} operations.

The communications process for each user pair can then be controlled as follows:

1. The user generates an independent random number X_i chosen uniformly from the interval $\{1, 2, ..., q-1\}$. X_i is kept secret, but the corresponding $Y_i = \alpha^{X_i} \bmod q$ is placed in a public file.

2. When users i and j wish to communicate they both use a common key computed as

$$K_{ij} = \alpha^{X_i X_j} \bmod q. \qquad (6.7)$$

   Sender i generates the key by using the receiver's public key Y_j and his or her own secret X_i to obtain $K_{ij} = Y_j^{X_i} \bmod q = (\alpha^{X_j})^{X_i} \bmod q = \alpha^{X_j X_i} \bmod q$. Receiver j obtains K_{ij} similarly from Y_i and X_j.

This system is secure because one of the secret pieces of information X_i or X_j must be known to generate the key K_{ij}. An outside user knows only the public numbers Y_i and Y_j, and would have to generate K_{ij} by computing a logarithm of the form

$$K_{ij} = Y_i^{(\log_\alpha Y_j)} \bmod q. \qquad (6.8)$$

However, the operation of expression (6.8) is computationally difficult. It should be noted that while a common key is used by each sender-receiver pair, no key transmission is involved since either party can generate the key information independently.

An alternative procedure, one not based on the use of common keys by senders and receivers, is provided by the well-known RSA cipher (named after its inventors, R.L. Rivest, A. Shamir, and L. Adleman). [23–25] That system also requires two types of keys, E and D, for enciphering and deciphering, respectively. Security is provided by guaranteeing that D cannot be computed easily from E without additional, secret trapdoor information. An enciphered message M^E has a form similar to that of the original message M. That is, the space of all enciphered messages is the same as the space of original messages. This makes it possible to use the decrypting key D on an original message before any enciphering has taken place. Since both M^E and M^D are thus legal operations, the RSA scheme can be used both for secrecy (requiring M^E) and for authentication (requiring M^D).

The RSA scheme calls for the following operations: [2]

1. Each user selects two large prime numbers P and Q at random, and multiplies them to obtain $N = P \cdot Q$. N should be about 200 digits long and can be made public; P and Q are kept secret.

2. Using P and Q, the user computes the Euler totient function $\Phi(N)$, representing the number of positive integers relatively prime to N. It is known that $\Phi(N) = \Phi(P) \cdot \Phi(Q) = (P-1)(Q-1)$.[1]

3. The user then chooses a quantity E at random from the interval 2 to $\Phi(N)-1$. The quantity E is made public.

4. Given a message M to be enciphered, M is broken down into a sequence of quantities $M_1, M_2, ..., M_p$, where each component M_i is represented by an integer between 0 and $N-1$. The enciphering is now done separately on each block M_i using the public information E and N to generate a cryptogram C_i as

$$C_i = M_i^E \bmod N. \qquad (6.9)$$

As previously noted, this computation requires at most $2 \cdot \log_2(N)$ multiplications.

5. Using the secret information $\Phi(N)$, the user can easily compute a quantity D such that $E \cdot D = 1 \bmod \Phi(N)$; this quantity can be used to decipher any message enciphered with the numbers E and N. Indeed if $E \cdot D = 1 \bmod \Phi(N) = k \Phi(N) + 1$, then $D = k\Phi(N)+1/E$ By Euler's generalization of a formula by Fermat, it is known that $M^{\Phi(N)} \bmod N = 1 \bmod N$, or $M^{k\Phi(N)+1} \bmod N = M \bmod N$. Since $E \cdot D = k \Phi(N) + 1$, a simple deciphering procedure can be carried out: Computing $C_i^D \bmod N$ to obtain the original message block M_i from the cipher block C_i. Thus

$$C_i^D \bmod N = M_i^{ED} \bmod N = M_i^{k\Phi(N)+1} \bmod N \qquad (6.10)$$
$$= M_i \bmod N = M_i.$$

---

1. It is easy to see that $\Phi(N)$, the number of positive integers relatively prime to N is equal to $(P-1)(Q-1)$. Indeed, consider the complete set of residues mod N { $0,1,...,PQ-1$ }. Since P and Q are prime, all of these residues are relatively prime to N except for the $P-1$ elements $\{Q,2Q,...(P-1)Q\}$ and the $Q-1$ elements $\{P,2P,...,(Q-1)P\}$, plus the number 0. Therefore $\Phi(N) = P \cdot Q - [(P-1) + (Q-1) + 1] = (P-1)(Q-1)$.

Note that when only the enciphering keys N and E are known, and not the secret trapdoor information P, Q, and $\Phi(N)$, the deciphering key D must be computed by factoring N into its prime factors P and Q, computing $\Phi(N)$ as $(P-1)(Q-1)$, and finally generating D from $\Phi(N)$ and E in such a way that $E \cdot D = k\,\Phi(N)+1$. All these operations but the factorization are simple. When a 200-digit number represents N, the fastest factorization method known is believed to require about 10^{23} operations, taking $3 \cdot 10^9$ years at the rate of a million operations per second.

To find D, the multiplicative inverse of E mod $\Phi(N)$, where $D \cdot E = k\,\Phi(N)+1$, the first step is to define $\Phi(N) = r_0$ and $E = r_1$. Then successively divide r_i/r_{i+1} for $i \geq 0$ to obtain equations of the following form:

$$
\begin{aligned}
r_0 - k_1 r_1 &= r_2 \\
r_1 - k_2 r_2 &= r_3 \\
&\;\;\vdots \\
r_{n-2} - k_{n-1} r_{n-1} &= r_n \\
r_{n-1} - k_n r_n &= 1 \\
\text{The last remainder, } r_{n+1}, &= 1.
\end{aligned}
$$

Starting with the bottommost equation, substitute for r_n the expression in the preceding equation (that is, $r_{n-2} - k_{n-1}r_{n-1}$). Continue substituting for r_{n-1}, r_{n-2}, etc. from the preceding equations until only r_0 and r_1 appear:

$$
\begin{aligned}
r_{n-1} - k_n[r_n-2 - k_{n-1}r_{n-1}] &= 1 \\
-k_n r_{n-2} - r_{n-1}(-1 - k_{n-1}) &= 1 \\
-k_n r_{n-2} - (-1 - k_{n-1})[r_{n-3} - k_{n-2}r_{n-2}] &= 1 \\
&\;\;\vdots
\end{aligned}
$$

Two cases are possible:

1. $xr_1 - kr_0 = 1$, corresponding to $xE - k\Phi(N) = 1$, in which case $x = D$.

2. $kr_0 - xr_1 = 1$, in which case x can be rewritten as $(r_0 - y)$ to obtain $yr_1 - (r_1 - k)r_0 = 1$ (corresponding to $yE - (E-k)\Phi(N) = 1$), in which case $y = D$.

For example, let $E = 2550$ and $\Phi(N) = 8443$ to find D such that $D \cdot 2550 = k \cdot 8443 + 1$:

$$8443 - 3 \cdot 2550 = 793$$
$$2550 - 3 \cdot 793 = 171$$
$$793 - 4 \cdot 171 = 109$$
$$171 - 1 \cdot 109 = 62$$
$$109 - 1 \cdot 62 = 47$$
$$62 - 1 \cdot 47 = 15$$
$$47 - 3 \cdot 15 = 2$$
$$15 - 7 \cdot 2 = 1$$

Substituting for $r_n = 2$, $r_{n-1} = 15$, $r_{n-3} = 47$, and so forth, the result is as follows:

$$15 - 7\,(47 - 3 \cdot 15) = 22 \cdot 15 - 7 \cdot 47 = 1$$
$$22\,(62 - 47) - 7 \cdot 47 = 22 \cdot 62 - 29 \cdot 47 = 1$$
$$22 \cdot 62 - 29(109 - 62) = 51 \cdot 62 - 29 \cdot 109 = 1$$
$$51 \cdot (171 - 109) - 29 \cdot 109 = 51 \cdot 171 - 80 \cdot 109 = 1$$
$$51 \cdot 171 - 80(793 - 4 \cdot 171) = 371 \cdot 171 - 80 \cdot 793 = 1$$
$$371\,(2550 - 3 \cdot 793) - 80 \cdot 793 = 371 \cdot 2550 - 1193 \cdot 793 = 1$$
$$371 \cdot 2550 - 1193(8443 - 3 \cdot 2550) = 3950 \cdot 2550 - 1193 \cdot 8443 = 1$$

$$D = 3950$$

Before a message block can actually be enciphered, it is necessary to choose a numeric representation. Since the computations are carried out modulo N, each block must appear as a number not larger than N. If $N \geq 2626$, a message could be divided into two character blocks, where the string AA could appear as 0101, BB as 0202, and ZZ as 2626. Consider the following simple example:

Assume that $P = 3$ and $Q = 13$.

Then $N = P \cdot Q = 39$ and $\Phi(N) = (P-1)(Q-1) = 24$.

If E is chosen as 7, then $D = 7$ because $7 \cdot 7 - 2 \cdot 24 = 1$.

Let message block $M_i = 2$. Cryptogram C_i is then defined as

$$C_i = M_i^E \bmod N = 2^7 \bmod 39 = 11.$$

To decipher the inverse transformation, C_i^D is used as follows:

$$M_i = C_i^D \bmod N$$
$$= 11^7 \bmod 39$$
$$= 19,487,171 \bmod 39$$
$$= 2 \bmod 39.$$

The security of the RSA system depends on using carefully selected prime numbers P and Q. Testing methods are available to ascertain with reasonable accuracy whether a given number is prime. [1] Even when the required prime numbers are available, the RSA method is not entirely attractive because substantial amounts of key information are needed to store the quantities N, D, E, P and Q, estimated at about 2000 bits per user when N, D, and E are 200-digits long. This can be compared with the key length of 56 bits in the DES system. Further, the computational requirements to encipher and decipher are also substantial, as suggested by the preceding sample computations. Therefore a system such as RSA will not replace more conventional methods based on substitutions and permutations until very fast enciphering and deciphering devices become available to carry out the needed exponentiation.

Another approach based on the notion of NP-completeness consists of using *knapsack* ciphers. [26] Because the form of encoded messages is not the same as that of original messages in a knapsack system, it may not be possible to provide both secrecy and authentication. However, secrecy without authentication can be assured by first applying an enciphering method to all messages before deciphering them. Similarly, authentication without secrecy is assured when all messages are deciphered before enciphering.

A one-dimensional knapsack consists of finding a subset of a set of positive integers whose sum is equal to a given positive integer C. More precisely, given a vector $a = (a_1, a_2, ..., a_n)$ of positive integers, a binary vector $X = (x_1, x_2, ..., x_n)$ is sought such that $\sum_{i=1}^{n} a_i x_i = C$ for a given positive integer C. For example, given $n = 5$, $C = 14$, and $a = (1, 10, 5, 22, 3)$, the vector $x = (1,1,0,0,1)$ provides a solution because $1 + 10 + 3 = 14$.

The knapsack problem is known to be NP-complete, the best-known algorithm requiring both exponential time and exponential space in the vector length n. However, there exist so-called *simple* knapsacks, in which successive integers in the vector are superincreasing — that is, each integer is larger than the sum of all preceding integers. Simple knapsacks can be solved trivially, as shown by the following example. Consider the simple knapsack $a' = (15, 17, 40, 121, 527)$ and let $C' = 582$. The vector a' is now scanned from right to left, one element at a time. The right-most element, 527, must necessarily be chosen for inclusion in the set, by setting $x'_5 = 1$, because the sum of all other vector elements is known to be smaller than 527, and hence too small to sum to 582. A number of additional vector elements must now be chosen from the remainder of a' whose sum equals $C' - a'_5$ or 55. Obviously $x'_4 = 0$ since 121 exceeds 55. However, $x'_3 = 1$ because the remaining elements again could not add up to 55. By continuing this argument one easily determines a' as $(1,0,1,0,1)$.

A knapsack vector $a = (a_1,a_2,...,a_n)$ can be used for message encipher-ing by dividing the message into n-bit blocks $X_1, X_2, \ldots, X_m$, and com-puting for each message block the vector product $S_i = a \cdot X_i = (a_1 x_{i_1} + a_2 x_{i_2} + ... + a_n x_{i_n})$. The sums S_i then constitute the ciphertext. To restore the plaintext, one needs to recover the binary blocks X_i from the sums S_i; this involves solving the knapsack problem because some of the elements of vector a must be chosen and others rejected. The knapsack problem cannot be solved in a reasonable time; hence a mes-sage encoded in this fashion cannot be easily deciphered. However, a message encoded with a simple knapsack is easily decipherable. To obtain a usable system, a simple knapsack then must be used for enci-phering; to prevent decoding by unauthorized persons, however, the structure of the simple knapsack used for enciphering must be hidden.

The following method suggests itself:

1. A random simple knapsack vector a' is chosen that exhibits several hundred components. Vector a' is kept secret.

2. A random number m is chosen that is larger than the sum of the vector elements a_i' ($m > \sum\limits_{i=1}^{n} a_i'$); m is also kept secret.

3. A random pair of integers w, w^{-1} is chosen such that $w \cdot w^{-1} = 1$ mod m; that is, w^{-1} is the multiplicative inverse of w modulo m. Both w and w^{-1} are kept confidential.

4. Using the confidential information a', m and w, a public knapsack vector a is then generated by multiplying each component of a' by w mod m, that is, $a = a' w \bmod m$.

5. Each user publishes his or her public enciphering vector a, which can then be used to encipher any message blocks X_i by computing the sums $S_i = \sum\limits_{i=1}^{n} a_i \cdot x_i$.

When a legitimate recipient receives an enciphered message, the se-cret information w^{-1} and m is now used to transform the ciphertext S into an altered cipher S' that can be solved using the simple knapsack vector a' as follows:

$$S' = w^{-1} S \bmod m$$

$$= w^{-1} \sum_{i=1}^{n} a_i \cdot x_i \bmod m$$

$$= w^{-1} \sum_{i=1}^{n} (w \, a_i' \bmod m) \, x_i \bmod m$$

$$= \sum_{i=1}^{n} (w^{-1} \, w \, a_i' \bmod m) \, x_i \bmod m$$

$$= \sum_{i=1}^{n} a_i' \, x_i \bmod m = a' \cdot x.$$

Since $m > \sum_{i=1}^{n} a_i'$, the simple knapsack problem is now easily solved.

Consider, as an example, the superincreasing vector $a' = (5,7,14,30,59)$, and let $m = 117$ ($m > \sum_{i=1}^{n} a_i'$). Then given the multiplier $w = 17$, the public vector a can be constructed by multiplying each element of a' by 17 modulo 117. This produces $a = (85,2,4,42,67)$. The sample message $(0,1,0,1,1)$ is now enciphered with the public vector a as $2 + 42 + 67 = 111$.

To decipher the message, it is necessary to use the multiplicative inverse w^{-1} corresponding to $w = 17$, and to transform S into S' using the formula $S' = w^{-1} S \bmod m$. The multiplicative inverse algorithm described previously can be used to determine w^{-1} as 62 because $w \cdot w^{-1} = 17 \cdot 62 = 1 \bmod 117$. S' is then computed as 96 ($62 \cdot 111 \bmod 117$), which is easily decoded using the simple knapsack a' as $(0,1,0,1,1)$.

There are indications that the knapsack ciphering system may not be as secure as some of the other public key cryptosystems. [27–30] The basic problem with all the ciphering methods that use computationally hard approaches, however, lies with the amount of computation required for enciphering and deciphering, and with the large amount of key information required. Both objections vanish when shorter keys are used in the system — for example, knapsack vectors of a few dozen elements instead of a few hundred. However, the computational security of these systems deteriorates in these circumstances, and decoding is no longer computationally difficult. At present, conventional ciphering methods based on iterated character substitutions and permutations are still preferred for most practical purposes.

References

1. D.E.R. Denning, *Cryptography and Data Security*, Addison-Wesley Publishing Company, Reading, MA, 1982.

2. W. Diffie and M.E. Hellman, Privacy and Authentication: An Introduction to Cryptography, *Proceedings of the IEEE*, 67:3, March 1979, 397–427.

3. W. Diffie and M.E. Hellman, New Directions in Cryptography, *IEEE Transactions on Information Theory*, IT-22:6, November 1976, 644–654.

4. A.G. Konheim, *Cryptography: A Primer*, John Wiley and Sons, New York, 1981.

5. H. Feistel, Cryptography and Computer Privacy, *Scientific American*, 228:5, May 1973, 15–23.

6. J. Saltzer, On Digital Signatures, *Operating Systems Review*, 12:2, April 1978, 12–14.

7. S.G. Akl, Digital Signatures: A Tutorial Survey, *Computer*, 16:2, February 1983, 15–24.

8. R.M. Needham and M.D. Schroeder, Using Encryption for Authentication in Large Networks of Computers, *Communications of the ACM*, 21:12, December 1978, 993–999.

9. A. Evans, Jr., W. Kantrowitz, and E. Weiss, A User Authentication Scheme Not Requiring Secrecy in the Computer, *Communications of the ACM*, 17:8, August 1974, 437–442.

10. R. Morris and K. Thompson, Password Security: A Case History, *Communications of the ACM*, 22:11, November 1979, 594–597.

11. A. Lempel, Cryptology in Transition, *Computing Surveys*, 11:4, December 1979, 285–303.

12. S. Peleg and A. Rosenfeld, Breaking Substitution Ciphers Using a Relaxation Algorithm, *Communications of the ACM*, 22:11, November 1979, 598–605.

13. G.R. Blakley, One Time Pads Are Key Safeguarding Schemes, Not Cryptosystems, *Proceedings 1981 Symposium on Security and Privacy*, IEEE Computer Society, April 1981, 75–88.

14. R.L. Rivest, Statistical Analysis of the Hagelin Cryptograph, *Cryptologia*, 5:1, January 1981, 27–32.

15. W.G. Barker, *Cryptanalysis of the Hagelin Cryptograph*, Aegean Park Press, Laguna Hills, CA, 1977.

16. G. Welchman, *The Hut Six Story — Breaking the Enigma Codes*, McGraw-Hill Book Co., New York, 1982.

17. W. Kozaczuk, *Enigma: How the German Machine Cipher Was Broken*, Arms and Armour Press, London, 1984.

18. R. Morris, N.J.A. Sloane, and A.D. Wyner, Assessment of the National Bureau of Standards Proposed Federal Data Encryption Standard, *Cryptologia*, 1:3, July 1977, 281–291.

19. R.C. Merkle and M.E. Hellman, On the Security of Multiple Encryption, *Communications of the ACM*, 27:7, July 1981, 465–467.

20. W. Diffie and M.E. Hellman, Exhaustive Cryptanalysis of the NBS Data Encryption Standard, *Computer*, 10:6, June 1977, 74–84.

21. M.E. Hellman, DES Will Be Totally Insecure within Ten Years, *IEEE Spectrum*, 16:7, July 1979, 32–39.

22. W.F. Ehrsam, S.M. Matyas, C.H. Meyer, and W.L. Tuchman, A Cryptographic Key Management Scheme for Implementing the Data Encryption Standard, *IBM Systems Journal*, 17:2, 1978, 106–125.

23. R.L. Rivest, A. Shamir, and L. Adleman, A Method for Obtaining Digital Signatures and Public Key Cryptosystems, *Communications of the ACM*, 21:2, February 1978, 120–126.

24. R.L. Rivest, A Description of a Single-Chip Implementation of the RSA Cipher, *Lambda*, 1:3, 1980, 14–18.

25. G.J. Simmons and J.N. Norris, Preliminary Comments on the MIT Public Key Cryptosystem, *Cryptologia*, 1:4, October 1977, 406–414.

26. R.C. Merkle and M.E. Hellman, Hiding Information and Signatures in Trapdoor Knapsacks, *IEEE Transactions on Information Theory*, IT-24:5, September 1978, 525–530.

27. A. Shamir, A Polynomial Time Algorithm for Breaking the Basic Merkle-Hellman Cryptosystem, *Proceedings 23rd Symposium on Foundations of Computer Science*, November 1982, 145–152.

28. A. Shamir and R.E. Zippel, On the Security of the Merkle-Hellman Cryptographic Scheme, *IEEE Transactions on Information Theory*, IT-26:3, May 1980, 339–340.

29. A. Shamir, On the Cryptocomplexity of Knapsack Systems, *Proceedings of 11th Annual ACM Symposium on the Theory of Computing*, Association for Computing Machinery, New York, May 1979, 118–129.

30. P.S. Henry, Fast Decryption Algorithm for the Knapsack Cryptographic System, *Bell System Technical Journal*, 60:5, May-June 1981, 767–773.

Chapter 7

File-Accessing Systems

7.1 Basic Concepts

Text-processing systems manipulate texts written in natural or artificial languages, and transform them using auxiliary morphological, syntactic, or structural information. For example, text-editing systems replace specific text excerpts with different, related text structures. Analogously, compression and encryption systems transform texts into new, condensed forms that hide the original structure or content.

Text manipulations are often carried out on individual text components, for example individual text characters or words; auxiliary information stored in tables and dictionaries is used in the process. Stored word-stem and word-affix lists are thus usually used as a basis for the decomposition of full words into word stems, and special tables may supply the codes that replace individual text words in cryptography, and may add syntactic and semantic data to particular word entries.

The effective use of dictionary information depends crucially on an appropriate choice of dictionary organization and on efficient file-search and file-access procedures. Such file-accessing methods, used to locate individual dictionary entries and to retrieve the information corresponding to particular file entries, are described in this chapter.

A *file* is a collection of records, each consisting of one or more *fields*. In an ordinary word dictionary, the records identify individual text words, and the fields contain information related to each word entry, such as pronunciation, decomposition into syllables, and grammatical indicators. To retrieve the dictionary information relating to particular entries, a search request must be formulated based on the contents of certain record fields. The fields used to specify the retrieval criteria are known as *key fields*, and the values contained in the key fields, as *search keys*. For example, access to a personnel file containing information about the employees of a particular organization can be obtained by using as search keys the names of employees, or job classifications, or salary levels. Similarly, a document file can be searched by using as keys the names of certain document authors, or the titles of particular documents, or certain words in the document texts. In each case, the file is searched by comparing the query specification with the contents of corresponding record fields; records whose key fields match the query specifications are retrieved.

Several types of query specifications can be distinguished. A *simple* query is one containing the value of a single search key. A *range* query contains a range of values for a single search key — for example, a request for all the records of employees ages 22 to 25. A *functional* query is specified by using a function of the values for certain search keys, for example the age of employees exceeding a given stated threshold.

From the point of view of file access, the most important distinction is between simple, *single-key* queries, and *multiple-key* queries. In the former case, the value of a single search key is used as the retrieval criterion, whereas for multiple-key queries a number of different search keys may be involved. For single-key queries, the record file can be maintained in order according to the values of the given single key. For example, a file of telephone service subscribers is normally maintained in alphabetic order of the subscriber names because the normal access is designed to obtain the telephone numbers corresponding to particular subscriber names. File access in multikey searches is complicated by the fact that it is obviously not possible to order the file simultaneously in accordance with the values of different search keys. Thus an employee file maintained in order by employee names cannot also be ordered by employee age or employee job-classification number.

Many different file-accessing methods have been proposed for both single- and multiple-key searches. The access methods used in a particular situation depend on the storage space required for the needed dictionaries and access structures, the speed of the file-search operations, the adaptability of the file-access method to the available hardware, and the usefulness of the file-search system in dynamic situations where the files grow or shrink. [1–4]

In practice, it is often necessary to carry out multikey searches and to process queries that are incompletely specified. In these circumstances, so-called *partial-match* retrieval strategies are used, in which the retrieved records are allowed to contain extraneous keys whose values are not specified in a search request, in addition to the normal search keys. The values of such extraneous, nonspecified record keys are disregarded in partial-match retrieval.

7.2 Single-Key Searching: Sequential Search

A *sequential search* is carried out by comparing each stored record in turn with an available query formulation, and retrieving appropriate stored data for all records whose key fields match the query keys. Since all records are eventually compared with the query, the record file need not be maintained in any particular order. The file-maintenance operations used to process the file are then substantially simplified, and storage overhead is reduced to a minimum because no auxiliary information is needed to access the file. Further, the sequential search can be used for both single-key and multiple-key searches — in either case one complete file traversal is necessary to retrieve the wanted records.

A typical sequential-search strategy for single-key searches is shown in Fig. 7.1. In the program, each record R_i is assumed to be identified by a key value K_i, the query key is designated as X, and a dummy record R_{n+1} with key K_{n+1} is appended to the file. The program of Fig. 7.1 requires a total of $(n+1)$ comparisons between query and record keys. If the search were programmed to stop after finding the first matching record and all record keys were distinct, the maximum search effort would still require $(n+1)$ key comparisons for unsuc-

---

Figure 7.1 Typical sequential-search strategy.

```
1. [Initialization]   K_{n+1} ← X

2. [Search file]      do for i = 1,2,...,n + 1
                         if K_i = X
                            then if i = n + 1
                               then print "unsuccessful"
                               else print R_i
                            end if
                         end do
```

---

cessful searches, those in which no matching record is found. Under the same assumptions, the average search effort for successful searches requires $(n+1)/2$ key comparisons because on average the needed record will be found after half the file has been traversed.

When retrieval probabilities of records vary from one record to another, the file can be ordered in decreasing order of retrieval probability, substantially reducing the average search effort needed to find a record. When retrieval probabilities are taken into account, the expected average effort for a sequential search is $\sum_{i=1}^{n} i \cdot p_i$ for a file of n records, where i is the number of query-record comparisons needed to find the ith record, and p_i is the access probability of the ith record.

Consider as an example a file of n records (with $n = 5$ in the illustrations that follow). When all records have a common probability p_i of being wanted, where $p_i = 1/n = 1/5$, the expected average search effort will be

$$\sum_{i=1}^{n} i \cdot p_i = 1 \cdot 1/5 + 2 \cdot 1/5 + ... + 5 \cdot 1/5 = 15/5 = 3.$$

On the other hand, when the five sample records exhibit varying access probabilities equal — for example, to $p_1 = 0.4$, $p_2 = 0.3$, $p_3 = 0.2$, $p_4 = 0.07$, and $p_5 = 0.03$ — the expected average search effort can be reduced by about one-third, to slightly over two query-record comparisons, by arranging the records in decreasing order of access probability:

$$\sum_{i=1}^{n} i \cdot p_i = 1 \cdot 0.4 + 2 \cdot 0.3 + 3 \cdot 0.2 + 4 \cdot 0.07 + 5 \cdot 0.03 = 2.03.$$

The lower search cost, of course, can be obtained only when the record-access probabilities are known and remain constant, and when the file is maintained in the appropriate order.

For large files, a sequential search will prove too time consuming even when the file can be appropriately ordered. It then becomes necessary to introduce auxiliary index structures that provide access to small subportions of the file.

7.3 Single-Key Indexed Searches

An *index file* is an auxiliary table, or file, containing the values of certain record keys together with pointers representing the addresses in the main file of records containing the corresponding key values. When the main file is ordered according to the values of the key field, a small *sparse index* may be used that includes only some of the key values, and for each such key value the address of only a single record carrying that key. To find other records with the same or related key values, the main file can be searched in the vicinity of the indicated address. Thus to carry out a search in a telephone directory, the index might be restricted to 26 entries, consisting of one entry for each distinct initial character of a subscriber name, together with the page numbers of the first subscriber whose name starts with the corresponding initial letter. To locate a particular telephone number, a sequential search is then started at the appropriate page specified in the index.

When the file is not maintained in order according to key values, or when the accessing time that can be obtained with the sparse index is too slow, a *full index* may be used; such an index contains all key values together with the addresses of all records corresponding to each particular key value. The index file may become very large, but a search of the main file may be completely avoided in some circumstances because all the required record addresses are contained in the index. Full indexes can be used with ordered or unordered main files. To simplify the search, the index itself is best maintained in order of key values. [2] The differences between sparse and full indexes are illustrated in the simplified example of Fig. 7.2, which shows only record keys and no other record information. In the sparse index, one pointer serves for all records whose key name starts with a particular character; in the full index, one pointer is used for each distinct record in the main file. [5]

The well-known *indexed sequential-access method* (ISAM) is a good example of a sparse index used to obtain access to a record file maintained in the order of increasing key value. The assumption is that the main file is maintained on disk, in which case the system of indexes can be tied to the disk technology. The disks are divided into sections, known as cylinders, and each cylinder is in turn subdivided into several tracks. As a result, *cylinder* and *track* indexes can be constructed containing in each case the keys of the last record included in a given cylinder, or track. With this index structure, access to the records can be contained by consulting the multilevel index system starting with the highest (cylinder) level to determine a particular cylinder, and then a track number within a cylinder. The specified track must eventually be scanned to find a particular record. [4–7]

An example of an indexed sequential search process is shown in Fig. 7.3 where the search key is assumed to be CAB. The cylinder index shows that if a CAB record actually exists, it must be stored in cylinder 01 since CAB precedes FAT in alphabetic order. The track index for cylinder 01 reveals that CAB must appear in track 02 since the record key is larger than the last key for track 01 (BLOCK) but smaller than the last key for track 02 (CAT). To find the CAB record, three different file accesses are thus required — to the cylinder index, a track index, and finally a particular record track. The ISAM process is efficient when each record appears in the regular (primary) track to which it is in principle assigned. Trouble arises, however, when additions must be made to a track that is already full. When this happens, the last record on the track must be moved to an overflow area, and other records stored on the overflow track may have to be moved downward to allow the new record to be inserted in the position corresponding to the alphabetic key order. When records are moved because of overflow, the track index must be changed and pointers to the overflow track must be maintained in addition to the regular track pointers.

An example of the overflow process is shown in Fig. 7.4 where CAB is added first, requiring the CAT record to be moved to the overflow track 16. The track index for track 02 now shows CAP as the last record in the track. When BUM is added next, CAP must in turn be moved, and the last record in track 02 is now CAN. In principle, the overflow area can itself be maintained in alphabetical key order, but in Fig. 7.4 the

Figure 7.2 Sparse- versus full-index organization.

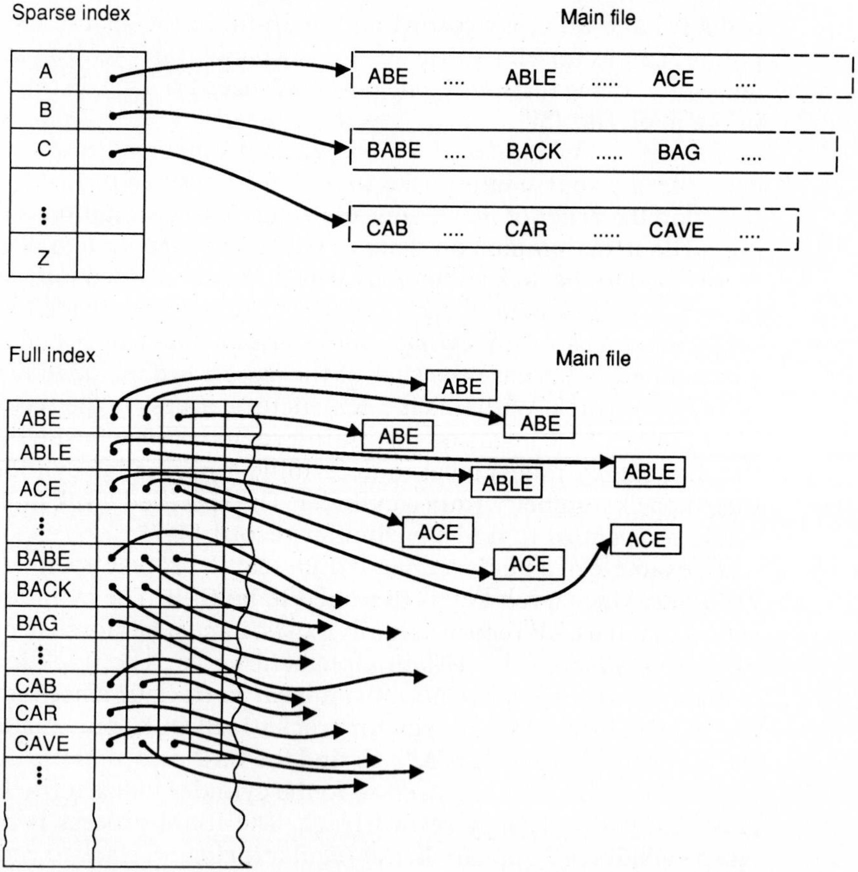

assumption is that the overflow tracks are filled in chronological order and must therefore be searched completely for each access. A typical indexed sequential search is outlined in Fig. 7.5. As the program shows, two accesses are required to the indexes followed by a search of a primary or an overflow track.

Dependence on hardware largely disappears in the so-called virtual sequential-access method (VSAM). A multilevel sparse index is used as before, but the storage subdivisions known as control areas and control intervals may span a variable number of physical tracks or cylinders. In VSAM, a free-space-allocation system is used that automatically creates a new control interval when a given interval becomes full — in which case, half the records from the old interval are allocated to

Figure 7.3 Basic indexed sequential access.

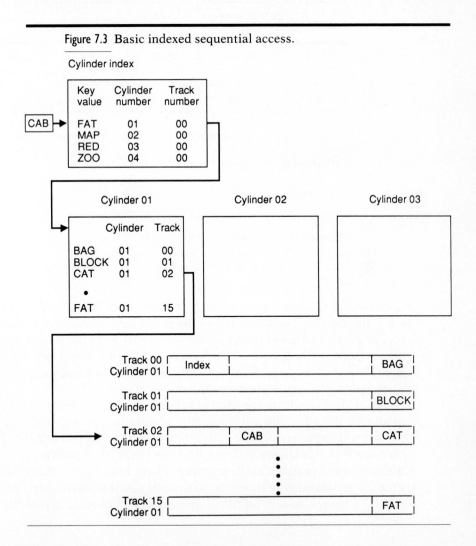

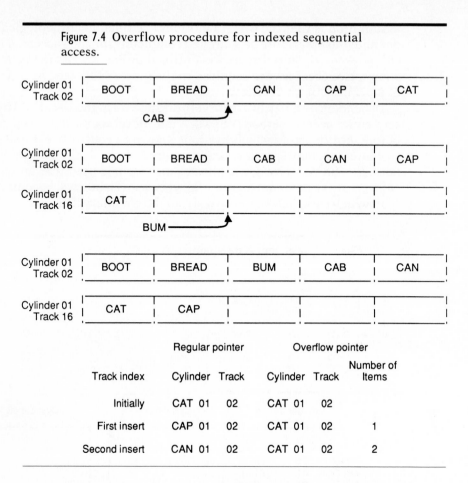

Figure 7.4 Overflow procedure for indexed sequential access.

the new control interval. Eventually control areas are also duplicated when necessary. Free space is usually provided at the end of each control interval, and some intervals are left empty in each control area to accommodate file growth. When records are removed from the file, the remaining records of the control interval are moved to the left so as to keep contiguous areas of empty space.

When "flat" indexes are used in tabular form as in ISAM, problems arise in a dynamic file environment because tables do not easily expand or shrink as required by the changes in the main record file. Further, both the auxiliary indexes and the main file require extensive maintenance because the file entries are kept in key order in each case. Index organizations in tree form are much easier to maintain than are tabular indexes, and in addition they generally provide faster file access.

Figure 7.5 Indexed sequential-search strategy.

---

1. [Examine cylinder index]

    do sequential search of cylinder index
    if record key = < key for cylinder (i)
        then set cylinder (i) as next access point

2. [Examine track index for cylinder (i)]

    do sequential search of track index
    if record key = < overflow key of track index (j)
        then if record key = < regular key of track index (j)
        then set access address to regular address
          of track index (j) and do step 3
        else set access address to overflow address
          of track index (j)

3. [Search track]

    locate record on regular track or overflow track
      (in regular track area keys appear in alphabetic order;
      in overflow area keys are chained and the whole overflow
      area must be searched)

7.4 Tree Searching

A tree structure consists of nodes, or vertices, containing node information together with pointers giving access to additional nodes of the tree. In a *binary tree*, each node carries the information pertaining to a particular record (especially the record key), in addition to at most two pointers giving access to two new tree nodes. The left pointer attached to a node gives access to another node with a smaller key value than the current node, while the right pointer gives access to a node with a larger key value. Either of the pointer values, or both, may be null for particular nodes. The structure of the nodes in a binary search tree is shown in simplified form in Fig. 7.6. In principle, the information stored with each node may include all the data for the corresponding file record. In practice, the record information is often stored in a separate file, and the tree structure serves only as an index giving access to the main record file. The node information then consists of key values and pointers to the corresponding records in the main file.

A typical binary search tree is shown in Fig. 7.7(a) for a set of records whose key values range from 5 to 18. Only the key values themselves are shown in the sample tree; the pointers to the corresponding records in the main file are omitted. A tree-search operation is performed by comparing the search key with the key values attached to

Figure 7.6 Node structure of binary tree.

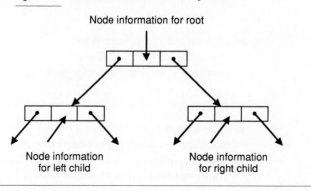

Node information for root

Node information
for left child

Node information
for right child

certain nodes of the tree starting with the root of the tree (node value 10 in Fig. 7.7a). If the search key is not equal to the current node key, the left or right path is taken from that node, depending on whether the search key is smaller or larger than the current node key. For example, to find the record with key value 13 in Fig. 7.7(a), search key 13 is compared with key value 10; this leads to the node with key value 14 using the right pointer, since 13 is larger than 10. From there the left path is taken since 13 is smaller than 14. Finally the right path from node 12 leads to node 13, which is equal to the search key. Node 13 is assumed to carry a pointer to the corresponding record address in the main file.

The maximum number of key comparisons needed to conduct a tree search is equal to the length of the longest path from the root to a leaf of the tree. In Fig. 7.7(a), the tree has four levels, and thus four key comparisons are needed to find the nodes with key values 13 or 15.

Figure 7.7 Binary search trees. (a) Typical binary search tree. (b) Search tree with node 10 removed.

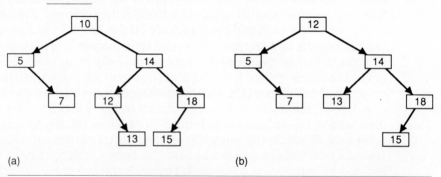

(a)

(b)

When the search tree is *full*, that is, when each node has two descendants (except for the leaf nodes on the lowest tree level), $\log_2 n$ levels are needed for search trees of n nodes. The search effort in a full binary tree search is therefore limited to $\log_2 n$, as opposed to n for a sequential file search. [6–14]

A tree organization easily supports operations such as searching for a stored record, inserting a new record, finding the stored record with the minimum key value, and deleting a record. Assuming that the number of tree levels in the search tree is approximately equal to $\log_2 n$, each of these operations requires approximately $\log_2 n$ key comparisons. To insert a new record, the given record key is used as a search key, and the new record information is then added as a new leaf node at the end of the search path. For example, to add a record with key value 16 to the tree of Fig. 7.7(a), the search path using 16 as a search key leads to node 15; the new record can then be added as a right child of node 15 on the next lower tree level. To find the record with the minimum key value, one moves as far to the left in the tree as possible. For the tree of Fig. 7.7(a), this leads to node 5.

Node deletion in a binary tree is more complicated than node searching or node addition because a proper binary tree structure must be preserved when a node is deleted. There are three possibilities:

1. If the node to be deleted is a leaf of the tree, the corresponding node is simply deleted: For example, node 7 can be deleted from the tree of Fig. 7.7(a) by inserting a null value for the right pointer of node 5.

2. If the node to be deleted has only one child, that is, if either the right or left pointer from that node is null, the node to be deleted may be replaced by the only available child node. In Fig. 7.7(a), node 18 may be deleted by replacing its node information with that of node 15. The right pointer from node 14 would then point directly to node 15.

3. If the deleted node has two children, the deleted node information is replaced by the node with the smallest key value in the right subtree. Thus node 10 can be removed from the tree of Fig. 7.7(a) by using node 12 as a replacement since 12 is the smallest key larger than 10. Since node 12 is not a leaf, its original position in the tree must in turn be replaced by its successor node 13. The tree obtained after deletion of node 10 from Fig. 7.7(a) is shown in Fig. 7.7(b).

To maintain files, it may be necessary to traverse a binary tree structure in such a way that each node is covered exactly once. Tree traversal is used, for example, to produce an ordered list of record keys or record addresses. Three traversal orders are common, all of which start at the root node and cover the nodes in a recursively defined manner:

1. The *symmetric*, or *inorder*, traversal strategy covers each node by taking at each point first the left child, then the root node, and finally the right child. For the sample tree of Fig. 7.7(a), this implies moving leftward from the root. Since node 5 has no left child, node 5 is listed first, followed by node 7. Since 7 has no children, one must retrace back to the root node 10. From there one takes the right child (node 14). But 14 is the root of a subtree with left child 12, so 12 is covered before 14. Since 12 has no left child, 12 can be listed before the right child 13. A final backtrack operation leads to 14 and finally to 15 and 18. The symmetric traversal order produces a node list in order of increasing key value (5,7,10,12,13,14,15,18).

2. For *preorder* traversal, one takes at each point the root followed by the left child followed by the right child. For the sample tree of Fig. 7.7(a), (10,5,7,14,12,13,18,15) is obtained.

3. Finally in *postorder* traversal, one takes the left child, right child, and root, in that order. For the sample tree, the postorder list is (7,5,13,12,15,18,14,10).

It may be noted that all tree-traversal methods require some back-tracking — that is, in going down the tree levels, it is important to re-member which paths higher up in the tree are still open, because these paths must be taken later on. For example, in preorder traversal it is necessary to pursue the leftward path from each node first by using the left pointers before pursuing the paths to the right. When follow-ing a left pointer, it is therefore necessary to remember that the corre-sponding right path from the same node remains to be followed later. This may be done conveniently by using a *stack*, consisting of a set of auxiliary storage registers, to store the right pointer addresses that remain to be processed. After a leftward path has been followed to the end, the stack addresses are read in a last-in-first-out (LIFO) mode. That is, the most recently stored stack address is read first, and the corresponding rightward path is followed. When the stack is empty after the end of a path is reached, traversal terminates. A preorder stack-traversal program is shown in Fig. 7.8, in which the left and right pointers from a node are denoted LLINK and RLINK.

Tree traversal can be simplified by using upward pointers to cer-tain nodes located higher up in the search tree. Upward pointers, also known as *threads*, can be added to a search tree by replacing normally empty left and right pointers of certain tree nodes by pointers to pre-decessor nodes higher up in the search tree. For example, empty left pointers can be replaced by threads to the corresponding predecessor nodes in symmetric traversal order, while empty right pointers can be replaced by threads to successor nodes in symmetric traversal order. By extension, the empty left pointer of the smallest (left-most) tree node and the empty right pointer of the largest (right-most) tree node are replaced by threads back to the root. The *threaded tree* obtained by adding upward pointers to the sample tree of Fig. 7.7(a) is shown in Fig. 7.9.

The symmetric traversal of threaded trees is much simplified because for all nodes that do not have a right child (RCHILD) on a lower level, the right pointer (RLINK) points upward to the successor node in symmetric order. This is notably the case for nodes 7, 13, and 15 of the tree in Fig. 7.9. A program for symmetric order traversal of threaded trees is shown in Fig. 7.10. Step 1 of the program determines the first node in symmetric order as the left-most node in the tree (node 5 in the sample tree of Fig. 7.9). Step 2 determines the set of successor nodes in symmetric order. In general the successor node is the node identified by the right pointer from a node. For example, in Fig. 7.9 the right pointer from node 5 points toward node 7. Similarly, the right pointer from 7 points upward to the successor node 10. Statement 2(b) of Fig. 7.10 identifies the right successor of a node as the potential successor node.

One exception to the basic rule of successor determination occurs when a node has a right link pointing downward to a successor node

---

Figure 7.8 Stack traversal of binary search tree in preorder.

1. [Initialize]

    S is an empty stack

    P is a pointer to the root of tree

2. [Is tree empty?]

    if P is empty

    then go to step 5

3. [Preorder visit]

    $X \leftarrow P$

    Record X on output

4. [Remember right path by storing address in stack and descend left]

    $S \leftarrow$ RLINK(P)

    $P \leftarrow$ LLINK(P)

    go to step 2

5. [Done? If not, read most recently stored address from stack]

    if S is empty

    then exit

    else $P \leftarrow S$

    go to step 2

Figure 7.9 Tree of Fig. 7.7(a) with added threads.

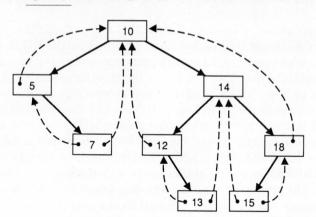

that itself has a left link also pointing downward. In that case these left links must be followed to find the successor of the original node. For example, in Fig. 7.9, the successor of node 10 is not node 14, but rather node 12, which is reachable from node 14 by a left link. Similarly, the successor of 14 is not 18, but 15. The program takes care of this special

Figure 7.10 Traversal of threaded tree in symmetric order.

1. Record left-most element in tree as the first element
   in symmetric list

   > $X \leftarrow$ HEAD
   > **while** LLINK(X) is DOWN
   > **do** $X \leftarrow$ LLINK(X)
   > Record X on list

2. Determine successor node S of node X

   (a) **do while** RLINK(X) ≠ HEAD
   (b) $S \leftarrow$ RCHILD(X)
   (c) **if** RLINK(X) is down
   (d)   **then while** LLINK(S) is down
   (e)   **do** $S \leftarrow$ LCHILD(S)
   (f)   **end while**
   (g) $X \leftarrow S$
   (h) RECORD X on list
   (i) **end do while**

case using statements (c)–(f) of step 2 in Fig. 7.10. When a right link is reached that points back to the head of the tree (statement 2(a) in Fig. 7.10), the symmetric-order traversal is complete.

The efficiency of tree-search operations varies with the number of tree levels needed to store the search tree. For n records (nodes) the number of tree levels in a binary tree can be as small as $\lfloor \log_2 n \rfloor + 1$, or as large as n, as shown in Fig. 7.11 for the sample records included in Fig. 7.7(b). Only three levels are needed to store the seven records in the tree of Fig. 7.11(a), but seven levels are used in the tree of Fig. 7.11(b). When the search tree is *complete*, as in Fig. 7.11(a) — that is, when all tree levels, except possibly the last, are fully occupied by assigned records — the left and right subtrees of each node contain approximately the same number of records. For example, the left and right subtrees of node 13 in Fig. 7.11(a) each contain three records.

Binary search can be represented by a complete search tree in which the comparison between search and record keys produces a split into two halves of the file remaining to be examined at each point. In a binary search, the initial key comparison is carried out with the key identifying the middle record (in increasing key-value order) of the file. When the n records of a file are assigned order numbers in increasing key-value order, the middle record has order number $\lfloor (n+1)/2 \rfloor$. If the search key is smaller than the key for the middle record, the key comparison is next carried out with the middle record of the first half of the file, that is, the record located halfway between record 1 and record $\lfloor (n+1)/2 \rfloor - 1$. Similarly, if the search key is larger than the key value of the middle record, the next key comparison is performed with the middle record of the second half of the file, that is, the record located halfway between record $\lfloor (n+1)/2 \rfloor + 1$ and record n. A program for a binary search is shown in Fig. 7.12, in which the records are assumed to be numbered from 1 to n, K_i repre-

Figure 7.11 Tree organizations for sample records of Fig. 7.7b. (a) Complete tree. (b) Unbalanced tree.

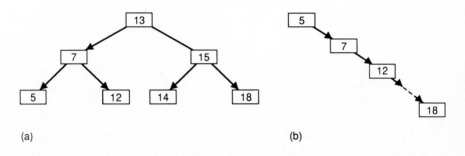

(a)   (b)

sents the key value of the ith record, and X is the search key. The characters B and E designate the beginning and end of the file segment remaining to be examined at each point.

Fig. 7.13 shows the search tree representing the binary search program of Fig. 7.12 for the eight records included in Fig. 7.7(a). The middle record is record number $\lfloor (1+8)/2 \rfloor = 4$. Similarly, the middle of the first half is determined as record number $\lfloor (1+3)/2 \rfloor = 2$, and the middle of the second half as record number $\lfloor (5+8)/2 \rfloor = 6$. In a binary search, the average number of key comparisons needed to locate an entry in a file of n records is $\lfloor \log_2 n \rfloor - 1$, while the maximum number of key comparisons is $\lfloor \log_2 n \rfloor + 1$. In the example of Fig. 7.13, a maximum of four key comparisons is needed to locate the eighth record with key value 18.

The search tree representing a binary search is *balanced* because the lengths of all search paths from the root of the tree to any of the leaves differ by one at most. In the tree of Fig. 7.13 all the leaves are located on two adjacent tree levels. Balanced search trees furnish the best average search time for a file of records. Even when a given search tree is initially balanced, however, the tree may rapidly become unbalanced in dynamic situations when new records are added to the file and old ones are deleted. For example, removing the record with

---

Figure 7.12 Program for binary search.

1. [Initialization]

    $B \leftarrow 1$

    $E \leftarrow n$

2. [Perform search]

    Repeat steps 3 and 4 while $B \leq E$

3. [Determine index of midpoint]

    $i \leftarrow \lfloor \dfrac{B + E}{2} \rfloor$

4. [Key comparison]

    if $X < K_i$

        then set $E \leftarrow i - 1$

    else if $X > K_i$

        then set $B \leftarrow i + 1$

    else print K_i and record information and exit

5. [Unsuccessful search]

    print "record not found" and exit

Figure 7.13 Binary search tree for records of Fig. 7.7(a) corresponding to program of Fig. 7.11.

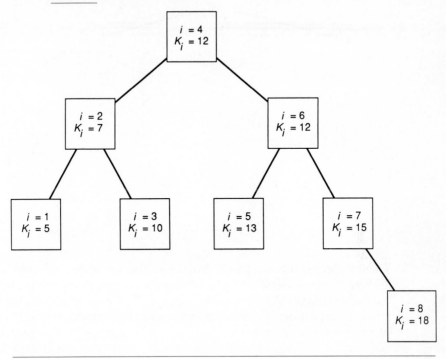

key value 7 and adding new records with key values 16 and 17 turns the tree of Fig. 7.7(a) into the new structure of Fig. 7.14, where two key comparisons are needed to access record 5, but six key comparisons are needed for record 17. This suggests that search trees should initially be generated in balanced form, and that this balance should be maintained when records are added and deleted.

7.5 Balanced Search Trees

A decision to use a balanced search tree rather than a random tree, and to maintain the tree in balance during file changes, must depend on the expected cost of the tree-balancing operations compared with the savings in search time because of the balanced trees. In considering whether to use tree balancing, one must be aware that rebalancing after node addition or deletion may involve structural changes of substantial complexity. For example, adding a record with key value 1 to the tree of Fig. 7.15(a) produces the search tree of Fig. 7-15(b). Figure

Figure 7.14 Unbalanced search tree.

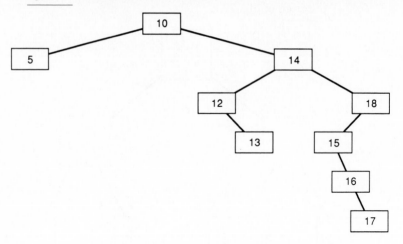

7.15(c) shows the balanced form for the records included in Fig. 7.15(b). A comparison of the two trees shows that every record receives a new position in the transition from Fig. 7.15(b) to 7.15(c). Indeed, only record 1 maintains the same parent node on the next-higher tree level in the two tree structures. To avoid the potentially high cost of frequent rebalancing, completely balanced trees need not always be provided. Instead, a certain imbalance in the search trees is normally tolerated, and balancing is performed only to correct overly unbalanced situations.

The well known *AVL tree* (after Adelson-Velskii and Landis [15]) is a compromise between a completely balanced binary tree and an

Figure 7.15 Complete tree rebalancing. (a) Original tree. (b) Tree with node 1 added. (c) Rebalanced tree.

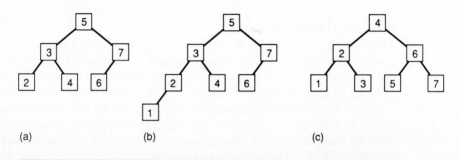

(a)　　　　　　　　(b)　　　　　　　　(c)

arbitrary binary tree. In an AVL tree, the height of the left subtree for each node differs from the height of the right subtree of the node by at most one. This implies that the longest search path to the right of a node differs from the longest search path to the left of that node by at most one.

In AVL trees, each tree node may be assigned to one of three classes according to its balance condition:

1. A node is in balance (designated B or 0) when the longest paths in the left and right subtrees of that node are of equal length.

2. A node is right heavy (R or $+1$) when the longest path to the right has a length that is one greater than the longest path to the left.

3. A node is left heavy (L or -1) when the longest path length to the left is one greater than the longest path length to the right.

When the *balance factors* of all nodes of a search tree fall into classes B, R, or L, it is an AVL tree and requires no rebalancing. This is the case for the sample tree of Fig. 7.15(b).

Consider now the problem of *node insertion* in AVL trees. As in ordinary binary trees, the key of a record to be inserted is treated as a search key, and the new record is inserted as a leaf at the end of the search path. After insertion of a node, the balance factors must be recomputed for all nodes on the search path from the root of the tree to the newly added node. For each node on that path, three possible cases may arise:

1. A node originally in classes R or L may have become balanced (B) after node insertion.

2. An originally balanced node (B) may have become left or right heavy (L or R).

3. A node originally in class L or R may have become *critical* (C) because the new record may have been inserted in a subtree that was already heavy.

Examples of these situations are shown in Fig. 7.16 where the added branch is shown in dashed lines and the old balance factors are in parentheses.

When a node insertion changes the balance factors of the nodes under cases 1 or 2, no action is needed because the new search tree is still in AVL form. Action must be taken when a node becomes critical, however, because the difference in path lengths between left and right subtrees is now two, and the tree is no longer an AVL tree. Two cases must be distinguished when nodes become critical after insertion, as illustrated in Figs. 7.17 and 7.18.

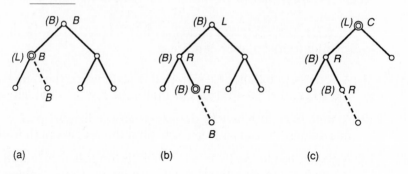

Figure 7.16 Node insertion in AVL trees. (a) Left-heavy node becomes balanced. (b) Balanced node becomes right heavy. (c) Left-heavy node becomes critical.

(a)　　　　　　(b)　　　　　　(c)

The first case applies when the descendant Y of a critical node X becomes unbalanced in the same direction in which the critical node was originally heavy. Before insertion, the descendant Y was balanced. In the example of Fig. 7.17(a), node X was originally left heavy and a new node was added to the left subtree of descendant Y. An analogous situation, also covered by case 1, occurs when the balances are heavy to the right. A single rotation around the critical node in a direction opposite to the existing imbalance corrects the case 1 problem. In particular, when a node is critical in case 1 because of a left imbalance (as in Fig. 7.17a), the rotation is carried out in a clockwise direction, and vice versa for right imbalances. The effect of the single rotation is

Figure 7.17 Rebalancing of AVL trees: case 1, single rotation (adapted from [7]). (a) Before single rotation. (b) After single rotation.

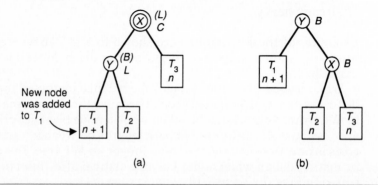

(a)　　　　　　(b)

illustrated in Fig. 7.17(b), where the box $\left[\begin{smallmatrix} T_i \\ n \end{smallmatrix}\right]$ represents a subtree T_i of height n. [7] The example shows that the descendant Y of the critical node becomes the new root of the rotated tree, and that all nodes are in balance after the rotation. The single rotation of Fig. 7.17 involves pointer changes for only nodes X and Y. In threaded trees, additional pointer changes are needed for the root of subtree T_2, whose father node changes from Y to X as a result of the rotation.

In case 2, the descendant Y of critical node X becomes heavy in a direction opposite to the one in which the critical node was originally heavy. In Fig. 7.18(a), the critical node X was originally left heavy, but a descendant Y that was originally balanced has become right heavy after addition of a new node. An analogous situation arises when the critical node is originally right heavy and a descendant node becomes unbalanced to the left.

For case 2 situations, a double rotation is needed to restore balance, as shown in Fig. 7.18. The first rotation is around the descendant Y of the critical node in a direction that creates imbalances in one direction only (leftward in Fig. 7.18). The result of this first rotation is shown in Fig. 7.18(b) for the example of Fig. 7.18(a). The situation after the first rotation, equivalent to a case 1 imbalance, can be corrected by another rotation in a direction opposite to the earlier one around the new descendant Z of node X. The second rotation restores a balanced tree, as

Figure 7.18 Rebalancing of AVL trees: case 2, double rotation (adapted from [7]). (a) Before double rotation. (b) After first rotation, counterclockwise around Y. (c) After second rotation, clockwise around Z.

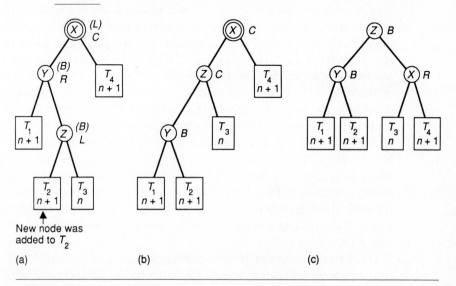

shown in Fig. 7.18(c). A comparison of the trees of Fig. 7.18(a) and (c) shows that the double rotation affects both pointers for node Z, as well as the right pointer of Y and the left pointer of X. In threaded trees, pointer changes are also needed for the root nodes of subtrees T_2 and T_3.

The following method can be used to test for rebalancing following node insertion in AVL trees. Let $u_0, u_1, ..., u_k$ represent the insertion sequence of a new record X, where u_0 represents the root node on level 0 of the tree, and u_i is a node on level i that is traversed in going from the root to the new node $x = u_k$. For each node in the sequence u_0 to u_k the balance is computed as the length of the longest path in the right subtree minus the length of the longest path in the left subtree. When the balances of all nodes in the sequence are 0, 1, or -1 (corresponding to balance factors B, R, and L), no action is taken. Otherwise the critical node u_i with the largest index i (that is, lowest in the tree) is considered, and single or double rotations are invoked according to the following rules:

- A single rotation is used if either the balance of $u_i = 2$ and the balance of $u_{i+1} = 1$, or the balance of $u_i = -2$ and the balance of $u_{i+1} = -1$.

- A double rotation is used if either the balance of $u_i = 2$ and the balance of $u_{i+1} = -1$, or the balance of $u_i = -2$ and the balance of $u_{i+1} = 1$.

Node deletions in AVL trees are carried out in the same way as deletion in ordinary binary trees. That is, nodes without children are simply removed, nodes with one child are replaced by the child node, and nodes with two children are replaced by the successor node in symmetric traversal order. However, AVL trees may require a rebalancing operation after node deletion. For this purpose the *insertion* sequence of the deleted node is examined, that is, the path from the root to the deleted node. Let u_i designate the lowest critical node in the tree (the node with the highest index i exhibiting balance factors of 2 or -2, and let v be a child of u_i. Then single or double rotations are carried out as for insertion: That is, single rotations when the imbalances are in the same direction for both u_i and v, and double rotations when the imbalances are in opposite directions. In addition, a new case may arise for node deletion when the balance of u_i is 2 or -2, and the balance of v is 0. In that case a single rotation around u_i suffices, as shown in Fig. 7.19.

On the average, very little more work is needed to search AVL trees than totally balanced trees. For the most unbalanced AVL tree possible, the maximum increase in the number of needed key comparisons is about 45 percent. [16]

AVL trees are examples of a more general class of *height-balanced* trees, which limit the differences in path lengths from a given node to the leaves of the tree. Differences in path length greater than those allowable for AVL trees may be introduced in terms of a bounded balance parameter α, chosen so as to avoid frequent rebalancing operations. [17]

Consider a binary search tree, and let the *root balance* RB(v) of an arbitrary node v reflect the relative number of nodes in the left and right subtrees of v, respectively. In particular, let

$$RB(v) = \frac{\text{Number of nodes in left subtree} + 1}{\text{Number of nodes in complete tree with root } v + 1}.$$

A tree is said to be in *bounded balance* with parameter α (BB(α)), for $0 \leq \alpha \leq 1/2$, if and only if for all nodes v, either size(v) = 1, or size(v) > 1, and the root balance RB(v) for all nodes of the tree is not smaller than α nor larger than $1 - \alpha$. A perfectly balanced tree will exhibit a bounded balance factor of 1/2 because the root balance factor of all nodes is 1/2. The greater the difference between the bounded balance factor α of a particular tree and 1/2, the more unbalanced the tree will appear. A sample tree in BB(1/4) is shown as in Fig. 7.20.

The notion of tree balance can also be applied to trees with weighted search paths. In that case, a weight attached to each node may reflect the probability with which the key for that node appears in a search request. The search operation will then be efficient when highly weighted nodes are placed close to the root of the tree, so that the search paths to those nodes remain short. Consider a binary search tree and let the weighted path length WPL be defined as $\Sigma \, \alpha_i \, h_i$,

Figure 7.19 Example of node deletion in AVL trees. (a) Before node deletion. (b) After node deletion. (c) After rotation.

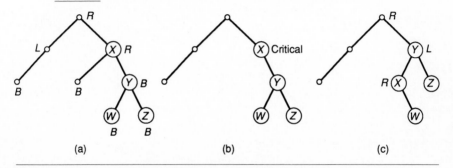

Figure 7.20 Tree in bounded balance; BB(1/4).

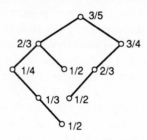

where α_i is the node weight of node i, h_i is the length of the search path from the root to node i (that is, the number of nodes to be traversed in reaching node i), and the sum is taken over all tree nodes. The best search tree is the one for which WPL is maximized or minimized, as the case may be, while preserving the lexicographic order of the nodes. Some typical weighted search trees and their weighted path lengths are shown in Fig. 7.21, where the assumed lexical order corresponds to the normal alphabetic order of the node labels. The three trees of Fig. 7.21 exhibit the same lexicographic ordering assuming symmetric-order traversal, but the weighted path lengths range from 24 for the middle tree to 13 for the right tree.

Generating optimum weighted search trees is unfortunately complex, and the methods for constructing minimum redundancy Huffman trees described in Chapter 5 do not apply here because no ordering requirement exists for the nodes of a Huffman tree. In practice, it may be easiest to use a simple heuristic process that produces reasonably good, but normally nonoptimal, trees. The following two methods

Figure 7.21 Weighted search trees; $\alpha(A)=1$, $\alpha(B)=6$, $\alpha(C)=4$, $\alpha(D)=3$. (a) WPL = 14. (b) WPL = 24. (c) WPL = 13.

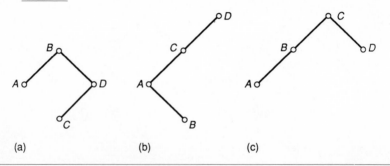

(a)   (b)   (c)

have been proposed for constructing efficient search trees with low weighted path lengths: [18–20]

1. Choose as the root the node with the maximum weight, and repeat for the left and right subtrees.

2. Choose as the root the node that produces left and right subtrees with nearly equal weights.

When large-volume search operations must be carried out, and the access statistics remain reasonably constant, an effort should be made to produce balanced search trees that are close to optimal. In all other cases, good quality, but nonoptimal, arrangements such as AVL or bounded-balance trees will be preferred.

7.6 Multiway Search Trees

In a complete binary search tree of n nodes, $\log_2(n+1)$ key comparisons may be required to find the key information associated with a leaf node. By packing a large number of keys into a single node of the search tree, the height of the tree, and consequently the number of key comparisons needed to find a given key node, may be substantially reduced. In particular, if each node is allowed to have m descendants instead of two as in a binary tree, the number of tree levels is decreased to $\log_m(n)$. Hence multiway tree searches will be more efficient than binary tree searches, assuming that the several keys stored in a single tree node can be scanned rapidly, and that efficient procedures are available to maintain the multiway trees.

To maintain search efficiency for dynamic files, height balancing of the kind used for binary trees could be considered. Alternatively, a multiway tree could be maintained at uniform depth, but the number of keys stored in a given node could be made to vary as keys are added or deleted. This latter strategy is used to maintain the well-known B-trees. [21–24] A B-tree of order m exhibits the following properties:

- The root has at least two descendants (two downward pointers) except if it is a leaf.

- Each interior node has a maximum of m descendants on the next lower tree level and a minimum of $\lceil m/2 \rceil$ descendants.

- All leaves appear on the same tree level.

- Each internal node with k descendants contains exactly $k-1$ keys.

The contents of a typical B-tree node including m pointers P_i and $m-1$ keys K_i are shown in Fig. 7.22. The assumption is that given a key

Figure 7.22 Typical node of B-tree of order m.

K_i, pointer P_i to the left of K_i points to a node containing keys that are smaller than K_i in the normal lexicographic key order, while pointer P_{i+1} to the right of K_i provides access to a node with keys larger than K_i. Figure 7.23 shows a sample B-tree of order 5 for which each interior node except the root contains between three and five descendants.

A B-tree search is conducted similarly to a binary tree search. Suppose that the search key value 22 is given for the tree of Fig. 7.23. Since 22 is less than 50, the left pointer is taken from the root to the first descendant on the next tree level. The keys stored in that node are then scanned, and since 22 falls between 20 and 30, the right pointer of key 20 is taken, leading to a leaf node that contains key 22. In principle, the record information associated with a particular key can be stored with the corresponding key information in the same node. In practice, the record information may be extensive and is better stored in a separate structure that is accessible from the B-tree nodes.

Node insertion into B-trees is handled as for binary trees: Each new key to be inserted is treated as a search key, and the new key is then inserted into the appropriate leaf node at the end of the search path. This operation is straightforward so long as the augmented leaf node does not contain more than $m-1$ keys. When the added key is the mth key of the node, it is necessary to reorganize the tree.

Consider an an example the B-tree of Fig. 7.23 following addition of a new key 12 (see Fig. 7.24a). Node B now contains five keys instead of

Figure 7.23 Typical B-tree of order 5.

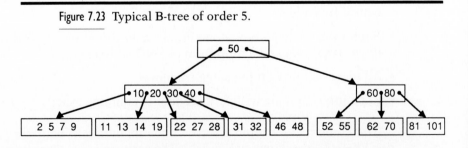

the permitted four, and must therefore be split into two parts. The splitting operation creates two new nodes, one for the left half and one for the right half of the keys. The middle key in the originally overflowing node (key 13 in Fig. 7.24(a)) is promoted to the parent node on the next-higher tree level as a separation criterion for the two newly created half nodes. The result of the splitting operation for node B of Fig. 7.24(a) is shown in Fig. 7.24(b). Since a new key has been added to the

Figure 7.24 Node insertion into B-tree. (a) B-tree following addition of key 12 and before split of node *B*. (b) B-tree following split of node B and before split of parent node. (c) Final tree configuration following addition of key value 12.

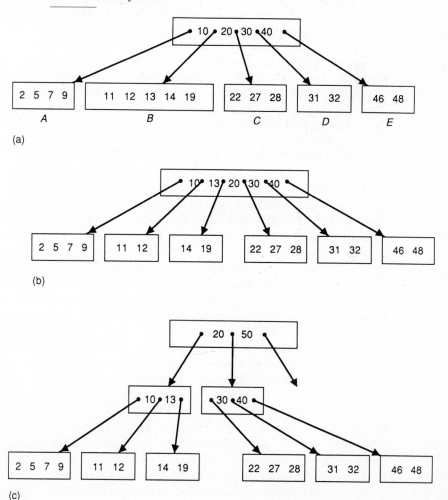

parent node of the split node pair, that parent node may itself overflow, causing a further split (see Fig. 7.24(c)). At most one node-
splitting operation may be needed on each tree level when a new key is
inserted into a B-tree, and at most one new tree level must be added at
the top of the tree containing a new root node.

Node deletion from B-trees may require node merging instead of
node splitting, and once again the node rearrangements may propa-
gate upward in the tree. Consider as an example the deletion of key 70
from the tree of Fig. 7.23. As shown in Fig. 7.25(a), the key removal
causes underflow in node G, which is now left with only one key instead of the minimum requirement of two. The underflow is remedied
by merging nodes F and G and bringing down the separating key (60)
from the parent node. Underflow now occurs in the parent node,
which is left with only one key (80), as shown in Fig. 7.25(b). A second
node-merge operation creates a new node with keys 10, 20, 30, 40, 50,
and 80. Since that node contains more than four keys, it is split by promoting the middle key (30) to the next higher level. The final tree structure after the deletion of key 70 is shown in Fig. 7.25(c).

When the key to be deleted from a B-tree is not located on the leaf
level of the tree, the deleted key is first replaced by the next larger key
from the bottom level of the tree, followed when necessary by node-
merging operation as described earlier. For example, if key 60 were to
be deleted from the tree of Fig. 7.23, it would first be replaced by the
successor key 62 from the bottom tree level. This causes underflow in
the leaf node, and requires that the two nodes containing keys 52 and
55 and key 70 be merged, and that the separating key 62 be demoted,
placing it with 52, 55, and 70 on the bottom-most tree level.

In some applications, fast sequential processing of the record keys
is important. For example, when keys represent dictionary entries, it
may be necessary to rapidly generate copies of the dictionary in alphabetic order of the entries. In that case it may be useful to store *all* the
keys in the bottom-most tree level, keeping only the indexing and
pointer information on the higher tree levels. A single left-to-right scan
of the leaf nodes will then list all key entries in lexicographic order
together with the related record information. The resulting modified
B-tree structure is known as a B^+ *tree*.

A typical *interior* node of a B^+ tree is shown in Fig. 7.26, where the
index entry K_i represents the smallest key value of any key in the subtree pointed to by pointer P_{i+1} to the right of K_i. A portion of a sample
B^+ tree is shown in Fig. 7.27. The set of all keys appears on the bottom-
most tree level in left-to-right order. The index entries on the higher
tree levels now duplicate certain key entries that also appear on the
bottom-most level of the B^+ tree. In searching a B^+ tree, one proceeds
as before by following the pointer to the left of an index entry if the
search key is smaller than the given index entry, and the pointer

to the right of an index entry if the search key is larger than or equal to the key entry.

The B-trees of order 3, also known as *2-3 trees*, exhibit particularly simple properties for searching and maintaining trees. [16,25] In that

Figure 7.25 Node deletion from B-tree of Fig. 7.23. (a) B-tree following removal of key value 70 with underflow in node *G*. (b) B-tree following merge operation of nodes *F* and *G* with underflow in parent node. (c) Final B-tree following node deletion in B-tree of Fig. 7.23.

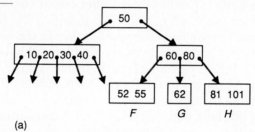

(a)

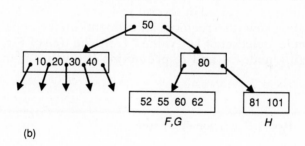

(b)

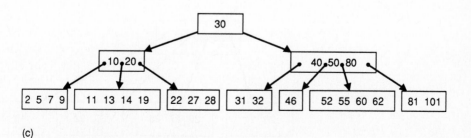

(c)

Figure 7.26 Interior node in B^+ tree (K_i is smallest key value in subtree pointed to by P_{i+1}).

$$P_i \quad K_i \quad P_{i+1} \quad K_{i+1} \quad P_{i+2}$$

case each node is used to store either one or two key values. A sample 2-3 (B^+) tree is shown in Fig. 7.28, in which the first key value of an interior node represents the smallest key in the second subtree reachable from that node, while the second key value is the smallest key in the third subtree reachable from the node. A dash represents an empty key entry. As shown in the figure, each node on the leaf level of a 2-3 tree contains the information for a single key value.

Node additions and deletions for 2-3 trees involve node splits and merges as for ordinary B-trees. For example, the addition of key value 10 as a leaf of the tree of Fig. 7.28 involves a splitting of node A (see Figs. 7.29a and b). When the middle key (10) is promoted to the parent level (Fig. 7.29b), node B overflows in turn, requiring a further split, and the eventual creation of a new tree level (Fig. 7.29c). Since some key values are stored in several nodes of a B^+ tree, deleting the corresponding keys also requires adjustments on the upper tree levels. For example, deletion of key value 7 from the tree of Fig. 7.29(c) involves merging nodes A and B, promoting key value 8, merging nodes C

Figure 7.27 Portion of B^+ tree.

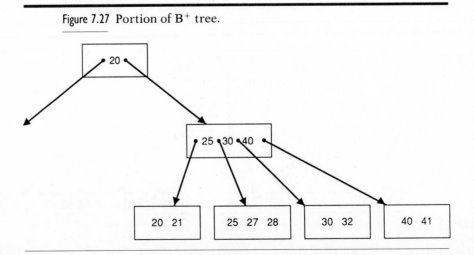

and D, and finally deleting node E with appropriate changes in the key values of the root node. The resulting tree appears in Fig. 7.30.

In practice, it is usually possible to store the set of keys attached to any node of a B-tree on the same track of a disk. In these cases it is advantageous to pack each node with a large number of keys, thereby reducing the number of tree levels and hence the number of disk accesses required to gain access to the B-tree. Since a B-tree is always maintained in perfect balance, a guaranteed worst-case performance is obtained for search, insertion, and deletion operations that varies with the logarithm of the number of key values stored in the tree. Indeed, the sparsest-possible B-tree contains one node on the root level, and 2, $2\lceil m/2\rceil$, $2\lceil m/2\rceil^2$, ... nodes on subsequent tree levels. On level k of the tree there will then be $2\lceil m/2\rceil^{k-1}$ leaves. Since the number of leaves is $n+1$, the result is: [26]

$$n + 1 \geq 2\lceil m/2\rceil^{k-1}$$

or

$$k \leq 1 + \log_{\lceil m/2\rceil}\left(\frac{n+1}{2}\right).$$

The number of node accesses needed for retrieval, or for node splitting and merging during maintenance, is limited to the number k of tree levels, that is a logarithmic function of the number of key entries. For 2-3 trees, the worst-case search time is not greater than $1 + \log_2 ((n+1)/2)$.

For many applications, it may be convenient to divide the search keys into several distinct portions. For example, alphabetic keys

Figure 7.28 Typical 2-3 (B$^+$) tree.

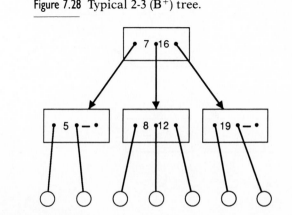

might be divided into individual key characters, and numeric keys into
individual key digits. In these circumstances a multiway tree can be

---

Figure 7.29 Node addition to 2-3 tree. (a) Overflow of node *A* following
addition of key value 10 to tree of Fig. 7.28. (b) Node-splitting operation followed by overflow in parent node *B*. (c) Final 2-3 tree following
addition of key value 10 to tree of Fig. 7.28.

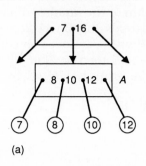

(a)

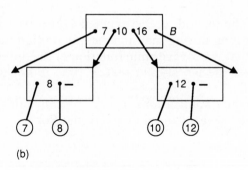

(b)

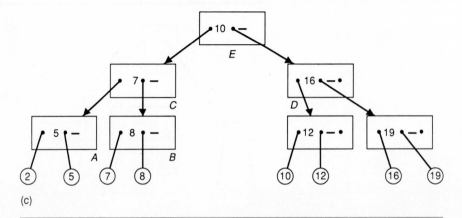

(c)

used as a search structure in which the various levels of the tree correspond to the individual key portions. For example, for alphabetic keys, the nth tree level might then correspond to the nth characters of the search keys. Such search trees are known as *digital search trees*, or *tries*. [27,28]

In principle, a 27-way tree may be used for alphabetic keys, where each node has 27 possible descendants on the next-lower tree level, corresponding to the 27 possible characters (26 letters plus a space or end-of-word symbol) that may occur in the next character position of the alphabetic keys. In practice, when natural-language words are used as search keys, the tries need not provide many letter sequences because these sequences do not exist in the language. For example, given the key character *Q*, it is not necessary to make provision for *Z* as a successor, since the combination *QZ* is not generally used in English. A typical trie for the keys *THE, THEN, THIN, THIS, TIN*, and *SING* appears in Fig. 7.31(a), where # is used as an end-of-word symbol. [16]

Search tries are efficient when many different search keys begin with the same character sequences. In such cases, the same initial search path will serve for many key values, and the branching factor, which determines the number of tests that must be carried out at each node, remains small. The tree of Fig. 7.31(a) can be reduced by eliminating search paths that correspond to branching factors of 1 and require no testing. For example, the key *SING* can be distinguished from the remaining keys by simply identifying an *S* instead of a *T* in the initial character position. Figure 7.31(b) shows the truncated trie obtained from Fig. 7.31(a) by eliminating unnecessary branches.

Digital search tries are useful when the total number of search keys is not too large — say a few hundred to a few thousand — and when the number and length of the search paths to distinguish these keys is relatively small. Typical applications include small dictionaries of function words, and dictionaries used to correct the spelling of common

Figure 7.30 2-3 tree after deletion of key 7 from tree of Fig. 7.29(c).

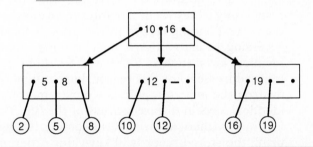

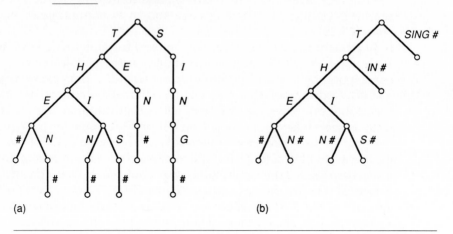

Figure 7.31 Typical alphabetic search trees. (a) Full digital-search tree. (b) Truncated digital-search tree.

words. For larger dictionaries with tens of thousands of different entries, balanced indexing structures such as B-trees are preferable.

7.7 Hash-Table Access

Balanced or nearly balanced tree structures are advantageous for file access because the resulting search effort is limited to approximately log n key comparisons for files of n records. The keys are available in lexicographic order within the tree structure, and the cost of maintaining files after file additions or deletions is also of order log n. However, faster file-access methods exist that ideally require only a single key transformation to find a stored record, or to add or delete a record. These methods are known as *key-to-address transformations*, or *scatter storage*, or *hash-table accessing*. [29–33]

To obtain file access with a hash-table system, the search key K_i is transformed into a hash-table address using a hashing or hash function h; the table address $h(K_i)$ stores either the record information corresponding to key K_i, or a pointer to an address in the main file where the corresponding record information is located. To be useful in file accessing, hash function h must be able to distinguish similar but nonidentical keys, such as *SAND* and *SANE*, by providing different hash-table addresses. For this reason, hash functions should be chosen that destroy the lexicographic key order and place records with nearly identical keys in different areas of the file. Thus normal file order is lost, and, without additional file sorting, it is impossible to read out, or print, the stored records in key-value order, or to find or delete records with the smallest or largest keys. Similarly, range searches designed to retrieve all records within a certain key range are difficult to implement. In principle, hashing is thus more efficient than tree access for finding particular stored records, or for adding or deleting specified records. However, the hash process cannot easily be used for operations that depend on file order.

Ideally, the size of a hash-table is larger than the number of different record keys available for the file under consideration. In these circumstances distinct hash-table addresses may correspond to distinct record keys. When the size of the table is large compared with the number of distinct keys, a *partial hashing* method may be used in which only parts of keys — for example, the first few key characters — determine the corresponding hash-table addresses. Alternatively, when the occupancy rate of the table is low, substantial space may be saved by deleting the actual key information for the corresponding records from the table. In that case, the assumption is made that each hash-table address automatically contains the information for the correct record.

However, the hashing function may not be able to distinguish between certain subsets of distinct keys. In that case $h(K_i) = h(K_j)$ for distinct keys K_i and K_j, and a *collision* is said to occur for the records corresponding to these distinct keys because all these records will be placed at the same hash-table address. A useful hash-table method must therefore include two main components:

1. A hash function $h(K)$ that has a low collision probability, given a particular input key distribution, and a given hash table of size M.

2. A collision-resolution technique that provides storage locations and retrieval strategies for distinct colliding records.

Two main collision-resolution techniques are in widespread use. The first relies on pointers stored with each record in the hash table that give the address in an overflow area of the next colliding record, if any. To retrieve a complete set of colliding records corresponding to a particular hash table address $h(K)$, it is then necessary to follow the pointer chain starting at the base address in the hash table. Figure 7.32 shows such a pointer chain system for a hash table of seven addresses (labeled 0 to 6) using a hash function that places record R_n in address $h(R_n) = n \bmod 7$. The assumed record-insertion order is $R_{11}, R_{16}, R_2, R_{19}, R_5$, and R_9.

The foregoing collision-resolution technique, *chaining*, provides a conceptually simple hash-table allocation that works well in dynamic situations in which many records are added and deleted. However, the retrieval operations are inefficient when the pointer chains are too long. The chains can be shortened by providing at each position enough storage locations for a complete *bucket* of records. In that case, the base address $h(K)$ identifies a bucket number, and a pointer chain is followed to an overflow bucket only when the original bucket is full. To locate a particular record in a bucket, either all the records stored in that bucket must be scanned, or each set of colliding records must be stored in increasing or decreasing order in the hash table.

When records are stored in decreasing key order in each pointer chain, the efficiency of unsuccessful searches (for keys that are not in the file) improves — a search carried out with search key K can stop as soon as a smaller key $K(i)$ stored in table position i is found. When a new key K must be inserted into an ordered pointer chain, an interchange process can be used that replaces $K(i)$ with K in the chain, and next inserts $K(i)$ into a new position later in the chain, possibly using additional key interchanges. In Fig. 7.32, an ordered pointer chain starting at table position 2 would give access first to R_{16}, followed by R_9 and R_2 in order.

Another collision-resolution technique consists of starting at the base address $h(K)$ in the hash table and computing the addresses of any overflow storage locations. In the basic *open-addressing* process, a base address b_o is first determined where $b_o = h(K)$. A *probe sequence* is then defined as a permutation of table addresses starting at address b_o and covering the entire hash table of size M. To retrieve a record with key K, the addresses are then scanned in probe sequence order starting with address $b_o = h(K)$, and the probe sequence is followed until the wanted record is found, or an empty slot or "table full" sign is met, in which case the search is unsuccessful. Figure 7.33 shows a program for hash-table access using open addressing with a linear traversal of memory.

Figure 7.32 Hash-table placement with collision resolution by chaining.

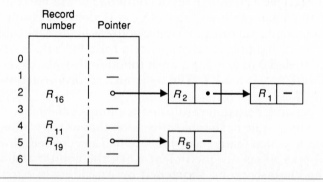

The probe sequence is typically constructed by using a hash function $p(K)$ to compute the next table address j from a given address i as $j = (i - p(K))$, and resetting j to $j + M$ when the original j turns negative for a table of size M. In the sample program of Fig. 7.33, the function $p(K)$ is replaced by the constant -1. The use of such linear probe sequences, however, is not recommended because sets of adjacent memory addresses are then filled rapidly, causing a clustering effect in the memory space. In particular, when position i becomes occupied, the probability that position $i + 1$ receives a record is twice as high as before, because now all the records with hash addresses i and $i + 1$ will be placed in table position $i + 1$. The clustering problem is mitigated by using a random probe sequence r_i obtained, for example, with a random number generator. This places records in positions $h(K) + 0$, $h(K) + r_1$, $h(K) + r_2, ..., h(K) + r_{M-1}$, where r_i represent a permutation of $0, 1, ..., M - 1$.

Table 7.1 displays typical performance figures for three types of hash-table searches; performance depends on the proportion of filled memory positions (or load factor) α of the table. [34,35] Chaining is the most efficient access method in terms of the number of accessed memory positions. Unfortunately, this technique requires a good deal of extra storage because the pointer chains must be stored and maintained when file items are added and deleted. The open addressing system, which requires no pointers, seems preferable for small memory load factors α. Released memory positions corresponding to deleted records cannot be recovered in an open address system, however, because the probe sequences would be destroyed. Also, when the load

---

Figure 7.33 Program for hash-table access with open address.

1. [Calculate initial address for search key X]
    $i = d \leftarrow h(X)$

2. [Is location i empty?]
    if K_i is empty
    then $K_i \leftarrow X$ and exit

3. [Increment and test]
    $i \leftarrow i + 1$
    if $i > M$
    then $i \leftarrow 1$
    if $i = d$
    then "overflow" and exit
    go to step 2

---

factor increases, some probing methods become very expensive, in part because of the previously mentioned clustering problems. The use of random probe sequences based on primary hash functions $h(X)$, followed by secondary hash functions $p(X)$ when needed, provides relatively efficient file access, especially for ordered chains where the probability is high that successful or unsuccessful searches can be terminated early.

No collision-resolution method is fully satisfactory when the hash table is nearly full. In that case, a rehashing process could be used that allocates space in a larger table. Rehashing is conceptually simple when the old and new tables are allocated in disjoint regions of the memory space. When only a limited amount of memory is available to be added to the original table, an "in-place" rehashing method can be used (see Fig. 7.34).

The program of Fig. 7.34 performs a linear sweep of the original table addresses, starting at address 0 and ending at address $M_1 - 1$. When an entry is found that has not yet been rehashed, its key K is used with hash functions $h(K)$ and $p(K)$ to generate a probe sequence defined as $(h(K) - ip(K))$ mod M_2, where $M_2 > M_1$ represents the new table size. The probe sequence is followed, and the entry corresponding to key K is put into the first table position in the sequence not yet rehashed. Next the displaced entry, if any, must be rehashed, possibly leading to a cascade of displaced entries. When no displaced entry is found, the original linear sweep of the old table is resumed until

Table 7.1 Typical performance figures for hash-table searches (average number of memory positions accessed for successful (S) and unsuccessful (U) searches given load factor α). [34]

Separate Chaining of Overflow Records			Open Addressing with Linear Probe			Random Probing with Double Hash Function		
$1 + \alpha/2$ S			$\dfrac{1}{2}\left(1 + \dfrac{1}{1-\alpha}\right)$ S			$-\dfrac{1}{\alpha}\ln(1-\alpha)$ S		
$\alpha + e^{-\alpha}$ U			$\dfrac{1}{2}\left(1 + \dfrac{1}{(1-\alpha)^2}\right)$ U			$\dfrac{1}{1-\alpha}$ U		
α	S	U	α	S	U	α	S	U
.10	1.050	1.005	.10	1.056	1.118	.10	1.054	1.111
.30	1.150	1.041	.30	1.214	1.520	.30	1.189	1.429
.50	1.250	1.107	.50	1.500	2.500	.50	1.386	2.000
.70	1.350	1.197	.70	2.167	6.060	.70	1.720	3.333
.90	1.450	1.307	.90	5.500	50.500	.90	2.558	10.000

memory position M_1 is reached, at which point the algorithm terminates.

Obviously, completely reorganizing memory as in Fig. 7.34 is too onerous to undertake frequently. An alternative method to maintain hash tables in dynamic files is provided by the *extensible* or *dynamic* hashing methods, which largely avoid repositioning hash-table entries. [36–39] An index, or directory, is interposed between the key terms and the final record addresses in the main file. The hashing operation then identifies an address in the index rather than in the main

Figure 7.34 In-place rehashing process.

1. [Initialize] $i \leftarrow 0$
   let X represent an empty table entry

2. [Is table entry if $T(i)$ is not empty, nor already rehashed
   $T(i)$ rehashable?] **then** exchange $T(i) \leftarrow\rightarrow X$
   go to step 4
   else continue enumeration at step 3

3. [Advance to next $i \leftarrow i + 1$
   table entry] if $i = M_1$ terminate
   else go back to step 2

4. [Compute hash $K \leftarrow \text{key}(X)$
   function values] $a \leftarrow h(K)$
   $c \leftarrow p(K)$

5. [Find unrehashed if $T(a)$ is already marked rehashed
   location] **then** compute new probe address
   $a \leftarrow (a - c) \bmod M_2$ until finding
   an address a such that $T(a)$ is not
   marked rehashed

6. [Insert in table] exchange $T(a) \leftarrow\rightarrow X$
   mark $T(a)$ rehashed;
   entry X now becomes displaced entry

7. [Processed displaced if displaced entry is empty
   entry] **go to** step 3 to resume enumeration
   else go to step 4 to rehash it
   and place it in table

file, and each index position in turn points to the main file addresses —
normally buckets — where the corresponding records are located. Instead of changing the main file configurations as new records are added, the index is made to grow: Thus when a given bucket overflows, the
index entry for that bucket is changed to produce two entries, corresponding to two new buckets replacing the single original bucket. Similarly when the file shrinks, two or more buckets are merged into a
single bucket by appropriate index-entry transformations.

Consider, as an example, a situation in which the records are stored
in buckets of size b, and an index of size 2^d is used to gain access to the
records. Given a key K, the appropriate bucket address is obtained in
two steps:

1. A hash function $h_d(K)$ is computed that produces a binary number
   in the range $0, 1,..., 2^d - 1$.

2. The binary number identifies an index entry that points to the
   bucket containing the record corresponding to search key K.

An example of this situation is shown in Fig. 7.35(a), where an index of
size $2^d = 8$ gives access to one of four storage buckets. Each bucket
exhibits a local depth $r \leq d$, where r identifies the key length associated with a given bucket. In the example, enough records were found
for hash address $h(K) = 010$ to allocate a separate bucket of local
depth 3 to the corresponding records. On the other hand, very few records were associated with index entries 100, 101, 110, and 111. All
these records are therefore assembled in a single bucket (number 4) of
local depth 1 characterized by the fact that the first, left-most index
address digit is a 1.

Three cases must be distinguished when inserting new records into
the file. If bucket B corresponding to key value K is not full, a new
record is simply inserted into the proper bucket. If bucket B is full, a
new bucket B′ must be created to accommodate the new record. If the
local depth r of B is smaller than the depth d of the index, it is sufficient to change the pointers of certain index entries to point to the
newly created bucket B′, and possibly to reallocate some records from
bucket B to B′ in accordance with the augmented index entries of
depth $r + 1$ of the corresponding records. This operation is illustrated
in Fig. 7.35(b), where bucket number 4 of depth 1 (index entry 1..) is
split into two buckets 4a and 4b of depth 2, identified by index entries
10 and 11, respectively. In rare cases, reallocating the records to the
split buckets causes bucket overflow when all records wind up in one
of the two split parts. In such cases, the bucket splitting must be
repeated.

When the bucket to be split has local depth equal to the depth of the index ($r = d$), the index itself must be increased in size. This is done by doubling the index size as shown in Fig. 7.35(c), and creating an index of 2^{d+1} entries of depth $d + 1$. At this point, the bucket of depth $r = d$ can be split into two parts of depth $r + 1 = d + 1$, as previously described. In Fig. 7.35(b), bucket 2 with index entry 010 was split by dou-

Figure 7.35 Memory allocation in dynamic hashing. (a) Initial bucket allocation. (b) Bucket allocation after split of bucket 5. (c) Bucket allocation after split of bucket 2.

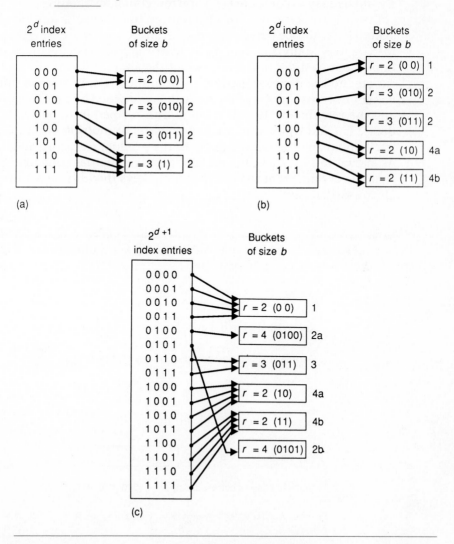

bling the index size and making available the new bucket addresses 0100 and 0101, assigned to buckets 2a and 2b, respectively. When the directory size is changed, many of the index pointers must be reallocated, but only the records in the split bucket may have to be moved.

After record deletion, a reverse process can be used to merge bucket pairs that jointly contain fewer than b records. If the merged buckets are the only ones of depth $r = d$, the index size can be halved and the depth reduced to $d - 1$.

The use of extensible hashing prevents large-scale record reallocation in dynamic file environments, but does not resolve the collision problem caused by a poor choice of hash function $h(K)$. Ideally, it should be easy to compute $h(K)$, and few collisions should occur. When collisions are detected, an efficient collision-resolution technique should be available that does not deteriorate with increasing memory-load factors. Many different methods are suggested in the literature to implement hashing functions, two of the simplest being the multiplication and the division methods. [34] In the division method, the key value, or some function of the key value, is divided by a prime number, and the remainder after division is transformed into the needed address. The multiplication method consists of multiplying the key by itself and using the middle digits of the product as record addresses. As shown in Fig. 7.36, this method avoids potential collisions by assigning very different table addresses to keys that differ only by a single low-order digit.

Figure 7.36 Typical hashing method using key multiplication. Assumed hash-table size is 64 positions.

Record *M*:   Key 11 01 01 00

Key squared   1 0 1 0 1 | 1 1 1 1 0 0 | 1 0 0 0 0

Decimal address corresponding to $(1\ 1\ 1\ 1\ 0\ 0)_2 =$

$$32 + 16 + 8 + 4 + 0 + 0 = 60$$

Record *N*:   Key 11 01 01 01

Key squared   1 0 1 1 0 | 0 0 1 0 0 1 | 1 1 0 0 1

Decimal address corresponding to $(0\ 0\ 1\ 0\ 0\ 1)_2 =$

$$0 + 0 + 8 + 0 + 0 + 1 = 9$$

Many hash functions have been proposed over the years, some specifically applicable to numeric or alphabetic key values. For example, the division method can be used with alphabetic keys by taking a numerical representation of each word, consisting of the concatenated order numbers of the alphabetic characters of the word, dividing this by the table size, and using the remainder of the division as an address for the corresponding record information. [40] Another interesting method is the *dispersed hash* strategy, where r different hash functions are applied to the key information, each producing a 1-bit address in a binary word of length n. The corresponding r bits of the word are then set equal to 1, producing a binary character string of length n of which r bits are set equal to 1. By using appropriate values of n and r as a function of file size, the probability of collision can be made very small. The dispersed hash strategy can construct bit strings that are valid for several distinct search keys simultaneously; it is examined in more detail later in this chapter.

In summary, hash tables afford fast file access when the collision probability is low, and provide for file additions and deletions. However, accurate guesses must be made in advance about required table sizes because restructuring large hash tables is expensive. Further, the hashing process destroys file ordering. When stored records must be processed in order, balanced tree procedures are usually preferable.

7.8 Indexed Searches for Multikey Access

The file-access procedures treated up to now apply primarily to single-key searches, in which the query consists of a single content term attached to a record, or of the value of a single attribute, such as a customer name in a file of telephone subscribers. For single-key searches, the record file can be ordered according to the values of the available search key — for example, the alphabetic order of the names of telephone subscribers. Alternatively, the index that gives access to the main file can be ordered, as in the previously described tree-access methods.

When multikey searches must be performed, a *principal key* can sometimes be identified, and the file can be ordered in accordance with the values of that key. When the principal key is used as part of a search statement, the subsection of the file corresponding to the given principal key value can then be isolated and subjected to a separate search based on the values of any *secondary keys* also included in the search query. For example, to find the records of telephone subscribers named SMITH who also live on STATE STREET, one isolates all the Smiths using the alphabetic file order, and then scans the output looking for those individuals living on State Street. When only secondary keys are included in a query statement, a sequential search of the entire file must be made, or a sparse or dense index must be available to provide the secondary key accesses. For example, the names of all subscribers living on State Street can be retrieved by scanning the complete subscriber file, or by constructing an index that provides file access by subscriber addresses.

A sample file of document authors and publisher names is shown in Fig. 7.37. The file is ordered in accordance with the principal key (author name), and a sparse index gives access to a chain of pointers for each publisher name. The set of all documents issued by a particular publisher can be found by following the appropriate pointer chain. When a pointer chain becomes too long for frequently used values, the chain for a secondary attribute can be broken up into several subchains, also known as *cellular lists*. When separate pointers are provided to each subchain, the partial chains corresponding to a common attribute value can then be searched in parallel to reduce search time.

Pointer chains can be provided for all secondary keys in addition to the primary keys attached to the records; each given record can be reached by following the pointer chain for any of its keys. The corresponding record organization is known as a *multilist*. [41,42] The

Figure 7.37 Chained access for secondary keys.

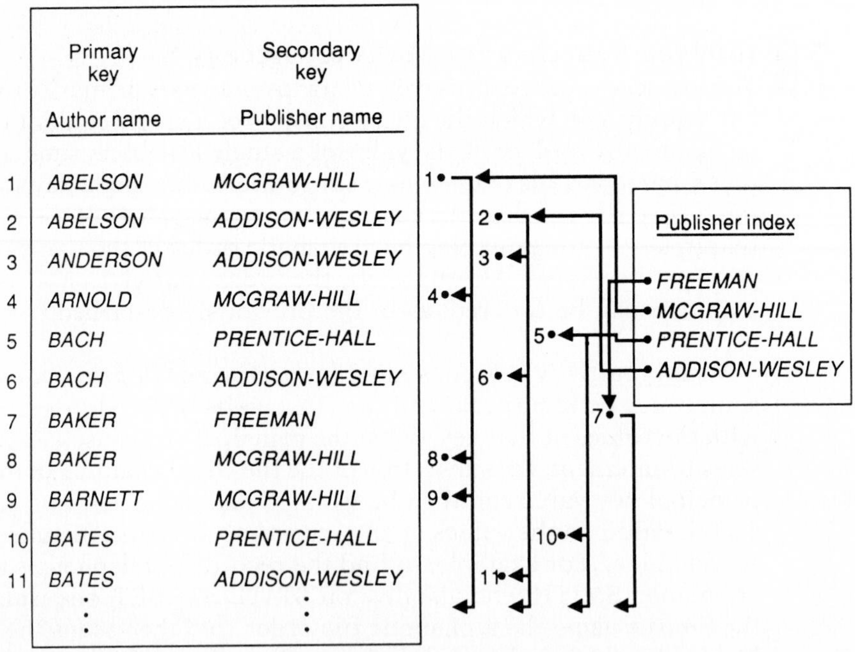

structure of a typical multilist record, identified by keys *A, B,* and *C,* appears in Fig. 7.38. To retrieve the records from a multilist in answer to a conjunctive query such as "*A* and *B* and *C*" (where all the stated key values must be present), it suffices to find the shortest list, corresponding to the query key with the smallest number of attached records. That pointer list can then be followed, and for each listed record, a test reveals whether pointers are also present for the remaining query keys, in which case the corresponding record is retrieved. If *C* happens to be the key with the smallest number of records in the example of Fig. 7.38, the *C* chain is followed, and for each *C* record, a test determines the presence of the other *A* and *B* pointers. For disjunctive queries such as "*A* or *B* or *C*," where any record present on any of the lists must be obtained, unfortunately all the pointer lists must be followed.

Multilist organization can be attractive when each query key is attached to a small number of records. When this is not the case, the list-traversal operations are very time consuming. If rapid responses are required, as is often the case, it is necessary to use large indexes that provide one pointer for each record exhibiting a given key value. Instead of storing a single pointer per key value identifying only the first record on a given list of records, as in Fig. 7.37, the same number of pointers are now stored in the index as the number of records for each key value. The resulting large index is known as an *inverted index* or *inverted file.* [2–7]

Inverted files are used almost universally in operational retrieval situations. The great advantage is that such files allow extremely rapid search and retrieval operations to be carried out, based only on the information provided in the index rather than data from the main record file. Thus to find the record addresses corresponding to keys "*A* and *B*," it suffices to look at the pointer lists for the two keys *A* and *B* in the inverted index and to identify the common elements from these two lists. This operation is illustrated in Fig. 7.39(b) for the inverted-

Figure 7.38 Record structure in multilist organization.

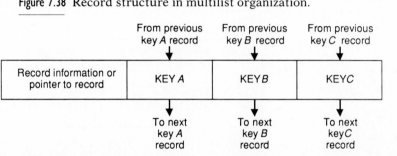

file organization shown in Fig. 7.39(a). To find the documents authored by "Bach" that are also published by "Addison-Wesley," the intersection of the "Bach" list in the author index (5,6), and the "Addison-Wesley" list in the publisher index (2,3,6,11) is used. The common elements from the two lists (record 6) constitute an answer to the query. Analogously, in response to an or-query, such as "author Bach or publisher Addison-Wesley," the union of the two lists — that is, the num-

Figure 7.39 Inverted index-file access. (a) Dense (inverted) index for all key values. (b) Intersection of pointer lists in index.

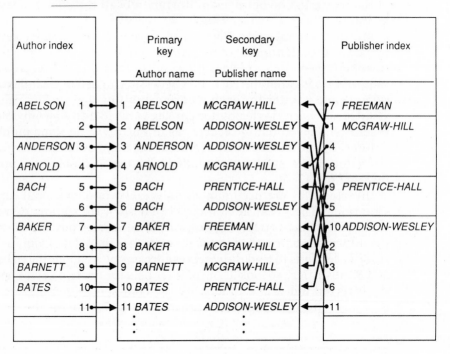

(a)

(b)

ber of distinct elements on both lists — is used to find records 2, 3, 5, 6, and 11 for the example of Fig. 7.39.

If the file organizations of Figs. 7.38 and 7.39 are compared, it is seen that the rapid search time possible with inverted files has been bought at the cost of a substantial increase in the index size. Obviously this large index must not only be stored, but also maintained when the file composition changes. When a complete dense index is used with pointers to every record from every applicable key, however, the records in the main file need not be stored in any special order because each record is individually accessible. In many commercial retrieval systems, the main records file is maintained in chronological order of record accession, not in order by any existing key.

In the file organizations discussed up to now, all the index entries correspond to individual key assignments. Thus the pointers included in the inverted indexes identify records containing a single key or attribute value. In many situations, queries consisting of single attribute values are rare; instead, the query formulations may cover combinations of attribute values. For the file previously used as an illustration, the query specifications may include, for example, both author and publisher names. In that case, the list manipulations illustrated in Fig. 7.39(b) can be avoided, and the retrieval operation speeded up by including in the inverted index pointer lists of combinations of attribute values, such as particular author-publisher pairs. [43–45]

The problem with using such *combined indexes* is the large number of combined index lists apparently required to answer the many possible multikey queries. Consider as an example the set of queries including three or fewer attribute values shown at the top of Table 7.2. A_i denotes the ith value of attribute A — for example, the name of the ith author in the author index. For n attributes, there are $n!$ possible permutations of the attributes, all of which are apparently required to answer the possible multiterm queries.

Consider as an example a list of record pointers for the combined keys A, B, and C. The (A,B,C) list is ordered according to the values of attribute A (with all records for attribute value A_1 preceding the records for attribute value A_2, and so on). Within the A ordering, the record pointers are ordered by the values of attribute B, and then C. Hence the combined list (A,B,C) can be used to answer the query formulations A_i, $(A_i$ and $B_j)$, and $(A_i$ and B_j and $C_k)$. Similarly, the combined list (B,A,C) would be used for the query set B_j, $(B_j$ and $A_i)$ — equivalent to $(A_i$ and $B_j)$ — and $(B_j$ and A_i and $C_k)$ equivalent to $(A_i$ and B_j and $C_k)$.

If any subset of attributes appears consecutively as the head of at least one of the combined lists included in the index, all possible conjunctive queries can be answered. As Table 7.2 shows, only three combined lists are needed for three attributes, instead of six, as projected.

Table 7.2 Combined index requirements for three attributes.

Possible Query Formulations (three attributes)

A_i
B_j
C_k
A_i and B_j
A_i and C_k
B_j and C_k
A_i and B_j and C_k

Possible Combined Index Lists (n ! lists)

List	Answerable Queries
A,B,C	1,4,7
A,C,B,	1,5,7
B,A,C	2,4,7
B,C,A	2,6,7
C,A,B	3,5,7
C,B,A	3,6,7

Sufficient Combined Index Lists $\begin{pmatrix} n \\ \lfloor (n+1)/2 \rfloor \end{pmatrix}$ lists

List	Answerable Queries
A,B,C	1,4,7
B,C,A	2,6,7
C,A,B	3,5,7

Reduction in Required Number of Combined Indexes

n	1	2	3	4	5	6
$n!$	1	2	6	24	120	720
$\begin{pmatrix} n \\ \lfloor (n+1)/2 \rfloor \end{pmatrix}$	1	2	3	6	10	20

It is known that the needed number of combined indexes for n attributes is equal to $\begin{pmatrix} n \\ \lfloor (n+1)/2 \rfloor \end{pmatrix}$. [43–45] While that number is much smaller than $n!$, as seen at the bottom of Table 7.2, the number of index-list combinations needed is nevertheless large enough to prevent the use of combined term lists in most operational situations.

7.9 Bitmap Encoding for Multikey Access

The inverted indexes described in the previous section provide fast access to the main record file. However, substantial storage and processing resources are required to generate and maintain the indexes. In many cases, the inverted indexes take as much space as the main record file itself, and smaller secondary indexes must be used to gain access to the main index. This, of course, increases the storage overhead of the inverted-index system even more. Further, to permit rapid merging of the pointer lists corresponding to different attribute values, these lists must normally be maintained in increasing or decreasing order of the document references (see Fig. 7.39(b)). The list-processing operations that manipulate and maintain these pointer lists become increasingly expensive as the lists become longer for frequently assigned key values.

This suggests that a different file-processing strategy should be used when pointer lists for certain key values become too long and expensive to process. The *bitmap* encoding system, an alternative accessing method, also involves fairly high initial storage and processing costs. However, overhead costs do not vary with the number of key values used to identify the records, nor with the number of records to which a given key value is assigned. Consider the collection represented in Fig. 7.40(a). Each document D_i is represented by a large binary string or vector, where the ith element is set equal to 1 when the ith attribute value is assigned to the corresponding document. The

Figure 7.40 Bitmap array system. (a) Bitmap encoding of collection. (b) Cost analysis comparing bitmap and inverted-file process.

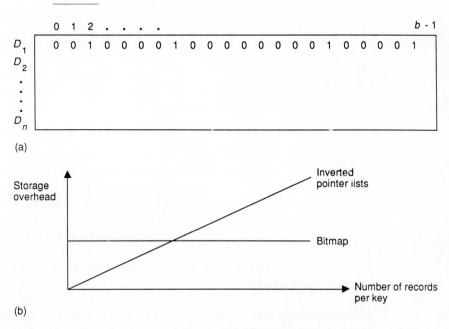

number of 1s in the *bit vector* (or bit string) representing a document is then equal to the number of assigned key values, and the vector length is the total number of distinct attribute values in the system.

The organization of Fig. 7.40(a) can be used for retrieval by constructing a bit vector $K(Q)$ for each given user query, and retrieving all documents D_i whose bit vectors exhibit 1 elements in all vector positions in which the query also exhibits a 1, that is, $K(Q) \subseteq K(D_i)$. It is also obvious that the processing cost of a document bitmap remains the same, no matter how the 1s are sprinkled over the document map. Thus the processing cost of inverted-file and bitmap processes can be represented by the graph of Fig. 7.40(b). While the bitmap costs of Fig. 7.40(b) remain constant with changes in the assignment frequencies of the keys, the cost of inverted list processing increases linearly with the length of the pointer lists.

Since the number of distinct attribute values b that can be assigned to the documents of a collection may be large — of the order of tens of thousands in some cases — the basic bitmap system of Fig. 7.40(a) may be too expensive for practical use. A bitmap encoding method can then be used in which each document is represented by a bit vector of length $n << b$, and the relevant attribute values are encoded into shorter bit vectors of length n. The best known of these encoding methods is the so-called *superimposed coding* system. [46–50] Superimposed coding represents a multikey hashing system in which each attribute is encoded into a bit vector of small dimensions in the following way:

- Each attribute, or key value, is represented by k 1s chosen from an n-bit binary field ($k < n$).

- The codes corresponding to the various attribute values attached to a record or a query, are superimposed using binary or operations to construct the vector for each record.

In Fig. 7.41(a), each key is encoded using two bit positions set equal to 1 in a field of 16 binary digits. To construct the bit vector corresponding to a record identified by the set of terms Data, Base, Management, and System, the corresponding bit vectors are added using or operations in such a way that the combined vector contains a 1 whenever any of the component term vectors has 1s in the same bit position. In Fig. 7.41(a), the record vector for the four keys contains six 1s out of 16.

The complete retrieval process for the superimposed coding system consists of four steps: [48]

1. Construct the superimposed code vector for the query as suggested by the illustration of Fig. 7.41(a).

2. Match the superimposed query vector with the superimposed code vectors of all documents in the collection, and identify those documents whose superimposed code vectors contain the superimposed query vector.

3. Retrieve the corresponding document records from the main file.

4. Check the corresponding record keys to ensure that the retrieved records in fact contain the requested query keys.

The last step is needed to ensure that each retrieved record is legitimate and does not belong to the class of so-called *false drops*, which are obtained because their combined key encodings fortuitously produce the same bit string as the combined legitimate keys.

Since the number of documents in a collection, and hence the number of bit vectors to be processed, may be large, indexing systems have

---

Figure 7.41 Processing of superimposed code vectors. (a) Example of superimposed coding. (b) Index file for access to bitmap file. (c) Compressed block code for file of (b).

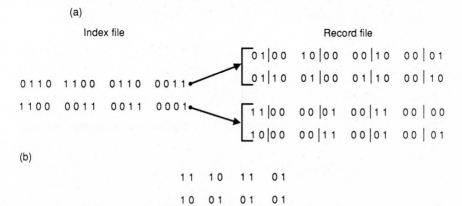

data	0000	0010	0000	1000
base	0100	0010	0000	0000
management	0000	0100	0001	0000
system	0000	0000	0101	0000

data base management system   0100   0110   0101   1000

(a)

Index file

0110   1100   0110   0011

1100   0011   0011   0001

Record file

$\begin{bmatrix} 0\,1|0\,0 & 1\,0|0\,0 & 0\,0|1\,0 & 0\,0\,|\,0\,1 \\ 0\,1|1\,0 & 0\,1|0\,0 & 0\,1|1\,0 & 0\,0\,|\,1\,0 \end{bmatrix}$

$\begin{bmatrix} 1\,1|0\,0 & 0\,0\,|0\,1 & 0\,0|1\,1 & 0\,0\,|\,0\,0 \\ 1\,0|0\,0 & 0\,0|1\,1 & 0\,0|0\,1 & 0\,0\,|\,0\,1 \end{bmatrix}$

(b)

11   10   11   01

10   01   01   01

(c)

been developed for access to the main bitmap, in which each index entry consists of dense bit vectors (vectors with more 1 bits than ordinary record vectors) that give access to all vectors in the main record file included in the corresponding dense index vectors. Two sample index vectors of this type are shown in Fig. 7.41(b). Various compression schemes have been devised to represent the bitmaps for large document collections economically. A typical example appears in Fig. 7.41(c), where a square block of four binary digits taken from two different record vectors is reduced to a single bit in compressed form. The compressed bit is equal to 0 when the original block of digits consists of four zeros, and is otherwise equal to 1. The compressed form of Fig. 7.41(c) requires four times fewer bits than the original record file in Fig. 7.41(b). [49]

To use a superimposed coding system, individual key values must be transformed into a form consisting of a randomly chosen k bits set equal to 1 in a bit vector of length n. One possibility consists of using a random number generator to determine the bit positions that must be set equal to 1. Figure 7.42 displays a program for generating the binary representations of the key values. [48] It should be noted that if two different key values produce the same initial setting H for the random number generator in that program, the sequence of generated bit positions, and hence the complete bit vectors, will all be identical.

As mentioned, the method of constructing the binary representation of the vectors by code superposition can produce unintended collisions, resulting in "false drops." In that case, completely different key combinations are represented by identical superimposed code vectors. The probability of a false drop can be computed as the probability $p(n,k,r,t)$ that the method of Fig. 7.42 sets a specific predetermined subset of t bit positions equal to 1, given that r binary code vectors are superimposed, when each key value is encoded as k 1s in a vector of length n. The probability $p(n,k,r,t)$ is given by [48,51]

$$p(n,k,r,t) = \sum_{j=0}^{t} (-1)^j \begin{bmatrix} t \\ j \end{bmatrix} \left[\frac{\begin{bmatrix} n-j \\ k \end{bmatrix}}{\begin{bmatrix} n \\ k \end{bmatrix}} \right]^r. \tag{7.1}$$

When k and t are small, expression (7.1) can be approximated as

$$p(n,k,r,t) \approx [p(n,k,r,1)]^t \approx [1 - (1 - (1 - \frac{k}{n})^r]^t. \tag{7.2}$$

This approximation can be justified informally by noting that in an n-bit vector with k bits set equal to 1, the probability that any vector element is equal to 1 is k/n. Hence the probability that all r binary code vectors will *not* hash into a particular chosen bit position is $(1-k/n)^r$. The probability that one of the chosen t-bit positions is identical to a position already set to 1 by one of the r code vectors is then $1 - (1-k/n)^r$. Finally, the probability that all t prespecified bit positions will be identical to positions already set to 1 by one of the r code vectors is $[1 - (1-k/n)^r]^t$, which is the approximation of expression (7.2). [52]

It is known that the probability of a false drop for superimposed code vectors is minimized when about half the bit positions are set equal to 1. Indeed, as the number k of bit positions in an n-bit vector is increased from 0, two competing effects are noticeable: [48]

1. The number w of 1s in a query bit vector increases as k increases; this *decreases* the probability that a random nonmatching record R will be falsely retrieved, since R must have all w query bit positions set equal to 1 before retrieval takes place.

Figure 7.42 Construction of binary code representations for key value.

1. [Initialize]	$b_j \leftarrow 0 \quad 1 \leq j \leq n$ $w \leftarrow 0 \quad$ (number of 1s in vector)
2. [Hashing of key value]	$H \leftarrow h(K) \quad$ use hash function h to generate an m-bit hash value H
3. [Initialize random number generator and generate numbers]	Use H to initialize random- number generator to generate a sequence of random numbers (called *random*)
4. [Determine next vector position in interval $[1,n]$]	next $j \leftarrow \lfloor n \cdot random \rfloor + 1$
5. [Is vector position already filled?]	if $b_j = 1$ **then** go back to step 4
6. [Set jth vector element equal to 1]	$b_j \leftarrow 1, w \leftarrow w + 1$
7. [Have enough elements been treated?]	if $w < k$ where k is desired number of 1s go back to step 4
8. [Exit]	Return completed binary code vector for key value K

2. The probability that any particular bit position in a superimposed code vector is equal to 1 increases as k increases, and this *increases* the number of falsely retrieved records. That latter effect predominates as k increases toward n.

Variations of the false drop probability with increasing values of k are shown in Fig. 7.43.

Superimposed coding systems have been widely used in experiments. They appear to be most effective when the records are identified by a relatively small number of key values. In one proposed system, each attribute value is hashed into a single bit position in a 16-bit vector. Assuming that a record carries six attribute values, each record is then represented by a 16-bit code vector, of which 6 bits are equal to 1. Since there are $\begin{bmatrix} 16 \\ 6 \end{bmatrix} = 8008$ different binary vectors with 6 of 16 bits equal to 1, a bucket number can be obtained for each stored record by simply converting the binary code representation of the records into a number in the range [0–8007]. [53] It is interesting to note that in an inverted-file environment the amount of work to search the file increases as the number of search keys included in the query grows. In the proposed multikey hashing system, the reverse is the case. For single-key queries where 1 bit is specified in a 16-bit word, it is necessary to search through $\begin{bmatrix} 16-1 \\ 6-1 \end{bmatrix} = 3003$ buckets; on the other hand, when three query keys are specified, only 3 of 6 bits are randomly specifiable, in which case only $\begin{bmatrix} 13 \\ 3 \end{bmatrix} = 286$ buckets must be searched. [53] Unfortunately, this elegant system becomes less attractive when the number of key values per record grows and varies from record to record.

In addition to the superimposed coding system, in which binary code vectors are added by logical or operations, a bitmap encoding

Figure 7.43 False drop probability for superimposed code vectors of length n with k of n bits set equal to 1.

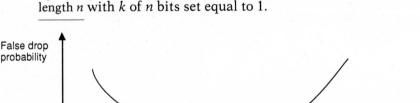

system can be implemented by *concatenating* the various code values to generate a record representation. [54–58] The concatenated code vectors are known as *word signatures*. An example of the signature construction for a record identified by the terms Data, Base, Management, and System is shown in Fig. 7.44.

Word-signature methods have been proposed to represent natural-language text messages; the individual words included in the messages are used to represent text content. The use of text words for content representation is in principle attractive. However, long texts may be converted into long signature vectors, and the signature-scanning operations needed to find coincidences between query and text signatures may then lead to unacceptably long waiting times for retrieval. Further, generating text signatures depends to some extent on word order: For example, the signatures for "data base management system," on the one hand, and "system for the management of data bases," on the other, may differ, implying that relevant records are rejected because the texts exhibit slightly different word orders.

The word-order problem can be eliminated by computing the signature for each significant text word — that is, each word not included on a special stop-word list — and listing the word signatures in the alphabetic order of the corresponding text words. If the query-word signatures are similarly reordered, correct comparisons are easy to implement between document and query signatures. However, reordering word signatures involves expensive sorting operations, and complicates the generation of text signatures.

All bitmap representations show the advantages of substantially compressed document representations. This is of special interest in environments where small microprocessors with limited storage capacity are used to manipulate text. A substantial number of disadvantages are also apparent for bit-vector representations:

- Signature-file searches may be slow unless special indexes are built that give access to certain file subsections.

- Signatures for variants of the same word may differ, as do the signatures of synonymous or otherwise equivalent text words; this complicates the construction of queries, as well as comparisons between queries and documents.

Figure 7.44 Word-signature example.

Term	data	base	management	system
Code	0000	0100	0111	1011

data base management system: 0000 0100 0111 1011

- The signature-file system may lead to false drops when completely different text words are assigned the same word signatures.

- Records containing more words are normally represented by longer text signatures, or by bit vectors with a larger number of 1s; as a result longer documents have a greater chance of being retrieved in response to a query than shorter items, and this may reduce the system's effectiveness at retrieving.

- When bit vectors are used to represent records, it is difficult to assign term weights in order of word importance; more generally, all the terms in a document signature will be treated as equally important. Once again this may not prove to be optimal in actual retrieval operations.

Bitmap representations may be most immediately useful to represent short messages, or telegrams, containing about the same number of terms, with homogeneous vocabularies. In that case, it may be possible to use the text words to represent content, and the bitmap system may prove inexpensive and effective.

In the normal bitmap representation of Fig. 7.40(a), a given document collection is represented by N document vectors of length n. To compare a query specification with the encoded documents, it is then necessary to process $n \cdot N$ binary digits. Instead of storing the file in row order — that is, in order by the document vectors — the bitmap could be stored in column order in a so-called *bit-slice* form (see Fig. 7.45a). It is obvious that the bit-slice format makes possible a much more economical query-document comparison, because it is necessary to use only those slices (columns) of the document representation that correspond to query components. The records that must be retrieved can then be easily identified by performing logical-and operations of the bit slices for all query components. Such a logical-and operation on the query columns is shown in Fig. 7.45(b). Assuming that there are w query terms in all, and that each is represented by k_q binary digits, a total of $w \cdot k_q \cdot N$ binary digits must be examined in the bit slice system instead of $n \cdot N$ as before.

The main disadvantage of the bit-slice system is the extra work involved in updating the file of binary code representations. Indeed when documents are added, deleted, or altered, it is no longer sufficient to access a single row of the bitmap at a time. Instead certain column elements must be changed for every slice, and hence all $n \cdot N$ bits must potentially be treated. Bit-slice organizations are therefore preferred for static files involving few updating operations.

Bit-slice representation can be combined with a multilevel index designed to gain fast access to the record file. [59,60] More specifically, the records could be divided into N_s segments, each containing N_r

records ($N_r \cdot N_s = N$), and records could then be retrieved by first identifying the segments matching a query specification, then accessing
the records belonging to the corresponding segments. If the segments
are characterized by binary representations of length n_s, of which approximately k_s bits are equal to 1, and the records are represented by
vectors of length n_r, of which k_r bits are equal to 1, the total required
storage for the index is $N_s \cdot n_s + N_r(n_r + \text{pointer size})$, as suggested in
Fig. 7.46.

Assuming that the segment representations are stored in bit-slice
form and that each of w query terms has k_s 1s in its binary representation, a total of $k_s \cdot w$ bit slices must be accessed in the coded segment
representations. Further, if the logical-and operations produce B
matching segments, and the N_r records for each segment fit on a single

Figure 7.45 Bit-slice string. (a) Bit-slice format. (b) Retrieval operation in
bit-slice organization.

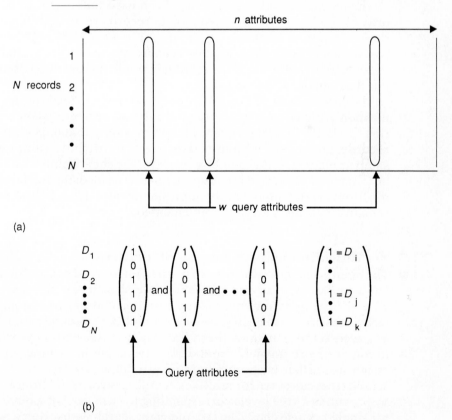

(a)

(b)

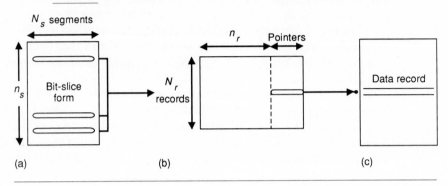

Figure 7.46 Multilevel bit-slice record storage. (a) Coded segment representation. (b) Coded record representation. (c) Main record file.

computer page, the total number of accesses to the coded index representations is $k_s \cdot w + B$.

The multilevel index system has been used for files of 25,000 records divided into 1000 segments of 25 records each, with typical parameters of $n_s = 4700$, $k_s = 2$, and $n_r = 128$, $k_r = 4$. [59,60] The major cost arises in updating segments because of the bit-slice format, and the principal limitation is the relatively small number of attribute values that can be accommodated.

The cost analysis of Fig. 7.40(b) suggests that a hybrid storage organization could be used in practical situations, with bitmap representations assigned to high-frequency attribute values that appear in many records, and inverted pointer lists used for attribute values with a small number of corresponding records. The short pointer lists could be efficiently converted into bitmap form as needed; the retrieval logic might be carried out entirely in bitmap form. Such a hybrid system remains to be designed and implemented.

7.10 ❖ Multidimensional Access Structures

The binary and multiway tree structures introduced earlier for single-key searches were advantageous because of their fast file access and efficient file updating in dynamic situations. Multidimensional tree structures have also been proposed for multikey, as opposed to single-key, access. Unfortunately the index structures for multikey representation are more unwieldy, and difficulties arise in manipulating the structures when large numbers of attributes are present. Binary search trees can serve for multikey searches involving k different keys by providing k tree levels corresponding to each level of a binary tree for single-key searches. The left and right search paths from a node at level i $(1 \leq i \leq k)$ are then designed to discriminate among the values of the ith key. The corresponding tree structure is known as a k-d tree. [61,62]

A typical k-d tree for two attributes $(k=2)$ appears in Fig. 7.47(a). The odd-numbered tree levels (1, 3, 5, etc.) provide discrimination for the first search key; the even-numbered levels do the same for the second key. Consider, as an example, the search path through nodes A,B,C,D of the tree of Fig. 7.47(a). Taking the right path from node A implies that the first query key x has a value larger than 5 (see Fig. 7.47b1). Taking the left path from B indicates that the second search key y is smaller than 9 (see Fig. 7.47b2). The search path next takes the left path from C, limiting the first key to the range $5 < x < 8$, followed by the right path from D, limiting the values of y to $7 < y < 9$. When the example ends in Fig. 7.47(b)(4), the search area is bounded by a small rectangle in a narrow range of values of the search keys x and y.

Although k-d trees provide logarithmic search and update times in the number n of records, $k \cdot \log n$ tree levels are needed to accommodate the nodes. The search effort then becomes large very rapidly for large values of k. An alternative possibility for multikey searches consists of using only $\log n$ tree levels, as in binary trees for single-key searching, but providing 2^k descendants from each node of the tree to ensure discrimination for all k attributes at each point. Such k-way trees are known as *quad trees*. [62,63]

Consider a typical node of a quad tree for two attributes x and y $(k=2)$, as shown in Fig. 7.48. In that case a four-way tree is needed since the four paths from each node depend on the values of the two search keys x and y. As illustrated in Fig. 7.48(a), each tree node subdivides the search space into four quadrants (instead of two quadrants as in k-d trees for $k=2$). The number of key comparisons needed to isolate a given area in the search space is therefore smaller for quad trees than for k-d trees, but the tree structure and comparison processes are correspondingly more complex.

Methods are available for maintaining k-way tree structures in approximately balanced form when new nodes are inserted, as shown in Figs. 7.48(c) and (d). Since each node of a quad tree partitions the remaining search space into 2^k subspaces, node deletions pose problems unless all nodes in the subtree below a deleted node are also removed. As k becomes large, the branching factor 2^k renders the quad-tree strategy less and less attractive. The use of multidimensional search trees is then restricted to "point" searches for single records, or to area searches for all records lying in a certain neighborhood in a key space of small dimensions. [64,65]

One additional multidimensional search structure deserves mention. In a *grid file*, the partitions of the search space are treated symmetrically for all dimensions — that is, the search space is split repeat-

Figure 7.47 k-d tree search. (a) Typical k-d tree (k = 2). (b) Search-area specification.

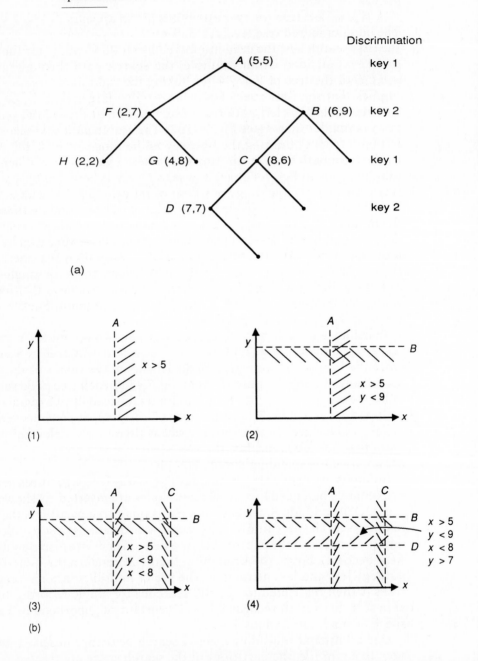

(a)

(b)

edly in half, using the values of each attribute in turn. [66] A two-dimensional grid file example is shown in Fig. 7.49, where the values of attribute 1 are associated with the x axis and the values of attribute 2 with the y axis, and a maximum bucket size of three records is assumed.

The complete value space of an attribute is first associated with a single bucket A. As records are added to the file, bucket A becomes full and the space is split in half along the x dimension, creating a new bucket (see Fig. 7.49b). As more items are added, bucket A becomes full once again, and a new split is made, this time in the y dimension. This creates four equal halves in the search space as shown in Fig. 7.49(c); however, only one new bucket must be added at this point (bucket C).

Figure 7.48 Quad tree examples. (a) Quad tree node ($k = 2$). (b) Corresponding space subdivision. (c) Single rotation of quad tree. (d) Double rotation of quad tree.

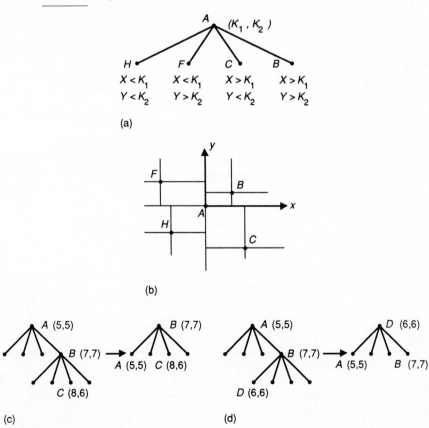

Because bucket B, covering records for which $x > x_1$, does not overflow, there is no point splitting bucket B into two pieces at this juncture. Instead another pointer is added for bucket B to cover both

Figure 7.49 Symmetric space partitioning in grid file. (a) Initial file. (b) File after one splitting operation. (c) File after two splitting operations. (d) File after three splitting operations.

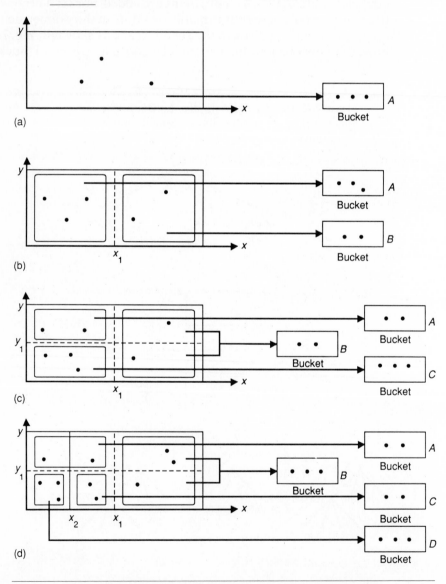

halves of the space for which $x > x_1$. Bucket C overflows next, and the next split is again made along the x dimension, creating a new bucket D for records with $x < x_2$ and $y < y_1$; bucket C keeps the items with $x_2 < x < x_1$, and $y < y_1$. Eventually the space is divided into grid blocks of dimension k, where k represents the number of different attributes used to identify the records. Each grid block carries pointers to the data buckets in which the corresponding records are stored. The full access mechanism consists of two parts:

1. k one-dimensional arrays, known as *linear scales*, specify the partitions along the attribute-value axis for the k attributes; a search of the linear scales for the record attributes identifies a particular grid block in the search space.
2. The pointer array associates a data bucket with each given grid block containing the records with the corresponding attribute values.

When the records are identified by relatively few attributes, and hence only a limited number of linear scales are needed, the grid-file system may provide more economical record access than multidimensional search trees.

References

1. D. Lefkovitz, The Large Data Base File Structure Dilemma, Conference on Large Data Bases, NAS/NCR Committee in Chemical Information, National Academy of Sciences, Washington, DC, May 1974.

2. D. Lefkovitz, *File Structures for On-line Systems*, Spartan Books, New York, 1969.

3. C.T. Meadow, *Applied Data Management*, John Wiley and Sons, New York, 1976.

4. I. Flores, *Data Structure and Management*, Prentice-Hall Inc., Englewood Cliffs, NJ, 1970.

5. J. Martin, *Computer Data Base Organization*, Prentice-Hall Inc., Englewood Cliffs, NJ, 1975.

6. T.A. Standish, *Data Structure Techniques*, Addison-Wesley Publishing Co., Reading, MA, 1980.

7. J.P. Tremblay and P.G. Sorenson, *An Introduction to Data Structures with Applications*, McGraw-Hill Book Co., New York, 1976.

8. D.E. Knuth, *The Art of Programming*, Vol. 1, *Fundamental Algorithms*, 2d ed., Addison-Wesley Publishing Co., Reading, MA, 1973.

9. D.E. Knuth, Optimum Binary Search Trees, *Acta Informatica*, 1:1, 1971, 14–25.

10. M. Elson, *Data Structures*, Science Research Associates, Chicago, 1975.

11. A.M. Tenenbaum and M.J. Augenstein, *Data Structures Using Pascal*, Prentice-Hall Inc., Englewood Cliffs, NJ, 1981.

12. N. Wirth, *Algorithms + Data Structures = Programs*, Prentice-Hall Inc., Englewood Cliffs, NJ, 1976.

13. J.L. Pfaltz, *Computer Data Structures*, McGraw-Hill Book Co., New York, 1977.

14. E. Horowitz and S. Sahni, *Fundamentals of Data Structures*, Computer Science Press, Woodland Hills, CA, 1976.

15. G.M. Adelson-Velskii and E.M. Landis, An Algorithm for the Organization of Information, *Doklady Academii Nauk SSSR, Matematicheskii Institut*, 146:2, 1962, 263–266.

16. A.V. Aho, J.E. Hopcroft, and J.D. Ullman, *Data Structures and Algorithms*, Addison-Wesley Publishing Co., Reading, MA, 1983.

17. J. Nievergelt and E.M. Reingold, Binary Search Trees of Bounded Balance, *SIAM Journal of Computing*, 2:1, March 1973, 33–43.

18. J. Nievergelt, Binary Search Trees and File Organization, *Computing Surveys*, 6:3, September 1974, 195–207.

19. W.A. Walker and C.C. Gotlieb, A Top-down Algorithm for Constructing Nearly Optimal Lexicographic Trees, in *Graph Theory and Computing*, R.C. Read, editor, Academic Press, New York, 1972, 303–323.

20. J.L. Baer and B. Schwab, A Comparison of Tree Balancing Algorithms, *Communications of the ACM*, 21:5, May 1977, 322–330.

21. R. Bayer and E. McCreight, Symmetric Binary B-trees: Data Structure and Maintenance Algorithms, *Acta Informatica*, 1:4, 1972, 290–306.

22. R. Bayer and E. McCreight, Organization and Maintenance of Large Ordered Indexes, *Acta Informatica*, 1:3, 1972, 173–189.

23. D. Comer, The Ubiquitous B-tree, *ACM Computing Surveys*, 11:2, June 1979, 121–137.

24. G. Held, and M. Stonebraker, B-Trees Reexamined, *Communications of the ACM*, 21:2, February 1978, 139–143.

25. A. Yao, On Random 2-3 Trees, *Acta Informatica*, 9:2, 1978, 159–170.

26. C.C. Gotlieb and L.R. Gotlieb, *Data Types and Structures*, Prentice-Hall Inc., Englewood Cliffs, NJ, 1978.

27. E. Fredkin, Trie Memory, *Communications of the ACM*, 3:9, September 1960, 490–499.

28. E.H. Sussenguth, Jr., Use of Tree Structures for Processing Files, *Communications of the ACM*, 6:5, May 1963, 272–279.

29. W.D. Maurer, An Improved Hash Code for Scatter Storage, *Communications of the ACM*, 11:1, January 1968, 35–38.

30. R. Morris, Scatter Storage Techniques, *Communications of the ACM*, 11:1, January 1968, 38–43.

31. W.D. Maurer and T.G. Lewis, Hash Table Methods, *Computing Surveys*, 7:1, March 1975, 5–20.

32. V.Y. Lum, General Performance Analysis of Key-to-Address Transformation Methods Using an Abstract File Concept, *Communications of the ACM*, 16:10, October 1973, 603–612.

33. V.Y. Lum, P.S.T. Yuen, and M. Dodd, Key to Address Transform Techniques: A Fundamental Performance Study on Large Existing Formatted Files, *Communications of the ACM*, 14:4, April 1971, 228–239.

34. D.E. Knuth, *The Art of Programming*, Vol. 3, Searching and Sorting, Addison-Wesley Publishing Co., Reading, MA, 1973.

35. D.G. Severance, Identifier Search Mechanisms: A Survey and Generalized Model, *Computing Surveys*, 6:3, September 1974, 175–194.

36. P. Larson, Dynamic Hashing, *BIT*, 18:2, 1978, 184–201.

37. M. Scholl, New File Organizations Based on Dynamic Hashing, *ACM Transactions on Database Systems*, 6:1, March 1981, 194–211.

38. R. Fagin, J. Nievergelt, N. Pippenger, and H.R. Strong, Extendible Hashing — A Fast Access Method for Dynamic Files, *ACM Transactions on Database Systems*, 4:3, September 1979, 315–344.

39. W. Litwin, Linear Hashing: A New Tool for File and Table Addressing, *Proceedings of Sixth Conference on Very Large Data Bases*, Montreal, Association for Computing Machinery, New York, 1980, 212–223.

40. K. Devine and F.J. Smith, Direct File Organization for Lemmatized Text Retrieval, *Information Technology*, 3:1, January 1984, 25–32.

41. N.S. Prywes, Man-Computer Problem Solving with Multilist, *Proceedings of the IEEE*, 54:12, December 1966, 1788–1801.

42. H.J.. Gray, W.I. Landauer, D. Lefkovitz, S. Litwin, and N.S. Prywes, The Multilist System, *Moore School Report* 62:10, 1:2, Moore School of Electrical Engineering, Philadelphia, PA, 1961.

43. B. Shneiderman, Reduced Combined Indexes for Efficient Multiple Attribute Retrieval, *Information Systems*, 2, 1977, 149–154.

44. V.Y. Lum, Multiattribute Retrieval with Combined Indexes, *Communications of the ACM*, 13:11, November 1970, 660–665.

45. M. Stonebraker, The Choice of Partial Inversions and Combined Indices, *International Journal of Computer and Information Sciences*, 3:2, 1974, 167–188.

46. C.N. Mooers, Zatocoding Applied to Mechanical Organization of Knowledge, *American Documentation*, 2:1, Winter 1951, 20–32.

47. J.R. Files and H.D. Huskey, An Information Retrieval System Based on Superimposed Coding, *Proceedings of the Fall Joint Computer Conference*, Vol. 35, AFIPS Press, Arlington, VA, 1969, 423–430.

48. C.S. Roberts, Partial Match Retrieval via the Method of Superimposed Codes, *Proceedings of the IEEE*, 67:12, December 1979, 1624–1642.

49. O. Vallarino, The Use of Bit Maps for Multiple Key Retrieval, *SIGPLAN Notices*, 10:3, March 1973, 108–114.

50. J.L. Pfaltz, W.J. Berman, and E.M. Cagley, Partial Match Retrieval Using Indexed Descriptor Files, *Communications of the ACM*, 23:9, September 1980, 522–528.

51. G. Orosz and L. Takacs, Some Probability Problems Concerning the Marking of Codes in the Superimposed Field, *Journal of Documentation*, 12:4, December 1956, 231–234.

52. A. Bookstein, On Harrison's Substring Testing Technique, *Communications of the ACM*, 16:3, March 1973, 180–181.

53. R.A. Gustafson, Elements of the Randomized Combinatorial File Structure, *Proceedings of the ACM/SIGIR Symposium on Information Storage and Retrieval*, Association for Computing Machinery, New York, April 1971, 163–174.

54. J.B. Rothnie and T. Lozano, Attribute Based File Organization in a Paged Memory Environment, *Communications of the ACM*, 17:2, February 1974, 63–69.

55. D. Tsichritzis and S. Christodoulakis, Message Files, *ACM Transactions on Office Information Systems*, 1:1, January 1983, 88–98.

56. C. Faloutsos, Access Methods for Text, *ACM Computing Surveys*, 17:1, March 1983, 49–74.

57. C. Faloutsos and S. Christodoulakis, Signature Files: An Access Method for Documents and Its Analytical Performance Evaluation, *ACM Transactions on Office Information Systems*, 2:4, October 1984, 267–288.

58. P.A. Larson, A Method for Speeding Up Text Retrieval, *Data Base*, 15:2, Winter 1984, 19–23.

59. R. Sacks-Davis, Performance of a Multi Key Access Method Based on Descriptors and Superimposed Coding Techniques, *Information Systems*, 10:4, 1985, 391–404.

60. R. Sacks-Davis and M. Ramamohanarao, A Two Level Superimposed Coding Scheme for Partial Match Retrieval, *Information Systems*, 8:4, 1983, 273–280.

61. J.L. Bentley, Multidimensional Binary Search Trees Used for Associative Searching, *Communications of the ACM*, 18:9, September 1975, 509–516.

62. J.L. Bentley and J.H. Friedman, Data Structures for Range Searching, *Computing Surveys*, 11:4, December 1979, 397–409.

63. R.A. Finkel and J.L. Bentley, Quad Trees: A Data Structure for Retrieval on Composite Keys, *Acta Informatica*, 4, 1974, 1–9.

64. S.V. N. Rao, S. S. Iyengar, and C.E.V. Madhavan, A Comparative Study of Multiattribute Tree and Inverted File Structures for Large Bibliographic Files, *Information Processing and Management*, 21:5, 1985, 433–442.

65. C.M. Eastman and S.F. Weiss, A Tree Algorithm for Nearest Neighbor Searching in Document Retrieval Systems, *SIGIR Forum*, 13:1, Summer 1978, 131–149.

66. J. Nievergelt, H. Hinterberger, and K.C. Sevcik, The Grid File: An Adaptable Symmetric Multikey File Structure, *ACM Transactions on Database Systems*, 9:1, March 1984, 38–71.

Part 3

Information Retrieval Systems

Chapter 8

Conventional Text-Retrieval Systems

8.1 Database Management and Information Retrieval

Information-retrieval systems process files of records and requests for information, and identify and retrieve from the files certain records in response to the information requests. The retrieval of particular records depends on the similarity between the records and the queries, which in turn is measured by comparing the values of certain attributes attached to records and information requests.

In most database management systems the files contain homogeneous records, with a specified set of attributes used to characterize each file item, and the values of the attributes attached to particular records assumed to describe these records unequivocally and completely. For example, a file of employee records maintained by a particular business organization can be characterized by employees' names, home addresses, job classifications, ages, and rates of pay. Each individual record is then identified by a particular name, address, job classification, age, and pay rate, and each of these attribute values pertains unequivocally to the corresponding employee record.

In processing databases, it is conceptually easy to identify records corresponding to particular search requests, because the query formulations must include some subset of the attribute values that also characterizes the file records. In these circumstances, the retrieval of records depends on an exact match between the attribute values used in the query formulations and those attached to the records being sought: Each retrieved record will contain the precise attribute values specified in the query (and possibly other attribute values not mentioned in the query), while each nonretrieved record will exhibit at least one mismatch between attribute values attached to the query and those attached to the stored records.

In text-based, or bibliographic, information processing, the retrieval activity can be conceptually similar to the search and retrieval of database records. This is notably the case when formal identifiers characterize the stored texts, such as the names of book publishers, the dates of publication, and the names of document authors. In that case, the retrieval of all publications written by particular authors is similar to the retrieval of personnel records for particular employee names. For text records, however, it is important to consider, in addition to the formal attributes characterizing each text item, a different set of more informal identifiers that deal with text content.

The *content* identifiers attached to the stored texts are known as *keywords, index terms,* or *descriptors*. Each index term is assumed to describe the text content only to some extent, not completely or unequivocally, and large numbers of different index terms may be attached to each particular document or text. In these circumstances, it may not be useful to insist on a complete match between query and document terms before particular documents are retrieved. Instead, the retrieval of an item may depend on a sufficient degree of coincidence between the sets of identifiers attached to queries and documents, produced by some approximate or partial matching method.

Because text-retrieval operations depend directly on the content representations used to describe the stored records, a substantial effort must necessarily be devoted to analyzing the content of the stored texts, dealing with the generation of the content identifiers, and comparing query and document descriptors. In database management, on the other hand, the content-analysis problem does not arise, at least not conceptually. The name of a person, or the age, address, job classification, salary, etc. are treated as unambiguous, and the retrieval decisions based on such criteria are simple. The problems treated in database environments therefore relate most often to higher-level processing problems, such as constructing abstract models to represent the data, and developing advanced languages for data definition and manipulation.

The remainder of this chapter outlines the conventional methods used for automatic document and text retrieval, as well as refinements and extensions leading to the construction of efficient text-retrieval systems.

8.2 Text Retrieval Using Inverted Indexing Methods

In principle, the retrieval of stored records in answer to information requests must be based on determining similarities between queries and stored items, and then retrieving those items that prove sufficiently similar to the corresponding queries. These operations are outlined Fig. 8.1(a). [1,2] In bibliographic information retrieval, the stored records and information requests may be unstructured text items, and the retrieval decision may depend on the content of the corresponding texts. In these circumstances, a direct comparison between records and queries is inconvenient; intermediate steps transform information requests into formal query statements and records into indexed representations before the comparison is actually carried out. An expanded view of the retrieval operations appears in Fig. 8.1(b). In that

Figure 8.1 Conceptual text retrieval. (a) Conceptual information retrieval. (b) Expanded text-retrieval system.

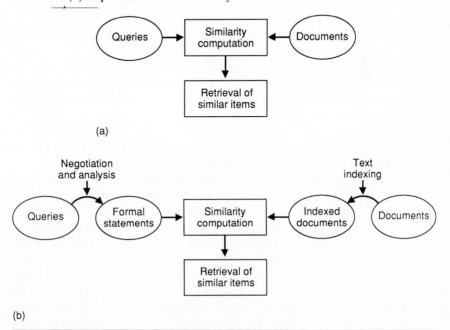

case, content analysis and query formulation steps appear before the query-record comparisons.

In operational environments, the stored records are represented by sets of *index terms*, sometimes called *term vectors*. Usually the terms are unweighted, although in some retrieval situations each term may be assigned a weight to reflects its relative importance. Queries may similarly be expressed by using sets of unweighted or weighted terms. In many practical systems, the query terms are joined by logical, or Boolean, operators that supply relationships between the query terms. Three types of operators are in current use:

1. The *or* operator treats two terms as effectively synonymous. In particular, given the query (term 1 or term 2), the presence of either term in a record suffices to retrieve that record.

2. The *and* operator combines terms into term phrases; thus the query (term 1 and term 2) indicates that both terms (or the complete term phrase consisting of terms 1 and 2) must be present for retrieval.

3. The *not* operator is a restriction, or term-narrowing, operator that is normally used in conjunction with the and operator to restrict the applicability of particular terms; thus the query (term 1 and not term 2) leads to the retrieval of all records containing term 1, provided that term 2 is not also present in the records.

Whether information requests are expressed as term sets or as Boolean combinations of terms, the search operations must effectively identify stored records containing certain term combinations. Various kinds of search strategies and data structures can be used for this purpose, including multilists, multidimensional trees, and combined indexes (see Chapter 7). In practice, operational retrieval environments are characterized by two main requirements: (1) Access to the files must be carried out more or less instantaneously, usually while users wait at computer terminals, and (2) the number of keywords or index terms to be accommodated in a given situation may be very large — of the order of tens of thousands.

The fast-access requirement eliminates sequential searches of the record file, as well as access methods based on pointer-chain tracing as in the multilist method, while the use of large numbers of terms effectively prevents file access based on combined indexes. The usual solution provides a separate dense index for each term or each attribute value used in the system. That is, for *each* term a separate index is constructed that stores the record identifiers, or record addresses, for *all* records identified by that term. The set of indexes for all allowable terms and attribute values is collectively known as an *inverted index* or *inverted file*. With an inverted index, the record set corresponding to a given query formulation is easily determined: The identifiers for all retrieved items can be obtained by extracting from the inverted index the list of record identifiers corresponding to each query term, and combining these record identifiers appropriately. A full inverted-file process can be described as follows:

1. The complete file is first represented as an array of indexed records, where each row represents a record, or document, and each column specifies the assignment of a particular term to the records of the collection.

2. The record-term array is inverted (actually transposed) in such a way that each row of the inverted array then specifies the records corresponding to some particular term.

3. The rows of the inverted term-record array are manipulated in accordance with a particular query specification to determine the set of records that respond to the query.

Consider, for example, the record-term array of Fig. 8.2(a), where four sample records are identified by four possible terms. A 1 at the intersection of row i and column j of the array signifies that term j is assigned to the corresponding record i, and a 0 correspondingly implies that the term is not assigned. Thus record 2 is represented by the term vector (row) (0,1,1,1), implying that term 1 is not assigned to the record but that the other three terms are assigned.

The inverted-index representation of the record file is obtained by transposing the record-term array in such a way that row i of the origi-

---

Figure 8.2 Relationship between record vectors and inverted index. (a) Original record specification. (b) Inverted view of collection.

	Term 1	Term 2	Term 3	Term 4
Record 1	1	1	0	1
Record 2	0	1	1	1
Record 3	1	0	1	1
Record 4	0	0	1	1

(a)

	Record 1	Record 2	Record 3	Record 4
Term 1	1	0	1	0
Term 2	1	1	0	0
Term 3	0	1	1	1
Term 4	1	1	1	1

(b)

nal array becomes column i of the inverted representation. Each row of the inverted array thus represents the list of record identifiers corresponding to a particular term. Thus row 2 of the inverted array of Fig. 8.2(b), represented as (1,1,0,0), indicates that term 2 is assigned to records 1 and 2 but not to records 3 and 4. The inverted-index operations required to obtain answers in response to information queries are based on a *list-merging* process capable of taking two or more rows of an inverted term-record array and producing a single combined list of record identifiers. For example, a list merging for rows 2 and 3 of the inverted array indicates that record 1 (R_1) is included in one of the two input lists, R_2 is present on both input lists, and R_3 and R_4 are each present on only one input list.

When the record identifiers included in the inverted array are ordered — for example, in increasing order of the record identifiers as in Fig. 8.2(b) — the list-merging operation can be carried out in a single scan of the input lists. A simplified program of a list-merging operation appears in Fig. 8.3, where the smallest element (the record with the next-smallest identifier) is successively transferred to the merged output list until both input lists are exhausted.

The following retrieval strategies can then be used to retrieve the records in response to various simple query statements:

- For vector queries consisting of terms without Boolean operators, such as (T_i, T_j, T_k), a merged record list is constructed for rows i, j, k

---

Figure 8.3 List-merging operation for two ordered lists.

Given two input lists of record identifiers in increasing record-number order

if both lists are empty **then** stop;

else if one of the input lists is empty

    then transfer onto the output list all
        items from the other list in order and stop;

    else take the next item R_i from list 1 and
        the next item R_j from list 2

    if $i < j$

        then transfer R_i onto the merged output list
            and read next item from list 1 before
            repeating the process;

        else transfer R_j onto merged output
            and read next item from list 2 before
            repeating the process

of the inverted index, and records are transferred to the output in decreasing order of the number of entries on the merged list; this retrieves items with n query terms before those with $n-1$ query terms, and so on down to the items containing only one query term that appear only once on the merged list.

- For Boolean *and-queries*, such as $(T_i$ and $T_j)$, a merged list is produced for rows i and j of the inverted index and all *duplicated* records (those containing both term T_i and term T_j) are transferred to the output.

- For *or-queries*, such as $(T_i$ or $T_j)$, the merged list is produced for rows i and j and all *distinct* items from the merged list are transferred to the output, corresponding to items having one term or the other, or both terms.

- For *not-queries*, such as $(T_i$ and not $T_j)$, the merged list for T_i and T_j is constructed as before, and items appearing only once on the merged list are removed to produce a list for $(T_i$ and $T_j)$; the T_i list is then merged with the $(T_i$ and $T_j)$ list, and items appearing more than once are removed before the remaining records are transferred to the output.

Typical examples of the list-merging operations carried out in the inverted index of Fig. 8.2(b) are shown in Fig. 8.4 for the query $((T_1$ or $T_2)$ and not $T_3)$.

In writing Boolean query statements, parentheses are needed to specify precedence among operations. The evaluation can then take place from the inside out as in ordinary algebra. Thus the expression $(T_1$ and T_2 or $T_3)$ is ambiguous in view of the distinct interpretations of $(T_1$ and $(T_2$ or $T_3))$ and $((T_1$ and $T_2)$ or $T_3)$:

Figure 8.4 Sample inverted-list operations for $((T_1$ **or** $T_2)$ **and not** $T_3)$.

Sample query	$((T_1$ or $T_2)$ and not $T_3)$
Lists from index	T_1 : $\{R_1,R_3\}$
	T_2 : $\{R_1,R_2\}$
	T_3 : $\{(R_2,R_3,R_4\}$
Merged (T_1,T_2) :	$\{R_1,R_1,R_2,R_3\}$
Output for $(T_1$ or $T_2)$:	$\{R_1,R_2,R_3\}$
Merged $((T_1$ or $T_2, T_3)$:	$\{R_1,R_2,R_2,R_3,R_3,R_4\}$
Output for $((T_1$ or $T_2)$ and $T_3)$:	$\{R_2,R_3\}$
Merged $((T_1$ or $T_2), ((T_1$ or $T_2)$ and $T_3))$:	$\{R_1,R_2,R_2,R_3,R_3\}$
Output for $((T_1$ or $T_2)$ and not $T_3)$:	$\{R_1\}$

$$T_1 \text{ and } (T_2 \text{ or } T_3) = (T_1 \text{ and } T_2) \text{ or } (T_1 \text{ and } T_3) \qquad (8.1a)$$

$$(T_1 \text{ and } T_2) \text{ or } T_3 = (T_1 \text{ and } T_2) \text{ or } (T_1 \text{ and } T_3) \text{ or } (T_2 \text{ and } T_3) \quad (8.1b)$$

The inverted-index process just described exhibits substantial advantages in terms of processing efficiency: A query can be constructed that can retrieve any desired subset of records; further, the query logic can be entirely evaluated in the inverted index using the previously outlined list-merging operations. Thus there is no need to gain access to the main record file, except to retrieve the record information for items already known to respond to the queries. This accounts for the speed with which responses can be obtained in operational search systems in which very large record files may be in use.

The conventional Boolean logic implemented by inverted-list operations also exhibits obvious disadvantages. First, the records are normally retrieved in the order in which they appear in the inverted lists (for example, in increasing record number order), rather than in some decreasing order of expected usefulness. In addition, the Boolean formulations cannot easily be related to particular desired output sizes: When the queries are broadly formulated with or operators, a large output set may overwhelm the user. On the other hand, narrowly formulated queries using and operators may generate very little output. In general, formulating useful Boolean queries is an art that is not accessible to uninitiated users.

8.3 Extensions of the Inverted Index Operations

Various extensions to the standard inverted-index technology have been proposed, or implemented, in attempts to simplify operations and improve retrieval. These extensions are outlined in the following subsections.

8.3.1 Distance Constraints

When stored records cover natural-language texts and documents, the terms used to characterize the records are frequently extracted from the actual document texts. This is the case in both manual and automatic indexing environments in which the terms are chosen by trained indexers or by some machine process. While the terms are usually assigned independently of each other, term relationships can be introduced in the query formulations by adding appropriate Boolean operators. Thus the query (information and retrieval) can be used to retrieve texts dealing with the general topic of information retrieval.

The relationship specified between two or more terms can be strengthened by adding *nearness* parameters to the query specification. Two possible parameters of this kind are the *within sentence* and *adjacency* specifications, where (*A* within sentence *B*) implies that terms *A* and *B* must cooccur in a common sentence of a retrieved text, whereas (*A* adjacent *B*) implies that terms *A* and *B* must occur adjacently in the text. When nearness parameters are included in a query specification, the topic is more narrowly defined, and the probable relevance of any retrieved item is larger.

Conceptually, the simplest way to implement a query specification constrained by nearness parameters is to process the broader and-query (*A* and *B*) and to reject retrieved items in which the specified relationship between terms *A* and *B* is not maintained. This apparently requires a text-scanning operation of all items retrieved by query (*A* and *B*), designed to reject those items in which the two terms are not in close proximity. As will be seen later, text-matching systems can be used to detect the presence or absence of particular character or word combinations in document texts. Text-scanning operations are expensive to carry out, however, and are usually too slow for general use.

The preferred solution to the problem of distance constraints consists of including term-location information in the inverted indexes. This makes it possible to verify the nearness conditions without actually accessing the record information in the main record file, and without scanning the document texts. A within sentence specification can be answered by extending the term lists in the inverted index to include sentence numbers for all term occurrences. Consider two standard lists for the terms "information" and "retrieval" as they might appear in an inverted index:

$$\text{information} \quad : \quad \{R_{345}, R_{348}, R_{350}, ...\}$$
$$\text{retrieval} \quad : \quad \{R_{123}, R_{128}, R_{345}, ...\}$$

When sentence location is added, the lists are extended as follows:

$$\text{information} \quad : \quad \{R_{345}, 25; R_{345}, 37; R_{348}, 10; R_{350}, 8; ...\}$$
$$\text{retrieval} \quad : \quad \{R_{123}, 5; R_{128}, 25; R_{345}, 37; R_{345}, 40; ...\}$$

indicating that the term "information" appears twice in record 345, in sentences number 25 and 37; once more in record 348, sentence 10; and in record 350, sentence 8. Using the preceding list specification for the terms "information" and "retrieval," the response to query (information within sentence retrieval) consists of record R_{345}, because both term lists contain the entry "$R_{345},37$," showing that sentence 37 of the record contains both terms.

A further extension of the inverted-index entries — covering, for example, paragraph numbers, sentence numbers within paragraphs, and word numbers within sentences — can provide answers to queries such as (information adjacent retrieval) or (information within five words retrieval), the latter implying that no more than four intervening words should occur in the document texts between the terms "information" and "retrieval." Thus the two list entries

information	:	$(R_{345}, 2, 3, 5)$
retrieval	:	$(R_{345}, 2, 3, 6)$

satisfy the adjacency restriction because the first term appears in paragraph 2, sentence 3, word 5 of the text of record R_{345}, and the second occurs adjacently in paragraph 2, sentence 3, word 6 of the same item.

Including term-location information in inverted-index lists expands the size of the indexes to a considerable extent — possibly by a factor of two or three — since each occurrence of each term in the text may have to be separately registered. However, such information allows much faster answers to be obtained to queries with location constraints than appears possible with text-scanning methods.

In some operational systems, additional location constraints may be imposed, indicating that the query terms must be restricted to specific portions of a document. Such location specifications may cover *within-title*, *within-bibliographic-citation*, or *within-abstract* constraints that may be satisfied by methods similar to those described earlier for term occurrences within sentences.

8.3.2 Term Weights

The introduction of term-importance weights for document terms and query terms may help distinguish terms that are more important for retrieval purposes from other, less important terms. A particular record could then appear as $R_i = \{T_{i1}, 0.2; T_{i2}, 0.5; T_{i3}, 0.6\}$ showing that term 3 of record R_i has an importance weight of 0.6, whereas term 1 has a much smaller importance weight of 0.2. When term weights are added to the inverted index, the records can be ranked at retrieval time in decreasing order of the weights of the matching terms between queries and documents.

The weighting strategy used to assign term weights to document terms must be simple to generate and easy to apply in a retrieval setting. Various term-weighting methods of this kind are outlined in the next chapter. When all document terms carry weight assignments, it is easy to rank the output documents in decreasing order of term weight. Vector queries, which express the query specification simply as a set of terms, can be distinguished from Boolean queries, which use logical operators to relate query terms. For vector queries, the retrieval weight of a document could be defined simply as the sum of the weights of all document terms that match the given query. Thus if a query Q consists of terms (T_i, T_j, T_k), the retrieval weight of a record R_n containing these terms would simply be computed as $w_{ni} + w_{nj} + w_{nk}$, where w_{np} is the weight of term p in record n. [3,4]

When Boolean queries are used, determining document-retrieval weights is more complex because of the many equivalent formulations of Boolean expressions. One possibility consists of transforming each query into a sum-of-products form, also known as the disjunctive normal form, where the query appears as a set of conjuncts of one or more terms (that is, terms interconnected by and operators such as $(T_i$ and T_j and $T_k)$), each conjunct being connected to the next one by an or operator. Sum-of-products forms were previously given in expression (8.1) for the two queries $(T_1$ and $(T_2$ or $T_3))$ and $((T_1$ and $T_2)$ or $T_3))$.

Given a particular query in disjunctive normal form, the retrieval weight of a document can be computed in two steps:

1. First, the document weight is computed with respect to each conjunct in the query as the minimum term weight of any document term in that conjunct.

2. Second, the document weight for the final query (the disjunction of all the conjuncts) is now established as the maximum of all the conjunct weights determined in step 1.

A typical assignment of retrieval weights is shown in Table 8.1 for two sample documents and a query in sum-of-products form. The example shows that the similarity score between the query $((T_1$ and $T_2)$ or $T_3)$ and record D_1 is 0.6, whereas the query-record similarity for record D_2 is 0.2. Thus D_1 would be retrieved before D_2 in a ranked retrieval system operating in decreasing order of query-record similarity.

Distance constraints and term weights usually result in a more precise specification of text content. That is, combinations of terms in close proximity, or terms distinguished by weight assignment, may represent more specific content descriptions than unweighted terms used alone. Other vocabulary modifications that are easily made in operational inverted indexes provide term transformations in the

---

Table 8.1 Sample evaluation of weighted documents with respect to Boolean query $((T_1$ and $T_2)$ or $T_3)$.

Document Vectors	Conjunct Weights		Query Weight
	$(T_1$ and $T_2)$	(T_3)	$(T_1$ and $T_2)$ or T_3
$D_1 = (T_1, 0.2; T_2, 0.5; T_3, 0.6)$	0.2	0.6	0.6
$D_2 = (T_1, 0.7; T_2, 0.2; T_3, 0.1)$	0.2	0.1	0.2

other direction, making excessively narrow content representations broader and more general. Two possible methods for doing this are synonym specification and term truncation.

8.3.3 Synonym Specification

In several operational retrieval systems, synonym specifications can be added to any query term in a query formulation. Each such synonym is then automatically substituted for the original term, and documents are retrieved with respect to both the original and the substituted terms. When Boolean query formulations are used, the synonym specifications can simply be joined to the original terms by or operators before a search is carried out. Thus the query ((T_1 and T_2) or T_3) is transformed into a broader statement (((T_1 or S_1) and T_2) or (T_3 or S_3)) when the user supplies S_1 as a synonym of T_1, and S_3 as a synonym of T_3. When synonyms are added to particular queries, the number of relevant items retrieved in a search may be larger than before.

8.3.4 Term Truncation

Content terms can be assigned to queries and stored records in *truncated* form by removing suffixes and/or prefixes before the term assignment. It is obvious that a truncated term represents a broader notion than the original nontruncated form, since the truncated term effectively includes a variety of different nontruncated terms. For example, the form PSYCH* (where * is a special sign representing a variable-length ending) represents psychiatrist, psychiatry, psychiatric, psychology, psychologist, psychological, and many other terms.

Various term-truncation methods can be used, including methods that remove particular word suffixes and prefixes, and those that remove a fixed number of terminal characters from the words, or reduce each word to word stems of a fixed size. Normally, certain specified word endings or word prefixes should be removed while still leaving a root form that appears reasonable to identify the words. Thus the suffix "ing" would be removed from a term like "indexing," but not from a term like "king."

How are truncated terms accommodated in systems based on inverted-index technologies? If only *suffix truncation* is allowed, the conventional inverted-index methodology can be maintained unchanged because all the record lists covered by particular truncated terms are adjacent in the index. In particular, given a query term such as PSYCH*, a combined list can easily be generated consisting of the distinct record identifiers on any of the lists for the subsumed nontruncated forms (including psychiatrist, psychology, and so on).

In principle, *prefix truncation* can be accommodated analogously by using an inverted index in which the term entries are inversely alphabetized. Thus the word "antisymmetry" would be entered as "yrtemmysitna," and "asymmetry" would similarly appear as "yrtemmysa." Given query term *SYMMETRY, the inversely alphabetized index is searched under YRTEMMYS*, and the search process is then reduced to the case of suffix truncation.

Word forms exhibiting both prefix and suffix truncation, such as *SYMM* (representing for example "antisymmetric" or "asymmetry,") require inverted-index entries that are alphabetized both forward and backward. A more complex solution, however, is needed to handle cases of *infix truncation*, such as WOM*N, which may stand, for example, for "woman" or "women." One possibility consists of supplying lists in the inverted index with entries for all possible "rotated" word forms. [5] The index might be constructed as follows:

1. Each term entry $X = x_1, x_2,...,x_n$ with individual characters x_i is augmented by adding a special terminal character such as a slash /.

2. Each augmented term $x_1, x_2,...,x_n/$ is rotated cyclically by wrapping the term around itself $n+1$ times. This produces $n+1$ different forms $x_1x_2...x_n/$, $/x_1x_2...x_n$, $x_n/x_1x_2...x_{n-1}$, and so on.

3. Each resulting word form is then augmented by appending a blank character.

4. Finally, the resulting file of word forms is sorted alphabetically, using the sort sequence $\wedge,/,a,b,...,z$, from the lowest-order to highest-order term.

The resulting dictionary now carries an entry that accounts for any kind of term truncation. The following retrieval strategies can be used to obtain the record identifiers corresponding to various forms of truncated terms: [5]

1. For query term X, representing an untruncated character string, the index entries $/X^\wedge$ or $X/^\wedge$ are picked up from the inverted index; the corresponding record identifiers all relate to term X augmented by the special characters / and $^\wedge$.

2. For query term $X*$, look for $/X$ in the index corresponding to all entries with a beginning / followed by string X, and possibly additional characters.

3. Query term $*X$ corresponds to search term $X/$; this retrieves list entries $X/^\wedge$, $X/Y_1,...,X/Y_n$, representing the original terms X, $Y_1X,...,Y_nX$ that contain arbitrary prefixes followed by X.

4. For query term $*X*$ the search term is X; this retrieves list entries $XY_1/Z_1,...,XY_n/Z_n$, corresponding to terms $Z_1XY_1,...,Z_nXY_n$, where X is the wanted infix in each case.

5. Finally, for the infix truncation $X*Y$ the search term is Y/X, which retrieves entries $Y/XZ_1,...,Y/XZ_n$, corresponding to terms $XZ_1Y,...,XZ_nY$, where the Z_is represent variable-length infixes.

Table 8.2 contains an example of the rotated index entries and a typical sample dictionary search. The right-most column of Table 8.2(a) shows that the original nonpermuted index is reproduced at the beginning of the fully rotated index with a slash / preceding each entry. The sample search process of Table 8.2(b) shows that output of the speci-

Table 8.2 Processing of truncated search terms (adapted from [5]). (a) Sample rotated index entries. (b) Sample query processing.

Original Dictionary	Augmented Entries	Cyclically Shifted Terms	Sorted Index Entries
ABC	ABC/	/ABC	/ABC
BABC	BABC/	C/AB	/BABC
BCAB	BCAB/	BC/A	/BCAB
		ABC/	
			AB/BC
		/BABC	ABC/
		C/BAB	ABC/B
		BC/AB	
		ABC/B	B/BCA
		BABC/	BABC/
			BC/A
		/BCAB	BC/BA
		B/BCA	BCAB/
		AB/BC	
		CAB/B	C/AB
		BCAB/	C/BAB
			CAB/B

(a)

Sample Query Form	Corresponding Search Term	Retrieved Terms	Corresponding Original Terms
B	B	B/BCA	BCAB
		BABC/	BABC
		BC/A	ABC
		BC/BA	BABC
		BCAB/	BCAB

(b)

fied dictionary sort sequence is not arranged in the normal alphabetic order. An added sorting operation is needed to retrieve record identifiers in alphabetic search-term order. Furthermore, the records corresponding to terms BABC and BCAB appear twice in the retrieved set.

The permuted dictionary method allows truncated terms to be used in query formulations, but at the cost of a substantial increase in index entries. The record identifier lists corresponding to the various index entries, and the records themselves, of course, need not be duplicated.

The term-modification procedures described in this section can be combined to produce a hierarchy of more or less specific query formulations. An appropriate choice of query formulations may then retrieve exactly the right number of records for each particular user.

8.4 Typical File Organization

A simplified illustration of the file organization used by the IBM STAIRS system (Storage and Information Retrieval System) is shown in Fig. 8.5. [6] There are two principal files: The inverted-term file, containing term entries with corresponding record identifiers, and the main record file, containing the record information itself. Separate indexes, known as the dictionary and the text index, are used to obtain access to the principal files.

The dictionary contains an entry for each term together with a pointer to the corresponding inverted list, as well as a pointer to a synonym file that stores the list addresses of all defined synonyms. When the dictionary contains many term entries, a small higher-level index not shown in Fig. 8.5, can be used to gain access to the dictionary entries. STAIRS maintains an inverted-term file — containing lists of record identifiers together with term location information (paragraph code, sentence number, and word number) for each term — in indexed sequential (ISAM) format, with record numbers listed in increasing order. This makes it possible to perform list-merging operations of the type shown in Fig. 8.3. For each term, the inverted index also contains the document frequency and the total number of term occurrences in the collection. This information can be used to compute term weights.

The text index contains one entry for each document or text record together with a privacy access code used to monitor possible access restrictions. The text index also lists the formatted fields containing objective document identifiers such as author names, dates of publication, and publisher names. STAIRS implements a separate SELECT access system for formatted fields, as opposed to the SEARCH mode used with normal content terms. Methods are provided to process queries containing both objective and content terms. The main text file contains document and paragraph headers in addition to document texts.

Many different text-retrieval systems have been implemented, each exhibiting its own special command structure. All systems, however, provide basic capabilities such as the following:

- Adding a search term to a query formulation;

- Combining an existing query formulation with previously constructed query forms;

- Displaying new terms that are related to specified existing terms, either by common subject or by closeness in the alphabetical sequence of the terms;

- Displaying complete hierarchical classification schedules for the indexing vocabulary in use;

Figure 8.5 STAIRS file organization.

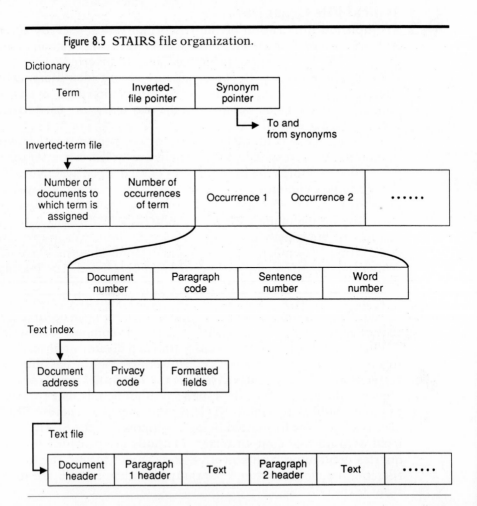

- Displaying retrieved document information at various levels of detail; and

- Supplying help and tutorial information to guide users through the search process.

More advanced systems may also include facilities for term weighting and for controlling the output size based on ranking retrieved items in decreasing order of presumed importance to users. Various vocabulary-expansion methods may be available based on the computation of term-association factors, as well as facilities for automatically rephrasing the user's query formulations. [7]

Among the well-known conventional text-retrieval systems are MEDLARS, implemented at the National Library of Medicine; BRS, developed by Bibliographic Retrieval Services; ORBIT, developed by the System Development Corporation; and DIALOG, designed by Lockheed Information Systems. [8-10] The more popular search services provide file access for tens of thousands of users every month, and many thousands of file searches may be carried out every day.

DIALOG, the largest such system, offers searches of more than 200 different databases, covering well over 100 million records. Remote access to the system can be obtained over various data-communications networks, at a connection cost of about $8 per hour, and typical 10-minute search costs may range from $5, for searching the relatively inexpensive government-sponsored databases, to more than $30, for expensive private databases. DIALOG, like many other online services, offers proximity and term-location searching, in which restrictions may be imposed on the location of search words in written texts. Also available are term-truncation and term-expansion features. In addition, the results of individual searches can be saved, and copies of the full texts of retrieved documents can sometimes be obtained.

Many advanced retrieval operations are covered in more detail in Chapter 10. The remainder of this chapter is devoted to describing optimization methods to streamline conventional inverted-file-processing methods.

8.5 ❖ Optimization of Inverted-List Procedures

❖ 8.5.1 Reducing the Number of Index Terms

The inverted-index approach gives users fast responses to their queries, at the substantial cost of storing and maintaining inverted lists of document identifiers for each allowable index term. In operational situations the inverted index may take up as much storage space as the main record file itself; maintaining the index as new records are added to the file is a major undertaking. Various methods designed to reduce the size of the index term set, and hence the inverted index itself, must therefore be given special attention.

Among the possibilities are using truncated terms instead of full word forms, implementing hash-table transformations that reduce variable-length word forms to short fixed-length codes, and replacing full term entries with word fragments of the type introduced in Chapter 5. [11,12] In each case, the total vocabulary size may be substantially reduced because many fewer short forms exist than complete index-term entries. The total number of record entries in the inverted lists may also be smaller for a vocabulary of reduced size because separate record entries appearing on related lists, such as those for psychology and psychologist, may be replaced by a single entry on a combined **PSYCH*** list. Reduced vocabularies can simplify the storage allocation problem that is inevitable when very long and very short lists of record identifiers are intermingled: Differences between the longest and the shortest lists are smaller for vocabularies of reduced size than for a full indexing vocabulary.

The disadvantage of reduced vocabularies is a loss of subject discrimination, possibly leading to reduced retrieval effectiveness, because the short forms of the terms do not always specify topics precisely. In a recent study, various term-shortening systems were evaluated, including term truncation by suffix removal; division hashing performed by dividing the first eight characters of each word by the desired vocabulary size and using the remainder after division as the term code; multiplication hashing performed by multiplying together two four-character segments contained in the original term and using part of the product as a term code; and code superposition obtained by successively combining four-character pieces of the original term using exclusive-or operations. [11,12] It appears that a term-truncation system that reduces each index term to four or five characters provides almost as good discrimination between relevant and nonrelevant documents as does a system that uses full terms. A division-hashing process performed on truncated terms containing five characters also gives good retrieval performance, as do redundant trigrams in which vocabulary terms are divided into overlapping segments of three characters each. Thus reduced-length vocabularies should be seriously considered in operational retrieval systems.

❖ 8.5.2 Quorum-level Searches

The standard use of Boolean query formulations presents many difficulties for users because retrieval output is sensitive to query formulations, and may vary severely with small changes in query statements. Moreover, the lack of simple controls over output size, and the generation of retrieval output not ranked in any order of presumed importance for users, complicate retrieval for most untrained people. Various proposals exist to simplify the search and retrieval operations while preserving the established retrieval technology based on Boolean query statements and standard list-merging methods. The so-called *quorum-level* search system is typical of moves in this direction. [13]

In a quorum-level search, an original Boolean query containing n terms is replaced by a new query chosen from a sequence of n-term Boolean queries ranging from very narrow formulations where all n terms are included in a single and clause (A and B and...) to very broad formulations where the n terms are interrelated by or operators (A or B or...). The intermediate query formulations consist first of a disjunction of n and clauses, with each and clause generated by removing one term from the and clause used in the original, most specific query formulation. The next, more relaxed query formulation is a disjunction of and clauses obtained by removing two terms each from the original and clause, and so on, until each and clause consists of a single term. The hierarchy of four-term queries, including terms A, B, C, and D, is shown in Table 8.3, where the most specific query consisting of a single and clause is labeled 0, and query i is generated by constructing all possible and clauses from which i terms are missing, and connecting these clauses by or operators.

In a query hierarchy of the type shown in the table, the number of retrieved documents can be expected to increase as the breadth of the query increases. The user can then choose a particular formulation from the query hierarchy designed to retrieve exactly the right amount of output for his or her purposes. When the chosen query is very narrow, the total number of retrieved items will be small, but most of the retrieved items will be relevant. On the other hand, for

Table 8.3 Four-term query hierarchy used in quorum search.

Query Number	Query Hierarchy (narrowest to broadest)	Number Retrieved	Relevant Number Retrieved
0	(A and B and C and D)	2	2
1	(A and B and C) or (A and B and D) or (A and C and D) or (B and C and D)	6	5
2	(A and B) or (A and C) or (A and D) or (B and C) or (B and D) or (C and D)	23	15
3	A or B or C or D	86	25

broad queries the amount of output is large, but the proportion of relevant items among the retrieved ones may be correspondingly smaller.

Two main parameters of retrieval effectiveness have been used over the years, defined as the proportion of relevant materials retrieved, or *recall* (R), and the proportion of retrieved materials that are relevant, or *precision* (P). [14,15] For narrow queries, the precision is high — almost everything retrieved is relevant — but the recall is low since very few items are in fact retrieved. As query statements are broadened, the total number of relevant items retrieved goes up, enhancing the recall; at the same time, the number of nonrelevant retrieved items also grows, decreasing the precision. That is, narrow searches produce high precision and low recall, whereas broader searches produce the reverse result. The situation is illustrated in Fig. 8.6, where the retrieval portion of the collection is shaded. The retrieval activity divides the collection into four parts, consisting of relevant retrieved items (a), relevant not retrieved (d), nonrelevant retrieved (b), and finally nonrelevant not retrieved (c). Recall and precision are then defined as $R = a/a+d$ and $P = a/a+b$.

In an evaluation of the quorum-level search system, the best formulation, producing both relatively high recall and relatively high precision, furnished an average recall of 0.74 and an average precision of 0.67 for the sample searches. This compares with an average recall of 0.30 and average precision of 0.51 for the original user-formulated Boolean queries. [10] The quorum-level system is thus especially useful because it does not burden the user with query formulation, and the performance level may be quite high.

❖ 8.5.3 Partial List Searching

In an inverted-list-processing system, the record lists corresponding to all distinct terms in the query formulation must be retrieved from the index. When the query formulations are complex and include many distinct search terms, the number of lists of record identifiers to be processed may be very large, even though the final number of retrieved items can be quite small. For "popular" terms, those attached to many documents in a collection, the lists may be quite long, and require substantial processing time to be merged.

However, it is not necessary in all circumstances to process all the inverted-term lists corresponding to terms in a query formulation. Indeed, when the user does not require a complete set of responses, but a subset of the best items matching the query is sufficient, processing time can be reduced by eliminating from consideration the record identifiers for certain query terms. In particular, when the query is formulated as a set of terms without Boolean operators (a vector query), and the query-document similarity is measured by the number of common terms between query- and document-term vectors, the *m* nearest neighbors to the query — that is, the *m* records with the great-

Figure 8.6 Recall-precision variations. (a) Narrow query formulations produce high precision, low recall. (b) Broad query formulations produce high recall, low precision.

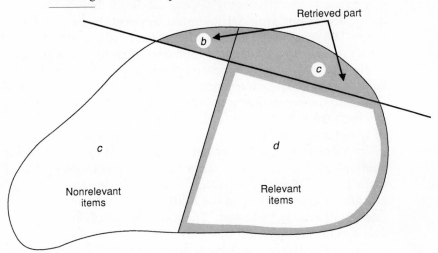

(a)

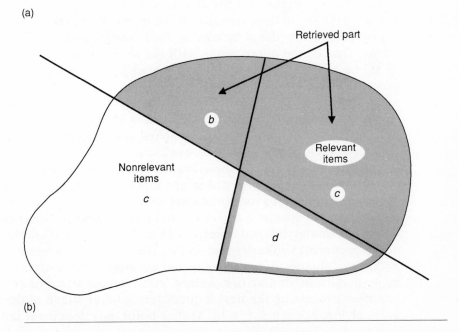

(b)

est similarity to the query — can be identified in substantially less time than the set of all n documents ($n >> m$) that may have terms in common with the query. [16,17]

In an inverted-file environment, one way to assess similarities between a query and the stored records of a collection consists of scanning the sets of record identifiers included in the inverted lists for all query terms and computing the corresponding query-record similarity for each record identifier included in one of these lists. Since a given record identifier may appear on many inverted lists, the same query-document similarities must apparently be computed many times. The repeated recomputation of particular query-document similarity measurements can be avoided by introducing auxiliary vector S of dimension N whose elements are initially set equal to 0, N being the collection size. The ith element of S, S_i, will be set equal to 1 after the similarity between query Q and document D_i has been computed for the first time. By checking the state of vector S, it is then possible to avoid recomputing the same similarity coefficients. The document identifiers for the m items with the largest query-document similarities are stored in another auxiliary response vector R of dimension m. If R is appropriately updated during the course of the operations, the identifiers of the m items of maximum similarity to the query will always be known. The minimal query-document similarity *min-sim* for an item in R must also be kept available.

A program to compute query-document similarities in an inverted-file organization that uses the auxiliary R and S vectors is shown in Fig. 8.7. [16] The assumption is that the query terms are arranged in query vector Q in order of increasing document frequency of the query terms: That is, the query terms with the shortest list lengths corresponding to the smallest number of stored document identifiers are processed first. For each query term T_j the corresponding list of document identifiers $(D_{j_1}, D_{j_2}, ..., D_{jn_j})$ is considered, and the similarities between Q and each D_{ji} computed. To do this easily, one must assume that the full set of content terms attached to each document (the full document vectors) are separately available.

The program of Fig. 8.7 traverses the lists of document identifiers corresponding to each query term one at a time, computes the query-document similarities for documents that have not yet been treated, and updates the vectors S and R to avoid recomputing the same query-document similarities and to keep track of the m items with the largest query-document similarity met so far. The program is unnecessarily long, even though it avoids repeated recomputations of the same query-document similarities. Indeed, consider the situation that exists after processing the first h query terms (after step 8 of the program of Fig. 8.7, when $j = h$). At that point, any document not yet treated (that is, for which the corresponding S element is still equal to 0) obviously lacks the first h query terms. Even if all $(k-h)$ query terms not yet seen are present in such a document D, the similarity between the query and such an item may never exceed the current min-sim value. In that case, it is obviously unnecessary to treat the lists of document identifiers for the $(k-h)$ query terms not yet seen, because none of the documents on any of these lists will exhibit a query-document similarity exceeding that of any of the m items already included in the R list. Since the query terms are arranged in order of increasing document frequency, the longest query term lists may then remain unprocessed, resulting in substantial decreases in processing time.

Figure 8.7 Query-document similarity computation [16].

Input: query $Q = (t_1, t_2, ..., t_k)$; terms listed in
            increasing document-frequency (list-length) order

            vector S [1:N] specifying documents D_i for which
            sim(D_i, Q) has already been computed

            vector R [1:m] specifying the m documents with largest
            similarities with query

            minimal similarity min-sim of any item in R

1. **for** j = 1 to k while not done (for each query term)

2.   **for** i = 1 to n_j (for each document on list for term j)

3.   **if** D_{ji} in S **then** ignore it;

4.   **else** compute sim(Q, D_{ji}) and set
               corresponding term in S equal to 1;

5.   if sim (Q, D_{ji}) > min-sim
               then replace item with lowest similarity in R
               by D_{ji} and adjust min-sim if necessary

6.   **end if**

7.   **end if**

8.   **end for**

9. **end for**

To achieve the projected savings, it is necessary to insert a test after step 8 of Fig. 8.7 that compares *min-sim*, the smallest similarity of any of the m best items, with the maximum reachable similarity of any item not yet seen after processing the hth query-term list. The maximum reachable similarity is obtained by assuming that all $k-h$ query terms not yet seen are indeed present in each unprocessed item. If the query-document similarity is computed by using, for example, the simple Dice coefficient [18]

$$\frac{2 \times (\text{number of matching terms in } Q \text{ and } D)}{(\text{number of terms in } D) \cdot (\text{number of terms in } Q)} \qquad (8.2)$$

the upper bound for the maximum reachable query-document similarity for unseen documents at step 8 of Fig. 8.7 is $2 \cdot (k-h)/(p+k)$, where k is the query length, and p is the assumed length of the shortest document (the one with the smallest number of terms in the collection). To limit the number of query-term lists to be processed, the test program of Fig. 8.8(a) can be inserted after step 8 in the program of Fig. 8.7.

The strategy of Fig. 8.8(a), which applies after reaching the end of each query-term list, can also be used in modified form when operating in the middle of a given list of document identifiers. Consider the situation arising after processing document D_{hi} (the ith document on query term list h). Any document D' on the hth list that has not yet been seen is known not to carry the first $h-1$ query terms. Hence the maximum possible similarity between any such document and query Q occurs for items that contain the remaining $k-h+1$ query terms. Assuming once again that the query-document similarity is measured by the Dice coefficient with unweighted terms (expression 8.2), the test of Fig. 8.8(b) can be inserted during the processing of new documents included in each inverted list following step 3 of the program of Fig. 8.7. [17] In Fig. 8.8(b), $|D'|$ represents the number of terms in each document D'.

The program of Fig. 8.7 identifies the m nearest neighbors of a given query Q, that is, the m documents exhibiting the highest query-document similarity. A related strategy can be used to find nearest neighbors for the documents of a collection rather than for the queries. For example, in constructing groups or clusters of related documents, or networks of related items, each stored item can be related to one or more close neighbors. The program of Fig. 8.9, a modification of those of Figs. 8.7 and 8.8, finds the one nearest neighbor for each of N documents. [19]

The program of Fig. 8.9 uses two auxiliary vectors of dimension N, known as NEIGHBOR and SIM(NEIGHBOR), respectively. The ith element of NEIGHBOR, that is NEIGHBOR(i), contains D_j if D_j is the nearest neighbor to D_i. Similarly, the ith element of SIM(NEIGHBOR) contains the actual similarity coefficient between D_i and D_j, where D_j is the nearest neighbor of D_i. The program takes up the term lists from the inverted index for terms included in each of the first $N-1$ documents. Given a list of document identifiers for a term in document D_d, all documents on that list with indices greater than d (that is, all documents between D_{d+1} and D_{dn_i}) are compared with D_d, and the nearest-neighbor information is updated as necessary. The upper bounds U_1 and U_2 are computed as before, and the processing stops when the level of similarity of the current nearest neighbor of each document cannot be reached by any document not yet processed.

The program does not use a vector S of the type included in Fig. 8.7 to store the indices of documents already seen. Since each document D_d is compared only against documents with higher indices from D_{d+1} to D_N, duplicate similarity computations will be performed only when such documents appear on several different term lists for a given document.

A related program can be constructed to obtain the k nearest neighbors for each of N items, instead of the single nearest neighbor as in Fig. 8.9. A system to compute the k nearest neighbors of each document in a collection can be used as an inexpensive document grouping or clustering system, where only the most important $N \cdot k/2$ similar document pairs are considered instead of all possible $N(N-1)/2$ pairs. [20]

Figure 8.8 Optimization procedures for inverted-list processes. (a) Test limiting the number of inverted lists to be processed [16]. (b) Test eliminating individual documents from consideration [17].

Insert after step 8 of Fig. 8.7

8a. Compute U_1 (upper bound 1)
$$U_1 = 2(k - h)/(p + k)$$

8b. **if** $(U_1 < \text{min-sim})$
        then stop

8c. **end if**

(a)

Insert after step 3 of Fig. 8.7

3a. **else** compute U_2 (upper bound 2)
$$U_2 = 2(k - h + 1)/|D'| + k)$$

3b. **if** $U_2 < \text{min-sim}$
        then ignore D' and take up next document

(b)

All the preceding programs are based on the assumption that, in addition to the usual inverted-term lists, the full indexing vectors (the full set of index terms) pertaining to the documents of a collection are separately available. These index vectors are needed to compute the query-document or document-document similarities in one operation. When index vectors for documents are not stored, partial similarities between documents must be accumulated little by little as the individual terms contained in these documents are processed one at a time. Thus when the jth term list is processed for a given document D_d, it is possible to obtain only a partial similarity attributable to the joint presence of term j in D_d and the other documents on the list. Since the full similarity between any pair of items cannot then be known before

---

Figure 8.9 Computation of nearest neighbor for each of N documents [19].

Set NEIGHBOR [1:N] and SIM(NEIGHBOR) [1:N) to 0

for d = 1 to N − 1 (for each document up to D_{N-1})

  for j = 1 to k (for the next term in document D_d)

    for i = d + 1 to d_{n_j} (for the next document D' on
    the jth term list of document D_d)
    compute $U_2 (D',D_d)$

    if $U_2 \leq$ SIM(NEIGHBOR(d))
      then take next document D' **end if**

    else compute $sim\ (D',D_d)$

      if $sim\ (D',D_d) >$ SIM(NEIGHBOR(d))
        then set NEIGHBOR (d) to D' and
        set SIM(NEIGHBOR(d)) to $sim\ (D',D_d)$ **end if**

      else if $sim\ (D',D_d) >$ sim(NEIGHBOR(i))
        then set NEIGHBOR(i) to D_d and
        set SIM(NEIGHBOR(i)) to $sim\ (D',D_d)$ **end if**

  end for

  compute $U_1 (D*, D_d)$ where $D*$ is document not yet
               seen with shortest term list

  if $U_1 <$ sim(NEIGHBOR(d))
    then take up next document D_{d+1} **end if**

  end for

end for

processing the list for the last common term, enough storage space must be allocated to accumulate the partial similarities for all distinct pairs of items. However, optimization steps based on the maximum possible similarity that remains to be computed at each step between a pair of items can be inserted as before. [21]

The programs of Figs. 8.7–8.9 are based on the assumption that similarity between items depends on the number (and possibly the weight) of jointly assigned terms. In modified form, the methodology can be extended to similarity computations between Boolean queries and document vectors by using an extended system of Boolean logic of the type described in Chapter 10.

8.6 Text-scanning Systems

8.6.1 General Considerations

All the retrieval procedures examined up to now are based on the use of inverted-term indexes for all terms or attribute values that characterize the items in a collection. Inverted indexes are attractive in operational situations where the file sizes are substantial, almost always the case, because fast response times can be achieved using information stored directly in the inverted index lists.

When file sizes are small and texts of stored items are limited in length, answers might be obtained in response to information requests by directly accessing the document texts in the main record file, without consulting any intermediary index. In these circumstances a text-scanning operation must be used to match the words or terms used in the information queries with the texts of the stored documents. For example, to find documents dealing with bananas, one might check the document texts to find those that contain the text word BANANA.

Text-scanning operations must be based on a comparison of individual characters in query formulations with words in stored document texts. As the number of characters in document texts increases, text scanning becomes more expensive, and a character-by-character comparison is then usually too inefficient for practical use. One must then either turn to inverted file technologies, or speed up the text-scanning systems as shown later in this section. Alternatively, the text sizes can be reduced by using text-compression systems, such as the superimposed coding or binary text signature systems previously described, before the text-scanning operations. [22,23]

All text-scanning systems suffer from the inflexibility inherent in any exact character-matching system. Clearly the query string APPLE does not match the text entry APPLES. When queries are formulated as multiword character strings, word order poses an additional problem, because a query on information retrieval does not, of course, directly match a document text containing the phrase "retrieval of information." Matching problems arise in such cases even when high-frequency words such as "of" are removed before the character comparisons. Text scanning usually proves most productive when short texts with stereotyped vocabularies are used.

8.6.2 Elementary String Matching

The elementary text-scanning operation, also known as a *string search*, is performed by scanning the query and document texts in normal left-to-right order, one character at a time, and performing pairwise character comparisons. The assumption is that each document consists of a character string $S = s_1 s_2 \ldots s_n$ of n individual characters (alphabetic symbols, numbers, or other special characters). Each query statement or search pattern $P = p_1 p_2 \ldots p_m$ is also represented as a character string of m characters, the assumption being that $m \leq n$.

The elementary pattern matcher traverses both S and P, starting with the left-most characters in each string. Two pointers keep track of the traversal sequence, denoted i and j for strings S and P, respectively. Initially i and j are set equal to 1, so that the first two characters compared are s_1 and p_1. Whenever a character match is detected, both pointers are incremented by 1, implying that the next character pairs to be matched are s_2 and p_2, followed by s_3 and p_3, and so on, until either a complete match is obtained between the characters in P and some substring of S, or a mismatch is found between some pair of characters of S and P. In the latter case the j pointer is reset to 1, but the i pointer is reset to a position one greater than its previous initial position. This effectively shifts the pattern P to the right by one position along the text string S, and readies the system for the comparison of s_2 with p_1, s_3 with p_2, and so on.

An elementary string-matching program appears in Fig. 8.10. [24] If a match is detected between S and P, the program returns i to indicate that P is the left-most substring of S starting at the ith character position of S. If P is not a substring of S, the program of Fig. 8.10 returns 0. This elementary character-match strategy is efficient when string P matches a substring of S early in the comparison process. When P matches the tail of a long text string, the number of needed character comparisons grows. The worst case occurs when strings P and S are nearly identical and a mismatch is discovered at the very end of the respective strings. In that case, the number of needed character comparisons between character pairs can be as high as the product of the string and pattern lengths $(n \cdot m)$. An example of this worst-case situation is shown in Fig. 8.11.

In most situations, the probability of a mismatch between a text string and a query pattern is much greater than the probability of a match. Hence a rough testing procedure capable of recognizing most mismatches very rapidly will allow more time to be spent processing cases in which a mismatch is not immediately detectable, and in which the possibility of a complete match actually exists. The substring test devised by Harrison provides such a rough test method. [25] In particular, the test determines whether a query pattern P can match some substring S_i of a string S: When the testing process $T(P,S_i)$ produces a negative result, P cannot possibly be a substring of S_i; on the other hand, when the test $T(P,S_i)$ is satisfied, P may or may not be equal to S_i, and a complete character-by-character match is then needed to determine the question unequivocally.

The substring test uses a bit vector of length p $(b_1,b_2,...,b_p)$ that is initially set to 0. For each of the two strings S and P, a *hashed k-signature* H^k is constructed by taking overlapping substrings s of length k, computing a hash function $i = \text{hash}(s)$ for each such substring, and setting the corresponding bit b_i equal to 1 in the p-digit bit vector. Thus given strings S and P of size n and m, respectively, L_1 overlapping segments of length k are recognized in S where $n = L_1+k-1$, and L_2 segments of length k in P, where $m = L_2 + k-1$. Each L_1 segment of S and each L_2 segment of P will turn on one bit in the hashed k-signatures $H^k(S)$ and $H^k(P)$, respectively. A sample hash transformation for segments of length 3 ($k=3$) is shown in Fig. 8.12.

Figure 8.10 Elementary string search.

1. Initialization :   set i and j equal to 1

2. Failure :   if $i > n - m + 1$

    then terminate with result 0

    (P is bigger than S, or P has been shifted to the right of S)

3. Test conditions :   else if $(p_j = s_{i + j - 1})$ and $(j = m)$

    then terminate with result i

    else if $(p_j = s_{i + j - 1})$ and $(j < m)$

    then increment j ($j \leftarrow j + 1$) and repeat test step 3

    else if $(p_j \neq s_{i + j - 1})$

    then reset j to 1 and increment i

    ($i \leftarrow i + 1$) and test for failure (step 2)

$S = s_1 s_2 \cdots s_n$ is a text string.

$P = p_1 p_2 \cdots p_m$ is a query pattern ($m \leq n$).

It is obvious that if P is a substring of S, all bits b_i set equal to 1 in $H^k(P)$ must also be set equal to 1 in $H^k(S)$. That is, there can be no match between P and S if $H^k(S)$ does not cover $H^k(P)$ (when at least one bit in $H^k(P) = 1$ and the corresponding bit in $H^k(S)=0$). When $H^k(S)$ covers $H^k(P)$ and all 1 bits in $H^k(P)$ are also equal to 1 in $H^k(S)$, P may or may not be a substring of S, the probability of a false match between $H^k(P)$ and $H^k(S)$ being $(1-(1 - 1/p)^{L_2})^{L_1}$. [25] In such a case, an exact string comparison is needed to ascertain whether an exact match actually exists.

A number of alternative string-matching methods are faster than the elementary character-by-character system, and at the same time do not rely on approximate substring tests of the type just described. These methods are briefly examined in the new few subsections.

Figure 8.11 Elementary string-match system.

step 1 S = a a a a a a .... a a b

           P = a a b

              ✓ ✓ ⊗

- -

step 2 P =   a a b

                ✓ ✓ ⊗

- -

step 3 P =   a a b

                 ✓ ✓ ⊗

- -

     .
     .
     .

step n - 3 P =   a a b

                         ✓ ✓ ⊗

- -

step n - 2 P =   a a b

                        ✓ ✓ ✓ (match)

     ✓ match
     ⊗ mismatch

Figure 8.12 Construction of hashed k signature $H^k(S)$.

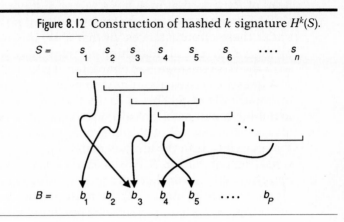

8.6.3 Fast String Matching

The elementary string matcher is characterized by a pattern shift of length 1 when a mismatch is detected between any character pair in S and P. Such a minimal displacement of P with respect to S presumes that nothing is known about the character composition of either P or S. One would expect, however, that if the query pattern P could be analyzed before the characters are compared, and if the occurrence patterns of the various string characters in P could be ascertained in advance, then the string-matching programs could be speeded up substantially. When P is preanalyzed, an exhaustive comparison of P and S is no longer necessary, and the string match can be performed by comparing the characters of P against only certain strategically located portions of S. [26-28]

The method originated by Knuth, Morris, and Pratt (the KMP method), as extended by Aho and Corasick, [26–27] scans the characters in a left-to-right mode, as described earlier for the elementary string matcher. However, when a mismatch occurs between a certain character pair, an optimum shift is carried out for the pattern P, instead of an automatic pattern shift by one character position. Consider the situation represented in Fig. 8.13, where an initial substring of P (a head of P) matches a substring of S before a pair of mismatched characters is detected (s_{i+6} and p_5). In view of the already matching substrings of P and S, it is evident that no new match can be obtained between any of the already matching parts of P and S except when some head of the matching part of P is identical to a tail of the matching part of S. For example, if p_1 and p_2 (a head of length 2 of P that is known to coincide with s_{i+2} and s_{i+3} in Fig. 8.13) also matches s_{i+4} and s_{i+5} (the tail of length 2 of the matching part of S), then a right shift by two positions produces a new coincidence between substrings of S and P. When no head of P exists that matches a tail of S, there is no point in a partial shift of P; the respective characters will not possibly be able to match under these circumstances. In that case, the pattern P can be shifted all the way across the matching portions, so as to bring p_1 into position with the first mismatched character of S (s_{i+6} in Fig. 8.13).

A question arises about how to detect coincidences between heads of P and tails of S. This is easily done by noting that since only the matching portions of S and P are involved, any matching tail of S is also a matching tail of P. The problem now consists of finding heads that match tails in the already matching part of P, that is, of detecting repeating portions in P. This is easily done by preanalyzing the query pattern P. Whenever there are no repeating character sequences in an already matching part of P, the pattern can always be shifted across the complete matching character portion. An illustration of the KMP pattern matcher appears in Fig. 8.14, [29] in which a shift by one character position in P is performed when no matching characters are detected in P and S (steps 1 and 3). In step 2, a full shift of P is made across the matching substring because no repeating parts exist in the matching portion of P (abc). Finally, in step 4 a partial shift of P is made to bring the repeating part of the matching pattern into position.

In actual pattern matching, the appropriate pattern shifts that occur in various circumstances must be known in advance. An output indicator signals three types of data: (1) when a pattern P completely matches a substring of S, (2) the needed shift pattern in P for a mismatched character pair at each character position of the pattern, and (3) the needed shift pattern in P for a matched character pair at each position. When a match exists between a character pair, the shift is predictable because the following character pair must be matched next (except, of course, when the end of the pattern is reached). When a mismatch is detected, the amount of shift in P depends on the configuration of the particular characters included in P. Table 8.4 contains the shift information for pattern P after a mismatch at a given character position for the sample pattern of Fig. 8.14 (abcabcacab).

Figure 8.13 KMP string matching.

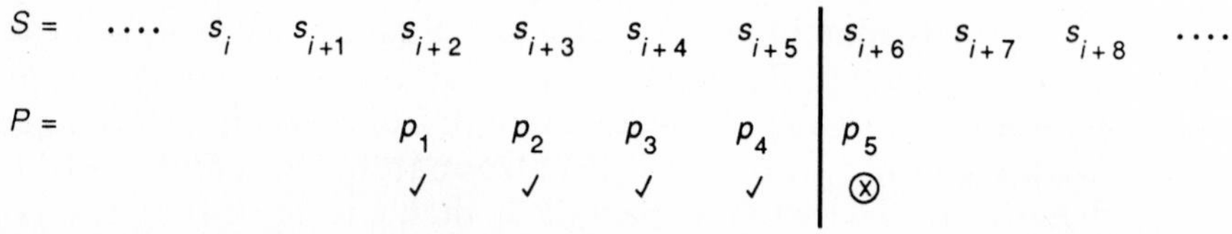

$S = \quad \cdots \quad s_i \quad s_{i+1} \quad s_{i+2} \quad s_{i+3} \quad s_{i+4} \quad s_{i+5} \quad \bigg| \quad s_{i+6} \quad s_{i+7} \quad s_{i+8} \quad \cdots$

$P = \qquad\qquad\qquad\qquad p_1 \quad p_2 \quad p_3 \quad p_4 \quad \bigg| \quad p_5$

$\qquad\qquad\qquad\qquad\quad \checkmark \quad\ \checkmark \quad\ \checkmark \quad\ \checkmark \quad \bigg| \quad \otimes$

Figure 8.14 String match using KMP method.

P : a b c a b c a c a b

S : b a b c b a b c a b c a a b c a

⊗

     step 1 : no match with character one of string *S* ;
                hence shift *P* right by one

P :   a b c a b c a c a b

S : b a b c b a b c a b c a a b c a

   ✓ ✓ ✓ ✓ ⊗

     step 2 : mismatch after three matching characters;
                no repeating portions in matching part abc;
                hence align first character of *P* with
                mismatched character in *S*

P :   a b c a b c a c a b

S : b a b c b a b c a b c a a b c a

        ⊗

     step 3 : mismatched first character pair implies
                shift of *P* by one character position

P :   a b c a b c a c a b

S : b a b c b a b c a b c a a b c a

      ✓ ✓ ✓ ✓ ✓ ✓ ⊗

     step 4 : matching substring abcabca : longest
                repeating portion in matching part is abca:
                hence shift pattern *P* right by three places to
                bring in coincidence with repeating portion

P :   a b c a b c a c a b

S : b a b c b a b c a b c a a b c a

         ✓ ✓ ✓ ✓ ⊗

     step 5 : matching status at end of sample string *S*

Table 8.4 shows that the amount of shift at each point depends on the character position of the mismatched character (i) and on the length of the repeating string in the already matched part of the pattern (L). A mismatch in the first character position of the pattern always entails a shift of 1. Thereafter the shift following the detection of a mismatch in character position i of the pattern entails a shift of length ($i-L+1$) in the pattern. Because the scanning method and the pattern shifts used in the KMP method are carried out uniformly from left to right, the process can be used for multiword patterns, as well as for comparisons of several different pattern strings P made in parallel with the same text string S. Such a parallel comparison becomes useful when an or query is processed — for example, (A or B or C). The solution then consists of constructing transition (shift) tables of the type shown in Table 8.4 for the individual query terms and performing all term comparisons in parallel. It can be shown that, using the KMP method, the expected number of character comparisons needed to match a string S and a query pattern P is of order ($n+m$) corresponding to the sum of the lengths of P and S. [26,27]

An alternative string-matching system, even faster than the KMP method, which also depends on preanalysis of the query pattern, is due to Boyer and Moore (BM). [28] Using the BM method, the pattern is scanned right to left, starting with the right-most character in the pattern. The advantage of the right-to-left shift is that large pattern shifts

Table 8.4 Computation of shift for mismatched character pair in KMP method for example of Fig. 8.14.

Mismatch in Character Position of Pattern P	Mismatched Character	Length of Repeating String in Matching Portion	Amount of Shift of Pattern P
1	a	0	1
2	b	0	1
3	c	0	2
4	a	0	3
5	b	1	3
6	c	2	3
7	a	3	3
8	c	4	3
9	a	0	8
10	b	1	8

become possible when a mismatched string character is known not to occur in particular positions of the pattern. Consider, for example, the pattern CREAM and the string BANANA ^ CREAM ^ PIE. In the BM method the right-most (fifth) character of the pattern (M) is matched against the fifth character of the text string (N). If these characters were identical, a leftward shift by one character position would next be used to compare the two preceding characters in position 4. Since M does not match N, however, the question is asked whether the mismatched string character N occurs elsewhere to the left of the mismatched character in the pattern. Since it does not, the pattern string can be shifted all the way across the mismatched character. This operation, known as a Δ_1 shift, is illustrated in step 1 of Fig. 8.15 for two sample text and pattern strings. The first Δ_1 shift carried out for the sample strings produces the situation shown in step 2 of the figure, where an attempt is made to match the last character of P with the 10th character of S. Since M does not match E, the query about the next occurrence of the mismatched string character E now reveals that E occurs two positions to the left in P. A Δ_1 shift of length 2 then produces the situation of step 3, where a right-to-left scan now detects five consecutive matching character pairs, signaling a complete match between S and P.

A second shift pattern, known as a Δ_2 shift, is used in the BM method when some tail of P already matches some substring of S, and a mismatched character pair is detected further to the left. In that case, any successful pattern shift must restore the match conditions for the already matching part of P. Hence the question is asked where else in the pattern the already matching part of P recurs further to the left; a Δ_2 shift is then carried out to bring this second occurrence of the matching substring in coincidence with the matching portion of S.

A Δ_2 shift is illustrated in Fig. 8.16(a), where the matching substring cab recurs five positions to the left in P. A Δ_2 shift of 5 thus restores the earlier match conditions. Since a mismatched character pair also exists, the Δ_1 test reveals that the mismatched string character (d) does not occur in P; hence a Δ_1 shift of 7 across the mismatched character pair is in order, as shown in Fig. 8.16(b). In the BM string-matching system, both Δ_1 and Δ_2 tests are made at each step to determine the next location in P of any mismatched string character (the Δ_1 test), as well as the next location of any already matching substring portion of P (the Δ_2 test). Since both test conditions must be satisfied to achieve complete coincidence between P and any substring of S, the pattern shift carried out at each step can be the maximum between the calculated Δ_1 and Δ_2 shifts. For the illustration of Fig. 8.16, the maximum shift is the Δ_1 shift of seven positions.

When an already matching part exists between P and S, but the Δ_1 shift across the mismatched character produces the maximum shift, as in Figs. 8.16(a) and (b), the Δ_1 shift across the mismatched character places in coincidence a head of P with the previously matching tail of P. Hence an extended Δ_1 shift can be used that places in coincidence any matching positions between heads and tails of P. If no such matching substrings exist in P, the Δ_1 shift can be extended across the previously matching string portions. In Fig. 8.16 a head of length 2 in P (ab) matches a tail of length 2; hence the Δ_1 shift can be extended beyond the mismatched character to bring the matching head in coincidence with the previously matching tail of P. This produces a shift of eight for the previous example, (see Fig. 8.16c).

Figure 8.15 Δ_1 shift in BM pattern matching.

S : B A N A N A$_\wedge$C R E A M

P : C R E A M

         $\otimes$

    step 1   mismatched string character N; N does not occur elsewhere in pattern; hence shift P to the right across mismatched character (Δ_1 shift)

S : B A N A N A$_\wedge$ C R E A M

P :   C R E A M

              $\otimes$

    step 2   mismatched string character E; E occurs two positions to the left; hence shift P by two positions

---

S : B A N A N A$_\wedge$C R E A M

P :   C R E A M

            $\checkmark$ $\checkmark$ $\checkmark$ $\checkmark$ $\checkmark$

    step 3   M matches M; take next character pair to left; A matches A; take next character pair to left; etc.

The BM string match, like the KMP method, is most effective when the query pattern contains few repeating portions. The expected number of character comparisons for BM is less than the string length n; this is substantially less than the number of comparisons needed for

---

Figure 8.16 Pattern shifting in BM string match. (a) Illustration of Δ_2 shift of five. (b) Illustration of Δ_1 shift of seven. (c) Illustration of extended Δ_1 shift of eight.

```
S :  b a b c b a d c a b c a a b c a

P :  a b c a b c a c a b

           ⊗✓ ✓ ✓
```

```
S :  b a b c b a d c a b c a a b c a

P :              a b c a b c a c a b

                   ✓ ✓ ✓
(a)
```

```
S :  b a b c b a d c a b c a a b c a

P :  a b c a b c a c a b

           ⊗✓ ✓ ✓
```

```
S :  b a b c b a d c a b c a a b c a

                 a b c a b c a c a b

                   ⊗
(b)
```

```
S :  b a b c b a d c a b c a a b c a

P :  a b c a b c a c a b

           ⊗✓ ✓ ✓
```

```
S :  b a b c b a d c a b c a a b c a

                   a b c a b c a c a b

                     ✓ ✓
(c)
```

string-matching methods that use left-to-right shifts. However, because of the complex mixture of leftward scanning and rightward shifts, the BM method is difficult to apply to situations in which several query terms must simultaneously be compared with a given text string. Furthermore, arbitrary "don't care" pattern portions — for example in M*N (representing MAN, MEN, MAIN, etc.) — are also not allowable because they do not allow the Δ_1 and Δ_2 tests in P to be carried out properly. The BM string-matching method is therefore effectively restricted to sequential searches of completely specified query patterns.

8.7 Hardware Aids to Text Searching

The text-search methods described previously are expensive to undertake when file sizes grow large. In practice, it is not unusual to be faced with files of millions of items described by tens of thousands of different terms. In these circumstances a good deal of processing time can be saved by using special-purpose hardware for text searching. For example, special equipment might be available to distribute large files among a number of parallel search mechanisms in such a way that a single search of one large file can be replaced by several parallel searches on smaller subfiles.

A typical text-search mechanism involves four main components [29–32]:

1. A general search controller that regulates machine functions, receives queries, and returns answers in the form of matching text portions.

2. A storage (or disk) subsystem that controls the storage accesses necessary to process the indexes and the main file.

3. A term comparator that actually carries out the comparisons between query patterns and text strings.

4. A query resolver that performs the logical operations necessary to determine whether an appropriate combination of different query terms is actually present in a query text.

A typical text-search device is shown in block diagram form in Fig. 8.17.

In designing a text-search device, various implementation decisions must be made that affect the method and speed of operation. Thus the entire database might be stored in a single search device, avoiding the complication of subdividing it. The records may be stored in more or less random fashion, or in order by record content. In the former case, usually the whole file must be compared against each query statement; in the latter, it may suffice to process only certain subsections of the file that exhibit some rough similarities with the query. Finally, searches can be conducted consecutively for each query, or the search operations can be overlapped or interleaved, minimizing the total search time for the entire query set.

Since query statements are often quite short, consisting of a small term set, short Boolean expressions, or short natural-language formulations, specialized text-search machines often provide a fixed store to hold a complete query formulation. The actual search is carried out by reading the main record file sequentially, and comparing the text strings on the fly with the contents of the query store. One possible implementation for the query store is a so-called *associative memory,* where all query terms can be simultaneously compared with a continuously varying text string, and full word matches are reported in the output. [33–35]

A typical associative search unit is shown in Fig. 8.18. Record text is continuously read from the main file into a data-input register, and comparisons are carried out in parallel with all cells of the associative store, and hence with all query terms simultaneously. The bit-control logic shown in the figure designates the particular character positions in the input that are actually used in the comparison operations, and

Figure 8.17 Text-search unit.

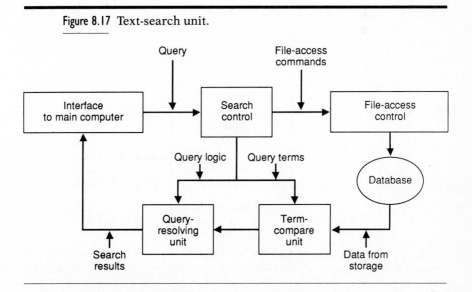

the word-control logic specifies the search conditions when multi-word text strings must be matched consecutively. Associative memories have been implemented experimentally by using logic-per-track disk technologies and fast random access memories.

An alternative string-comparison unit that can also be implemented in hardware, or in special programs using table manipulations, is based on a conceptual machine known as a *finite-state automaton* (FSA). [29–32] An FSA is characterized by individual states, usually represented on a diagram by nodes or circles; transitions between states are represented by branches between certain nodes. Transitions are controlled by the appearance of certain inputs such as individual characters of text words. The input symbols that trigger particular transitions from one state to another are usually listed along the corresponding branches of the finite-state-machine diagram. An FSA set up to recognize the occurrence of the term WIN is shown in Fig. 8.19(a). Four machine states are needed, labeled 1 to 4, including a beginning state (1) before the first input is received, and a final state (4) reached after the full input word is recognized. The three transitions are made when the three inputs W, I, and N are received consecutively.

Figure 8.18 Typical implementation of associative search device.

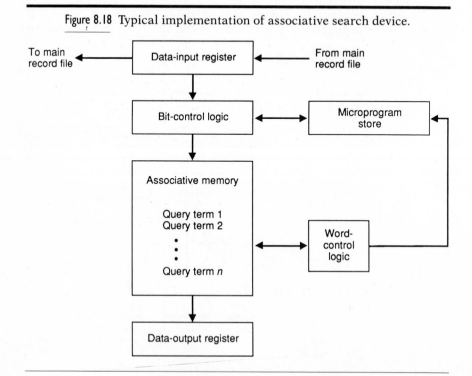

Figure 8.19(a) is incomplete because it does not include instructions for the machine actions to be followed when inputs other than W, I, and N are received. A more complete automaton for the recognition of □WIN□ is shown in Fig. 8.19(b), where □ is used to designate an inter-word boundary character such as a space; a default symbol # indicates a transition taken when any character other than a specifically desig-nated one appears at the input. The normal input characters □,W,I,N,□ produce transitions from input state 1 to output state 6. When an interword symbol is received, the transitions lead back to state 2, where the machine is ready to recognize the next character W; finally, when a symbol other than □,W,I,N is received, the transitions are made back to input state 1. In particular, when the machine is al-

Figure 8.19 Finite-state automaton configuration for term recognition (adapted from [2]). (a) Basic FSA diagram for recognition of WIN. (b) Complete automaton for recognition of □WIN□. (c) Automaton for recognition of □W*N□.

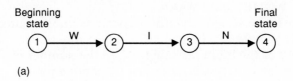

(a)

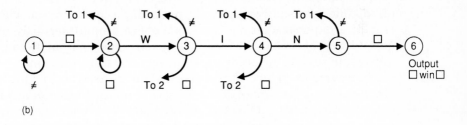

(b)

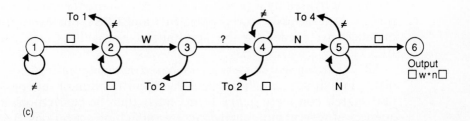

(c)

ready in state 1 and a symbol other than □ is received, the machine remains in state 1, where it is ready to recognize the full input term.

The finite-state approach can be used to recognize alternative terms because multiple transitions can be made from particular states to several successor states. Thus to recognize either WIN or WON, after the recognition of W, two successor states can be provided that apply when either I or O appears at the input, respectively. Further, arbitrary input-character strings of varying lengths can be accepted by simply remaining in a given state until a new significant input symbol is received. Thus the node arrangement of Fig. 8.19(c) can be used to recognize □W*N□, where * represents an arbitrary substring of length 1 or greater. The transition symbol ? in Fig. 8.19(c) represents a single arbitrary character whose recognition moves the automaton from state 3 to state 4. Thereafter the appearance of additional input characters other than N leaves the machine in state 4. The first N causes a transition to state 5, where the machine remains if further Ns appear. All additional N characters except the last are then treated as part of the substring of arbitrary length between W and N that is to be disregarded. The arrangement of Fig. 8.19(c) applies to strings such as WIN, WOMEN, and WARN.

The finite-state recognition system is implemented by using stored tables specifying the transitions that must occur for each possible symbol of the input alphabet. When the number of states needed in a particular situation is large, and the input alphabet is not tightly limited, the storage requirements for an FSA implementation may be substantial. Some storage space can then be saved by not storing default transitions, and by using different storage structures for different types of states. When a number of different input terms must be recognized, time can usually be saved by providing a configuration with several different character matchers that operate simultaneously and independently of each other. [36] Such "partitioned" automata can actually rest in several different states at the same time. Care must be taken, however, to insure that different states assigned to the same character matcher cannot both be active simultaneously for any input character sequence. In Fig. 8.20, the appearance of character E following B causes a transition from state 2 to states 3 and 10; the subsequent appearance of S leads from state 3 to 4 but not from 6 to 7, since state 6 was not activated by a preceding E. Hence character matcher 1 can serve simultaneously to recognize SET and BEST, but two different matchers are needed for the simultaneous recognition of BEST and BENT.

All text-string search systems are based on manipulating and recognizing individual text characters. The identification of text passages that match complete query terms must then be carried out as sequences of several individual character-matching operations. Because

Figure 8.20 Use of multiple character matchers [36].

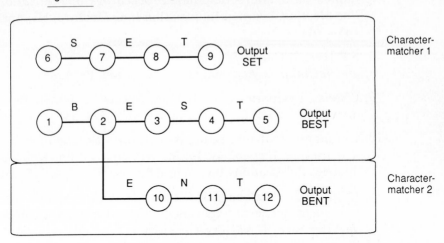

of the time needed for character matching, text-scanning systems are used principally for short texts and for files of restricted size.

References

1. F.W. Lancaster, *Information Retrieval Systems: Characteristics, Testing and Evaluation*, Second Edition, John Wiley and Sons, New York, 1979.

2. G. Salton and M.J. McGill, *Introduction to Modern Information Retrieval*, McGraw-Hill Book Co., New York, 1983.

3. G. Salton and C.S. Yang, On the Specification of Term Values in Automatic Indexing, *Journal of Documentation*, 29:4, December 1973, 351–372.

4. G. Salton, C.S. Yang, and C.T. Yu, A Theory of Term Importance in Automatic Indexing, *Journal of the ASIS*, 26:1, January-February 1975, 33–44.

5. P. Bratley and Y. Choueka, Processing Truncated Terms in Document Retrieval Systems, *Information Processing and Management*, 18:5, 1982, 257–266.

6. IBM World Trade Corp., Storage and Information Retrieval System (STAIRS) — General Information Manual, Second Edition, IBM Germany, Stuttgart, April 1972.

7. M.B. Koll, T. Noreault, and M.J. McGill, Enhanced Retrieval Techniques on a Microcomputer, *Proceedings of the National Online Meeting*, Learned Information Inc., Medford, NJ, April 1984, 165–170.

8. S.P. Harter, *Online Information Retrieval — Concepts, Principles, and Techniques*, Academic Press, Orlando, FL, 1986.

9. I. Weiss, Evaluation of ORBIT and DIALOG Using Six Data Bases, *Special Libraries*, 67:12, December 1976, 574–581.

10. C. Tenopir, Full-Text Databases, *Annual Review of Information Science and Technology*, 19, M. Williams, editor, Knowledge Industries Publications Inc., White Plains, NY, 1984, 215–246.

11. J.E. Burnett, D. Cooper, M.F. Lynch, P. Willett, and M. Wycherley, Document Retrieval Experiments Using Indexing Vocabularies of Varying Size, I. Variety Generation Symbols Assigned to the Fronts of Index Terms, *Journal of Documentation*, 35:3, 1979, 197–206.

12. P. Willett, Document Retrieval Experiments Using Indexing Vocabularies of Varying Size, II. Hashing, Truncation, Digram and Trigram Encoding of Index Terms, *Journal of Documentation*, 35:4, December 1979, 296–305.

13. C.W. Cleverdon, Optimizing Convenient On-line Access to Bibliographic Data Bases, *Information Services and Use*, 4:1, 1984, 37–47.

14. C.W. Cleverdon, J. Mills and E.M. Keen, Factors Determining the Performance of Indexing Systems, Volume 1 — Design, Aslib Cranfield Research Project, Cranfield, England, 1966.

15. S. Treu, Testing and Evaluation — Literature Review, *Electronic Handling of Information: Testing and Evaluation*, A. Kent, O.E. Taulbee, J. Belzer, and G.D. Goldstein, editors, Thompson Book Co., Washington, DC, 1967, 71–88.

16. A.F. Smeaton and C.J. van Rijsbergen, Nearest Neighbor Problem in Information Retrieval, *SIGIR Forum*, 16:1, Summer 1981, 83–87.

17. F. Murtagh, A Very Fast Exact Nearest-Neighbor Algorithm for Use in Information Retrieval, *Information Technology: Research and Development*, 1:4, October 1982, 275–283.

18. C.J. van Rijsbergen, *Information Retrieval*, Second Edition, Butterworths, London, 1979.

19. W.B. Croft, R. Wolf, and R. Thompson, A Network Organization Used for Document Retrieval, Proceedings of the 6th International ACM SIGIR Conference on Research and Development in Information Retrieval, *SIGIR Forum*, 17:4, Summer 1983, 178–188.

20. P. Willett, A Note on the Use of Nearest Neighbors for Implementing Single Linkage Document Classifications, *Journal of the ASIS*, 35:3, May 1984, 149–152.

21. C. Buckley and A.F. Lewit, Optimization of Inverted Vector Searches, *Proceedings of the Eighth International ACM SIGIR Conference on Research and Development in Information Retrieval*, Montreal, June 1985, Association for Computing Machinery, New York, 1985, 97–110.

22. P.A. Larson, A Method for Speeding Up Text Retrieval, *Data Base*, 15:2, Winter 1984, 19–23.

23. D. Tsichritzis and S. Christodoulakis, Message Files, *ACM Transactions on Office Information Systems*, 1:1, January 1983, 88–89.

24. A.V. Aho, J.E. Hopcroft, and J.D. Ullman, *The Design and Analysis of Computer Algorithms*, Addison-Wesley Publishing Co., Reading, MA, 1974.

25. M.C. Harrison, Implementation of the Substring Test by Hashing, *Communications of the ACM*, 14:12, December 1971, 777–779.

26. A.V. Aho and M.J. Corasick, Efficient String Matching: An Aid to Bibliographic Search, *Communications of the ACM*, 18:6, June 1975, 333–340.

27. D.E. Knuth, J.H. Morris, and V.R. Pratt, Fast Pattern Matching In Strings, *SIAM Journal of Computing*, 6:2, June 1977, 323–350.

28. R.S. Boyer and J.S. Moore, A Fast String Searching Algorithm, *Communications of the ACM*, 20:10, October 1977, 762–772.

29. G. Salton, Automatic Information Retrieval, *Computer*, 13:9, September 1980, 41–57.

30. L.A. Hollaar, Hardware Systems for Text Information Retrieval, Proceedings of the Sixth Annual ACM SIGIR Conference on Research and Development in Information Retrieval, *SIGIR Forum*, 17:4, Summer 1983, 3–9.

31. R. Haskin, Hardware for Searching Very Large Text Databases, *Proceedings of the Fifth Workshop on Computer Architecture for Non-Numeric Processing*, Association for Computing Machinery, New York, March 1980, 49–56.

32. D.C. Roberts, A Specialized Computer Architecture for Text Retrieval, *Proceedings of the Fourth Workshop on Computer Architecture for Non-Numeric Processing*, Association for Computing Machinery, New York, August 1978, 51–59.

33. E.J. Schuegraf and R.M. Lee, A Proposal for Associative File Store with Run Time Indexing, Part I: System Description, *Information Technology: Research and Development*, 2:2/3, July 1983, 73–88.

34. B. Parhami, Associative Memories and Processors: An Overview and Selected Bibliography, *Proceedings of the IEEE*, 61:6, June 1973, 722–730.

35. F.J. Burkowski, A Hardware Hashing Scheme in the Design of a Multiterm String Comparator, *IEEE Transactions on Computers*, C-31:9, September 1982, 825–834.

36. R.L. Haskin and L.A. Hollaar, Operational Characteristics of a Hardware Based Pattern Matcher, *Transactions on Data Base Systems*, 8:1, March 1983, 15–40.

Chapter 9

Automatic Indexing

9.1 Indexing Environment

It was seen in the last chapter that the identification and subsequent retrieval of records in response to incoming information requests usually depends on the degree of coincidence between document texts and query formulations. In principle, the computation of query-record similarities might involve a direct comparison of words or sentences used in information items. In reality, the vocabularies of normal information items show substantial variety. Also, the number of words or sentences included in many items may be so large that a complete text comparison between different information items becomes impossible. In these circumstances, it is advisable first to characterize record and query content by assigning special content descriptions, or profiles, identifying the items and representing text content. The text profiles can be used as short-form descriptions; they also serve as document, or query, surrogates during the text-search and -retrieval operations.

The process of constructing document surrogates by assigning identifiers to text items is known as *indexing*. In the past, indexing operations were normally performed intellectually by subject experts, or by trained persons with experience in assigning content descriptions. More recently, the original text of information items has frequently been used as a basis for indexing, and text analysis is now often controlled by automatic, machine-performed procedures. In either case, indexing assigns content identifiers to information items that can lead users to particular items in response to specific information requests. The assignment of well-chosen content identifiers may also be useful in relating items to each other — distinct items with largely overlapping content identifications usually cover similar or related information.

In describing the indexing environment, it is useful to make a number of basic distinctions. The first relates to the differences between *objective* and *nonobjective* text identifiers. Objective identifiers, such as author names, publisher names, dates of publications, and page numbering, apply integrally to the information items, and in general there is no dispute about how to assign them. Elaborate cataloging rules control the form and the method of assignment of these terms. [1,2] In contrast, there is no agreement about the choice and the degree of applicability of the nonobjective identifiers which relate to information or text content. This chapter is concerned largely with the choice of effective content identifiers and with automatic methods for determining the usefulness of terms.

The second distinction made in indexing concerns the use of *manual* versus *automatic* indexing methods, and the related differences between the structure of *controlled* and *uncontrolled* indexing vocabularies. When indexing is performed manually by human experts in a subject, these indexers often consult auxiliary schedules in the form of terminology lists and "scope notes" describing allowable vocabulary entries and giving instructions for the use of terms. When a knowledgeable person utilizes these indexing aids, a considerable degree of indexing uniformity can be achieved, and high-quality is sometimes obtained.

Instruction manuals and terminology schedules are hard to utilize in automatic-indexing environments. For this reason, most automatic indexing is based on manipulating the texts of the information items. In these circumstances, the indexing vocabulary is less tightly controlled than in manual indexing, and a great variety of index descriptions are normally assignable. Each text item can be retrieved with respect to a great diversity of information requests, and users have much greater freedom in formulating query statements than in systems that use controlled vocabularies.

Another major distinction in indexing context relates to the use of *single-term* indexing methods, compared with the use of *terms in context*. In the former case, the indexing products attached to the information items consist of sets of single terms, each pertaining to some aspect of text content, and term-relationship indicators are not available in the indexing products. However, indications of term relationship may be added at search time by using appropriate term combinations in query formulations. In some circumstances, the indexing vocabulary is *precoordinated* by assigning complex identifying units to the information items consisting of term phrases, or term groupings with specified relationship indications. Properly choosing and assigning precoordinated term groups is obviously much more demanding than using single-term indexing vocabularies.

In view of the complexity of indexing, any machine-indexing operation will necessarily perform imperfectly. However, the need to use a variety of different indexing experts in manual indexing environments also introduces unwanted variabilities and uncertainties that may adversely affect retrieval effectiveness. In automatic indexing environments, the lack of human expertise can be overcome by intelligent use of the free-text vocabularies in stored records and information requests. In fact, the retrieval results that can be obtained with advanced automatic indexing products are not inferior to the output generated in controlled, manually performed indexing environments. [3,4]

9.2 Indexing Aims

The effectiveness of any content analysis or indexing system is controlled by two main parameters, *indexing exhaustivity* and *term specificity*. Indexing exhaustivity reflects the degree to which all aspects of the subject matter of a text item are actually recognized in the indexing product. When indexing is exhaustive, a large number of terms are often assigned, and even minor aspects of the subject area are reflected by corresponding term assignments. The reverse obtains for nonexhaustive indexing, in which only main aspects of subject content are recognized.

Term specificity refers to the degree of breadth or narrowness of the terms. When broad terms are used for indexing, many useful information items are likely to be retrieved for the user — together with a substantial proportion of useless materials. Normally, broad terms cannot distinguish relevant from nonrelevant items. Narrow terms, on the other hand, retrieve relatively fewer items, but most of the retrieved materials are likely to be helpful to users.

In judging the effect of indexing exhaustivity and term specificity, it is convenient to refer to the previously introduced parameters of retrieval effectiveness, recall and precision. Recall (R) is the proportion of relevant material retrieved, defined as

$$R = \frac{\text{Number of relevant items retrieved}}{\text{Total number of relevant items in collection}}, \qquad (9.1)$$

while precision (*P*) is the proportion of retrieved material that is relevant, defined as

$$P = \frac{\text{Number of relevant items retrieved}}{\text{Total number of items retrieved}}. \qquad (9.2)$$

It is clear that recall and precision both vary from 0 to 1, or equivalently from 0 percent to 100 percent, and that in principle the average user wants to achieve both high recall and high precision: That is, a large proportion of the useful materials should preferably be retrieved, and at the same time a large proportion of the extraneous items should be rejected. In practice, a compromise must be reached because simultaneously optimizing recall and precision is not normally achievable. Indeed when the indexing vocabulary is narrow and specific, retrieval precision is favored at the expense of recall, since many extraneous items are then rejected, but many useful ones are as well. The reverse obtains when the indexing vocabulary is broad and nonspecific; in that case recall is favored at the expense of precision.

The average user often prefers a middle point in the performance spectrum, where neither recall nor precision is disastrously low. In that case, the indexing vocabulary must be neither too broad nor too specific. Although the term specificity may favor either recall or precision, indexing exhaustivity may affect both evaluation parameters in the same direction. A lack of exhaustivity in indexing certainly affects recall because many relevant items may not be recognized in the absence of certain kinds of index terms. At the same time, precision may be affected when the terms actually assigned are too broad to provide appropriate discrimination among terms.

In actual tests of operational retrieval services, particular choices of indexing and search policies have produced variations in performance ranging from 80 percent precision and 20 percent recall to about 10 percent precision and 80 percent recall. In many circumstances, an intermediate performance level, at which both the recall and the precision vary between 50 and 60 percent, is more satisfactory for the average user than either of the limiting performance levels that favor high recall or high precision exclusively. [5]

When a choice must be made between extreme term specificity and extreme term breadth, the former is generally preferable because the output produced by the high-recall, low-precision alternative tends to burden the user with unmanageably large piles of retrieved materials. In contrast, high-precision searches retrieve fewer items that are more easily examined. Lack of search precision is also more easily remedied than lack of recall, because precision can be ascertained by assessing the usefulness of the retrieved materials, whereas recall also depends on the relevant items in the collection that were not retrieved. Estimation methods and sampling techniques must then be used to compute recall, while precision can be obtained directly from search results. [6]

9.3 Single-term Indexing Theories

9.3.1 Term-frequency Considerations

The assignment of index terms to documents and queries is carried out in the hope of distinguishing materials that are relevant for information users from others that are extraneous. Such a characterization is unfortunately useless for purposes of actual indexing: In the absence of specific sample queries and user relevance assessments, little is known a priori about what renders an item relevant or not relevant. Instead of concentrating on the relevance or nonrelevance of particular documents, it seems reasonable first to consider the occurrence properties of the terms in complete document collections.

As noted earlier, in the composition of written texts, grammatical function words such as "and," "of," "or," and "but" exhibit approximately equal frequencies of occurrence in all the documents of a collection. Moreover, most function words are characterized by high occurrence frequencies in ordinary texts. On the other hand, nonfunction words that may actually relate to document content tend to occur with greatly varying frequencies in the different texts of a collection. Furthermore, the frequency of occurrence of nonfunction words may actually be used to indicate term importance for content representation. The following indexing method is based on the number of occurrences of particular terms in the documents of a collection: [7]

1. Eliminate common function words from the document texts by consulting a special dictionary, or stop list, containing a list of high-frequency function words.

2. Compute the term frequency tf_{ij} for all remaining terms T_j in each document D_i, specifying the number of occurrences of T_j in D_i.

3. Choose a threshold frequency T, and assign to each document D_i all terms T_j for which $tf_{ij} > T$.

Indexing policies based on computations of term frequency were used in many early indexing experiments. However, as the considerations previously mentioned about the recall and precision function of information retrieval demonstrate, the term frequency measure fulfills only one of the basic retrieval aims, recall. Indeed, a term such as "apple" occurring with reasonable frequency in particular documents certainly indicates that the corresponding items deal with apples. The assignment of the term "apple" with a high frequency weight will then help to retrieve these documents in response to appropriate queries.

Unfortunately, the precision function of retrieval is not well served by assigning high-frequency terms to document texts, because high precision implies the ability to distinguish individual documents from each other to prevent unwanted retrievals of extraneous items. A high-frequency term is therefore acceptable for indexing purposes only if its occurrence frequency is not equally high in all the documents of a collection. More concretely, the word "apple" may not be an ideal index term even though its occurrence frequency may be high in particular items. This is true in particular for a pomology collection, where almost all documents contain the word "apple" many times.

The precision function is in fact better served by terms that occur rarely in individual document collections, because such terms are certainly able to distinguish the few documents in which they occur from the many from which they are absent. If the document frequency df_j is defined as the number of documents in a collection of N documents in which term T_j occurs, then an appropriate indication of term value as a document discriminator can be given by using an inverse function of the document frequency of the term. A typical inverse document frequency (idf) factor of this type is given by log N/df_j. [8]

The two preceding observations can be combined into a single frequency-based indexing model by postulating that the best indexing terms — those that fulfill both the recall and the precision functions of retrieval — are those that occur frequently in individual documents but rarely in the remainder of the collection. A typical combined term importance indicator of this type is the product ($tf \cdot idf$) where the importance, or weight, w_{ij} of a term T_j in a document D_i is defined as the term frequency multiplied by the inverse document frequency: [9,10]

$$w_{ij} = tf_{ij} \cdot \log \frac{N}{df_j} \tag{9.3}$$

Thus an improved indexing policy consists of eliminating common function words as before, computing the value of w_{ij} for each term T_j in each document D_i, and assigning to the documents of a collection all terms with sufficiently high ($tf \cdot idf$) factors. The available experimental evidence indicates that the use of combined term frequency and document frequency factors provides a high level of retrieval.

A different but related viewpoint about automatic indexing uses the concepts of information theory, introduced in Chapter 5. In information theory, the least predictable terms in a running text — those exhibiting the smallest occurrence probabilities — carry the greatest information value. In particular, the information value of a text word with occurrence probability p is given as $-\log_2 p$, and the average information value per word for t distinct words occurring with probabilities $p_1, p_2, ..., p_t$, respectively, is

$$\bar{H} = - \sum_{k=1}^{t} p_k \log_2 p_k. \qquad (9.4)$$

The average information value of expression (9.4) has been used to derive a measure of term usefulness for indexing purposes known as the *signal-noise ratio*. [11,12] The signal-noise ratio favors terms that are perfectly concentrated in particular documents, and that do not therefore occur in the remaining documents of a collection. On the other hand, the least-useful terms are those which occur evenly in all documents of the collection. In practice, the most concentrated terms tend to be low-frequency terms, whereas the terms with even occurrence characteristics generally exhibit high frequency in a collection. The signal-noise ratio thus exhibits properties somewhat similar to those of the inverse document-frequency factor, and available data show that little is gained by replacing the frequency-based measures of term value with related concepts of information theory. [10]

9.3.2 Term-discrimination Value

It was mentioned earlier that a desirable property of useful index terms is the ability to distinguish the documents of a collection from each other. In the previous section the discrimination value of the terms was approximated by using term specificity, evaluated as a function of inverse document frequency.

Consider the collection representation of Fig. 9.1, in which each x represents a particular document of a collection, and the distance between two xs in the figure is assumed to be inversely proportional to the similarity between the respective term assignments. That is, when two documents are assigned very similar term sets, the corresponding points in the document configuration appear close together; the reverse occurs when the corresponding term sets are dissimilar. Given the space configuration of Fig. 9.1, it appears reasonable to approximate the value of a term as a document discriminator by using for this purpose the type of change occurring in the space configuration when a term is assigned to the documents of a collection. In particular, when a good discriminator is assigned to the documents of a collection, the few items to which the term is assigned will be distinguished from the rest of the collection; this should increase the average distance between the items in the collection and hence produce a document space less dense than before (see Fig. 9.1b). On the other hand, when a high-frequency term is assigned that does not discriminate between the items of a collection, such a term will appear in many of the documents, and its assignment will render the documents more similar. This is reflected in an increase in document *space density* (see Fig. 9.1c).

This argument suggests that the term discrimination value dv_j of term j be computed as the difference of the space densities before and after term assignment of term j to the documents of a collection: [9,10,13]

$$dv_j = Q - Q_j.$$

The space densities Q and Q_j, before and after the assignment of term T_j, respectively, can be computed in various ways, the conceptually simplest one being to use simply the average pairwise similarity between all pairs of distinct items:

$$Q = \frac{1}{N(N-1)} \sum_{\substack{i=1}}^{N} \sum_{\substack{k=1 \\ i \neq k}}^{N} \text{sim}(D_i, D_k) \tag{9.5}$$

where $\text{sim}(D_i, D_k)$ represents a similarity coefficient between documents D_i and D_k based on the similarity of the respective index-term assignments.

The formula of expression (9.5) shows that good discriminators capable of spreading out the document space are assigned positive discrimination values, dv_j, because the average similarity between the items will be smaller after assignment of term T_j than before. Positive

Figure 9.1 Document space configuration illustrating discrimination value of terms. (a) Before term assignment. (b) After assignment of good discriminator. (c) After assignment of poor discriminator.

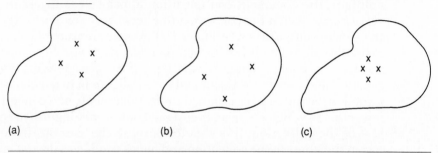

(a)   (b)   (c)

discrimination values are usually associated with certain medium-frequency terms that appear neither too rarely nor too frequently in a collection. High-frequency terms, assigned to many documents of a collection, are analogously assigned negative discrimination values. Finally, very low-frequency terms that appear in only one or two documents do not affect space density one way or the other; the corresponding term discrimination values are then close to zero. The main variations of term-discrimination values with document frequencies of the terms are represented in Fig. 9.2. The illustration shows that unlike the inverse document frequency factor, N/df_j, which decreases steadily with increasing document frequency, the discrimination value of a term first increases from zero to positive as the document frequency of the term increases, and then decreases sharply as the document frequency becomes still larger. This indicates that a term-weighting formula such as

$$w_{ij} = tf_{ij} \cdot dv_j, \qquad\qquad (9.6)$$

which combines the term frequency of term T_j inside a particular document D_i with the term-discrimination value, can produce a somewhat different ranking of term usefulness than the previously used $(tf \cdot idf)$ function of expression (9.3).

The space-density computation of expression (9.5) is based on the use of the $N(N-1)$ pairwise similarities between distinct document pairs. A more efficient space-density computation is based on the use of a dummy document, known as the *document centroid*, defined as the average document located in the center of the document space. In particular, if a document is represented by a document vector of the form $D_i = (d_{i1}, d_{i2}, \ldots., d_{it})$, and the centroid C appears as $C = (c_1, c_2, \ldots, c_t)$, the jth centroid element c_j may simply be assigned the average value of

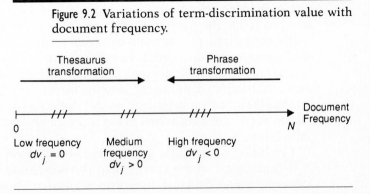

Figure 9.2 Variations of term-discrimination value with document frequency.

the jth terms in all the documents of the collection, that is,

$$c_j = \sum_{k=1}^{N} d_{kj}. \tag{9.7}$$

Given a centroid C for the document collection, the space density Q can then be redefined as

$$Q = \frac{1}{N} \sum_{k=1}^{N} \text{sim}\,(C,D_k) \tag{9.8}$$

Evaluating expression (9.8) involves only the N similarity coefficients between the centroid and each document in the collection. Available evidence indicates that the simplified formula of expression (9.8) produces term-discrimination values generally similar to those obtainable with the more complex formula of expression (9.5). [14]

The term-discrimination value, like the previously used inverse document frequency, depends on the global properties of the terms in a complete document collection. In actual fact, a desirable parameter of term value for indexing purposes would measure the differences in term characteristics that occur between relevant and nonrelevant items of a collection — or equivalently the inverse in the average distance between relevant and nonrelevant items in the document space — rather than increases in the pairwise distance between *all* documents of a collection. In practice, relevance properties of documents are not sufficiently well known at the time documents are indexed to make the use of an exact formula reasonable. Thus in practice the simplified assumptions inherent in the definition of expression (9.6) must be used.

❖ 9.3.3 Probabilistic Term Weighting

When inverse document frequency or term-discrimination value is used to judge the usefulness of a term for indexing purposes, potentially important distinctions between term occurrences in relevant and nonrelevant documents are disregarded. This may be surprising in view of the aim of indexing, that is, distinguishing relevant and nonrelevant items in order to retrieve the former and reject the latter. The *probabilistic* term-weighting model makes explicit distinctions between occurrences of terms in the relevant and nonrelevant items of a collection.

Consider in particular a collection of document vectors of the form $x = (x_1,x_2,...,x_t)$, where x_i represent the individual terms contained in document x. A decision-theoretic argument shows that an optimal document-ranking function that minimizes retrieval errors will arrange the documents in order according to the function $g(x)$, defined as follows: [15,16]

$$g(x) = \log \frac{Pr(x|\text{rel})}{Pr(x|\text{nonrel})} + \log \frac{Pr(\text{rel})}{Pr(\text{nonrel})} \cdot \qquad (9.9)$$

Factors $Pr(x|\text{rel})$ and $Pr(x|\text{nonrel})$ in expression (9.9) represent the occurrence probabilities of item x in the relevant and nonrelevant document sets, respectively, and constants $Pr(\text{rel})$ and $Pr(\text{nonrel})$ are an item's a priori probabilities of relevance and nonrelevance.

The occurrence probabilities of the documents in the relevant and nonrelevant parts of the collection must be estimated by looking at the corresponding occurrences of the individual terms x_i included in these documents. If the not entirely realistic assumption is made that the terms occur independently in the relevant and nonrelevant document portions, the probabilistic equivalences of expression (9.10) are valid:

$$Pr(x|\text{rel}) = \prod_{i=1}^{t} Pr(x_i|\text{rel})$$

$$\qquad (9.10)$$

$$Pr(x|\text{nonrel}) = \prod_{i=1}^{t} Pr(x_i|\text{nonrel}).$$

The insertion of expressions (9.10) into the earlier formula for $g(x)$ produces the following new ranking function:

$$g(x) = \sum_{i=1}^{t} \log \frac{Pr(x_i|\text{rel})}{Pr(x_i|\text{nonrel})} + \text{constants}. \qquad (9.11)$$

More specifically, given a document $D = (d_1, d_2, ..., d_t)$ where d_i represent the term weights of terms x_i (in particular, $d_i = 0$ when term x_i is absent from D), the retrieval value of D will be given by

$$g(D) = \sum_{i=1}^{t} \log \frac{Pr(x_i = d_i|\text{rel})}{Pr(x_i = d_i|\text{nonrel})} + \text{constants}. \qquad (9.12)$$

When term weights d_i are restricted to either 0 or 1, depending on whether the ith term is present in a document, one obtains

$$Pr(x_i = d_i|\text{rel}) = p_i^{d_i} (1 - p_i)^{1 - d_i} \qquad (9.13a)$$

and

$$Pr(x_i = d_i|\text{nonrel}) = q_i^{d_i}(1-q_i)^{1-d_i}, \tag{9.13b}$$

where $p_i = Pr(x_i=1|\text{rel})$, $1-p_i = Pr(x_i=0|\text{rel})$, $q_i = Pr(x_i=1|\text{nonrel})$, and $1-q_i = Pr(x_i=0|\text{nonrel})$. By inserting expressions (9.13) into (9.12), a final document-ranking function is obtained:

$$g(D) = \sum_{i=1}^{t} \log\frac{1-p_i}{1-q_i} + \sum_{i=1}^{t} d_i \log\frac{p_i(1-q_i)}{q_i(1-p_i)} + \text{constants}. \tag{9.14}$$

Expression (9.14) shows that the retrieval value of each term T_j present in a document (for which $d_j=1$) will be

$$tr_j = \log\frac{p_j(1-q_j)}{q_j(1-p_j)} = \log\frac{Pr(x_j=d_j|\text{rel})Pr(x_j=0|\text{nonrel})}{Pr(x_j=d_j|\text{nonrel})Pr(x_j=0|\text{rel})} \tag{9.15}$$

The term value tr_j is known as the *term-relevance* weight of term T_j in the collection, and its value is determined by the occurrence probabilities of the term in the relevant and nonrelevant items of a collection. [17,18] By analogy with expressions (9.3) and (9.6), which were based on the previously introduced term-frequency and discrimination-value models, the indexing value of term T_j in document D_i can be defined as

$$w_{ij} = tf_{ij} \cdot tr_j. \tag{9.16}$$

To use the term-relevance weights, tr_j, it is necessary to characterize both the relevant and nonrelevant documents of a collection, a difficult task in the absence of reliable relevance assessments for at least a representative document sample. The use of a few previously retrieved documents that have been judged for relevance may not always produce good values for tr_j, because the relevant documents retrieved may not constitute a sufficiently good sample of the complete set of relevant items. The difficulty of estimating the relevance properties of the terms and thus of obtaining reliable term-relevance weights is a principal disadvantage of the probabilistic approach in indexing.

Various proposals have been made for generating the occurrence probabilities p_j and q_j of terms in the relevant and nonrelevant document sets. When little is known about the relevance or nonrelevance of any particular document with respect to any query, the occurrence probability of a term in the nonrelevant documents (q_j) can be approximated by the occurrence probability of the term in the entire document collection (that is, $q_j = df_j/N$), because the large majority of the documents in the collection will be nonrelevant to the average query. At the same time, the occurrence probabilities of the terms in the small number of relevant items can all be assumed to be equal by using a typical constant value such as $p_j = 0.5$ for all j. [19] Using these simple assumptions, the term relevance of expression (9.15) reduces to $tr_j = \log{(N - df_j)/df_j}$, which is a form of the inverse document frequency. Thus when little is known about the relevance properties of the terms, a reasonable indexing policy consists of using the term-frequency expression (9.3) to determine the indexing value of a term.

An alternative approach to obtaining the values of p_j and q_j in the absence of information about document relevance consists of estimating the number of relevant items r_j in the collection that contain term T_j as a function of the known document frequency tf_j of term T_j. Once r_j is available, the probabilistic parameters p_j and q_j can immediately be computed as

$$p_j = \frac{r_j}{R} \qquad\qquad (9.17a)$$

and

$$q_j = \frac{df_j - r_j}{N - R}, \qquad\qquad (9.17b)$$

where R is an estimate of the total number of relevant items in the collection.

In attempting to estimate r_j given document frequency df_j, it is reasonable first to consider the situation for an ideal term that occurs only in the relevant documents. In that case, one has $r_j = df_j$. Considering next the case of a poor term, unsuitable for indexing, that is randomly sprinkled among the relevant and the nonrelevant documents of the collection, for such a term $r_j = (R/N) \cdot df_j$, where R/N is the proportion of relevant documents in the collection. In practice, an intermediate position may be taken by assuming that a suitable index term follows rules somewhere between those of the ideal and randomly occurring terms.

The graph of Fig. 9.3 shows assumed variations of r_j with document frequency df_j of a typical term T_j. (To avoid the confusion created by multiple symbols, df_j is labeled f in the figure.) The N documents of the collection are listed along the abscissa in normal retrieval order. The perfect case occurs when the first R retrieved documents containing a particular term T_j are also the R relevant documents in the collections. In that case, the variations of r with increasing document frequencies f

are expressed by equations

$$r = f \text{ when } 0 \le f \le R$$

and

$$r = R \text{ when } R < f \le N,$$

corresponding to the upper line segments in Fig. 9.3. The case of the randomly occurring term is represented by the lower line in the triangle of the figure, that is, by line $r = (R/N)f$.

The model under consideration assumes that, for a useful index term, occurrences in relevant documents are concentrated more in the first few retrieved items than in the documents retrieved late in a search. This situation is represented by the dashed line of Fig. 9.3, defined as: [20]

$$r = af \quad \text{for } 0 \le f \le R \text{ and } R/N < a < 1 \qquad (9.18a)$$

and

$$r = b + cf \quad \text{for } R < f \le N \text{ and } 0 < c < R/N. \qquad (9.18b)$$

Using the assumptions of expressions (9.18), the values of r_j can be obtained from the document frequencies f_j of the terms, which in turn leads to appropriate estimates for relevance probabilities p_j and q_j according to expressions (9.17). It can be shown that for medium values of the parameter a (that is, $a \approx 1/2$), the term relevance weight tr_j can once again be approximated by a form of the inverse document frequency. [21] This situation is based on the assumption that nothing is

---

Figure 9.3 Occurrence pattern of a typical term T_j in the relevant documents [20].

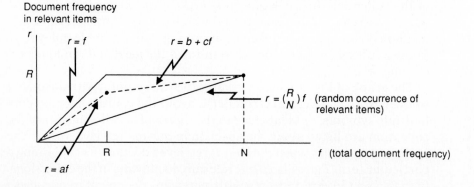

Document frequency
in relevant items

known about term occurrences in the relevant or nonrelevant documents of a collection. However, when complete relevance information is available for all term occurrences in the collection, the term occurrences for each term T_j can be characterized by an occurrence table of the kind shown in Table 9.1. Using the frequency data of the table, the occurrence probabilities p_j and q_j can be computed by expressions (9.17), and the term-relevance weight is then obtained as

$$tr_j = \log \frac{p_j(1-q_j)}{q_j(1-p_j)} = \log \left(\frac{r_j}{R-r_j} \right) \div \left(\frac{(f_j-r_j)}{N-R-f_j+r_j} \right). \qquad (9.19)$$

In operational conditions, of course, complete relevance assessments are not available for all documents in a collection, and hence the term-occurrence array of Table 9.1 cannot be constructed accurately. In most retrieval situations, however, it is customary to conduct searches iteratively as a sequence of partial search operations, which allows the results of earlier searches to be used to improve the output of later searches. One possibility consists of asking the user to assess the relevance of certain terms retrieved in earlier search operations, and using these assessments to construct improved query formulations. This process, known as *relevance feedback*, has been shown experimentally to improve retrieval effectiveness greatly.

In a relevance-feedback environment, occurrence tables like Table 9.1 can be constructed by using the term occurrences in the retrieved part of the collection, and assuming that the occurrence characteristics in the retrieved part are valid for the entire collection. From the data produced with the retrieved subset of documents, term-relevance weights can then be obtained in accordance with expression (9.19), and query terms can be weighted using the combined term-frequency and term-relevance weight of expression (9.16). Relevance feedback is described in more detail at the end of this chapter.

Table 9.1 Term occurrence frequencies for term T_j in collection of N documents.

Occurrence Pattern of Terms	Relevant Documents	Nonrelevant Documents	Total Number of Documents
Term x_j is present	r_j	f_j-r_j	f_j
Term x_j is absent	$R-r_j$	$N-R-f_j+r_j$.	$N-f_j$
Total Number of Documents	R	$N-R$	N

9.4 Term Relationships in Indexing

The indexing approaches described previously were based on assigning single-term indexing elements to information items. In such circumstances the stored records are identified by sets of single terms that are used collectively to represent the information content of each record. The use of single-term indexing units, however, is justified only by operational considerations. Actually, assigning single terms to the items in a collection is not ideal — first, because single terms used out of context often carry ambiguous meanings, and, second, because many single terms are either too specific or too broad to be useful in indexing.

When content analysis and indexing are performed manually by subject experts and trained indexers, the indexing units usually consist of groupings of terms, such as noun phrases, that are specific enough to permit reasonably unambiguous interpretations. Further, vocabulary-control tools may be available in the form of thesauruses, or hierarchical term arrangements, which control the specificity of indexing units by providing cross-references between terms, and pointers from specific term entries to other, related broader or narrower concepts.

The use of complex text identifiers consisting of groupings or classes of single terms presents difficulties because the tools needed to generate useful complex text identifiers are not readily available. Among the methods suggested to generate complex identifiers are linguistic-analysis procedures capable of recognizing linguistically related units in document texts; term-grouping or term-clustering methods that generate groups of related words by observing word cooccurrence patterns in the documents of a collection; and probabilistic indexing methods that incorporate term-dependence information.

Consider first the extension of the previously described probabilistic indexing system to a case in which the index terms no longer occur independently in the relevant and nonrelevant documents of the collection. In that case, the term-independence assumptions of expression (9.10) do not apply, and more complex formulas must be used to express the probabilities of occurrence of any item x in the relevant and nonrelevant document subsets. In particular, the formulas for $Pr(x|\text{rel})$ and $Pr(x|\text{nonrel})$, which involve only parameters p_i and q_i under the term-independence assumption, must be replaced by the following expressions:

$$Pr(x|\text{rel}) = \prod_{i=1}^{t} p_i^{x_i} (1-p_i)^{1-x_i}\{1 + A\} \qquad (9.20a)$$

and

$$Pr(x|\text{nonrel}) = \prod_{i=1}^{t} q_i^{x_i} (1-q_i)^{1-x_i} \{1 + B\}, \qquad (9.20b)$$

where factors *A* and *B* also include the occurrence probabilities for higher-order term subsets, such as joint occurrence probabilities p_{ij} and q_{ij} for terms T_i and T_j, probabilities p_{ijk} and q_{ijk} for triples T_i, T_j and T_k, and so on for all higher-order subsets. [22,23]

In the extended probabilistic model, then, it is necessary to consider an exponential number of term combinations, and for each combination to estimate the joint occurrence probabilities in relevant and nonrelevant document subsets. In practice, it is extremely difficult to obtain reliable information about the occurrences of term groups in the documents of a collection. Hence it is difficult to accurately estimate the probabilistic parameters for the higher-order dependent term combinations. Furthermore, no practical methods exist for actually utilizing a large number of term dependencies even if parameters could be estimated easily.

For this reason the probabilistic term-dependence systems that have actually been considered are based on simplified models using only a few of the more important term dependencies. Thus in the so-called *tree-dependence* model, only certain dependent term pairs are actually included, the other term pairs and all higher-order term combinations being disregarded. [24] A tree-dependence example derived for a document collection in education is shown in Fig. 9.4, in which a downward-pointing connection from an upper-level term to a lower-level term implies that these terms are related. The tree graph used as an example thus specifies a pairwise dependency between "school" and "girls," "school" and "boys," and "school" and "children." However, there is no analogous relation between "children" and either "boys" or "girls." Many important term relationships are necessarily excluded in the tree-dependence model.

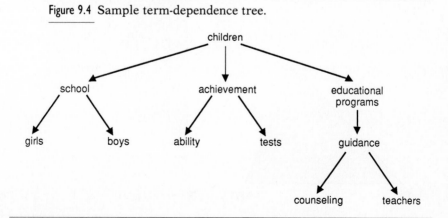

Figure 9.4 Sample term-dependence tree.

The problem of missing term relations noted for the tree-dependence system also exists in the somewhat more refined *generalized term-dependence* model, which can incorporate some higher-order dependencies, such as the three-term dependencies among "school," "girls," and "boys," and among "children," "achievement," and "ability," which are represented in the sample structure of Fig. 9.5. [25]

Unfortunately, all the known probabilistic term-dependency models suffer from the absence of some important higher-order term dependencies, as well as from the previously mentioned difficulties of estimating the required probabilistic parameters. It is not surprising, then, that available evaluation results indicate that the probabilistic approaches are not reliable enough to generate useful higher-order indexing units. [26]

An alternative method to identify higher-order term combinations consists of using *term classification* or *clustering* systems capable of generating important groupings of related terms. Automatic classification methods are examined in more detail in the next chapter. For now, it is sufficient to note that most automatic term-classification methods use an existing indexed document collection as the basis for grouping or clustering those terms that cooccur most often in the documents of the collection.

Given the sample term-document array shown in Fig. 9.6, where d_{ij} represents the value or importance of term T_j assigned to document

Figure 9.5 Generalized term-dependence example.

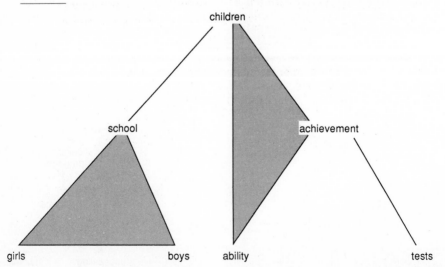

D_i, two main approaches can be used to generate classes of related terms:

1. First, it is possible to compare the columns of the array with each other, and to group terms whose corresponding column representations reveal similar assignments to the documents of the collection. In particular, when two terms are jointly assigned to many documents of the collection (that is, when the corresponding d_{ij} factors are nonzero), the terms are assumed to be related and are therefore grouped into common classes.

2. Alternatively, the term-document array can be processed by using the rows of the matrix; in that case documents are grouped into common classes that exhibit sufficiently similar term assignments. Once a document classification is constructed, it is possible to group those terms that cooccur frequently in the previously generated document classes.

The difficulty with term classes constructed from sample document collections is that the cooccurring terms are not necessarily closely related. Further, even if a relationship can be demonstrated, it may be local to the collection from which the terms were obtained. Thus a grouping of cooccurring terms into complex indexing units may be invalid outside the environment from which the term groups were originally obtained. [27]

Thus the use of only statistical and probabilistic methodologies to generate valid higher-order indexing units is not likely to lead to high-quality indexing units. The main problem is that reliable procedures do not exist for distinguishing cooccurring term groups that provide useful indexing units. This suggests that additional nonquantitative methods should be used to determine term relationships and the assignment of complex indexing units.

Figure 9.6 Basic term-document matrix.

		Terms			
		T_1	T_2	....	T_t
	D_1	d_{11}	d_{12}	....	d_{1t}
	D_2	d_{21}	d_{22}	....	d_{2t}
	.	.	.		.
	.	.	.		.
Documents	.	.	.		.
	.	.	.		.
	.	.	.		.
	D_n	d_{n1}	d_{n2}	....	d_{nt}

d_{ij} = value of T_j in D_i

Linguistic methodologies have been proposed in the indexing frame-work mainly for the identification and subsequent assignment of in-dexing *phrases*, that is, of nominal constructions including adjectives and nouns. In principle, it is relatively simple to consult a dictionary to assign syntactic class indicators (for example, noun, adjective, and adverb) to the words occurring in document texts, and to construct word phrases from sequences of words exhibiting certain allowed syn-tactic markers (such as noun-noun and adjective-noun sequences).

Such an assignment of syntactic function indicators can identify a number of useful term phrases as well as many extraneous or erron-eous phrases. The difficulty is that the mere occurrence of certain word types in a particular context does not guarantee that definite syntactic or semantic relationships are actually present. Thus in a sequence such as "high frequency transistor oscillator," which might be charac-terized by the syntactic chain adjective-noun-noun-noun, it is not possible to easily determine the existing word dependencies. Using word adjacency as an additional criterion does not always help: Cer-tainly "high" and "frequency" could properly be grouped to form "high frequency"; however, the next two words, "frequency" and "transistor," should certainly not be grouped because "frequency transistor" is not a meaningful entity in the language.

It is clear that constructing complex content identifiers for assign-ment to document texts raises issues of substantial difficulty, no matter what methodology is used. Because of the questionable use-fulness of many single terms, however, attempts must nevertheless be made to broaden overly specific terms, and make specific terms more general.

A principal method for narrowing terms is the generation of phrases consisting of sequences of single terms. Thesauruses, on the other hand, can be used for term broadening by replacing individual narrow terms with the thesaurus groups in which the terms are in-cluded. Methods for phrase generation and thesaurus generation are covered in the next two sections.

9.5 Term-phrase Formation

Term phrases consisting of sequences of related text words carry a more specific meaning than the single terms included in the phrases. For example, "computer science" or "computer program" is more spe-cific than "computer." When phrases are introduced as content identi-fiers, the intent must thus be to refine the meaning of single-term iden-tifiers that would be too broad to be used alone. Using the frequency spectrum of Fig. 9.2, the phrase-formation process carries out a right-to-left transformation that transforms higher-frequency nondis-criminating terms into medium-frequency phrases with greater discriminating power. This implies that term phrases should not be randomly constructed or assigned: In particular, phrases that include only low-frequency specific components from the left side of the frequency scale of Fig. 9.2 will receive a still lower document frequency further to the left, and their value for indexing purposes will be even smaller than that of the single-term components they replace.

The following simple phrase-formation process might be used as a starting point:

1. The principal phrase component, known as the *phrase head*, should be a term with a document frequency exceeding a stated threshold (for example, $df > 2$), or should exhibit a negative discrimination value.

2. The other components of the phrase should be medium- or low-frequency terms with stated cooccurrence relationships with the phrase head. For example, the phrase components should cooccur in a common document sentence with the phrase head within a stated number of words of each other.

3. Common function words that are entered on a special list of excluded words (a stop list) are not used in the phrase-formation process.

In choosing phrase-formation parameters, a compromise is needed between strict criteria that lead to the rejection of many useful phrases, and lax criteria that lead to the creation and assignment of many false term combinations. Consider, as an example, a typical sentence such as

> *Effective retrieval systems are essential for people in need of information.*

Assuming that the words "are," "for," "in," and "of" are common function words to be disregarded in the phrase-formation process, and that the words "systems," "people," and "information" exhibit sufficiently high document frequencies to be usable as phrase heads, a variety of two-word phrases can be formed as shown in Table 9.2. The left column of the table shows the phrases produced by requiring adjacency in the text between phrase heads and components (after removal of common function words); the additional phrases produced by extending the context to cooccurrences within the complete sentence are shown in the right column. Phrases assumed to be useful for content identification are marked with an asterisk in the table. The sample output shows that two of the five basic phrases obtained with the adjacency criterion are certainly pertinent. As the specified context is extended, some additional important phrases are obtained, including especially phrase 11 ("retrieval information"). However, a number of questionable phrases are also added, such as "effective people" and "systems need," that are not likely to be useful in retrieval.

Table 9.2 shows that a phrase-formation process controlled only by word cooccurrences and the document frequencies of certain words is not likely to generate a large number of high-quality phrases. The addition of syntactic criteria for phrase heads and phrase components may provide further control in phrase formation. In each case, syntactic considerations can replace the earlier strategy, or can be used in addition to the earlier steps:

4. Syntactic class indicators (adjective, noun, adverb, etc.) are assigned to the terms by consulting a suitable word dictionary, and phrase formation is then limited to sequences of specified syntactic markers, such as adjective-noun and noun-noun sequences. [28–30]

5. A simple syntactic analysis process can also be used to recognize basic syntactic sentence units such as subject phrase, object phrase, and verb phrase; the phrase elements may then all be chosen from within the same syntactic unit.

The use of step 4 alone does not change the phrase-formation results for the example of Table 9.2 because all listed phrases are in fact proper noun phrases that would certainly be allowed on syntactic grounds. However, the process outlined in step 4 may be helpful and may lead to the elimination of questionable sequences such as adverb-adjective or adverb-noun combinations. The syntactic-analysis process specified in step 5 should also be helpful in principle. Unfortunately, many syntactic ambiguities inherent in the language cannot be resolved by simple syntactic methods, so that it is not always possible

Table 9.2 Sample phrases generated by nonlinguistic methods.

Phrase Heads and Components Must Be Adjacent	Phrase Heads and Components Co-occur in Sentence
1. retrieval systems*	6. effective systems
2. systems essential	7. systems need
3. essential people	8. effective people
4. people need	9. retrieval people
5. need information*	10. effective information*
	11. retrieval information*
	12. essential information*

to obtain unique, and correct syntactic decompositions for all input sentences. For many sentences, however, reasonable syntactic decompositions can be generated that may be useful in document indexing.

Consider again the typical input sentence "effective retrieval systems are essential for people in need of information." The following main sentence components can be recognized:

- Subject phrase: effective retrieval systems;

- Verb phrase: are essential; and

- Object phrase: people in need of information.

If the phrase-formation process is based on component cooccurrence within common subphrases, the complete process of steps 1–5 will produce the results of Table 9.3. A comparison with Table 9.2 shows that the proportion of useful phrases generated by the adjacency requirement within syntactic components is now larger (two out of three) than when the syntactic constraints were not used (two out of five). However, the syntactic phrase requirement also eliminates a number of good phrases, such as phrases 10–12 of Table 9.2, that were found in the wider cooccurrence context.

The preceding example demonstrates that more stringent phrase-formation criteria produce fewer phrases, both good and bad, than less stringent methodologies. Beyond this, it is not clear which phrase-formation process should actually be used, since no procedure currently known is likely to produce a large proportion of the wanted phrases while also rejecting most of the extraneous ones. The simple syntactic process postulated in step 5 of the phrase-formation process does not always produce correct syntactic attachments for prepositional phrases, nor can syntax alone handle pronominal references unequivocally. Thus in the sentence "the man saw the girl *with the telescope*," the prepositional phrase could modify either "man" or "girl," and in the sentence "he dropped the plate on his foot and broke it," the

---

Table 9.3 Sample phrases for co-occurrences within syntactic components.

Adjacent Phrase Heads and Components within Syntactic Components	Phrase Heads and Components Co-occur within Syntactic Components
retrieval systems*	effective systems
people need	
need information*	

pronoun "it" cannot be interpreted unless the context indicates whether a broken plate or a broken foot is present.

Refined syntactic-analysis processes that include semantic components may become generally available in the future. In that case, some ambiguous interpretations may be eliminated in certain contexts. [31,32] For example, in the noun phrase "high frequency transistor oscillator," a built-in semantic component valid for the electronics field might reveal that "high" refers to "frequency," and that "frequency" modifies "oscillator" rather than the adjacent word "transistor." This type of information could be used to reject a number of phrases proposed by conventional syntactic phrase-generation systems, such as "high frequency transistor" and "frequency transistor." However, it is not clear whether even sophisticated semantic components would lead to the rejection of phrases such as "high transistor" and "high oscillator," where "high" is interpreted as "tall." Clearly, a "tall oscillator" may in fact represent a semantically plausible entity. [31] Thus the available options in phrase-generation appear limited, and the introduction of costly and refined methodologies may bring only marginal improvements.

Two additional issues are the actual interpretation of phrase meaning, and the recognition of semantically equivalent but structurally distinct phrases. Concerning phrase interpretation, a complete semantic phrase analysis may well be superfluous for indexing, in which the main idea is simply to assign similar units to both documents and information requests, leading to useful matches between query and document terms. Full semantic interpretations of noun phrases are not easy to render, and certainly cannot be obtained by superficially determining syntactic structure.

In an indexing environment, the matching of semantically identical but syntactically distinct phrases is of greater interest than generating complete semantic interpretations, because correct phrase matching depends on normalizing phrase formulations. Obviously, phrases such as "information retrieval" and "retrieval of information" cannot be directly matched without various term adjustments. In particular, any phrase-matching system must be able to deal with the problems of synonym recognition, differing word orders, intervening extraneous words (as in "retrieval *of* information"), and with many kinds of syntactic and semantic transformations. [33,34] No phrase-classification system yet devised can reduce to a single canonical form the many equivalent forms of even simple expressions of the type shown in Table 9.4.

Instead of attempting to reduce equivalent phrases to a common canonical form, the reverse approach might be taken by adding to each available phrase all possible variant forms. [31] Even though programs for this purpose can actually be built, the need to store and ma-

Table 9.4 Equivalent phrase formulations.

Base form	text analysis system
Variants	system analyzes the text
	text is analyzed by the system
	system carries out text analysis
	text is subjected to analysis by the system
	text is subjected to system analysis
Related term substitution	text → documents, information items
	analysis → processing, transformation, manipulation
	system → program, process

nipulate hundreds of variants for each phrase appears to make this possibility impracticable.

9.6 Thesaurus-Group Generation

Phrase generation improves the specificity, and hence the discrimination value, of indexing units that would otherwise be too general or too broad. The reverse process, *thesaurus transformation*, broadens index terms whose scope is too narrow to be useful in retrieval. Considering the frequency spectrum of Fig. 9.2 once again, the thesaurus transformation takes low-frequency, overly specific terms and replaces them with less-specific, medium-frequency thesaurus "heads" with a positive discrimination value. To be useful, a thesaurus must then assemble groups of related specific terms under more general, higher-level class indicators. A typical thesaurus excerpt used with an engineering collection is shown in Table 9.5. [35] When a thesaurus of this type is available, terms such as "prohibition" or "veto," for example, can be replaced by the thesaurus class indicator 761, which can then be assigned to any text containing one of the word entries under that class. Using a thesaurus in a text-analysis system can improve recall because the thesaurus classes have better matching capabilities than the original indexing vocabulary.

The matching capability of thesaurus classes can be improved further by using reduced word forms as thesaurus entries, for example *word stems*. For English-language texts, the thesaurus-consulting process must then be preceded by a suffix-deletion system that removes common suffixes from text words before replacing them with thesaurus class indicators. Various automatic word-stem generation systems have been designed; their basic idea is to remove suffixes recursively from the tail ends of words until a stem remains that is at least three characters long. [36] A word such as "effectiveness" is first reduced to "effective" by removing "ness," and then to "effect" by deleting "ive." "King" is not reduced to "k," however, because that operation does not leave a stem of the required length.

Typically, a small dictionary of suffixes controls the suffix-deletion process, and additional morphological rules are invoked to handle operations such as the following:

- Restore a silent e after suffix removal from certain words to produce "hope" from the original form "hoping," rather than "hop."

- Delete certain doubled consonants such as b, d, g, l, m, n, p, r, s, and t after suffix removal, so as to generate "hop" from "hopping," rather than "hopp."

- Use a final y for an i in forms such as "easier," so as to generate "easy" instead of "easi."

Table 9.5 Typical thesaurus excerpt (from [35]).

Class Indicator	Entry	Class Indicator	Entry
760	(permission) permission leave sanction allowance tolerance authorization warrant	763	(offer) offer presentation tender overture advance submission proposal proposition invitation
761	(prohibition) prohibition veto disallowance injunction ban taboo	764	(refusal) refusal declining noncompliance rejection denial
762	(consent) consent acquiescence compliance agreement acceptance	765	(request) request requisition petition suit solicitation application invitation

Special rules are also used to delete suffixes from certain exceptional words such as "metallic," which is not reduced to "met" even though "allic" is an acceptable suffix. Instead "metallic" must be reduced to "metal" by removing "ic," followed by removal of the doubled terminal consonant l. An exceptions dictionary can be used to identify entries to which the normal rules do not apply. [36]

Word-stem-generation programs may also be used when a thesaurus is not involved. In such a case, normal index entries are assigned in word-stem form rather than as full words. Suffix deletion then increases the matching possibilities between stored texts and query formulations and produces higher recall in many circumstances. Suffix-removal and word-stem-generation routines are useful in indexing systems even when large-scale improvements in recall and precision cannot be obtained, because an indexing vocabulary in word-stem form is much smaller than a full-word vocabulary, thus reducing the size of the needed dictionaries or thesauruses.

Obviously, a thesaurus can be used only if practical methods exist for thesaurus construction. Most well-known thesauruses valid for subject areas of reasonable scope are constructed manually, or intellectually, by committees of experts who review the subject matter and propose reasonable class arrangements for their topic. Some basic principles exist for constructing useful thesauruses — for example, the thesaurus classes should cover restricted topics of specified scope, and collectively the classes should cover the complete subject area evenly. Thesaurus classes representing reasonably narrow topic areas might then correspond to medium-frequency concepts with positive discrimination values.

Constructing a thesaurus in a given subject area is always demanding. Automatic aids can be provided, however, to simplify the task for human subject experts. For example, a *concordance* of terms can be produced representing an alphabetical listing of term occurrences in a collection, together with the contexts in which the terms occur. The use of concordances may simplify the detection of ambiguous terms that occur in several distinct contexts. The concordance may also help identify distinct terms with similar contexts for inclusion in common thesaurus classes.

Various automatic methods of thesaurus construction have also been proposed, which in some cases could produce usable term arrangements. Thus starting with a basic term-document matrix representing the index-term assignment for a sample document collection, (see Fig. 9.6), similarity coefficients can be obtained between pairs of distinct terms based on coincidences in the term assignments to the documents of the collection. Letting d_{ij} represent the weight, or value of term T_j in document D_i, a typical similarity measure between T_j and

T_k is given by

$$\text{sim}\,(T_j, T_k) = \sum_{i=1}^{n} d_{ij} \cdot d_{ik}, \qquad\qquad (9.21)$$

where n documents are taken into account. Alternatively, a cosine computation can be used to generate normalized term similarities between 0 and 1. In that case,

$$\text{sim}\,(T_j, T_k) = \frac{\displaystyle\sum_{i=1}^{n} d_{ij} \cdot d_{ik}}{\sqrt{\displaystyle\sum_{i=1}^{n} (d_{ij})^2 \cdot \sum_{i=1}^{n} (d_{ik})^2}}. \qquad\qquad (9.22)$$

When pairwise similarities are available between all useful term pairs, an automatic term-classification process can collect into common classes all terms with sufficiently large pairwise similarities. [37,38] Among these term-classification strategies are *single-link* and *complete-link* or *clique* class-construction methods, defined as follows

- In a single-link classification system, each term must have a similarity exceeding a stated threshold value with at least one other term in the same class.

- In a complete-link classification, each term has a similarity to all other terms in the same class that exceeds the threshold value.

The complete link process usually produces a large number of small classes because the classification criterion is very stringent, requiring each term to be similar to every other term in the same class. The single-link method, on the other hand, produces fewer, much larger term classes; certain terms may be grouped into common classes even though the terms may in fact be quite dissimilar.

When thesauruses are derived from the term occurrences and cooccurrences in particular document collections, recall improvements of the order of 10 to 20 percent may be possible, provided that the thesaurus is used in an environment similar to that when the original thesaurus was constructed. [39,40] When the sample document collection used for thesaurus construction differs substantially from the thesaurus application area, the thesaurus classes may be less valid. Automatically constructed term-class arrangements must therefore be tested with various document collections before their validity can be assumed.

Several automatic thesaurus-construction systems are based on the existence of tentative, initially existing term classes that must be refined. For example, each initial thesaurus class can tentatively be constructed by collecting all low-frequency terms that cooccur in particular documents of a collection. Such a process generates as many initial term classes as the number of documents in the specified subcollection. The initial term classes can then be refined by merging term classes with a sufficiently similar composition, and by associating terms from new documents with the closest existing classes. [41,42]

A last possibility for automatic thesaurus construction is so-called *pseudoclassification*, which consists of using a sample document collection for which representative relevance judgments between documents and sample queries have previously been obtained. That is, for each sample query, the relevance of the documents in the sample collection is assumed to be known. Given particular query-document pairs, it is then possible dynamically to construct a term thesaurus with the aim of increasing the similarity of query-document pairs known to be relevant to each other, while simultaneously decreasing the similarity of nonrelevant pairs.

Consider, in particular, some term T_j occurring in a given query Q, and a different term T_k occurring in a document D relevant to Q. The inclusion of T_j and T_k in a common term class of a thesaurus will increase the similarity between Q and D, since they will be assigned the same thesaurus class identifier. By proceeding iteratively, and considering the various (Q,D) pairs in turn, it may be possible to place into common thesaurus classes the vocabularies for the relevant (Q,D) pairs, while ensuring at the same time that the vocabularies of nonrelevant query-document pairs do not appear in common thesaurus classes. [42]

Pseudoclassification, like all other automatic term-class-generation methods, can be useful only if the term assignments to the document collection used as an initial sample, as well as the available query-document relevance assessments, are representative of random texts in the subject area. Experience to date with automatically constructed thesauruses indicates that their effectiveness is questionable outside the special environments in which they are generated.

9.7 A Blueprint for Automatic Indexing

The preceding discussion can be summarized by presenting a blueprint for generating effective indexing representations from available document texts. [43] In most practical situations a single-term word extraction system such as the following produces index term sets that outperform more elaborate systems based on controlled index terms and vocabulary normalization tools such as synonym lists and tables of term relationships:

1. Identify the individual words occurring in the documents of a collection.

2. Use a *stop list* of common function words (and, of, or, but, the, etc.) to delete from the texts the high-frequency function words that are insufficiently specific to represent content.

3. Use an automatic *suffix-stripping* routine to reduce each remaining word to *word-stem* form; this reduces to a common form all words exhibiting the same stem (for example, analysis, analyzer, and analyzing are all reduced to stem ANALY).

4. For each remaining word stem T_j in document D_i, compute a weighting factor w_{ij} composed in part of the term frequency and in part of the inverse document-frequency factor for the term, for example

$$w_{ij} = tf_{ij} \cdot \log (N/df_j).$$

5. Represent each document D_i by the set of word stems together with the corresponding weighting factors, that is,

$$D_i = (T_1, w_{i1}; T_2, w_{i2}; \ldots,; T_t, w_{it}).$$

This procedure uses a stop list to remove common function words from the texts of documents, and a suffix-stripping method to generate word stems for the remaining entries. A weight is next assigned to each word stem, and each document is represented by the vector of weighted word stems. This easily implemented system can function without further refinement.

In situations where a thesaurus or word-grouping tool is available, and where term phrases can be constructed, an indexing system can be used that is based on the standard methods previously outlined for single terms, followed by a thesaurus transformation for the low-frequency terms with small discrimination values, and a phrase transformation for the high-frequency terms with negative discrimination values:

1. Identify individual text words.

2. Use stop list to delete common function words.

3. Use automatic suffix stripping to produce word stems.

4. Compute term-discrimination value for all word stems.

5. Use thesaurus class replacement for all low-frequency terms with discrimination values near zero.

6. Use phrase-formation process for all high-frequency terms with negative discrimination values.

7. Compute weighting factors for the complex indexing units represented by thesaurus classes and term phrases (for example, use the average of the weights of all component terms).

8. Assign to each document the existing single terms, term phrases, and thesaurus classes with the corresponding weights.

When a thesaurus is not available, the phrase process can be used alone without the thesaurus transformation of step 5.

The two systems just outlined can be applied to queries as well as document texts, assuming that query statements are originally available in natural-language form. Both queries and documents are then represented by weighted term vectors. To construct information queries in Boolean form, the choice of query terms must be followed by a grouping of terms into clauses and the assignment of Boolean operators. The processing of Boolean queries in conventional retrieval environments was outlined in Chapter 8, and methods for handling weighted terms in Boolean query environments, and other advanced systems, are described in Chapter 10. For present purposes, the assumption is that user statements of information need are available in natural-language form and that queries are expressed by weighted term sets.

One minor difference between query- and document-term assignment relates to the choice of term-weighting functions. Because most query texts are relatively short, and relatively fewer terms are assigned to queries than to documents, the occurrence frequency of the query terms rarely exceeds 1. In these circumstances, the term-frequency component of the query-term weights can be eliminated. Given query- and document-term vectors of the form

$$Q = (w_{q1}, w_{q2}, ..., w_{qt}) \qquad (9.23a)$$

and

$$D_i = (d_{i1}, d_{i2}, ..., d_{it}) \qquad (9.23b)$$

where the w_{qj} represent inverse document-frequency weights, and the d_{ij} are defined as combined term-frequency and inverse document-frequency weights, a typical query-document similarity coefficient can be obtained by using the conventional inner-product formula

$$\text{sim}(Q,D) = \sum_{j=1}^{t} w_{qj} \cdot d_{ij}. \tag{9.24}$$

The formula of expression (9.24) can be used with variable-length vectors, exhibiting a variable number of included terms. When non-normalized document vectors are used, the longer documents with more assigned terms have a greater chance of matching particular query terms than do the shorter document vectors. This advantage does not necessarily produce the best retrieval effectiveness. A vector-normalization process may not be as important for the query vectors as for document vectors, because the query vectors are short and the length differences for different queries are small. It is known, however, that in most retrieval environments, normalized document vectors whose length is reduced to a common value of 1 are preferred over nonnormalized vectors. The query-document similarity formula of expression (9.24) is then replaced advantageously by the normalized formulas of expression (9.25):

$$\text{sim}(Q,D_i) = \frac{\displaystyle\sum_{j=1}^{t} w_{qj} \cdot d_{ij}}{\sqrt{\displaystyle\sum_{j=1}^{t} (d_{ij})^2}} \tag{9.25a}$$

or

$$\text{sim}(Q,D_i) = \frac{\displaystyle\sum_{j=1}^{t} w_{qj} \cdot d_{ij}}{\sqrt{\displaystyle\sum_{j=1}^{t} (d_{ij})^2 \cdot \sum_{j=1}^{t} (w_{qj})^2}}. \tag{9.25b}$$

The preceding formula represents the cosine of the angle between the query and document vectors considered as vectors in a space of t dimensions, where t is the number of distinct terms in the system.

When a similarity coefficient is computed between query and document vectors, the retrieved documents can be ranked in decreasing order of query-document similarity, and the user can be made aware of citations or abstracts of the top-ranked documents. This enables the user to assess the usefulness of some of the previously retrieved items. Given such relevance assessments for a few of the retrieved items, the query formulation can now be altered by adding new terms to the queries and changing the query-term weights of the existing terms. [44,45]

The well-known *relevance feedback* process can be used to improve query formulations by altering the original queries in two substantial ways:

1. Terms present in previously retrieved documents that have been identified as relevant to the user's query are added to the original query formulations.

2. The weights of the original query terms are altered by replacing the inverse document-frequency portion of the weights with term-relevance weights obtained by using the occurrence characteristics of the terms in the previously retrieved relevant and nonrelevant documents of the collection.

Normally, relevance feedback improves retrieval effectiveness greatly — of the order of 50 percent in average retrieval precision evaluated at certain fixed levels of the recall. [46]

Assuming that the initial query is available in the form specified in expression (9.23), a reformulated query will take the following form:

$$Q' = \alpha \{w_{q1}, w_{q2}, ..., w_{qt}\} + \beta \{w'_{q_{t+1}}, w'_{q_{t+2}}, ..., w'_{q_{t+m}}\}. \qquad (9.26)$$

In expression (9.26), α and β may take values between 0 and 1, and the weights of the t initial terms may be generated by taking combined term-frequency and inverse-document-frequency weights. The weights of the newly added terms T_{t+1} to T_{t+m} on the other hand, may consist of a combined term-frequency and term-relevance weight of the kind given in expression (9.16). In the next chapter, procedures are given for applying relevance feedback to the reformulation of Boolean rather than vector queries.

The final indexing prescription, which includes the two basic methods outlined earlier in this section, plus the relevance-feedback system for query reformulations is carried out as follows:

1. Identify individual text words.

2. Use a stop list to delete common words.

3. Use suffix stripping to produce word stems.

4. Replace low-frequency terms with thesaurus classes.

5. Replace high-frequency terms with phrases.

6. Compute term weights for all single terms, phrases, and thesaurus classes.

7. Compare query statements with document vectors.

8. Identify some retrieved documents as relevant and some as non-relevant to the query.

9. Compute term-relevance factors based on available relevance assessments.

10. Construct new queries with added terms from relevant documents and term weights based on combined frequency and term-relevance weights.

11. Return to step 7.

Each section of the indexing system can be used by itself without any of the subsequent steps. The best results are likely to be produced when relevance feedback is used for at least one reformulation step following an initial retrieval activity.

A summary of the expected effectiveness of the previously described indexing steps appears in Table 9.6. The data in the table indicate only the improvements that can be achieved for average document collections with the various indexing methodologies. Usually the

Table 9.6 Summary of expected effectiveness of automatic indexing procedures.

Indexing Methodology	Improvement in Search Precision Calculated at Certain Recall Levels and Averaged over a Number of User Queries
Basic single-term automatic indexing	–
Use of thesaurus to group related terms in the given topic area	+10% to +20%
Use of automatically derived term associations obtained from joint term assignments found in sample document collections	0% to −10%
Use of automatically derived term phrases obtained by using co-occurring terms found in the texts of sample collections	+5% to +10%
Use of one iteration of relevance feedback to add new query terms extracted from previously retrieved relevant documents	+30% to +60%

improvements provided by thesaurus use and automatic phrase construction are relatively modest. The use of automatically constructed term associations obtained from joint term occurrences in sample document collections is not recommended. The relevance-feedback process, on the other hand, may produce substantial advantages in query indexing and retrieval effectiveness, and should be incorporated in any on-line search environment in which users' opinions about the relevance of previously retrieved materials can be easily obtained.

References

1. E.M. Keen, On the Generation and Searching of Entries in Printed Subject Indexes, *Journal of Documentation*, 33:1, March 1977, 15–45.

2. B.C. Vickery, *Techniques of Information Retrieval*, Archon Books, Hamden, CT, 1970.

3. C.W. Cleverdon, Optimizing Convenient On-line Access to Bibliographic Databases, *Information Service and Use*, 4:1, 1984, 37–47.

4. G. Salton, Another Look at Automatic Text Retrieval, *Communications of the ACM*, 29:7, July 1986, 648–656.

5. F.W. Lancaster, *Evaluation of the Medlars Demand Search Service*, National Library of Medicine, Bethesda, MD, January 1968.

6. G. Salton, *Automatic Information Organization and Retrieval*, McGraw-Hill Book Co., New York, 1968.

7. H.P. Luhn, A Statistical Approach to the Mechanized Encoding and Searching of Literary Information, *IBM Journal of Research and Development*, 1:4, October 1957, 309–317.

8. K. Sparck Jones, A Statistical Interpretation of Term Specificity and Its Application in Retrieval, *Journal of Documentation*, 28:1, March 1972, 11–21.

9. G. Salton and C.S. Yang, On the Specification of Term Values in Automatic Indexing, *Journal of Documentation*, 29:4, December 1973, 351–372.

10. G. Salton, *A Theory of Indexing*, Regional Conference Series in Applied Mathematics No. 18, Society for Industrial and Applied Mathematics, Philadelphia, PA, 1975.

11. C.E. Shannon, Prediction and Entropy in Printed English, *Bell System Technical Journal*, 30:1, January 1951, 50–65.

12. S.F. Dennis, The Design and Testing of a Fully Automatic Indexing Searching System for Documents Consisting of Expository Text, in *Information Retrieval: A Critical Review*, G. Schecter, editor, Thompson Book Co., Washington, DC, 1967, 67–94.

13. G. Salton, C.S. Yang, and C.T. Yu, A Theory of Term Importance in Automatic Text Analysis, *Journal of the ASIS*, 26:1, January-February 1975, 33–44.

14. P. Willett, An Algorithm for the Calculation of Exact Term Discrimination Values, *Information Processing and Management*, 21:3, 1985, 225–232.

15. A. Bookstein and D.R. Swanson, A Decision Theoretic Foundation for Indexing, *Journal of the ASIS*, 26:1, 1975, 45–50.

16. W.S. Cooper and M.E. Maron, Foundation of Probabilistic and Utility Theoretic Indexing, *Journal of the ACM*, 25:1, 1978, 67–80.

17. S.E. Robertson and K. Sparck Jones, Relevance Weighting of Search Terms, *Journal of the ASIS*, 27:3, 1976, 129–146.

18. C.J. van Rijsbergen, *Information Retrieval*, Second Edition, Butterworths, London, 1979.

19. W.B. Croft and D.J. Harper, Using Probabilistic Models of Information Retrieval without Relevance Information, *Journal of Documentation*, 35:4, December 1979, 285–295.

20. C.T. Yu, K. Lam, and G. Salton, Term Weighting in Information Retrieval Using the Term Precision Model, *Journal of the ACM*, 19:1, January 1982, 152–170.

21. H. Wu and G. Salton, A Comparison of Search Term Weighting: Term Relevance versus Inverse Document Frequency, *ACM SIGIR Forum*, 16:1, Summer 1981, 30–39.

22. R.O. Duda and P.E. Hart, *Pattern Classification and Scene Analysis*, John Wiley and Sons, New York, 1973.

23. C.T. Yu, W.S. Luk, and M.K. Siu, On Models of Information Retrieval Processes, *Information Systems*, 4:3, 1979, 205–218.

24. C.J. van Rijsbergen, A Theoretical Basis for the Use of Cooccurrence Data in Information Retrieval, *Journal of Documentation*, 33:2, June 1977, 106–119.

25. C.T. Yu, C. Buckley, K. Lam, and G. Salton, A Generalized Term Dependence Model in Information Retrieval, *Information Technology: Research and Development*, 2:4, October 1983, 129–154.

26. G. Salton, C. Buckley, and C.T. Yu, An Evaluation of Term Dependence Models in Information Retrieval, *Lecture Notes in Computer Science*, G. Salton and H.J. Schneider, editors, 146, Springer Verlag, Berlin 1983, 151–173.

27. M.E. Lesk, Word-Word Associations in Document Retrieval Systems, *American Documentation*, 20:1, January 1969, 27–38.

28. P.H. Klingbiel, Machine Aided Indexing of Technical Literature, *Information Storage and Retrieval*, 9:2, February 1973, 79–84.

29. P.H. Klingbiel, A Technique for Machine Aided Indexing, *Information Storage and Retrieval*, 9:9, September 1973, 477–494.

30. M. Dillon and A. Gray, Fully Automatic Syntax-based Indexing, *Journal of the ASIS*, 34:2, March 1983, 99–108.

31. K. Sparck Jones and J.I. Tait, Automatic Search Term Variant Generation, *Journal of Documentation*, 40:1, March 1984, 50–66.

32. B.K. Boguraev and K. Sparck Jones, A Natural Language Analyzer for Database Access, *Information Technology: Research and Development*, 1:1, 1982, 23–29.

33. C.D. Paice and V. Aragon-Ramirez, The Calculation of Similarities between Multiword Strings Using a Thesaurus, *RIAO Conference Proceedings*, University of Grenoble, March 1985, 293–320.

34. G. Salton, Automatic Phrase Matching, in *Readings in Computational Linguistics*, D.G. Hays, editor, American Elsevier Publishing Co., New York, 1966, 169–188.

35. *Roget's International Thesaurus*, Thomas Y. Crowell Co., New York, 1946.

36. J.B. Lovins, Development of a Stemming Algorithm, *Mechanical Translation and Computational Linguistics*, 11:1-2, March and June 1968, 11–31.

37. K. Sparck Jones, *Automatic Keyword Classification for Information Retrieval*, Butterworths, London, 1971.

38. G. Salton, Generation and Search of Clustered Files, *ACM Transactions on Database Systems*, 3:4, December 1978, 321–346.

39. G. Salton and M.E. Lesk, Information Analysis and Dictionary Construction, in *The Smart Retrieval System — Experiments in Automatic Document Processing*, G. Salton, editor, Prentice-Hall, Inc., Englewood Cliffs, NJ, 1971, 115–142.

40. G. Salton, Experiments in Automatic Thesaurus Construction for Information Retrieval, *Information Processing 71*, North Holland Publishing Co., Amsterdam, 1972, 115–123.

41. R.T. Dattola, Experiments with Fast Algorithms for Automatic Classification, in *The Smart Retrieval System — Experiments in Automatic Document Processing*, G. Salton, editor, Prentice-Hall, Inc., Englewood Cliffs, NJ, 1971, 265–297.

42. G. Salton, Automatic Term Class Construction Using Relevance — A Summary of Work in Automatic Pseudoclassification, *Information Processing and Management*, 16:1, 1980, 1–15.

43. G. Salton, A Blueprint for Automatic Indexing, *ACM SIGIR Forum*, 16:2, Fall 1981, 22–38.

44. J.J. Rocchio, Jr., Relevance Feedback in Information Retrieval, in *The Smart Retrieval System — Experiments in Automatic Document Processing*, G. Salton, editor, Prentice-Hall Inc., Englewood Cliffs, NJ, 1971, 324–336.

45. E. Ide, New Experiments in Relevance Feedback, in *The Smart Retrieval System — Experiments in Automatic Document Processing*, G. Salton, editor, Prentice-Hall, Inc., Englewood Cliffs, NJ, 1971, 373–393.

46. H. Wu and G. Salton, The Estimation of Term Relevance Weights Using Relevance Feedback, *Journal of Documentation*, 37:4, December 1981, 157–228.

Chapter 10

Advanced Information-Retrieval Models

10.1   The Vector Space Model

❖ 10.1.1   Basic Vector-processing Model

Various mathematical models have been proposed to represent information-retrieval systems and procedures, including the Boolean model, which compares Boolean query statements with the term sets used to identify document content; a probabilistic model based on the computation of relevance probabilities for the documents of a collection; and the *vector-space* model, which represents both queries and documents by term sets and computes global similarities between queries and documents. Of these, the vector-space model is the simplest to use and in some ways the most productive.

    The vector-space model assumes that an available term set is used to identify both stored records and information requests. [1,2] Both queries and documents can then be represented as *term vectors* of

313

the form

$$D_i = (a_{i1}, a_{i2}, \ldots, a_{it}) \qquad (10.1a)$$

and

$$Q_j = (q_{j1}, q_{j2}, \ldots, q_{jt}) \qquad (10.1b)$$

where the coefficients a_{ik} and q_{jk} represent the values of term k in document D_i or query Q_j, respectively. Typically a_{ik} (or q_{jk}) is set equal to 1 when term k appears in document D_i (or in query Q_j), and to 0 when the term is absent from the vector. Alternatively, the vector coefficients could take on numeric values, the size of the coefficient depending on the importance of the term in the respective document or query.

Consider now a situation in which t distinct terms are available to characterize record content. Each of the t terms can then be identified with a term vector T, and a vector space is defined whenever the T vectors are linearly independent. In such a space, any vector can be represented as a linear combination of the t term vectors. Hence the rth document D_r can be written as

$$D_r = \sum_{i=1}^{t} a_{ri} T_i \qquad (10.2)$$

where the a_{ri}s are interpreted as the components of D_r along the vector T_i. Figure 10.1 represents a typical document vector in a two-dimensional vector space. [3]

In a vector space, the similarity between vectors x and y can be measured by the product $x \cdot y = |x|\,|y| \cos\alpha$, where $|x|$ is the length of x and α is the angle between the two vectors. Hence given a document D_r and a query Q_j represented in the form specified by expression (10.2), the document-query similarity can be computed as

$$D_r \cdot Q_s = \sum_{i,j=1}^{t} a_{ri}\, q_{sj}\, T_i \cdot T_j. \qquad (10.3)$$

Computing the similarity values of expression (10.3) thus depends on a specification of the document and query components, as well as knowledge of the term correlations $T_i \cdot T_j$ for all term pairs. The vector components are usually generated by an indexing operation from which a term-document matrix is obtained like the one shown in Fig. 10.2 for a collection of N documents. The term correlations, on the other hand, are not usually available a priori, and it is not simple to generate useful term associations.

Figure 10.1 Document representation in vector space.

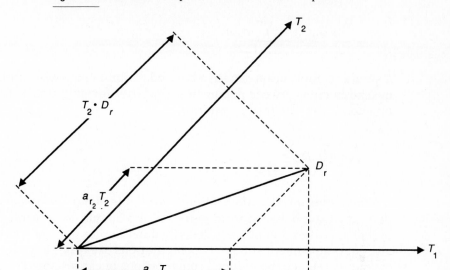

In practice the term-correlation problem is often solved, or circumvented, by assuming that the terms are in fact uncorrelated, in which case the term vectors are orthogonal (that is, $T_i \cdot T_j = 0$, except when $i = j$ and $T_i \cdot T_i = 1$). When the t term vectors are orthogonal, linear independence follows automatically, and the t term vectors form a proper basis for the vector space. Assuming that the terms are uncorrelated, the term-document similarity computation of expression (10.3) is reduced to the simple sum-of-products form of expression

Figure 10.2 Term-document matrix A.

$$A = \begin{array}{c} \\ D_1 \\ D_2 \\ \cdot \\ \cdot \\ \cdot \\ D_N \end{array} \begin{array}{ccc} T_1 & T_2 & T_t \\ \left[\begin{array}{ccc} a_{11} & a_{12} & a_{1t} \\ a_{21} & a_{22} & a_{2t} \\ & & \\ & & \\ & & \\ a_{N1} & a_{N2} & a_{Nt} \end{array}\right] \end{array}$$

(10.4):

$$\text{sim}(D_r, Q_s) = \sum_{i,j=1}^{t} a_{r_i} q_{s_j} .$$

(10.4)

A similar computation can then be used to obtain pair-wise similarity measurements between documents, the latter forming a basis for certain document-clustering systems:

$$\text{sim}(D_r, D_s) = \sum_{i,j=1}^{t} a_{r_i} a_{s_j} .$$

(10.5)

When appropriate information is available about the associations that may exist between term pairs — for example, as a result of the pseudoclassification process described in Chapter 9 — the more precise query-document similarity computations of expression (10.3) can, of course, replace the reduced computations of expressions (10.4) and (10.5).

Consider as an example the sample computation of Fig. 10.3. [3] The standard sum-of-products form of Fig. 10.3(c) produces similarity coefficients of 10 and 2 between the query and documents D_1 and D_2, respectively. When the term correlations specified in Fig. 10.3(b) are incorporated, reduced similarity measurements of 8.8 and -0.8 are obtained for the two documents because of the presence in the documents of term T_2, which is negatively correlated with query term T_3.

It should be pointed out that term correlations can in principle be computed from the term-document matrix of Fig. 10.2 by noting that each term is implicitly specified by its assignment to the documents of the collection. In that case term T_i is specified as the ith column of the term-document matrix:

$$T_i = \sum_{r=1}^{N} b_{ir} D_r$$

(10.6)

The correlation between two columns of the matrix produces a term-term similarity between T_i and T_j as in expression (10.7):

$$T_i \cdot T_j = \sum_{r,s=1}^{N} b_{ir} b_{js} D_r \cdot D_s .$$

(10.7)

To actually obtain the term-term similarities from the data of Fig. 10.2, it is then necessary to assume that the document vectors are themselves orthogonal (that is, $D_r \cdot D_s = 0$ when $r \neq s$). However, such an assumption is clearly unreasonable for any kind of practical document collection. [3]

As a matter of practice, the vector-space model can then be used to obtain correlations, or similarities, between pairs of stored documents, or between queries and documents, under the assumption that the t term vectors are orthogonal, or that the term vectors are linearly independent, so that a proper basis exists for the vector space. When term dependencies or associations are available from outside sources, they can be taken into account (see the sample computations of Fig. 10.3).

There are three main reasons why it is advantageous to generate similarity coefficients between queries and documents in information-retrieval environments:

1. The documents can be arranged in decreasing order of corresponding similarity with the query, making it possible to display retrieved items in decreasing order of presumed importance.

Figure 10.3 Sample query-document similarity computations (from [3]). (a) Sample documents and query. (b) Assumed term correlations. (c) Similarity computations for uncorrelated terms. (d) Similarity computations for correlated terms.

	T_1	T_2	T_3
T_1	1	0.5	0
T_2	0.5	1	-0.2
T_3	0	-0.2	1

$D_1 = 2T_1 + 3T_2 + 5T_3$

$D_2 = 3T_1 + 7T_2 + 1T_3$

$Q = 0T_1 + 0T_2 + 2T_3$

(a)

(b)

$$\text{sim}(D_1, Q) = 2 \cdot 0 + 3 \cdot 0 + 5 \cdot 2 = 10$$
$$\text{sim}(D_2, Q) = 3 \cdot 0 + 7 \cdot 0 + 1 \cdot 2 = 2$$

(c)

$$\text{sim}(D_1, Q) = (2T_1 + 3T_2 + 5T_3) \cdot (2T_3)$$
$$= 4T_1 \cdot T_3 + 6T_2 \cdot T_3 + 10T_3 \cdot T_3$$
$$= \quad -6 \cdot 0.2 + 10 \cdot 1$$
$$= \quad 8.8$$

$$\text{sim}(D_2, Q) = (3T_1 + 7T_2 + 1T_3) \cdot (2T_3)$$
$$= 6T_1 \cdot T_3 + 14T_2 \cdot T_3 + 2T_3 \cdot T_3$$
$$= \quad -14 \cdot 0.2 + 2 \cdot 1$$
$$= \quad -0.8$$

(d)

2. The size of the retrieved set can be adapted to the users' requirements by retrieving only the top few items in the ranked order when
casual users are involved, while providing a more exhaustive group
of items to specialized users who may require high-recall performance.

3. Items retrieved early in a search, which are most similar to the
queries, may help generate improved query formulations using relevance feedback.

A list of typical vector-similarity measures appears in Table 10.1.
The first row shows the inner product (or sum-of-products) formula
introduced in expressions (10.4) and (10.5). For binary vectors, the inner product measures the number of matching terms in the two vectors, whereas for weighted term vectors, it corresponds to the sum of
the products of the weights for equivalent terms. Because this last co-

Table 10.1 Measures of vector similarity.

Similarity Measure $\text{sim}(X, Y)$	Evaluation for Binary Term Vectors	Evaluation for Weighted Term Vectors
Inner product	$\lvert X \cap Y \rvert$	$\displaystyle\sum_{i=1}^{t} x_i \cdot y_i$
Dice coefficient	$2 \dfrac{\lvert X \cap Y \rvert}{\lvert X \rvert + \lvert Y \rvert}$	$\dfrac{2 \displaystyle\sum_{i=1}^{t} x_i y_i}{\displaystyle\sum_{i=1}^{t} x_i^2 + \sum_{i=1}^{t} y_i^2}$
Cosine coefficient	$\dfrac{\lvert X \cap Y \rvert}{\lvert X \rvert^{1/2} \cdot \lvert Y \rvert^{1/2}}$	$\dfrac{\displaystyle\sum_{i=1}^{t} x_i y_i}{\sqrt{\displaystyle\sum_{i=1}^{t} x_i^2 \cdot \sum_{i=1}^{t} y_i^2}}$
Jaccard coefficient	$\dfrac{\lvert X \cap Y \rvert}{\lvert X \rvert + \lvert Y \rvert - \lvert X \cap Y \rvert}$	$\dfrac{\displaystyle\sum_{i=1}^{t} x_i y_i}{\displaystyle\sum_{i=1}^{t} x_i^2 + \sum_{i=1}^{t} y_i^2 - \sum_{i=1}^{t} x_i y_i}$

$X = (x_1, x_2, \ldots, x_t)$
$\lvert X \rvert$ = number of terms in X
$\lvert X \cap Y \rvert$ = number of terms appearing jointly in X and Y

efficient is in principle unbounded, it is customary in most applications to use normalized similarity coefficients whose values vary between 0 and 1 when the vector elements are nonnegative. Three typical normalized similarity coefficients of this kind are the Dice, cosine, and Jaccard coefficients, also included in the table. [4]

The disadvantages of the basic vector-processing model relate to the assumed orthogonality, and hence independence between terms, and the lack of theoretical justification for some of the vector-manipulation operations. For example, the choice of a particular vector-similarity measure for a certain application is not prescribed by any theoretical considerations, and is left to the user. Some of the advantages are the model's simplicity, the ease with which it accommodates weighted terms, and its provision of ranked retrieval output in decreasing order of query-document similarity. A main virtue of this approach is the ease with which individual vectors can be modified, making it possible to adapt the query and document vectors to a dynamic environment as described in the next subsection.

10.1.2 Vector Modifications

One of the most important and difficult operations in information retrieval is generating useful query statements that can extract materials wanted by users and reject the remainder. Since usually an ideal query representation cannot be generated without knowing a great deal about the composition of the collection, it is customary to conduct searches iteratively, first operating with a tentative query formulation, and then improving formulations for subsequent searches based on evaluations of the previously retrieved materials. One method for automatically generating improved query formulations is the well-known relevance-feedback process. [5–7]

The main assumption behind relevance feedback is that documents relevant to a particular query resemble each other in the sense that they are represented by reasonably similar vectors. This implies that if a retrieved document has been identified as relevant to a given query, the query formulation can be improved by increasing its similarity to such a previously retrieved relevant item. The reformulated query is expected to retrieve additional relevant items that are similar to the originally identified relevant item.

It remains to find an effective method for "moving" a given query toward the relevant items and away from the nonrelevant ones. Consider first the construction of an ideal query which maximizes the average query document similarity for the relevant documents, at the same time minimizing the average query-document similarity for the nonrelevant documents. It is known that under appropriate assumptions such a query has the form

$$Q_{\text{opt}} = k \left\{ \frac{1}{R} \sum_{\text{Rel}} \frac{D_i}{|D_i|} - \frac{1}{N-R} \sum_{\text{Nonrel}} \frac{D_i}{|D_i|} \right\}, \qquad (10.8)$$

where R and $N-R$ are the assumed number of relevant and non-relevant documents, and the two summations range over the sets of normalized relevant and nonrelevant documents, respectively. [5]

The summation of expression (10.8) is not immediately useful for constructing queries because the sets of relevant and nonrelevant documents with respect to the queries are not known, of course, before an exhaustive search. Hence the relevant and nonrelevant document vectors cannot be summed to construct the desired query vector. Expression (10.8) can be approximated after an initial search operation, however, by asking the user to assess the relevance of some of the previously retrieved items. This identifies some subset R' of the R items relevant to the query, and some subset N' of the $N-R$ nonrelevant documents. An approximation of the optimal formulation of expression (10.8) is then obtained by taking an available query formulation $Q^{(i)}$ and adding the vector elements for the items identified as relevant, while subtracting the vectors for the items identified as nonrelevant:

$$Q^{(i+1)} = Q^{(i)} + \frac{1}{|R'|} \sum_{D_i \epsilon R'} D_i - \frac{1}{|N'|} \sum_{D_i \epsilon N'} D_i \qquad (10.9)$$

or alternatively,

$$Q^{(i+1)} = Q^{(i)} + \alpha \sum_{D_i \epsilon R'} D_i - \beta \sum_{D_i \epsilon N'} D_i \qquad (10.10)$$

for suitable multipliers α and β.

As indicated by the form of expressions (10.9) and (10.10), the steps in relevance feedback can be carried out iteratively in such a way that the query statement is made to approach the optimal query little by little as the relevance status of more and more documents becomes known. Also, multipliers α and β in (10.10) can be chosen in various ways to reflect techniques that give equal weight to relevant and nonrelevant items ($\alpha = \beta = 0.5$), or that favor only the relevant items ($\alpha = 1$, $\beta = 0$). An especially effective feedback technique is the so-called "dec hi" method, which uses all positive (that is, relevant) information for feedback purposes but subtracts only the highest ranked nonrelevant document. [6,7]

Figure 10.4(a) illustrates a positive relevance-feedback technique, with the t-dimensional vector space rendered in two dimensions, and the distance between two items assumed to be inversely proportional to the similarity between corresponding vectors. The transformation of expression (10.10) effectively moves the query toward the area of the vector space where the relevant items are located.

In some cases, the basic relevance feedback process does not operate satisfactorily because the relevant documents identified do not form a tight cluster in the document space, or because nonrelevant documents are scattered among certain relevant ones. One way to detect such conditions is by clustering the previously identified relevant items and calling for remedial action whenever more than one homo-

---

Figure 10.4 Relevance-feedback illustration. (a) Positive relevance feedback. (b) Feedback with query splitting.

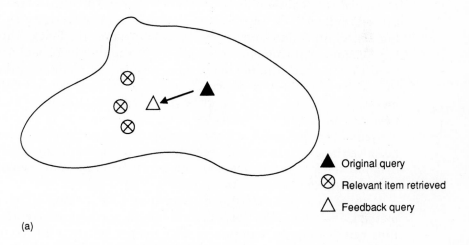

Original query
Relevant item retrieved
Feedback query

(a)

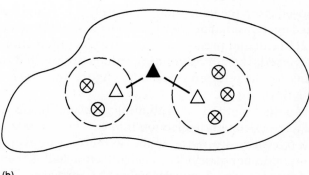

(b)

geneous relevant document cluster is detected. Such action could consist of splitting the original query into several pieces by constructing one new feedback query for each subset of identified, homogeneous relevant items. Figure 10.4(b) illustrates such a *query-splitting* operation; two new feedback queries are generated from a single original query because the previously identified relevant items are separated into two subgroups. [8]

By assuming that the query-document and the document-document similarity coefficients for a collection follow certain specified probabilistic assumptions, formal conditions can be given for the construction of improved feedback queries using relevance feedback. [9] A single iteration of relevance feedback usually produces improvements of from 40 to 60 percent in the search precision, evaluated at certain fixed levels of the recall and averaged over a number of user queries. [10,11] In evaluating the relevance feedback process, care must be taken to disregard the effect of gains in recall and precision due to improved ranking in the retrieval of relevant documents retrieved in earlier search iterations, and subsequently used for feedback. Thus in Fig. 10.5(a) two documents originally retrieved in ranks 2 and 5 were used to construct the feedback query. Since the feedback process forces the new query to approach to two previously retrieved documents, these items will probably be retrieved in the top two ranks in a new search conducted with the reformulated query. The rank improvement from 2 and 5 to 1 and 2 is not of genuine interest, however, because the user has already seen these two relevant items after the original search, and hence does not profit from the subsequent retrieval with improved ranks.

Various methods exist for disregarding this ranking effect. One method, residual collection evaluation with partial rank freezing, is illustrated in Fig. 10.5. In this method, the previously retrieved items identified as relevant are kept "frozen" in their original retrieval ranks, and the previously retrieved nonrelevant items are simply removed from the collection, their ranks (1, 3, and 4 in Fig. 10.5a) occupied by items that are newly retrieved in subsequent search iterations. [12] Recall and precision values are computed after each document is retrieved; the corresponding values are plotted in Fig. 10.5(c). The ranks of the relevant items in the figure improve from 2, 5, 7, and 8 to 2, 3, 5, 6, and 7.

Another method for evaluating relevance feedback consists of splitting the document collection into two pieces, taking care to even out the relevance properties of the two halves (the average number of relevant items per query). The test-collection half is then used to construct modified feedback queries using the normal relevance-feedback process, while the control half serves for the evaluation (see Fig. 10.6). [12]

Figure 10.5 Residual collection evaluation with partial rank freezing. (a) Initial query performance. (b) Feedback query performance. (c) Recall-precision graph.

Rank	Document number	Recall	Precision	Rank number	Document number	Recall	Precision
1	x 1	0	0	1	x 4	0	0
2	• 1	1/10	1/2	2	• 1	1/10	1/2
3	x 2	1/10	1/3	3	• 3	2/10	2/3
4	x 3	1/10	1/4	4	x 5	2/10	2/4
5	• 2	2/10	2/5	5	• 2	3/10	3/5
6	x 4	2/10	2/6	6	• 4	4/10	4/6
7	• 3	3/10	3/7	7	• 5	5/10	5/7
8	• 4	4/10	4/8	8	x 6	5/10	5/8
9	x 5	4/10	4/9	9	x 7	5/10	5/9
10	x 6	4/10	4/10	10	x 8	5/10	5/10

Retrieval cutoff (between ranks 5 and 6, left table)

• Relevant items
x Nonrelevant items

(a)   (b)

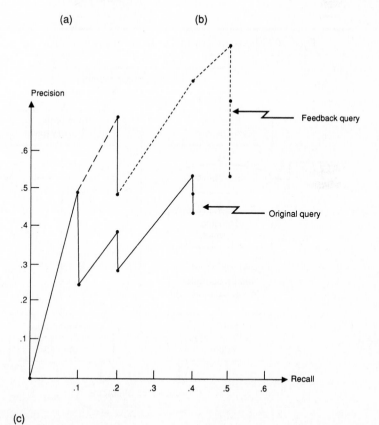

Precision

.6
.5
.4
.3
.2
.1

Feedback query

Original query

Recall

.1 .2 .3 .4 .5 .6

(c)

The test-and-control evaluation method poses fewer conceptual problems than residual-collection evaluation, but splitting the collection into halves with similar relevance properties is not always easy to do.

The relevance feedback process generates improved query formulations without modifying the document vectors themselves. A similar approach, however, can be used to also alter the document vectors in the course of operations. Such a *document-space modification* operation improves document indexes, reflecting the experiences of prior collection processing. [13,14] In one such operation, the vectors of documents previously retrieved in response to a common query are modified by moving documents identified as relevant closer to the common query, and at the same time moving documents identified as nonrelevant away from the query. This operation is represented in simplified form in Fig. 10.7. It is clear from the illustration that when the relevant items approach a common query location, these documents will resemble each other more closely than before, and therefore can be retrieved more easily in response to a similar query submitted lat-

Figure 10.6 Test-and-control collection evaluation.

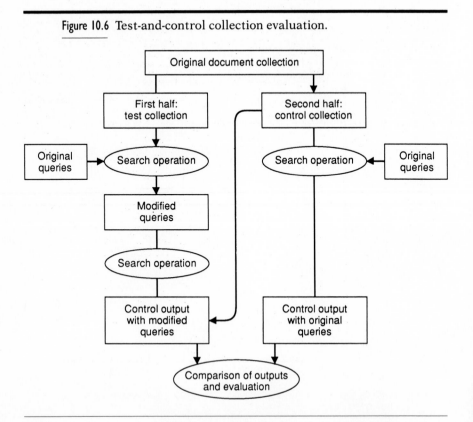

er. The converse is true for the nonrelevant documents that are shifted away from the query.

The easiest way to modify the vectors of the desired documents is to add the terms from the query vector to the documents previously identified as relevant, and subtract the query terms from the documents identified as nonrelevant. [13] Care must be taken to control the movements of the documents in the vector space. Since relevance assessments by users are necessarily subjective, each individual document movement must remain small, ensuring that substantial changes in document position reflect the effects of many small individual modifications performed by different users. In practice, then, only small modifications of the term weights are allowed at each iteration.

The automatic document-space-modification process can be used to control a collection by "promoting" documents deemed important, at the same time "demoting" those considered extraneous. Such an approach serves to control a collection's growth by identifying unimportant items — those never requested during previous searches — and eventually removing them from the collection, or shifting them to an auxiliary portion of the files. [15,16]

Various document-retirement algorithms have been used experimentally, including procedures in which the weights of all promotable documents — those retrieved early in a search, or deemed relevant by users — are multiplied by a small positive quantity in each search iteration, while demotable documents — those retrieved at the bottom of

---

Figure 10.7 Document-space modification.

● Relevant document
■ Nonrelevant document
▲ Query

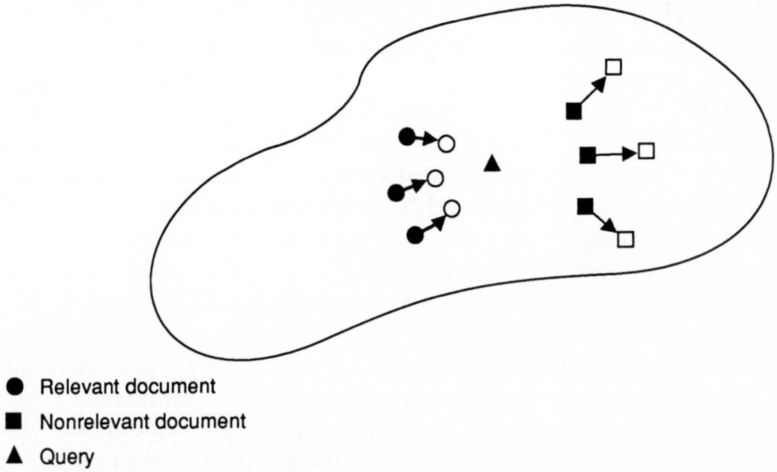

the ranked output lists — are multiplied by a small negative quantity. Instead of altering the term weights directly, a separate usage indicator attached to each document can be modified appropriately. In any case, documents are retired from the collection when the value of the document usage indicator, or the average term weight, falls below a given threshold. Retirement algorithms can also be based on conventional document-space-modification methods of the kind illustrated in Fig. 10.7, in which items that have been moved out to the far periphery of the document space are eliminated.

Document-space-modification methods are difficult to evaluate in the laboratory, where no users are available to dynamically control the space modifications by submitting queries. However, indications are that substantial growth in a collection can be accommodated without requiring basic changes in the collection's organization, and that document-retirement rates of up to 10 percent will affect search recall and precision only minimally. [15,16]

10.2 Automatic Document Classification

10.2.1 General Considerations

A disadvantage of conventional information-retrieval methodology, using inverted index files, is that the information pertaining to a document is scattered among many different inverted-term lists. Further, information relating to different documents with similar term assignments is not in close proximity in the file system. If browsing is to be permitted in the document collection, however, data about related items should appear close together. Browsing operations become possible when collection grouping, or *clustering* operations, group into common areas items judged to be similar. Clustered document collections can be maintained in addition to the normal inverted-index files. In that case, collection searches can be conducted conventionally, and browsing operations carried out using the special cluster structure. Alternatively, inverted indexes may be completely abandoned when a clustered file organization is available — the cluster structure can in fact be used for both searching and browsing.

In general, a clustered file provides efficient file access by limiting the searches to those document clusters which appear to be most similar to the corresponding queries. At the same time, clustered file searches may also be effective in retrieving the wanted items whenever the so-called *cluster hypothesis* holds — that is, when associations between documents, measured by document-document similarity coefficients, convey information about the joint relevance of documents to queries in a collection. [4,17,18]

The outline of a typical clustered file appears in Fig. 10.8, in which the main file is assumed to be grouped into three large clusters, each subdivided into a number of smaller, lower-level clusters that in turn contain individual documents, each represented by an x. Depending on the subject areas covered, a collection may be divided into many different clustering levels, instead of only the three levels in Fig. 10.8. In a clustered file, each cluster, or supercluster, can be represented by a special term vector, known as the *cluster centroid*. The centroid may actually be identical to a particular document included in the corresponding cluster; more usually, it is a special dummy item separately constructed from the remaining vectors in the cluster and located in the center of the corresponding cluster. The centroids in Fig. 10.8 include a hypercentroid, representing the center for the complete space; supercentroids, representing the next level of the structure; and the lower-level centroids, representing regular clusters. Using a file organization like the one shown in the figure, a file search can be conducted by comparing the query first against the highest-level centroids (supercentroids in the figure). For higher-level centroids that prove sufficiently similar to the query, a query-centroid comparison is then carried out with the lower-level centroids. This operation is re-

Figure 10.8 Typical clustered file organization.

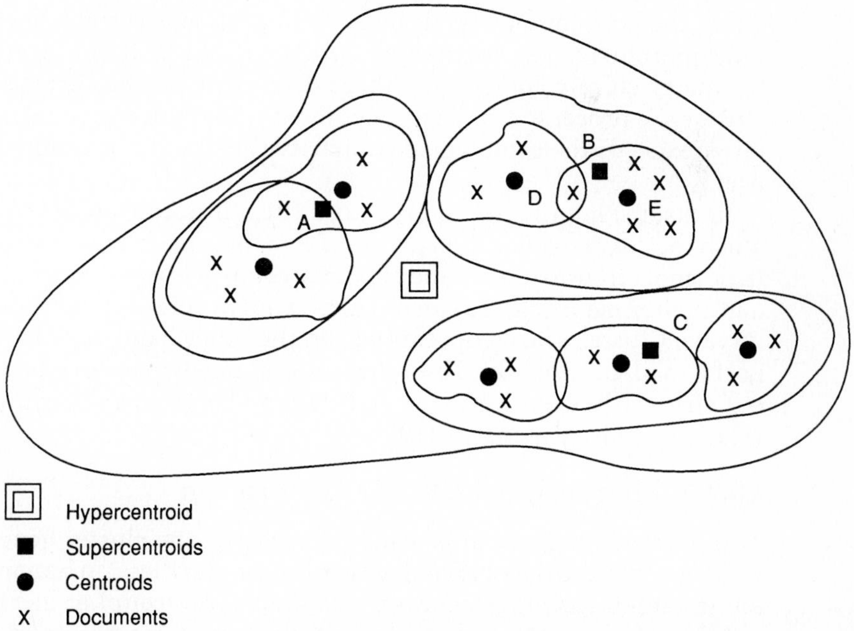

	Hypercentroid
■	Supercentroids
●	Centroids
X	Documents

Figure 10.9 Search strategy for clustered file of Figure 10.8.

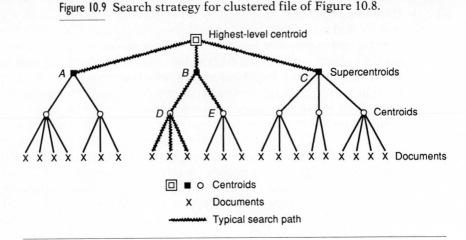

peated until eventually some actual documents are identified that are included in some of the low-level clusters.

A search tree for the cluster organization of Fig. 10.8 is shown in Fig. 10.9. A typical search carried out with this cluster structure first compares the query with the three supercentroids, labeled A, B, and C in Fig. 10.9. Assuming that supercentroid B is similar to the sample query, the next comparison is made with centroids D and E, located in the supercluster represented by supercentroid B. If D now matches the query closely enough, the three documents in the corresponding cluster are processed, and any document whose query-document similarity exceeds the established similarity threshold is presented to the user.

In discussing the use of clustered files, it is convenient to distinguish the *cluster-generation* process from the *cluster-search* strategies. In normal circumstances, the cluster structure is generated only once, and cluster maintenance can be carried out at relatively infrequent intervals. Cluster-search operations, on the other hand, may have to be performed continually. These operations must therefore be carried out efficiently, even while the generation process may be slower and relatively more expensive. [19]

10.2.2 Hierarchical Cluster Generation

Two main strategies can be used to carry out the cluster generation. First, a complete list of all pairwise item similarities can be constructed, in which case it is necessary to employ a grouping mechanism capable of assembling into common clusters items with sufficiently large pairwise similarities. Alternatively, *heuristic methods* can be used that do not require pairwise item similarities to be computed. When clustering does depend on pairwise item similarities, a term-document matrix such as that of Fig. 10.2 is conveniently used as a starting point, followed by a comparison of all distinct pairs of matrix rows to be used for document clustering (or of matrix columns to be used for term clustering). The pairwise comparison of matrix columns produces $N(N-1)/2$ different pairwise similarity coefficients for the documents (or $t(t-1)/2$ different pairwise term similarities). No matter what specific clustering method is used, the clustering process can be carried out either *divisively* or *agglomeratively.* In the former case, the complete collection is assumed to represent one complete cluster that is subsequently broken down into smaller pieces. In the latter, individual item similarities are used as a starting point, and a gluing operation collects similar items, or groups, into larger groups.

A simple program outline for a hierarchical, agglomerative clustering process appears in Fig. 10.10. [20] Each item is placed in a class by itself and then the two most similar items are combined into a class; the combining process is continued until only a single class of objects remains. The crucial step is combination — step 3 of Fig. 10.10. When two single documents are combined into a class, the clustering criterion is simply the size of the similarity coefficient between them. When larger clusters must be combined, a criterion of closeness between clusters must be specified. Several possibilities present themselves: [20,21]

- In *single-link* clustering, the similarity between a pair of clusters is taken to be the similarity between the *most similar* pair of items, one of which appears in each cluster; thus each cluster member will be more similar to at least one member in that same cluster than to any member of another cluster.

Figure 10.10 Basic program for hierarchical agglomerative clustering (adapted from [20]).

1. Compute all pairwise document-document similarity coefficients ($N(N - 1)/2$ coefficients)

2. Place each of N documents into a class of its own

3. Form a new cluster by combining the most similar pair of current clusters i and j; update similarity matrix by deleting the rows and columns corresponding to i and j; calculate the entries in the row corresponding to the new cluster $i + j$

4. Repeat step 3 if the number of clusters left is greater than 1

- In *complete-link* clustering, the similarity between the *least similar* pair of items from the two clusters is used as the cluster similarity; thus each cluster member is more similar to the most dissimilar member of that cluster than to the most dissimilar member of any other cluster.

- *Group-average* clustering is a compromise between the extremes of the single-link and complete-link systems, in that each cluster member has a greater average similarity to the remaining members of that cluster than it does to all members of any other cluster.

Consider, for example, the ordered pairwise similarity coefficients of Table 10.2 for six items labeled A to F. [22] For N items, there will be $N(N-1)/2$ pairwise similarities, and any sorting operation necessary to arrange the similarity pairs in decreasing order of similarity will require of the order of $N^2 \log N^2$ operations. Table 10.3 shows a single-link clustering process for the sample items of Table 10.2. The similarity pairs are processed in decreasing order of pairwise similarity. The hierarchical nature of the clustering operations is displayed in tree form in Table 10.3 The smallest, tightest clusters appear at the bottom

Table 10.2 Ordered pairwise similarity coefficients for six items labeled to A to F.

Step	Pair	Similarity
1	AF	0.9
2	AE	0.8
3	BF	0.8
4	BE	0.7
5	AD	0.6
6	AC	0.5
7	BD	0.5
8	CE	0.5
9	BC	0.4
10	DE	0.4
11	AB	0.3
12	CD	0.3
13	EF	0.3
14	CF	0.2
15	DF	0.1

Table 10.3 Single-link cluster generation.

Step Number	Similarity Pair	Single-link Structure	Items Covered	Similarity Matrix

1. AF 0.9 — structure: 0.9 over A, F — Items Covered: A, F

	A	B	C	D	E	F
A	.	.3	.5	.6	.8	.9
B	.3	.	.4	.5	.7	.8
C	.5	.4	.	.3	.5	.2
D	.6	.5	.3	.	.4	.1
E	.8	.7	.5	.4	.	.3
F	.9	.8	.2	.1	.3	.

2. AE 0.8 — structure: 0.8 over (0.9 over A, F) and E — Items Covered: A, E, F

	AF	B	C	D	E
AF	.	.8	.5	.6	.8
B	.8	.	.4	.5	.7
C	.5	.4	.	.3	.5
D	.6	.5	.3	.	.4
E	.8	.7	.5	.4	.

3. BF 0.8 — structure: 0.8 over (0.9 over A, F) and E, B — Items Covered: A, B, E, F

	AEF	B	C	D
AEF	.	.8	.5	.6
B	.8	.	.4	.5
C	.5	.4	.	.3
D	.6	.5	.3	.

4. BE 0.7 — no change —

	ABEF	C	D
ABEF	.	.5	.6
C	.5	.	.3
D	.6	.3	.

5. AD 0.6 — structure: 0.6 over (0.8 over (0.9 over A, F) and E, B) and D — Items Covered: A, B, D, E, F

6. AC 0.5 — structure: 0.5 over (0.6 over (0.8 over (0.9 over A, F) and E, B) and D) and C — Items Covered: A, B, C, D, E, F

	ABDEF	B
ABDEF	.	.5
C	.5	.

of the cluster tree, and increasingly larger clusters are formed at lower similarity levels as one proceeds upward in the tree.

Table 10.3 illustrates the following cluster-formation process: [22]

1. A cluster is first formed of items A and F at a similarity level of 0.9; the matrix manipulation of step 3 of Fig. 10.10 consists of replacing rows A and F of the matrix by a combined row AF, and columns A and F of the matrix by a combined column AF. In constructing the new AF row and column, the similarity between AF and each remaining document is the maximum of the similarities between either A or F and each third item. Thus, since sim(A,B) = 0.3 and sim(F,B) = 0.8, sim(AF,B) is defined as 0.8. Similar considerations control the formation of sim (AF,C), sim (AF,D), and sim (AF,E).

2. A larger three-item cluster is formed next that includes A, E, and F at a similarity level of 0.8. This step is represented by merging rows AF and E of the similarity matrix.

3. A larger cluster of the four items A, B, E, and F appears next at a similarity level of 0.8 obtained from pair (B,F), and generated by combining rows AEF and B of the similarity matrix.

4. A cluster of the five items A, B, D, E and F is then formed at a similarity level of 0.6; this cluster is generated after reaching pair (A,D).

5. A final six-item cluster at level 0.5 can be formed after processing pair (A,C).

The single-link clustering process stops after step 6 of the table since all six existing items are now clustered. Note that no change occurs in the cluster structure when the similarity pair (B,E) is taken up at step 4, because both items B and item E are already present in the cluster hierarchy at a higher similarity level than specified by (B,E). Two sample single-link cluster structures produced by the process of the table are shown in Fig. 10.11 for assumed similarity thresholds of 0.7 and 0.5, respectively. As the example shows, the single-link process tends to produce a small number of large clusters that are characterized by a *chaining* effect, in which each element is usually attached to only one other member of the same cluster at each similarity level.

In a single-link clustering process, it is sufficient to remember the list of previously clustered single items; the process can be stopped when all single items are included in the clustered tree. In a complete-link clustering system, on the other hand, the clustering steps depend on the similarity coefficients between each item and all other elements in the same cluster, making it necessary to remember the list of all item pairs previously considered in the clustering process. The example of Table 10.4 illustrates the data shown earlier in Table 10.2. [22]

As shown in Table 10.4, the first processed pair (A,F) immediately leads to the formation of a complete-link cluster, since neither item A nor item F has previously been seen. In eliminating matrix rows A and F to create row AF, the minimum similarities between A or F and each third item must be used to specify the coefficients of the combined row AF. In particular, since $sim(A,B) = 0.3$ and $sim(F,B) = 0.8$, the similarity between B and the combined AF is computed as $sim(AF,B) = min(0.3, 0.8) = 0.3$.

When the next similarity pair (A,E) is considered, no change is produced in the cluster structure because item E cannot be added to cluster AF without knowing the similarities for both pair (A,E) and pair (E,F). The same is true when pair (B,F) is processed because the similarity between B and AF depends on $sim(A,B)$ as well as $sim(B,F)$. If a checklist is kept of all similarity pairs previously considered, as in column 3 of Table 10.4, actual clustering can be confined to instances when two completely new items are encountered, or when all related similarity pairs have previously been seen.

Several complete-link clusters are represented in Fig. 10.12 for the example of Table 10.4. After step 4, two clusters of two items each are formed at a similarity threshold of 0.7 (see Fig. 10.12a). It is necessary to wait until step 9 before enlarging the (B,E) cluster by inclusion of item C at a similarity level of 0.4. The resulting structure is shown in Fig. 10.12(b). A further enlargement occurs at step 12, when cluster (B,C,D,E) is formed at a similarity level of 0.3. A comparison of Figs. 10.11 and 10.12 shows that the complete-link and single-link clustering methods lead to very different cluster structures. A single-link system produces a small number of large, poorly linked clusters, whereas the complete-link process produces a much larger number of small,

Figure 10.11 Single-link clusters for example of Table 10.3. (a) Similarity level 0.7. (b) Similarity level 0.5.

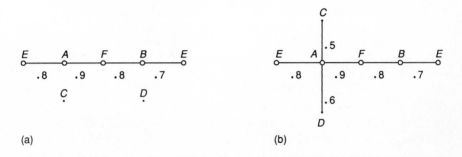

(a)

(b)

Table 10.4 Complete-link cluster generation.

Step Number and Similarity Pair	Check Operations	Complete Link Structure and Pairs Covered	Similarity Matrix

			A	B	C	D	E	F
1. *AF* 0.9	new	0.9 / A F	A	.	.3	.5	.6	.8	.9
			B	.3	.	.4	.5	.7	.8
			C	.5	.4	.	.3	.5	.2
			D	.6	.5	.3	.	.4	.1
2. *AE* 0.8	check *EF* ×	(A, E)	E	.8	.7	.5	.4	.	.3
		(A, F)	F	.9	.8	.2	.1	.3	.

3. *BF* 0.8 — check *AB* × — (A, E) (A, F) / (B, F)

4. *BE* 0.7	new	0.7 / B E		AF	B	C	D	E

			AF	.	.3	.2	.1	.3
			B	.3	.	.4	.5	.7
			C	.2	.4	.	.3	.5
5. *AD* 0.6	check *DF* ×	(A, D) (A, E) (A, F)	D	.1	.5	.3	.	.4
		(B, E) (B, F)	E	.3	.7	.5	.4	.

6. *AC* 0.6 — check *CF* × — (A, C) (A, D) (A, E) (A, F) / (B, E) (B, F)

7. *BD* 0.5 — check *DE* × — (A, C) (A, D) (A, E) (A, F) / (B, D) (B, E) (B, F)

8. *CE* 0.5	check *BC* ×	0.4		AF	BE	C	D

			AF	.	.3	.2	.1
			BE	.3	.	.4	.4
9. *BC* 0.4	check *CE* 0.5	0.7 C / B E	C	.2	.4	.	.3
			D	.1	.4	.3	.

10. *DE* 0.4	check *BD* 0.5	(A, C) (A, D) (A, E) (A, F)
	check *CD* ×	(B, C) (B, D) (B, E) (B, F)
		(C, E) (D, E)

11. *AB* 0.3	check *AC* 0.5	(A, B) (A, C) (A, D) (A, E) (A, F)
	AE 0.8	(B, C) (B, D) (B, E) (B, F)
	BF 0.8	(C, E) (D, E)
	CF ×	
	EF ×	

Table 10.4 (continued) Complete-link cluster generation.

Step Number and Similarity Pair	Check Operations	Complete Link Structure	Similarity Matrix
12. CD 0.3	check BD 0.5 DE 0.4		AF BCE D AF . .2 .1 BCE .2 . .3 D .1 .3 .
13. EF 0.3	check BF 0.8 CF × DF ×	(A, B) (A, C) (A, D) (A, E) (A, F) (B, C) (B, D) (B, E) (B, F) (C, D) (C, E) (D, E) (E, F)	
14. CF 0.2	check BF 0.8 EF 0.3 DF ×	(A, B) (A, C) (A, D) (A, E) (A, F) (B, C) (B, D) (B, E) (B, F) (C, D) (C, E) (C, F) (D, E) (E, F)	
15. DF 0.1	last pair		AF BCDE AF . .1 BCDE .1 .

tightly linked groupings. Because each item in a complete-link cluster is guaranteed to resemble all other items in that cluster at the stated similarity level, the complete-link clustering system may be better adapted to retrieval than the single-link clusters, where similarities between items may be very low. Unfortunately, a complete-link cluster generation is more expensive to perform than a comparable single-link process as shown by the comparison of the procedures in Tables 10.3 and 10.4.

All the hierarchical clustering methods described up to now are based on full knowledge of all pairwise item similarities. The computation of item similarities can be based on document-vector representations and the corresponding inverted-term lists. Conceptually, the simplest method consists of taking each available list from the inverted index and computing the pairwise similarities for all pairs of distinct items appearing on each list. [23] The corresponding program is outlined in Fig. 10.13. This performs a similarity computation whenever two item identifiers appear jointly on any common term list.

When two items share several terms in common, the corresponding item identifiers will appear on several term lists, and the same similarity values will be recomputed many times. Recomputing similarities for the same pairs of items can be avoided by maintaining an auxiliary vector S_j of length N for each document D_j, and setting S_{ji}, the ith element of S_j, equal to 1 whenever $sim(D_j,D_i)$ is first computed. A check of the S_j vector carried out before each similarity computation is initiated reveals whether a particular coefficient must be generated. [24] The corresponding program is shown in Fig. 10.14.

An even faster process uses an auxiliary vector V of dimension N for each item in the collection. However, instead of identifying the documents already matched against a particular item D_i, the vector element V_{ji} specifies the number of term matches (or the sum of the weights of the matching terms) between the given item D_j and all other items D_i. [25] When the V_j vector is available for a given item D_j, it is easy to generate the similarities between D_j and all other items D_i ($i > j$) that have common terms with D_j. For example, using the Dice coefficient of Table 10.1, the item similarities can be defined in terms of the coefficients of vector V_j as follows:

$$sim(D_j,D_i) = \frac{2 \cdot V_{ji}}{|D_j| + |D_i|} \qquad (10.11)$$

Figure 10.12 Complete link clusters for example of Table 10.4. (a) Similarity level 0.7. (b) Similarity level 0.4. (c) Similarity level 0.3.

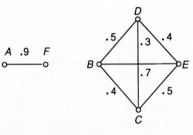

(a)

(b)

(c)

Figure 10.13 Basic generation of pairwise item similarities [23].

$D_i = (d_{i1},d_{i2},...,d_{it})$ document vector for D_i

$L_j = (l_{j1},l_{j2},...,l_{jnj})$ inverted list for term T_j

$\quad l_{ji}$ document identifier (and weight) of ith document listed under term T_j

$\quad n_j$ number of postings (or list length $|L_j|$) for term T_j

$\quad$ **for** $j = 1$ to t (for each of t possible terms)

$\quad\quad$ **for** $i = 1$ to n_j (for all n_j entries on the jth list)

$\quad\quad\quad$ compute sim $(D_{l_{ji}},D_{l_{j,i+k}})$ $i + 1 \leq k \leq n_j$

$\quad\quad$ **end for**

$\quad$ **end for**

---

in which $|D_i|$ and $|D_j|$ represent the number of terms assigned to D_i and D_j respectively. [25]

It should be noted that when an auxiliary vector such as S or V is used to compute item similarities, substantial additional storage and processing resources are required — in particular, N different vectors

---

Figure 10.14 Generation of pairwise item similarities without recomputations [24].

---

for $j = 1$ to N (for each document in collection)

$\quad$ set $S(j) = 0, 1 \leq j \leq N$

$\quad$ **for** $k = 1$ to n_j (for each term in document)

$\quad\quad$ take up inverted list L_k

$\quad\quad$ **for** $i = 1$ to n_k (for each document identifier on list)

$\quad\quad\quad$ **if** $i < j$ or **if** $S_{ji} = 1$

$\quad\quad\quad\quad$ take up next document D_i

$\quad\quad\quad$ **else** compute sim(D_j,D_i)

$\quad\quad\quad\quad$ set $S_{ji} = 1$

$\quad\quad$ **end for**

$\quad$ **end for**

end for

---

of length N. Since each vector must be completely scanned for each document, the number of needed scans is of order N^2. However, when the similarity coefficients between items depend on only the number of common terms between the two items, or the sum of the weights of the common terms (as is the case for the Dice coefficient of expression (10.11)), the item vectors themselves need not be fetched from memory because the relevant information can be obtained from the V vectors directly.

10.2.3 Heuristic Clustering Methods

The hierarchical clustering strategies just described are based on prior knowledge of all pairwise similarities between items. Therefore the corresponding cluster-generation methods are relatively expensive to perform. In return, these methods produce a unique set of well-formed clusters for each set of data, regardless of the order in which the similarity pairs are introduced into the clustering process. Furthermore, the resulting cluster hierarchy is stable in that small changes in input data do not lead to large rearrangements in the cluster structure.

These desirable clustering properties are given up when heuristic clustering methods are used; heuristic methods produce rough cluster arrangements rapidly at relatively little expense. The simplest heuristic process, a *one-pass* procedure, takes the elements to be clustered one at a time in arbitrary order, requiring no advance knowledge of item similarities. [19,26] Item 1 is first taken and placed into a cluster of its own. Each subsequent item is then compared against all existing clusters (initially against item 1 only), and is placed in a previously existing cluster whenever it is similar enough to that cluster. If a new item is not sufficiently similar to any existing cluster, the new item forms a cluster of its own. This process is continued until the last element is processed. To determine the similarity between an established cluster and a newly introduced element, it is convenient to represent each cluster by a centroid. The relevant clusters are then determined at each point by computing the similarities between all existing centroids and each new, incoming item. When an item is added to an existing cluster, the corresponding centroid must then be appropriately updated.

This single-pass process usually produces uneven and probably undesirable cluster structures. In particular, certain generated clusters may become very large, whereas others will consist of single items. For this reason, controls must be introduced over cluster sizes, the number of clusters, and the proportion of overlap (that is, the number of common items) between clusters. Cluster size is most easily controlled by using parameters specifying a desirable average cluster size, and splitting clusters into separate pieces when the maximum permitted size is exceeded. Figure 10.15 shows a cluster-splitting operation in which the maximum cluster size allowed is four. When a new item is added to cluster A (see Fig. 10.15b), the size limitations are exceeded and two new clusters, labeled A' and A", are formed, as shown in Fig. 10.15(c). This splitting operation affects supercluster S, which now includes five subclusters instead of the four allowed. Hence supercluster S must itself be split into two pieces S' and S", as shown in Fig. 10.15(d). [19]

Cluster splitting is easy to perform by comparing the elements in the oversize cluster with each other and placing in a common subcluster all sufficiently similar elements. Reverse cluster merging can also be implemented to collect into larger groups any isolated items that do not fit into existing cluster structures. The number of clusters to be formed and the overlap among clusters can be controlled by variable similarity thresholds that help enlarge relatively empty clusters, while preventing new additions to clusters that are almost full. In the former case, the clustering thresholds used are quite low, while higher cluster thresholds are used when the clusters are almost full.

Single-pass clustering produces cluster arrangements that vary according to the order in which individual items are introduced. It is therefore not certain that the cluster hierarchy in fact accurately represents the similarity properties of individual items. Available experimental evidence indicates, however, that in many retrieval settings this system produces results about as effective as those based on hierarchical agglomerative methodologies.

A somewhat different heuristic clustering method is based on identifying individual items that lie in dense regions of the document space, that is, items surrounded by many other items in close proximity. [5,27,28] When such an item is located, it is used as a cluster seed, and all sufficiently similar items in the same general vicinity then form a common class of items. More specifically, a *density test* is performed sequentially for all items not yet clustered. Whenever an item passes the density test by exhibiting a sufficient number of close neighbors, a clustering operation forms a new cluster around the item. The density-test process is then resumed with the next item not yet clustered. At the end of the process, some items remain unclustered either because they failed the density test, or because they were too far removed from cluster seeds to fit into any existing cluster. Such "loose" items may be left unclustered, or they may be assembled into cluster structures of their own.

Another heuristic clustering method consists of *refining* any existing cluster arrangement that may already be defined for a set of items. Thus given a collection of existing clusters and cluster centroids, each item can be compared against all existing cluster centroids; an item

Figure 10.15 Example of cluster-splitting process. ▣ Top level centroid ▢ Second level centroid • Third level centroid × Individual file item [19]. (a) Initial state of cluster structure. (b) Addition of one more item to cluster *A*. (c) Splitting cluster *A* into two pieces *A'* and *A"*. (d) Splitting superclusters *S* into two pieces *S'* and *S"*. (Reprinted from ACM/TODS, Vol. 3, No. 4, December 1978. Courtesy of ACM Publications.)

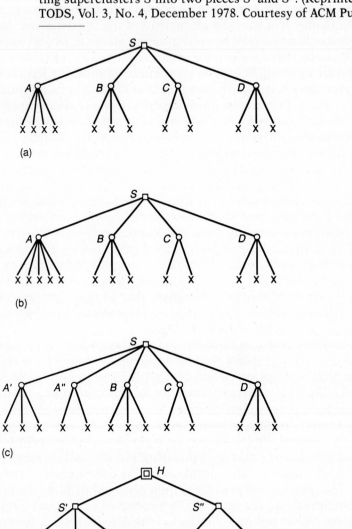

can then be placed into the cluster with the maximum item-centroid similarity. If this entails a shift of any item from one cluster to another, the corresponding centroids are recomputed, and the item-centroid comparisons repeated in a subsequent iteration until no further shifting between clusters occurs for any item. It can be shown that, with appropriate parameter settings, this cluster-refinement process converges in a small number of iterations. [29]

A somewhat related adaptive-clustering method first assigns to each item an arbitrary, randomly chosen position in the cluster structure. Whenever two positively related items are identified — for example, they may be jointly retrieved in response to a common query, or designated as relevant to a given query in a feedback process — their positions in the structure are slightly shifted to decrease the distance between them and increase their similarity. Whenever two particular items are shifted toward each other, two other, arbitrarily chosen items are moved slightly apart to make them more dissimilar. This iterative item-shifting operation, reminiscent of document-space modification, produces collection arrangements that directly depend on the judgments of users obtained during collection processing. It has been shown that the adaptive process converges rapidly to produce cluster structures. [30]

10.2.4 Cluster Searching

Clustered files sometimes allow rapid file searches by confining the actual query-document searches to small portions of the file. Clustered file searching is conceptually simpler than cluster generation. Whereas cluster generation can sometimes be performed without constructing formal cluster centroids, cluster search is usually based on an auxiliary file of *cluster centroids*. A cluster centroid is typically constructed as the average vector of all the documents in a given cluster; that is, the weight of centroid term j is defined as the average of the weights of the jth terms in the clustered documents. When a stored centroid file is available, a cluster search proceeds by comparing some of the centroid vectors with the available queries, while retrieving certain documents located in clusters with sufficiently high query-centroid similarities.

Two main strategies are distinguished for searching a cluster hierarchy, known respectively as *top down* and *bottom up*. In a top-down search, the query is first compared with the highest-level centroids, as suggested earlier in Fig. 10.9, and the search proceeds downward in the cluster tree until eventually some individual items in the lowest-level clusters are chosen for retrieval. In a bottom-up search, only the lowest-level centroids are stored — that is, those containing specific items of the collection — and the higher-level cluster structure is disregarded. Starting with the low-level centroids, the best clusters (those with the highest query-centroid similarity) are identified, and some of the documents located in these clusters are then retrieved.

In the sample cluster tree of Fig. 10.16, the centroids are numbered and the individual documents are identified by alphabetic characters. [22] In the figure the query-centroid or query-document similarities are entered next to the corresponding centroid or document symbols. Low-level centroids which directly contain specific documents are shaded. Because the number of low-level centroids may be very large in operational files, it is often useful to build an auxiliary index, such as an inverted index of low-level centroid terms, for use in a bottom-up search. In comparing top-down and bottom-up cluster searches, a tradeoff is apparent between the small expense of storing the centroids in a bottom-up search, and the added cost of storing and maintaining the low-level centroid index.

Two possible retrieval disciplines can be used with either a top-down or bottom-up search. Certain complete clusters can be retrieved consisting of all documents included in these clusters; alternatively, each item included in certain low-level clusters can be individually compared with the queries, and only selected items withdrawn from each cluster. Searches that retrieve individual documents as opposed to complete clusters are more expensive to perform, but usually produce better results.

Two sample searches are illustrated in Figs. 10.17 and 10.18, covering a top-down entire cluster strategy and a bottom-up individual item

Figure 10.16 Sample cluster hierarchy (adapted from [22]). Cluster centroids are numbered; individual documents are identified by letters; similarity coefficients with query are shown in parentheses; and low-level centroids are shaded. (Courtesy of Dr. Ellen Voorhees, Siemens Research Laboratory.)

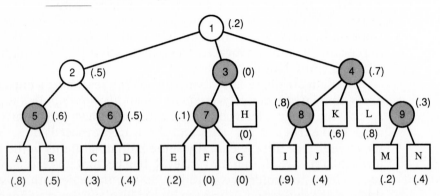

search, respectively. In both cases, the sample cluster hierarchy of Fig. 10.16 is used under the assumption that three documents must be retrieved. The top-down entire cluster search of Fig. 10.17 proceeds downward in the cluster tree and enters the best centroid at each point on an active node list. The downward movement continues until a cluster is located that contains not more than the number of wanted items. This strategy first locates cluster 8 containing two items (I and J); the next-best centroid is then taken up, and cluster 5 is eventually retrieved with items A and B. In the individual bottom-up search of Fig. 10.18, the items located in the three best bottom-level clusters are ranked in order, and the three best items picked for retrieval. This strategy retrieves items I, L, and A.

Figure 10.17 Top-down entire-cluster search strategy (adapted from [22]). (a) Program. (b) Sample top-down entire-cluster search. (Courtesy of Dr. Ellen Voorhees, Siemens Research Laboratory.)

1. Initialize by adding top item to active node list;

2. Take centroid with highest query similarity from active node list;

   if the number of singleton items in subtree headed by that centroid is not larger than number of items wanted,

   then retrieve these singleton items and eliminate the centroid from active node list;

   else eliminate the centroid with highest query similarity from active node list and add its sons to active node list;

3. **if** number retrieved ≥ number wanted **then** stop

   else repeat step 2

(a)

Active node list	Number of single items in subtree	Retrieved items
(1, .2)	14 (too big)	
(2, .5), (4, .7), (3, 0)	6 (too big)	
(2, .5), (8, .8), (9, .3), (3, 0)	2	I,J
(2, .5), (9, .3), (3, 0)	4 (too big)	
(5, .6), (6, .5), (9, .3), (3, 0)	2	A,B

(b)

Since the upper levels of the cluster hierarchy are disregarded in a bottom-up search, the number of needed query-centroid comparisons, and hence the retrieval effort, is smaller for bottom-up than for top-down searches. On the other hand, when small tight clusters are used as in a complete-link clustering system, a top-down cluster search simplifies the identification of useful bottom-level clusters because a definite search path is followed from one level to the next.

Most cluster-search strategies have not been used widely because of the conceptual problems that arise in clustering very large files and maintaining the clustered organizations in a dynamic file environment. A comparison of clustered file searches with the more widely used inverted-file technologies involves aspects of file usage that are difficult to measure. In general, the efficiencies of inverted-file search techniques are difficult to match with any other file-search system because the only documents directly handled in the inverted-list approach are those included in certain inverted lists that are known in advance to have at least one term in common with the queries. In a clustered organization, on the other hand, many cluster centroids, and ultimately many documents, must be compared with query formulations that may have little in common with the queries. However, since similar records are collected in common groups in a clustered file, browsing is easy, and records similar to specific items can be located rapidly. The value of such a browsing capability is unfortunately difficult to assess in objective terms.

When the search efficiency of the top-down cluster search strategy is compared with that of an inverted-file search, it is found that cluster search requires about 50 percent more storage than inverted-file

---

Figure 10.18 Bottom-up individual-cluster search (adapted from [22]). (a) Program. (b) Sample search. (Courtesy of Dr. Ellen Voorhees, Siemens Research Laboratory.)

Take a specified number of low-level centroids

  if there are enough singleton items in those clusters to equal the number of items wanted,
    then retrieve the number of items wanted in ranked order;

  else add additional low-level centroids to list and repeat test

(a)

Active centroid list	Ranked documents from clusters	Retrieved items
$(8,.8), (4,.7), (5,.6)$	$(I,.9) (L,.8), (A,.8), (K,.6)$ $(B,.5) (J,.4), (N,.4), (M,.2)$	I,L,A

(b)

search, and that inverted-file search is substantially faster. The difference in memory requirements is not crucial because normal processing environments usually provide enough storage to accommodate either type of search. A comparison of the average number of pages of data (that is, cluster centroids or inverted lists of document identifiers) brought into internal memory shows that about five times more page accesses are needed for certain collections using a clustered search than using a comparable inverted-file search. Thus it is likely that inverted file searches will always remain faster than cluster searches, no matter how refined a cluster organization is available. However, the inverted-file strategy does not provide easy access to the complete record information, nor does it have a browsing capability.

10.3 ❖ Probabilistic Retrieval Model

In the vector-space model the assumption is made that the terms forming the basis for the vector space are orthogonal, and that existing term relationships need not be taken into account. Furthermore, many of the parameters that control the vector-space operations, such as the query-document similarity measure, are not specified within the model and must be chosen somewhat arbitrarily. The probabilistic model can include term dependencies and relationships, and major parameters such as the weighting of query terms and the form of the query-document similarity are determined by the model itself. [31,32]

The probabilistic approach is based on two main parameters, $\Pr(rel)$, the probability of relevance, and $\Pr(nonrel)$, the probability of nonrelevance of a record. If relevance is assumed to be a binary property, $\Pr(nonrel) = 1 - \Pr(rel)$. In addition, two cost parameters are used, designated a_1 and a_2, representing the loss associated with the retrieval of a nonrelevant record and the nonretrieval of a relevant record, respectively. Because the retrieval of a nonrelevant record carries a loss of $a_1 \cdot [1 - \Pr(rel)]$, and the rejection of a nonrelevant item has an associated loss factor of $a_2 \cdot \Pr(rel)$, the total loss caused by a given retrieval process will be minimized if an item is retrieved whenever

$$a_2 \cdot \Pr(rel) \geq a_1 [1 - \Pr(rel)]. \tag{10.15}$$

Equivalently, a retrieval function g may be introduced, where

$$g = \frac{\Pr(rel)}{1 - \Pr(rel)} - \frac{a_1}{a_2}, \tag{10.16}$$

and an item may then be retrieved whenever its g value is nonnegative.

Function g cannot be evaluated without relating it to other design parameters. In particular, the relevance properties of records must be related to the relevance properties of various terms attached to records. In particular, using Bayes' theorem to replace $\Pr(rel|x)$ with $\Pr(x|rel)\Pr(rel)/\Pr(x)$ for each record x, and assuming that the loss parameters a_1 and a_2 are equal, one obtains

$$\log g(x) = \log \frac{\Pr(x|rel)}{\Pr(x|nonrel)} + \log \frac{\Pr(rel)}{\Pr(nonrel)}, \qquad (10.17)$$

where $\Pr(rel)$ and $\Pr(nonrel)$ are the a priori probabilities of relevance or nonrelevance of any record. The retrieval function of expression (10.17) was used in Chapter 9 to obtain an optimal term weight under the assumption that the terms are independently assigned to the relevant and nonrelevant parts of the collection.

Various formulations are suggested in the literature for expressing the occurrence properties of records $\Pr(x|rel)$ and $\Pr(x|nonrel)$ in terms of the individual term probabilities $\Pr(x_i|rel)$ and $\Pr(x_i|nonrel)$. One can assume, for example, that the term distributions in the records of the collection follow one of the well-known probabilistic models such as the Poisson, normal, or binomial distributions, and derive appropriate expressions valid for each case. [33] When the term distribution is exponential in the relevant and nonrelevant items, an exact formula for $\Pr(x|rel)$ (and analogously for $\Pr(x|nonrel)$) is given by the Bahadur and Lazarsfeld expansion (BL) [34,35]

$$\Pr(x|rel) = \prod_{k=1}^{t} p_k{}^{x_k}(1-p_k)^{1-x_k}\,[1+A] \qquad (10.18)$$

where

$$A = \sum_{i<j} \rho_{ij}\delta_i\delta_j - \sum_{i<j<k} \rho_{ijk}\delta_i\delta_j\delta_k + \ldots - \rho_{1,2\ldots t}\,\delta_1\delta_2\ldots\delta_t.$$

In expression (10.18), the assumption is made that each record x is identified by a collection of t binary terms $x = (x_1, x_2 ,\ldots, x_t)$, and p_i is defined as the occurrence probability of term T_i in the relevant items. That is,

$$p_i = \Pr(x_i=1|rel).$$

Furthermore,

$$\delta_i = (x_i-p_i) / \sqrt{p_i(1-p_i)},$$

and the term correlation coefficients are

$$\rho_{ij} = (p_{ij} - p_i p_j)/\sqrt{p_i(1-p_i)p_j(1-p_j)},$$
$$\rho_{ijk} = (p_{ijk} - p_{ij}p_k - p_{ik}p_j - p_{jk}p_i + 2p_ip_jp_k)/\sqrt{p_i(1-p_i)p_j(1-p_j)p_k(1-p_k)},$$

and so on. The pairwise correlations ρ_{ij} were expressed in vector notation as $T_i \cdot T_j$ at the beginning of this chapter; similarly, $\rho_{ijk} = T_i \cdot T_j \cdot T_k$, and so on.

The form of expression (10.18) shows that the evaluation of the BL formula presupposes a knowledge of the occurrence probabilities of all single terms p_i, p_j, p_k, all term pairs p_{ij}, p_{ik}, p_{jk}, all term triples p_{ijk}, and so on, for all subsets of the t terms. In practice, there is no hope of accumulating enough data to estimate all these needed probabilities. Hence the BL formula of expression (10.18) must be simplified. When term A in expression (10.18) is assumed to be 0, that is, when all term correlations are disregarded, the BL formula reduces to the form of Eq. (9.13) of Chapter 9. In that case, the probabilistic model becomes a form of the vector-space model where term orthogonality is assumed, as suggested in the discussion of probabilistic indexing in Chapter 9.

Less drastic simplifications in the BL formulation are obtained by taking into account only some of the more important pairwise term correlations, disregarding all the other multiterm correlations. One possibility consists of using the well-known *tree-dependence* model, where all terms (except a single distinguished term x_k) are assumed to depend on exactly one other term in the term set. [36,37] In that case, $\Pr(x|rel)$ (and analogously $\Pr(x|nonrel)$) can be represented as

$$\Pr(x|rel) = \prod_{i=1}^{t} \Pr(x_{m_i}|x_{m_{j(i)}}) \quad 0 \le j(i) < i, \qquad (10.19)$$

where $\Pr(x_k|x_{m_o}) = \Pr(x_k)$.

If p_i is then defined as $\Pr(x_i=1|x_{j(i)}=1)$ and q_i as $\Pr(x_i=1|x_{j(i)}=0)$, each term in expression (10.19) can be written as

$$\Pr(x_i|x_{j(i)}) = [p_i^{x_i}(1-p_i)^{1-x_i}]^{x_{j(i)}}[q_i^{x_i}(1-q_i)^{1-x_i}]^{1-x_{j(i)}}.$$

This in turn leads to a reduced but nonlinear formulation of the BL expression (10.18):

$$\log \Pr(x|rel) = \sum_{i=1}^{t} (x_i \log p_i + (1-x_i) \log (1-p_i))$$

$$+ \sum_{i=1}^{t} \left[x_{j(i)} \log \frac{1-p_i}{1-q_i} + x_i x_{j(i)} \log \frac{p_i(1-q_i)}{q_i(1-p_i)} \right] + \text{constants.} \quad (10.20)$$

The term-dependence model can be extended by including the effects not only of certain selected pairwise term dependencies, but also of some term triples and higher-order term dependencies. [38] However, the basic problem of all reduced term-dependency models remains the difficulty of including exactly the right subsets of terms in the computations, and of estimating the corresponding needed probabilistic parameters. Available evidence indicates that retrieval effectiveness can be improved substantially if it is assumed that all needed probabilistic parameters are known for all term subsets. However, not enough reliable term-occurrence information can be extracted from available document collections to produce improvements for reduced dependency models. [37–39]

Probabilistic models have been extended to cover the use of weighted terms, where the weights of the terms x_i are no longer restricted to 1 for terms that are present and 0 for terms that are absent. [40] One way to do this is to use the expected value of the retrieval function $g(x)$, that is, $E(g(x))$, instead of $g(x)$, as in formula (10.17)

$$E(g(x_i)) = \Pr(x_i=1|D) \, g(x_i=1) + \Pr(x_i=0|D) \, g(x_i=0). \quad (10.21)$$

Since $g(x_i=0) = 0$ when $x_i=0$, expression (10.21) reduces to

$$E(g(x_i)) = \Pr(x_i=1|D) \, g(x_i=1), \quad (10.22)$$

where the first term represents the probability that term x_i is assigned to document D. The corresponding probability can be interpreted as a term-significance weight of term x_i in document D. Croft estimates $\Pr(x_k=1|D)$ as $K+(1-K)n_{x_i}$, $0 \le K \le 1$, where $n_{x_i} = w_{x_i}/\max w_{x_i}$, and w_{x_i} is a normalized frequency weight of term x_i in the document under consideration. Since $g(x_i=1)$ can be reduced to a form of the inverse document frequency, as shown in Chapter 9, the formulation of expression (10.22) is interpretable as the well-known $(tf \cdot idf)$ term-weighting factor, introduced previously. Probabilistic approaches have also been used to control cluster-search strategies. [41,42]

Probabilistic retrieval models provide an important guide for characterizing retrieval processes, as well as a theoretical justification for practices previously used on an empirical basis, such as the introduction of certain term-weighting systems. The probabilistic methodology has not led to large improvements in retrieval effectiveness, however, because of the difficulties of obtaining representative values for the required term-occurrence parameters. In practice, term-occurrence probabilities in the relevant and nonrelevant parts of the collection have been estimated by using the set of relevant and nonrelevant items retrieved in earlier search operations. The relevant retrieved items may not, however, provide accurate samples of the complete set of relevant items. In these circumstances, probabilistic approaches are likely to approximate actual retrieval operations poorly.

10.4 ❖ Extended Boolean Retrieval Model

❖ 10.4.1 Fuzzy Set Extensions

In a practical retrieval environment, Boolean query formulations must normally be compared with the index term sets attached to the documents of a collection. Various measures designed to reflect the similarity, or distance, between queries and documents were introduced in Table 10.1. Those measures, however, cannot be used when the queries are formulated in a Boolean framework. Indeed, for normal Boolean queries only two values of query-document similarity are valid: 1 when the document indexing precisely matches the query formulation, and 0 when it does not. In conventional Boolean environments, then, it is impossible to generate a ranked output of the documents in decreasing order of query-document similarity because variable similarity coefficients cannot be computed between queries and documents.

Because of the practical importance of the Boolean query system, the global matching operations used in the vector model could be usefully extended to Boolean query formulations. This would guarantee that dynamic query-modification techniques such as relevance feedback could be applied to Boolean query formulations. The extended Boolean processing logic introduced in this section generalizes both the vector-processing and the Boolean query models and covers both these models as special cases.

Consider first the operations in the conventional Boolean framework, in which query formulations consist of term sets interrelated by the Boolean operators and, or, and and not. A pair of operands together with an interrelating operator constitutes a *Boolean clause* expressing term relationships, such as synonym relations for or, term-phrase relations for and, and restriction relations for and not. For each Boolean query Q and document D a two-step procedure can, in principle, be used to compute the query-document similarity sim(D,Q): [43]

1. Each query term q_i in Q is first replaced by a function $F(D,q_i)$ that in the conventional Boolean system evaluates to 1 if term q_i is present in D, and to 0 otherwise.

2. The resulting expression is processed using an evaluation table such as the one in Table 10.5 for the standard Boolean system; for Boolean statements containing more than one operator, the evaluation proceeds recursively one clause at a time starting with the innermost clause.

For a query Q such as ((t or s) and not r) and a document D containing terms t but not term s or term r, the functions $F(D,q)$ are defined as $F(D,t) = 1$ and $F(D,s) = F(D,r) = 0$. The first clause $F(D, t$ or $s)$ then evaluates to 1, and the complete formula becomes $1 \cdot (1-0) = 1$, showing that the value of D with respect to Q is 1.

Various extensions have been proposed to the Boolean processing system, the most important the introduction of document-term weights reflecting the importance of the individual terms attached to the documents of a collection. Assuming that the weight of a query term q_i in a document D is equal to k, the function $F(D,q_i)$ now evaluates to k, where k may take any value in the interval from 0 to 1. When document-term weights are introduced into a Boolean environment, the *fuzzy-set* methodology can be applied to the retrieval problem. [44–46] In a fuzzy-set environment, function $F(D,q)$ is known as the membership function of the term q in the set of documents indexed by q. The evaluation formulas of Table 10.5 remain unchanged, but the values of retrieval output for the documents can now range from 0 to 1. The fuzzy-set model is thus compatible with, and reduces to, a pure Boolean system when the document-term values are limited to 0 and 1.

Table 10.5 Query-document similarity evaluation for Boolean query forms (adapted from [43]).

Boolean Formulation	Evaluation Formula
$f(D,t$ and $s)$	min $(F(D,t),F(D,s))$ $F(D,t) \cdot F(D,s)$
$F(D,t$ or $s)$	max $(F(D,t),F(D,s))$ $F(D,t) + F(D,s) - (F(D,t) \cdot F(D,s))$
$F(D,t$ and not $s)$	$F(D,t) \cdot (1 - F(D,s))$

Consider the previous sample query ((*t* or *s*) and not *r*) and assume that $F(D,t) = 0.7$, $F(D,s) = 0.2$, and $F(D,r) = 0.1$. Then $F(D,t$ or $s)$ evaluates to max($F(D,t)$, $F(D,s)$) = 0.7, and the complete document-output value becomes $0.7 \cdot (1 - 0.1) = 0.63$. The fuzzy-set system is much less restrictive than the pure Boolean system because it provides ranked retrieval output in decreasing order of query-document similarities, while preserving the structured query formulations of the normal Boolean environment. The ranking feature can also control the size of the retrieval output by retrieving in each case a restricted number of the top-ranked documents as specified by individual users' requirements.

The fuzzy-set system is not as flexible as desired, however, because it does not assign term weights to the query terms (as opposed to document terms), and because the retrieval values of the documents depend on the values of only some document terms. In particular, in response to an or-query such as (*A* or *B* or ... or *Z*), the retrieval value of any document *D* is defined as the maximum value of any of the query terms *A*,*B*,...,*Z* in the document, whereas for an and-query (*A* and *B* and ... and *Z*), the retrieval value of *D* is the minimum of the query-term values in the document (see Table 10.5). Exclusive dependence on the term of maximum or minimum weight is remedied by introducing term weights for query terms as well as document terms.

In the vector-processing system, no conceptual distinction needs to be made between query and document terms, since both queries and documents are represented by identical constructs. In the Boolean and fuzzy-set models, distinctions necessarily arise because the query structure demands different evaluation procedures for query terms and document terms. In introducing the effects of weighted query terms in a Boolean context, care must be taken to preserve certain desirable properties of the basic Boolean system, such as compatibility with the pure Boolean output when term weights are restricted to 0 and 1, the consistency implied by producing equal document output values for logically equivalent queries (such as ((*A* or *B*) and *C*) and ((*A* and *C*) or (*B* and *C*))), and finally the separability that makes it possible to evaluate functions $F(D,q)$ without considering the type of query clause containing term *q*. [47]

In a Boolean environment, one way to use query-term weights as well as document-term weights that also preserves the essential evaluation properties is to multiply the weights of query and document terms in calculating the retrieval values of the documents with respect to the queries. Specifically, the value of $f(F(D,p),a)$, where *a* is the weight of term *p* in query *Q* could be defined as

$$f(F(D,p),a) = a \cdot F(D,p). \qquad (10.23)$$

An evaluation of a typical query-document similarity function for a sample document D and query Q based on an evaluation of formula (10.23) is shown in Table 10.6. [43] In the sample query, weights are assigned to individual document terms as well as to query terms; also, as shown in Table 10.6(b), the query clauses are separately weighted. The evaluation consists of a repeated application of formula (10.23) used in conjunction with the maximum and minimum functions of Table 10.5 for or and and clauses, respectively. The corresponding details are presented in Table 10.6(c). The final document-retrieval value, 0.01512, reflects the fact that all quantities used in the multiplicative steps are bounded by 1, and that the presence of an and operator produces the minimum of the input values joined by that operator.

Table 10.6 Evaluation of weighted Boolean expression (adapted from [43]). (a) Sample expression. (b) Assumed term weights. (c) Computation.

Document $D = (p,q,r,s,t)$

Query $Q = ((((p,a)$ and $(q,b)),c)$ or $(r,d),e)$ and $((s,f)$ or $(t,g),h),i)$

(a)

Document-term Weight	Query-term Weight	Query-clause Definition	Query-clause Weight
$F(D,p) = 0.6$	$a = 0.5$	$C_1 = (p$ and $q)$	$c = 0.7$
$F(D,q) = 0.3$	$b = 0.9$	$C_2 = (C_1$ or $r)$	$e = 0.1$
$F(D,r) = 0.7$	$d = 0.2$	$C_3 = (s$ or $t)$	$h = 1.0$
$F(D,s) = 0.8$	$f = 0.6$	$C_4 = (C_2$ and $C_3)$	$i = 0.8$
$F(D,t) = 0.9$	$g = 0.4$		

(b)

Elementary Terms		Clause Evaluation	Standard Values
(p,a)	0.3	(p,a) and (q,b)	0.27
(q,b)	0.27	$(((p,a)$ and $(q,b)),c)$	0.189
(r,d)	0.14	$(0.189$ or $(r,d))$	0.189
(s,f)	0.48	$((0.189$ or $(r,d),e)$	0.0189
(t,g)	0.36	(s,f) or (t,g)	0.48
		$(((s,f)$ or $(t,g)),h)$	0.48
		$(0.0189$ and $0.48)$	0.0189
		$((0.0189$ and $0.48), 0.8)$	0.01512

(c)

The disadvantages of this method are well illustrated by the sample evaluation: The size of the retrieval output value for each document depends on the query length and the number of multiplication operations performed. Thus document-output values are controlled by small values of supposedly unimportant terms used in and-clauses. One way to avoid computing very small document-output values is to use different evaluation formulas depending on the type of Boolean operator under consideration. Thus formula (10.23) might be replaced by the following definitions: [48]

$$f(F(D,p),a) = a \cdot F(D,p) \text{ when term } p \text{ appears in an or-clause.}$$
$$(10.24a)$$

$$f(F(D,p),a) = \frac{1}{a} \cdot F(D,p) \text{ when term } p \text{ appears in an and-clause.}$$
$$(10.24b)$$

Unfortunately the evaluation system of expressions (10.24) violates the previously stated separability requirements: It is no longer feasible to evaluate document output values from the inside out, one term at a time, but instead complete query clauses must be considered from the start.

Another possibility consists of using separate strategies to handle the weights for document and query terms. The former may still be considered to indicate the importance of the terms assigned to the documents of a collection. The latter, on the other hand, are now used as *threshold values* that reduce the effect of the document term values to zero when these values fall below a threshold specified in the query formulation. The following interpretation can be used as an example: [43,44,49]

$$f(F(D,p),m) = F(D,p) \quad \text{if } F(D,p) \geq m$$
$$(10.25)$$
$$f(F(D,p),m) = 0 \quad \text{if } F(D,p) < m$$

where m is the value of term p in query Q, interpreted as a threshold. The formulas in expression (10.25) produce retrieval-output values of zero for and-clauses in which the query-term values fall below the stated threshold. When the query-term values are large enough, the output values of the documents are determined directly by the document-term values.

❖ 10.4.2 Extended Boolean System

The conceptual difficulties outlined in the previous section are not present in an extended logic system based on generalized distance functions reflecting the similarity between weighted Boolean queries and weighted document vectors. [50,51] In the extended Boolean system, query- and document-term weights are treated in a completely parallel manner, and computations of similarity between documents and queries are adjusted under the control of a special parameter, known as the *p-value*, to produce a variety of different document-output values. Document-output values can thus be obtained that correspond to the results produced by a conventional Boolean system. Alternatively, the results of a vector-processing system can be obtained when the effect of Boolean operators is disregarded. Finally, results can be generated corresponding to systems intermediate between the Boolean and vector-processing models.

The notion of generalized distance between a Boolean query and a document vector can be clarified by considering the two-dimensional case, in which only two terms, A and B, are attached to documents and queries. In two dimensions, a typical Boolean query is expressed as (A and B), or (A or B), and a document D can be represented by the vector (d_A, d_B), d_i designating the weight of term T_i in D. Assuming that all term weights are limited to the range from 0 to 1, a document can be represented by a point in the one-square, as shown in Fig. 10.19 for document ($d_A = 0.4$, $d_B = 0.9$).

Considering first the value of document $D = (d_A, d_B)$ with respect to query (A or B), and assuming that d_A and d_B are restricted to values 0 and 1, it is obvious that documents (0,1), (1,0), and (1,1) will be retrieved

Figure 10.19 Distance measurements for Boolean queries. (a) Distances from point (0,0) for query (A **or** B). (b) Similarities to point (1,1) for query (A **and** B).

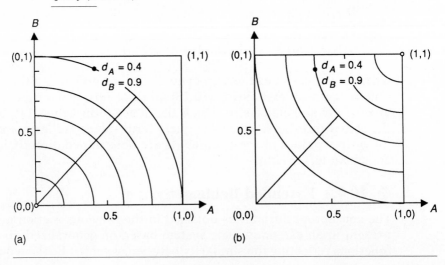

(a)

(b)

by the query because all these documents contain either term A, or term B, or both A and B. The only document rejected by query (A or B) is document (0,0), which lacks both term A and term B. This suggests that the retrieval value of a document with respect to the or-query (A or B) can be measured by using the distance between the document point in the one-square and the (0,0) point, as outlined in Fig. 10.19. The more the separation between a document and the point (0,0), the more chance that the document will be retrieved with respect to query (A or B).

The case for query (A and B) is analogous. Here the desirable point leading to retrieval is the (1,1) point in the square where both term A and term B are present in the document. The bad documents rejected by query (A and B) are represented by vectors (0,1), (1,0), and (0,0), where either terms A or B, or both terms, are absent. With respect to query (A and B), the good documents should therefore be located close to the (1,1) point, suggesting that the similarity to the (1,1) point, or equivalently the inverse distance from (1,1), be used to measure the retrieval value of a document for query (A and B).

The retrieval-output values for the documents are conveniently limited to the range 0 to 1. To obtain distance values normalized to values between 0 and 1, a normalization factor equal to $\sqrt{2}$ must be used because the maximum distance from (0,0) to the (1,1) point in the one-square of Fig. 10.19 is $\sqrt{2}$. The following distance measurements are then appropriate to reflect the similarity of a document $D = (d_A, d_B)$ for queries (A or B) and (A and B), respectively:

$$\text{sim}(D, Q_{(A \text{ or } B)}) = \sqrt{\frac{(d_A - 0)^2 + (d_B - 0)^2}{2}} \qquad (10.26a)$$

$$\text{sim}(D, Q_{(A \text{ and } B)}) = 1 - \sqrt{\frac{(1 - d_A)^2 + (1 - d_B)^2}{2}}. \qquad (10.26b)$$

It is easy to verify that the formulas of expressions (10.26), measuring the normalized Euclidian distance from the (0,0) point, and the inverse normalized Euclidian distance from the (1,1) point, respectively, provide the correct retrieval values when document weights d_A and d_B are restricted to values 0 and 1. In that case one obtains a value of 1 for documents that are to be retrieved, and 0 for items that must be rejected.

The formulas of expression (10.26) are easy to extend to the case of weighted or- and and-queries ((A,a) or (B,b)) and ((A,a) and B,b)), where a

and b represent the weights of query terms A and B, respectively. The normalized distances appropriate in that case are as follows:

$$\text{sim}(D,Q_{(A,a \text{ or } B,b)}) = \sqrt{\frac{a^2 d_A^2 + b^2 d_B^2}{a^2 + b^2}} \tag{10.27a}$$

$$\text{sim}(D,Q_{(A,a \text{ and } B,b)}) = 1 - \sqrt{\frac{a^2(1-d_A)^2 + b^2(1-d_B)^2}{a^2 + b^2}} \tag{10.27b}$$

Extensions of formulas (10.26) and (10.27) covering situations with more than two terms present in the queries are also quite straightforward.

In the preceding discussion, Euclidian distances represented document-retrieval values. A generalized distance measure is obtained by using the well known L_p-vector norm with a special parameter p limited to the range from 1 to infinity. [50,51] The generalized distances between documents $D = (d_t,d_s)$ and queries $Q = (q_t \text{ or } q_s)$ and $Q = (q_t \text{ and } q_s)$, are given by

$$\text{sim}(D,Q_{(q_t \text{ or } q_s)}) = \left[\frac{q_t^p d_t^p + q_s^p d_s^p}{q_t^p + q_s^p}\right]^{1/p} \tag{10.28a}$$

$$\text{sim}(D,Q_{(q_t \text{ or } q_s)}) = 1 - \left[\frac{q_t^p(1-d_t)^p + q_s^p(1-d_s)^p}{q_t^p + q_s^p}\right]^{1/p}. \tag{10.28b}$$

In expressions (10.28) q_t and q_s represent the weights of query terms T_t and T_s, respectively. Expressions (10.28) are identical with the earlier formulations of expression (10.27) except that value 2, used to measure the Euclidian distance, is replaced by variable parameter p.

What follows is a summary of the query-document evaluation formulas of the extended Boolean system, using the notation introduced in Table 10.5 for the conventional Boolean system.

$$F(D,q_t \text{ and } q_s) = 1 - \left[\frac{q_t^p(1-F(D,t))^p + q_s^p(1-F(D,s))^p}{q_t^p + q_s^p}\right]^{1/p}$$

$$F(D,q_t \text{ or } q_s) = \left[\frac{q_t^p F(D,t)^p + q_s^p F(D,s)^p}{q_t^p + q_s^p}\right]^{1/p}$$

$$F(D,q_t \text{ and not } q_s) = F(D,t) \cdot (1 - F(D,s))$$

Consider now the evaluation of the preceding formulas for the special cases when $p = \infty$, $p = 1$, and $1 < p < \infty$:

1. For $p = \infty$,

$$F(D, Q_{(q_t \text{ and } q_s)}) = 1 - \frac{\max[q_t(1 - F(D,t)), q_s(1 - F(D,s))]}{\max(q_t, q_s)}.$$

When binary query weights are used, that is, $q_t = q_s = 1$, this expression reduces to

$$F(D, Q_{(q_t \text{ and } q_s)}) = \min(F(D,t), F(D,s)). \qquad (10.29a)$$

Similarly, for $p = \infty$

$$F(D, Q_{(q_t \text{ or } q_s)}) = \frac{\max[q_t F(D,t), q_s F(D,s)]}{\max(q_t, q_s)}. \qquad (10.29b)$$

This reduces to $\max(F(D,t), F(D,s))$ for the special case when $q_t = q_s = 1$.

Expressions (10.29a) and (10.29b) are identical to those in Table 10.5 for the conventional Boolean model and the fuzzy-set model. One concludes that for $p = \infty$, the extended Boolean-processing model reduces to a normal Boolean system when the term weights are disregarded.

2. For $p = 1$, expressions (10.28a) and (10.28b) are reduced as follows

$$F(D, Q_{(q_t \text{ and } q_s)}) = \frac{q_t F(D,t) + q_s F(D,s)}{q_t + q_s}$$

$$F(D, Q_{(q_t \text{ or } q_s)}) = \frac{q_t F(D,t) + q_s F(D,s)}{q_t + q_s}$$

That is,

$$F(D, Q_{(q_t \text{ and } q_s)}) = F(D, Q_{(q_t \text{ or } q_s)}) = \frac{q}{q_t + q_s} \cdot F(D,q).$$

When $p = 1$, the results obtained with both an and-query and or-query are identical; they are equivalent to the output produced by a vector-processing system in which the retrieval-output values of the documents are determined as a simple inner-vector product (Σ $q_i d_i$) with normalized query weights.

3. When values of p are intermediate between ∞ and 1, a soft Boolean system is created in which the interpretation of the Boolean operators is relaxed. The strict Boolean phrases conventionally specified by using and operators, and the strict synonym chains specified by or operators, are then replaced by fuzzy, tentative phrases, and chains of approximately similar terms.

When the retrieval results obtainable in the extended Boolean system are compared with those of a conventional Boolean system that interprets operators strictly, retrieval effectiveness is greatly improved, as suggested by Table 10.7, which shows average search precision values for certain fixed recall levels, averaged over a number of user queries for four different document collections. As the results of the table indicate, retrieval results are somewhat better when the query structure is preserved by setting the values of p equal to 2 (instead of 1) The improvements over the strict Boolean case range from 62 percent in average precision for the CISI collection, to 167 percent for the MED collection. When p values much larger than 2 are used, the results become progressively worse, approximating those of the pure Boolean system for p values larger than 10. [50]

The extended Boolean system preserves the advantages of the structured Boolean query formulations, and eliminates the disadvantages relating to the lack of ranked output and the absence of control over the number of retrieved items. The relaxed interpretation of Boolean

Table 10.7 Evaluation and retrieval effectiveness of extended Boolean retrieval.

Collection	Standard Boolean Binary Weights ($p=\infty$)	Standard Boolean tf·idf Weights ($p=\infty$)	Extended Boolean $p=1$ Weighted Terms	Extended Boolean $p=2$ Weighted Terms	Extended Boolean Mixed p [1.2–2.5] Weighted Terms
CACM 3204 (52 queries)	0.1789	0.1551 (−14%)	0.3090 (+72%)	0.3314 (+84%)	0.3166 (+76%)
CISI 1460 (35 queries)	0.1118	0.1000 (−11%)	0.1835 (+64%)	0.1806 (+62%)	0.1771 (+159%)
INSPEC 12684 (77 queries)	0.1159	0.1314 (+13%)	0.2747 (+136%)	0.2700 (+133%)	–
MED 1033 (30 queries)	0.2065	0.2368 (+15%)	0.5505 (+167%)	0.5573 (+167%)	–

logic also seems more appropriate for text retrieval than the relatively unforgiving nature of conventional Boolean logic:

- When users submit and-queries, such as (A and B), they prefer items containing both terms rather than only one. This does not imply, however, that items containing only one of the terms should necessarily be rejected.

- Analogously, for or-queries such as (A or B), items containing either term alone should certainly be retrieved. However, items containing both terms are generally even more appropriate than items containing only one term.

In the extended Boolean model, documents containing only one term of an and-clause can be retrieved with a low retrieval value. Furthermore, document containing several terms of an or-clause are preferred over those containing only one term.

The disadvantages of the extended model are twofold. First, most of the basic Boolean processing laws, such as the associative and distributive laws, are not strictly valid in the extended system. [50,51] This implies that different retrieval output values may be obtainable for seemingly equivalent queries such as (A and (B and C)) and ((A and B) and C). The differences in values obtained in practice are very small, however, and do not appear to affect the quality of the output.

The second, more serious problem inherent in extended Boolean logic relates to the complexity of the formulas that must be evaluated to obtain the output values for the documents. In particular, recursive application of formulas (10.28) produces complicated expressions for Boolean statements with a large number of operators. Thus for a sample document $D = (d_A, d_E, d_F)$ and a sample query $Q = \{(A,a) \text{ or } (b[(E,e) \text{ and } (F,f)])\}$, where b represents a clause weight attached to clause (E and F), the appropriate evaluation formula is

$$\text{sim}(D,Q) = \left\{ \frac{a^p d_A^p + b^p \left[1 - \frac{(e^p(1-d_E)^p + f^p(1-d_F)^p)^{1/p}}{[e^p + f^p]^{1/p}} \right]^p}{a^p + b^p} \right\}^{1/p} . \qquad (10.30)$$

Thus in the extended Boolean system, the large improvements in retrieval effectiveness are somewhat decreased by losses in computational efficiency, compared with the strict Boolean methodology based on inverted files. In practical implementations, it may be necessary to give up the flexibility inherent in a completely free choice of p values, and use instead special-purpose evaluations prepared for a few fixed values of p. For example, the computations can be limited to p values of 1, 2, and ∞, in which case maximum and minimum operators can be used for p equal to ∞, and multiplication and square root operations will replace the exponential factors for $p = 2$. Such a reduced evaluation process should be much more efficient.

In the extended Boolean system, generating retrieval output values for documents is based on a comparison between each stored document and the corresponding p-valued query formulations. Obviously, it is impossible to perform the computations specified by expressions (10.28) for the complete set of documents in a large collection. Thus an appropriate subcollection to be searched must first be identified. Such a subcollection can be obtained by taking the output of a broad, conventional Boolean query formulation operating in the conventional way with inverted-file methods, using a suitable document collection. Each item included in such a previously retrieved subcollection can then be processed in a subsequent search operation against a refined p-valued query in the extended Boolean system to produce a final ranked output. A simple outline of such a practical implementation follows: [52]

1. Take initial Boolean query statement or initial natural-language query formulation.

2. Run an initial *broad* search using conventional methodology, designed to retrieve a subset of potentially relevant items.

3. Formulate a more refined p-valued Boolean query and assign weights to document and query terms. Use higher p values for clauses considered important by the user, and lower p values for the remaining clauses.

4. Run p-valued search in extended system, comparing refined query against items retrieved in step 2.

5. Rank items in proper output order, obtain relevance assessments for some retrieved items, and reformulate p-valued query if desired. Go back to step 3.

The assumption made in step 3, query construction, is that the user can distinguish important query clauses from less important ones, so that higher p values (say $p = 2.5$) are assigned to the former, implying a stricter interpretation of the Boolean operators, while lower p values (say $p = 1.5$) are used for remaining clauses. [53] An experiment using variable p values with two sample document collections is evaluated in the right-most column of Table 10.7. When users do not participate directly in query formulation, it is best to use a preestablished p-value such as $p = 2$ for all operators.

The preceding outline also includes a relevance-feedback process that generates improved Boolean query formulations by incorporating terms from previously retrieved documents designated as relevant by users. The Boolean query-feedback process can be performed in a manner analogous to that used for vector queries. [54,55] In particular, consider the case in which sample terms T_i, T_j, T_k are first extracted from previously retrieved relevant documents. Conjunctive Boolean clauses can then be formed from those terms, including clauses $(T_i$ and $T_j)$, $(T_i$ and $T_k)$, $(T_j$ and $T_k)$, and $(T_i$ and T_j and $T_k)$. For each clause, it is possible to estimate the number of documents that can be retrieved when the corresponding clause is included in a query. Specifically, if n_i is the postings frequency of term T_i in a collection of N documents (that is, the number of documents indexed by T_i), the number of items retrievable by clause $(T_i$ and $T_j)$ can be estimated as $n_i \cdot n_j / N + 1$; similarly, the number retrieved by $(T_i$ and T_j and $T_k)$ will be $n_i \cdot n_j \cdot n_k / (N+1)^2$. Using or operators, enough new query clauses can then be added to the original query formulations to retrieve a previously specified number of new documents.

Consider, for example, a case when 10 new documents are wanted, applying a relevance feedback procedure to Boolean queries. If the estimate of output size indicates that two particular clauses $(T_i$ and $T_j)$ and $(T_i$ and $T_k)$ will retrieve four and six documents, respectively, a new query Q' can be constructed from original query Q as $Q' = Q$ or $(T_i$ and $T_j)$ or $(T_i$ and $T_k)$. Available evaluation results for the Boolean query relevance feedback indicate that retrieval effectiveness is improved greatly for the first few feedback iterations. [55]

10.5 Integrated Systems for Processing Text and Data

Many environments include records consisting of text as well as factual data of the type usually handled in data-management systems. This is the case, for example, when processing survey data in which respondents answer specific questions factually, and pieces of text are added to elaborate and explain the factual data. Similarly, medical charts and summaries use formal components as well as dictated text excerpts that describe patients' conditions. The data and text portions of such integrated documents are described in somewhat different terms, leading to differing retrieval strategies. The formal data part of the items can usually be characterized by values of prespecified attributes, whereas the text portion is identified by index terms or keywords, possibly supplemented by importance weights.

Retrieval strategies for various document components differ because usually an exact match is required between the data portions contained in the query specifications and the attribute values attached to the stored records, whereas approximate global comparisons are more effective for the keyword sets that identify text content. Various retrieval systems can handle integrated records including both text and data. One solution consists of providing different system components to handle the data and text portions of the records, and reconnecting the components in such a way that the results obtained with the data-retrieval system are made available to the text-retrieval section, or vice versa. [56,57] Typically, the data-retrieval operations are performed first, isolating a specific set of records whose attribute values precisely match the specified query attributes; the retrieved part of the file is then passed to the text-retrieval component for processing in a subsequent search. An alternative, normally preferred approach is to transform the text portion into a formal structure of the type normally used for records processed by standard database management systems. This approach makes the text data accessible to database processing operations. The usual way to adapt text to database procedures is the relational database, in which files are represented by two-dimensional tables. [58–61]

In the relational model, term assignment to the documents of a collection is in principle characterized by a table in which each row contains a document number, a term, and a term weight, the number of rows being equal to the number of documents multiplied by the average number of terms per document. A complete document collection, then, is represented by a number of different tables (or relations), including those representing the document title, term assignment to the documents, inverted index, thesaurus, and author specifications. In such a system, the information pertaining to a common item can be assembled by joining the rows of different tables using a common attribute, such as a document number or term, as described in Chapter 3.

The problem with decomposing the document information is that certain aspects of the document — such as the text itself — are not easily compressed into tabular form. Furthermore, enormous table sizes may be needed: Typically the table specifying the assignment of terms to documents requires hundreds of thousands of rows for even a modest-size collection. Most importantly, the usual relational operations that assemble the data items included in different tables, or in different rows or columns of the same table, are not especially useful in document processing and retrieval. For these and related reasons, extensions to the normal relational processing model have been introduced, designed to represent document information appealingly and to simplify processing operations. Among the components of such extended systems, the following are most important: [59–61]

- "Long fields" to store and process actual text items of variable length, such as the individual sentences of documents. [60,61]

- Special operations to manipulate the information stored in long fields, capable of recognizing document sentences containing particular text words or components, and of breaking up long text strings into short pieces.

- Structured objects such as hierarchically organized texts (for example, documents broken down into chapters themselves divided into paragraphs, sentences, and individual words), and operations capable of manipulating complex objects as single entities. [60,61]

- Ordered relations in which the order of the rows of the tables is specified by line-identification numbers attached to each row; such ordering makes it possible to process the texts in normal text order. [60]

- New operations to facilitate interactive file access, such as ranked retrieval of items in decreasing order of similarity with the queries, as well as browsing operations through indexes and record files. [62]

- Systems that provide concurrent file access for a number of different users, and methods that allow access to distributed databases where the files are broken up into pieces located or processed in a number of different locations. [63]

The justification for basing a text-retrieval system on a modified relational technology, and on strategies used with conventional database management systems, is the widespread use and understanding, and degree of sophistication, of current data-manipulation systems. Unfortunately, the different characterizations of text-based and data-based records suggest that it may not be advantageous to embed a text-based system into a data-retrieval framework. A new approach for handling text and data records consists of not distinguishing fundamentally between various types of record identifiers, and instead supplying separate comparison techniques for query and document identifiers of different types. One possibility is to represent each item by an extended vector that includes various types of identifiers. [64] Consider in particular a typical record identified by objective identifiers, such as author names or publication dates, index terms used for content representation, and citation identifiers designating bibliographic references attached to the record. Such a record can be represented in extended vector form as

$$D = (d_1,...,d_k,o_{k+1},...,o_n,c_{n+1},...,c_t) \tag{10.31}$$

where d_i, o_j, and c_k represent the weights of the ith content term, the jth objective identifier, and the kth bibliographic citation attached to item D, respectively.

In an extended vector system, the query-document similarity can be specified as

$$\text{sim}(D,Q) = \alpha \left\{ \begin{array}{c} \text{content-term} \\ \text{similarity} \end{array} \right\} + \beta \left\{ \begin{array}{c} \text{objective-term} \\ \text{similarity} \end{array} \right\} + \delta \left\{ \begin{array}{c} \text{citation} \\ \text{similarity} \end{array} \right\},$$

$$(10.32)$$

where α, β and δ are appropriately chosen multipliers controlling the contribution made by each vector component. The content-term and citation-term similarities can be computed using global vector similarities such as the Dice or cosine coefficients, and an exact match method might be used for the similarity between objective-term components. If relevance assessments are available for samples of previously retrieved documents, optimal values of parameters α, β, and δ can be calculated that will discriminate best between the relevant and nonrelevant sample documents. Such optimal parameter values can then be used to control retrieval operations in subsequent searches performed with similar data. [64]

An elegant way to implement retrieval operations for the extended-item representations of expression (10.31) is the extended Boolean logic used to formulate query statements with mixed p value assignments. High p values could be used for objective terms considered compulsory, whereas much lower p values would serve to process the content terms. A typical formulation of this type, requesting documents originating with a certain author and publisher, is shown in expression (10.33).

$$Q = [(\text{author} = \text{van Rijsbergen}; (0.9)) \text{ and}^{\infty} (\text{publisher} =$$
$$\text{Butterworths}; (0.8))]$$
$$\text{and}^2 [(\text{term} = \text{information retrieval}; (0.7))$$
$$\text{or}^{1.5} (\text{term} = \text{automatic documentation}; (0.5))] \qquad (10.33)$$

Experiments using such global similarity computations with extended vector formulations remain to be carried out in actual user environments.

10.6 Advanced Interface Systems

At present, many hundreds of potentially useful databases and collections are available for automatic searching, and at least half a dozen major retrieval services offer access to these databases. These retrieval services all use conceptually similar methodologies, usually based on dense inverted indexes representing all term assignments to the records. However, the actual command structures and the methodologies used to gain access to the files are all different, and generally incompatible. Also, the various services provide somewhat different facilities. Thus, a typical user is confronted with the problem of identifying a service that actually makes available the needed databases, and then learning the command structures and rules that access the retrieval system chosen.

To help in such an apparently discouraging situation, so-called access *gateways* have been designed that aid users in formulating search requests, locating the appropriate databases and retrieval services, and finally routing requests to the proper services for handling. A typical gateway system includes the following retrieval aids: [65]

- Automatic convertors that translate query formulations and access protocols from one system language to another, or from some common specified input language to the individual languages specified by each system.

- Automatic routing systems that dial up and log on to an automatic system, and call the proper directory and applications package needed to formulate and process queries.

- Automatic selectors, capable of locating the appropriate retrieval-service vendor, the appropriate telecommunications system to gain access to the retrieval service, and finally the proper database to be searched.

- Automatic search aids capable of managing off-line or online searches by providing menus of system commands, giving advice at particular times during the search process, and generally offering search expertise.

- Evaluators and analyzers that assess the user's characteristics and needs before a search, and evaluate the quality of the information obtained in response to particular query formulations.

The existing gateway systems are often used with intelligent terminals and local microprocessors that conduct the query-negotiation and -formulation process locally before long-distance networks and vendor's host computers are actually accessed. Conit, a well-known advanced interface systems, provides a common command language that is automatically converted to the access language used by a particular retrieval system. In addition, a simple user-interface system is available that explains what is done at each step, and offers advice about what the user should do next during a particular search effort. [66] In the IIDA system, user behavior is monitored, and questionable search strategies, such as the formulation of several near-identical queries with similar output, are prevented by asking the user to take remedial action. [67] Other advanced intermediary systems provide flexible access to particular search systems and particular subject areas. [68–70]

Various interface designs are based on advanced graphic techniques; split-screen displays and multiple windows make it possible to simultaneously display thesauruses and indexes, protocols of previously executed commands, and other special messages. [71,72] Automatic cursor-positioning devices may be used to control the operations, and displays may suggest new operations and additional actions. Graphic display units are especially useful to display complex structures, such as hierarchical outlines of the available search vocabulary, and, by means of overlapping or simultaneous displays on different parts of the screen, to interrelate different portions of the system.

In the future such approaches may lead to the design of automated search experts that can understand and interpret unrestricted natural-language input, supply knowledge and information about the subject of interest, assess the special needs of particular users, and disambiguate and formalize the user's statements before beginning the search process. Figure 10.20 is a simplified representation of such a search expert system. [73] As more becomes known about the construction of knowledge bases in particular subject areas, and about language-processing methods to handle user-system interactions, expert system approaches to text processing may become widespread. For the moment, less ambitious automatic-interface methods are likely to be used to operate automatic search and retrieval systems.

Figure 10.20 Expert interface system for text retrieval [73].

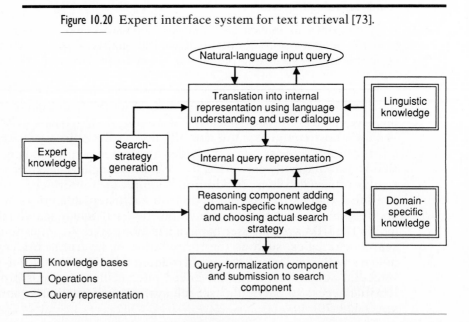

References

1. G. Salton, *Automatic Information Organization and Retrieval*, McGraw-Hill Book Co., NY, 1968, Chapter 2, 21–65.

2. G. Salton, A. Wong, and C.S. Yang, A Vector Space Model for Automatic Indexing, *Communications of the ACM*, 18:11, November 1975, 613–620.

3. V.V. Raghavan and S.K.M. Wong, A Critical Analysis of the Vector Space Model for Information Retrieval, *Journal of the American Society for Information Science (JASIS)*, 37:5, September 1986, 279–287.

4. C.J. van Rijsbergen, *Information Retrieval*, Butterworths, London, Second Edition, 1979.

5. J.J. Rocchio, Jr., Relevance Feedback in Information Retrieval, in *The Smart System — Experiments in Automatic Document Processing*, G. Salton editor, Prentice-Hall Inc., Englewood Cliffs, NJ, 1971, 313–323.

6. E. Ide, New Experiments in Relevance Feedback, in *The Smart Retrieval System — Experiments in Automatic Document Processing*, G. Salton, editor, Prentice-Hall, Inc., Englewood Cliffs, NJ, 1971, 337–354.

7. E. Ide and G. Salton, Interactive Search Strategies and Dynamic File Organization in Information Retrieval, in *The Smart Retrieval System — Experiments in Automatic Document Processing*, G. Salton, editor, Prentice-Hall Inc., Englewood Cliffs, NJ, 1971, 373–393.

8. A. Borodin, L. Kerr, and F. Lewis, Query Splitting in Relevance Feedback Systems, Scientific Report No. ISR-14, Section XII, Department of Computer Science, Cornell University, Ithaca, NY, October 1968.

9. C.T. Yu, W.S. Luk, and T.Y. Cheung, A Statistical Model for Relevance Feedback in Information Retrieval, *Journal of the ACM*, 23:2, April 1976, 273–286.

10. G. Salton, The Performance of Interactive Information Retrieval, *Information Processing Letters*, 1:2, July 1971, 35–41.

11. G. Salton, Relevance Feedback and the Optimization of Retrieval Effectiveness, in *The Smart Retrieval System — Experiments in Automatic Document Processing*, G. Salton, editor, Prentice-Hall, Inc., Englewood Cliffs, NJ, 324–336.

12. C. Cirillo, Y.K. Chang, and J. Razon, Evaluation of Feedback Retrieval Using Modified Rank Freezing, Residual Collection, and Test and Control Groups, Scientific Report No. ISR-16, Section X, Department of Computer Science, Cornell University, Ithaca, NY, September 1969.

13. T.L. Brauen, Document Vector Modification, in *The Smart Retrieval System — Experiments in Automatic Document Processing*, G. Salton, editor, Prentice-Hall Inc., Englewood Cliffs, NJ, 1971, 456–484.

14. C.S. Yang, On Dynamic Document Space Modification Using Term Discrimination Values, Scientific Report No. ISR-22, Section X, Department of Computer Science, Cornell University, Ithaca, NY, November 1974.

15. K. Sardana, Automatic Document Retirement Algorithms, Scientific Report No. ISR-22, Section XII, Department of Computer Science, Cornell University, Ithaca, NY, November 1974.

16. M.D. Kerchner, Dynamic Document Processing in Clustered Collections, Doctoral Dissertation, Scientific Report No. ISR-19, Department of Computer Science, Cornell University, Ithaca, NY, October 1971.

17. N. Jardine and C.J. van Rijsbergen, The Use of Hierarchic Clustering in Information Retrieval, *Information Storage and Retrieval*, 7:5, December 1971, 217–240.

18. E.M. Voorhees, The Cluster Hypothesis Revisited, *Proceedings of the Eighth Annual International ACM SIGIR Conference on Research and Development in Information Retrieval*, Association for Computing Machinery, New York, June 1985, 188–196.

19. G. Salton and A. Wong, Generation and Search of Clustered Files, *ACM Transactions on Database Systems*, 3:4, December 1978, 321–346.

20. A. Griffiths, L.A. Robinson, and P. Willett, Hierarchic Agglomerative Clustering Methods for Automatic Document Classification, *Journal of Documentation*, 40:3, September 1984, 175–205.

21. F. Murtagh, A Survey of Recent Advances in Hierarchical Clustering Algorithms, *The Computer Journal*, 26:4, 1982, 354–360.

22. E. M. Voorhees, The Effectiveness and Efficiency of Agglomerative Hierarchic Clustering in Document Retrieval, Doctoral Dissertation, Cornell University, Ithaca, NY, January 1986.

23. W.B. Croft, Clustering Large Files of Documents Using the Single Link Method, *Journal of the American Society for Information Science (JASIS)*, 28:6, November 1977, 341–344.

24. A.F. Harding and P. Willett, Indexing Exhaustivity and the Computation of Similarity Matrices, *Journal of the American Society for Information Science (JASIS)*, 31:4, July 1980, 298–300.

25. P. Willett, A Fast Procedure for the Calculation of Similarity Coefficients in Automatic Classification, *Information Processing and Management*, 17:2, 1981, 53–60.

26. R.E. Williamson, Real Time Document Retrieval, Doctoral Dissertation, Cornell University, Ithaca, NY, June 1974.

27. J.J. Rocchio, Jr., Document Retrieval Systems — Optimization and Evaluation, Doctoral Dissertation, Harvard University, Cambridge, MA, March 1966.

28. R.T. Grauer and M. Messier, An Evaluation of Rocchio's Clustering Algorithm, in *The Smart Retrieval System — Experiments in Automatic Document Processing*, G. Salton, editor, Prentice-Hall, Inc., Englewood Cliffs, NJ, 1971, 243–264.

29. R.T. Dattola, Automatic Classification in Document Retrieval Systems, Doctoral Dissertation, Cornell University, Ithaca, NY, May 1973.

30. C.T. Yu, C.M. Suen, K. Lam, and M.K. Siu, Adaptive Record Clustering, *ACM Transactions on Database Systems*, 10:2, June 1985, 180–204.

31. M.E. Maron and J.L. Kuhns, On Relevance, Probabilistic Indexing and Information Retrieval, *Journal of the ACM*, 7:3, July 1960, 216–243.

32. A. Bookstein and D.R. Swanson, Probabilistic Models for Automatic Indexing, *Journal of the American Society for Information Science (JASIS)*, 26:1, January-February 1975, 45–50.

33. A. Bookstein, Explanation and Generalization of Vector Models in Information Retrieval, *Lecture Notes in Computer Science*, 146, G. Salton and H.J. Schneider, editors, Springer Verlag, Berlin, 1983, 118–132.

34. R.O. Duda and P.E. Hart, *Pattern Classification and Scene Analysis*, John Wiley and Sons, New York, 1973.

35. C.T. Yu, W.S. Luk, and M.K. Siu, On Models of Information Retrieval Processes, *Information Systems*, 4:3, 1979, 205–218.

36. C.J. van Rijsbergen, A Theoretical Basis for the Use of Cooccurrence Data in Retrieval, *Journal of Documentation*, 33:2, June 1977, 106–119.

37. D.J. Harper and C.J. van Rijsbergen, An Evaluation of Feedback in Document Retrieval Using Cooccurrence Data, *Journal of Documentation*, 34:3, September 1978, 189–216.

38. C.T. Yu, C. Buckley, K. Lam, and G. Salton, A Generalized Term Dependence Model in Information Retrieval, *Information Technology: Research and Development*, 2:4, October 1983, 129–154.

39. G. Salton, C. Buckley, and C.T. Yu, An Evaluation of Term Dependence Models in Information Retrieval, *Lecture Notes in Computer Science*, 146, G. Salton and H.J. Schneider, editors, Springer Verlag, Berlin, 1983, 151–173.

40. W.B. Croft, Document Representation in Probabilistic Models in Information Retrieval, *Journal of the American Society for Information Science (JASIS)*, 31:6, November 1981, 451–457.

41. C.T. Yu and W.S. Luk, Analysis of the Effectiveness of Retrieval in Clustered Files, *Journal of the ACM*, 24:4, October 1977, 607–622.

42. W.B. Croft, A Model of Cluster Searching Based on Classification, *Information Systems*, 5:3, 1980, 189–195.

43. D.A. Buell, A General Model of Query Processing in Information Retrieval, *Information Processing and Management*, 17:5, 1981, 249–262.

44. T. Radecki, Fuzzy Set Theoretical Approach to Document Retrieval, *Information Processing and Management*, 15:5, 1979, 247–259.

45. A. Bookstein, Fuzzy Requests: An Approach to Weighted Boolean Searches, *Journal of the American Society for Information Science (JASIS)*, 30:4, July 1980, 240–247.

46. V. Tahani, A Fuzzy Model of Document Retrieval Systems, *Information Processing and Management*, 12:3, 1976, 177–188.

47. W.G. Waller and D.H. Kraft, A Mathematical Model for a Weighted Boolean Retrieval System, *Information Processing and Management*, 15:5, 1979, 235–245.

48. A. Bookstein, A Comparison of Two Weighting Schemes for Boolean Retrieval, *Journal of the American Society for Information Science (JASIS)*, 32:4, July 1981, 275–279.

49. D.A. Buell and D.H. Kraft, Threshold Values and Boolean Retrieval System, *Information Processing and Management*, 17:3, 1981, 127–136.

50. G. Salton, E.A. Fox, and H. Wu, Extended Boolean Information Retrieval, *Communications of the ACM*, 26:11, November 1983, 1022–1036.

51. H. Wu, On Query Formulation in Information Retrieval, Doctoral Dissertation, Cornell University, Ithaca, NY, 1981.

52. G. Salton, A. Blueprint for Automatic Boolean Processing, *ACM SIGIR Forum*, 17:2, Fall 1982, 6–25.

53. G. Salton and E. Voorhees, Automatic Assignment of Soft Boolean Operators, *Proceedings of the Eighth Annual International ACM SIGIR Conference on Research and Development in Information Retrieval*, Association for Computing Machinery, New York, June 1985, 54–69.

54. G. Salton, C. Buckley and E.A. Fox, Automatic Query Formulations in Information Retrieval, *Journal of the American Society for Information Science (JASIS)*, 34:4, July 1983, 262–280.

55. G. Salton, E.A. Fox and E. Voorhees, Advanced Feedback Methods in Information Retrieval, *Journal of the American Society for Information Science (JASIS)*, 36:3, 1983, 200–210.

56. IBM Corporation, Storage and Information Retrieval System for OS/VS (Stairs/VS), Program Reference Manual, Publication SH 12-5400, White Plains, NY, 1979.

57. R.T. Dattola, First: Flexible Information Retrieval System for Text, *Journal of the American Society for Information Science (JASIS)*, 30:1, January 1979, 9–19.

58. I.A. Macleod, Toward an Information Retrieval Language Based on a Relational View of Data, *Information Processing and Management*, 13:3, 1977, 167–175.

59. H.J. Schek, Methods for the Administration of Textual Data in Database Systems, in *Information Retrieval Research*, R.N. Oddy, S.E. Robertson, C.J. van Rijsbergen, and P. W. Williams, editors, Butterworths, London, 1981, 218–235.

60. M. Stonebraker, H. Stettner, N. Lynn, J. Kalash, and A. Guttman, Document Processing in a Retrieval Database System, *ACM Transactions on Database Systems*, 1:2, April 1983, 143–158.

61. R.L. Haskin and R.A. Laurie, On Extending the Functions of a Relational Database System, *Proceedings of ACM SIGMOD Conference*, Association for Computing Machinery, New York, 1982, 207–212.

62. E.A. Fox, Implementing Smart for Minicomputers via Relational Processing with Abstract Data Types, *ACM SIGMOD/SIGSMALL*

Workshop on Data Bases for Small Systems, Association for Computing Machinery, New York, October 1981.

63. I.A. Macleod, P. Martin, and B. Nordin, A Design of a Distributed Full Text Retrieval System, *Proceedings of the 1986 ACM Conference on Research and Development in Information Retrieval*, F. Rabitti, editor, Pisa, Italy, September 1986, 131–137.

64. E.A. Fox, Extending the Boolean and Vector Space Models of Information Retrieval with p-Norm Queries and Multiple Concept Types, Doctoral Dissertation, Cornell University, Ithaca, NY, August 1983.

65. M.E. Williams, Transparent Information Systems through Gateways, Front Ends, Intermediaries, and Interfaces, *Journal of the American Society for Information Science (JASIS)*, 37:4, July 1986, 204–214.

66. R.S. Marcus, An Experimental Comparison of the Effectiveness of Computers and Humans as Search Intermediaries, *Journal of the American Society for Information Science (JASIS)*, 34:6, 1983, 381–404.

67. C.T. Meadow, T.T. Hewett, and E.S. Aversa, A Computer Intermediary for Interactive Database Searching, Part 1: Design, Part II: Evaluation, *Journal of the American Society for Information Science (JASIS)*, 33:5, 1982, 325–332 and 357–364.

68. C.M. Goldstein and W.H. Ford, The User-Cordial Interface, *On-Line Review*, 2:3, 1978, 269–275.

69. E.G. Fayen and M. Cochran, A New User Interface for the Dartmouth On-Line Catalog, *Proceedings of 1982 National On-Line Meeting*, Learned Information Inc., Medford, NJ, March 1982, 87–97.

70. M.J. McGill, G.E. Brown, and S. Siegel, The Chemical Substances Information Network: Its Evaluation and Evolution, *Proceedings of 1983 National On-Line Meeting*, Learned Information Inc., Medford, NJ, August 1983, 367–376.

71. H.P. Frei and J.F. Jauslin, Graphical Presentation of Information and Services: A User Oriented Interface, *Information Technology: Research and Development*, 2:1, January 1983, 23–42.

72. G.E. Heidorn, K. Jensen, L.A. Miller, R.J. Byrd, and M.S. Chodorow, The Epistle Text Critiquing System, *IBM Systems Journal*, 21:3, 1982, 305–326.

73. G. Guida and C. Tasso, IR-NLI: An Expert Natural Language Interface to On-Line Data Bases, *Conference on Applied Natural Language Processing*, Association for Computational Linguistics, Santa Monica, CA, 1983, 31–38.

Part 4

Text Analysis and Language Processing

Chapter 11

Language Analysis and Understanding

11.1   The Linguistic Approach

The information-retrieval models described in Chapter 10 are based on simplified treatments of natural-language text input. Every text-retrieval approach in use is limited by the absence of a refined content analysis. Text records are generally represented by single words, or sometimes groups of words, extracted from the document texts: no refined linguistic procedures are included in the text-processing packages. However, texts are necessarily available in the form of natural-language constructs; some form of natural language analysis should improve text retrieval and other text-processing operations. In considering the linguistic techniques that might be used in text processing, one must be mindful that different types of analyses may be appropriate for different applications. Thus only a limited amount of linguistic input may be needed to build programs to automatically correct spelling errors in written texts. On the other hand, more extensive linguistic capabilities would presumably be incorporated into automatic systems for text abstracting or machine translation.

In information-retrieval environments, a linguistic component could indicate term relationships between indexing units, which might be used to generate more complete and representative text descriptions than can be obtained from single terms alone. More refined content analysis might improve retrieval effectiveness, and replace reference retrieval systems with limited question-answering capabilities that provide specific responses to certain questions. Alternatively, passage-retrieval systems might be developed, capable of recognizing specific passages of text that contain information relevant to particular user queries. A natural-language capability might also facilitate interaction between user and system by giving the user natural-language access tools to replace the usual formalized query languages.

Consider first a total approach to text analysis, with the aim of understanding text content completely. In this case, text sentences cannot be treated in isolation. Indeed, substantial knowledge is needed about the discourse area under consideration, and about the world at large, to ensure that the written records are properly interpreted. [1-3] A prescription for a complete language-analysis package might be based on the following components:

- A *knowledge base* consisting of stored entities and predicates, the latter used to characterize and relate the entities. Inference rules might also be called upon to generate new facts and information from already existing data.

- A *text-analysis* module consisting of a syntactic component for structural decomposition of the text, and a *semantic-interpretation* module that transforms syntactic constructs into formal frameworks representing text meaning.

- A *search and comparison* module that takes elements of the formalized text structure and supplements them, or transforms them, using portions of the stored knowledge base.

- Finally, a *problem solving* module that takes the available descriptions derived from the texts and from the knowledge base, and performs specific application tasks such as generating formalized queries to be submitted to a database or text-retrieval system.

Unfortunately, in most environments such a prescription is difficult to follow. In particular, most discourse areas are not confined to a small number of facts and entities that are easily mapped into an unambiguous topic arrangement. Even when the discourse area is limited to the contents of a small number of documents, the structure of the required knowledge base is likely to remain elusive. Finally, even if the relevant knowledge bases should somehow be available, the search and matching operations needed to compare text excerpts with stored databases are not easily specified. Analyzed texts and stored data may include different terminologies and different forms of term relationships, making it impossible to locate the relevant related data in the knowledge base.

Even though it is desirable in principle to use complete language understanding systems for text processing, fundamental problems must be resolved before such an approach is practicable. Thus for the immediate future, simplified linguistic methodologies must be pursued. In designing a linguistic-analysis system, program portability is an important consideration, in the sense that the analysis should apply not only to the sample texts used to prepare the data and operations, but also to new texts, or related texts in similar topic areas. Portability can be achieved by using a syntax-driven analysis that separates the semantic component from the structural decomposition of the texts. The same syntactic-analysis component could then produce syntactic decompositions for many document collections, while distinct semantic interpretation steps could be added for each distinct topic area under consideration. Unfortunately, in many cases available syntax-based methods do not furnish unambiguous text decompositions without additional semantic specifications. There is some hope, however, that in most instances, syntactic analysis systems supplemented by limited, partly domain-independent semantic processes could suffice for text analysis. For example, in text retrieval, gross characterizations of text content might generate indexing products even when all text phrases and sentences are not completely understood.

In the remainder of this chapter several language-analysis components are introduced, including their morphological, syntactic and semantic processing steps. Although these aspects are interrelated, the portability criterion makes it desirable to conceptually separate the language-analysis components. Specialized analysis methods that can be used with incomplete or incorrect text input, and with sublanguages valid only in specific domains, are briefly introduced at the end of the chapter.

11.2 Dictionary Operations

11.2.1 Morphological Decomposition

The first step of any language-analysis system is necessarily recognizing and identifying individual text words. The procedures used to recognize or generate individual words must be based on *word morphology*, that is, the forms of individual words. The word forms determine to some extent the type and hence the function of the individual words; furthermore, word-form identification makes it possible to consult dictionaries and to extract linguistic information from them.

An especially important aspect of morphology is the decomposition of words into word stems and word affixes. Reducing full words to word-stem form leads to substantial storage economies — the number of distinct root forms plus the number of distinct affixes is much smaller than the number of distinct complete words. Word-decomposition systems are also useful in determining word-formation methods and word derivations. [4,5] In decomposing English text into stems and affixes, the same basic process can be used for prefix and suffix determination: A stored affix list is used, and a word stem is constructed by removing from each word the longest possible affix — either prefix or suffix — that matches an entry in the affix table. In English, only about 75 prefixes and about 250 suffixes are distinguishable. Hence the required affix lists can be stored and searched quite inexpensively. [6] A small excerpt from a typical English suffix list is shown in column 1 of Table 11.1(a). Table 11.1(b) contains an excerpt from a list of typical "stop words" — that is, the words that should receive special treatment during analysis. In general, common function words, such as prepositions, conjunctions, and pronouns, that do not reflect document content are used as stop-word entries.

The basic affix-decomposition rule — removal of the longest matching entry in an affix dictionary — will not always generate satisfactory word stems. For example, removing the prefix a- is appropriate for "asymmetry" but not for "able." Similarly, deleting the suffix -ing is proper for "interesting" but not for "king." Two main types of exceptions must be made to the basic affix deletion rule:

1. Contextual rules must be invoked to modify the affix-deletion process for special word forms embedded in particular contexts. Thus, contextual rule is used to prevent the deletion of "eature" from "feature," while allowing deletion of the same suffix from "creature." Similarly, the suffix "allic" is not removed from "metallic," preventing the formation of word stem "met" rather than "metal."

2. Spelling rules must be used in some cases to recode the stems produced by the standard suffix-removal rules and thus restore proper English word forms. For example, when adding a suffix to an English word that ends in b, d, g, m, n, p, r, s, or t, the final consonant must be doubled whenever the last syllable of the word is stressed. When such suffixes are deleted during word-stem generation, these doubled consonants must be converted back to simple occurrences. Thus "hopping" produces "hop" and not "hopp," and "canning" produces "can." A typical excerpt from a list of recoding rules is shown in Table 11.2, together with examples illustrating the rules. [7]

The extent of special processing required in an affix-deletion system depends to some extent on the aims and applications envisioned. In some cases, it may be sufficient to use consistent suffix-deletion

Table 11.1 Excerpt from typical English suffix and stop-word lists. (a) Suffix list (endings in 'ic' and 'ed'). (b) Stop-word list.

(a)	(b)
aged	m
aic	many
ailistic	may
aitric	me
alistic	meanwhile
allic	might
anced	more
antic	moreover
aric	most
aristic	mostly
arized	much
ated	must
atic	my
enced	myself
ened	n
ented	name
entific	namely
ered	near
erized	necessary
etic	neither
fic	never
fied	nevertheless
icated	new
ied	next
ified	nine
inated	no
ined	nobody
ioned	none
ished	noone
istic	

Table 11.2 Typical word-stem transformation rules (adapted from [7]). (J.B. Lovins, Development of a Stemming Algorithm, *Mechanical Translation and Computational Linguistics*, 11:1-2, March and June 1968. Used by permission of the Association for Computational Linguistics; copies of the publication from which this material is derived can be obtained from Dr. Donald E. Walker (ACL), Bell Communications Research, 445 South Street, MRE 2A379, Morristown, NJ 07960, USA.)

Stem-transformation Rule	Input	Resulting Stem
uct → uc	producer production	produc
umpt → um	consumer consumption	consum
olut → olv	resolve resolution	resolv
ond → ons	responding responsive	respons
metr → meter	metrical metering	meter

rules without attempting to produce morphologically perfect English stems. In such circumstances, strong affix-removal systems that leave short root forms and do not involve many exceptional contextual or spelling rules may prove effective. A flowchart for a basic suffix-removal program for English is shown in Fig. 11.1. [7]

11.2.2 Dictionary Types

In addition to the suffix and prefix tables used in word-stem-generation systems, several kinds of lexicons and dictionaries may prove useful for different text-processing purposes. A distinction must be made in this connection between term characterizations derived by analyzing particular text samples, which may be valid only in restricted environments, and large, complete compendiums similar to desk dictionaries, which represent major portions of the language and reflect the properties of unknown texts in unspecified subject areas. In recent years, as the size of available computer memories has grown, efforts have been made to make available mechanized versions of major desk dictionaries such as the New Oxford English Dictionary and Longman's Dictionary of Contemporary English. [8–10] Large mechanized dictionaries provide information about word spelling, syllabification, pronunciation, lexical word categories and syntactic features, word etymology, distinctions of word sense, word definitions, word usage specifications, sample sentences incorporating various words,

Figure 11.1 Typical word stem generation process [7]. (J.B. Lovins, Development of a Stemming Algorithm, *Mechanical Translation and Computational Linguistics*, 11:1-2, March and June 1968. Used by permission of the Association for Computational Linguistics; copies of the publication from which this material is derived can be obtained from Dr. Donald E. Walker (ACL), Bell Communications Research, 445 South Street, MRE 2A379, Morristown, NJ 07960, USA.).

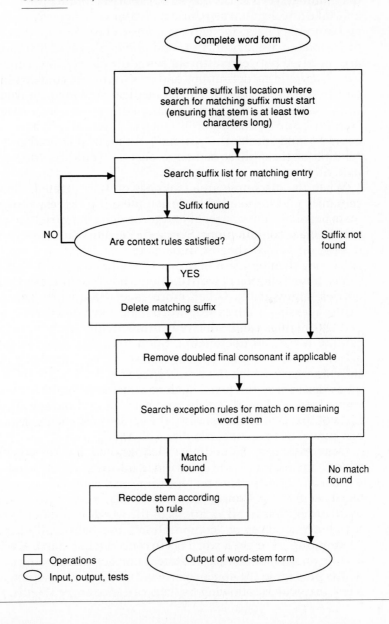

and word synonyms. Dictionaries can correct spelling by providing phonetic access to entries, allowing homograph recognition by distinguishing various meanings of homographic word entries, and allowing term relationships to be recognized based on the definitions listed.

Simple text-analysis methods are primarily based on syntactic information, including lexical word categories (noun, pronoun, conjunction, preposition, and so on) and syntactic feature information (gender, number, verb tense, and so on). More elaborate linguistic systems also take into account semantic indicators extracted from dictionaries and authority lists. Typically, semantic class information is attached to various dictionary entries, and allowable relationship indications are specified between different semantic classes in the form of predications providing definitions and specifying the contexts in which the entries are used. [11–13] Thus a medical sublanguage would include the semantic classes "doctor" (for which typical word entries would be "doctor" and "consultant"), "medical action" ("admission," "discharge"), and "patient" ("patient"). An allowable predicate-argument relation of these three semantic classes would be "doctor admitted patient."

When the discourse area is not severely restricted, the number of semantic classes needed to derive meaning representations for the texts becomes unmanageably large, as does the variety of possible semantic class combinations. Semantic decomposition into primitive semantic units may then be undertaken, and semantic interpretation rules may then be given in terms of available semantic primitives.

The main function of word dictionaries is to characterize dictionary entries linguistically. Other, more specialized word lists are used in text processing, such as stop-word lists, discussed earlier. Some word and text listings can be derived automatically from initially available sample texts and documents. Such lists may provide information about the number and types of distinct words appearing in the texts, the contexts in which the words appear, and the statistical characteristics describing the texts, such as word and sentence length, occurrence frequencies of words, and section and paragraph structure. Lists of text words that specify the context for each word occurrence are known as text concordances. [14–16]

Concordances, sometimes also known as keyword-in-context (KWIC) indexes, provide occurrence information for some or all text words, including precise text locations and context for each individual word occurrence. Concordances are usually arranged in alphabetical word order, that is, all locations of the word "computer" are listed after all occurrences of "computation", but before all occurrences of "computing". For each word occurrence included in a KWIC index, a certain amount of context is stated, normally consisting of a few text words preceding the concordance entry in the normal text order, plus a few text words following the concordance entry. Figure 11.2 shows

Figure 11.2 Excerpt from keyword-in-context index [16].

Keyword-in-context bibliographical index		Document identifier
LIST OF	ABBREVIATED AND FULL TITLES OF TECHN	INSTSI-57-LAF
ENT AND PROOF SERVICES,	ABERDEEN PROVING GROUND.	PERRJW-57-NIS
URING COUNTRY, MACHINES	ABOARD UNEARTH INFORMATION BURIED IN	BENSLC-55-DCI
CARDS TO SORT INFRARED	ABSORPTION AND CHEMICAL STRUCTURE DA	KUEN L-51-NCH
CARDS INDEXING INFRARED	ABSORPTION SPECTROGRAMS.	KEUNLE-52-CIW
GRAPHIC SCHEME BASED ON	ABSTRACT AND INDEX CARDS.	BISHC - -BSB
TIC INFORMATION.* USING	ABSTRACT AND INDEX PUBLICATIONS.	SEWEW -57-RTI
	ABSTRACT ARCHIVE OF ALCOHOL LITERATU	JELLEM-48-AAA
PUBLISHING MODERN	ABSTRACT BULLETINS.	WEILBH- -PMA
COMPANY PHARMACEUTICAL	ABSTRACT BULLETIN.	SEWEW -54-PIC
A PUNCHED CARD	ABSTRACT FILE ON SOLID STATE AND TRA	PATTLD-55-PCA
THE	ABSTRACT OF THE TECHNICAL REPORT.	CORTE -55-ATR
RELATION OF AN	ABSTRACT TO ITS ORIGINAL.	MALOCJ- -ATR
FROM JOURNAL ARTICLE TO	ABSTRACT.	DYSOG -51-RAI
ID SYSTEM OF CODING AND	ABSTRACTING CHEMICAL LITERATURE USING	BIOLAB-56-BRJ
SYMPOSIUM ON	ABSTRACTING AND INDEXING.	KIRSS -56-SRS
THE ORGANIZATION OF AN	ABSTRACTING SERVICE.	CHEMEN-52-SAI
WABASH CUTS WAY BILL	ABSTRACTING EXPENSE.	MCGEJH- -OAS
IL OF SCIENTIFIC UNIONS	ABSTRACTING BOARD.	EASTWR-50-WCW
	ABSTRACTING AND INDEXING SERVICES IN	BOUTPR-56-ICS
AN EVALUATION OF	ABSTRACTING JOURNALS AND INDEXES.	MILEJT-57-AIS
SLANTING IN SCIENTIFIC	ABSTRACTING PUBLICATIONS.	SMITMH- -EAJ
TERNATIONAL COOPERATIVE	ABSTRACTING ON BUILDING.* AN APPRAIS	HERNS - -SSS
ION AND COORDINATION IN	ABSTRACTING AND DOCUMENTATION.	EVANAB- -ICA
THE ICSU	ABSTRACTING BOARD.* THE STORY OF A V	FRANO -6 -CCA
Y OF CURRENT PERIODICAL	ABSTRACTING AND BIBLIOGRAPHIES.	BOYTGA- -IAB
OVERAGE BY INDEXING AND	ABSTRACTING SERVICE.	BESTT -52-IBD
	ABSTRACTING BOARD OF INTERNATIONAL C	HIMWWA-54-SWM
A RUSSIAN	ABSTRACTING SERVICE IN THE FIELD OF	BOYTGA-56-ABI
DOMLY PUNCHED CARDS FOR	ABSTRACTING PUBLICATIONS AND REPORTS	BEYEE -56-RAS
	ABSTRACTING AND LIBRARY WORK IN THE	SHERJ -53-U4H
TECHNICAL	ABSTRACTING AND CHEMICAL INDEXING IN	NATURE-53-ALW
CIENTIFIC AND TECHNICAL	ABSTRACTING AND INDEXING SERVICES.	INSTSI- -TAC
ION PROCESSING- SCIENCE	ABSTRACTING.	CONFAS- -PCA
COOPERATION IN PHYSICS	ABSTRACTING.	HUTCE -56-CIP
PHYSICS	ABSTRACTING.	CROWBM- -ICP
AN EXPERIMENT IN AUTO	ABSTRACTING.	GRAYDE-50-PA
L CONFERENCE ON SCIENCE	ABSTRACTING, 1949, FINAL REPORT.	IBM RC-58-EAA
D FOR THE BIBLIOGRAPHY,	ABSTRACTING, AND INDEXING OF CHEMICA	UNESPA-49-ICS
IBLIOGRAPHIC, INDEXING,	ABSTRACTING, AND REVIEW MEDIA.	GULLC -46-PCM
VARIATION IN CONTENT OF	ABSTRACTS ACCORDING TO USE.	FLEMTP-58-RDK
A SURVEY OF SCIENTIFIC	ABSTRACTS AND INDEXING SERVICES.	FLEIM -56-VCA
YPES OF CHEMICAL PATENT	ABSTRACTS FOR PUNCH CARD USE.	VAROWW-49-SSA
BIOLOGICAL	ABSTRACTS IN AN ERA OF AUTOMATION.	TAPIEW- -CST
	ABSTRACTS OF DOCUMENTATION LITERATUR	GARFE - -BAE

an excerpt from a KWIC index automatically produced from document titles. Each title is listed under each significant title word, together with a document identifier derived from the author names, year of publication, and beginning letters of the first three title words. [16] Automatically produced concordances are useful in detecting word ambiguities when certain word forms occur in several different contexts. Concordances that list the text words in reverse alphabetic order are often used to construct suffix dictionaries to detect rhyming words in poetry.

Additional word lists automatically generated as by-products of normal processing include lists of "words not found" during dictionary consultation or "look-up". Such lists usually contain misspellings and other entries for which special provisions must be made. Although it is easy to generate word lists of many kinds when sample text collections are provided, any dictionary actually used must be stored and maintained, and dictionary-handling procedures are inevitably onerous when many large dictionaries are needed. In practice, large dictionaries of all text words, or all words in the language, are sometimes replaced by word lists of restricted scope, including lists of common function words, lists of word endings, and lists of exceptional word occurrences.

11.3 Syntactic Analysis

Syntax deals with the structural properties of texts. *Syntactic text-generation* methods construct well-formed text statements by assembling individual text components into larger constructs, whereas *syntactic-analysis* systems decompose complete utterances into simpler phrases, and characterize the structural relations between sentence components. In principle, it is sometimes possible to disregard completely any structural properties of text composition. For example, when a subject matter is narrowly specified, it may be possible to translate a text by transforming the semantic entities directly without performing explicit structural decompositions. The variety of semantic entities available in any natural language is such that semantic interpretation of natural-language texts is generally simplified when structural decompositions are performed that constrain the task of semantic interpretation.

In designing a syntactic analysis system, two main considerations must be kept in mind:

1. Applying any syntactic decomposition rule — such as the decomposition of a verb phrase into a verb followed by a noun phrase — depends to some extent on the context in which the phrase occurs. For example, the verb form may have to agree in number with the previously occurring subject if a given phrase decomposition is to apply. An attempt to replace a syntactic constituent by other constituents

without considering the context is likely to produce ambiguous output.

2. All syntactic-analysis systems must eventually use semantic constraints to eliminate ambiguities that cannot be resolved by purely structural considerations. Semantic input can also be used to deal with extra-grammatical input, ellipses, and constructions involving conjunctions, comparatives, pronominal referents, and ambiguous prepositions. Sentences such as "they are flying planes" cannot be interpreted without outside information giving the referent of the pronoun "they".

Language analysis that makes hard distinctions between syntax, on the one hand, and semantics, on the other, is therefore not completely realistic: A useful analysis must include a variety of suitably integrated components. Nevertheless, presentation is simplified if mainly syntactic approaches are distinguished from methods that use substantially semantic ingredients.

To perform a structural text decomposition, two main parsing strategies are available in principle: [17,18]

1. A top-down, hypothesis-driven approach in which the main clause structure and subject-verb-object decompositions are generated first, followed by a more refined decomposition of each subclause into individual clause components.

2. A bottom-up, data-driven approach in which the individual text words are initially considered, and attempts are made to group them into successively larger, more comprehensive components.

In practice, neither of these strategies is completely satisfactory. A strictly top-down, left-to-right parsing strategy is inefficient when initial expectations are not met as the actual sentence components are encountered. It becomes necessary to abandon the analysis and start over with a new set of hypotheses concerning the structure of the available input. Such a situation is illustrated by the sentences of example (11.1), where the interpretations do not become clear until the form of the verb "take" is considered: [19]

> Have the students take the make-up examination today! *(11.1a)*
> Have the students taken the make-up
> examination today? *(11.1b)*

Backtracking operations — that is, abandoning the current analysis and considering new interpretations — can be avoided to some extent by using look-ahead features that anticipate the sentence structures to the right of the current analysis point. However, both backtracking and look-ahead features substantially complicate the analysis system.

A strictly bottom-up analysis process may also be inefficient because a hypothesis that is confirmed early during a structural analysis can substantially simplify the later analysis steps. Thus in example (11.2), the phrase "to make Sue feel better" can be appropriately interpreted by noting that the main verb "want" will accept an infinitive complement, whereas "call" will not: [19]

> I called (John) (to make Sue feel better). *(11.2a)*
>
> I wanted (John to make Sue feel better). *(11.2b)*

In (11.2a), the confirmed hypothesis derived from the interpretation of the main verb ("want" or "call") then leads to the identification of "John" as the verb complement, whereas in (11.2b) the complete infinitive phrase "John to make Sue feel better" is the complement.

A third approach to syntactic recognition consists of using a partly data-driven analysis that also reflects global expectations derived from previously occurring structures. A typical parser of this kind uses an *active node stack* to store partially built syntactic trees that have been generated in the course of the analysis, plus a *constituent buffer*, a work space for assembling the individual elements into larger structures. Based on the partial structures stored in the node stack, the derived hypotheses are then checked by looking at the contents of the buffer. A mixed data-driven and hypothesis-driven approach to language analysis may be more efficient than either of the pure strategies: The use of previously generated hypotheses eliminates many possible later interpretations, while the look-ahead feature provided by a multiplace buffer furnishes the data needed to determine whether the hypotheses are applicable. [19,20]

11.3.1 Typical Syntactic-Analysis Systems

Conceptually, the simplest approach to language analysis consists of avoiding all theories of language structure, and basing sentence interpretation simply on the presence of certain word patterns, possibly supplemented by the characterization of particular word functions. This reduces the analysis process to a *pattern-matching* system in which the presence of particular patterns in the input leads to corresponding output responses.

The well-known ELIZA program simulates a conversation between user and automatic system, where the presence of a specified word pattern in the user's input directly generates corresponding system output. [21,22] Typically, the input patterns are specified as occurrences of function words, embedded in certain variable contexts; appropriate responses are constructed that incorporate the stated input context. Some sample input-output patterns of this type are shown in Table 11.3 for the input "— always —" and "— he — me —". ELIZA usually specifies several different responses for each input pattern, ensuring that the same response will not appear each time a particular input pattern is detected. The variable response system guarantees that a person conversing with the system will not detect the lack of genuine contribution in the system's response, at least not immediately.

As mentioned in Chapter 9, pattern-matching techniques have been widely used in automatic indexing for the assignment of complex content identifiers consisting of multiword phrases. [23–25] In that case, syntactic class markers, such as nominal, adjective, and pronoun, are first attached to the text words. Syntactic class patterns are then specified, such as "noun-noun", or "adjective-adjective-noun," and groups of text words corresponding to permissible syntactic class patterns are assigned to the texts for content identification. Word-frequency and word-distance constraints may also be used to refine phrase construction.

The problem with all pattern-matching approaches to language analysis is the lack of real understanding, and hence the lack of discrimination in the output. Pattern-matching systems recognize many useful constructs, but also many questionable ones, and the balance of effectiveness is not always obvious. Consider, for example, a word pattern such as

$$\text{Adjective — Noun 1 — Preposition — Noun 2 — Noun 3} \quad (11.3)$$

and assume that the phrase-formation rules identify the phrases Adjective-Noun 1, Noun 2-Noun 3, and Noun 1-Noun 3 as appropriate

---

Table 11.3 Typical ELIZA pattern match (adapted from [21]). (P.J. Hayes and J.G. Carbonell, A Tutorial on Techniques and Applications for Natural Language Processing, Technical Report CMU-CS-83-158, Carnegie-Mellon University, Pittsburgh, PA, October 1983. Reprinted with permission.)

Typical Input Pattern	Sample Input	Sample System Responses
X *always* Y	My brother *always* fights with me.	Can you think of a specific example?
		Really, always?
X *he* Y *me*	Because *he* hates *me*.	Why do you think he hates you?
		Suppose he did hate you? What would that mean?

units to identify content. Even though the specified phrase patterns may be syntactically valid, their usefulness for content identification depends on the particular context and the meaning of the phrase components.

A sample word sequence for the input pattern of example (11.3) appears in Table 11.4. The first two of the three generated phrases are acceptable both syntactically and semantically, and even the third phrase cannot be rejected on syntactic grounds. However, only the second phrase, "pseudotumor formation," is completely appropriate for content identification of the sample word sequence. Pattern-matching techniques thus appear most useful in restricted areas of discourse in which stereotyped language constructs are used, and in which the presence of word patterns automatically indicates text content.

A conventional syntactic-analysis system provides more reliable output when the detection of word phrases and other content-identifying units depends not only on specific word patterns, but also on the structure of complete sentences. In particular, when a complete sentence decomposition is available, a fragmentary word pattern can be accepted as a plausible sentence unit only when that pattern actually fits into the larger sentence structure. Syntactic-analysis systems assign syntactic features to sentence components and decompose sentences into substructures using decomposition rules that identify the allowable structural patterns. The set of syntactic decomposition rules is known as a *grammar*.

A particularly simple type of grammar, the so-called *phrase-structure grammar*, can be used for both sentence generation and sentence analysis. Phrase-structure grammars are specified by rewrite rules of the form

$$w A x \rightarrow w \delta x, \qquad (11.4)$$

where A is a single input element (normally a single word, or a phrase of a particular type), and δ is a sequence or string of words or phrases.

Table 11.4 Phrase generation with pattern-matching approach.

Input Pattern	Input Example	Phrase Output	Examples
Article-Adjective-Noun 1-	The specific complication	Adjective-Noun 1	specific complication
Preposition-Noun 2-	of pseudotumor	Noun 2-Noun 3	pseudotumor formation
Noun 3	formation	Noun 1-Noun 3	complication formation

The rule of expression (11.4) specifies that input element A can be replaced with the string of elements δ when A is preceded by structure w and followed by structure x. For example, a particular noun phrase A may be replaced by a word string consisting of an adjective followed by another noun phrase. When the context w and x is absent from a rule and word replacement $A \rightarrow \delta$ applies regardless of context, the grammar is known as *context free*; otherwise as *context sensitive*.

A typical context-free grammar is shown in Fig. 11.3 together with the decomposition of a sample sentence. The analysis starts by using a dictionary-consulting procedure to attach syntactic class identifiers to all input words. The input text is then scanned from left to right, and a syntax rule is invoked whenever the right-hand side of a rule matches a syntactic class pattern in the input text. When several different syntax rules are applicable simultaneously, the first rule in the ordered list of rules is used. Figure 11.3 shows that the noun phrase combining rule (rule 2 in the grammar of Fig. 11.3a) becomes available first to build the noun phrase "the man," followed by the noun phrase "the ball." Rule 5 is used next to combine the verb "hits" with the phrase "the ball," generating the verb phrase "hits the ball." Finally, the initially constructed noun phrase "the man" is combined with the verb phrase "hits the ball," using rule 1 to generate the final sentence symbol S. When S is reached and all the input words are properly accounted for, a complete analysis is obtained that is correct according to the grammar in use.

Fig. 11.3(b) represents the analyzed sentence in two ways: a parenthesized form in which each pair of parentheses represents a phrase, and an equivalent tree decomposition in which the phrases are represented by subtrees. The tree representation of a complete sentence is known as a phrase marker. When rule 5 was invoked in Fig. 11.3(a) to combine the word "hits" with the phrase "the ball," "hits" was automatically interpreted as a verb V. "Hits," however, is also coded as a noun N in the dictionary. This does not cause difficulties in the sample derivation because the grammar does not contain a rule combining a noun N with a noun phrase NP. When analyses are carried out using operational grammars, however, multiple syntactic interpretations are often generated depending on the choice in assigning syntactic function indicators to the input words. The sample grammar of Fig. 11.3 will also accept as correct the sentence "the ball hits the man," even though that sentence appears less plausible semantically than "the man hits the ball." Assuming that grammar rules 4 and 6 are expanded to cover plural forms as well as singular, by using rules such as

N → man or men or ball or balls

Figure 11.3 Sample analysis with context-free grammar. (a) Context-free grammar excerpt. (b) Sample sentence analysis.

Rule number	Grammar Rule	Explanation
1	S → NP, VP	Sentence is transformed into a noun phrase followed by a verb phrase
2	NP → T, N	Noun phrase is transformed into an article followed by a noun
3	T → the	Article becomes "the"
4	N → man or ball	Noun becomes "man" or "ball"
5	VP → V, NP	Verb phrase is transformed into a verb followed by a noun phrase
6	VP → hits or took	Verb phrase becomes "hits" or "took"

(a)

Transformed sentence	Rule number	Tree representation
The man hits the ball	initial input	
T N V,N T N | | | | | The man hits the ball	dictionary lookup	
(The man) hits the ball	2	
(The man) hits (the ball)	2	
(The man) (hits (the ball))	5	
((The man) (hits (the ball)))	1	

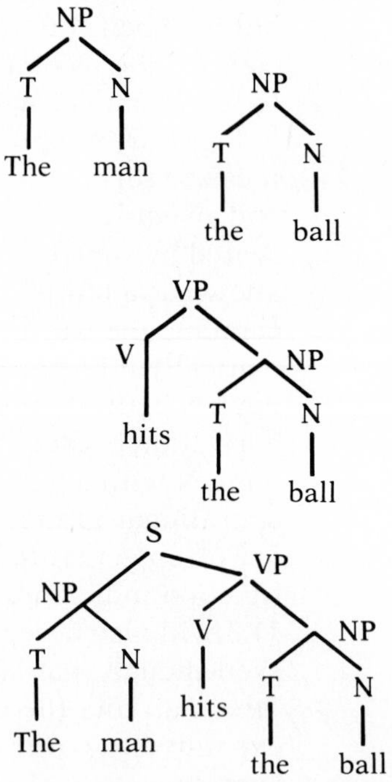

(b)

or

$$VP \rightarrow hit \ or \ hits \ or \ took \ ,$$

grammatically incorrect sentences such as "the men hits the ball" would also prove acceptable.

Such simple context-free phrase-structure grammars do not account for many linguistic facts. Refinements can be added to ensure, for example, that sentence subjects and verbs agree in number by using separate phrase-structure rules for singular and plural forms, such as

$$S_1 \rightarrow NP_s \ , \ VP_s$$

and

$$S_2 \rightarrow NP_p \ , \ VP_p \ ,$$

where the S_1 rule applies to the analysis of "the man hits the ball," whereas the S_2 rule would serve for "the men hit the ball." However, there is no "quick fix" to account for the so-called discontinuous constituents, where the different components of a single phrase are split up in the English formulation, as in "he called Mary up" ("call" and "up" do not appear adjacently). In general, phrase-structure grammars can deal with nestings and juxtapositions of phrases, but not with interleaved constituents or with grammatical transformations such as active-passive shifts.

To handle changes in word order and other linguistic phenomena beyond the capabilities of simple phrase-structure grammars, more elaborate grammatical systems have been developed. The well-known *transformational grammars* generate a so-called deep structure representing all semantically equivalent forms of each utterance. This deep structure can be transformed into standard English output by using one or more steps chosen from an approved list of transformations. The transformations produce specific surface structures reflecting active and passive moods, affirmative and negated statements, declarative and interrogative forms, and so on.

Sentence generation by transformational grammars is outlined in Fig. 11.4. A *base* component of the grammar first generates the deep structure, representing the syntactic and semantic interpretation of an utterance. This is followed by a *transformational* step that obtains the surface structure, reflecting the actual English form, from the deep-structure representation. [26] When the transformational approach is applied to language analysis instead of generation, reverse transformations must be applied to the surface structures to obtain the deep-structure representations. Unfortunately, while only a small number of direct transformations can turn a particular deep structure into the desired surface structure during sentence generation, hundreds of different reverse transformations potentially apply to each given surface structure in the analysis step. Experience with transformational analysis shows that the process is inefficient except when the number of generated surface trees is very small, or when enough information is provided in each surface tree node to select only those inverse transformations likely to lead to correct deep structures.

An alternative grammatical model that carries the same power as a transformational grammar but is simpler to use is the *augmented transition network* (ATN) model. [27–29] In the ATN system, the grammar is represented by a network consisting of nodes representing states, and branches specifying transitions between states. The branches are labeled with syntactic class indicators implying that a transition is made from one state to the next whenever the network branch label corresponds to the structure currently available in the input sentence. There is an initial network state that starts the analysis, and one or more final states. When a final state is reached and all input components are exhausted, the corresponding sentence analysis is accepted as correct according to the grammar.

An excerpt from an ATN grammar is shown in Fig. 11.5 with initial state S_1 and final state S_5. [21] Instead of using formal transformations to account for equivalent forms of the input, different paths are provided in the network for distinct surface structures. For example, if a particular input sentence begins with a noun phrase, the transition

Figure 11.4 Sentence generation using transformational grammar.

Input

Grammar and lexicon

Base component of transformational grammar

Generalized phrase marker
representing deep structure

Transformational component of grammar

Derived phrase marker
representing surface structure

Output

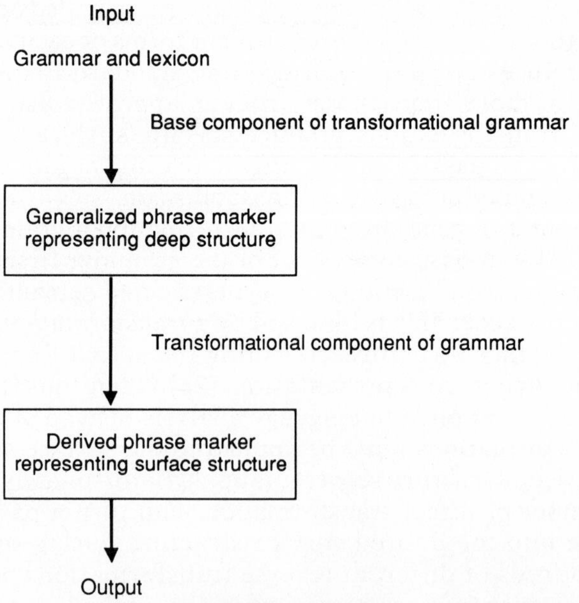

from S_1 to S_3 is taken; if an auxiliary verb is encountered first, the transition would be made from S_1 to S_2. It is easy to verify that the final state S_5 can be reached in Fig. 11.5 for input pattern NP-V-NP ("the man hits the ball"), or alternatively for the sequence AUX-NP-V-by-NP ("was the ball hit by the man").

The specifications of Fig. 11.5 reflect the rules normally included in context-free grammars. Additional flexibility is obtained in an ATN environment by using temporary storage registers to save information that can be recalled when needed. This makes it possible to handle intermediate substructures, such as prepositional phrases or subclauses, by storing current status information before treating intermediate structures, and then resuming the original analysis at the interrupted point. "Push" and "pop" arcs designate the transitions between main structures and substructures in an ATN network, respectively, indicating that the current information is pushed onto storage before the substructure analysis is initiated, and popped from storage when the main analysis resumes. Figure 11.6 shows a stylized example of push and pop operations.

In addition to providing auxiliary storage facilities, the ATN system performs tests whose outcome controls the transitions from one state to the next. This makes it possible to deal with agreement in number between subject and verb, and to prevent multiple transitions through a given subset of arcs. Thus an improper input sequence such as "was the ball hit by the man by the woman" can be rejected by setting a flag when the first "by" is encountered, corresponding to the transition from state S_5 to state S_6 in Fig. 11.5. A test condition is then attached to the "by" arc, and a second occurrence of "by" is disallowed if the flag is found to have been turned on earlier. A typical set of test conditions that might apply to the network of Fig. 11.5 is shown in Table 11.5. For declarative utterances such as "the man hits the ball," the tests cover agreement in number between subject and verb and verification of

Figure 11.5 Excerpt of transition network grammar. (P.J. Hayes and J.G. Carbonell, A Tutorial on Techniques and Applications for Natural Language Processing, Technical Report CMU-CS-83-158, Carnegie-Mellon University, Pittsburgh, PA, October 1983. Reprinted with permission.)

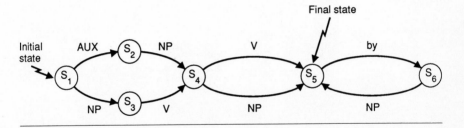

transitivity for the verb, ensuring that a verb complement is acceptable in a given context. For interrogative sentences such as "was the ball hit by the man", additional tests can be performed to ensure that the verb consists of a form of "to be" followed by a past participle, and that only one prepositional phrase terminates the sentence.

The examples of Fig. 11.5 and Table 11.5 demonstrate that the ATN methodology reflects substantial complexities in the input. Reasonably large networks, however, are required to cover meaningful portions of natural-language utterances, and large networks are not easily manipulated. This proves especially disadvantageous when ambiguous or difficult inputs are treated that require backtracking and tracing many parallel analysis paths. In addition, ATN provides little semantic control, and thus meaningless parses are easily generated. For example, a grammar that accepts "the man throws the ball" will normally also accept "the ball throws the man," even though this last utterance may be improbable.

A number of new, context-dependent grammars have recently been developed that account for substantial linguistic complexities but are not based on constructing or manipulating large transition networks. *Generalized phrase structure* grammars use a rule-based system that replaces various kinds of operations included in the transformational model. [30,31] Complex categories are assigned to the input words specifying various syntactic features, and metarules reflect transformations such as passivization and topicalization (a device to shift the emphasis in the discourse). *Lexical functional grammars* produce normal constituent phrase structures similar to those shown in Fig. 11.3(b). These grammars also use functional specifications consisting of detailed feature lists for subject, predicate, and object constituents, and functional descriptions of syntactic relationships between all sentence components. [32]

Another method of supplementing conventional phrase-structure grammars consists of adding condition specifications to the left sides

---

Figure 11.6 Operations of push and pop branches in ATN grammar.

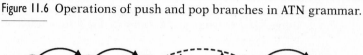
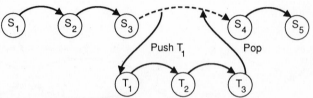

and creation specifications to the right sides of the grammatical rules. The so-called augmented phrase-structure grammar (APSG) is a bottom-up, data-driven analysis system that follows all allowable analysis paths in parallel to avoid possible backtracking. [33] Because the analysis system operates from the bottom up, normal phrase-generation rules (illustrated in Fig. 11.3), are used in reverse order — that is, right to left. Rules 2 and 5 of Fig. 11.3(a) would be written as

$$T \text{ (condition specifications), NP (condition specifications)} \rightarrow$$
$$\text{NP (creation specifications)} \qquad (11.5a)$$

and

$$V \text{ (condition specifications), NP (condition specifications)} \rightarrow$$
$$\text{VP (creation specifications)} \qquad (11.5b)$$

The following rule interpretation takes place for the rules of expression (11.5): First a test is made to verify that the input pattern matches the left side of some particular rule; when a matching pattern is found, a test verifies that the condition specifications are also fulfilled. For

Table 11.5 Tests and register settings for ATN network of Figure 11.5 (adapted from [21]).

Transition	Test Condition	Register Settings
$S_1 - S_2$	—	Set verb register to current input Set type register to "question"
$S_1 - S_3$	—	Set subject register to current input Set type register to "declarative"
$S_3 - S_4$	Test that current input agrees with verb	Set verb register to current input
$S_2 - S_4$	Test that current input agrees with subject	Set subject register to current input
$S_4 - S_5 (V)$	Test that verb register is "be" and input is past participle	Put contents of subject register into object register Set verb register to current input Set subject register to "someone" Set flag register to "true"
$S_4 - S_5 (NP)$	Test that verb register specifies "transitive"	Set object register to current input
$S_5 - S_6$	Test flag register for value "true"	Set flag register to "false" to prevent second traversal
$S_6 - S_5$	—	Set subject register to current input

each matching input pattern for which the condition specifications are met, an output record is created in accordance with the specifications on the right side of the rules.

Table 11.6 contains five sample APSG rules, labeled A through E, which are used in Fig. 11.7 to analyze the sample sentence "your dog eats red dog food." [34] A dictionary-consulting process first assigns grammatical class indicators to the input words. The five rules of Table 11.6 then combine a determiner (for example, an article or a pronoun) followed by a noun phrase, into a new noun phrase (rule A); a noun phrase followed by another noun phrase into a new combined noun phrase (rule B); an adjective phrase followed by a noun phrase into a new combined noun phrase (rule C); a verb phrase followed by a noun phrase into a verb phrase (rule D); and finally a noun phrase followed by a verb phrase into a combined verb phrase (rule E). For the example of Fig. 11.7, these five rules generate the following phrases: "your dog," "dog food," "red dog food," "eats red dog food," and finally "your dog eats red dog food."

The condition and creation specifications that apply to the sample rules are shown in columns 1 and 2 of Table 11.6; comments appear in column 3. For example, rule A — forming a noun phrase by combining a determiner with a noun phrase — applies only when the noun phrase does not already contain a determiner and when both determiner and noun phrase agree in number. The first condition is needed to avoid the formation of noun phrases with multiple determiners (such as "this your dog"), and the second to prevent the attachment of singular determiners to plural nouns or vice versa (such as "this dogs"). The reasons for the other conditions listed are equally obvious.

Syntactic considerations govern all the linguistic-analysis systems examined in this subsection. These systems avoid a great many analysis paths by storing syntactic word features with input elements, and adding conditions to the grammar rules as well as tests to verify that the conditions are in fact fulfilled. The syntactic approach cannot prevent the generation of semantically implausible output, however, nor can syntactic ambiguities be resolved in the absence of semantic specifications. Semantic-type grammars have been introduced to control both syntactic and semantic aspects of language generation and analysis.

11.3.2 Semantic Grammars

In introducing semantic controls for language analysis, an important question is the scope of the semantic apparatus actually needed to obtain effective analyzed output. In principle, a vast amount of semantic knowledge is required to analyze and disambiguate completely arbitrary input statements: A good deal is taken for granted in ordinary

Table 11.6 Rules in augmented phrase-structure grammar.

Left Side of APSG Rule	Right Side of APSG Rule	Comments
A. DET,NP(¬DETRM, DET.AGREE.NP)	NP(copy NP, DETRM = DET, PRMODS = DET...PRMODS)	Formation of "your dog"
1. There is a determiner followed by a noun phrase	a. Form a single noun phrase by copying the current noun phrase	Condition 2 avoids formation of the your dog this that dog
2. The noun phrase is not yet preceded by a determiner	b. The determiner is specified by a pointer to the DET node	Condition 3 avoids formation of those dog these dog
3. There is agreement in number between the determiner and the noun phrase	c. Any premodifiers of the noun phrase are concatenated to the determiner	
B. NP1(¬ PRMODS), NP2(¬DETRM)	NP(copy NP2, PRMODS = NP1...PRMODS)	Formation of "dog food"
1. There is a noun phrase followed by another noun phrase	a. Form a single noun phrase by copying the noun phrase 2	Condition 2 avoids multiple passes by forcing attachment of premodifiers in right to left order
2. The first noun phrase has no premodifiers	b. The premodifiers of the noun phrase consist of noun phrase 1 followed by any existing premodifiers of noun phrase 2	Condition 3 avoids formation of dog the food
3. The second noun phrase has no determiner		
C. AJP, NP(¬DETRM)	NP (copy NP, PRMODS = AJP...PRMODS)	Formation of "red dog food"
1. There is an adjective phrase followed by a noun phrase	a. Form a single noun phrase by copying the noun phrase	Condition 2 avoids formation of red the dog food
2. The noun phrase has no determiner	b. The premodifiers consist of the adjective phrase followed by any premodifiers of the noun phrase	*(continued)*

Table 11.6 (Continued.)

Left Side of APSG Rule	Right Side of APSG Rule	Comments
D. VP (TRANS, ¬OBJ, ¬SUBJ), NP	VP (copy VP, OBJ = NP, PSMODS = PSMODS ...NP)	Formation of "eats red dog food"
1. There is a verb phrase followed by a noun phrase	a. Form a single verb phrase by copying the verb phrase	Condition 2 avoids sleep red dog food
2. The verb is transitive	b. The object is defined by the current noun phrase	Condition 3 avoids eats the food the trash
3. The verb does not yet have an object		
	c. The postmodifiers are the postmodifiers of the verb phrase followed by the noun phrase	Condition 4 avoids multiple passes by forcing attachment of object before subject
4. The verb does not yet have a subject		
E. NP, VP(NP.AGREE.VP, ¬SUBJ)	VP (copy VP, SUBJ = NP, PRMODS = NP... PRMODS)	Formation of "your dog eats red dog food"
1. There is a noun phrase followed by a verb phrase	a. Form a verb phrase by copying current verb phrase	Condition 2 avoids the dogs eats the food
2. There is agreement in number between noun phrase and verb phrase	b. The subject of the verb phrase is defined as the noun phrase	Condition 3 avoids the dogs the cats eat the food
3. The verb phrase does not already have a subject	c. The premodifiers of the verb phrase are the noun phrase followed by the current premodifiers of the verb phrase	

discourse, implying that a complete analysis system must deal with unmentioned assumptions, unstated facts, and implications of the input. It seems inappropriate to operate in an environment of unrestricted semantic input, however, because so little is known about generating, representing, and manipulating large knowledge structures. The practical possibilities of using semantic information in language analysis are thus somewhat limited.

Two main approaches must be examined: (1) Operate with relatively shallow knowledge covering a reasonably wide area, or (2) use deeper, more detailed knowledge structures that are valid only locally. In either case, the idea is to supplement lexical-class and syntactic-feature indicators of the text words by semantic-class identifiers, and to incorporate semantic criteria into rules for text generation and analysis.

Figure 11.7 Sample analysis for augmented phrase structure grammar [34].

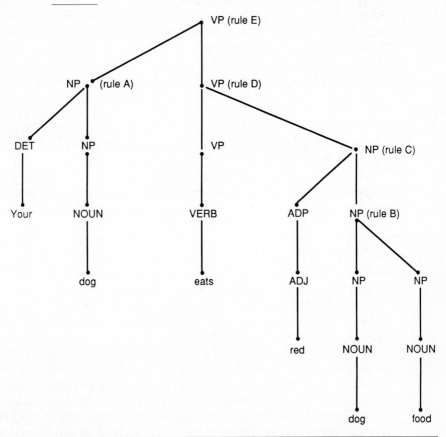

Case grammar is the best known of the relatively shallow, domain-independent approaches to semantic processing. [35] The case system characterizes every construction, including complete sentences, by a particular lexical head. Nouns normally function as heads of noun phrases and verbs as heads of sentences. Each head concept is associated in a well-defined manner with certain roles also known as cases. Individual cases are specified as quasi-semantic characteristics such as agent, object, or instrument. A word of a particular syntactic class can usually fill many individual case specifications.

A case-grammar analysis operates by comparing the expectations embodied in *case frames* attached to the individual head concepts with the case identifiers attached to the elements of the sentence. This makes it possible to assign appropriate sentence elements to case frames when a match occurs. More specifically, each significant word is identified in the lexicon by one or more case identifiers of the type shown in Table 11.7, and each head concept is characterized by a case frame such as the one shown in Table 11.8 for the verb "to break". [36] To analyze an input statement, an attempt is made to fill the "slots" in the case frame with appropriate sentence elements using the available case specifications and special markers ("to" and "from" for location, "with" for an instrument) attached to the case definitions. Thus given an input statement such as "John violently broke the window on Main Street with his fist," the subject and object of the sentence represent, respectively, AGENT and PATIENT. The preposition "with" identifies "fist" as the INNER MEANS, and "on" identifies "Main Street" as the LOCUS. Finally "violence" is labeled as a possible OUTER MEANS. The completed case analysis for the sample sentence is shown in column 3 of Table 11.8.

When a case-grammar analysis is completed by filling the case frame slots with appropriate sentence elements, most of the syntactic ambiguities are automatically eliminated. For example, the input "the man throws the ball" might be analyzed by a case-frame system into the sequence AGENT-HEAD-PATIENT. However, "the ball throws the man" could be rejected by insisting that the AGENT of "throw" be characterized as animate. On the other hand, semantically ambiguous statements that are normally resolvable only by contextual information can still not be uniquely analyzed by a case grammar, and neither can statements whose understanding requires the specialized knowledge of a particular discourse area.

In a case grammar, individual sentence elements are supplemented by case identifiers, but there is no attempt to analyze the meaning of the various concepts in detail. In principle, it is possible to use small numbers of semantic primitives to perform a more detailed semantic analysis that characterizes the meaning of each object. [37,38] The notion of "drinking" might thus be characterized as the ingestion of a

Table 11.7 Typical case identifiers (adapted from [36]).

Case Name	Case Definition
AGENT	Perceived external instigator, initiator, or experiencer of an event or state
PATIENT	Perceived central participant in an event or state (also called OBJECT or THEME)
INNER LOCUS (from, in)	Perceived source, goal, or location of the PATIENT
OUTER LOCUS (in, at, on)	Perceived abstract or concrete spatial setting of an action or state
INNER CORRESPONDENT	Perceived entity corresponding to the PATIENT (EXPERIENCER)
OUTER CORRESPONDENT	Perceived external frame of reference or standard for the state or action
INNER MEANS (with, by means of)	Perceived immediate effector of an event or state (INSTRUMENT)
OUTER MEANS	Abstract method by which an external influence impinges on the situation (MANNER)
TIME (at, on)	Temporal setting of a state or event

liquid substance by an animate subject, the liquid being eventually absorbed by the subject. Similarly, a "crook" becomes a "no-good" person who harms other persons, or alternatively an object used by a person to force animals to stay in line. Analysis systems based on the use of primitive semantic categories have actually been incorporated into

Table 11.8 Case frame for "BREAK" and analysis of "John violently broke the window on Main Street with his fist."

Head Concept	Case Identifiers and Definition	Filler
BREAK	AGENT who does the breaking	JOHN
	PATIENT that is being broken	WINDOW
	INNER LOCUS: location of PATIENT	
	OUTER LOCUS: location of ACTION	MAIN STREET
	INNER MEANS: instrument used for breaking	FIST
	OUTER MEANS: manner of breaking	VIOLENCE
	TIME: time of action	

automatic question-answering facilities. [39] Even such a relatively sophisticated approach, however, cannot deal with ambiguities where specialized subject knowledge and commonsense information are needed for language understanding. Thus a decomposition of the terms "transistor" and "oscillator" into primitive semantic concepts still might not lead to a proper interpretation of the phrase "high frequency transistor oscillator," because electronic know-how is needed to determine whether "high frequency" modifies "transistor" or "oscillator" or both. Furthermore, both commonsense and subject knowledge are needed to reject the idea of a high (in the sense of tall) transistor, or of a high oscillator. [40]

The best way to master complexities of this type is to build specialized grammars capable of analyzing only certain kinds of texts in restricted subject areas. All the necessary syntactic and semantic information could then be included in advance in the grammatical system, which could then analyze texts fitting the narrow subject specifications. Typical systems of this kind have been built to analyze queries submitted to retrieve information from specialized databases. [41,42] In such situations, the syntactic-recognition system can be restricted to the treatment of certain interrogative statements (such as "can you tell me about such and such," or "what is known about such and such"), and semantic interpretations must be provided only for small selections of interesting concepts. Table 11.9 shows a typical semantic grammar for a sample database dealing with ships and their attributes. As this illustration makes clear, normally ambiguous notions

Table 11.9 Illustration of semantic grammar. (a) Sample semantic grammar. (b) Generation of information requests (adapted from [21]).

1. S	→	(present) the (attribute) of (ship)
2. (present)	→	what is or tell me
3. (attribute)	→	length or beam or class
4. (ship)	→	the (shipname) or ships of class (classname)
5. (shipname)	→	kennedy or enterprise
6. (classname)	→	kitty hawk or lafayette

(a)

Rule Sequence	Sample Information Query
1, 2, 3, 4, 5	what is the length of the kennedy
1, 2, 3, 4, 6	tell me the beam of ships of class lafayette

(b)

such as "length" or "class" are now unambiguous, since they can refer only to ship attributes in the context of the sample grammar. The same is true of ship and class names. Thus neither "kennedy" nor "lafayette" is interpretable as the name of a person, but only as a ship or a class name, respectively. The usefulness of this type of semantic grammar is limited because the system becomes unmanageable when the number of rules grows large. When system aims change, it is usually easier to write a new semantic grammar than to adapt an existing one with its relative lack of flexibility and unique interpretations of all concepts included.

In some situations, a given task must be performed for a number of different databases or different semantic environments. For example, the same stereotyped query formulation might be addressed to databases covering different classes of objects. In these circumstances, the syntactic portions of the query generation (exemplified by rules 1 and 2 in the sample grammar of Table 11.9a) could be separated from the semantic portion of the grammar, and only the latter would have to be newly generated for each distinct domain. In general, however, the lack of ambiguity and relative conceptual simplicity of the semantic approach is bought at the price of substantial inflexibility and severe restrictions in a particular area.

11.4 Knowledge-based Processing

11.4.1 Knowledge Structures

As mentioned earlier, the syntactic approach cannot deal with many problems of linguistic ambiguity, and plausible interpretations of linguistic utterances often cannot be attained without substantial amounts of outside knowledge. The context necessary to interpret natural-language statements can sometimes be inferred from the remainder of the discourse. In a syntactic framework, however, the analysis cannot normally be extended outside the boundaries of single sentences. Further, it is not usually easy to predetermine what type of outside knowledge may be needed for particular semantic interpretations.

To help furnish semantic interpretations outside specialized or restricted environments, the existence of a *knowledge base* is often postulated. Such a knowledge base classifies the principal entities or concepts of interest and specifies certain relationships between the entities. [43–45] The knowledge base may also contain a system of inference rules designed to extend the available knowledge by supplying new facts and relations from already available information.

The literature includes a wide variety of different knowledge representations, ranging from formal systems based on propositional and predicate calculus that define only restricted logical relationships between entities, to large network structures that describe the entities by different types of attributes and that include many different relationships between entities. The best-known knowledge-representation techniques are the *semantic-net* and *frame* or *script* systems.

A semantic net is a graph structure in which the nodes represent concepts or entities of interest, and the branches between pairs of nodes supply relationships between the entities, or suitable property specifications for the entities. In generating a semantic network, it is necessary to decide on a method of representation for each entity, and to relate or characterize the entities. The following types of knowledge representation levels are recognized: [46–48]

- A logical form in which the nodes represent propositions (such as "Jack is the father of Jim") or predicates (such as "X is the father of Y"), and the links represent logical relationships that modify or combine predicates and propositions using operators such as "and," "subset," and "there exists."

- A knowledge-representation level in which the nodes represent concept types or concept elements, each identified by attributes and properties, and the links represent either knowledge inheritance from one concept to the next, or knowledge modification.

- A conceptual level in which the nodes are concepts and the links are case relations (such as instrument, recipient, and location) connecting different concepts, or primitive acts (such as grasp, ingest, and transform) relating different concepts.

- A linguistic level in which the elements are language specific and the links represent arbitrary relationships between concepts that exist in the area under consideration.

Some of these models are obviously much less constrained than others: On the linguistic level, any concept type and any conceptual relationship is representable, whereas on the conceptual level only case relations and a small number of primitive acts are allowed. Inconsistencies may complicate the use and interpretation of the semantic data, however, no matter what level of representation is chosen. In particular, the same configuration of network nodes and branches can usually be interpreted in many different ways, depending on the context and the needs of information representation. The following difficulties must be considered: [46]

- The distinction between general statements applying to complete generic classes ("all swans are white") and specific statements applying only to certain individual members of a class ("a white swan was gliding in the water").

- The confusion between intension (a reference to the properties of a particular dog) and extension (a description of the properties that all dogs have in common).

- The difference between an assertion ("there is a ball that is red") and a description ("the red ball rolled down the hill").

- The distinction between an attributive statement that introduces a property for a given entity ("this man is Norwegian") and a referential statement ("a Norwegian landed in the United States") in which the nominal serves simply as a reference to a given person.

Thus to interpret stored information clearly, differentiations must be made in network types, or among different nodes of the same network. One possibility for simplifying the interpretation of the stored information consists of introducing a more flexible model to represent information, one that accommodates a greater variety of data structures than a conceptual network. The use of frame or script models may be a step in this direction. [49, 50]

A frame is a structure that describes a particular entity, theme, or situation by listing elements of interest in the particular context, and implicitly answering questions that could be asked in connection with that entity. Scripts have similar aims, although they may also include expectations and anticipated developments from particular situations. [1] A "restaurant" frame might thus describe the locale (chairs, tables, counters), the participants in the situation (cooks, cashiers, waiters, patrons), the activities (ordering food, eating food, paying the bill), and other special developments that could occur in the restaurant world. Different frame types may represent surface syntactic frames similar to the case frames for head verbs used in the case-grammar model; surface semantic frames describing the context, actions, and qualifications for certain concept interpretations; thematic frames listing topics, activities, and strategies connected with particular topics; and narrative frames describing stories, explanations, arguments, conventions, and developments of particular events or plots.

Slots, similar in spirit to the slots in a case frame, store the information attached to particular frames. Each slot is filled with a particular type of information element. The values of certain attributes, or the names of subframes that themselves contain more detailed information about particular aspects of the situation described in the main frame, can fill the open frame slots. Frames can be related to each other, representing, for example, superconcepts or subconcepts, parts of other frames, or related events. Frame relationships thus constitute conceptual frame networks like semantic networks, except that individual node structures are more complex and represent greater varieties of information. Because information describing particular events and situations is not always available, frames are often specified incompletely. Many slot positions will therefore be filled only when the corresponding information becomes available. The use of incompletely specified information structures can cause problems in comparing the information extracted from particular linguistic statements with stored data in the frame structure, and more generally in matching different elements of the knowledge structure.

Some of the problems of knowledge representation mentioned for semantic nets also arise in the frame model. Thus different types of information must be included in the frame structures — including assertions and descriptions; general statements that are always valid and specific ones that apply only to particular instances; and attributions and references. Specific problems may arise in deciding, for example, whether a given piece of information should fill a slot in an existing frame, or should be represented by a separate frame, or a subframe of another frame. In general, determining information relationships is not easier in the frame model than in the semantic network structures.

One suggestion is to separate so-called terminological (T) boxes, containing structured descriptions of concepts and concept relations, from assertional (A) boxes, representing descriptions of themes and events. [47] While much can be done to standardize the representation and manipulation of knowledge, as yet there is no agreement about the best way to represent knowledge, nor about the primitive knowledge elements needed and the manner in which these elements should be processed to derive semantic interpretations of linguistic formulations. Some long-range studies, currently under way, are expected to derive acceptable and consistent representations for large areas. [51] In practice, however, it is wise to restrict semantic processing to well-circumscribed restricted situations with a stereotyped discourse structure and a well-understood linguistic domain.

11.4.2 Prospects for Knowledge-based Processing

The various attempts to interpret text based on structured knowledge representations all rest on a rationalistic tradition — the assumption that an objective reality exists, consisting of objects with well-defined properties that enter relationships with each other in particular situations. In these circumstances, general rules can be stated that apply to particular situations, and these rules can generate logical conclusions about new events that follow from particular premises and new inferences to be drawn at particular times.

There is a substantial antirationalist tradition, however, which denies the idea of objective reality, and does not accept the existence of objects that bear properties independent of particular interpretations. [52–54] In this view, one cannot coherently talk about an external world without also furnishing the background and contexts that control the events in each circumstance. Knowledge and understanding are not believed to result from formal operations on mental representations of particular objects, but to require each individual's immediate participation, controlled by a socially shared background of concerns, actions, and beliefs. The antirationalist position asserts that a question cannot be answered unequivocally without considering the context in which it may be uttered, as well as the background of questioners and responders, and also asserts that statements are not either true or false, but only more or less appropriate in various contexts. These premises lead to the conclusion that concrete representations of knowledge and particular rules of interpretation necessarily exhibit a greater or lesser degree of blindness that restricts them to limited sets of potentially relevant actions. It follows that the environment actually controlling objects and activities in the real world can never be reflected in artificial structures of the type usable in a computer, and that semantic interpretations of meaning based on objective constructs — such as knowledge bases, frames, slots, and scripts — must fail in most circumstances. Furthermore, because the essence of intelligence is the ability to act appropriately when simple predefinitions of the problem do not exist, and when the areas of knowledge that may lead to a solution are not determined, preconstructed knowledge bases necessarily fail to replace human intelligence when it counts most.

In these circumstances, one might ask whether expert human informers could not help construct extended formal frameworks that reflect the richness of human background. Obviously human experts do function in a complex world, unbothered by blindness and limited intelligence in most circumstances. [55,56] In the antirationalist view, however, experts cannot transfer deep knowledge to an automatic system for the simple reason that experts do not need formalized representations in order to act. Experts do not consider facts and rules to reach particular goals; they do what comes naturally and what they know from experience will work.

An alternative possibility is to build *learning programs* that start with simple structures and attempt to represent knowledge more completely as the system operates and gains experience in solving problems. Learning systems have worked well in simple, structured environments such as the solution of puzzles and games. In the area of language understanding, the fear is that learning will adjust the initially programmed representation only slightly, and that the basic problem of fixed object representation and blindness to context and circumstances cannot be avoided.

Whether meaningful progress can be made in designing intelligent systems to analyze text and interpret language thus remains an open question.

11.5 Specialized Language Processing

❖ 11.5.1 Robust Parsing

In many situations the linguistic data available for analysis are incomplete or flawed. For example, texts may contain misspellings, or text words may be missing from the lexicon, making it impossible to assign syntactic- and semantic-feature indicators. Texts may also contain spurious phrases, interpolations, and unusual word orders, and there may be missing text elements and fragmentary utterances. The incomplete or fragmentary statements may be perfectly comprehensible in context, but cannot of course be analyzed by conventional grammars designed to process syntactically acceptable input.

When problems arise for single words, such as misspellings and unknown word uses, spelling-correction routines might be invoked; alternatively, syntactic and semantic markers might be assigned in accordance with expectations derived from the surrounding context. Sometimes the available suffix and other morphological specifications also provide clues about the function of particular words. More elaborate approaches are needed to treat problems on a sentential level, at which large portions of text would be rejected by conventional grammars. The following suggestions, among others, have been made for the treatment of ill-formed input: [57–59]

- The same grammar might be used to analyze both well-formed and ill-formed inputs. However, the constraints that restrict the applicability of rules (for example, the condition specifications of APSG grammars) might be dropped to interpret the ill-formed inputs. Such an approach takes care of certain irregularities, but leads to misinterpretations when the dropped constraints are essential to obtain correct interpretations.

- Different sets of constraints might be developed to handle well-formed and ill-formed inputs, while using a common grammar in both cases. This solution could work for many types of ill formation, but would exclude unusual interpretations that are automatically treated by the ill-formed version of the syntactic rules.

- A metric might be developed to determine the amount of deviation between a postulated interpretation for some questionable input and a related interpretation for some well-formed input. The well-formed interpretation with the smallest distance from the postulated one might then be assumed to apply.

- In appropriately constrained situations, attempts can be made to guess the user's intent in submitting certain kinds of questionable inputs. Correction factors could then be automatically applied before generating final interpretations.

A procedure that should work for a variety of unusual inputs consists of using a conventional grammar to analyze all types of input. When the input is ambiguous and several different analyses are produced, a ranking process arranges the interpretations in decreasing order of likelihood. When, on the other hand, the input deviates sufficiently from any usually accepted grammatical form and an acceptable analysis cannot be obtained, peripheral procedures are used to resolve the normal parsing failures as simply as possible. The so-called *fitted* parsing system attempts to do that in the following way: [60,61]

1. A head constituent is first chosen for the available input, preferably a verb phrase characterized by a tense indication and an identifiable subject. Alternatively, a tensed verb phrase without subject indication is used as the head; another segment is used if no tensed verb phrase can be identified.

2. Once the head constituent is chosen, the other constituents are "fitted" into the available context; in particular, subject and object phrases are used to complement the head constituent. When a question arises about the extent of any constituent, the widest segment covering the greatest length of text is picked at each point. The fitting process is complete when all open segments have been added to the head and the head constituent covers the complete input string.

Examples of analyzed output using the fitted parsing system appear in Fig. 11.8. In Fig. 11.8(a), the head constituent is the tensed verb phrase with subject stating "75 percent of $250 is $187.50." The string portion "$250 is $187.50" also obeys the head-constituent specification; however, the wider context given earlier is preferred. Once the head verb phrase is analyzed conventionally, the prefix "Example:" is specified as a simple noun phrase. Figure 11.8(b) represents a noun phrase with a conjunction and an attached clause. Since the clause "I wish you the best" contains a tensed verb, it is used as the head constituent. The

Figure 11.8 Examples of fitted parse trees for irregular input (adapted from [60]). (a) "Example: 75 percent of $250 is $187.50." (b) "Good luck to you and yours and I wish you the best."

NP : Noun phrase
PP : Prepositional phrase
AJP : Adjective phrase
PRON : Pronoun
CONJ : Conjunction
ADJ : Adjective
QUANT : Quantifier
VP : Verb phrase
PREP: Preposition

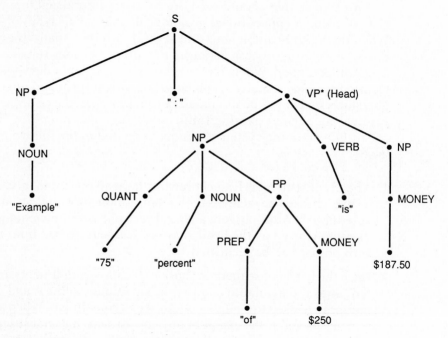

(a)

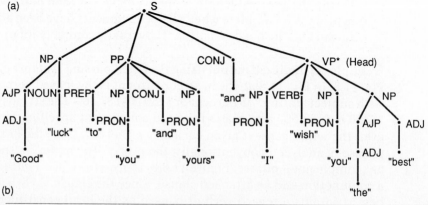

(b)

remainder, "good luck to you and yours," is then interpreted as a noun phrase followed by a prepositional phrase. A fragment without any verb such as "best wishes to you all" would also be interpreted as a noun phrase followed by a prepositional phrase. In the absence of additional contextual information, fitted parsing may result in reasonable interpretations for flawed inputs of the type shown in the illustrations.

❖ 11.5.2 Sublanguage Analysis

As mentioned earlier, substantial advantages may accrue in language analysis and semantic interpretation when restricted inputs are available that do not encompass the full scope of all natural-language phenomena. Special, relatively simple analysis systems might be used in the following circumstances:

- When the full extent of the grammatical complexity is absent, for example when processing lists of noun-phrase structures or special word lists rather than ordinary running text.

- When the discourse area is limited to particular disciplines, such as law, biology, or mathematics, in which the vocabulary may be stereotyped and the variety of language structures to be dealt with is smaller than in unrestricted environments.

- When special-purpose texts are analyzed, such as instruction manuals, job advertisements, or patent applications.

For texts of type 1 most complexities of ordinary syntax can be disregarded, and the analysis can be carried out with a simple syntactic system. In case 2, when the discourse area is limited, the problem of determining conceptual entities and term relations may not exist. In particular, if only a small number of semantic classes are dealt with, the large diversity of semantic relationships normally present in ordinary language can be replaced by a few well-determined patterns. In that case, semantic interpretation can be generated without major difficulty.

Finally, for texts of type 3, most lexical ambiguities may be absent because each word will then be used in the specialized sense peculiar to the text function under consideration. In addition, only limited amounts of outside knowledge may be necessary for semantic interpretation. For example, in technical texts the term "eccentric" might be used only for inanimate objects. Similarly, in a technical context, "ball" may always be interpreted as a spherical object and never as a dancing party, and terms such as "spring" and "race" may be used only concretely. In such special circumstances, simple semantic interpretations can sometimes be generated in tabular formats, as shown in Table 11.10 for descriptions of plants and for medical summaries of patients' conditions. [62,63] In these situations, text analysis is less complex than for unrestricted input because syntactic constructions are stereotyped and applicable semantic restrictions are more severe. Even comparatively difficult input can sometimes be dealt with by referring to existing syntactic and semantic restrictions. Consider as an example a medical report excerpt of the following form: "cultures were obtained in the visit to the emergency room prior to admission." [13] In this case, no problem arises for the phrase "cultures were obtained in the visit," which follows the schema TEST–TREATMENT VERB–MEDICAL ACTION, or with the location information "visit to the emergency room" (MEDICAL ACTION IN MEDICAL INSTITUTION). A decision must be made, however, about the point of attachment of the prepositional phrase "prior to admission." This normally difficult problem is solved by consulting the list of allowable semantic class patterns for time prepositions such as "during," "after," and "prior to." In this case, the pattern TIME PREPOSITION — MEDICAL ACTION is allowed to modify semantic class components such as SIGN/SYMPTOM, TEST, MEDICAL ACTION, PATIENT VERB, and

---

Table 11.10 Sample tabular frameworks for special document types. (a) Tabular specification of plant descriptions (adapted from [63]). (b) Tabular specification of medical test data (adapted from [62]). (From Grishman and Hirschman, Question Answering from Natural Language Medical Data Bases, *Artificial Intelligence*, Volume 11. Copyright © 1978 Elsevier Science Publishers. Reprinted with permission.)

General Specifications		Flower Description			Leaf Description			Habitat	
Name	*Size*	*Color*	*Shape*	*Size*	*Color*	*Shape*	*Size*	*Location*	*Season*
small bugloss	a foot high	blue	–	small	–	wavy	–	widespread	April onward
.		.		.		.			
.		.		.		.			
.		.		.		.			

(a)

Test Information			Medical Verb	Finding
Test Type	*Test Location*	*Date*		
films	of chest	5/25/70	exhibit	no callus formation
xray film	of chest	6/17/72	reveal	multiple pulmonary metastasis

(b)

TREATMENT VERB, but not the class MEDICAL INSTITUTION (hospital, emergency room, and so on). This allows "visit prior to admission" as an attachment point, but not "emergency room prior to admission". [13]

It is not clear to what extent it is possible to standardize the construction of allowable semantic pattern schemes for different subject areas, nor to what extent this type of analysis can be applied to large document classes. Substantial intellectual efforts appear needed to construct the semantic class schedules and decide on allowable semantic patterns in each area. It is conceivable that the insights gained in one area may apply to other fields, at least in part. In that case, this special-purpose approach to language analysis may well become more widely used.

11.5.3 Natural-Language Interface to Information Systems

One area of language analysis that has proved of particular interest is the design of natural-language interfaces to data-retrieval systems. [39,41,64–73] Two main reasons exist for the popularity of interface designs. First, database management systems are widely used, normally by people without special technical training who find it hard to use the technical interface procedures and formal query-manipulation methods usually provided. If a flexible user-system interaction process were provided allowing query formulations and other user inputs in relatively unrestricted natural-language form, the DBMSs would be much more useful. The argument for the design of natural-language interfaces is the relative simplicity of the processing environment. Analyzing natural-language database queries is less complex than analyzing totally free natural-language text, and ambiguities can sometimes be eliminated by referring to the contents of the particular database. For example, the query "list the names of New York secretaries" may be interpreted unambiguously as a request for the names of secretaries living in New York City if the query phrase "New York" matches an address attribute entry in the file being interrogated. On the other hand, if "New York" matches a birthplace attribute, a different interpretation would be used. [69]

Figure 11.9 shows a typical translation system from natural-language query input to actual database access operations. The first step is a standard language analysis, using a dictionary consultation to produce syntactic tree structures annotated with syntactic and semantic features. Many types of language-analysis systems have been proposed for this purpose, their unifying trend being a concern with domain and data independence that allows the analysis system to apply to many different data-retrieval environments.

The syntactic tree structures produced in step 1 of Fig. 11.9 must be translated into a form accessible to the data-management system before they are submitted to the retrieval component. This translation is conveniently broken down into several steps. The first step, labeled "mapping system" in Fig. 11.9, transforms the tree representation into a linear, logical expression that may be similar in structure to a formula in the predicate calculus. By using the main subject-verb-object structure obtained in the language-analysis step together with appropriate semantic-function indications, the query can be transformed

Figure 11.9 Conversion from natural language query input to database operations (adapted from [39]). (Reprinted with permission from *Information Technology: Research and Development*, 1:1 January, B.K. Boguraev and K. Sparck Jones, "A Natural Language Analyzer for Database Access." Copyright 1982, Pergamon Press plc.)

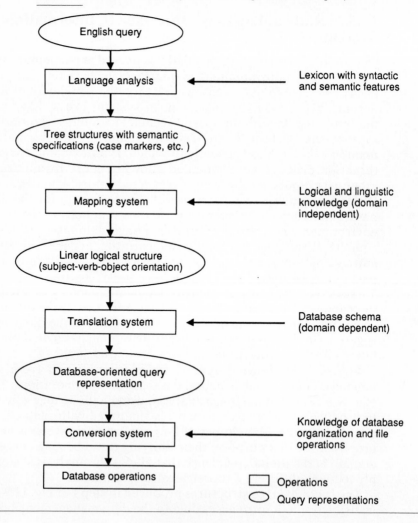

into a logical statement with predicates and quantified variables. In the query-conversion system of Fig. 11.9, the mapping step is performed without direct reference to the database contents by identifying referents to semantically unspecified items such as "what," "how much," and "who," and attempting to reject semantically anomalous interpretations. Thus by turning "who" into a nominal corresponding to the predicate "supplies," and noting that "green" is a value of a "color" attribute, the input "who supplies green parts" can be transformed into a logical expression of the following form:

> for every x_1 where x_1 is supplier
> and for every x_2 where x_2 is a part
> and where color of x_2 is green
> display x_1 if x_1 supplies x_2

The logical statements produced by a database-independent mapping system cannot be submitted to the retrieval component directly because the concepts and predicates used in the query may not correspond to recognizable entities in the database. For example, the predicate "supplies" in the previous example may not be present in the available file system, and may have to be replaced by a term such as "manufactures." Furthermore, the attributes included in a query may refer to the entities ambiguously, as in "state the location of suppliers x and parts y." In that case, the mapping system could supply various interpretations such as "give the location for suppliers x," "give the location of parts y," or "give the location for suppliers x who are capable of supplying parts y." To resolve such problems, a database-dependent translation step is added to the query-conversion system; this step supplies the terminology peculiar to the database environment under consideration, and removes ambiguities by referring to the stored file information.

Query disambiguation using information derived from the database is shown in Table 11.11. [73] In that case, "supplier" is identified as an attribute in a Supply file; "locate" is a verb with the subject "supplier" in the Supply file, or the subject "part number" in a Parts file; and "city" and "Paris" represent an attribute and attribute value referring to the location of either suppliers or part numbers. The fact that "supplier" is identified as the subject of "locate" makes it possible to decide that the first of the two interpretations given in Table 11.11 is correct in this case.

The last step in the query-translation system of Fig. 11.9 takes the form supplied by the database-specific translation and converts it into actual search and retrieval commands that can be submitted to an operational retrieval system. This step, of course, must be tailored to the retrieval service in use and to the file structures available for searching.

Table 11.11 Sample database query translation (adapted from [73]). (a) Sample data base specification. (b) Query interpretation.

"City"   Noun (((attribute in Supply file) and (city is Supply location)) or ((attribute in Parts file) and (city is Parts location)))

"Paris"   Noun ((value of attribute city in Supply file) or (value of attribute city in Parts file))

"locate"   Verb ((subject is part number in Parts file) or (subject is supplier in Supply file))

"supplier"   Noun (attribute in Supply file)

(a)

Initial query	:	Which suppliers are located in Paris
Interpreted queries	:	a. for every x_1, where x_1 is supplier and supply location is Paris
		b. for every x_2, where x_2 is supplier and parts location is Paris

(b)

It was seen earlier that a useful query-translation system tailors the query vocabulary to the terminology used in a file environment. This "customization" might be streamlined by letting the user contribute to data acquisition. [67–69] For example, when a new term such as "earn" is introduced, the user could be asked to specify the syntactic category (verb), the third-person-singular present tense (earns), the past tense (earned), and so on. In addition, sample statements incorporating the new word could be supplied to characterize the word usages. In customizing databases through user inputs, the assumption is that the user knows the database terminology, but does not possess linguistic expertise.

The design of natural-language query-processing systems has greatly simplified access to databases and retrieval systems. What remains to be seen is whether the insights gained in this area can be used to simplify the problems of understanding language in unrestricted discourse environments.

References

1. R.C. Schank and R.P. Abelson, *Scripts, Plans, Goals, and Understanding*, Lawrence Erlbaum Associates, Hillsdale, NJ, 1977.

2. T.R. Addis, Machine Understanding of Natural Language, *International Journal of Man-Machine Studies*, 9:2, March 1977, 207–222.

3. K. Sparck Jones and M. Kay, Linguistics and Information Science: A Postscript, in *Natural Language and Information Science*, D.E. Walker, H. Karlgren, and M. Kay, editors, FID Publication 551, Skiptor, Stockholm, 1977, 183–192.

4. P.H. Mathews, *Morphology — An Introduction to the Theory of Word Structure*, Cambridge University Press, Cambridge, 1974.

5. N. Cercone, Morphological Analysis and Lexicon Design for Natural Language Processing, *Computers and the Humanities*, 11:4, July-August 1977, 235–258.

6. C.J. van Rijsbergen, *Information Retrieval*, Second Edition, Butterworths, London, 1979.

7. J.B. Lovins, Development of a Stemming Algorithm, *Mechanical Translation and Computational Linguistics*, 11:1–2, March and June 1968, 11–31.

8. D.E. Walker, Knowledge Resource Tools for Accessing Large Text Files, *Information in Data*, First Conference of the University of Waterloo Centre for the New Oxford English Dictionary, Waterloo, Canada, November 1985, 11–24.

9. H. Kucera, Uses of On-line Lexicons, *Information in Data*, First Conference of the University of Waterloo Centre for the New Oxford English Dictionary, Waterloo, Canada, November 1985, 7–10.

10. H. Alshawi, B. Boguraev, and T. Briscoe, Towards a Dictionary Support Environment for Real Time Parsing, *Proceedings of the Second Conference of the European Chapter of the ACL*, University of Geneva, Switzerland, March 1985, 27–29.

11. N. Sager and R. Grishman, The Restriction Language for Computer Grammars of Natural Language, *Communications of the ACM*, 18:7, July 1975, 390–400.

12. N. Sager, Sublanguage Grammars in Science Information Processing, *Journal of the ASIS*, 26:1, January-February 1975, 10–16.

13. R. Grishman, L. Hirschman and C. Friedman, Isolating Domain Dependencies, in *Natural Language Interfaces*, Conference on Applied Natural Language Analysis, Association for Computational Linguistics, Santa Monica, CA, 1983, 46–53.

14. D.M. Barton, Automated Concordances and Word Indexes: Machine Decisions and Editorial Revisions, *Computers and the Humanities*, 16:4, December 1982, 195–218.

15. A.B. Tucker, Jr., *Text Processing: Algorithms, Languages and Applications*, Academic Press, New York, 1979.

16. H.P. Luhn, Keyword-in-Context for Technical Literature (KWIC Index), ASDD Report No. RC-127, IBM Corporation, Yorktown Heights, NY, August 1959.

17. N. Sager, Perspective Paper: Computational Linguistics, in *Natural Language in Information Science*, D.E. Walker, H. Karlgren, and M. Kay, editors, FID Publication 551, Skiptor AB, Stockholm, Sweden, 1977, 75–100.

18. R.W. Blanning, Conversing with Management Information Systems in Natural Language, *Communications of the ACM*, 27:3, March 1984, 201–207.

19. M.P. Marcus, *A Theory of Syntactic Recognition for Natural Language*, MIT Press, Cambridge, MA, 1980.

20. E.J. Briscoe, Determinism and Its Implementation in PARSIFAL, in *Automatic Language Parsing*, K. Sparck Jones and Y. Wilks, editors, Ellis Horwood Ltd., Chichester, England, 1983.

21. P.J. Hayes and J.G. Carbonell, A Tutorial on Techniques and Applications for Natural Language Processing, Technical Report CMU-CS-83-158, Carnegie-Mellon University, Pittsburgh, PA, October 1983.

22. J. Weizenbaum, ELIZA — A Computer Program for the Study of Natural Language Communication between Man and Machine, *Communications of the ACM*, 9:1, January 1966, 36–45.

23. P.H. Klingbiel, Machine-Aided Indexing of Technical Literature, *Information Storage and Retrieval*, 9:2, February 1973, 79–84, and 9:9, September 1973, 477–494.

24. G. Salton, Automatic Phrase Matching, in *Readings in Computational Linguistics*, D.G. Hays, editor, American Elsevier Publishing Co., New York, 1966, 169–188.

25. M.Dillon and A.S. Gray, "FASIT: A Fully Automatic Syntactically Based Indexing System", *Journal of the ASIS*, 34:2, 1983, 99–108.

26. N. Chomsky, *Aspects of the Theory of Syntax*, MIT Press, Cambridge, MA, 1965.

27. W.A. Woods, Transition Network Grammars for Natural Language Analysis, *Communications of the ACM*, 13:10, October 1970, 591–606.

28. M. Bates, The Theory and Practice of Augmented Transition Network Grammars, in *Natural Language Communication via Computer*, L. Bolc, editor, Lecture Notes in Computer Science, Springer-Verlag, Berlin, 1978, 191–260.

29. R. Grishman, A Survey of Syntactic Analysis Procedures for Natural Language, *American Journal of Computational Linguistics*, 13:5, 1976 (Microfiche 47).

30. G. Gazdar, Natural Languages, Context-Free Languages and Context-Free Phrase Structure Languages, in *Automatic Natural Language Parsing*, K. Sparck Jones and Y. Wilks, editors, Ellis Horwood Ltd., Chichester, England, 1983.

31. G. Gazdar, Unbounded Dependencies, *Linguistic Inquiry*, 12:2, 1981, 155–184.

32. R.M. Kaplan and J. Bresnan, Lexical-Functional Grammar: A Formal System for Grammatical Representation, in *The Mental Representation of Grammatical Relations*, J. Bresnan, editor, MIT Press, Cambridge, MA, 1982, 173–281.

33. G.E. Heidorn, K. Jensen, L.A. Miller, R.J. Byrd, and M.S. Chodorow, The EPISTLE Text Critiquing System, *IBM Systems Journal*, 21:3, 1982, 305–326.

34. J. Fagan, Notes on Augmented Phrase Structure Grammars, Department of Computer Science, Cornell University, Ithaca, NY, 1986.

35. C.J. Fillmore, The Case for Case, in *Universals in Linguistic Theory*, E. Bach and R.T. Harris, editors, Holt, Rinehart and Winston, New York, 1968, 1–88.

36. S. Starosta, Case Relations, Perspective and Patient Centrality, Working Papers in Linguistics, 14:1, University of Hawaii at Manoa, January-April 1982.

37. E. Charniak and Y. Wilks, *Computational Semantics*, North Holland Publishing Co., Amsterdam, 1976.

38. Y. Wilks, An Intelligent Analyzer and Understander of English, *Communications of the ACM*, 18:5, May 1975, 264–275.

39. B.K. Boguraev and K. Sparck Jones, A Natural Language Analyzer for Database Access, *Information Technology: Research and Development*, 1:1, January 1982, 23–39.

40. J.I. Tait and K. Sparck Jones, Automatic Search Term Variant Generation for Document Retrieval, British Library R and D Report 5793, Computer Laboratory, University of Cambridge, Cambridge, 1983.

41. G.G. Hendrix, E.D. Sacerdoti, D. Sagalowicz, and J. Slocum, Developing a Natural Language Interface to Complex Data, *ACM Transactions on Database Systems*, 3:2, June 1978, 105–147.

42. G.G. Hendrix, Human Engineering for Applied Natural Language Processing, *Proceedings of the Fifth International Joint Conference on Artificial Intelligence*, Massachusetts Institute of Technology, Cambridge, MA, 1977, 183–191.

43. D.E. Walker, The Organization and Use of Information — Computational Linguistics and Artificial Intelligence, *Journal of the ASIS*, 32:5, September 1981, 347–363.

44. G. Silva and C.A. Montgomery, Knowledge Representation for Automatic Understanding of Natural Language Discourse, *Computers and the Humanities*, 11:4, July-August 1977, 223–234.

45. W.A. Woods, What's Important about Knowledge Representation, *Computer*, 16:10, October 1983, 22–29.

46. R.J. Brachman, *On the Epistemological Status of Semantic Networks*, Academic Press, New York, 1979.

47. G.D. Ritchie and F.K. Hanna, Semantic Networks — A General Definition and Survey, *Information Technology: Research and Development*, 2:4, October 1983, 187–231.

48. R.J. Brachman, What IS-A Is and Isn't: An Analysis of Taxonomic Links in Semantic Networks, *Computer*, 16:10, October 1983, 30–36.

49. M. Minsky, A Framework for Representing Knowledge, in *The Psychology of Computer Vision*, P. Winston, editor, McGraw-Hill Book Co., New York, 1975.

50. R.J. Brachman, R.E. Fikes, and H.J. Levesque, Krypton: A Functional Approach to Knowledge Representation, *Computer*, 16:10, October 1983, 67–73.

51. D. Lenat, M. Prakash, and M. Shepherd, CYC: Using Common Sense Knowledge to Overcome Brittleness and Knowledge Acquisition Bottlenecks, *The AI Magazine*, Winter 1986, 65–84.

52. J. Weizenbaum, *Computer Power and Human Reason*, W.H. Freeman and Co., San Francisco, 1976.

53. T. Winograd and F. Flores, *Understanding Computers and Cognition*, Ablex Publishing Corporation, Norwood, NJ, 1986.

54. H.L. Dreyfus and S.E. Dreyfus, *Mind over Machine*, The Free Press, New York, 1986.

55. W.B. Croft, User Specified Domain Knowledge for Document Retrieval, *Proceedings of the ACM Conference on Research and Development in Information Retrieval*, F. Rabitti, editor, Pisa, Italy, September 1986, 201–206.

56. G. Guida and C. Tasso, IR-NLI: An Expert Natural Language Interface to Online Data Bases, *Conference on Applied Natural Language Processing*, Association for Computational Linguistics, Santa Monica, CA, 1983, 31–38.

57. J.G. Carbonell and P.J. Hayes, Recovery Strategies for Parsing Extragrammatical Language, *American Journal of Computational Linguistics*, 9:3–4, July-December, 1983, 123–146.

58. R.M. Weischedel and N.K. Sondheimer, Meta-rules as a Basis for Processing Ill-formed Input, *American Journal of Computational Linguistics*, 9:3–4, July-December 1983, 161–177.

59. S.C. Kwasny and N.K. Sondheimer, Relaxation Techniques for Parsing Ill-formed Input, *American Journal of Computational Linguistics*, 4:2, 1981, 99–108.

60. K. Jensen, G.E. Heidorn, L.A. Miller, and Y. Ravin, Parse Fitting and Prose Fitting: Getting a Hold of Ill-formedness, *American Journal of Computational Linguistics*, 9:3–4, July-December 1983, 147–160.

61. G.E. Heidorn, Experience with an Easily Computed Metric for Ranking Alternative Parses, *Proceedings of the 20th Annual ACL Meeting*, Association for Computational Linguistics, Toronto, Canada, 1982, 82–84.

62. R. Grishman and L. Hirschman, Question Answering from Natural Language Medical Data Bases, *Artificial Intelligence*, 11:1,2, August 1978, 25–43.

63. J.R. Cowie, Automatic Analysis of Descriptive Texts, *Proceedings of Conference on Applied Natural Language Processing*, Association for Computational Linguistics, Santa Monica, CA, 1983, 117–123.

64. M. Templeton and J. Burger, Problems in Natural Language Interface to Data Base Management Systems with Examples from Eufid, *Proceedings of Conference on Applied Natural Language Processing*, Association for Computational Linguistics, Santa Monica, CA, 1983, 3–16.

65. B.W. Ballard, J.C. Lusth, and N.L. Tinkham, LDC-1: A Transportable, Knowledge-based Natural Language Processor for Office Environments, *ACM Transactions on Office Information Systems*, 2:1, January 1984, 1–25.

66. M. Bates and R. Bobrow, A Transportable Natural Language Interface for Information Retrieval, *ACM SIGIR Forum*, 17:1, 1983, 81–86.

67. B. Grosz, TEAM: A Transportable Natural Language Interface System, *Proceedings of Conference on Applied Natural Language Processing*, Association for Computational Linguistics, Santa Monica, CA, 1983, 39–45.

68. B. Thompson and F. Thompson, Introducing ASK — A Simple Knowledgeable System, *Proceedings of Conference on Applied Natural Language Processing*, Association for Computational Linguistics, Santa Monica, CA, 1983, 17–24.

69. L. Harris, User-oriented Database Query with the ROBOT Natural Language System, *International Journal of Man-Machine Studies*, 9, 1977, 697–713.

70. W.A. Martin, Some Comments on EQS, A Near Term Natural Language Data Base Query System, *Proceedings of the ACM 1978 Annual Conference*, December 1978, 156–164.

71. D.L. Waltz, An English Language Question Answering System for a Large Relational Data Base, *Communications of the ACM*, 21:7, July 1978, 526–539.

72. J. Mylopoulos, A. Borgida, P. Cohen, N. Roussopoulos, J. Tsotsos, and H.K.T. Wong, TORUS: A Step toward Bridging the Gap between Databases and the Casual User, *Information Systems*, 2:1, 1976, 49–64.

73. D.E. Johnson, Design of a Robust, Portable Natural Language Interface Grammar, IBM Research Report No. RC 10867, IBM Corporation, Yorktown Heights, NY, December 1984.

Chapter 12

Automatic Text Transformations

12.1 Text Transformations

Many automatic text-processing systems take some form of text input and transform it into output of a different form. Texts can be edited and formatted in various ways; they can be shortened by constructing abstracts and summaries, and can be lengthened by supplying new information related to the original data. Texts can also be compressed, encrypted, and translated from one language to another.

Most text transformations must be based on a thorough comprehension of text content — certainly complex transformations such as abstracting or translation cannot be completed successfully without accurate, complete descriptions of content. In view of the difficulties inherent in text understanding, in an unrestricted processing environment it may be impossible to obtain entirely satisfactory text products. However, useful text products can be generated by limiting discourse areas and using simple, well-understood methodologies to replace missing language understanding. Thus instead of attempting to construct free-form abstracts more or less independently of the original text forms, reduced text versions might be produced by excerpting certain critical passages from the original full document texts. Analogously, translated text versions might be prepared that are flawed but nevertheless can be understood by speakers of the output languages.

12.2 Automatic Writing Aids

The production and transmission of machine-readable text has increased enormously in the last few years; text items such as messages and memorandums are often manipulated with word-processing and computer-network equipment. Because of the informal nature of many text-processing environments, the text items are often imperfect in orthography and style. This explains the popularity of systems that standardize the nature and form of text elements by eliminating spelling errors, and checking grammar and/or style.

Ten years ago, most systems for text normalization handled input from optical character readers and voice-recognition systems. Thus attention was paid chiefly to correction methods that would resolve character-substitution errors that gave incorrect output interpretations to particular input characters. Interest has now shifted to more general text-handling systems capable of processing unrestricted machine-readable text. This accounts for the development of sophisticated systems that furnish writers with a large variety of automatic aids, including the detection and correction of spelling errors and the verification of grammar and style. [1–3]

Most automatic systems for text verification and correction are based on stored dictionaries and tables containing the accepted forms of linguistic units such as word stems, word suffixes, and complete words and phrases. When spelling-correction dictionaries are used, the incoming texts are compared with the dictionary entries; matching word forms are accepted as correct. Thus a principal problem in handling text errors is designing and preparing dictionaries to detect and correct spelling errors. If the dictionary contains partial word entries, attention must also be paid to automatic text-reduction and text-encoding methods, such as the affix-removal process described in Chapter 11. When complete matches cannot be obtained between dictionary entries and incoming word forms, approximate string-matching systems must be used to find closely matching dictionary entries.

12.2.1 Automatic Spelling Checkers

Many natural languages are characterized by notoriously complex spelling conventions. This is especially true of nonphonetic languages, such as English, which have little connection between spelling and sound, and of languages with many borrowed foreign words that cannot be accommodated by normal spelling conventions. In English, the following morphological problems make spelling troublesome: [4]

- Words with quite different phonetic characteristics may exhibit the same spelling ("bough," "enough").

- Different word fragments may serve the same purpose and may be pronounced similarly, but may nevertheless exhibit distinct spellings (the suffixes "ible" and "able," and the prefixes "en" and "in").

- Several different spellings may be acceptable for the same word ("neighbor" and "neighbour").

- Many different spelling conventions may be equally acceptable for multiword groups ("online," "on-line," "on line").

- Foreign words may pose special transliteration problems ("Tchebycheff," "Chebysheff," "Chebycheff").

- Morphological word transformation rules complicate the spelling problems ("absorb" and "absorption," "hop" and "hopping," "easy" and "easier").

- Different conventions may be used to formulate abbreviations of the same word ("v." and "vs."; "approx." and "approxn.").

In principle, orthography-resolution programs can be based on complete language-analysis systems that take into account the syntactic and semantic requirements characterizing a particular language. In practice, simpler methods are usually used to detect spelling errors, especially statistical analysis of word occurrences that reject word forms that are statistically improbable. In addition, stored dictionaries containing either full words or word fragments may be used to verify spelling.

The statistical-analysis method generally consists of performing a frequency analysis of the texts under consideration, and then applying threshold frequencies that lead to the acceptance of word forms with appropriate occurrence frequencies. Small, preconstructed dictionaries of high-frequency words can be used instead of threshold frequencies, and text words that match a dictionary entry can once again be accepted as correct.

A word-frequency analysis cannot be performed for the large number of low-frequency words included in normal texts because these words do not occur often enough to make it possible to distinguish correct and faulty word forms. A statistical analysis of word *fragments*, however, can be used for both high-frequency and low-frequency words. In particular, if the words are represented by sets of adjacent character pairs (digrams) or character triples (trigrams), the frequency spectrum of such character combinations may provide information about words with unusual character combinations.

A typical spelling-verification system based on a word-fragment analysis uses a preconstructed dictionary containing the expected occurrence frequencies of character pairs and character triples in ordinary running text. In principle, 676 different character pairs (26 · 26) exist for normal alphabetic character sequences and 17,576 character triples (26 · 26 · 26). In practice, frequency tables are much smaller because only about 500 different pairs and 5000 different triples are actually used in languages such as English. Given the expected frequency characterization of character pairs and triples, a composite frequency score can be computed for each incoming text word by using the corresponding dictionary frequencies for the included character sequences. Text words with unusual frequency spectra can then be rejected or brought to the user's attention for further processing. Thus, for the word "string" the frequency spectrum would consist of the dictionary frequencies of fragments ST, TR, RI, IN, NG, STR, TRI, RIN, and ING. If the sample word were misspelled (for example as SRTING), the infrequent character combinations SR and SRT could produce a low-frequency spectrum that leads to rejection of the corresponding word. [5]

In the TYPO program, which operates without preconstructed dictionaries, each word is first decomposed into character triples, and for each triple a *peculiarity index* is computed measuring the probability that the particular trigram was computed from the same source as the rest of the text. A combined word-peculiarity index is then computed as the root-mean-square of the indexes of the individual trigrams, and words with unusually high peculiarity indexes are rejected. [6,7] Specifically, each trigram XYZ occurring in a given text word is considered together with the corresponding digrams XY and YZ. Fragment frequencies $f(XYZ)$, $f(XY)$, and $f(YZ)$, representing the frequencies of occurrence of the corresponding character combinations in the texts under consideration, are then used to obtain a fragment peculiarity index PI:

$$PI(XYZ) = \frac{[\log(f(XY)-1) + \log(f(YZ)-1)]}{2} - \log(f(XYZ)-1). \quad (12.1)$$

A logarithm of 0 is interpreted as -10 in expression (12.1).

A misspelled word is likely to have a high peculiarity index because acceptable character-pair frequencies will be combined with unusually low frequencies for the corresponding character triples. For example, if the triple ING is misspelled NGI, the pairwise frequencies $f(NG)$ and $f(GI)$ may be high in the text under consideration, but the frequency of NGI is likely to be very low. This leads to a high value of

PI(*NGI*), and hence to a high value of the index for words containing unusual character combinations such as *NGI*. TYPO program produces a list of words sorted in decreasing order of their peculiarity indexes, making it easy to spot questionable word forms, which appear near the top of the list.

Most other spelling checkers use some form of dictionary containing correct, or acceptable, word entries. Dictionaries of full words tend to be large, and expensive to process and to store; a compromise solution consists of using *word-stem* dictionaries in which the entries appear in truncated form. The following kind of dictionary-consulting strategy can be used:

1. Identify individual word forms in the texts under consideration.

2. Sort the word forms and eliminate duplicate word occurrences.

3. Use a special dictionary to detect exceptional or high-frequency word forms and accept as correct all words that match entries in the special dictionary.

4. Remove suffixes and prefixes from the remaining words and accept the remaining word stems if they appear in a previously constructed word-stem dictionary.

5. Print out the remaining words that are not found in the special exceptions dictionary or the word-stem dictionary.

Obviously, a dictionary-based spelling detection system cannot detect correctly spelled words that are misused in their environments, such as "accept" instead of "except," or "affect" instead of "effect." Neither can a dictionary system recognize erroneous word repetitions such as "had had". The use of word-stem dictionaries instead of full-word dictionaries leads to special errors when apparently correct word fragments are combined into erroneous full words. The examples of Table 12.1 illustrate this point. Such errors can be avoided by using dictionaries of complete instead of truncated word forms. Alternatively, the stem dictionaries can be improved by including unusual root forms such as "bookkeep" that can generate acceptable full words such as "bookkeeper" and "bookkeeping." Specialized dictionaries may be used in addition to word-stem dictionaries to process irregular words and exceptional cases that cannot be handled by normal stem-suffix juxtaposition rules. [8]

Full-word dictionaries involve tradeoffs between size and usefulness. Large, reasonably complete dictionaries will miss few text words, but are expensive to build and to process; smaller dictionaries are much less costly to handle, but necessarily lead to some undetected text errors because of missing entries. Dictionaries that detect

Table 12.1 Incorrect words produced by correct stem-suffix rules.

Affix		Stem	Incorrect Combination	Correct Form
dis	+	spell	disspell	dispell
ance	+	occur	occurrance	occurrence
in	+	mature	inmature	immature
er	+	begin	beginer	beginner
ly	+	bar	barly	barely
ity	+	special	speciality	specialty
s	+	stress	stresss	stress

spelling errors must also include special-purpose terminology such as proper nouns of interest in the given discourse area, abbreviations, and novel technical terms. [8] With a well-designed dictionary, the vast majority of the most common spelling errors can be detected and brought to the user's attention.

12.2.2 Automatic Spelling Correction

The methods just described only detect potential misspellings, leaving the actual substitution of correct entries to the user. Procedures have also been developed that will both correct and detect misspelled text words. Two main approaches must be distinguished. The *absolute* error-correction approach consists of using a dictionary of commonly misspelled words, and replacing any misspelling detected in a text by the corrected version listed in the dictionary. The alternative *relative* error-correction method consists of using a conventional dictionary with correctly spelled word entries, and assuming that the "closest" dictionary entry provides the correct form for any word that does not completely match a dictionary entry. Thus the absolute-correction methods make exact comparisons between text words and dictionary entries, while the relative-correction methods perform partial, or approximate, matches.

When the origin of the incoming text is known, the error-correction problem may be much simplified because some errors will be much more common than others. For example, in typewritten texts the most common problems are single-character substitution errors — one character is erroneously replaced by another character located in the same general vicinity of the keyboard. Other common types of errors are phonetic substitutions such as "f" instead of "ph," or "k" instead of "qu." Finally, special dictionaries can include many commonly misspelled words, such as "greatful" instead of "grateful," "prehaps" instead of "perhaps," and "hte" instead of "the."

Special-purpose procedures can be used even without specific information about the nature of the texts under consideration. Evidence indicates that a very large proportion of the misspelled words in ordinary texts — more than 80 percent — are single-character errors. This includes words with a missing character, an extra character, a wrong character, or a transposition of two adjacent characters. [9,10] Thus, several well known error-correcting methods are confined to detecting and subsequently correcting such single-character errors.

All error-correcting systems operate in two main steps:

1. A comparison of either the original text, or some transformed version of the text, with prestored word forms listed in a dictionary.

2. An approximate matching process to find the "closest" possible dictionary entry for words without an exact correspondent in the dictionary.

In any system to correct spelling errors, the most crucial part is the automatic matching procedures between text words and stored dictionary entries. [6] One possibility consists of using an encoding process to reduce similar text words to a common form that is checked against an encoded dictionary. The phonetic "Soundex" system is a coding system sometimes used to correct spelling errors. In this system, phonetically similar words (such as "Dickson," "Dixon," and "Diksen") receive the same encoded form. The first consonant of a word is used, followed by a numeric code that represents the consonants in the remainder of the word. This picks up many common spelling errors because the variant forms are all replaced by a common encoded form. However, other misspellings are not detectable by the Soundex code — for example, "Rogers" is encoded as R262, whereas the very similar "Rodgers" is transformed into R326. Various alternative word-coding systems have been used with some success for specialized texts. In a proposed scheme for chemical compounds, the first character of the word is used, followed by the unique consonants in their order of occurrence, followed by the unique vowels in their order of occurrence. Consecutive occurrences of the same character are reduced to a single character. Thus the following sample entries for the term "chemical" appear: CHEMICAL is encoded as CHMLEIA; CHEMCIAL, as CHMLEIA; CHEMCAL, as CHMLEA; and CHIMICAL, as CHMLIA. [11,12]

After constructing the similarity code of a text word, it suffices to find a dictionary entry whose similarity code is close to the coded form of the text word. Such a system works well for vowel errors and for certain transpositions, but fails when erroneous consonants are used early in a word. Suggestions have been made to improve the code by making special provisions for consonants (such as R and S) that are often missing in ordinary text. Early consonants cannot be disregarded, however, since they often characterize distinct words such as "run," "sun," "bun," and "pun."

An alternative approximate matching system uses a similarity measure based on the number of common n-grams (that is, runs of n characters) in the words. The use of single characters (one-grams) would obviously produce too many matches between distinct words, such as "bun" and "nub," while long character strings (four-grams or longer runs) would not detect the common roots of many short words. For this reason, matching character pairs and triples usually serve to compute similarities between text words and dictionary entries. [13,14] A typical matching process of this type uses three main steps:

1. The number of matching two-grams and three-grams is computed between a text word and a dictionary entry.

2. A similarity coefficient is obtained based on the number of matching n-grams compared with the total number of distinct n-grams.

3. If the matching coefficient exceeds a predetermined threshold, the dictionary entry is assumed to represent the correct form of the text word.

A number of obvious refinements suggest themselves to limit the amount of work and to improve the discriminatory power of the method:

4. A stop-word list of common words can be used to eliminate the common words, thereby limiting the comparison procedure to content words.

5. Very high-frequency n-grams that occur in many different words (for example, AN, AD, TH, and HE) can be eliminated before computing the similarity coefficients.

6. The remaining n-grams can be weighted using an inverse-frequency coefficient that assigns the highest values to the least frequent n-grams; this ensures that matches between less frequent n-grams will contribute more to word similarity than matches between frequent n-grams.

7. Common suffixes can be deleted before the comparison operations, because suffixes such as ING and NESS occur in many quite distinct words that should not be confused with each other.

Table 12.2 shows a matching operation for overlapping character triples included in the input word RECEIEVE and the dictionary entries REACTIVE, RECEIVE, RECEIVER, REPRIEVE, and RETRIEVE. As shown, when similarity coefficients are computed as the number of common triples divided by the number of distinct triples, the highest values are obtained for dictionary entries RECEIVE (3/8) and RECEIVER (3/9). If a grammatical-analysis system were incorporated in the spelling correction program, a choice could be made between RECEIVE and RECEIVER to replace RECEIEVE, based on the available syntactic specification. If a noun were specified in the text, RECEIVER would be used as a replacement for RECEIEVE; if not, RECEIVE would be chosen. The latter entry would also be used in a system without syntax, under the assumption that the computed similarity of 3/8 between RECEIEVE and RECEIVE exceeds the predetermined similarity value.

Experimental data indicate that up to 70 percent of common orthographic mistakes can be corrected by n-gram encoding methods; while about 20 to 30 percent of the errors remain uncorrected, and about 10

Table 12.2 Word comparison based on overlapping character triples.

Trigrams	Input	Dictionary Entries				
	RECEIEVE	*RECEIVE*	*RECEIVER*	*REPRIEVE*	*RETRIEVE*	*REACTIVE*
REC	1	1	1			
ECE	1	1	1			
CEI	1	1	1			
EIE	1					
IEV	1			1	1	
EVE	1			1	1	
EIV		1	1			1
IVE		1	1			
VER			1			
REP				1		
EPR				1		
PRI				1		
RIE				1	1	
RET					1	
ETR					1	
TRI					1	
REA						1
EAC						1
ACT						1
TIV						1
Similarity coefficient		3/8	3/9	2/10	2/10	0/11

percent are miscorrected because the wrong dictionary correspondent is chosen. [11–14]

If mistakes are assumed to be single-character errors consisting of insertions, deletions, or substitutions of single characters, or of transpositions of two adjacent characters, it is in principle possible to obtain a list of all *variants* of a word not found in the dictionary, and to compare these variants with the dictionary entries. [9] For a word of n characters and an alphabet of k characters, there are $(n+1)k$ possible single-character insertions, n single-character deletions, $n(k-1)$ single-character substitutions and $(n-1)$ transpositions of adjacent characters. The total number of variants due to single-character errors, then, can be as large as $k(2n+1)+n-1$. In practice, many variants can be discarded because the corresponding character sequences do not occur in the language. The number of possible variants may still be very large, however, and the corresponding dictionary comparisons will be onerous.

Instead of generating all variants of a text word before consulting the dictionary, a nonmatching text item can be compared with a dictionary directly, using an iterative character-by-character matching scheme that determines the smallest number of single-character operations (insertions, deletions, substitutions, and transpositions) required to transform one of the words into the other. Using the so-called *Damerau-Levenshtein* (DL) metric, such a similarity coefficient between words can be obtained. When DL coefficients are available for a given nonmatching text word and the related dictionary entries, the closest dictionary entry can be chosen to replace the erroneous word. [9,15]

The DL coefficient between two character strings S and T is computed recursively by scanning inputs S and T from left to right, one character at a time, and using one of the four possible single-character operations when a mismatch exists between two particular characters. Let $f(i,j)$ represent the computed string difference between a substring of length i in S and a substring of length j in T. A minimum cost function is then obtained as

$$f(0,0) = 0 \tag{12.2}$$
$$f(i,j) = \min \{f(i-1,j)+1, f(i,j-1)+1, f(i-1,j-1)+d(s_i,t_j),$$
$$f(i-2, j-2)+d(s_{i-1},t_j)+d(s_i,t_{j-1})+1\},$$

where $d(s_i,t_j) = 0$ if the ith character in S is equal to the jth character in T — that is, if $s_i = t_j$, and is equal to 1 otherwise. The assumption in formula (12.2) is that each single-character operation for nonmatching characters can be performed at a cost of 1, and that for string S of length p and string T of length q, the final DL cost is given by $f(p,q)$.

The first term in computing f(i,j) accounts for the insertion of an extra letter in string T; the second is an insertion of one character in S. The third term, corresponding to the comparison of the ith character in S and the jth character in T, is performed at a cost of 0 when the characters match and a cost of 1 when a substitution is necessary. The last represents a transposition between characters $i-1$ and i of S and $j-1$ and j of T, the total cost once again being defined as 1.

Figure 12.1 shows a sample computation of the Damerau-Levenshtein formula for the strings MONSTER and CENTRE, respectively. The cost computation is represented by a path from the upper left corner to the lower right corner of the rectangle of Fig. 12.1(a). A

Figure 12.1 Character-string comparison using Damerau-Levenshtein metric (adapted from [9]). (a) Graphical example of minimum-cost character-string comparison. (b) Character operations for the example.

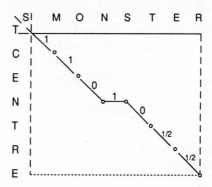

(a)

Character number		Operation	Cost
S	T		
M	C	substitution	1
O	E	substitution	1
N	N	match	0
S	—	insertion	1
T	T	match	0
E	R	half transposition	1/2
R	E	half transposition	1/2

(b)

horizontal move represents an insertion in string S; a vertical move, an insertion in T. Diagonal moves are character comparisons that cost nothing when the corresponding characters match, 0.5 for each half of a transposition, and 1 for a substitution. As the example shows, the total cost of bringing the two strings MONSTER and CENTRE in coincidence is equal to 4, consisting of two substitutions (characters M and C, and O and E, respectively), one character insertion (character S), and one transposition (ER and RE, respectively).

12.2.3 Syntax and Style Checking

Most syntax- and style-checking systems are based on an automatic analysis of the input texts, followed by the computation of measurements reflecting the differences between the given input texts and the linguistic patterns characterizing well-written text samples. Deviations from the norm are brought to the user's attention, and suggestions may be made to improve the presentation.

In one approach, complicated linguistic-analysis procedures are avoided in favor of a series of relatively inexpensive tools that can collectively detect a vast number of exceptional conditions. In the Writer's Workbench available under the UNIX operating system, the information is processed at various levels of detail: [16–19]

- Word-level processing that bring questionable words or poor word usage to the user's attention.

- Phrase-level processing relating to questionable or empty phrases ("accounted for by the fact that," "collect together"), noun phrases with too many modifiers ("disk pack holder mount support"), too many adverbial or adjectival modifiers, split infinitives, and so on.

- Sentence-level critiques that flag sentences considered to be too long or too short, and those with too many verbs or too many negatives. Sentences with an excessive distance between subject and verb may also be noted, as well as those with several dependent clauses.

- Paragraph-level comments that list paragraphs with too many passive sentences, passages with many compound or complex sentences, and paragraphs with a low readability score.

A list of sample word- and phrase-level programs used with the Writer's Workbench appears in Table 12.3. These programs use small dictionaries of acronyms, trademarks, negative words, function words, and so on that are inexpensive to store and process. Like the other higher-level programs, the Parts program that assigns parts of speech to text words, is similarly designed to operate rapidly and inexpensively: Only a small dictionary of function words is needed, and words

---

Table 12.3 Word- and phrase-level style-checking programs incorporated into the Writer's Workbench.

1. Printout of special condition not using dictionary information

CAPITALIZATION	capitalized words that also appear in lowercase or with initial capitals only
DOUBLE	consecutive occurrences of the same word
PUNCTUATION	inconsistencies in punctuation such as space use and unbalanced quotes

2. Printout of entries found in special dictionaries

ABSTRACTNESS	abstract words
ACRONYMS	acronyms
CONSISTENCY	various inconsistencies such as differences between British and American spelling
DICTION	awkward phrases ("as to," "as to whether," "join together," etc.)
FIND BE	occurrences of "to be" indicating passive tense, nominalizations, etc.
GRAM	misused articles
NEG	negative words
SEXIST	sexist terms ("girl," "businessman," etc.)
WORD USE	commonly confused or misused words and phrases

3. Printout of error conditions based on special text analysis

CONTINGENCY	analysis of contingency words such as "if," "when," "except," "unless," etc. to determine proper grammatical use
DIVERSITY	type-token ratio of words in text to determine diversity of vocabulary
SPELL	words not found in a dictionary and not derivable by simple rules based on word-suffix analysis
SPLIT	detects split infinitives based on Parts program
SWITCH	finds words used as both nouns and verbs based on results of Parts program
TMARK	determines proper use of trademarks and service marks
TOPIC	determines document topic by printing the 20-most-frequent nouns and adjective-noun pairs

are assigned to syntactic classes based on the recognition of special word forms and word endings. Although each component of the Writer's Workbench is conceptually simple, the complete collection of programs constitutes a powerful system that may be more useful, and certainly more cost effective, than alternative approaches based on more sophisticated syntactic- and semantic-analysis methods.

The EPISTLE system has similar aims as the Writer's Workbench. However, EPISTLE uses a complete syntactic analysis based on augmented phrase-structure grammars to determine text structure before the analysis. [20] The applicability of the grammatical rules is based in part on the syntactic functions of the words and in part on semantic features, such as indications of time, place, and measurement. When acceptable syntactic interpretations cannot be obtained for a particular text sentence, the restrictions imposed on grammatical rules are relaxed until a successful interpretation is produced for that sentence. This relaxation of conditions is used later to generate comments about the structure of the texts under consideration.

The following *syntactic* error conditions may be brought to the user's attention as a result of the input analysis in the EPISTLE system:

- Subject-verb disagreement ("your statement of deficiencies *have* not been completed").

- Erroneous pronoun cases ("the company will sell the product to *whomever* asks for it").

- Noun-modifier disagreement ("these *report* must be checked").

- Nonstandard verb forms ("the complete manuscript was *wrote* by Tom").

- Nonparallel structures ("we will accept the funds and *crediting* their account").

Grammatical-analysis methods may also be used in *style* checking: Simple sentences with a single verb and no dependent structures are distinguished from compound sentences that include several verbs, and from complex sentences that also use subordinate clauses. Style-checking systems usually perform objective measurements relating to sentence and word length that are later transformed into sentence "readability grades." The idea is to reject long sentences containing long words that are more difficult to understand than shorter, crisper versions. Attempts are also often made to compute the distribution of word types and the number of passive constructions, and to note other interesting stylistic features.

If a syntax- and style-checking system is implemented interactively using an advanced console display, errors and imperfections in the text can be highlighted, and special colors can signal the gravity of the error. [20,21] For example, a green display could be used for faultless passages; questionable sentence components for which an adjustment is not compulsory might be shown in yellow; and faulty text that must be corrected, in red. When the system suggests stylistic improvement, the user could be asked to accept the system's determination by selecting one of the displayed menu alternatives to correct the text. Alternatively, the user might request additional information about the error by pointing to a "help" window, or could override the system's suggestions by entering appropriate corrections in place of the highlighted text or by selecting the highlighted text a second time.

The available systems for correcting spelling errors are widely used. Automatic methods for grammar and style checking, which are more complex and more expensive to implement, are not yet widely used.

12.3 Automatic Abstracting Systems

12.3.1 Automatic Extracting

Generating text summaries and abstracts is an important theoretical and practical problem. Text abstracts, serving as surrogates for the complete, unabridged version of a document, are needed for many purposes. Some abstracts actually inform the reader of the main contents of the document; others may simply indicate whether the complete text version should be of interest without explaining the text in detail. Abstracts are also used as text surrogates in abstracting publications, and replace full texts in some automatic text-search systems.

Since an abstract must reflect the contents of the original, a reasonably complete specification of document content is required. When such a specification is not available, short-cut abstracting methods must be used. The most widely used simplified abstracting method consists of computing a value, or weight, for each sentence of an original document, based on the types of words and phrases included in the sentences, and then using the most highly weighted sentences to generate an abstract. [22–24]

Figure 12.2 outlines a typical *automatic extracting* system that distinguishes between words occurring in the text body, and words occurring in titles, captions, and section headings. The former may be subjected to a standard term-weighting process, whereas the latter may receive special treatment based in part on the location of the terms in the specific document. Special provisions may also be made for high-frequency function words occurring in the texts, as well as for very rare words that occur only once in a collection of documents.

After individual text words are identified, a term-weighting system similar to that described for automatic indexing can assign term weights as a function of the frequency of occurrence of the words in the texts and the number of documents in a collection to which the terms are assigned. As mentioned in Chapter 9, a high order of indexing performance is obtained by using a term weight that varies directly with the frequency of occurrence of the terms in individual documents and inversely with the number of documents in which the terms occur (*tf* · *idf* weight). Term *phrases* may also be generated consisting of groups of words that cooccur in the sentences of the texts,

Figure 12.2 Typical sentence-extracting system (adapted from [23]).

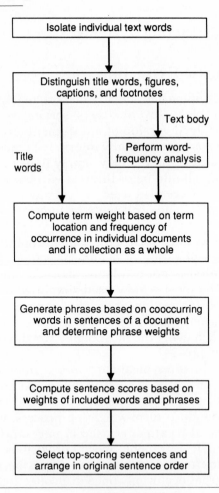

and phrase weights can be assigned, for example, as the average weights of the component terms.

Once the term and phrase weights have been computed, a composite *sentence score* can be generated based on these weights. Such a sentence score could be computed as the average weight of the included single words and phrases; alternatively, the term phrases may receive extra weight, or extra importance may be assigned to sentences in which many highly weighted terms and phrases are close together. The last step of sentence extracting consists of choosing for inclusion in the text abstract a certain number of highly scoring sentences, or a certain proportion of the text sentences exhibiting the highest sentence scores. A typical automatically constructed sentence extract follows: [22]

Document Citation

A.S. Marrazzi, Messenger of the Nervous System, *Scientific American*, 196:2, February 1957, 86–94.

Automatic Sentence Extract (sentence significance scores in parentheses)

It seems reasonable to credit the single-celled organisms also with a system of chemical communication by diffusion of stimulating substances through the cell, and these correspond to the chemical messengers (e.g., hormones) that carry stimuli from cell to cell in the more complex organisms. (7.0)

Finally, in the vertebrate animals there are special glands (e.g., the adrenals) for producing chemical messengers, and the nervous and chemical communication systems are intertwined: for instance, release of adrenalin by the adrenal gland is subject to control both by nerve impulses and by chemicals brought to the gland by the blood. (6.4)

The experiments clearly demonstrated that acetylcholine (and related substances) and adrenalin (and its relatives) exert opposing actions which maintain a balanced regulation of the transmission of nerve impulses. (6.3)

It is reasonable to suppose that the tranquilizing drugs counteract the inhibitory effect of excessive adrenalin or serotonin or some related inhibitor in the human nervous system. (7.3)

A document extract constructed in accordance with the preceding specification is likely to contain a large number of sentences that indicate the document's content. On the other hand, as the example shows, it is highly unlikely that such an extract can compete in readability and coherence with a properly constructed text abstract. The extracted sentences will probably be disconnected from each other, and readability and ultimately comprehension may be impaired. For this reason, it may be wise to supplement the basic sentence-extracting system by using criteria not based on word-frequency computations alone. [25,26] Three kinds of considerations may be important in this connection:

1. Certain *cue words* or *cue phrases* in text sentences may indicate a sentence's importance regardless of the actual sentence or word scores. Sentences containing phrases such as "our work," "this paper," "the present research," and so on might be automatically used for abstracting purposes.

2. *Syntactic-coherence* considerations suggest that sentences referring to earlier passages already used in the abstract should also be included. For example, sentences containing passages such as "presented earlier," and "stated above" could be included in the abstract if the preceding text has already been chosen.

3. Finally, the *location* of a sentence in a text may be used to adjust the normal sentence score. For example, the first sentence of a paragraph may be chosen automatically regardless of the computed sentence score.

Elaborate rules have been devised to identify contextual clues of sentence importance, based in part on the identification of word (or word-stem) classes of the type illustrated in Fig. 12.3(a), and in part on sentence templates such as that illustrated in Fig. 12.3(b). [26] In the template illustration, permissible distances between sentence compounds are shown in square brackets, and incremental component weights are shown as superscripts. When a particular document sentence fits one of the prescribed sentence templates, a complete sentence score is computed by adding up the prescribed weights for sentence components that match the corresponding template specifications, as in the following examples (italicized portions match the template of Fig. 12.3b):

In this **first** *paper we* **will** *discuss* **a simple** *method* **for**....

$$+3 \qquad\qquad +2 \qquad\qquad\qquad\qquad (+7)$$

In this investigation **a new automatic process** *is* **briefly** *discussed*....

$$+3 \qquad\qquad\qquad\qquad +2 \qquad (+5)$$

After sentence scoring is completed, an extract of the prescribed length can be constructed by choosing high-scoring sentences from the original paper together with adjacent text sentences that are related to the chosen excerpts by appropriate exophoric references (that is, reference words or phrases that point to text portions outside the immediate context). In unrestricted linguistic contexts, identifying and disambiguating exophoric references is a largely unsolved process. However, a partial identification of exophora can be made based on the presence of particular reference patterns ("hence," "besides," "more to the point," and so on), and this in turn can augment the original text excerpts. [26]

Sentence-extraction methods such as those just outlined and those shown in Fig. 12.3 will identify many useful sentences for inclusion in the extract. However, a substantial lack of coherence may still be evident. It has been suggested therefore that a text abstract could be constructed by choosing one or more complete paragraphs from the texts of original documents. [27] In particular, an association measure $M(i,j)$

Figure 12.3 Typical sentence-scoring criteria for "discuss" sentences [26]. (a) Typical word-class entries. Hyphens denote variable length endings; numbers in parentheses are minor weight deviations. (b) Typical sentence template. Bracketed numbers are number of permissible intervening words; positive numbers denote partial weights; word followed by question mark is optional. (C.D. Paice, Automatic Generation of Literature Abstracts — An Approach based on the Identification of Self Indicating Phrases, in *Information Retrieval Research*, R.N. Oddy, S.E. Robertson, C.J. van Rijsbergen and P.W. Williams, editors, Butterworths, London, 1981. Reprinted with permission.)

Class	Class elements
"discuss" words	discuss-, introduce, present, develop, examine, describe, review, report, outline, consider, investigate, explore, assess-, analy-, synthesi-, stud-, survey, ask, simplif-, deal-, trace(-2), cover(-2)

(a)

(b)

can be computed between any two text paragraphs $P(i)$ and $P(j)$, based on the number of common words or word phrases contained in these paragraphs. Given all pairwise paragraph similarity measures, a global closeness measure $m(i)$ can then be generated for each paragraph $P(i)$ as the average closeness between that paragraph and all other paragraphs in a document of N paragraphs:

$$m(i) = \sum_{j=1}^{N} \frac{M(i,j)}{N} \qquad (12.3)$$

A document abstract can then be built by assuming that the most important paragraphs are those closest on average to all other paragraphs in the document. Typically a particular number of high-scoring paragraphs could be chosen whose total length equals a stated threshold length for the extract. Alternatively, the paragraphs could be clustered by grouping paragraphs with high $M(i,j)$ values, and a complete cluster of similar paragraphs could then be chosen for inclusion in the extract, or one important paragraph could be chosen from each paragraph cluster. [27]

The identification of interesting passages in particular documents can be used not only to abstract these documents, but also to retrieve them. In the so-called *passage-retrieval* systems, particular document extracts that appear similar to an available query statement are retrieved and submitted to the user in answer to the query. [28,29] A passage may be chosen for retrieval when it contains one or more sentences, titles, headings, or figure captions that collectively include a sufficient number of query terms. A passage-retrieval system is intermediate between a standard full-text document retrieval system, which retrieves complete documents (or document abstracts) in answer to incoming queries, and a question-answering system, which constructs a direct response to each incoming query.

One passage-retrieval system makes the following distinctions between relevant passage types: [28]

- A *connected* passage is a sequence of two or more sentences such that every sentence except the first contains a "connection" word ("however," "on the other hand," "these," and so on) to a sentence occurring earlier in the passage. Also, each sentence in the passage requires a minimal number of matches to the query statement.

- A *concentrated* passage is a sequence of several sentences exhibiting a concentration of query words so that collectively a match exists for each query word and the total number of query-passage term matches exceeds some given threshold.

- A *compound* passage is a combination of a figure caption, title, or section heading with an appropriate passage that collectively obey the restrictions for the concentrated passages.

A passage-retrieval system must compute the matching coefficients between the query statements and the connected, concentrated, and compound passages, and must then retrieve appropriate combinations of passages in answer to incoming queries. Available experience indicates that about 70 percent of the relevant sentences contained in document texts can be identified and retrieved using the criteria established for connected and concentrated passages (recall = 0.70); in addition, about 30 percent of the retrieved sentences are extraneous (precision = 0.70). The false retrievals are due largely to false coordination of query terms in the retrieved passages, and to query terms occurring in the texts with a different meaning from that intended in the queries. Instead of identifying the relevant passages by matching document texts and incoming query statements, a passage-retrieval system can also be based on a deep indexing approach that generates index terms for particular document sentences, rather than for complete documents. Such an indexing system can produce output reminiscent of conventional "back-of-the book" indexes, which identify document passages matching corresponding index entries.

12.3.2 Abstracting Based on Text Understanding

The text-extracting systems just described often produce useful text representations that are closely related to the corresponding document texts. On the other hand, when polished, comprehensive abstracts are needed, even a comparatively refined extracting method will not always perform satisfactorily. In that case, it is necessary to analyze the texts more thoroughly, reducing them to a canonical form representing the content as completely as possible. Such a canonical text representation can then be turned into a text abstract or summary by identifying certain essential passages that follow a preestablished theme pattern.

Since a deep text analysis cannot be undertaken in an unrestricted semantic environment, the approach must be to limit the area of discourse, representing some particular topic area to analyze the texts of incoming documents. Among the methods used to represent topics are logical propositions composed of predicates and entities [30], concept frames containing characterizations of entities and entity relationships, [31,32], and stored scripts describing sequences of events and inferences about additional events that may occur in the future. [33–35]

After the knowledge base is constructed — for example, in terms of concept triples — the texts of incoming documents must be related to the canonical form triples. This can be done in various ways: [30]

- A direct match may exist between a stored knowledge base triple and an incoming text excerpt.

- An incoming text excerpt can match a synonym of some canonical form predicate; synonymous predicates are identified by prestored relational expressions such as [relapse (x,y)] $<=>$ [reactivate (x,y)].

- Inferential techniques can produce a match between the incoming texts and the stored knowledge base; the needed inferences must be derived from stored inference rules such as [diagnose (x,y,p)] $=>$ [confirm $(x,p(y))$], indicating that "if x diagnoses y as p, then x confirms that p is true of y."

Once the relevant portions of the knowledge base have been identified for a given piece of text, a text summary can be generated using hierarchical navigation operations to extract appropriate concept triples from the knowledge base and assemble them into semantically significant concept chains. Thus for a given matching proposition, more general concepts can be obtained by moving upward in the hierarchy, and more specific ones by moving downward. The final text summary would consist of appropriately related excerpts extracted from the knowledge base.

It is plausible that for a well-circumscribed and controlled field, a useful knowledge base can in fact be constructed in advance. In general, the fuzzy, indirect matching system needed to relate arbitrary input texts to the preconstructed knowledge base will give uncertain results even when the semantic contexts can be properly circumscribed. Moreover, it is hard to imagine that such an approach can be extended to cover a substantial variety of texts in different subject areas.

A conceptually related approach to text condensation and summarization consists of using a *frame-relation* model to encode the knowledge base. The entities under consideration are described by complex representations that include equivalence relations as well as association pointers relating attributes to the entities they characterize, and joining entities to each other. Before the incoming texts are compared with the information stored in the knowledge base, the texts must be broken down into text constituents using a deep syntactic-semantic analysis that incorporates macrotextual *coherence* methods in addition to microtextual *cohesion* considerations. The coherence criteria account for theme progression and focus identification and supply the technical knowledge to understand the argument structures. The cohesion part includes the recognition of ellipses, the identification of pronoun referents, and the proper interpretation of coordination in the text. [31,32]

If a text analysis recognizes the dominant concepts of the incoming text structures, these in turn can activate the corresponding frames in the knowledge base, as well as the relationship between different sections of a single frame and between different frames. Assuming that frame identification and activation are correctly handled, various kinds of text products can be constructed automatically:

- The main themes of the text may be used to build indicative abstracts that provide information about the topic areas under discussion.

- Additional theme aspects may be included in an expanded summary providing more detailed information about text contents.

- Related facts not directly mentioned in the text can also be added to produce even more detailed text versions.

When the text contents are properly understood, output can be produced in various formats according to circumstances, including ordinary text, tabular forms where the information is used to fill preformatted spaces, and various types of graphics. In view of the difficulties relating to frame-based knowledge representation, as well as to analyzing unrestricted natural-language texts unambiguously, frame analysis is once again unlikely to provide useful solutions to the problem of abstracting texts.

A last approach to text summarization consists of using stored *scripts* of important facts characterizing particular situations. [33–35] Each script is a repository of a restricted set of events that may occur, or that are related to particular contexts. Thus an automobile-accident script may contain information about the type of vehicle involved, the objects involved in a collision with a vehicle, the location of the accident, the type of injuries sustained, the number of people involved, the fault determination, if any, and so on. Because each script is specific and circumscribed, the text analysis to relate text portions to particular scripts may be relatively shallow. In particular, dictionaries may specify context tests that must be satisfied by text elements if the dictionary entry is to be applied to particular text excerpts. After applicable scripts are identified, the script structures can be used to produce formalized paraphrases of the story. When available input matches script information closely enough — in the sense that a sufficient number of relevant words and phrases are found in the text — a correct choice of useful scripts may then lead to construction of reasonable text summaries. This solution is once again likely to produce questionable output for texts that straddle different scripts, or texts that lie somewhat outside available knowledge structures.

Until more progress is made in developing useful methods to represent knowledge and to analyze and understand language, it appears that the enhanced text-extracting methods discussed in the previous subsection will be more useful for constructing shortened text representations than the methods based on complete knowledge representations and content analyses.

12.4 ❖ Automatic Text Generation

❖ 12.4.1 Approaches to Text Generation

In many text-processing situations such as abstracting, output must be furnished as excerpts from a natural-language text. Users are more likely to accept a system if database or bibliographic queries are answered with natural-language responses instead of obscure formalized statements. Thus substantial efforts are devoted to producing natural-language text forms in many situations. Text-generation methods are also needed to generate automatic reports, and in automatic story-telling systems. [36–38]

All automatic text-generation systems must begin by extracting some relevant parts from a stored knowledge base. The criteria controlling the choice of information extracted differ according to the application. In constrained systems where a specific task must be performed, such as generating responses to information requests, relevant areas of the knowledge base may be easy to identify. In more general situations, the data needed to generate the output may not be easy to define. For example, in open-ended text-writing systems no specific goal or specific input text may be available a priori. Furthermore, certain knowledge bases cannot be used easily to generate sentences when the entities and descriptions in the knowledge base do not directly correspond to sentence-size pieces that can be transferred directly to the output.

One possibility consists of extracting a large number of small fragments from the knowledge base, each fragment representing some minimal information unit such as an entity-attribute pair, or an information triple consisting of two entities and a relationship indication between the two entities. [38] The text-generation system then assembles and composes knowledge-base fragments into usable text excerpts.

A text generation system is outlined in Fig. 12.4. After the knowledge-base fragments are identified, a *problem solving* module selects a particular outline and style for the text to be generated. The stylistic composition of the output depends on a set of goals that characterize the expected effect of the text excerpt on the reader. Given particular goals, such as presenting the salient facts of a story, rules must be available relating the goal satisfaction to the effects that can be derived from certain stylistic forms. The problem-solving module uses these rules to generate an ordered set of text prescriptions to be filled later by particular text sentences. The next module, a *discourse organizer*, relates the available information fragments to the chosen text prescription. This module uses aggregation rules and grammatical specifications to transform individual facts and sentence fragments into well-formed natural-language clauses. It also uses preference rules to determine a preferred sentence order depending on the presumed importance of the terms in the sentences. Finally, a *sentence generation* module constructs the final text in paragraph form. This module inserts punctuation, replaces nouns or noun phrases with pronoun referents, and selects specific syntactic forms and clause arrangements within paragraphs.

Figure 12.4 Typical text-generation system.

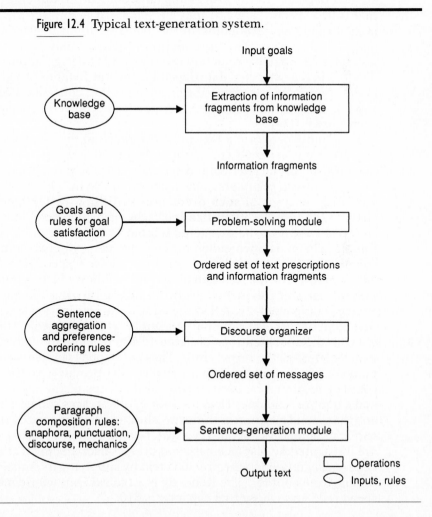

As Fig. 12.4 indicates, two kinds of knowledge are needed in the text-generation system: static knowledge that describes a particular discourse area, and a dynamic system of rules that uses the available knowledge to produce corresponding messages. The knowledge base may once again appear as a hierarchical arrangement of facts and entities, together with attribute specifications for the various entities, and links indicating various kinds of entity relationships. [37]

The dynamic rule system used to control text production must first make inferences to elicit new facts from data previously incorporated in the knowledge base. In addition, linguistic know-how is needed to select and order phrases, to select syntax, to specify anaphora and verb morphologies, to select punctuation, and to specify the general type of discourse. The choice of the relevant knowledge pool to generate text depends on the processing environment. In directed systems that fulfill specific aims, it may be sufficient to extract the specific facts directly corresponding to the available input queries or input texts. In more general text-production systems, it may be useful to extract all facts that are remotely relevant, and to assign importance indicators to the extracted data depending on the distance of a given fact in the knowledge base from the more important concepts. The importance indicators can filter the text portions required in a particular environment. [39]

To actually generate a text prescription from the available knowledge base, it is necessary to combine rhetorical techniques that satisfy the purposes of the particular discourse. One approach consists of defining *rhetorical predicates* such as those shown in Table 12.4 and constructing schemas of such predicates fulfilling the text-generation goals. [37] A typical "identification" schema, which describes a given entity, is shown in the example of Table 12.5(a). As can be seen, the sample schema is open ended in the sense that only two compulsory components are included: the identification itself, specifying the class and attributes, or the function of the entity, followed by an illustrative example or some evidence useful in characterizing the entity. The analogy component, as well as the terminal amplification and illustration components, are optional. A sample set of knowledge fragments obeying the specifications of Table 12.5(a) is shown in Table 12.5(b), which identifies the term "ship." These sentence fragments cannot be immediately assembled into a polished text product. Additional discourse rules must be used to control the focus of the discourse and make it more readable. Thus the first two sentences can be combined, and the second mention of the term "ship" can be replaced by the referent "its" as follows: "A ship is a water-going vehicle...; *its* capabilities are illustrated by displacement and draft." Also, the illustration must be properly related to the previous text by supplying its function — by saying, for example, "The Kennedy is a typical ship whose maximum speed is 25 and whose fuel capacity is 810...."

Table 12.4 Typical rhetorical predicates used for text generation (adapted from [37]). (K.R. McKeown, the Text System for Natural Language Generation — An Overview, *Proceedings of the 20th Annual ACM Conference*, Association for Computational Linguistics, Toronto, Canada, 1982. Used by permission of the Association for Computational Linguistics; copies of the publication from which this material is derived can be obtained from Dr. Donald E. Walker (ACL), Bell Communications Research, 445 South Street, MRE 2A379, Morristown, NJ, 07960, USA.)

Name	Function
Identification	Defines a particular entity or event
Attributive	Provides properties associated with an entity or event
Constituency	Describes subparts or subtypes of particular entities
Analogy	Compares a particular entity to some other familiar entity
Contrast	Provides differences between pairs of entities
Illustration	Provides a particular example — e.g., describes a particular object included in an object class

Rules to transform the text fragments corresponding to a particular discourse schema into polished text are necessarily complex. One text-generation system uses separate rules to combine clauses; modify the sequence of messages to conform to desired focus requirements; control the length of sentences and paragraphs; introduce hyponyms (weakened references to previously introduced concepts) and anaphoric references (pronouns); and supply other useful linguistic devices. [36] Reasonably polished text samples can be produced when the discourse area is well defined and the text function is properly understood.

❖ 12.4.2 Typical Text-generation Systems

Some early "novel-writing" systems used selected sequences of grammatical rules and tightly specified relationships between the grammatical rules and certain corresponding semantic structures from the stored database. Thus a particular syntactic rule sequence could be produced by one of a number of corresponding stored semantic patterns extracted from the knowledge base. [40] While such a procedure may generate readable text when well-structured knowledge bases are available, the resulting text-generation system does not demonstrate deep understanding of the content.

It is preferable to base the production of semantically interesting text that includes reasoned sequences of events on a problem-solving approach in which the chosen entities are expected to satisfy certain goals, and chosen events give rise to new events and hence to additional goals. A typical story-generating system based on problem-

Table 12.5 Sample schema construction using rhetorical predicates (adapted from [37]). (a) Sample schema for entity identification. (b) Sample text fragments for "ship" identification. (K.R. McKeown, the Text System for Natural Language Generation — An Overview, *Proceedings of the 20th Annual ACM Conference*, Association for Computional Linguistics, Toronto, Canada, 1982. Used by permission of the Association for Computational Linguistics; copies of the publication from which this material is derived can be obtained from Dr. Donald E. Walker (ACL), Bell Communications Research, 445 South Street, MRE 2A379, Morristown, NJ, 07960, USA.)

Schema Component	Remarks
[(class and attributes of entity) or (function of entity)]	compulsory component
[analogy or constituency or attributive]	may appear 0 to n times
[particular-illustration or evidence]	may appear 1 to n times
[amplification or analogy or attributive]	optional
[particular-illustration or evidence]	optional

(a)

Typical Selected Schema	Corresponding Sample Text Fragment
Identification	A ship is a water-going vehicle that travels on the surface of the water.
Evidence	The ship's surface-going capabilities are specified by the attributes displacement and draft.
Attributive	Other attributes of a ship include the maximum speed, the propulsion, the fuel capacity, the dimensions, the name.
Particular-illustration	The ship Kennedy has maximum speed 29, fuel capacity 810, draft 25, beam 46, length 440.

(b)

solving considerations is outlined in Fig. 12.5. [41] The system first retrieves a fragment from the stored knowledge base and passes it on to the problem solver. The problem solver uses the knowledge fragment together with an available goal specification to generate one or more events. The generated events are then added to the available knowledge base using an assertion mechanism. Additional events that can be inferred from the newly added events may also be generated. The newly asserted events are then passed to the problem solver for additional event and goal specification.

Consider as an example the initial assertion "a bear moves through the woods" with the goal "the bear wants to eat." A new assertion might then specify "the woods contain trees," and the subgoals could specify that "the bear wants to find honey." This leads to still other events such as "the bear climbs a tree" with the subgoal "the bear wants to find a beehive," and so on. It is likely that this type of iterative inference and event assertion process can generate plausible stories in which each event is properly related to credible antecedent and consequent events. On the other hand, this problem-solving approach is unlikely to provide the intuitions and creativity associated with the writing of intelligent human beings. In principle, random disturbances could be introduced in an automatic event-production system to simulate unexpected author intentions, but even if this were done, the interest and variety of the output is not likely to compare to the writings of gifted human authors. This suggests that an interactive automatic-writing system might be implemented in which human writers make suggestions to the system at certain critical junctures. Such cooperative writing systems remain to be tried out in a serious way.

While creative automatic text-writing systems are not available in unrestricted discourse areas, relatively polished text output can be obtained for specialized areas. A typical example is a stock market report generator that takes as input simple facts contained on a stock exchange ticker tape, and produces natural-language reports outlining the movements and current conditions of the market (see Fig. 12.6). [36] The input facts may consist of market indicator values, such as the Dow-Jones Index valid for certain times of the day, as well as information about the proportion of stocks with rising and falling prices. The corresponding natural-language report may then state, "the market meandered upward during the day...the market turned in a mixed

Figure 12.5 Typical story-writing system based on problem solving (adapted from [41]). (J.R. Meehan, The Meta-Novel: Writing Stories by Computer, Doctoral Dissertation and Research Report No. 74, Computer Science Department, Yale University, New Haven, CT, 1976. Reprinted with permission.)

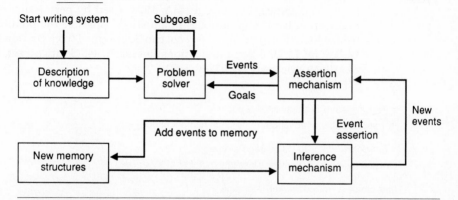

Figure 12.6 Typical automatically produced stock market report [36]. (K. Kukich, Design of a Knowledge-based Report Generator, *Proceedings of the 21st Annual ACM Conference*, Association for Computational Linguistics, Cambridge, MA, 1983. Used by permission of the Association for Computational Linguistics; copies of the publication from which this material is derived can be obtained from Dr. Donald E. Walker (ACL), Bell Communications Research, 445 South Street, MRE 2A379, Morristown, NJ 07960, USA.)

Wall Street's securities markets meandered upward through most of the morning, before being pushed downhill late in the day yesterday. The stock market closed out the day with a small loss and turned in a mixed showing in moderate trading.

The Dow Jones average of 30 industrials declined slightly, finishing the day at 810.41, off 2.76 points. The transportation and utility indicators edged higher.

Volume on the big board was 55860000 shares compared with 62710000 shares on Wednesday. Advances were ahead by about 8 to 7 at the final bell.

showing in moderate trading...and the Dow-Jones average declined slightly." To generate such texts, the knowledge base must contain domain-specific linguistic knowledge-defining expressions such as "over the counter," "selling short," and "odd lot." In addition, definitions must be provided for expressions relating to market behavior such as "meandering upward," "mixed showing," "broad and steep decline," and "in heavy trading." Two principal kinds of rule systems can

Figure 12.7 Message-generating rule for "mixed market" message [36]. (K. Kukich, Design of a Knowledge-based Report Generator, *Proceedings of the 21st Annual ACM Conference*, Association for Computational Linguistics, Cambridge, MA, 1983. Used by permission of the Association for Computational Linguistics; copies of the publication from which this material is derived can be obtained from Dr. Donald E. Walker (ACL), Bell Communications Research, 445 South Street, MRE 2A379, Morristown, NJ 07960, USA.)

if

  [(closing status of DJ average is up)

    and (number of advances is less than number of declines)]

  or [(closing status of DJ average is down)

    and (number of declines is less than number of advances)]

then create a "mixed market" message

transform facts extracted from the available knowledge base into appropriate linguistic expressions:

1. A message-generating system that chooses one or more applicable message types from a prestored message collection.

2. A discourse generator that collects messages into groups and produces an ordered stream of combined messages in accordance with predefined discourse-organizing rules.

Among the message classes used to generate stock market reports are those relating to "closing market status," "volume of trading," "interesting fluctuations," and "mixed market performance." A typical rule specifying the conditions of choice for a mixed-market message is shown in Fig. 12.7. Analogous rules lead to the choice of additional messages from the stored message inventory. The discourse rules used to assemble individual messages into complete stock reports provide a default ordering for the messages, and a set of exception specifications can be used to alter the normal default ordering. Thus when an unusual event occurs, such as when the averages hit a new high or a new low for the preceding 12 months, this event may be given top billing in the message stream, regardless of the originally specified order.

After message order is determined, a complicated sentence-generation program produces actual output sentences. This module uses lexical, syntactic, and rhetorical constraints to determine syntactic structure, usage of pronouns and other anaphoric referents, verb-tense specifications, constraints on sentence and paragraph length, and other criteria of text structure. The quality of the automatic stock market report system can be evaluated using fluency criteria for such characteristics as rhetoric (criteria include appropriate use of pronouns, ellipses, and hyponyms; variety of sentence lengths; and consistent use of tenses) and syntax (criteria include appropriate syntactic choice, use of conjunctions, and clause structure). The automatic stock-reporting system is apparently quite fluent and accurate. [42]

When the rule system is carefully constructed, false messages will be chosen only in extraordinary circumstances. On the other hand, it will always be difficult for any automatic report-generating system to provide the completeness of the manually prepared reports published in the financial press. A study of stock market reports included in the *Wall Street Journal* reveals that a substantial portion of the published sentences refer to events external to the stock market itself. These external events, which may explain stock market behavior, remain inaccessible to automatic report generators unless stored knowledge bases covering these external events are available to the system.

12.5 Automatic Translation

12.5.1 Main Approaches

Efforts to construct automatic language-translation systems go back to the early 1950s. At first simple, mechanized bilingual dictionaries were implemented and word-for-word translation systems were built, initially restricted to translating only a few sample sentences. Later syntactic analysis systems were based on context-free phrase-structure grammars, and it was predicted that satisfactory automatic translation soon would be widely used in operational environments. By 1960, at least 50 different machine-translation groups were at work around the world and various commercial automatic-translation projects had started. [43,44]

As the work progressed, it was realized that the dictionary consulting systems and the simple syntactic approaches to language analysis could not cope with the many complexities of natural-language texts, and that there was little chance of ever producing high-quality translations in a fully automatic way. In 1966, a National Academy of Science committee questioned the entire machine-translation effort. [45] As funding sources became scarce, interest shifted from implementing practical translation programs toward developing theoretical text-analysis systems that might prove useful for automatic translation in the long term, but were not immediately directed at translation.

More recently interest in mechanical translation has been renewed — due in part to the increasing availability of machine-readable text, as well as the existence of international communication networks that simplify the transmission of text. The study of text-understanding and language-translation systems was a principal component of the well-known Japanese "Fifth Generation" project. There is now a general perception among many experts that research into automatic translation might also benefit related text-processing activities such as automatic indexing and automatic abstracting. [46–49]

The following main approaches to machine translation must be distinguished:

1. *Direct* translation systems based on specialized methods that directly convert input in a specific source language to output in another specific target language (see Fig. 12.8a).

2. *Indirect* translation systems, which may analyze the source language independent of the synthesis in the target language. An indirect system thus uses certain analysis steps independent of the target language, and certain synthesis steps independent of the source language.

Two main possibilities have been considered for indirect translation systems: [46,47]

1. The *interlingual* approach uses a formal representation language that is independent of the source language (see Fig. 12.8b). This formal representation synthesizes the desired target language.

2. The *transfer* system first transforms the source text into some underlying meaning representation whose form and structure may depend on the input. A separate transfer step then converts the language-specific meaning representation of the source text into a target-language-specific output representation, which is eventually used to synthesize the output (see Fig. 12.8c).

Because of the difficulties of building universal formal meaning representations that are valid for all natural languages, the transfer ap-

---

Figure 12.8 Types of language-translation processes [51]. (a) Direct translation process. (b) Interlingual translation process. (c) Transfer translation process.

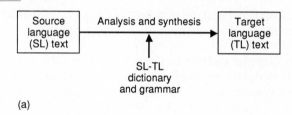

(a)

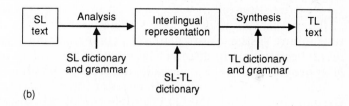

(b)

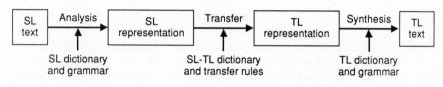

(c)

proach is used in most currently operating machine-translation systems. All of these systems include the following principal components:

- Dictionaries specifying the morphological variants of the input, as well as syntactic word functions and semantic features useful for analysis, together with the translated equivalents and the target-language constraints needed for synthesis.

- Morphological analysis methods used when the dictionaries contain uninflected base forms instead of complete words.

- Syntactic-analysis systems that construct the parse trees representing the analyzed word-class sequences and the functional groupings of the input.

- Semantic-analysis systems based on available semantic features (such as "animate," "male," and "liquid,") that resolve input ambiguities and assign semantic roles to the input constructs.

- Synthesis procedures for the target language that supply the correct correspondents and appropriate morphological forms for the output, as well as proper output structures.

- Optional preediting and postediting systems that standardize input and streamline output.

Among the desirable properties of a language-translation system are fidelity to the original version, intelligibility of the output, cost effectiveness, variety of output formats obtainable, and of course correctness of the output. In view of the difficulties inherent in all language understanding systems, it is not surprising that a perfect text-translation system cannot be built. In many cases, the correct correspondents of the input may depend on extralinguistic factors such as the situation in which a given utterance is placed, the focus of the utterance, or social context. These factors are difficult to capture in any system. More generally, corresponding syntactic and semantic constructs in different languages vary widely, and the choice of appropriate target-language forms is correspondingly difficult.

Table 12.6 illustrates the difficulties of translating directly between German and English. [50,51] The table completely disregards text focus, stress, discourse features, and social context; the problems stem entirely from the lexical properties of the words and the structural properties of the two languages. In particular, only three of the eight German input words have unique English correspondents. The needed disambiguation for the short sample excerpt depends on a variety of devices, including semantic coding of the input to distinguish animate from nonanimate entities, agreement in gender between pronoun and corresponding noun, and knowledge of idiomatic target-language expressions such as "to tell the truth".

Table 12.6 Translation example [50]. (a) Source-language analysis. (b) Target-language synthesis.

Input: Er hätte seiner Frau die Wahrheit nicht gesagt

Lexical correspondence:

Er	he/it
hätte	would have/had
seiner	his/its
Frau	woman/wife
die	the
Wahrheit	truth
nicht	not
gesagt	said/told

Source-language rules:

1. hätte + gesagt	:	analytic form of "sagen"
2. hätte gesagt + nicht	:	negation of verb
3. seiner + Frau	:	adjective + noun
4. die + Wahrheit	:	article + noun
5. hätte gesagt + seiner Frau	:	verb + dative object
6. hätte gesagt + die Wahrheit	:	verb + accusative object
7. er + hätte gesagt	:	subject + predicate

(a)

Target-language rules:
1. pluperfect subjunctive formed with "would" + infinitive
2. negative particle comes after personal form of verb
3. adjective comes before noun
4. article comes before noun
5. direct object used without preposition follows verb
6. indirect object can precede or follow direct object;
   if it follows, "to" is needed
7. subject precedes predicate

Intermediate output:

he/it would not have said/told his/its woman/wife the truth

Variant rules:

1. he/it	:	"sagen" refers to a human being; hence "er" → "he"
2. woman/wife	:	related to a male person; hence "wife"
3. his/its	:	"seiner" must refer to a male person; hence "his"
4. say/tell	:	verb complemented by dative object; "to tell the truth" is common in English

Final output: he would not have told his wife the truth

(b)

As noted earlier, indirect-translation systems are now used in most practical applications. Indirect-translation strategies became popular when it was realized that by separating input-language analysis from output-language synthesis, only one input and one output system would have to be designed for each language in the translation system. By separating the translation programs into modules, changes would be easier to introduce without affecting the complete system. At first, it was believed that the large variety of "surface" formalisms found in different natural languages could be reduced to some common "deep" structure, and attempts were made to adapt Chomsky's transformational grammar as a common pivot language in a translation system. [52,53] For reasons explained in Chapter 11, the formalism of transformational grammar was difficult to use, and problems arose in finding sets of linguistic primitives that could represent content and structure. At present, the transfer approach to natural-language translation is generally preferred.

A transfer system is usually based on three subsystems: [54]

1. A set of monolingual features that determine the surface structure of the source text.

2 A transfer process, designed for the specific language pair under consideration, that converts the input language's features into appropriate output structures. The transfer process uses syntactic and semantic properties as well as other contextual features to derive the required level of language understanding.

3. A set of monolingual features that determine the surface structure of the target text.

Using the transfer approach, different deep-structure representations can be used for source and target languages, and no attempt need be made to derive representative sets of linguistic primitives reflecting text context.

In recent years, artificial intelligence approaches have been applied to language translation. [55] It has been suggested that the construction of formal syntactic patterns should be replaced by the use of semantic fragments expressing text content. Typically the input words would be defined by predetermined primitive semantic units, and the text expressed by semantic statements representing relationships between primitive units. Thus the notion of "drinking" might be expressed as "animate thing ingests liquid via a particular aperture." The corresponding meaning might be expressed by a semantic triple such as "animate thing contains liquid." When a complete text is interpreted as a set of semantic relationships, the corresponding semantic fragments might be converted into running text using available rules to choose the proper lexical items in the target language. The use of semantic primitives and semantic grammars may be most productive in restricted situations with narrow text functions and discourse areas.

The modern computing environment provides a number of additional possibilities for implementing machine-translation systems. Use could be made of one of the large, recently developed machine-readable dictionaries and encyclopedias covering major portions of natural language, and offering detailed information about the syntactic and the semantic properties of the entries. It is conceivable that the use of large terminological data banks may help in recognizing synonyms and in resolving many types of source-text ambiguities. Appropriately detailed dictionary information might also help assign semantic features and characterize the input text semantically. [56]

Another possibility is the use of human intelligence in analyzing input and in choosing operations during analysis. Since many translation activities take place in interactive user-system environments, the user might be asked to verify system decisions and interpretations or to supply actual data as needed. [57] In such a situation, menus might allow the user to choose among alternative possibilities for interpreting certain words, or among alternative suggested text analyses.

12.5.2 Typical Machine-translation Systems

Two approaches are apparent in the current implementations of translation systems. The first attempts to produce polished special purpose systems that operate in restricted subject areas, or else require a human being to participate in the input analysis. The second approach generates somewhat imperfect output, but covers much wider subject areas. Among the best known of the former systems are TAUM-METEO and TAUM-AVIATION, which perform English-to-French translations of weather reports and aircraft maintenance manuals, respectively. [58,59] These systems are implemented as conventional transfer systems, but also utilize special features adapted to their specialized environments. Thus the weather-report system subdivides each report into well-defined sections, including special heading, title of forecast, list of localities and regions, and main forecast sections. In addition, elaborate provisions are made for processing dates and hours of the day, as well as temperature measurements and other important facts in weather forecasting. Complete sets of idioms used in weather reporting are also available, together with translations in the output language. On the other hand, there is no special effort to include external, pragmatic knowledge and other discourse features.

The TAUM-METEO weather-forecast translation system is outlined in Fig. 12.9. As shown, TAUM-METEO is a transfer system with clearly separated stages. It uses distinct dictionaries for analysis, transfer, and synthesis, and emphasizes morphological and syntactic transfer procedures. The syntactic transfer system converts analyzed syntactic input trees or graphs into syntactic output trees, based in part on the presence or absence of semantic markers in the input trees. Because of the special nature of the input, only those syntactic transformations useful for weather report production are actually included. Provisions are made, however, to detect input errors and missing dictionary entries.

The TITUS 4 system, another special-purpose translation system, simultaneously translates materials dealing with textiles into four different languages (French, English, German, Spanish). [60] Many of the

Figure 12.9 Transfer system for weather forecast production [51,59].

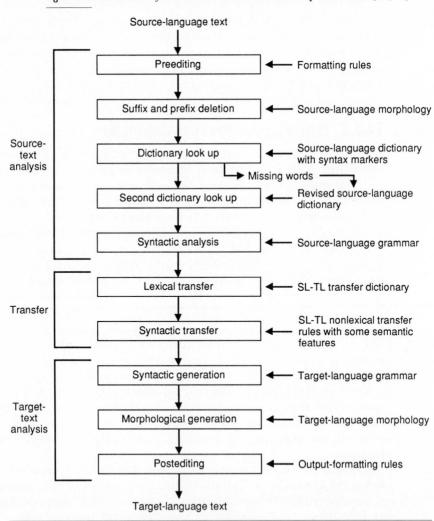

complexities of the source-language analysis are avoided by tailoring the system to documents that follow a specially controlled syntax, consisting chiefly of nominal groupings used as subject and complement structures plus verbal groups used for complementation. Prepositional phrases are also allowed, as are coordinating conjunctions ("and") used for enumeration, and negated statements. By excluding complex and compound sentences from the source text, the difficulties of the language analysis are of course greatly reduced. The TITUS system uses a transformational analysis to convert the input into a formal analyzed representation, and subsequent synthesis steps convert the analyzed input into the translated output in the various languages. Because of the restricted form of input, the intermediate pivot representation is constructed relatively easily. Figure 12.10 shows some typical output obtained with the system. It can be seen that the restricted syntax produces somewhat stilted but easily comprehensible output.

The Weidner system, an interactive, machine-aided translation system, transforms English input into either French, German, or Spanish output. [61] Competent human operators guide the translation system. The following main tasks are based on user-supplied information:

- Correcting and editing submitted input texts.

- Updating dictionary entries by additions to, deletions from, and alterations of the existing dictionary structure.

- Submitting synonyms and modifying the computer-produced translated output.

The dictionaries supply the usual information on syntactic roles and features as well as the needed semantic features. The more frequently occurring idioms can also be processed. The Weidner system uses a relatively simple linguistic analysis and produces imperfect output. However, a competent human intermediary can greatly affect both the quality of the output and the general performance of the system.

Existing general-purpose systems, such as Systran and the more recently developed METAL, are based on the use of large grammars containing several hundred grammatical rules, and impressively large dictionaries that may include several tens of thousands of word entries. [51,62] Syntactic and semantic features determine the applicability of particular grammatical rules, and attempts are made to deal with some of the more complicated issues in language analysis, such as homograph resolution, compound-noun identification, phrase identification, and the treatment of prepositional and coordinate structures. Since it is impossible to resolve all possible ambiguities in unrestricted environments, a number of analysis paths are sometimes followed in parallel, with plausibility scores used to distinguish different output analyses based on their probability of correctness.

Most existing large-scale systems will tolerate somewhat imperfect input and bring obvious faults and problems to the user's attention.

Figure 12.10 Typical output of the TITUS 4 translation system [60].

DATE 12/05/82   ****TITUS 4 SYSTEM****   FILE NAME: DEMO

SENTENCE NR: 02 INPUT LANGUAGE (DE < EN < ES < FR)= = > FR

INPUT SENTENCE = = > LES PROGRES RECENTS DES LOGICIELS APPROPRIES AU TRAITEMENT ON-LINE DES SYSTEMES D'IN-FORMATION ONT FAVORISE LE DEVELOPPE-MENT DES BASES DE DONNEES DANS TOUS LES DOMAINES DES SCIENCES ET DES TECH-NIQUES.

FRANCAIS ******* LES PROGRES RECENTS DES LOGICIELS APPROPRIES AU TRAITEMENT ON-LINE DES SYSTEMES D'INFORMATION ONT FAVORISE LE DEVELOPPEMENT DES BASES DE DONNEES DANS TOUS LES DO-MAINES DES SCIENCES ET DES TECHNIQUES.

ENGLISH ******* THE RECENT PROGRESS OF THE SOFTWARE SUITABLE FOR THE ON-LINE TREATMENT OF INFORMATION SYSTEMS HAS FAVORED THE DEVELOPMENT OF DATA BASES IN ALL THE FIELDS OF SCIENCES AND TECH-NIQUES.

DEUTSCH ******* DIE NEUEN FORTSCHRITTE DER FUER DIE ON-LINE VERARBEITUNG DER INFORMATIONSSYSTEME GEEIGNETEN SOFT-WARE HABEN DIE ENTWICKLUNG DER DATENBASEN IN ALLEN BEREICHEN DER WISSENSCHAFTEN UND DER TECHNIKEN BEGUENSTIGT.

ESPAGNOL ******* LOS PROGRESOS RE-CIENTES DEL SOFTWARE APPOPRIADO PARA EL TRATAMIENTO ON-LINE DE LOS SISTEMAS DE DOCUMENTACION FAVORECIERON EL DE-SARROLLO DE LAS BASES DE DATOS EN TODOS LOS CAMPOS DE LAS CIENCIAS Y DE LAS TEC-NICAS.

NEXT STEP COMMAND = = >

Because these systems are based largely on a syntactic framework, the level of understanding used to characterize the texts may be relatively shallow. This implies that less than perfect output may be produced in some instances. However, semantic-based methodologies are not available and, as two well-known machine-translation experts say, the idea of generating such systems in unrestricted domains is not appealing: [62]

> The thought of writing complex models of even one technical domain is staggering...if such models are indeed required for our [machine translation] application, we will never succeed.

Fortunately, useful machine translations can be generated even under the limitations imposed by currently available levels of language understanding. Current systems produce about 10,000 words (or about 40 typewritten pages) per day, and major faults are detected in only about 20 percent of the output sentences. The processing cost of these systems is still relatively high, but will decrease in time. The development of machine-translation systems is expected to accelerate, and translation systems will receive increasing use and attention even if no fundamental progress is made in developing new theories of language structure and understanding.

References

1. E.J. Galli and H.M. Yamada, Experimental Studies in Computer-assisted Correction of Unorthographic Text, *IEEE Transactions on Engineering Writing and Speech*, EWS-11:2, August 1968, 57–62.

2. J.J. Pollock, Spelling Error Detection and Correction by Computer: Some Notes and a Bibliography, *Journal of Documentation*, 38:4, December 1982, 282–291.

3. A. Zamora, Automatic Detection and Correction of Spelling Errors in a Large Data Base, *Journal of the ASIS*, 31:1, January 1980, 51–57.

4. T.N. Turba, Checking for Spelling and Typographical Errors in Computer Based Text, Proceedings of the ACM SIGPLAN SIGOA Symposium on Text Manipulation, *ACM SIGPLAN Notices*, 16:6, June 1981, 51–60.

5. E.M. Zamora, J.J. Pollock, and A. Zamora, The Use of Trigram Analysis for Spelling Error Detection, *Information Processing and Management*, 17:6, 1981, 305–316.

6. J.L. Peterson, Computer Program for Detecting and Correcting Spelling Errors, *Communications of the ACM*, 23:12, December 1980, 676–687.

7. R. Morris and L.L. Cherry, Computer Detection of Typographical Errors, *IEEE Transactions on Professional Communication*, PC-18:1, March 1975, 54–64.

8. M.D. McIlroy, Development of a Spelling List, *IEEE Transactions on Communications*, COM-30:1, January 1982, 91–99.

9. F.J. Damerau, A Technique for Computer Detection and Correction of Spelling Errors, *Communications of the ACM*, 7:3, March 1964, 171–176.

10. P.A.V. Hall and G.R. Dowling, Approximate String Matching, *Computing Surveys*, 12:4, December 1980, 381–402.

11. J.J. Pollock and A. Zamora, Automatic Spelling Correction in Scientific and Scholarly Text, *Communications of the ACM*, 27:4, April 1984, 358–368.

12. J.J. Pollock and A. Zamora, System Design for Detection and Correction of Spelling Errors in Scientific and Scholarly Text, *Journal of the ASIS*, 35:2, 1984, 104–109.

13. R.C. Angell, G.E. Freund, and P. Willett, Automatic Spelling Correction Using a Trigram Similarity Measure, *Information Processing and Management*, 19:4, 1983, 255–261.

14. G.E. Freund and P. Willett, Online Identification of Word Variants and Arbitrary Truncation Searching Using a String Similarity Measure, *Information Technology: Research and Development*, 1:3, July 1982, 177–187.

15. R.A. Wagner and M.J. Fischer, The String-to-String Correction Problem, *Journal of the ACM*, 21:1, January 1974, 168–173.

16. UNIX System, Writer's Workbench Software, User's Guide, Report 995-805-00615, 1985.

17. N.H. Macdonald, L.T. Frase, P. Gingrich, and S.A. Keenan, The Writer's Workbench: Computer Aids for Text Analysis, *IEEE Transactions on Communications*, 30:1, 1982, 105–110.

18. L.L. Cherry, A Toolbox for Writers and Editors, *Proceedings of AFIPS Office Automation Conference*, AFIPS Press, Arlington, VA, March 1981, 221–227.

19. L.L. Cherry, Computer Aids for Writers, Proceedings of the ACM SIGPLAN-SIGOA Sympoium on Text Manipulation, *ACM SIGPLAN Notices*, 16:6, June 1981, 62–67.

20. G.E. Heidorn, K. Jensen, L.A. Miller, F.J. Byrd, and M.S. Chodorow, The EPISTLE Text-Critiquing System, *IBM Systems Journal*, 21:3, 1982, 305–326.

21. I. Durham, D.A. Lamb, and S.B. Saxe, Spelling Correction in User Interfaces, *Communications of the ACM*, 26:10, October 1983, 764–773.

22. H.P. Luhn, The Automatic Creation of Literature Abstracts, *IBM Journal of Research and Development*, 2:2, April 1958, 159–165.

23. H.P. Edmundson and R.E. Wyllys, Automatic Abstracting and Indexing — Survey and Recommendations, *Communications of the ACM*, 4:5, May 1961, 226–234.

24. H.P. Edmundson, Problems in Automatic Abstracting, *Communications of the ACM*, 7:4, April 1964, 259–263.

25. J.E. Rush, R. Salvador, and A. Zamora, Automatic Abstracting and Indexing — Production of Indicative Abstracts by Application of Contextual Inference and Syntactic Coherence Criteria, *Journal of the ASIS*, 22:4, July-August 1964, 260–274.

26. C.D. Paice, Automatic Generation of Literature Abstracts — An Approach Based on the Identification of Self Indicating Phrases, in *Information Retrieval Research*, R.N. Oddy, S.E. Robertson, C.J. van Rijsbergen and P.W. Williams, editors, Butterworths, London, 1981, 172–191.

27. J.W. McInroy, A Concept Vector Representation of the Paragraphs in a Document Applied to Automatic Extracting, Report TR 78-001, Computer Science Department, University of North Carolina, Chapel Hill, NC, 1978.

28. J. O'Connor, Answer Passage Retrieval by Text Searching, *Journal of the ASIS*, 32:4, July 1980, 227–239.

29. J. O'Connor, Retrieval of Answer-Sentences and Answer-Figures from Papers by Text Searching, *Information Processing and Management*, 11:5/7, 1975, 155–164.

30. D.E. Walker and J.R. Hobbs, Natural Language Access to Medical Text, Technical Note 240, SRI International, Menlo Park, CA, March 1981.

31. U. Hahn, R. Kuhlen, and U. Reimer, Konzeption und Aufbau des Automatischen Textkondensierungssystems TOPIC, Report TOPIC 1/82, University of Konstanz, Germany, September 1982.

32. U. Hahn and U. Reimer, Entwurfsprinzipien und Architektur des Textkondensierungssystems TOPIC, Report TOPIC 14/85, University of Konstanz, Germany, April 1985.

33. G. deJong, An Overview of the FRUMP System, in *Strategies for Natural Language Processing*, W.G. Lehnert and M.H. Ringle, editors, L. Erlbaum Associates, Hillsdale, NJ, 1982, 149–176.

34. R.C. Schank, Reminding and Memory Organization: An Introduction to MOPS, in *Strategies for Natural Language Processing*, W.G. Lehnert and M.H. Ringle, editors, L. Erlbaum Associates, Hillsdale, NJ, 1982, 455–493.

35. J.L. Kolodner, Indexing and Retrieval Strategies for Natural Language Fact Retrieval, *ACM Transactions on Database Systems*, 8:3, September 1983, 434–464.

36. K. Kukich, Design of a Knowledge-based Report Generator, *Proceedings of the 21st Annual ACL Conference*, Association for Computational Linguistics, Cambridge, MA, 1983, 145–150.

37. K.R. McKeown, The Text System for Natural Language Generation — An Overview, *Proceedings of the 20th Annual ACL Conference*, Association for Computational Linguistics, Toronto, Canada, 1982, 113–120.

38. W.C. Mann and J.A. Moore, Computer Generation of Multiparagraph English Text, *American Journal of Computational Linguistics*, 7:1, January-March 1981, 17–29.

39. E.J. Conklin and D.D. McDonald, Salience: The Key to the Selection Problem in Natural Language Generation, *Proceedings of the 20th Annual ACM Conference*, Association for Computational Linguistics, Toronto, Canada, 1982, 129–135.

40. S. Klein, J.F. Aeschlimann, D.F. Balsiger, S.L. Converse, C. Court, M. Foster, R. Lao, J.D. Oakley, and J. Smith, Automatic Novel Writing — A Status Report, Technical Report 186, University of Wisconsin, Madison, WI, July 1976.

41. J.R. Meehan, The Meta-Novel: Writing Stories by Computer, Doctoral Dissertation and Research Report No. 74, Computer Science Department, Yale University, New Haven, CT, 1976.

42. K. Kukich, Fluency in Natural Language Reports, Technical Report, Computer Science Department, Carnegie-Mellon University, Pittsburgh, PA, 1984.

43. W.N. Locke and A.D. Booth, editors, *Machine Translation of Languages*, John Wiley and Sons, New York, 1955.

44. Y. Bar Hillel, The Present State of Automatic Translation of Languages, in *Advances in Computers*, F. Alt, editor, Academic Press, NY, 1960, 91–163.

45. Automatic Language Processing Advisory Committee (ALPAC), *Language and Machines*, Publication 1416, National Academy of Sciences, Washington, DC, 1966.

46. W.J. Hutchins, Machine Translation and Machine-Aided Translation, *Journal of Documentation*, 34:2, June 1978, 119–149.

47. J. Slocum, A Survey of Machine Translation: Its History, Current Status, and Future Prospects, *Computational Linguistics*, 11:1, January-March 1985, 1–36.

48. M. King, Eurotra: An Attempt to Achieve Multilingual MT, in *Practical Experience of Machine Translation*, V. Lawson, editor, North Holland Publishing Company, Amsterdam, 1982.

49. M. Nagao, J. Tsujii, and J. Nakamura, The Japanese Government Project for Machine Translation, *Computational Linguistics*, 11:2–3, April-September 1985, 91–110.

50. S. Perschke, Automatic Language Translation — Its Possibilities and Limitations, *Euratom Bulletin*, 6:2, June 1967, 54–60.

51. J.W. Hutchins, The Evaluation of Machine Translation Systems, in *Practical Experience of Machine Translation*, V. Lawson, editor, North Holland Publishing Company, Amsterdam, 1982, 21–37.

52. N. Chomsky, *Syntactic Structures*, Mouton and Company, The Hague, Netherlands, 1957.

53. B. Vauquois and C. Boitet, Automatic Translation at Grenoble University, *Computational Linguistics*, 11:1, January-March 1985, 28–36.

54. J.I. Tsujii, Future Directions of Machine Translation, *Proceedings of COLING-86, Eleventh International Conference on Computational Linguistics*, University of Bonn, Bonn, Germany, August 1986, 655–668.

55. Y. Wilks, An Artificial Intelligence Approach to MT, in *Computer Models of Thought and Language*, R.C. Schank and K.M. Colby, editors, W.H. Freeman, San Francisco, CA, 1973, 114–151.

56. M.E. Lesk, What Use Are Machine Readable Dictionaries? A Summary of the "Automating the Lexicon" Workshop, Bell Communications Research, Morristown, NJ, 1986.

57. M. Kay, The MIND System, in *Natural Language Processing*, R. Rustin, editor, Courant Computer Science Symposium No. 8, Algorithmics Press, NY, 1973, 155–188.

58. P. Isabelle and L. Bourbeau, TAUM-Aviation: Its Technical Features and Some Experimental Results, *Computational Linguistics*, 11:1, January-March 1985, 18–27.

59. B. Thouin, The METEO System, in *Practical Experience of Machine Translation*, V. Lawson, editor, North Holland Publishing Co., Amsterdam, 1982.

60. J.M. Ducrot, The TITUS 4 System, Institut Textile de France, Paris, May 1982.

61. M.G. Hundt, Working with the Weidner Aided Translation System, in *Practical Experience of Machine Translation*, V. Lawson, editor, North Holland Publishing Company, Amsterdam, 1982.

62. W.S. Bennett and J. Slocum, The LRC Machine Translation System (METAL), *Computational Linguistics*, 11:2–3, April-September 1985, 111–121.

Chapter 13

Paperless Information Systems

13.1 Paperless Processing

Processing paper documents and forms has many disadvantages. Paper products tend to be bulky, and when information is fragmented among different documents, usually voluminous paper files are needed that are inconvenient and expensive to manipulate. Handling large paper files is labor intensive and requires slow, complicated operations. Paper is most useful as a static recording medium when the recorded information is not subjected to large-scale changes. Many document files are volatile, however, requiring frequent updating and maintenance. In such situations, paper files may be unsuitable because information recorded on paper is difficult to erase and replace. Most important — as everyone knows who has had to shuffle through large stacks of paper documents — finding particular items of information in paper files can be unpleasant, frustrating, and extremely time consuming. For all these reasons, paper is often usefully replaced by a more flexible information-recording medium, one more easily manipulated and updated. [1–4]

With the advent of computer networks that electronically link large classes of information producers and users, and of inexpensive workstations that create and manipulate machine-readable information, the role and importance of paper as a carrier of information have substantially changed. Electronically readable information is much cheaper to store than paper products, and machine-readable information is now universally produced with word-processing technology. Certain novel technologies such as optical disks have also been introduced that provide a unified medium for bulk storage of different types of information, such as written texts, graphic images, and digitized speech; optical technology can be interfaced easily with existing computer networks. Finally, electronically recorded information is manipulated much more easily than information recorded on paper, especially when files are frequently modified and updated.

Because of the versatility of the electronic recording media, many automatic information-processing applications are planned, or have already been implemented, including the following:

- Electronic mail and messaging systems, replacing ordinary letters, telephone calls, face-to-face conversations, and personal visits.

- Electronic information-dissemination services, handling document delivery to both individuals and entire classes of recipients.

- Electronic notebooks and bulletin boards, replacing ordinary file folders on desktops.

- Electronic information-accessing methods, handling the creation of, and access to, directories, dictionaries, catalogs, reviews, indexes, and other auxiliary information files.

- Electronic-publishing systems, helping to generate and issue documents, using display screens to compose text and lay out pages, and editing and formatting commands to prepare and correct text.

- Electronic-conferencing systems, providing interfaces that permit free-form interactions among participants in different locations.

While electronic-processing methods have many attractions, the long-predicted demise of conventional paper-handling systems has not yet occurred. The conventional print medium has advantages over alternative information-recording methods, such as the integrity and historical value of written information recorded on paper, portability, and the convenience and easy readability of high-resolution printing and graphics recorded on paper. Another advantage of conventional paper handling relates to the fact that, to gain access to and use the information recorded on paper, there is no need to learn the intricacies of electronic equipment and of electronic information-handling methods. Obviously, the need to learn electronic processing techniques constitutes a drawback for the untrained user. A number of more intangible problems also arise — relating, for example, to the ownership of information and the compensation provided to information owners for the use of recorded information, the safeguarding of protected information that should remain inaccessible to unauthorized users, and the preservation of the interests of industrial segments, like publishing, that have a substantial stake in the operations of information-processing systems.

13.2 Processing Complex Documents

In practical information-processing systems, the data of interest take on a variety of different forms, especially written texts and formatted records of many types. Texts are often supplemented by pictorial data, including graphs and other illustrative images. In modern environments, it is also possible to process speech, music, and other types of audiovisual information. Thus the processing environment should make it possible to manipulate different types of objects, including natural-language text strings, graphic data and images, and recorded speech. Specifically, the electronic system should furnish tools for acquiring, composing, editing, storing, and retrieving information items, including written texts, graphic images, and recorded sound elements. Such items are generally known as *multimedia* objects. In addition, real-time methods should also be available for distributing and exchanging stored information among the users of a system. [5–7]

In considering the design of multimedia document-processing systems, provisions must be made for manipulating various portions of documents: [6]

- Content identifiers consisting of attribute names, attribute values, and other types of content identifiers.

- Images represented by collections of picture points, or directly defined as graphic objects of certain types.

- Voice segments that may refer to particular image or text sections of the document.

- Text portions that may represent titles, headings, chapters and sections, references, and other text segments.

- Annotations providing additional information about a document's structure or content.

In the environment of multimedia documents, methods must be available for submitting and processing information requests, browsing through the document database, and relating various document portions to each other. Normally this implies that the related information objects are linked in various ways and that these links are followed in searching and retrieving document information. For example, the text paragraphs can be linked separately from graphic illustrations and speech samples. Text, graphs, and audio portions referring to common topics or located in adjacent document areas can be linked. One implementation idea consists of defining information "chunks," and providing special processing capabilities tailored to the individual chunks rather than documents as a whole. [8] Once again, pointer and link structures represent the element associations and the document components and help process the structured objects.

Several types of document decompositions can be recognized. [9] The first is a *conceptual* layout in which the document chunks represent particular notions or semantic contexts. Figure 13.1(a) shows the conceptual layout of a sample document representing a call for papers to a professional conference. The layout decomposes the document into principal topics, with semantic connections making it possible to create unified entities from a variety of distinct information chunks. In addition to conceptual layouts, *logical* layouts can be defined that reflect the object structure in terms of actual text components, such as sections and paragraphs, figure captions and image portions, and table rows and columns (see Fig. 13.1b). Finally, *physical* layouts break down the document into individual boxes and blocks on various parts of the physical page (see Fig. 13.1c).

The chunk format enables the user to create individual object associations by linking chunks together in various ways, and defining paths through a collection of related chunks. The linking mechanism also makes it possible to define auxiliary chunks representing annotations, cross-references, and citations, and to attach these auxiliary elements to their corresponding principal chunks. The chunk model described here for text fragments applies equally to the decomposition of figures, tables, graphs, and sound segments, and to the description of sequences of related elements.

To process structured objects, structure-manipulation operations must be defined for node or chunk creation, node linking, structure display, and structure alteration. A typical scheme, shown in Fig. 13.2, displays a portion of a document structure on a screen, together with related chunks that could be linked to the main objects. A menu of operations for use in performing relevant structure modification and display operations may also be available. [7]

Many actual or proposed structure-processing systems described in the literature manipulate complex "hypertext" document structures, including structure-editing operations, [10–12] chunk- and tree-manipulation systems that carry out the copying, pasting, and linking operations that process the document portions, [13–18] and auxiliary link attachments that can explain the system and can define auxiliary

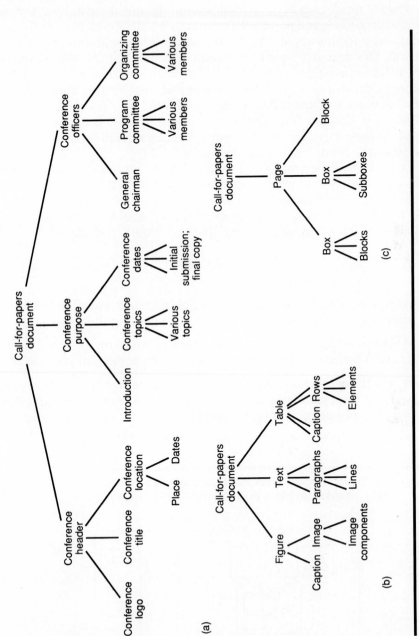

Figure 13.1 Various object decompositions (adapted from [9]). (a) Excerpt from conceptual layout of a call for papers. (b) Excerpt from logical layout. (c) Excerpt from physical layout. (F. Barbic, Retrieval of Office Documents via Structured Trees, Report, Dipartimento di Eletronica, Politecnico di Milan, Italy, 1985. Reprinted with permission.)

concepts extracted from related documents. [19–21] Sophisticated workstations, with substantial computational and local-storage capabilities, usually interact with the system. Extensive user-interface software must also be provided, including special graphics and/or sound recording and playback facilities, as well as connections to specialized peripherals and to local and remote communications networks. One recently proposed system, based on optical disk technology, offers almost unlimited storage at very low cost, and very high storage densities. Optical disks are useful to store text materials, as well as voice and image data in digitized form. Access times, however, tend to be slow for information not stored in close proximity on the disk. In these circumstances, it pays to group related information and to store the related items contiguously. [22,23]

A multimedia system must include an object-recognition handler that, for each type of object, provides lists of procedures applicable to the object under consideration. In addition, the query-specification interface must provide a variety of different search and retrieval options. The following search strategies are usually considered:

- A sequential search through objects of a given type (text only, or graphic images only).

- A sequential search in which related objects (text, voice, and images) that refer to a common subject are retrieved simultaneously.

- A search relative to a particular storage position, designed to retrieve information stored in the vicinity of the current position.

- A search by logical components of a document where effort is restricted to particular document sections — for example, tables or figures only, or certain text sections.

Figure 13.2 Typical structured text display. (a) Auxiliary chunks. (b) Main display area. (c) Possible commands.

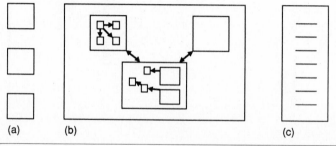

(a) (b) (c)

- A pattern-matching search that retrieves document excerpts satisfy-
ing a stated content prescription. However, pattern matching is not
straightforward for voice and image data.

   The voice and image portions of complex documents require special
treatment by methods substantially different from those used for text
materials. Some basic available graphics- and speech-processing
methods are examined in the next two sections.

13.3 Graphics Processing

13.3.1 Basic Display Systems

Since the 1960's, computers have been used to process pictorial information in the form of graphs and images. Compared with ordinary
text, manipulating graphic information requires much greater computational resources and uses more extensive storage areas. Furthermore, complex software systems are required to generate lifelike pictures that accurately model the normal visual relationships among
elements of the picture. Because in an interactive computer graphics
environment the user controls the picture generation and manipulation, the graphic-processing step must be fast enough to permit useful
interaction with the human controller. Graphic-processing systems
thus require computational resources of substantial complexity and
power. [24–27]
   Many current interactive graphic-display systems are based on the
use of cathode ray tube (CRT) technology, in which an electron beam
strikes a phosphor-coated screen that emits light with an intensity depending on the kinetic energy of the electrons. Since the light output
produced by the phosphor fades rapidly, the displayed image must be
redrawn frequently, typically at a rate of 30 times per second or more.
This *image-refreshing* operation is normally based on a stored digital
representation of the picture, maintained in a special buffer known as
the *refresh buffer.*
   Two principal methods exist for directing the electron beam of the
CRT unit to the desired place on the display screen. In a *vector-display*
system, the beam actually traces certain primitive graphical figures,
such as lines, arcs, and alphabetic characters, by following a simple
prescription. Thus, to trace a line segment, only the coordinates of the
two endpoints are required; this makes it possible to deflect the beam
continuously between the two corresponding points, thereby tracing
the desired line segment. A vector-display system is obviously parsimonious of memory because the actual images need not be stored,
only their mathematical definitions. On the other hand, only certain

simple graphical structures can be defined easily by coordinate measurements. In any case, complex figures are difficult to draw in the limited time available between refresh cycles, even if they could be defined mathematically. In a *raster-display* system, the beam is not deflected in a pattern determined by the image under construction. Instead, a regular pattern is traced, usually horizontal lines starting at the top of the screen. As each line is traced, the intensity of the beam is controlled in accordance with the requirements of the particular image. Raster-display systems are simpler and less expensive to implement than vector-display systems because the beam traces only regular left-to-right horizontal patterns. Furthermore, a raster-scan system can easily construct solid objects and other complex visual scenes. On the other hand, raster systems require large refresh buffers because every display point (pixel) of a complete display screen must be stored for display and refresh purposes. This makes it difficult to carry out dynamic display changes — it is usually necessary to respecify a large number of image points instead of only the few coordinate points that are normally specified in vector displays.

A graphic-display system may include many kinds of *input devices* to let the user introduce objects and alter the displayed information. *Locator* devices, such as hand-held mice with buttons, track balls, joysticks, and touch panels, specify positions or locations on the screen. Entire displayed objects can often be manipulated by using a stylus, mouse, or light pen that points at a particular screen area. Valuators consisting of dials and knobs may be available to introduce particular values into the display. Finally, conventional input characters may be specified on the keyboard, and special-function keys may be provided to make choices, select actions, and enter particular commands.

A *display processor* usually generates images, constructing the pictures and storing the finished product in the refresh buffer for transfer to the display device. A typical display-processing system is outlined in Fig. 13.3. The display processor usually receives picture-

Figure 13.3 Typical-display-processing unit.

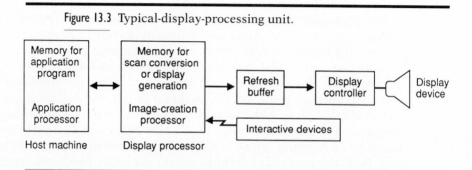

drawing commands from a host machine, or directly from the user by means of controlled input devices. To generate the images, the digital coordinate-point specifications in a vector system are converted into analog form, and these analog values are used to drive the deflection coils of the CRT display unit. In a raster-scan display system, a *scan-conversion* program converts the image specification to a raster scan format to be stored in the refresh buffer. In both cases, the display controller interprets the display instructions, and activates the display unit in accordance with specifications.

Most graphic-processing systems utilize high-level instructions to model a wanted object or scene, which can be displayed and appropriately modified until the desired image is actually obtained. The model can be generated by using geometric coordinates to specify object positions, then adding display color attributes, stating object relationships, and supplying related data such as text elements that must be processed with the object. To view an object on the display screen, the object coordinates must be mapped into corresponding display-device coordinates, and object portions outside the available viewing window must be removed, or clipped. Objects initially specified in three dimensions must also be reduced to two dimensions before being displayed, and smoothing algorithms must be used to create lifelike images. General object-manipulation programs shift objects from one place to another, alter the object scale, perform rotation and stretching operations, and supply shadings, color, shadows, highlights, and textures.

In conventional object-modeling systems, the high-level processing operations are designed to transform each object as a unit, with no provision for carrying out low-level operations at the level of the individual display points of the screen. For some applications, such as design and art work, it is useful to work at the individual pixel level; a special "painter's" approach may be available to transform individual picture points. In some situations, different operations may be performed simultaneously, using distinct screen portions; window-managing systems are often provided to control the displays of several related applications. The system manager then defines and moves overlapping displays, and scales and clips the displayed information to fit into visible parts of available windows.

13.3.2 Object Transformations

The objects in a graphic-processing system may be initially defined in a world-coordinate system that measures the units in centimeters or inches. Before the screen display can begin, the object coordinates must be transferred into a screen domain measured in raster units. A further transformation into a selected window within the screen domain may also become necessary if window and screen domains are not identical. For three-dimensional world domains, a projectional transformation is then added to map the three-dimensional world onto the two-dimensional screen, the projection depending on the viewpoint chosen.

Consider the well-known *central* projection with a defined viewpoint on the z-axis of a three-dimensional space. The central projection transforms a conventional three-dimensional window into a viewing pyramid with its apex at the viewpoint, as shown in the example of Fig. 13.4, where a cube is transformed into a truncated pyramid. To obtain the display coordinates of an object under a projection system, each object point must be mapped onto the image plane using the assumed viewpoint. The image of an object point $p(x,y,z)$ will then lie at the intersection of the image plane with a line that joins the point p with the viewpoint. Assuming that the viewpoint lies at point z_0 on the z-axis of the coordinate system, and that the image plane intersects the z-axis at z_I, the coordinates of the image point $P(X,Y)$ may be defined as

$$X = x \cdot \frac{z_0 - z_I}{z_0 - z}$$

and

$$Y = y \frac{z_0 - z_I}{z_0 - z}.$$

A sample central-projection operation is illustrated in Fig. 13.5. When the viewpoint is moved to infinity, an *orthographic* projection is obtained in which parallel lines in the object are transformed into parallel lines in the image plane. In that case, $x = X$ and $y = Y$.

Figure 13.4 Transformation of cube using central project with assumed viewpoint at z_0.

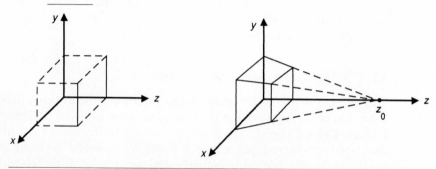

Many additional routine object transformations can change the orientation and shape of displayed objects. Among these transformations are rotations, translations, and scale transformations. Rotations of objects around the point of origin from an old coordinate system (x,y) to a new system (x',y') are defined by the following equations:

$$x' = x \cos \alpha + y \sin \alpha$$

and

$$y' = -x \sin \alpha + y \cos \alpha,$$

where α is the angle between the original and the new coordinate axes, respectively. Assuming that the z-axis is not moved, the rotation operation is defined in matrix notation as

$$[x'\ y'\ z'] = [x\ y\ z] \cdot \begin{bmatrix} \cos \alpha & \sin \alpha & 0 \\ -\sin \alpha & \cos \alpha & 0 \\ 0 & 0 & 1 \end{bmatrix}$$

A sample rotation operation around the origin is illustrated in Fig. 13.6.

Translations are performed by adding a positive or negative constant to each coordinate of an object point, so that

$$x' = x + c_x,$$
$$y' = y + c_y,$$

and

$$z' = z + c_z.$$

Figure 13.5 Central project of $p(x,y,z)$ onto $P(X,Y)$ on image plane.

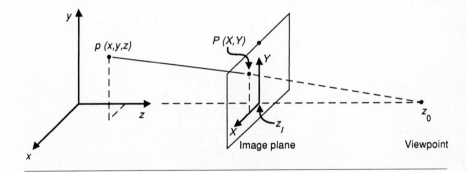

Scale transformations are similarly executed by multiplying the coordinates by scale factors s_x, s_y, and s_z, respectively:

$$x' = x \cdot s_x,$$
$$y' = y \cdot s_y,$$

and

$$z' = z \cdot s_z.$$

One problem faced in all object-display systems is the need to identify areas of an object that are invisible from the point of view of the observer when the corresponding points are hidden by other areas of the same object or by different objects. Such points must be suppressed from the displayed image. For example, if the cube of Fig. 13.4 is assumed to be solid and nontransparent, the origin of the coordinate system is invisible to the observer. A great many *hidden-line* algorithms have been devised whose underlying principle is to search and sort through collections of object surfaces to determine which surfaces are located closest to the observer and cannot therefore be hidden by other surfaces. [28] In performing the sorting operations, the coherence of the environment can be assumed. This implies that it is unnecessary to distinguish between many points that lie on the same edges or surfaces, assuming that the object surfaces hang together properly, without random discontinuities.

Two main image-generation systems are used to solve the hidden-line problem. In the *painter's algorithm*, objects are broken down into

Figure 13.6 Rotation of coordinate system from (x,y) to (x',y').

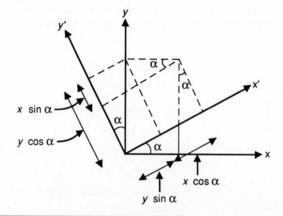

polygons ordered from back to front according to their distances from the viewpoint. The polygons are then projected into the refresh buffer in back-to-front order so that new polygons overlapping objects previously placed in the buffer are superimposed on the older images, erasing in part the previously recorded information. The sequential construction of a cube using the painter's method is illustrated in Fig. 13.7.

In the alternative *z-buffer* method, each picture element of an object is characterized by four values x, y, z, and v, where x, y, and z represent the coordinate values and v is the corresponding pixel intensity of the element. Assuming that the image plane has the value $z = 0$, it is necessary, for each fixed pair of values of x and y, to find the corresponding picture element with the smallest z value. That picture element will eventually be in view in the displayed image, and its corresponding z value z_i and pixel intensity v_i will be placed in the refresh buffer. As mentioned earlier, object-coherence criteria make it possible to avoid sorting for many (x,y) points.

Somewhat similar considerations are used to control the placement of shadows, shadings, and highlights in the image plane. Like the painter's method of object generation, shadow placement depends on a classification of surfaces. Surfaces visible both from the viewpoint

Figure 13.7 Object generation using Painter's algorithm. (a) Individual polygons. (b) Partly assembled object.

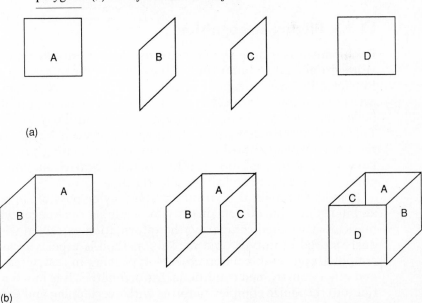

(a)

(b)

and from points at which light sources are placed do not appear in shadow. On the other hand, shadows must be generated for surfaces visible from the viewpoint but not from the light sources. The computation of shadings takes into account both the properties of the surface — for example, color, texture, and reflection properties — and the relative location and orientation of light sources and other surfaces. Distinctions can be made in the shading method between various light sources — for example, point sources such as lamps, ambient light sources, and distributed light sources such as windows. Special computational methods can also deal with transparent or translucent surfaces such as glass, and can handle shiny surfaces characterized by mirrorlike reflections known as *highlights*. In that case, the amount of light reflected depends on the angle formed by the light source and the viewpoint with respect to the surface of the object. When these two angles are approximately equal, the surface acts like a mirror and special provisions must be made to represent the corresponding reflections.

In summary, sophisticated image-generation systems are now available in many environments. While processing complex scenes and three-dimensional objects tends to be expensive, simple graphs can be handled efficiently using high-level graphic packages to perform the more frequently executed operations on points, lines, and surfaces. [29] The automatic manipulation of objects that include both text and images is expected to become increasingly common in the foreseeable future.

13.3.3 Picture Recognition

Document-processing systems are useful not only to generate and store graphic information, but also to retrieve the images on demand. Retrieval involves questions of pattern matching and automatic picture recognition. In principle, graphic pattern-matching problems can be avoided entirely by indexing each image similarly to text items. This method attaches a set of keywords to each image, reducing the image-retrieval problem to a keyword-matching problem. The keyword-indexing solution is often used in libraries and museums to characterize picture and slide collections.

In modern retrieval environments, it may be possible to recognize and index graphic objects directly by scanning the images with automatic devices, then comparing the information extracted with previously stored prototype objects. This method is especially useful for simple graphs and isolated objects appearing in restricted lighting and other constrained conditions. Unfortunately, it is much more difficult to recognize complex pictures with overlapping and extraneous features that contribute to the appearance of the objects.

Two main approaches are current for recognizing graphic data. The first one, a *low-level* approach, consists of detecting certain simple features such as edges or particular surfaces with specified properties. The recognition of individual features then leads to conclusions about the nature of the complete objects. The low-level approach is often used in alphabetic character-recognition systems, which identify characters by the properties of particular character components, or to recognize simple objects that differ sufficiently from all other objects in a picture.

Consider as an example the recognition of alphabetic characters in printed text. A scanning device can be used first to distinguish the black picture points, which are covered in part by a character from the white ones, which are not. The scanning resolution, measured by the number of distinguishable pixels per square inch, must be high enough to characterize the input with reasonable completeness, and the pixel-classification system used to distinguish the white and black areas must be accurate enough to preserve the main properties of each character. The output of a character scanner using two different scanning resolutions is shown in Figs. 13.8(a) and (b). It is clear that Fig. 13.8(b) is much more representative of the letter A than Fig. 13.8(a). After the scanning operation, a feature-detection system determines the important characteristics of each input pattern. Thus edges and curves can be traced by following the outlines of the picture points, leading to the identification of features such as line intersections, angles, and curves. When the shapes of input patterns are closely controlled, characterizing a given class of input patterns will be comparatively simple, and recognizing the unknown input is reasonably straightforward. On the other hand, when faulty or variable input must be processed, the features used for classification may be distorted, and character recognition is correspondingly much more difficult.

Figure 13.8 Black-and-white picture-point recognition for character A. (a) Low resolution. (b) Higher resolution. (c) Malformed character.

(a) (b) (c)

Thus the misshapen character A of Fig. 13.8(c) does not exhibit the usual intersection of vertical line segments; a recognition system using that feature may then decide that the pattern represents an H rather than an A.

Most automatic-character recognition systems can recognize printed input consisting of numbers and characters in a given typefont with better than 95 percent accuracy. On the other hand, this equipment cannot recognize handwritten material and other uncontrolled input with variable character shapes and ill-defined boundaries between characters.

An alternative to the feature-based recognition system is a *model-based* system, in which the objects to be recognized in a picture must be narrowly specified in advance. Typically a detailed model of the objects under consideration is built, and input patterns are compared with the model. The problem with model-based recognition is that objects embedded in a complex background may have unusual appearances that defeat the comparison with the stored models. In principle, the model-based approach could be extended by storing a variety of different object models, each corresponding to distinct viewpoints of the same object. The available image would then be compared with the several possible stored model representations. Because of the variety of possible object representations, however, complete identification of arbitrary scenes and images with this method remains elusive.

13.4 Speech Processing

It is often useful to include voice data with graphic and textual information items. Voice output tends to be more immediate than written texts, because texts must be read before they can be understood, whereas spoken versions are absorbed immediately. Furthermore, text cannot be easily processed by persons unable to read or see, while speech is easily processed even by small children.

Recently, substantial progress has been made in developing so-called "talking chips," which store and play back recorded audio information on demand. Also, advances in speech synthesis have led to the design of usable text-to-speech systems that convert arbitrary written input into understandable spoken output. Unfortunately, the inverse speech-recognition problem — which would permit relevant speech samples to be identified and retrieved from a store of spoken information, or spoken information to be converted to written information — is under much less control. In fact, the available speech-recognition systems are still generally restricted to manipulating small speech samples produced by speakers with known speech characteristics.

13.4.1 Speech Synthesis

Speech-synthesis systems produce spoken output from some form of stored speech representation. [30–32] Speech is usually represented by analog waveforms reflecting the variations of sound frequency and intensity over time. In principle, analog speech waveforms can be sampled at frequent intervals, and the sample readings can be converted to digital form and the result stored in a computer. Before retrieval and eventual playback, the stored digital representation must be reconverted into analog form. Unfortunately, the standard pulse-code modulation method of speech storage requires 64K bits of storage for each second of speech. Thus for a spoken text message two minutes long, the uncompressed digitized storage uses 7.68 million bits of memory, compared with about 0.02 million bits for the corresponding alphabetic form of the text.

Memory cost can be reduced substantially by using some form of *speech coding* to produce a compressed speech representation. The well-known linear predictive coding (LPC) attempts to model the human voice system by using a time-varying recursive filter with time-varying coefficients. Good-quality speech can be produced by LPC coding using only 5000 bits of storage per second of speech; some other forms of speech coding require only 1000 bits. [33]

In applications handling only a small number of distinct words or sentences, such as talking computer terminals and various talking instruments, it is possible to store the complete digitized forms of the desired output utterances. For applications involving the production of arbitrary and initially unknown speech output, the desired output must be synthesized from a small number of prestored sound units. This solution is used in text-to-speech conversion for the visually handicapped and in inquiry systems with flexible speech output. Only about 40 recognizable speech sounds, or phonemes, are actually used in English. While synthesis from the basic phonemes requires little storage for speech data, however, increased computational resources are inevitably needed to generate the contextual features such as stress, intonation, and intermediary sounds that produce understandable speech from individual sounds. Consider as an example a typical text-to-speech conversion system that takes mail, message, or document input to produce corresponding speech output. [34,35] The text-to-speech system outlined in Fig. 13.9 is based on the conversion of text letters to sound units. The initial phonological component converts English letters into speech sounds. This step raises difficult problems, however, because individual letters do not correspond to specific sounds on a one-to-one basis — for example, there are only five vowels in English, but 16 different vowel sounds.

While letters cannot be converted into speech sounds directly, additional information about word spelling and word sequences can be used to derive phonemes and stress patterns for the text. The ideal beginning would be to decompose the input text into meaningful linguistic units, isolating individual words and using compound words such as "backache" and "hothouse" to produce semantic units such as "back," "ache," "hot," and "house." Such a morphemic decomposition is difficult to provide without a large word dictionary storing all individual morphemes. However, decomposition into semantic units is necessary to avoid transforming the "th" in "hothouse" into the "th" sound of "rather" or "bother", as well as interpreting "backache" as "ba-cake."

After morphemic decomposition, a set of several hundred contextual letter-to-phoneme rules might be used to guess the pronunciation of certain letter sequences occurring in certain contexts. Experience indicates that with a good set of basic rules, a success rate of some 70 percent may be achieved. Because many of the most frequent English words have exceptional pronunciations, an exceptions dictionary of several thousand words would have to be used in addition to the basic rule set.

In most languages, the pronunciation of individual words depends on their context. In particular, clause structure determines pauses, stress patterns, rhythm, and intonation. Thus a pause is often inserted

Figure 13.9 Typical text-to-speech system.

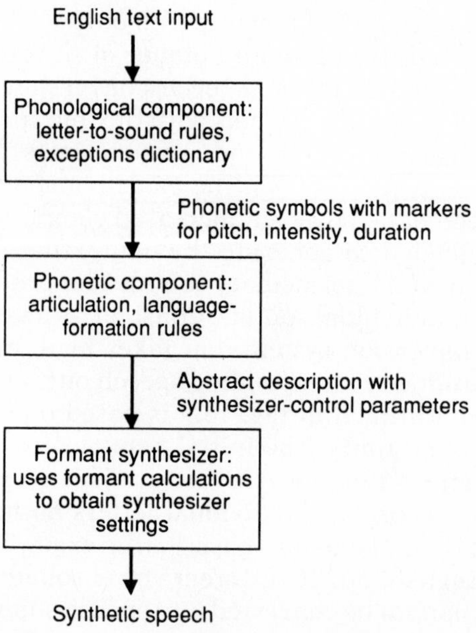

English text input

↓

Phonological component:
letter-to-sound rules,
exceptions dictionary

↓ Phonetic symbols with markers
for pitch, intensity, duration

Phonetic component:
articulation, language-
formation rules

↓ Abstract description with
synthesizer-control parameters

Formant synthesizer:
uses formant calculations
to obtain synthesizer
settings

↓

Synthetic speech

at the end of clauses, and unstressed components are shortened while stressed ones are lengthened. Determining useful pronunciation patterns must be based on sufficiently complete syntactic information to identify clause boundaries, and if possible noun-phrase and verb-phrase boundaries. Because recognizing noun and verb phrases is complicated and subject to erroneous interpretations in English, a completely accurate formal linguistic description cannot always be produced for an unrestricted input text.

To generate final speech output, the linguistic descriptions in terms of basic phonemes, stress, duration, and other phenomena must be converted into control parameters for each pitch period, which in turn produce correct settings for the speech synthesizers. In view of the complexity of language analysis for ordinary unrestricted texts, it is not surprising that existing speech-synthesis systems, which are necessarily based on concatenating discrete speech units, do not always produce very natural-sounding output.

These language-analysis problems can be avoided to a large extent, and the quality of speech output correspondingly enhanced, by restricting the speech-synthesis system to situations with restricted vocabularies, and simple sentence structures. This explains why many practical speech-production systems have been built and used commercially in recent years, even though the total problem of language analysis remains unsolved. A particularly successful application is an automatic telephone-inquiry system whose users communicate with a stored database by means of standard touch-tone telephone sets; voice output is generated that can be heard on the same telephones used for input. [36] Buttons on the telephone are used to introduce commands and respond to requests made by the system. A flowchart for a typical telephone-inquiry system is shown in Fig. 13.10.

Typical inquiry services with speech output can be used to obtain weather information, to listen to specific recordings on demand, to obtain directory information, and to order merchandise listed in a catalog — in general, to interact with a limited store of information maintained and processed by a computer. A typical interactive sequence

Figure 13.10 Typical telephone inquiry system.

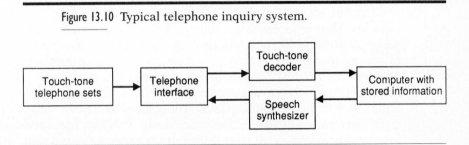

Table 13.1 Sample interaction for telephone inquiry system [36].

User:	dials service
Computer:	"hello, this is the telephone inquiry service; please enter your user number"
User:	enters number
Computer:	"please enter your password"
User:	enters password
Computer:	"which service do you require"
User:	enters service number (number 101 reaches the Stores Information Service)
Computer:	"Stores Information Service; please enter component name"
User:	SN7406#
Computer:	"the component name is SN7406; is this correct"
User:	*1# (* is command prefix, 1 means "yes")
Computer:	"this component is in stores"
User:	*7# (7 is the command for "price")
Computer:	"the component price is 35 cents"
User:	*8# (8 is the command for minimum number that can be ordered)

between a user and a catalog sale service is shown in Table 13.1. [36] Although the computer responses are generated from a phonetic representation by using appropriate conversion rules, these rules are tailored to the small set of stereotypical responses needed to run the specific services provided by the system. In such restricted circumstances, a high order of speech quality can usually be achieved.

13.4.2 Speech Recognition

Analyzing and transforming speech input into some alternative output form is much more difficult than the inverse operation, speech synthesis. For one thing, the quality and characteristics of speech sounds depend on the identity of the speakers and on the context of the speech samples. Thus whereas in speech synthesis it is normally sufficient to generate one type of speech output for a given linguistic input pattern, in speech recognition it may be necessary to analyze hundreds of different speech forms for any given utterance. Furthermore, unlike a fingerprint, which is unique to an individual, a single voice print is not uniquely attached to each speaker. Indeed, speakers can substantially alter their voices as the occasion demands. This fact has not deterred intelligence agencies from training human experts to read voice prints in an effort to identify the origin of speech samples obtained by hidden microphones and "bugging" devices. [37]

The speech-recognition problem is characterized by the following complex circumstances:

- Many different speech waveforms exist for identical utterances. See, for example, Fig. 13.11, which shows quite different speech waveforms (spectrograms) for utterances of the word "science" obtained by different speakers. [38]

- No clear differentiation can be made between those features in a particular spectrogram that are speaker independent and hence utterance specific, and those that are not.

- The form of a spectrogram depends greatly on the environment in which the utterance is placed. Thus continuous speech patterns differ from discrete patterns, and noisy environments produce characteristics different from quiet ones. A sample spectrogram for the utterance "science" produced in a noisy room appears in Fig. 13.12.

The obvious conclusion is that the problem of recognizing unrestricted speech does not have a simple solution. In particular, the model-based approach used for image recognition cannot be used, because no standard model exists for particular utterances with which the many incoming utterances from arbitrary speakers can be compared. Furthermore, no practicable speech-analysis system can possibly store in advance the thousands of possible versions of each utterance.

Two main approaches are used in speech recognition. [30,39–41] The first handles the recognition of voice input from a small number

Figure 13.11 Spectrograms of the utterance "science" by two different speakers [38].

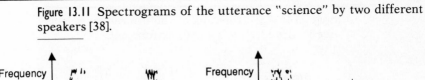
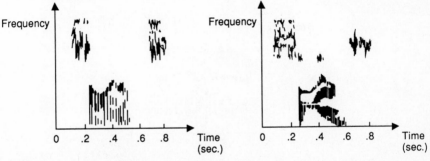

of known subjects. A *learning phase* can store templates of speech patterns for particular speakers. After a speaker is characterized, a second template-matching phase compares the unknown, incoming speech samples with the known, stored speech patterns obtained from the available subjects.

The learning-phase system is not useful for recognizing speech samples produced by unknown speakers not under the control of the system's operators. In that case a phonetically oriented method can be tried, based on the recognition of minimal speech units such as individual phonemes, groups of phonemes, particular syllables, or particular words. This approach raises complex problems of locating and identifying features, and the further problem of constructing rules based on the feature information. Given the great variability of speech input, and the lack of a detailed theory of speech production and perception, it is very difficult to construct rules relating message content and speaker classification to observed phonetic sound patterns.

Since the ability to identify unrestricted vocabularies of continuous speech is not imminent, the industrial and commercial applications of speech recognition are restricted to treating relatively large vocabularies in systems trained to specific users, or small vocabularies in speaker-independent systems. When isolated words are available as input rather than continuous speech, the scope of the vocabulary that can be handled increases greatly. [42]

A typical system for recognizing isolated words is outlined in Fig. 13.13. First a sampling of the input speech waveform converts the analog input to digital form. Next the boundaries between speech samples corresponding to individual words are identified by subtracting the ambient noise and detecting the areas of low energy output that represent silences in the incoming patterns. The feature-extraction system then assigns attributes to the speech samples, consisting of phonetic

Figure 13.12 Spectrograms of the utterance "science" (see Figure 13.11) in a noisy environment.

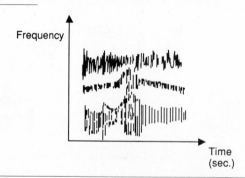

Frequency

Time
(sec.)

features identifying vowels, pauses, or unvoiced consonants, as well as spectral shape features such as slope and maximum or minimum measurements of the speech waveforms. These features are then incorporated into a subsequent pattern-matching operation that compares the input samples with the features characterizing known speech samples stored in a reference dictionary.

The pattern matching may include a technique known as *time warping*, which allows for time and distance variations in the occurrences of feature patterns extracted from speech samples. This normalization accounts for differences in utterance speeds for various sample speakers. The pattern-matching system can be based on a "best-fit" technique that uses the closest dictionary entries to identify the presumed correspondents for the voice input. It is also useful to include an additional syntactic-processing step to verify the decisions made by the low-level feature-analysis system, and to resolve output ambiguities. If, for example, an input sample is recognized as either "mine" or "nine," then "mine" might be recognized rather than "nine" when a noun is expected at that point in the utterance. The language-analysis

Figure 13.13 Typical system for recognizing isolated words [30].

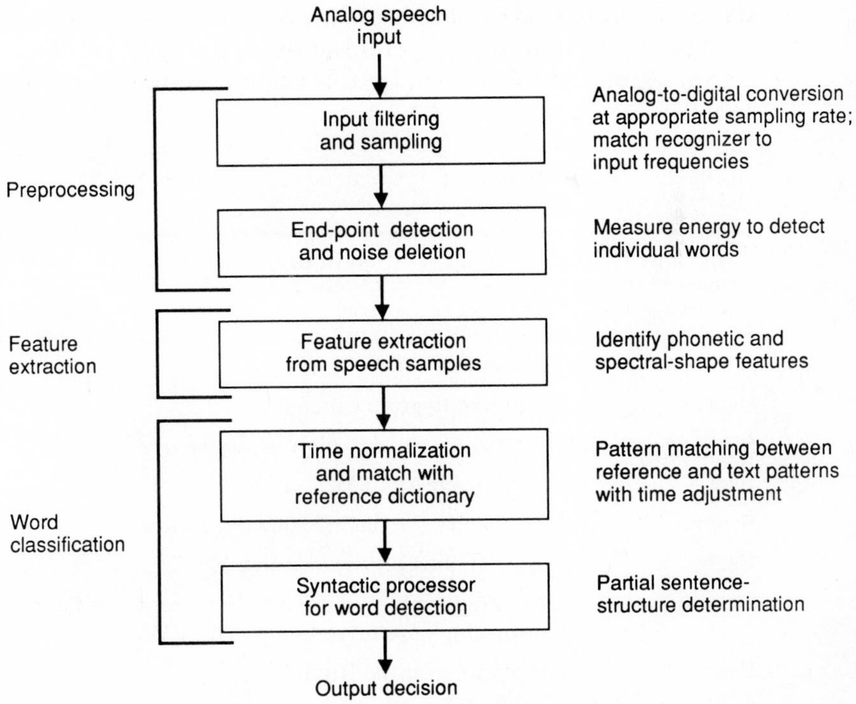

step could be used iteratively (as suggested by the loop in Fig. 13.12) to hypothesize about matching patterns and then verify the assumed analysis linguistically. As more and more input words are correctly identified, analyzing the complete utterance becomes more constrained and hence easier to manage.

At present, it is possible to recognize connected speech from several different speakers produced in a quiet room over a high-quality microphone, using a total vocabulary of about 1000 words. Only a minimum of speaker cooperation is needed, and relatively little training is required by the system for adaptation to the speakers. [42,43] Unconstrained connected speech cannot be recognized yet. However, in many environments, such as database management systems covering specific subject areas, or catalog sales, somewhat restricted vocabularies and restricted speech patterns are the norm, and the speech-recognition problem is much easier to tackle.

As an example of a constrained system that combines speech recognition and speech synthesis, consider a conversational flight-information system based on data stored in the well-known *Official Airline Guide*. [44] That system uses an acoustic word recognizer for about 150 words dealing with reservation systems, travel plans, aircraft types, flight choices, seat selection, meal service, fare information, and so on. A syntactic analysis is used that recognizes sentences employed in making airline reservations; semantic-category specifications help resolve potential linguistic ambiguities. A sample conversation for the automatic reservation system is reproduced in Table 13.2.

Table 13.2 Sample conversation in flight-information system [44].

System:	"This is the Bell Laboratories Flight Information System. May I help you"
User:	"I would like to go to Chicago"
System:	"Please specify the day of your departure"
User:	"I want to leave at 4 PM"
System:	"Please specify the day of your departure"
User:	"I want to depart on the two-five May"
System:	"Flight number nine-two leaves New York at 4 PM arrives in Chicago at five-twenty-five PM"
User:	"What plane is on the flight"
System:	"The aircraft is a Boeing seven twenty seven"

13.5 Automatic Teleconferencing Systems

A teleconferencing system is a multimedia information-interchange system with substantial voice and graphics capability that allows a group of participants to communicate with each other interactively. [45–49] Teleconferencing uses various group-communication devices, including video cameras and screens to transmit and view pictures, electronic blackboards capable of recording the information written on them, microphones and loudspeakers to transmit sound, graphic printers, and several kinds of recording equipment. When enough bandwidth is provided in the communications channels, simultaneous interactions between several participating groups can be assured in real time. Alternatively, asynchronous interactions can be implemented, as in conventional mail systems, in which participants receive and send data at their own convenience.

Telecommunication systems may be helpful for many purposes: Emergencies when people on the scene cannot reach decisions without outside help; situations when someone needs information but is physically unable to move; and many other environments when teleconferencing is less expensive than face-to-face meetings. [46] Many different teleconferencing environments can be considered. [49] In full-motion video conferencing, the complete interaction of all participants is continuously recorded. In freeze-frame video conferencing, on the other hand, pictorial and other graphic aids are transmitted as still pictures, and the participants are not continuously visible. An audio-teleconferencing system uses only minimal picture transmission, but voice data are transmitted, and graphic data may be stored locally and displayed on demand. Finally, an audio teleconference proceeds without graphic transmissions.

Full-motion video-conferencing systems require large bandwidths to transmit many different types of data. Three display screens are usually used. The first displays images of the remotely located participants, while images of the most recently transmitted picture and of locally kept images recalled from storage can be displayed on the second and third screens. In full-motion video conferencing, a conference monitor usually controls the equipment that receives incoming information and the corresponding broadcasting equipment. A full teleconferencing facility may cost up to a million dollars, and data transmission may cost several thousand dollars per hour. A typical teleconferencing facility is shown in simplified form in Fig. 13.14.

Audio conferencing requires much smaller bandwidths for transmission, and costs are correspondingly lower. Unlike a conventional conference telephone call, however, audio conferencing may include the transmission of text — or facsimile data — and the use of information recorded on electronic blackboards. A compromise between a full video conference and an audio conference consists of designating a principal participant, such as a senior management person, who is visible continuously by all remote points; only audio information is transmitted by the other participants.

Figure 13.14 Typical video teleconferencing facility.

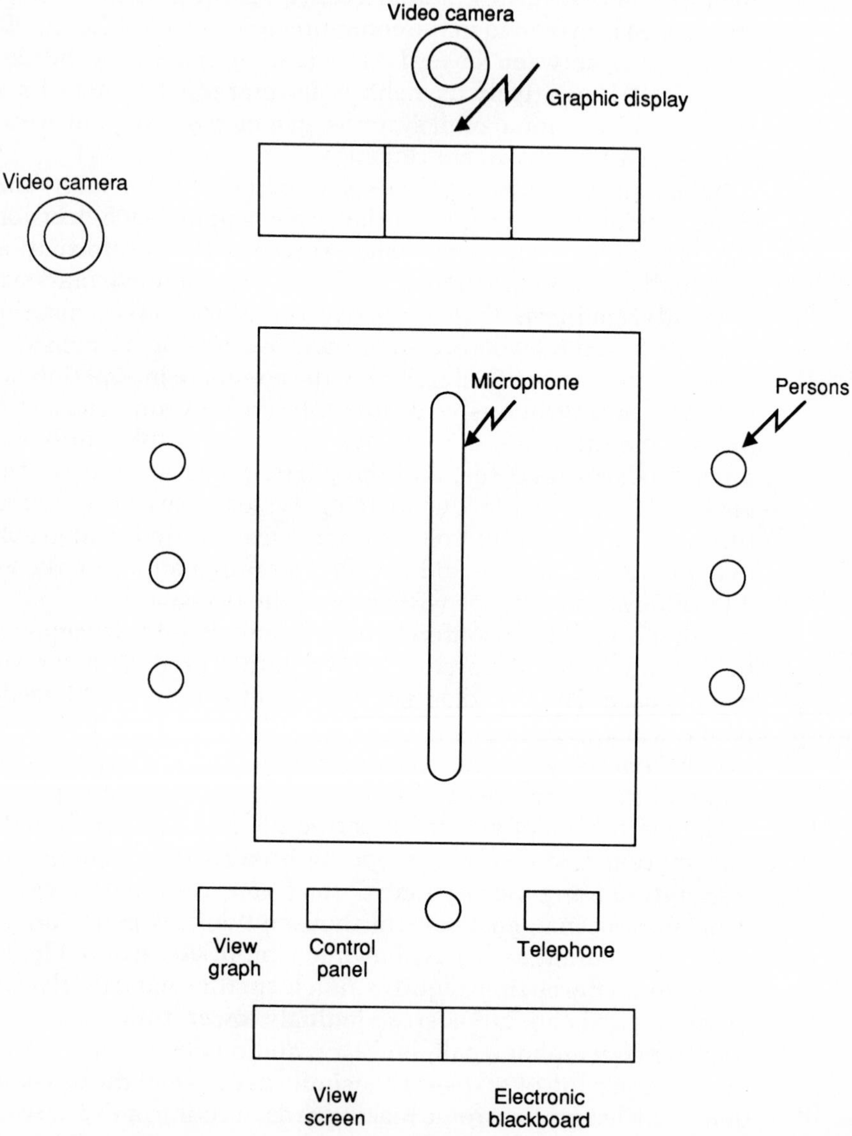

Another inexpensive alternative is a text-based group communications system in which the participants transmit text messages, often asynchronously rather than simultaneously. This system requires only relatively simple devices, including keyboard terminals to send and receive information, modems to connect the terminals to telephone-transmission lines, a host computer to store, retrieve, and distribute written materials within the system, and a data communications network that allows the users to communicate over local telephone-access lines. This type of system can provide private mail and messaging services, manage personal notebooks, provide directory and index services, organize bulletin boards for public notices, and handle balloting and polling among various participants.

Unlike complete teleconferencing, simple group communication is used widely. Implementing such systems, however, raises a number of technical, social, and legal issues. [50] Technically, access and concurrency control methods must be used to accommodate potentially large groups of users who want simultaneous access to files and services. Decisions must also be made about file management and file location: The participants may share various centrally located files, or the files may be distributed among participating sites, and possibly duplicated, so that copies can be held at individual workstations. The latter alternative saves a good deal of communications expense but requires consistency controls to ensure that the multiple file copies carry identical information. Among the social problems are preserving individual privacy — presumably no conference participant wishes to be seen in compromising situations by outsiders — and safeguarding individual autonomy. There are also legal questions about the liability of conference participants for advice and opinions voiced over long-distance channels, and about the admissibility in court of testimony obtained from witnesses using teleconferencing methods. These questions and many others must be resolved before electronic group communications are used more widely.

13.6 Electronic Mail and Messages

An electronic mail facility is a communications system that allows participants to send each other mail and messages using electronic methods of information transmission. Among the main features of such systems are provisions for entering text messages, mailing messages, informing the intended recipients of the arrival of messages, and allowing the recipients to read, file, or discard incoming mail. Electronic-messaging systems are popular among many users because they simplify the composition and transmission of messages, while also increasing the transmission speed and reducing the cost of communication. Automatic mail systems may also increase users' productivity — the sender avoids the inconvenience of dealing with busy telephone lines and unanswered telephones. Furthermore, since mail can be forwarded and received at any time, electronic mail-handling systems need not interrupt other activities.

A successful electronic-mail system must be based on a simple, easy-to-operate user interface. The system should be reliable and available on demand. Obviously its usefulness increases with the number of participants. Ideally, all potential correspondents should be attached to the system, and the security and reliability of conventional mail environments should be maintained. Because of the widespread use in some organizations of existing computer networks, the universality requirement is generally met. The first such network, ARPANET, was designed in the late 1960s. Today the vast majority of computer science organizations, and organizations in many other fields, are attached to one or more of the networks offering electronic mail and messaging.

The following computer networks developed over the past few years are of special interest in this connection: [51]

- CSNET supports collaborative research in computer science, but offered electronic mail as its initial service. Centrally administered, CSNET contains about 180 host nodes, many serving as gateways to internal company or national networks.

- BITNET, a decentralized network, contains 1300 hosts in 21 countries, most at universities and research centers. BITNET supports communication and collaboration among programmers, offering unrestricted access without network membership fees. New organizations can join the network at minimum cost by acquiring a leased communications line that allows it to connect to some other network node.

- USENET, another decentralized network, began in the early 1980's. With about 2000 host machines, it is devoted principally to disseminating news and messages. Various news groups are defined that cover both technical and nontechnical subjects, and recipients can subscribe to news items in specified subject areas. USENET also has computer conferencing and mailing-list facilities.

A useful automatic message-processing system includes the following components: [52,53]

- An interface program between the user's applications programs and the communications system that actually transmits information. The interface system should save incoming messages temporarily until the user's applications program is ready to take over, and should maintain queues of outgoing messages ready for transmission but not yet delivered to the network.

- A message-editing system that packs messages into segments, and interprets the destination and routing information in the message headers.

- A mailbox service that classifies messages in priority order, lists incoming messages, counts and inspects mailbox contents, stores particular messages, handles mail inquiries, releases messages, and eliminates items to be discarded.

Various designs are available to implement a mail and messaging system. A system dedicated to mail handling is highly reliable; other processes are unlikely to interfere with the mail function. A word-processor-based system uses conventional user-terminal equipment tied together by a communications network to handle mail; one or more local processors maintain local mailboxes and carry out communications access. Finally, a central processor can maintain mailboxes and handle communications, in which case users can obtain access through any terminal with dial-up capabilities.

Figure 13.15 shows a typical message-processing system, including the following components: [23]

- The *originating-user interface* interacts with users in preparing outgoing messages, checks message format, consults the name directory for addressing information if necessary, and establishes routes to the receiving processor.

- The *name-directory processor* handles the mapping between user names and user mailbox addresses and updates directories. It also administers user mailboxes.

Figure 13.15 Typical message-processing system (adapted from [23]).

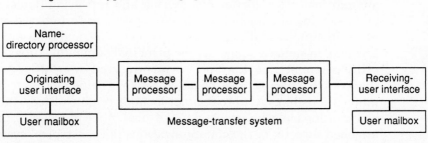

- The *message-transfer system* may consist of a variable number of message processors that receive messages from originating users and other message processors, and forward these messages to other message processors or to destination users in accordance with available routing information.

- The *receiving-user interface* allows users to retrieve messages from their mailboxes and to receive messages from other users.

Communications between the user interface and message processor must follow a standard protocol. The originating-user program first places the message information in a special file accessible to the message processor. The message processor then extracts routing information from the message, assigns a transaction number, and forms a delivery command. When a message processor receives a message addressed to a user under its control, the message is entered into a file available to the receiving user's interface programs, and returns an acknowledgment to the originating message processor.

A message-processing system depends crucially on the correctness and accessibility of the name *directory*. The directory consists of tables specifying bindings between user names and corresponding low-level user objects. Thus given a user name, the directory produces the user-interface address to which mail must be addressed for that user. In principle, routing messages — that is, determining the links used to forward messages — can be carried out independently of the addressing system. Various methods exist for reaching routing decisions, including systems with memory that reach routing decisions based on information about previously processed messages, and coordinated systems in which the routing of particular messages depends on the handling of other messages that enter the system at the same time. [54,55] No matter the routing method, provisions must be made to detect unusual conditions such as trapped messages at a nonterminal node, and message shuttling around a loop in the forwarding path.

The modern electronic office constitutes a principal application for electronic mail services. In an office, the main tasks include creating and editing office documents, storing and retrieving items, sending and receiving documents, and handling various form-based office applications such as billing, inventory processing, and sales processing. The mail system can serve as the principal communications path for office personnel. [56] Each office can be served by an office processor that controls the user mailboxes, and also provides access to the communications lines used to contact local or remote offices. Individual workstations may be attached to the local office processors, or can be attached directly to the communications lines. A typical system configuration of this kind is shown in Fig. 13.16.

In an office environment, the automated system is charged with forwarding messages between individuals. The system also handles message circulation to multiple recipients, message forwarding from one user to another in a specified sequence, messages that must be delivered within a stated time frame, and message acknowledgments and replies. Thus the addressing system must accommodate multiple destination addresses and circulation and forwarding lists, as well as alternative recipient lists to replace the names of primary recipients who are unavailable. In addition, service functions must be performed that specify delivery times and handle reply requests and receipt notifications. Private passwords are generally used to ensure confidentiality and to restrict the participants to authorized operations.

Preserving the confidentiality of messages can pose a major problem in automated mail systems — it is often relatively easy to breach the security of computer files. Additional social and legal problems can also affect the operations of automatic mail systems. On the one hand, electronic letters are often not treated as seriously as more formal paper correspondence, and are assumed to be informal and transitory. On the other, legal and regulatory rules must apply when electronic mail systems replace conventional paper systems.

The information overload caused by the misuse of electronic mail systems to transmit trivial or useless subject matter represents another serious problem. Because it is much easier to prepare messages and transmit multiple copies to diverse recipients in an electronic environment than in a conventional system, participants tend to be less

Figure 13.16 Typical office-system configuration [56].

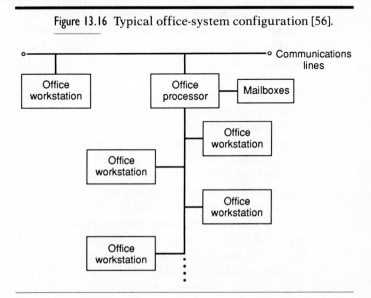

restrained in their use of the mailing privilege. This produces unhappy recipients who are swamped with unwanted materials that they must process. [57] At present, most electronic messages are not properly indexed, and it is difficult to apply content screens to identify and weed out extraneous items. Also, in most environments no distinction is made between personal and public messages, or between messages produced by important and unimportant correspondents. The information-overload problem may eventually be solved by installing special private mail channels and private mailboxes accessible only to designated users, and by introducing special message classes that recipients can use in dealing with messages. In view of the convenience and speed of electronic mail, further expansion and development of automatic-messaging systems is certain to take place.

13.7 Electronic Information Services

The notion of combining data processing technologies with information display and telecommunications capabilities — introduced in the discussion of speech processing earlier in this chapter — can be extended to more generalized electronic-information services for a wide range of applications of interest to many kinds of users. These services are based on the electronic dissemination of textual, graphic, or audio information for display or reception on low-cost terminals, optionally followed by responses from users. [58,59]

There are two main classes of services. In the first, a one-way information-dissemination system, selected items are brought to the user's attention by one-way television cables, or over-the-air broadcast channels. Because of the one-way nature of the communications system, continuous interactions are not maintained between user and system, and the user's responses are not returned after the information display. This service, known as *teletext*, supplements or replaces existing information-dissemination sources such as radio, television, and newspapers.

The other type of service, a fully interactive two-way system, is implemented over the telephone network, or a two-way cable TV system; information returned to the system by the user is used for further data processing. The two-way system, known as *videotex* or *viewdata*, can also supplement existing information sources. In addition, it provides sophisticated services such as electronic home banking, home computing services and video games, remote shopping services, mail and message facilities, and electronic-sensing systems to detect fires, manage home energy use, and read utility meters.

The usefulness of both teletext and videotex ultimately depends on a number of different factors, such as the technology used to implement these systems, the ease of learning them, and the reliability of the equipment. Such user considerations as the need for the service and the cost of using the system also play a role in determining whether these systems will be accepted.

13.7.1 Teletext

Teletext, a one-way information service, normally uses ordinary television technology. Typically, alphanumeric and graphic information is transmitted over television cables in the form of bit streams of digital data at a bit rate compatible with TV technology. The encoded digital data are normally inserted into, or multiplexed onto, the TV signal waveform in such a way that the data are placed on the unused lines in the vertical blanking intervals between the normal scans that form pictures. The teletext data are detected by a special decoder that stores them in a buffer memory for eventual display on the TV screen as directed by the user.

Usually the transmitted teletext data are divided into pages that are continuously and repetitively transmitted in sequence, at the rate of 4 pages per second. To view a particular page, the viewer must punch the desired page number on a special keypad. When that page reaches the local TV set in the sequence of transmitted pages, the decoder automatically picks out the page, holds it in the special buffer, and displays it on the screen. Assuming that the maximum waiting time for most users is 25 seconds, between 100 and 200 pages of teletext information can be handled by the system at any one time. Users determine the pages of interest to them by consulting special index pages stored with the other teletext pages. A sample index page is shown in Table 13.3, and a typical teletext communications system is presented in

Table 13.3 Sample teletext index page.

News Headlines	101	Food Guide	161
News in Detail	102–119	Farming	168
News Flash	150	TV and Radio	171–174
News Index	190	Tomorrow's TV	177–178
Newsreel	199	Weather and Travel Index	180
Finance Headlines	120		
Financial News	121–139	Full Index	
Sport Headlines	140	A–F	193
		G–O	194
Sport Pages	141–159	P–Z	195

Figure 13.17 Typical teletext system.

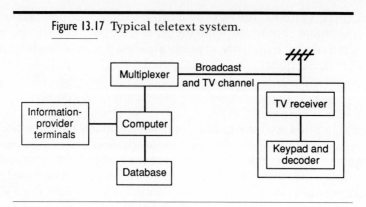

Fig. 13.17. In principle, teletext pages can be transmitted without piggybacking on the standard TV system by using all the available TV scan lines for teletext pages only. This allows the number of transmitted pages to be greatly increased without substantially increasing the average waiting time to access the information. However, the advantage of simultaneous ordinary TV service is obviously lost. Faster access can also be obtained by increasing the capacity of the storage buffers in the decoder, in which case the index pages can be permanently stored in the decoder and made accessible instantaneously.

The major advantages of teletext are widespread availability to users owning TV equipment, and low cost. The bandwidth normally used for TV transmission accommodates the additional teletext pages without extra cost, and transmission does not require specialized equipment or extra power. Thus most of the costs incurred are to compensate the information providers, as well as a one-time acquisition of the keypad and decoder at a cost of less than $200. Also, a teletext service can be kept current by replacing information pages whenever the displayed information becomes obsolete. The disadvantages are the relatively small number of available information pages, and the lack of personalized service. Teletext services have been provided on a trial basis, but no continuing service is currently in operation.

13.7.2 Videotex

The significant difference between videotex and teletext is the two-way nature of the communications system controlling the videotex transmissions. Videotex data are not routinely cycled in a broadcast mode, but instead are kept in a computer store until requested by individual users. A videotex system is comparable in operation to a standard text-retrieval system, except that the retrieval capabilities are routinely extended to graphic data, and potentially to audio information. [60–63] A typical videotex system is outlined in Fig. 13.18.

A videotex system consists of a large computer capable of storing hundreds of thousands or even millions of pages, software to find and retrieve specific pages on demand, transmission lines to send information back and forth between user and computer, and display and retrieval terminals at the user end. Data transmission can be handled by telephone lines, or by cable TV with two-way capabilities, as shown in Fig. 13.18; alternatively, special microwave links can be used. TV terminals or modified computer terminals are used to display information.

The best-known videotex development, the Prestel service, has been available in Great Britain for several years. Prestel can process 250,000 pages of information and can accommodate up to 200 user calls simultaneously. The maximum waiting time before a user receives the first output page is approximately 2 seconds. A Prestel page consists of 24 lines of 40 characters, received at a speed of 1200 bits per second. Data transmission from the user back to the system takes place at 75 bits per second.

Videotex is burdened by two main problems not confronted by teletext: the difficulty of access to the system, and the high cost of service. Three possibilities suggest themselves to solve the access problem:

1. Menu-based access, which leads the user through a sequence of increasingly refined topic classes using options from a set of dis-

Figure 13.18 Typical videotex system.

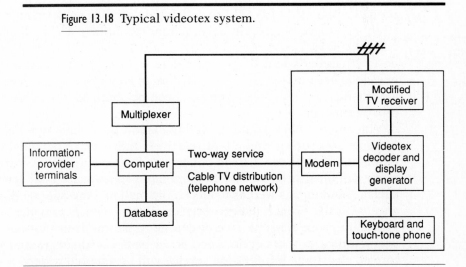

played alternatives. Menu-based systems are simple to use, but can lead the user astray when false paths are chosen through the access network of available topics.

2. Alphabetic subject lists can also be used to access the data, but do not help users who cannot find a wanted topic in the subject index.

3. Keyword systems can be designed with conventional Boolean query formulations similar to those used in text retrieval. Keywords must be assigned to the stored data — a difficult task with graphic data, as previously explained.

Existing videotex systems are not based on the deep content indexing sometimes used in text-based retrieval systems. As a result, the users must gain access using a hierarchical subject index or alphabetic subject lists, which, as just explained, do not always lead to the information desired. The information provider faces the related problem of how to subdivide the available information into pages, and where to store the pages in the subject schedules to ensure that users can actually find what they need.

A videotex service is much more expensive than a comparable teletext system because the cost includes the line charges incurred while the user's equipment is connected to the central computer. In addition, the user must pay for local equipment, as well as the service cost for displayed information.

In principle, videotex has vast potential for changing the social habits of viewers by bringing the power of computing to the home and using it for home shopping, opinion polling, banking, and information acquisition. In actual fact, experience with videotex experiments has been disappointing. [63,64] The dedicated decoding equipment is relatively expensive — typically several hundred dollars. The high-quality color displays used experimentally resulted in slow display speeds — up to 20 seconds to display a complete information page. Questions have also been raised about the wisdom of emphasizing the news service facilities of videotex when news can be obtained less expensively by other means.

Videotex services would do well to exploit the momentum built up in home computing, and adapt relatively inexpensive personal computers to videotex use instead of using dedicated equipment. Furthermore, emphasis can be shifted from news to transactional services such as banking, as well as to electronic mail and messaging. Experience with the French teletext service, Teletel, which provides small special-purpose consoles free of charge to hundreds of thousands of users, indicates that service costs must be reduced substantially before an electronic information service will be adopted widely.

The public policy questions mentioned for mail and message systems must also be considered for videotex. Among these questions are the potential for abuse by network managers in collecting private information about service subscribers, and problems arising from the distribution of misinformation, or from ignoring rights of information ownership and privacy. Proposals have been made to extend to the videotex services the regulations governing the standard common carrier services such as broadcasting. So far, these policy questions have not been resolved in the United States.

13.8 Electronic Publications and the Electronic Library

Several drawbacks of conventional journal- and book-publishing systems were outlined at the beginning of this chapter. [65] Among these drawbacks are the complexities of the information chain that must be followed to ready a document for publication. Usually this chain starts with the author, who sends a manuscript to an editor, who in turn contacts one or more reviewers, who may return the manuscript with advice about further steps. The editor may then return the paper to the author with instructions for revising and returning the manuscript. Finally, after a lengthy approval and editing process, the paper may be sent to a printer, who may disseminate the publication to the reading public.

Conventional publication processes are also too expensive for many purposes, not only because of the complexities of the publication process, but also because packaging into journal or book form forces the reader to pay for unwanted materials. It has also been claimed that space limitations in conventional publications cause potentially valuable items to be hopelessly delayed during publication, or sometimes completely suppressed.

The proposed solution to these problems, known as *desktop publishing*, is based on the direct preparation and composition of original materials by the author, using a combination of automatic text- and graphic-processing techniques. Dissemination to intended users can take place over existing electronic information-processing networks. In addition, the finished materials can be printed either locally or remotely, using laser-printing equipment. [66,67] Various implementations of desktop publishing have been proposed, starting at the low end with local microcomputers and laser printers, up to mainframe computer systems with elaborate electronic composition and high-quality printed output at the high end. Even on microcomputers, sophisticated document-preparation software can be used to manipulate graphs and pictures as well as text, and to transform the information into attractive published products.

Proposals have also been made for disseminating published information to intended recipients. Typically, authors place the finished materials in a publicly accessible file, together with titles, abstracts, and indexing information such as keywords and subject indicators. Subscribers to the electronic dissemination service can then search this information, retrieving a complete document only if the keyword information is sufficiently promising. When a document is actually retrieved, the reader is automatically assessed a royalty fee, based on the number of accesses to the stored information and the amount of material actually utilized.

An automatic publication system ensures that all released materials are instantly available, and reduces the expense of publication by eliminating delays and avoiding the packaging of heterogeneous materials into common journal covers. Furthermore, all readers tied to the automatic information-dissemination network have an equal chance to see materials of interest, whereas at present "insiders" in particular disciplines have an unfair advantage in finding materials in their areas.

Although in a paperless environment the role of the information specialist who helps access and handle electronically stored information probably increases, there is less certainty about the future function of information publishers and of information repositories such as libraries. Publishers might deal only with specialized materials that are not subject to instant dissemination, or are too bulky for electronic storage. Analogously, libraries would be converted into training centers for information specialists, and learning centers for non-expert users who need help in accessing electronic data files. The only paper documents maintained locally might be items of interest in that area for which a conversion to electronic form would not be rational. [2–4]

Many interesting questions are raised in the literature about the eventual abandonment of paper documents. [65,68,69] For example, the social functions fulfilled by the traditional journal- and book-publishing system would have to be replaced. Under current conditions, editors and referees control to some extent the amount and type of information published. In so doing, they help prevent information overload, and at the same time confer status on the materials accepted for publication. In many situations, authors depend on that stamp of approval for advancement and reward; the incentive to publish new results might diminish when the publication is no longer rewarded.

Additional questions have been raised about the preservation of copyrights and the issue of information ownership. For example, in an electronic dissemination system, individual information users might copy from the centralized files large sections of the stored documents that appear of special interest. The local files could be used later without further compensation to the original information provider. Furthermore, once information is accessible in machine-readable form and available through a communications network, it is much more difficult to maintain the trade, business, financial, and other kinds of restrictions often placed on information dissemination. An inevitable conflict then arises between the advocates of free information flow and universal availability of information, and others who look on information as a commodity or resource whose value must be protected.

Some observers suggest that solutions can be found for all these problems and that any current objections to the paperless society will disappear in time. The following quotation is typical of this line of thought: "We are so far along the road toward a paperless society that it is difficult to see what might occur that would permanently reverse the trend." [70] These experts are also impatient with arguments that stress the satisfaction of holding a book in one's hand and reading it, rather than sitting at an electronic display screen: [71,72] "This (convenience) argument, of course, is complete nonsense. The printed book has lasted for only 500 years, which is a mere dot in the history of human communication. . . ." [70]

The age of the printing industry, however, has little to do with whether it is in danger of demise. Many useful implements in current use, such as the wheel, the bathtub, or running water distribution systems, have been with us for many thousands of years, and there is no indication that they are about to be replaced. Paper documents will disappear when a more convenient medium comes along for the dissemination of information, one that preserves the advantages of print on paper. That time has not yet arrived. For now, electronic systems do not offer advantages when the document texts are not subjected to complex searching or processing. It is safe to predict that paper items will be around for a long time to come, and that poetry, novels, and detective stories will continue to appear in paper form.

Very likely, the electronic and paper forms will coexist for the foreseeable future. The electronic form will be appreciated for its speed of dissemination, easy access, and low cost, and the paper form will be found to be more convenient and easier to use in many situations. One is tempted to agree with the following argument for a compromise position: [72]

> I do not believe that electronic dissemination of information will replace print in any important way, but rather it will enhance the use of print through making print less costly and more efficient. As did microfilm, it is likely to raise the threshold below which publishing on demand is more efficient than the printing of editions. This may affect some highly specialized, small circulation journals as microfilm did with doctoral theses that once required printing. I have no fear for the general future of books, magazines and newspapers, but I do anticipate that eventually a far larger proportion of the long-term storage of materials will be done in electronic rather than print formats.

References

1. V. Bush, As We May Think, *Atlantic Monthly*, 176:1, 1945, 101–108.

2. J.G. Kemeny, A Library for 2000 A.D., in *Management and the Computer of the Future*, M. Greenberger, editor, MIT Press, Cambridge, MA, 1962, 134–178.

3. F.W. Lancaster, *Toward Paperless Information Systems*, Academic Press, New York, 1978.

4. J.C.R. Licklider, *Libraries of the Future*, MIT Press, Cambridge, MA, 1965.

5. A. Poggio, J.J. Garcia Luna Aceves, E.J. Craighill, D. Moran, L. Aguilar, D. Worthington, and J. Hight, CCWS: A Computer-based Multimedia Information System, *Computer*, 18:10, October 1985, 92–103.

6. S. Christodoulakis, M. Theodoridou, F. Ho, M. Papa, and A. Pathria, Multimedia Document Presentation, Information Extraction, and Document Formation in MINOS: A Model and a System, *ACM Transactions in Office Information Systems*, 4:4, October 1986, 345–383.

7. N. Yankelovich, N. Meyrowitz, and A. van Dam, Reading and Writing the Electronic Book, *Computer*, 18:10, October 1985, 15–30.

8. R.H. Trigg and M. Weiser, Text Net: A Network Based Approach to Text Handling, *ACM Transactions on Office Information Systems*, 4:1, January 1986, 1–23.

9. F. Barbic, Retrieval of Office Documents via Structured Trees, Report, Dipartimento di Elettronica, Politecnico di Milano, Milan, Italy, 1985.

10. N. Meyrowitz and A. van Dam, Interactive Editing Systems, *ACM Computing Surveys*, 14:3, September 1982, 321–415.

11. C.W. Fraser, Syntax Directed Editing of General Data Structures, *Proceedings of the ACM SIGPLAN/SIGOA Conference on Text Manipulation*, Association for Computing Machinery, New York, 1981, 17–21.

12. J. Walker, The Document Editor: A Support Environment for Preparing Technical Documents, *Proceedings of the ACM SIGPLAN/SIGOA Conference on Text Manipulation*, Association for Computing Machinery, New York, 1981, 44–50.

13. S. Carmody, W. Gross, T.H. Nelson, D. Rice, and A. van Dam, A Hypertext Editing System for the 360, in *Pertinent Concepts in Com-*

puter Graphics, M. Faiman and J. Nievergelt, editors, University of Illinois Press, Urbana, IL, 1969, 291–330.

14. D.C. Engelbart and W.K. English, A Research Center for Augmenting Human Intellect, in *Proceedings of the Fall Joint Computer Conference*, 33, AFIPS Press, Reston, VA, 1968, 395–410.

15. T.H. Nelson, Getting It Out of Our System, in *Information Retrieval: A Critical View*, G. Schecter, editor, Thompson Books, Washington, DC, 1967, 191–210.

16. D.C. Engelbart, R.W. Watson, and J.C. Norton, The Augmented Knowledge Workshop, *Proceedings of the National Computer Conference*, 42, AFIPS Press, Reston, VA, 1973, 9–21.

17. C. Robertson, D. McCracken, and A. Newell, The ZOG Approach to Man-Machine Communications, *International Journal of Man-Machine Studies*, 14:4, May 1981, 461–488.

18. L. McCracken and R.M. Akscyn, Experience with the ZOG Human Computer Interface, *International Journal of Man-Machine Studies*, 21:2, August 1984, 293–310.

19. H.G. Bohnert and M. Kochen, The Automated Multilevel Encylopedia as a New Mode of Scientific Communication, *Proceedings of the American Documentation Institute*, October 1963, 269–270.

20. D. Soergel, An Automated Encylopedia — A Solution to the Information Problem, *International Classification*, 4:1–2, 1977, 4–10 and 81–89.

21. S.A. Weyer and A.H. Borning, A Prototype Electronic Encylopedia, *ACM Transactions on Office Information Systems*, 3:1, January 1985, 63–88.

22. S. Christodoulakis and C. Faloutsos, Design and Performance Considerations for an Optical Disk-based Multimedia Object Server, *Computer*, 19:12, December 1986, 45–56.

23. N. Naffah and A. Karmouch, AGORA — An Experiment in Multimedia Message Systems, *Computer*, 19:5, May 1986, 56–66.

24. C. Machover and W. Myers, Interactive Computer Graphics, *Computer*, 17:10, October 1984, 145–161.

25. A. van Dam, Computer Software for Graphics, *Scientific American*, 251:3, September 1984, 146–151.

26. W.K. Giloi, *Interactive Computer Graphics — Data Structures, Algorithms, Languages*, Prentice-Hall Inc., Englewood Cliffs, NJ, 1978.

27. W.M. Newman and R.F. Sproull, *Principles of Interactive Computer Graphics*, McGraw-Hill Book Co., NY, 1979.

28. I.E. Sutherland, R.F. Sproull, and R.A. Schumacher, A Characterization of Ten Hidden-Surface Algorithms, *Computing Surveys*, 6:1, March 1974, 1–55.

29. W.M. Newman and R.F. Sproull, An Approach to Graphics System Design, *Proceedings of the IEEE*, 64:4, April 1974, 471–484.

30. H.L. Andrews, Speech Processing, *Computer*, 17:10, October 1984, 315–324.

31. F.J. Smith and R.J. Linggard, Information Retrieval by Voice Input and Output, *Lecture Notes in Computer Science*, 146, G. Salton and H.J. Schneider, editors, Springer-Verlag, Berlin, 1983, 275–288.

32. A.F. Smeaton and C.J. van Rijsbergen, Information Retrieval in an Office Filing Facility and Future Work in Project Minstrel, *Information Processing and Management*, 22:2, 1986, 135–150.

33. N.F. Maxemchuk, An Experimental Speech Storage and Editing Facility, *Bell System Techical Journal*, 59:8, October 1980, 1383–1396.

34. D.H. Klatt, A Text-to-Speech Conversion System, *Proceedings of the AFIPS Office Automation Conference*, AFIPS Press, Montvale, NJ, March 1981.

35. G. Kaplan and E.J. Lerner, Realism in Synthetic Speech, *IEEE Spectrum*, 22:4, April 1985, 32–37.

36. I.H. Whitten and P.H.C. Madams, The Telephone Inquiry Service: A Man-Machine System Using Synthetic Speech, *International Journal of Man-Machine Studies*, 9, 1977, 449–464.

37. A.I. Solzhenitsyn, *The First Circle*, Harper & Row Publishers, New York, 1968.

38. R.H. Bolt, F.S. Cooper, E.E. David Jr., P.B. Denes, J.M. Pickett, and K.N. Stevens, Identification of Speaker by Speech Spectrograms, *Science*, 166:3903, 17 October 1969, 338–343.

39. G.E. Peterson, Automatic Speech Recognition Procedures, *Language and Speech*, 4:4, October-December 1961, 200–219.

40. D.B. Fry and P. Denes, The Solution of Some Fundamental Problems in Mechanical Speech Recognition, *Language and Speech*, 1:1, January-March 1958, 35–58.

41. J.R. Welch, Automatic Speech Recognition — Putting it to Work in Industry, *Computer*, 13:5, May 1980, 65–73.

42. P. Wallich, Putting Speech Recognizers to Work, *IEEE Spectrum*, 24:4, April 1987, 55–57.

43. D.H. Klatt, Review of the ARPA Speech Understanding Project, *Journal of the Acoustical Society of America*, 62:6, December 1977, 1345–1366.

44. S.E. Levinson and K.L. Shipley, A Conversational-Mode Airline Information and Reservation System Using Speech Input and Output, *Bell System Technical Journal*, 50:1, January 1980, 119–137.

45. S. Saxin, Computer-based Real-time Conferencing System, *Computer*, 17:10, October 1985, 33–45.

46. J.A. Lifsey, 101 Applications of Teleconferencing, *Proceedings of the 47th Annual ASIS Meeting*, 21, Knowledge Industry Publications, White Plains, NY, 1984, 184–186.

47. L. McCartney, Teleconferencing Comes Down to Earth, *Datamation*, 29:1, January 1983, 76–81.

48. D. Livingston, Computer Conferencing, *Datamation*, 30:14, July 15, 1984, 111–116.

49. D. Anastassiou, M.K. Brown, H.C. Jones, J.L. Mitchell, W.B. Pennebaker, and K.S. Pennington, Series 1 Based Videoconferencing System, *IBM Systems Journal*, 22:1/2, 1983, 97–110.

50. S.R. Hiltz and M. Turoff, The Evaluation of User Behavior in a Computerized Conferencing System, *Communications of the ACM*, 24:11, November 1981, 739–751.

51. J.S. Quarterman and J.C. Hoskins, Notable Computer Networks, *Communications of the ACM*, 29:10, October 1986, 932–970.

52. W.E. Ulrich, Introduction to Electronic Mail and Implementation Considerations in Electronic Mail, *AFIPS Conference Proceedings*, 49, AFIPS Press, Arlington, VA, 1980, 485–488, 489–492.

53. J. Hogg and S. Gamvroulas, An Active Mail System, *ACM SIGMOD Record*, 14:2, June 1984, 215–222.

54. P. Schicker, Naming and Addressing in a Computer-based Mail Environment, *IEEE Transactions on Communications*, COM-30:1, January 1982, 46–62.

55. D. Tsichritzis, Message Addressing Schemes, *ACM Transactions on Database Systems*, 2:1, January 1984, 58–87.

56. S. Sakata and T. Ueda, A Distributed Office Mail System, *Computer*, 18:10, October 1985, 106–116.

57. P.J. Denning, Electronic Junk, *Communications of the ACM*, 25:3, March 1982, 163–165.

58. J. Martin, *The Wired Society: A Challenge for Tomorrow*, Prentice-Hall, Englewood Cliffs, NJ, 1978.

59. J. Tydeman, H. Lipinski, R. Adler, M. Nyhan, and L. Zwimpfer, *Teletext and Videotex in the United States — Market Potential, Technology, Public Policy Issues*, McGraw-Hill Book Co., New York, 1982.

60. A. Buscain, Videotex Systems and Data Access Methods: A State-of-the-Art Review, *Aslib Proceedings*, 37:6-7, June-July 1985, 249–256.

61. C.H. Jacobs, Fourth Generation Videotex, *Aslib Proceedings*, 37:6-7, June-July 1985, 273–276.

62. P. Linton, Designing a Viewdata System, *Aslib Proceedings*, 35:8, August 1983, 312–318.

63. C. Fletcher, Videotex: Return Engagement, *IEEE Spectrum*, 22:10, October 1985, 34–38.

64. E. Sigel, The Software Publishing Phenomenon: New Perspectives on Software and Electronic Publishing, in *Electronic Publishing Plus: Media for a Technological Future*, M. Greenberger, editor, Knowledge Industry Publications, White Plains, NY, 1985, 95–111.

65. M. Turoff and S.R. Hiltz, The Electronic Journal: A Progress Report, *Journal of the ASIS*, 33:4, July 1982, 195–202.

66. C. Winkler, Desktop Publishing, *Datamation*, 32:23, December 1, 1986, 92–96.

67. D.S. Backer, Prototype for the Electronic Book, in *Electronic Publishing Plus: Media for a Technological Future*, M. Greenberger, editor, Knowledge Industry Publications, White Plains, NY, 1985, 137–139.

68. J.S. Rubin, Unmet Expectations: Online Systems for Professionals, in *Electronic Publishing Plus: Media for a Technological Future*, M. Greenberger, editor, Knowledge Industry Publications, White Plains, NY, 1985, 125–129.

69. M.E. Williams, Electronic Databases, *Science*, 228, 26 April 1985, 445–456.

70. F.W. Lancaster, The Paperless Society Revisited, *American Libraries*, 16:8, September 1985, 553–555.

71. P.A. Strassmann, Illusion of the Paperless Office, in *Electronic Publishing Plus: Media for a Technological Future*, M. Greenberger, editor, Knowledge Industry Publications, White Plains, NY, 1985, 343–351.

72. D. Lacy, Libraries and Access to Information, in *Electronic Publishing Plus: Media for a Technological Future*, M. Greenberger, editor, Knowledge Industry Publications, White Plains, NY, 1985, 325–332.

Author Index

Subject Index